श्रीमद्वाल्मीकीय रामायणम्
VAALMEEKI RAAMAAYANA

बाल काण्ड
baala kaanda

VAALMEEKI RAAMAAYANA

A Study and Translation by
LOKNATH SWAMINATHAN

1. Vaalmeeki Raamaayana — A Revelation

2. Vaalmeeki Raamaayana — A Treasury (3 Parts)
   (Collection of Slokas from Raamaayana with Commentary in English)
   Baala Kaanda, Ayodhya Kaanda, Aranya Kaanda— (Part 1)
   Kishkindha Kaanda, Sundara Kaanda — (Part 2)
   and *Lanka Kaanda* — (Part 3)

3. Vaalmeeki Ramayana — Full Text with English Rendering in 14 Vols.

ॐ

आनो भद्राः क्रतवो यन्तु विश्वतः
Let noble thoughts come to us from all over the GLOBE

श्रीमद्वाल्मीकीय रामायणम्
VAALMEEKI RAAMAAYANA

बाल काण्ड
baala kaanda

by

L. Swaminathan

Sanskrit text edited by Smt. Shantha Srinivasam
English Translation by L. Swaminathan

MLBD PUBLICATIONS

Motilal Banarsidass Publications

MOTILAL BANARSIDASS
PUBLICATIONS
4741/23, Ansari Road, Daryaganj, New Delhi - 110002 (India)
Email: *mlbd@mlbd.com* | *sales@mlbd.com* | *exports@mlbd.com*
Website: *www.mlbd.com*

Vaalmeeki Raamaayana
by
L. Swaminathan

First Edition Published in 2022

Published in India by Motilal Banarsidass Publications

ISBN : 978-93-91759-49-0 (PB)

Printed and bound in India

Benediction

I BOW TO HIS HOLINESS SWARGIYA SRI SRI ABHINAVA VIDYA THEERTHA MAHAA SANNIDHAANAM WHO STIMULATED MY INTEREST IN VAALMEEKI RAAMAAYANA BY ENLIGHTENING ME ABOUT USAGE OF ONE WORD SHARANAM – refuge- BY MAHARISHI VAALMEEKI IN KISHKINDA KAANDA THAT HAD SOME WHAT DISTURBED ME EARLIER IN IGNORANCE

I BOW TO MY KULA AACHAARYA Sri Sri BHARATHITHEERTHA Sri SANNIDHANAM, JAGADGURU SHANKARACHARYA SARADA PEET SRINGERI

I BOW TO MY LORD SUBRAHMANYA THE SKANDATHE DHEVA SENAPATHI, THE SHANMUGA
I BOW TO MAHARISHI VAALMEEKI

—Lokanatha Swaminathan

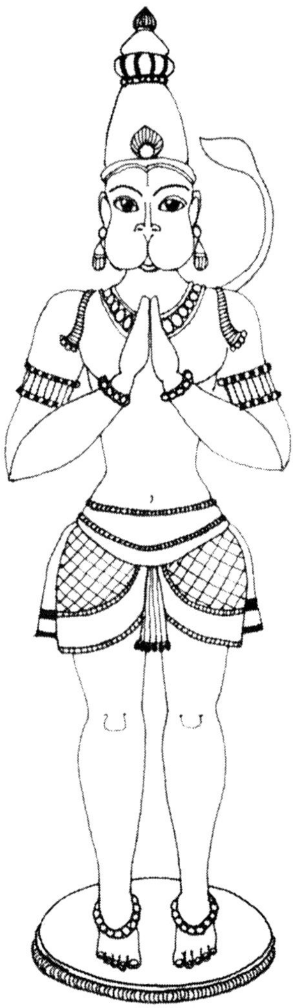

Foreword

DR. KARAN SINGH

3, NYAYA MARG,
CHANAKYAPURI
NEW DELHI - 110 021

Yavat sthasyanti girayah saritashcha mahitale
Tavad-Ramayani katha lokeshu pracharishyati
As long as the mountains and the rivers exist on the earth,
The story of Ramayana will be popular amongst the people

The above maxim aptly captures the long-lasting and the wide ranging influence of Ramayana on the Indian psyche. To quote MacDonnell, "Probably no work of world literature, secular in its origin, has ever produced so profound an influence on the life and thought of a people as the Ramayana" (Encyclopaedia of Religion and Ethics, Vol. X, p.574).

Valmiki's Ramayana not only incorporates all the facets of human existence in a lucid manner but also expounds the moral values of an ideal life, with all its ups and downs. Right from the *Balakanda*and up to the *Uttarakanda*, Ramayana symbolizes various aspects of the journey of human life, be it the most mundane and material or the most sacred and spiritual. The beauty of vast natural and agricultural resources across the lands, the efficiency of intricate military measures, the depth of moral dilemmas, the sanctity of Dharma in family life, the trials and tribulations of a righteous person and his psychic travesties are all manifested through the principal characters portrayed by Valmiki in his Ramayana. It is not without reason then that it has been suggested by some scholars, no less than the great Shankaracharya himself, that the Ramayana is not just a simple story, it has an allegorical significance :

Tirtva moharavanam hatva dveshadirakshasan
Shanti-Sita-samayuktaatma-ramovirajate
The human self, in the form of Rama, after crossing
The forest of moha or delusion, and after killing the
Rakshasas in the form of raga or passion and dvesha
Or hatred, radiates resplendently as
He is united with Shanti or peace in the form of Sita

The eternal and universal appeal of Ramayana is visible in several parts of India as well as various countries of Southeast Asia. To retain the original essence but to spread the message of Ramayana in diverse

TEL. : (011) 2611-5291 2611-1744
Email : karansingh@karansingh.com

Dr. KARAN SINGH

3, NYAYA MARG,
CHANAKYAPURI
NEW DELHI - 110 021

dictions has been very popular in the Indian literary tradition since ancient times to contemporary climes. I am very pleased to know that the nonagenarian Sri Lokanath Swaminathan of Chennai, a technologist by profession, has delved deep into the text of Valmiki Ramayana and has been studying it as a passion for the past 20 years.

No wonder that his Kulaguru, His Holiness Sri Shankarachaya of Sharada Peetham, Shringeri has expressed his desire that the Epic should be published along with a rendering in English, Shloka by Shloka in 14 Volumes, and his worthy disciple Sri Swaminathan has taken it as a command. I pray for the realization of his endeavour and to the accomplishment and fulfillment of his monumental project.

The whole set is being published by the veteran Indology publisher Motilal Banarsidass Publications. This first volume begins, of course, with the Bala Kanda which covers the birth, childhood and youth of Sri Rama. It is a great pleasure for me to be involved in the release of this volume which, I am sure, will soon be followed by others.

My warm congratulations to Sri Lokanath Swaminathan for this great achievement. He has completed the work and I pray to Sri Rama that he may see the full set in his own life time.

Karan Singh

Vijaya Dashmi
5 October 2022

TEL. : (011) 2611-5291 2611-1744
Email : karansingh@karansingh.com

SALUTATION

TO
THE RAMCO GROUP OF INDUSTRIES
founded by

Sri P.A.C. Ramasamy Raja of Rajapalayam

who was a man of Dharma
who tried to live by RAAMA's VALUES.

We offer our thanks to
Sri PR Raamasubrahmaneya Rajha, Chairman,
RAMCO GROUP

Who has been source of inspiration and support in
our studies on Vaalmeeki Raamaayana
for over two decades.

Introduction

The Inspiration for presenting this mammoth work is his Holiness Sri Sri Shankaracharya, Sarada Peet, Sringeri. Vaalmeeki Raamaayana carries about Slokas in Six Books (Kaandams) and covered in various chapters.

Vaalmeeki Raamaayana is not just a story book, nor a mythological extravaganza that can be ignored.

For children it is a story book.

For youngsters it is poetry & romanace.

For the common man it is a guide for day to day life.

For religious minded it is book of prayer.

For elders it is a book on philosophy & dharma.

AND IT IS VEDHA recognized as such along with the unwritten vedhas like Rik, Yajur, Saama and Atharvana.

Every Cultivated Indian should have this at home. It is our heritage. Even in this high tech world, we can find solace through this epic that is ETERNAL.

Rt Hon'ble VS SRINIVASA SASTRY on VAALMEEKI RAAMAAYANA

There was this noble man, who was a teacher, scholar, orator and a statesman who took on the onerous task of serving the cause of Indians in South Africa and alleviating their suffering.

Mahatma Gandhi considered him his 'brother' and mentor.

Let us read what he says about Raamaayana.

"....but it appears to me that there is a way of studying the Raamaayana with reverence, with adoration of the great qualities of the hero and heroine and with full appreciation of the unparalleled influence that it has exerted in ages past and will still exert for ages to come on the lives and characters of our people. EVERY DAY I READ THAT EPIC, MY OPINION GAINS STRENGTH THAT IT IS ONE OF THE GREATEST EPICS EVER COMPOSED BY MAN....

"I Should call it the greatest epic, but I shrink from that statement because I have no acquaintance with the originals of epics comparable to it in date and extent."

For those people who shun reading this epic because of lack of knowledge of Sanskrit, Rt.Hon'ble says that one need not be a mountaineer to enjoy the mountains. Of course only a mountaineer will know the extent of beauty and all what it offers. Himalayas is always beautiful even if one gazes at it from foot hills.

Banana – Jack Fruit – Coconut

Before presenting this book, your author would like to set your mind at rest. He begs readers not to stay away from reading Vaalmeeki Raamaayana because it is mythology, a myth and so on.

"What have we got to do with myth. What can we possibly learn from such an epic."

Dear readers, till recently we had a great son in India. His name was Chakravarthy Rajagopalachari, endearingly called Rajaji he was a lawyer, a freedom fighter, Chief Minister of a state, first Indian Governor General of India, founded a liberal political party... In spite of such a busy schedule, he found time not only to read Raamaayana and Mahaabharatha but also wrote beautiful books that is read and enjoyed by readers of age 8 to 80. When some one questioned the utility of such epics on the ground they are mythology, and won't serve our purpose today, Rajaji was quick with his rejoinder. In a style only he can!

"You have to peel the skin before you enjoy the Banana" Mythology clothes the epic. But, what is 'Inside' is what matters. Taking the cue from Rajaji, your writer who is fond of Jackfruit and its juice has this to say.

You have to skin the Jack fruit (no mean task) and throw the skin away. After a tiring exercise, what do you have? The juicy jack fruit. In case of coconut you need even an axe to cut the shell and fibre. On a hot day surely the drink is most welcome. It is worth your effort.

Yes, study of Vaalmeeki is worth your labour. Vaalmeeki Raamaayana is no newspaper or magazine.

IT IS VEDHA. IT IS DHARMA. IT IS SALVATION

Guru Parampara

H.H. (S.S.) Narasimha Bharati
(1879-1912) (33)

H.H. Chandrasekhara Bharati
(1912-1954) (34)

H.H. Abhinava Vidyatirtha
(1954-1989) (35)

H.H. Sri Bharati Tirtha
(1989 -) (36)

SRIMUKHAM
from
Shri JAGADGURU SRINGERI SHRIMAD BHARATHEE THEERTHA MAHAA SWAAMIGAL

May these blessings offered, after invoking the benign Presence of Lord NAARAAYANA, shower Luminescence, in the endevour of our most devoted disciple Sri. Swaminathan, the son of Sri (Dr. P.S.) Lokanathan.

"To save and protect the good, to destroy evil forces to establish Dharma, I am born (in the world, time and again) Yuga after Yuga."

Thus, The Lord declared.

As a consequence, in Thretha Yuga, for protecting good people like Vishwaamithra and to destroy evil persons like Raavana, the Lord descended (on earth) as incarnation in the form of Ramachandra.

The first amongst poets, the great sage VAALMEEKI, composed to holy story of Lord Ramachandra, in Srimad Raamaayana in 24,000 slokas.

This became renowned as the first composition of its kind.

This is accepted as The Foremost by followers of Sanaathana Dharma.

In this great work, each sloka excels the other in grandeur.

Translation of Srimad Raamaayana have been rendered in almost all languages.

Many great poets have found fulfillment by authoring poetic works, Drama and Dance, based on the story of Sri Raama in Srimad Raamaayana.

Having obtained Grace under the (Lotus) feet of our Guru (Sri Sri Abhinava Vidya Theertha Maha Sannidhaanam), having thus become worthy of his compassion and blessings, you have carefully translated each verse in English.

This exposition of this great epic in many chapters, has become repository for pious people.

Now again, you have given elevating expression and translation to some selective slokas from Raamaayana.

Those who are impatient to go through the entire epic will obtain enjoyment of the history of Raama be beholding this (four new) book.

Your effort is praiseworthy.

With unlimited grace of Sri Shaaradaamba and Sri Chandramouleeswarar, may this book that is to be released soon, bring enjoyment to the heat of good people.

We pray and bless you for your well being and prosperity.

Sringagiri
Baargava Vaasara
(30.9.2005)

By grace of Naaraayana

Contents

BAALA KAANDA

Chapter 1

(In 100 verses that follow, the entire Raamaayana is condensed: Sage Naaradha gives the gist of Raamaayana to sage Vaalmeeki)

❍ ❍ ❍

१. तपःस्वाध्यायनिरतं तपस्वी वाग्विदां वरम् ।
नारदं परिपप्रच्छ वाल्मीकिर्मुनिपुङ्गवम् ॥

1. (Vaalmeeki asks Naaradha): (Seeking enlightenment) the austere & ascetic Vaalmeeki beseeched the foremost amongst sages, (the 'tiger' amongst sages), Naaradha, who was foremost amongst men of eloquence & who was ever in meditation and contemplation of Vedhas.

❍ ❍ ❍

२. को न्वस्मिन् सांप्रतं लोके गुणवान् कश्च वीर्यवान् ।
धर्मज्ञश्च कृतज्ञश्च सत्यवाक्यो दृढव्रतः ॥

2. (Vaalmeeki asks) Who, in this world, at present, is adorned with good qualities, is brave, knows Dharma, is truthful, resolute (steadfast) in vows (service), & is a man of gratitude.

❍ ❍ ❍

३. चारित्रेण च को युक्तः सर्वभूतेषु को हितः ।
विद्वान् कः कः समर्थश्च कश्चैकप्रियदर्शनः ॥

3. Who, is endowed with good conduct, is compassionate to all living beings, foremost in knowledge (most learned), most capable, whose pleasant looks are unique.

❍ ❍ ❍

४. आत्मवान् को जितक्रोधो द्युतिमान् कोऽनसूयकः ।
कस्य बिभ्यति देवाश्च जातरोषस्य संयुगे ।।

4. Who, is a man of courage, bright, free from jealousy, controls anger, but when provoked (to war), is a terror even to Dhevas.

❍ ❍ ❍

५. एतदिच्छाम्यहं श्रोतुं परं कौतूहलं हि मे ।
महर्षेत्वं समर्थोऽसि ज्ञातुमेवंविधं नरम् ।।

5: I wish to know this; my desire & curiosity is great; If there be such a man, you are indeed the fit person (to describe him to me).

❍ ❍ ❍

६. श्रुत्वा चैतत् त्रिलोकज्ञो वाल्मीकेर्नारदो वचः ।
श्रूयतामिति चामन्त्रय प्रहृष्टो वाक्यमब्रवीत् ।।

6. (Naaradha replies to Vaalmeeki) Having listened to these words (questions) of Vaalmeeki, sage Naaradha the knower of three worlds, was pleased and immediately replied.

❍ ❍ ❍

७. बहवो दुर्लभाश्चैव ये त्वया कीर्तिता गुणाः ।
मुने वक्ष्याम्यहं बुद्ध्वा तैर्युक्तः श्रूयतां नरः ।।

7. Oh Muni (Vaalmeeki)! Rare indeed (is a person endowed with) so many qualities enumerated by you; I am telling you, having given some thought; May you hear about such a man endowed with such qualities.

❍ ❍ ❍

८. इक्ष्वाकुवंशप्रभवो रामो नाम जनैः श्रुतः ।
नियतात्मा महावीर्यो द्युतिमान्धृतिमान् वशी ।।

8. He is called Raama by people:; born in Ikshwaaku family: Resolute, he is a man of immense strength and

composure People endear to him & willingly surrender to him: Very brave, brilliant.

❍ ❍ ❍

९. बुद्धिमान्नीतिमान् वाग्मी श्रीमान् शत्रुनिबर्हणः ।
विपुलांसो महाबाहुः कम्बुग्रीवो महाहनुः ।।

9. He is a wise man; man of justice; has command over speech; is endowed with riches; is destroyer of enemies; has broad shoulders; large hands; neck conch shaped; possesses robust cheeks.

❍ ❍ ❍

१०. महोरस्को महेष्वासो गूढजत्रुररिन्दमः ।
आजानुबाहुः सुशिराः सुललाटः सुविक्रमः ।।

10. He is broad chested; his long hands reach as far as his knees; collar bones well concealed; has nice forehead, lovely head; Skilled in archery, he subjugates foes; He has nice gait.

❍ ❍ ❍

११. समः समविभक्ताङ्गः स्निग्धवर्णः प्रतापवान् ।
पीनवक्षा विशालाक्षो लक्ष्मीवान् शुभलक्षणः ।।

11. He is of good height, (Sama-well balanced), with well proportioned body; has a glossy complexion* (snigda varna); he is ever radiant; With broad shoulders, wide eyes, good features, he is handsome (Lakshmivaan-resplendent): (Vaalmeeki uses word =* snigda varna = to describe Raama's complexion-literal meaning is 'sticky' complexion, endearing complexion).

❍ ❍ ❍

१२. धर्मज्ञः सत्यसन्धश्च प्रजानां च हिते रतः ।
यशस्वी ज्ञानसम्पन्नः शुचिर्वश्यः समाधिमान् ।।
प्रजापतिसमः श्रीमान्धाता रिपुनिषूदनः ।।

12. He is knower of Dharma (moral code); upholder of Truth, Virtuous; full of wisdom; highly venerated; is ever concerned with welfare of his subjects; richly blessed, he is (like) God Bramma (on earth): he is destroyer of enemies; He is the 'Giver'; a great conciliator, dutiful, people subject to his 'will' (lovingly)..

❍ ❍ ❍

१३. रक्षिता जीवलोकस्य धर्मस्य परिरक्षिता ।
रक्षिता स्वस्य धर्मस्य स्वजनस्य च रक्षिता ।।

13. Protector of all life (ecology); protector of Dharma; protector of his own Dharma, (himself not above laws of Dharma), he is protector of people.

❍ ❍ ❍

१४. वेदवेदाङ्गतत्त्वज्ञो धनुर्वेदे च निष्ठितः ।
सर्वशास्त्रार्थतत्वज्ञः स्मृतिमान् प्रतिभानवान् ।।

14. Knows essence of Vedhas and every part of Vedha (Holy Texts); is master of Dhanur Vedha (Science of war) Knows the truths of Shaasthra-s (Sacred books, compendium of rules, codes) Is endowed with tremendous memory; brilliant (Clarity of thought crosses his mind).

❍ ❍ ❍

१५. सर्वलोकप्रियः साधुरदीनात्मा विचक्षणः ।
सर्वदाऽभिगतः सद्भिः समुद्र इव सिन्धुभिः ।।

15. Loved by all the worlds, he is a good man; strong in spirit; far sighted; good men flock to him like rivers heading towards ocean.

❍ ❍ ❍

१६. आर्यः सर्वसमश्चैव सदैकप्रियदर्शनः ।
स च सर्वगुणोपेतः कौसल्यानन्दवर्धनः ।।

16. An honorable man (An Aryan); ever bestows a pleasing eye on one & all; Considerate to one & all without

discrimination; endowed with diverse rich qualities; And to (his mother) Kowsalya he radiates happiness.

❍ ❍ ❍

१७. समुद्र इव गाम्भीर्ये धैर्येण हिमवानिव ।
विष्णुना सदृशो वीर्येसोमवत् प्रियदर्शनः ।।

17. In generosity, he is like ocean; in patience and fortitude, he is like Himaalayas; in valour, he is verily like God Vishnu; in appearance, pleasant looking like moon.

❍ ❍ ❍

१८. कालाग्निसदृशः क्रोधे क्षमया पृथिवीसमः ।
धनदेन समस्त्यागे सत्ये धर्म इवापरः ।।

18. In composure (forbearance), he is like mother earth; In charity, like Kubhaera (the lord of wealth); In anger, he is like Pralaya fire (at the end of total annihilation of universe); in Truth, like Dharma (personified).

❍ ❍ ❍

१९. तमेवंगुणसम्पन्नं रामं सत्यपराक्रमम् ।
ज्येष्ठं श्रेष्ठगुणैर्युक्तं प्रियं दशरथः सुतम् ।।

19. A man endowed with above mentioned character (& virtues); truly valiant, ever in service of people, such a man was Raama, the eldest son, the loving son of Dhascharatha; Endowed with foremost qualities.

❍ ❍ ❍

२०. प्रकृतीनां हितैर्युक्तं प्रकृतिप्रियकाम्यया ।
यौवराज्येन संयोक्तुमैच्छत् प्रीत्या महीपतिः ।।

20. (After describing Raama's qualities, Naaradha continues) To further the cause of service to the people & out of love towards (Raama), king Dhascharatha desired to anoint (appoint) Raama as Crown prince (to succeed the throne).

❍ ❍ ❍

२१. तस्याभिषेकसंभारान्दृष्ट्वा भार्याऽथ कैकयी ।
पूर्वं दत्तवरा देवी वरमेनमयाचत ।।
विवासनं च रामस्य भरतस्याभिषेचनम् ।।

21. (But Dhascharatha's third wife, queen Kaikeyi wants her own son Bharatha to become crown prince instead of Raama) Seeing preparations & arrangements like holy baths (for Raama's coronation) taking place, his wife Kaikeyi, who had earlier (years back) obtained boons, (commitment from her husband Dhascharatha), demanded Raama's banishment (from kingdom) & (her own son) Bharatha's appointment (as crown prince instead).

❍ ❍ ❍

२२. स सत्यवचनाद्राजा धर्मपाशेन संयतः ।
विवासयामास सुतं रामं दशरथः प्रियम् ।।

22. (Wife Kaikeyi had once helped her husband & he had promised her any wish she may chose and Kaikeyi exercised her options to avail the boons at a moment most suited to her interests & schemes and she pressed her husband with these demands now) Bound by Truth & commitment and tied by "ropes" of Dharma, king Dhascharatha, banished his most beloved son Raama from his kingdom (A king never breaks a promise even after years).

❍ ❍ ❍

२३. स जगाम वनं वीरः प्रतिज्ञामनुपालयन् ।
पितुर्वचननिर्देशात् कैकेय्याः प्रियकारणात् ।।

23. The brave (Raama), bound by his father's command & also to please (his step mother) Kaikeyi, left for forest (on exile), to uphold (his father's) honour & command.

❍ ❍ ❍

२४. तं व्रजन्तं प्रियो भ्राता लक्ष्मणोऽनुजगाम ह ।
स्नेहाद्विनयसंपन्नः सुमित्रानन्दवर्धनः ।।
भ्रातरं दयितो भ्रातुः सौभ्रात्रमनुदर्शयन् ।।

24. The endearing Lakshmana, who was endowed with qualities of high born (like good breeding, education), who increased the joy of (his mother) Sumithra, who was the beloved of his brother (Raama), exhibiting his deep affection and friendship for his brother (Raama), accompanied his brother Raama as he was going on exile (Sumithra was the second wife & queen of Dhascharatha).

❍ ❍ ❍

२५. रामस्य दयिता भार्या नित्यं प्राणसमा हिता ।
जनकस्य कुले देवमायेव निर्मिता ।।

25. Dear to him as life itself, the loving & endearing Seetha, the wife of Raama, who was born in (King) Janaka's household and (who looked like a celestial woman), an illusory celestial created (on earth)......... .

❍ ❍ ❍

२६. सर्वलक्षणसंपन्ना नारीणामुत्तमा वधूः ।
सीताऽप्यनुगता रामं शशिनं रोहिणी यथा ।।

26. Who was endowed with good qualities and who was foremost amongst women, accompanied Raama, following him ever, like Rohini following the Moon: (Rohini is divine consort of Moon as per mythology).

❍ ❍ ❍

२७. पौरैरनुगतो दूरं पित्रा दशरथेन च ।
श्रृङ्गिबेरपुरे सूतं गङ्गाकूले व्यसर्जयत् ।।
गुहमासाद्य धर्मात्मा निषादाधिपतिं प्रियम् ।।

27. (Raama's) father Dhascharatha and citizens followed them a distance, (and then returned to Ayodhya). The noble soul Raama (who continued the journey with his brother Lakshmana & wife Seetha to the forest) met his dear friend Guha chief of hunters. Then on the banks of Ganges at Sringabhaerapura, he sent back his charioteer (along with chariot) to the capital (Ayodhya).

❍ ❍ ❍

२८. गुहेन सहितो रामो लक्ष्मणेन च सीतया ।।

28. (Raama's acceptance of his banishment is total & he would want nothing from his kingdom No chariots, nor comforts of a prince of Ayodhya) Raama, with his wife Seetha and brother Lakshmana, spent (some time) with Guha.

❍ ❍ ❍

२९. ते वनेन वनं गत्वा नदीस्तीर्त्वा बहूदकाः ।
चित्रकूटमनुप्राप्य भरद्वाजस्य शासनात् ।।

29. (Then leaving his friend Guha) they crossed forest after forest, crossed mighty rivers (that were full of waters); and under advice of sage Bharadhwaj, reached Chithrakoot.

❍ ❍ ❍

३०. रम्यमावसथं कृत्वा रममाणा वने त्रयः ।
देवगन्धर्वसमाशास्तत्र ते न्यवसन् सुखम् ।।

30. (At Chithrakoot) these three who were looking radiant like heavenly beings, set up a lovely cottage and were enjoying life in forest.

❍ ❍ ❍

३१. चित्रकूटं गते रामे पुत्रशोकातुरस्तथा ।
राजा दशरथः स्वर्गं जगाम विलपन् सुतम् ।।

31. When Raama was at Chithrakoot, unable to stand the pangs of separation from his son (Raama), king (Dhascharatha), crying miserably over his son, in utter grief, died. (reached heavenly abode).

❍ ❍ ❍

३२. मृते तु तस्मिन् भरतो वसिष्ठप्रमुखैर्द्विजैः ।
नियुज्यमानो राज्याय नैच्छद्राज्यं महाबलः ।।

32. (King Dhascharatha paid the penalty of having given an open boon to Kaikeyi in a moment of impulse long, long ago) On his death, in spite of Vasishta and other

senior (Brahmin) counselors' offer of Crown to him, the mightily strong Bharatha, (on whose account Raama was banished by Kaikeyi, (the mother of Bharatha), did not desire the kingdom: (Bharatha refused the throne).

❍ ❍ ❍

३३. स जगाम वनं वीरो रामपादप्रसादकः ।।

33. (Raama is indeed very fortunate; his brother Lakshmana & wife Seetha accompany him on his exile And his other brother Bharatha refuses to usurp the throne) Bharatha, the brave, immediately left for forest to get Raama's blessings (and seek his return from forest immediately) to accept the kingdom.

❍ ❍ ❍

३४. गत्वा तु सुमहात्मानं रामं सत्यपराक्रमम् ।
अयाचद् भ्रातरं राममार्यभावपुरस्कृतः ।।

34. Meeting the great soul Raama who was truly valiant, (his brother Bharatha) whose character & behaviour was most exemplary, begged his brother Raama (to return to Ayodhya to take over the kingdom, to forget about his exile).

❍ ❍ ❍

३५. त्वमेव राजा धर्मज्ञ इति रामं वचोऽब्रवीत् ।
रामोऽपि परमोदारः सुमुखः सुमहायशाः ।।
न चैच्छत् पितुरादेशाद्राज्यं रामो महाबलः ।।

35. (And Bharatha pleads): = Oh knower of Dharma (Oh Raama) You (alone) are (fit to be) king= He told Raama these words (But) Raama who was most generous (to every one), who was mightily strong and famous, who was ever pleasant, out of commitment to his father, (refused to yield) and refused to accept the kingdom (till the period of his banishment from kingdom was over).

❍ ❍ ❍

३६. पादुके चास्य राज्याय न्यासं दत्त्वा पुनः पुनः ।
निवर्तयामास ततो भरतं भरताग्रजः ।।

36. However, this Raama the elder brother of Bharatha, gave his Sandals to Bharatha as token and pledge for him to rule the kingdom (as his representative). And further, he sent him back from there (immediately: Ayodhya cannot be without a ruler).

❍ ❍ ❍

३७. स काममनवाप्यैव रामपादावुपस्पृशन् ।
नन्दिग्रामेऽकरोद्राज्यं रामागमनकाङ्क्षया ।।

37. (Readers may see the cleverness of Raama; he cannot go back as he was banished for 14 years and Bharatha does not want to rule during his absence. A tight situation! So he asks Bharatha to rule as Regent, drawing inspiration and authority from him with his Sandals as token).

Although his wishes were not fully fulfilled, Bharatha, (worshipping and) taking Raama's Sandals (as Raama's authority on him, prayed for Raama's safe return), looking forward to his return (after 14 years of exile). He, (Bharatha), established a (new, temporary) capital at Nandhigram.

(Bharatha did not want to rule the kingdom from Ayodhya because, as far as he was concerned, only Raama was the rightful king after their father's death. So he decides to rule from Nandigram, a village outside capital Ayodhya).

❍ ❍ ❍

३८. गते तु भरते श्रीमान् सत्यसन्धो जितेन्द्रियः ।
रामस्तु पुनरालक्ष्य नागरस्य जनस्य च ।।
तत्रागमनमेकाग्रो दण्डकान् प्रविवेश ह ।।

38. After Bharatha left, the resplendent Raama who was resolute, truthful, and who ever controlled his senses (& overcame passions), anticipating more such visits

from citizens (of his kingdom if he stayed nearby, left Chithrakoot) & entered forest of Dhandaka.

❍ ❍ ❍

३९. प्रविश्य तु महारण्यं रामो राजीवलोचनः ।
विराधं राक्षसं हत्वा शरभङ्गं ददर्श ह ।।
सुतीक्ष्णं चाप्यगस्त्यं च अगस्त्यभ्रातरं तथा ।।

39. Lotus eyed Raama, entering the wild forest, destroyed demon Viradha. He then met Sages Scharabhanga, Sutheekshana, Agasthya and also Agasthya's brother.

❍ ❍ ❍

४०. अगस्त्यवचनाच्चैव जग्राहैन्द्रं शरासनम् ।
खड्गं च परमप्रीतस्तूणी चाक्षयसायकौ ।।

40. Under Agasthya's advice, he acquired bow, sword, hallowed weapons (like Aindhram), together with two quivers full with "Inexhaustible" arrows, in great joy.

❍ ❍ ❍

४१. वसतस्तस्य रामस्य वने वनचरैः सह ।
ऋषयोऽभ्यागमन् सर्वेवधायासुररक्षसाम् ।।

41. The Muni-s (the sages) and all of them who were living in forest, approached Raama who was (living) in forest, for (seeking his help for) the destruction of demons and Asura-s (in forests).

❍ ❍ ❍

४२. स तेषां प्रतिशुश्राव राक्षसानां तथा वने ।।

42. He assured them (protection) from demons thus (he promised).

❍ ❍ ❍

४३. प्रतिज्ञातश्च रामेण वधः संयति रक्षसाम् ।
ऋषीणामग्निकल्पानां दण्डकारण्यवासिनाम् ।।

43. A vow was taken by Raama there before the Rishi-s (sages & Muni-s) who were residing: at Dhandaka

forest and who were radiant like fire, (the vow of) killing of demons in battle.

❍ ❍ ❍

४४. तेन तत्रैव वसता जनस्थाननिवासिनी ।
विरूपिता शूर्पणखा राक्षसी कामरूपिणी ।।

44. Living there, Raama maimed a (devil of a woman), a demoness* (named) Schoorpanaka, who was living in the forests of Janasthana This (wicked woman) could take on any form she pleased (* For a woman demon, we have used =Demoness =).

❍ ❍ ❍

४५. ततः शूर्पणखावाक्यादुद्युक्तान् सर्वराक्षसान् ।
खरं त्रिशिरसं चैव दूषणं चैव राक्षसम् ।।
निजघान रणे रामस्तेषां चैव पदानुगान् ।।

45. Instigated by Schoorpanaka (who wanted revenge upon Raama & Lakshmana because they had maimed her & rejected her amorous advances) the zealous demons (and their chiefs) & Dhooshana and Thrischiras and their gang were all destroyed by Raama (when they attacked Raama), single handedly, in war.

❍ ❍ ❍

४६. वने तस्मिन्निवसता जनस्थाननिवासिनाम् ।
रक्षसां निहतान्यासन् सहस्राणि चतुर्दश ।।

46. 14,000 demons who were residents of Janasthana were all killed by (Raama) who was (then) residing in Janasthana.

❍ ❍ ❍

४७. ततो ज्ञातिवधं श्रुत्वा रावणः क्रोधमूर्च्छितः ।
सहायं वरयामास मारीचं नाम राक्षसम् ।।

47. Raavana, (the king of Lanka), hearing the destruction of his friends & cousins, was in mad rage and sought (his demon friend) Maareecha's assistance.

❍ ❍ ❍

४८. वार्यमाणः सुबहुशो मारीचेन स रावणः ।
न विरोधो बलवता क्षमो रावण तेन ते ।।

48. (But Maareecha advises Raavana not to confront Raama)=Oh Raavana! You must be tolerant Must not bear enmity with the very strong Raama= This Raavana was restrained in many ways by Maareecha (Maareecha, his demon friend tried his best to prevent Raavana to go anywhere near Raama; alas, in vain).

❍ ❍ ❍

४९. अनादृत्य तु तद्वाक्यं रावणः कालचोदितः ।
जगाम सहमारीचस्तस्याश्रमपदं तदा ।।

49. Yet, succumbing to fate, ignoring Maareecha's advice, Raavana reached the hermitage of Raama) accompanied by Maareecha.

❍ ❍ ❍

५०. तेन मायाविना दूरमपवाह्य नृपात्मजौ ।
जहार भार्यां रामस्य गृध्रं हत्वा जटायुषम् ।।

50. Using him, (using Maareecha's services), who was an expert in magic, he made the two princes (Raama & Lakshmana) go far away (from their abode), and he kidnapped (Seetha) the wife of Raama after (mortally) wounding the big bird Jataayu (on the way, when Jataayu tried to save Seetha from Raavana's clutches).

❍ ❍ ❍

५१. गृध्रं च निहतं दृष्ट्वा हृतां श्रुत्वा च मैथिलीम् ।
राघवः शोकसन्तप्तो विललापाकुलेन्द्रियः ।।

51. (Raama the) Raaghava, when he came to know of the abduction (of his wife Seetha the) Maithili and when he saw the beaten up (and dying Jataayu the) vulture bird, was tormented by grief; Losing control of himself, (losing his senses), he wailed.

❍ ❍ ❍

५२. ततस्तेनैव शोकेन गृध्रं दग्ध्वा जटायुषम् ।।

52. In great grief he performed the Last Rites of vulture Jataayu.

❍ ❍ ❍

५३. मार्गमाणो वने सीतां राक्षसं सन्ददर्श ह ।
कबन्धं नाम रूपेण विकृतं घोरदर्शनम् ।।

53. Then, (going about) in search of Seetha, he saw Kabhandha in forest, a demon who presented a strange sight, gruesome to look at.

❍ ❍ ❍

५४. तं निहत्य महाबाहुर्ददाह स्वर्गतश्च सः ।।

54. Then the mighty limbed (Raama) killed him and he (this Kabhandha) went to heaven after he was cremated (by Raama).

❍ ❍ ❍

५५. स चास्य कथयामास शबरीं धर्मचारिणीम् ।
श्रमणीं धर्मनिपुणामभिगच्छेति राघवम् ।।

55. (While going up in the sky towards heaven) he stayed (for a while there) and he told (Raama), the Raaghava: = You meet woman saint Schabari, the expert in Dharma, who practices Dharma =.

५६. सोऽभ्यगच्छन्महातेजाः शबरीं शत्रुसूदनः ।
शबर्या पूजितः सम्यग्रामो दशरथात्मजः ।।

56. The most brilliant Raama the destroyer of enemies, saw Schabari; This (Raama) the son of Dhascharatha, was well honoured by Schabari (with hospitality).

❍ ❍ ❍

५७. पंपातीरे हनुमता सङ्गतो वानरेण ह ।
हनुमद्वचनाच्चैव सुग्रीवेण समागतः ।।

57. (Later on) On the banks of Pampa river, he was met by

Hanumaan: By Hanumaan's words (of request) he met with Sugreeva (& befriended him)

❍ ❍ ❍

५८. सुग्रीवाय च तत्सर्वं शंसद्रामो महाबलः ।
आदितस्तद्यथावृत्तं सीतायाश्च विशेषतः ।।

58. The mightily strong Raama enumerated from beginning all the events, particularly Seetha's (kidnapping), to Sugreeva.

❍ ❍ ❍

५९. सुग्रीवश्चापि तत्सर्वं श्रुत्वा रामस्य वानरः ।
चकार सख्यं रामेण प्रीतश्चैवाग्निसाक्षिकम् ।।

59. Monkey Sugreeva too, listened to all of Raama's (story) and being pleased with Raama, formed friendship with him, with fire as witness.

❍ ❍ ❍

६०. ततो वानरराजेन वैरानुकथनं प्रति ।
रामायावेदितं सर्वं प्रणयाद्दुःखितेन च ।।

61. And by the grief stricken monkey prince (Sugreeva) everything was told to Raama in confidence; about the story of hostility (by his brother Vaali towards him).

Raama vowed to kill (Sugreeva's brother) Vaali; the monkey (Sugreeva) then narrated about Vaali's strength.

❍ ❍ ❍

६२. सुग्रीवः शमितश्चासीन्नित्यं वीर्येण राघवे ।।

62. (But) Sugreeva entertained the usual doubt about the valour in (Raama) the Raaghava.

(Can Raama match his brother Vaali, doubted Sugreeva).

❍ ❍ ❍

६३. राघवप्रत्ययार्थं तु दुन्दुभेः कायमुत्तमम् ।
दर्शयामास सुग्रीवो महापर्वतसन्निभम् ।।

63. To test (Raama) the Raaghava and build confidence in himself (about Raama's capability), Sugreeva pointed at the mighty (dead) body of (Demon) Dhundhubi which was like a big mountain.

❍ ❍ ❍

६४. उत्स्मयित्वा महाबाहुः प्रेक्ष्य चास्थि महाबलः ।
पादाङ्गुष्ठेन चिक्षेप संपूर्णं दशयोजनम् ।।

64. The mightily strong mighty limbed (Raama), then looking at the big body & skeleton (of Dhundhubi), kicked it to a full distance of 10 yojanas (about 90 miles), with the toes of his foot, smiling (sarcastically).

❍ ❍ ❍

६५. बिभेद च पुनः सालान् सप्तैकेन महेषुणा ।
गिरिं रसातलं चैव जनयन् प्रत्ययं तदा ।।

65. And further, with one big arrow, he split up seven huge trees, mountain, subterranean earth, to instill confidence (in Sugreeva).

❍ ❍ ❍

६६. ततः प्रीतमनास्तेन विश्वस्तः स महाकपिः ।
किष्किन्धां रामसहितो जगाम च गुहां तदा ।।

66. Then, because of all this, (Sugreeva) became happy with confidence (about Raama's valour); The big monkey then went back to the caves of Kishkindha along with Raama.

❍ ❍ ❍

६७. ततोऽगर्जद्धरिवरः सुग्रीवो हेमपिङ्गलः ।
तेन नादेन महता निर्जगाम हरीश्वरः ।।

67. There, the great monkey Sugreeva who was of golden hue, sent out a roar (War cry); By this mighty roar, the

lord of monkeys (his brother Vaali) came out (of his abode in Kishkindha).

❍ ❍ ❍

६८. अनुमान्य तदा तारां सुग्रीवेण समागतः ।
निजघान च तत्रैनं शरेणैकेन राघवः ।।

68. After consoling (his wife) Thaara and taking leave of her, (Vaali) confronted (his brother) Sugreeva; and Raama then and there killed him, with just one arrow.

❍ ❍ ❍

६९. ततः सुग्रीववचनाद्धत्वा वालिनमाहवे ।
सुग्रीवमेव तद्राज्ये राघवः प्रत्यपादयत् ।।

69. Raama, having killed Vaali in battle at the bidding of Sugreeva, then installed Sugreeva (as king of monkeys) in the kingdom (of Kishkindha).

❍ ❍ ❍

७०. स च सर्वान् समानीय वानरान् वानरर्षभः ।
दिशः प्रस्थापयामास दिदृक्षुर्जनकात्मजाम् ।।

70. The noble monkey (Sugreeva, the "Bull" amongst monkeys), desirous of seeing (and finding) Seetha the daughter of Janaka, dispatched all the monkeys in all directions after summoning (them all).

❍ ❍ ❍

७१. ततो गृध्रस्य वचनात् संपातेर्हनुमान् बली ।
शतयोजनविस्तीर्णं पुप्लुवे लवणार्णवम् ।।

71. Then the strong Hanumaan, under the words of (advice) of vulture Sampaathi, crossed over 100 yojana-s (about 900 miles) over the ocean.

❍ ❍ ❍

७२. निवेदयित्वाऽभिज्ञानं प्रवृत्तिं च निवेद्य च ।
समाश्वास्य च वैदेहीं मर्दयामास तोरणम् ।।

72. Reaching the city of Lanka that was ruled by Raavana,

(Hanumaan) went to Asoka forest where he saw Seetha (pining away) in deep thought.

❍ ❍ ❍

७३. निवेदयित्वाऽभिज्ञानं प्रवृत्तिं च निवेद्य च ।
समाश्वास्य च वैदेहीं मर्दयामास तोरणम् ॥

73. (Disclosing his identity by) Delivering the token (of Remembrance given to him by Raama), informing her about the news and efforts (taken by Raama and others to find her and retrieve her), and after consoling (Seetha) the Vaidhehi, (Hanumaan), (single handedly) destroyed the Gates (of Lanka).

❍ ❍ ❍

७४. पञ्च सेनाग्रगान् हत्वा सप्त मन्त्रिसुतानपि ।
शूरमक्षं च निष्पिष्य ग्रहणं समुपागमत् ॥

74. (Hanumaan was the first to discover Seetha in captivity in Lanka; After consoling her, he plays havoc on Lanka before getting back to India to inform Sugreeva and Raama that he had found Seetha a prisoner in Raavana's Lanka).

Destroying five commanders (of Raavana) and also seven of his ministers and crushing the brave Aksha, he was (eventually) trapped (captured by Raavana's demons)

❍ ❍ ❍

७५. अस्त्रेणोन्मुक्तमात्मानं ज्ञात्वा पैतामहाद्वरात् ।
मर्षयन् राक्षसान् वीरो यन्त्रिणस्तान् यदृच्छया ॥

75. (But) The brave mighty monkey (Hanumaan), realising that he was spontaneously released (from shackles) by (the power of) weapons obtained as boon from God Bramma, forgave these demons who had bound him........ .

❍ ❍ ❍

७६. ततो दग्ध्वा पुरीं लमामृते सीतां च मैथिलीम् ।
रामाय प्रियमाख्यातुं पुनरायान्महाकपिः ।।

76. With ropes then he set fire to Lanka city without (harming) Seetha, the Maithili; and then after, returned (to India) to inform the happy (news) to Raama.

❍ ❍ ❍

७७. सोऽभिगम्य महात्मानं कृत्वा रामं प्रदक्षिणम् ।
न्यवेदयदमेयात्मा दृष्टा सीतेति तत्त्वतः ।।

77. (Returning and) approaching the great soul Raama and going round him in circumbumbulation, (Hanumaan) who possessed immense power, informed him=SEETHA SEEN=(by me; he said this and told him all) exactly (as it had happened during his visit to Lanka).

❍ ❍ ❍

७८. ततः सुग्रीवसहितो गत्वा तीरं महोदधेः ।
समुद्रं क्षोभयामास शरैरादित्यसन्निभैः ।।

78. Thereupon (Raama), along with Sugreeva, reached the sea coast (at southern tip of India) and shook up the ocean Mahodadhi with his powerful arrows that were like Sun's rays.

❍ ❍ ❍

७९. दर्शयामास चात्मानं समुद्रः सरितां पतिः ।
समुद्रवचनाच्चैव नलं सेतुमकारयत् ।।

79. The lord of rivers, the Ocean, showed himself up (to Raama); Under the words (of advice) of the ocean king, he built a bridge across the ocean with Nala's aid.

❍ ❍ ❍

८०. तेन गत्वा पुरीं लमां हत्वा रावणमाहवे ।
रामः सीतामनुप्राप्य परां व्रीडामुपागमत् ।।

80. Going over to Lanka over this (bridge), Raama then

killed Raavana in (a great) war and retrieved Seetha Then he became ashamed (of himself), a rare (sight in him).

(Quite understandable: for, as a husband, Raama was not sure of his wife who had lived long in Raavana's place away from him; Of course Seetha never gave encouragement to Raavana during her captivity).

❍ ❍ ❍

८१. तामुवाच ततो रामः परुषं जनसंसदि ।
अमृष्यमाणा सा सीता विवेश ज्वलनं सती ॥

81. Therefore Raama spoke harsh words (to Seetha) in front of the multitude. The pure (& virtuous) Seetha, unable to bear this, entered fire (to prove to the world her chastity).

❍ ❍ ❍

८२. ततोऽग्निवचनात् सीतां ज्ञात्वा विगतकल्मषाम् ।
बभौ रामः संप्रहृष्टः पूजितः सर्वदैवतैः ॥

82. (But Seetha comes out of fire, untouched by fire) By the words of Agni (Lord of fire), Seetha was (proved to be) without blemish; Raama realising this, became very joyous; he was honoured by all Dhevas.

❍ ❍ ❍

८३. कर्मणा तेन महता त्रैलोक्यं सचराचरम् ।
सदेवर्षिगणं तुष्टं राघवस्य महात्मनः ॥

83. By noble soul Raama's achievements, the three worlds comprising animate & inanimate objects (& hallowed by) multitude of Rishis, became happy (& tranquil).

❍ ❍ ❍

८४. अभिषिच्य च लमायां राक्षसेन्द्रं विभीषणम् ।
कृतकृत्यस्तदा रामो विज्वरः प्रमुमोद ह ॥

84. And Raama then appointed Vibheeshana in Lanka as lord of demons (to succeed Raavana) Having

completed the tasks undertaken, free from worries, (Raama) rejoiced (and became happy).

❍ ❍ ❍

८५. देवताभ्यो वरं प्राप्य समुत्थाप्य च वानरान् ।
अयोध्यां प्रस्थितो रामः पुष्पकेण सुहृद्वृतः ।।

85. Having received blessings (and boons) from various Dheva-s, he made the (dead) monkeys get up (from the battle field as they were lying down slain in the bloody war); And surrounded (& accompanied) by his friends, started back to Ayodhya (in India from Lanka) in Pushpak Aircraft-Station.

❍ ❍ ❍

८६. भरद्वाजाश्रमं गत्वा रामः सत्यपराक्रमः ।
भरतस्यान्तिकं रामो हनूमन्तं व्यसर्जयत् ।।

86. (Courageous) Raama who was truly valiant, reached the hermitage of (Sage) Bharadhwaj and he sent (in advance) Hanumaan to Bharatha's place (in Nandhigram near Ayodhya).

❍ ❍ ❍

८७. पुनराख्यायिकां जल्पन् सुग्रीवसहितस्तदा ।
पुष्पकं तत् समारुह्य नन्दिग्रामं ययौ तदा ।।

87. While flying in the Pushpak Airstation accompanied by Sugreeva, Raama reminisced about olden times; he reached Nandhigram.

❍ ❍ ❍

८८. नन्दिग्रामे जटां हित्वा भ्रातृभिः सहितोऽनघः ।
रामः सीतामनुप्राप्य राज्यं पुनरवाप्तवान् ।।

88. Along with his (three) brothers, the sinless Raama discarded his (forest style of) 'Hair do" at Nandigram; and along with Seetha, took back the kingdom (of Ayodhya from his brother Bharatha who had ruled during his 14 years exile).

❍ ❍ ❍

८९. प्रहृष्टमुदितो लोकस्तुष्टः पुष्टः सुधार्मिकः ।
निरामयो ह्यरोगश्च दुर्भिक्षभयवर्जितः ।।

89. (Naaradha continues the story: Talks about Raama's rule)

(Under his rule) People became thrilled (with joy); very happy; prosperous; free from mental & physical ailments; they were men of Dharma; were free from wants.

❍ ❍ ❍

९०. न पुत्रमरणं किञ्चिद्द्रक्ष्यन्ति पुरुषाः क्वचित् ।
नार्यश्चाविधवा नित्यं भविष्यन्ति पतिव्रताः ।।

90. Men never saw anywhere seeing their sons dead; women had no fear of losing their husbands; they were faithful to their husbands always.

❍ ❍ ❍

९१. न चाग्निजं भयं किञ्चिन्नाप्सु मज्जन्ति जन्तवः ।
न वातजं भयं किञ्चिन्नापि ज्वरकृतं तथा ।।

91. No fear of fire; no fear of drowning in waters; no fear from Air (typhoons); no fear of sickness (diseases).

❍ ❍ ❍

९२. न चापि क्षुद्भयं तत्र न तस्करभयं तथा ।।

92. No fear of starvation; no fear from robbers.

❍ ❍ ❍

९३. नगराणि च राष्ट्राणि धनधान्ययुतानि च ।
नित्यं प्रमुदिताः सर्वेयथा कृतयुगे तथा ।।

93. In villages and towns, the granaries were full with grains, food stuffs etc; like in Krithi Yuga, every one was happy always.

(Mythology says that the Age of Universe is: The Krithi yuga- 1,728,000: Thretha yuga:- 1,297,000: Dwaapara yuga-864,000 and Kali yuga-432,000: A total of 4,32 million years We are now in Kali yuga).

❍ ❍ ❍

९४. अश्वमेधशतैरिष्टा तथा बहुसुवर्णकैः ।
गवां कोट्ययुतं दत्त्वा ब्रह्मलोकं प्रयास्यति ।।

94. (Raama), by performing hundreds of Ashwamedha (Horse) Sacrifices, and likewise by offering gold, millions of cows etc during sacrifices, will (eventually) obtain the world of (God) Bramma...... .

❍ ❍ ❍

९५. असफ्ख्येयं धनं दत्त्वा ब्राह्मणेभ्यो महायशाः ।।

95. the most famous (Raama will go to heaven) having given gifts innumerous to Braamins (during his rule).

❍ ❍ ❍

९६. राजवंशञ्छतगुणान् स्थापयिष्यति राघवः ।
चातुर्वर्ण्यं च लोकेऽस्मिन् स्वे स्वे धर्मेनियोक्ष्यति ।।

96. (Raama will foster & develop his kingdom 100 times).

Raama the Raaghava, will increase the Royal dynasty 100 fold; And Raama will "yoke" every one amongst the four caste-s in their respective Dharma (duties) in this world.

(Readers may know that there are mainly four caste-s in India: A sort of division of labour The Braamin-teacher, priest etc: The Kshathriya- warrior, soldier, protector etc: The Vysya -Business class: And Schoodhra-the working class).

❍ ❍ ❍

९७. दशवर्षसहस्राणि दशवर्षशतानि च ।
रामो राज्यमुपासित्वा ब्रह्मलोकं प्रयास्यति ।।

97. Raama will rule for 10,000 years and yet another 1,000 years And then will obtain the world of Heaven- The Bramma Loka.

❍ ❍ ❍

९८. इदं पवित्रं पापघ्नं पुण्यं वेदैश्च संमितम् ।
यः पठेद्रामचरितं सर्वपापैः प्रमुच्यते ।।

98. (And Naaradha, after summarising the story of Raama, has this to say to Vaalmeeki who had sought enlightenment from him).

Whoever reads the history of Raama which is pure, which will bring forth goodness, which will destroy evil and which is comparable to Vedhas, will be released from all sins.

❍ ❍ ❍

९९. एतदाख्यानमायुष्यं पठन् रामायणं नरः ।
सपुत्रपौत्रः सगणः प्रेत्य स्वर्गेमहीयते ।।

99. Whoever reads this work of Raama's history which will give long life, will (live long enough) with his sons and grandsons and amongst good men; (When he departs from earth) discards his mortal body, will be honoured in heaven.

❍ ❍ ❍

१००. पठन् द्विजो वागृषभत्वमीयात् स्यात् क्षत्रियो भूमिपतित्वमीयात्।
वणिग्जनः पण्यफलत्वमीयाज्जनश्च शूद्रोऽपि महत्त्वमीयात् ।।

100. If a Braamin reads, he will become master of speech; If a Kshathriya reads, he will imbibe qualities of a ruler; If a Vysya reads, he will become prosperous in business; If a Schoodhra reads, he will attain stature.

(After being enlightened by Naaradha, Vaalmeeki wrote the Raamaayana with blessings of God Bramma).

❍ ❍ ❍

Chapter 2

God Bramma's Visit (HE appears before Vaalmeeki)

(Naaradha departs after enlightening Vaalmeeki about Raama: Vaalmeeki is enchanted; his interest in Raama is kindled; God Bramma appears before Vaalmeeki & blesses him).

❍ ❍ ❍

१. नारदस्य तु तद्वाक्यं श्रुत्वा वाक्यविशारदः ।
पूजयामास धर्मात्मा सहशिष्यो महामुनिः ।।

1. Having listened to these words from Naaradha, the great sage Vaalmeeki the noble soul (man of Dharma) who was proficient in speech, paid his respects to Naaradha along with his disciples.

❍ ❍ ❍

२. यथावत् पूजितस्तेन देवर्षिर्नारदस्तदा ।
आपृष्ट्वैवाभ्यनुज्ञातः स जगाम विहायसम् ।।

2. Then the divine sage Naaradha, after receiving due honours from him, went over to the sky, having said farewell & taken leave.

❍ ❍ ❍

३. स मुहूर्तं गते तस्मिन् देवलोकं मुनिस्तदा ।
जगाम तमसातीरं जाह्नव्यास्त्वविदूरतः ।।

3. Soon after (Naaradha) had reached the celestial world, the Muni (Vaalmeeki) reached the banks of Thamasa, not far from Ganges river.

❍ ❍ ❍

४. स तु तीरं समासाद्य तमसाया मुनिस्तदा ।
शिष्यमाह स्थितं पार्श्वे दृष्ट्वा तीर्थमकर्दमम् ।।

4. Standing on the banks of Thamasa river, the sage (Vaalmeeki), observing the purity of its waters,

remarked to his disciple who was standing close (to him).

❍ ❍ ❍

५. अकर्दममिदं तीर्थं भरद्वाज निशामय ।
रमणीयं प्रसन्नाम्बु सन्मनुष्यमनो यथा ।।

5. Oh Bharadhwaj! See this beautiful bathing place; With pure clear waters, like the heart of a pure man.

(Bharadhwaj, not to be confused with Sage Bharadhwaj).

❍ ❍ ❍

६. न्यस्यतां कलशस्तात दीयतां वल्कलं मम ।
इदमेवावगाहिष्ये तमसातीर्थमुत्तमम् ।।

6. Oh (Bharadhwaj): Keep down the water pitcher; let me have my (bathing costume) of Bark material; I am going to have bath in this foremost Thamasa waters.

❍ ❍ ❍

७. एवमुक्तो भरद्वाजो वाल्मीकेन महात्मना ।
प्रायच्छत मुनेस्तस्य वल्कलं नियतो गुरोः ।।

7. When told thus by the great soul Vaalmeeki, Bharadhwaj who was devoted to his Guru (teacher Vaalmeeki), handed over the dress (made) of bark materials.

❍ ❍ ❍

८. स शिष्यहस्तादादाय वल्कलं नियतेन्द्रियः ।
विचचार ह पश्यंस्तत् सर्वतो विपुलं वनम् ।।

8. (Vaalmeeki) the conqueror of passion & senses, took the costume from the hands of his disciple and wandered happily, looking on all sides of the vast forest.

❍ ❍ ❍

९. तस्याभ्याशे तु मिथुनं चरन्तमनपायिनम् ।
ददर्श भगवांस्तत्र क्रौञ्चयोश्चारुनिस्वनम् ।।

9. The Lord (Vaalmeeki) saw nearby, two Kraunchi birds,

a pair of male & female birds with sweet voice, roaming about there & very close together (making love).

❍ ❍ ❍

१०. तस्मात्तु मिथुनादेकं पुमांसं पापनिश्चयः ।
जघान वैरनिलयो निषादस्तस्य पश्यतः ।।

10. (At that moment) A sinful & inimical hunter, marking out the male (bird) from the couple, 'shot' it dead, even as he was looking on.

❍ ❍ ❍

११. तं शोणितपरीताङ्गं वेष्टमानं महीतले ।
भार्या तु निहतं दृष्ट्वा रुराव करुणां गिरम् ।।

11. The female bird, seeing (the male partner) fallen down on earth & rolling over with blood besmeared on its body, began to wail pitiably.

❍ ❍ ❍

१२. वियुक्ता पतिना तेन द्विजेन सहचारिणा ।
ताम्रशीर्षेण मत्तेन पत्रिणा सहितेन वै ।।

12. The (female bird) with copper hued wings & robust body, was thus separated from this bird, its companion, lover, and lord.

❍ ❍ ❍

१३. तथा तु तं द्विजं दृष्ट्वा निषादेन निपातितम् ।
ऋषेर्धर्मात्मनस्तस्य कारुण्यं समपद्यत ।।

13. On seeing the fallen bird felled by the hunter, great compassion (pity) seized the great soul sage (Vaalmeeki, the Dharma-Aathma).

❍ ❍ ❍

१४. ततः करुणवेदित्वादधर्मोऽयमिति द्विजः ।
निशाम्य रुदतीं क्रौञ्चीमिदं वचनमब्रवीत् ।।

14. Out of compassion, the Braamin (Vaalmeeki), facing the sobbing female bird, addressed thus:=This is not

Dharma = (This unnecessary killing) And further said these words.

❍ ❍ ❍

१५. मा निषाद प्रतिष्ठां त्वमगमः शाश्वतीः समाः ।
यत्क्रौञ्चमिथुनादेकमवधीः काममोहितम् ।।
(मानिषाद प्रतिष्ठां त्वमगमः शाश्वतीः समाः ।
यत् क्रौञ्चमिथुनादेकमवधीः काममोहितम् ।।)

15. (And to the hunter, he said): Oh Hunter! When the Krauncha bird was making love & was stupefied by passion (of love) you killed this one Therefore you will not live long (You will not dwell for many seasons in this world) (This is repeated by Vaalmeeki: The Sanskrit version is).

Maanishaadha Prathishtaam Thwam Agamaha Shaashwathi Samaaha Yath Krauncha Mithunaath Ekam Avadheehi Kaama Mohitham (The meaning is the same as in stanza above).

❍ ❍ ❍

१६. तस्यैवं ब्रुवतश्चिन्ता बभूव हृदि वीक्षतः ।
शोकार्तेनास्य शकुनेः किमिदं व्याहृतं मया ।।

16. =What is this that was uttered by me who is afflicted by grief over this bird = Such a thought seized his mind who told (& repeated) this stanza, looking (at the wailing bird).

❍ ❍ ❍

१७. चिन्तयन् स महाप्राज्ञश्चकार मतिमान् मतिम् ।
शिष्यं चैवाब्रवीद्वाक्यमिदं स मुनिपुङ्गवः ।।

17. The very wise & sacred (Vaalmeeki) began to ponder in his mind; This "tiger" amongst sages, (this Vaalmeeki) repeated these words (of poetry) to his disciple.

❍ ❍ ❍

१८. पादबद्धोऽक्षरसमस्तन्त्रीलयसमन्वितः ।
शोकार्तस्य प्रवृत्तो मे श्लोको भवतु नान्यथा ।।

18. "May the words that have come out from me out of grief, may these words with proper syllables, may these words with proper meter and rhyme like (the musical instrument) Veena which carries music & rhythm in its strings, be verily Sloka (Poetry): It is nothing else."

(Vaalmeeki could never get over it; How could he have "composed" poetry when he knew his limitations But what he told this hunter was no prose but poetry The answer to this was given by God Bramma who appears before him to affirm that it was poetry This was the turning point & Vaalmeeki became first amongst poets when he wrote the Epic Raamaayana in poetry).

❍ ❍ ❍

१९. शिष्यस्तु तस्य ब्रुवतो मुनेर्वाक्यमनुत्तमम् ।
प्रतिजग्राहं संहृष्टस्तस्य तुष्टोऽभवद्गुरुः ।।

19. The disciple also started learning this (by repeating it) happily when this sage (Vaalmeeki) uttered the foremost (words); And his teacher (Guru Vaalmeeki) became pleased with him.

(To a teacher his student should appreciate what he says!)

❍ ❍ ❍

२०. सोऽभिषेकं ततः कृत्वा तीर्थे तस्मिन् यथाविधि ।
तमेव चिन्तयन्नर्थमुपावर्तत वै मुनिः ।।

20. After bathing in waters as per norms, the Muni (Vaalmeeki) kept on thinking and returned (to his hermitage).

❍ ❍ ❍

२१. भरद्वाजस्ततः शिष्यो विनीतः श्रुतवान् मुनिः ।
कलशं पूर्णमादाय पृष्ठतोऽनुजगाम ह ।।

21. Highly educated and knowledgeable in Shaasthra-s (Holy Texts etc), this disciple, Muni Bharadhwaj, followed his master, carrying pot full (of water).

❍ ❍ ❍

२२. स प्रविश्याश्रमपदं शिष्येण सह धर्मवित् ।
उपविष्टः कथाश्चान्याश्चकार ध्यानमास्थितः ।।

22. This knower of Dharma (Vaalmeeki), entered the hermitage along with his disciple and sat down, started meditation and then began study of various (holy) Texts.

❍ ❍ ❍

२३. आजगाम ततो ब्रह्मा लोककर्ता स्वयं प्रभुः ।
चतुर्मुखो महातेजा द्रष्टुं तं मुनिपुङ्गवम् ।।

23. At that moment, God Bramma the creator of The Worlds, this most brilliant Lord with four faces, Himself came to see the noble sage (Vaalmeeki), who was a "tiger" amongst sages.

❍ ❍ ❍

२४. वाल्मीकिरथ तं दृष्ट्वा सहसोत्थाय वाग्यतः ।
प्राञ्जलिः प्रणतो भूत्वा तस्थौ परमविस्मितः ।।

24. (When good and noble men are agitated The Lord appears before them in many ways; God Bramma appears before Vaalmeeki).

Greatly surprised on seeing Him there, Vaalmeeki got up at once He stood there with his arms cupped in Anjali, modestly restraining himself to a few words (of Greetings).

❍ ❍ ❍

२५. पूजयामास तं देवं पाद्यार्घ्यासनवन्दनैः ।
प्रणम्य विधिवच्चैनं पृष्ट्वाऽनामयमव्ययम् ।।

25. He honoured this celestial (God Bramma) with (traditional hospitality of) Arghya, Paadhya and

offered Him a seat Bowing before Him as per norms, he enquired about His Eternal Welfare.

❍ ❍ ❍

२६. अथोपविश्य भगवानासने परमार्चिते ।
वाल्मीकये महर्षये संदिदेशासनं ततः ॥

26. After the Lord (Bramma) who was greatly worshipped by (Vaalmeeki) had sat down in his seat, God directed the great sage Vaalmeeki to a seat.

❍ ❍ ❍

२७. ब्रह्मणा समनुज्ञातः सोऽप्युपाविशदासने ॥

27. So ordered by God Bramma, (Vaalmeeki) also sat in a seat.

❍ ❍ ❍

२८. उपविष्टे तदा तस्मिन् साक्षाल्लोकपितामहे ।
तद्गतेनैव मनसा वाल्मीकिर्ध्यानमास्थितः ॥

28. (Even) While The Father of The Universe (Bramma) was sitting (before him), in His very presence, Vaalmeeki went into (a state of) deep thinking, with his mind engrossed (in the bird affair).

❍ ❍ ❍

२९. पापात्मना कृतं कष्टं वैरग्रहणबुद्धिना ।
यस्तादृशं चारुरवं क्रौञ्चं हन्यादकारणात् ॥

29. (Vaalmeeki's thoughts never left him even before God!)

(He thought): By an evil minded (hunter) whose mind was seized with hostility, this cruelty was inflicted; Who will (have the heart to) kill such a sweet voiced Kraunchi bird without reason.

❍ ❍ ❍

३०. शोचन्नेव मुहुः क्रौञ्चीमुप श्लोकमिमं पुनः ।
जगावन्तर्गतमना भूत्वा शोकपरायणः ॥

30. Permeated by grief, his mind grieving over (the fate of

the) female bird, he repeated the stanza for sometime in his mind (totally oblivious of the presence of God Bramma).

❍ ❍ ❍

३१. तमुवाच ततो ब्रह्मा प्रहसन् मुनिपुङ्गवम् ।
श्लोक एव त्वया बद्धो नात्र कार्या विचारणा ।।

31. Then God Bramma said to this foremost (Vaalmeeki) who was a "tiger" amongst sages, smilingly: = What was composed by you is indeed Sloka (Poetry); In this matter (over the fate of the bird) no purpose will be served by (your) pondering = (Dont brood, because a great task awaits you, says God Bramma to Vaalmeeki. You have become a poet!)

❍ ❍ ❍

३२. मच्छन्दादेव ते ब्रह्मन् प्रवृत्तेयं सरस्वती ।
रामस्य चरितं सर्वं कुरु त्वमृषिसत्तम ।।

32. Oh Braamin (Oh Vaalmeeki): Your, these words (of Poetry) came (out of your mouth) as per my wish (& my Grace) Oh noble Rishi! You undertake (to render) The Entire History of Raama.

❍ ❍ ❍

३३. धर्मात्मनो गुणवतो लोके रामस्य धीमतः ।
वृत्तं कथय धीरस्य यथा ते नारदाच्छ्रुतम् ।।

33. The history of this wise noble soul brave Raama who is endowed with (great) qualities in this world, was heard by you from Naaradha. Just (as you heard) you narrate (in detail).

❍ ❍ ❍

३४. रहस्यं च प्रकाशं च यद्वृत्तं तस्य धीमतः ।
रामस्य सहसौमित्रे राक्षसानां च सर्वशः ।।

34. The known & unknown (to you) about the story of the

wise Raama who is (ever) with (Lakshmana) the son of Sumithra, the story about the demons and all........ .

❍ ❍ ❍

३५. वैदेह्याश्चैव यद्वृत्तं प्रकाशं यदि वा रहः ।
तच्चाप्यविदितं सर्वं विदितं ते भविष्यति ।।

35. Likewise the known & unknown (to you) about the story of (Seetha the) Vaidhehi, (all these) will become known to you even if you do not know them all (as you start writing this History).

❍ ❍ ❍

३६. न ते वागनृता काव्ये काचिदत्र भविष्यति ।
कुरु रामकथां पुण्यां श्लोकबद्धां मनोरमाम् ।।

36. In this (your) Epic, words will never but be True (to history) May you do the holy story of Raama in Sloka (Poetry) of pleasing style.

❍ ❍ ❍

३७. यावत् स्थास्यन्ति गिरयः सरितश्च महीतले ।
तावद्रामायणकथा लोकेषु प्रचरिष्यति ।।

37. Your work of Raamaayana will reach all parts of the globe; will extend to wherever there are rivers & mountains (and all till they exist).

❍ ❍ ❍

३८. यावद्रामस्य च कथा त्वत्कृता प्रचरिष्यति ।
तावदूर्ध्वमधश्च त्वं मल्लोकेषु निवत्स्यसि ।।

38. As long as The Raamaayana done by you shines, your (name) will ever live in my worlds, up & down (Heaven & Earth).

❍ ❍ ❍

३९. इत्युक्त्वा भगवान् ब्रह्मा तत्रैवान्तरधीयत ।
ततः सशिष्यो भगवान् मुनिर्विस्मयमाययौ ।।

39. Having said thus, God Bramma soon left (disappeared);

At that moment the sage (Vaalmeeki) who was with his disciples, was astounded.

(God Bramma wants Vaalmeeki to write The Epic for posterity; As Bramma's grace will be on Vaalmeeki, the entire History of Raama will reveal itself to Vaalmeeki as he begins his work; And God Bramma admonishes Vaalmeeki when he wastes too much grief on the Krauncha bird).

❍ ❍ ❍

४०. तस्य शिष्यास्ततः सर्वेजगुः श्लोकमिमं पुनः ।
मुहुर्मुहुः प्रीयमाणाः प्राहुश्च भृशविस्मिताः ॥

40. And all his disciples who were all amazed, uttered this stanza again and again. They also sang the stanza in sheer delight.

❍ ❍ ❍

४१. समाक्षरैश्चतुर्भिर्यः पादैर्गीतो महात्मना ।
सोऽनुव्याहरणाद्भूयः शोकः श्लोकत्वमागतः ॥

41. When that (Stanza) which was set to four meter scale & which had equal number of syllables, was recited by the great soul (Vaalmeeki), this grief (of his over the Krauncha bird), turned into sheer poetry when it was uttered repeatedly.

❍ ❍ ❍

४२. तस्य बुद्धिरियं जाता वाल्मीकेर्भावितात्मनः ।
कृत्स्नं रामायणं काव्यमीदृशैः करवाण्यहम् ॥

42. This decision = I Must Do This Epic of Raamaayana Like This = arose in Vaalmeeki, whose soul was purified thinking about* The Universal Soul (*Bhaavithaathamana).

❍ ❍ ❍

४३. उदारवृत्तार्थपदैर्मनोरमैस्तदस्य रामस्य चकार कीर्तिमान् ।
समाक्षरैः श्लोकशतैर्यशस्विनो यशस्करं काव्यमुदारधीर्मुनिः ॥

43. The famous & exalted Muni (Vaalmeeki) expounded & spread the famous Raama's Epic Poem that highlighted (Raama's) fame, in numerous delightful stanzas, couched with proper syllables, full of meaning, foremost anecdotes, & in proper meter.

❍ ❍ ❍

४४. तद्रुपगतसमाससन्धियोगं सममधुरोपनतार्थवाक्यबद्धम् ।
रघुवरचरितं मुनिप्रणीतं दशशिरसश्च वधं निशामयध्वम् ॥

44. May you (make all) listen to this Epic about the foremost (Raama) the Raaghava that is expounded by the Muni (Vaalmeeki) with proper sweet words full of meaning, with proper conjunction of words, well combined and which (describes also) the killing of the ten headed (Raavana).

❍ ❍ ❍

Chapter 3

Vaalmeeki perceives the History of Raama:

(By the Grace of God Bramma Vaalmeeki is able to perceive the entire history of Raama through his spiritual power).

❍ ❍ ❍

१. श्रुत्वा वस्तु समग्रं तद्धर्मात्मा धर्मसंहितम् ।
व्यक्तमन्वेषते भूयो यद्वृत्तं तस्य धीमतः ॥

1. Hearing the essence of the story of Raama that is full of Dharma totally, the noble soul (Vaalmeeki) investigated further and further to know clearly about this story, (this history) of the wise (Raama).

❍ ❍ ❍

२. उपस्पृश्योदकं सम्यग्मुनिः स्थित्वा कृताञ्जलिः ।
प्राचीनाग्रेषु दर्भेषु धर्मेणान्वेषते गतिम् ॥

2. Muni (Vaalmeeki) sipped water as per norms, sitting on Dharbha grass (mat) whose ends were pointed towards the east Cupping his hands in Anjali, he investigated (& meditated) upon the efficacy (& power) through Dharma.

❍ ❍ ❍

३. रामलक्ष्मणसीताभी राज्ञा दशरथेन च ।
सभार्येण सराष्ट्रेण यत्प्राप्तं तत्र तत्त्वतः ।।

3. What all was obtained by King Dhascharatha along with his wives, and with Raama & Lakshmana and Seetha and with his subjects, the true state of affairs.......

❍ ❍ ❍

४. हसितं भाषितं चैव गतिर्या यच्च चेष्टितम् ।
तत्सर्वं धर्मवीर्येण यथावत् संप्रपश्यति ।।

4. The laughter, the conversations, (the Government &) other activities, his movements all these he perceived as one who could perceive through the power of Dharma.

(History of Raama slowly "unfolds" before Vaalmeeki).

❍ ❍ ❍

५. स्त्रीतृतीयेन च तदा यत्प्राप्तं चरता वने ।
सत्यसन्धेन रामेण तत्सर्वं चान्ववैक्षत ।।

5. At that time (Vaalmeeki) perceived all that was obtained by the man of Truth, Raama, who was roaming about the forest with his wife (Seetha), as the third (in the three some group that went on exile).

❍ ❍ ❍

६. ततः पश्यति धर्मात्मा तत्सर्वं योगमास्थितः ।
पुरा यत्तत्र निर्वृत्तं पाणावामलकं यथा ।।

6. And further, the noble soul (Vaalmeeki), the man of Dharma who was in a state of Yoga (meditation), saw everything that happened to them before, like seeing a

small (Aamalaka) fruit in his palm (Like Action Replay in TV!).

❍ ❍ ❍

७. तत्सर्वं तत्त्वतो दृष्ट्वा धर्मेण स महाद्युतिः ।
अभिरामस्य रामस्य चरितं कर्तुमुद्यतः ।।

7. This most illustrious (Vaalmeeki) seeing all those that had happened, by the power of his) Dharma, became stimulated to do the (full) story of Raama, (the Raama) who delights...... .

❍ ❍ ❍

८. कामार्थगुणसंयुक्तं धर्मार्थगुणविस्तरम् ।
समुद्रमिव रत्नाढ्यं सर्वश्रुतिमनोहरम् ।।

8. (Vaalmeeki decides to write the Story) that was full of substance, character, passion, that was sweet on the ears of all, that was like ocean full of pearls and which was characterised by Kaama (passion) and Artha (substance).

❍ ❍ ❍

९. यथावत् कथितं पूर्वं नारदेन महर्षिणा ।
रघुवंशस्य चरितं चकार भगवानृषिः ।।

9. The Rishi (Vaalmeeki), this lord, as he had been told =earlier (and enlightened) by the great sage Naaradha, expounded the story of the dynasty of Raghu-s ..... .

❍ ❍ ❍

१०. जन्म रामस्य सुमहद्वीर्यं सर्वानुकूलताम् ।
लोकस्य प्रियतां क्षान्तिं सौम्यतां सत्यशीलताम् ।।

10. (The story) of the great birth of Raama, his valour, likewise his friendly disposition to all; his endearment with (citizens of) the world, his serene sweet temperament, his truthfulness, his indulgence (& forbearance).

❍ ❍ ❍

११. नानाविधाः कथाश्चान्या विश्वामित्रसमागमे ।
जानक्याश्च विवाहं च धनुषो भेदनं तथा ।।

11. (Vaalmeeki contemplates about Raama's history; many events about the history reveal itself; Stanzas 10 to 39 describe some of the important events in this history; events that crosses his mind).

❍ ❍ ❍

१२. रामरामविवादं च गुणान् दाशरथेस्तथा ।
तथाऽभिषेकं रामस्य कैकेय्या दुष्टभावताम् ।।

12. Confrontation between Raama & ParashuRaama; The qualities of (his father) Dhascharatha; Likewise, the anointment of Raama (as crown prince that did not take place), Kaikeyi's wickedness.

❍ ❍ ❍

१३. विघातं चाभिषेकस्य रामस्य च विवासनम् ।
राज्ञः शोकविलापं च परलोकस्य चाश्रयम् ।।

13. The failure (and impediments to) the crowning ceremony; Raama's exile; The King (Dhascharatha's) wailing (over Raama's exile and consequently) his death (and going over to heaven).

❍ ❍ ❍

१४. प्रकृतीनां विषादं च प्रकृतीनां विसर्जनम् ।
निषादाधिपसंवादं सूतोपावर्तनं तथा ।।

14. The people's sorrow; People turned back (from following Raama); The charioteer being sent back (by Raama); His conversation with (his friend Guha), the chief of hunters.

❍ ❍ ❍

१५. गङ्गायाश्चापि तरणं भरद्वाजस्य दर्शनम् ।
भारद्वाजाभ्यनुज्ञानाच्चित्रकूटस्य दर्शनम् ।।

15. The crossing over river Ganges; His meeting sage

Bharadhwaj; Under advice of Bharadhwaaj, his visit to Chithrakoot.

❍ ❍ ❍

१६. वास्तुकर्म निवेशं च भरतागमनं तथा ।
प्रसादनं च रामस्य पितुश्च सलिलक्रियाम् ॥

16. Construction of abode (at Chithrakoot) and his stay: Bharatha's visit; Raama's tranquility (and grace); His performance of water Rituals (for his dead father).

❍ ❍ ❍

१७. पादुकाग्र्याभिषेकं च नन्दिग्रामनिवासनम् ।
दण्डकारण्यगमनं विराधस्य वधं तथा ॥

17. (Raama's) Sandals being anointed (by Bharatha) who stays (and establishes a temporary capital) at Nandhigram (near Ayodhya): (Raama) going to Dhandakaaranya (forest); The killing of Viraadha.

❍ ❍ ❍

१८. दर्शनं शरभङ्गस्य सुतीक्ष्णेन समागमम् ।
अनसूयासमस्यां च अङ्गरागस्य चार्पणम् ॥

18. His seeing Scharabhanga; and meeting with Sutheekshana; Their stay with Anasooya & offer of Sandal paste.

❍ ❍ ❍

१९. अगस्त्यदर्शनं चैव दर्शनं च जटायुषः ॥

19. Meeting with sage Agasthya: His seeing (big bird) Jataayu.

❍ ❍ ❍

२०. शूर्पणख्याश्च संवादं विरूपकरणं तथा ।
वधं खरत्रिशिरसोरुत्थानं रावणस्य च ॥

20. Encounter with Schoorpanaka; Like wise, his maiming of her; Killing of (demons) Khara & Thrischiras; Raavana's efforts.

❍ ❍ ❍

२१. मारीचस्य वधं चैव वैदेह्या हरणं तथा ।
राघवस्य विलापं च गृध्रराजनिबर्हणम् ।।

21. The killing of Maareecha; likewise the abduction of (his wife Seetha the) Vaidhehi: (Raama, the) Raaghava's wailing The king of birds (Jataayu's) death.

❍ ❍ ❍

२२. कबन्धदर्शनं चैव पंपायाश्चापि दर्शनम् ।
शबर्या दर्शनं चैव हनूमद्दर्शनं तथा ।।

22. His seeing (demon) Kabhandha; Seeing the river Pampa His meeting with Schabari; Likewise his meeting Hanumaan.

❍ ❍ ❍

२३. विलापं चैव पंपायां राघवस्य महात्मनः ।।

23. The great soul (Raama the) Raaghava's wailing at Pampa.

❍ ❍ ❍

२४. ऋश्यमूकस्य गमनं सुग्रीवेण समागमम् ।
प्रत्ययोत्पादनं सख्यं वालिसुग्रीवविग्रहम् ।।

24. His visit to Rischyamukh; His association with Sugreeva; Building confidence (in Sugreeva) and forming friendship with him; Combat between Vaali & Sugreeva.

❍ ❍ ❍

२५. वालिप्रमथनं चैव सुग्रीवप्रतिपादनम् ।
ताराविलापं समयं वर्षरात्रनिवासनम् ।।

25. Destruction of Vaali; The restoration (of kingdom) to Sugreeva: (Vaali's wife) Thaara's wailing; The agreement & stay (and the inactivity) during the rainy season.

❍ ❍ ❍

२६. कोपं राघवसिंहस्य बलानामुपसंग्रहम् ।
दिशः प्रस्थापनं चैव पृथिव्याश्च निवेदनम् ।।

26. The wrath of (Raama) the "Lion" amongst Raghu-s; Assembly of the Army (of monkeys & bears) Despatch of (various) armies (to various places) in various directions (for the search of Seetha); The description of the Earth (The Globe).

❍ ❍ ❍

२७. अङ्गुलीयकदानं च ऋक्षस्य बिलदर्शनम् ।
प्रायोपवेशनं चैव संपातेश्चापि दर्शनम् ।।

27. The Giving of the Ring (The Insignia of Raama); The sight of the caves of Riksha mountain (The resolution of monkeys) to fast unto death (unable to find Seetha) The meeting with Sampaathi.

❍ ❍ ❍

२८. पर्वतारोहणं चापि सागरस्य च लङ्घनम् ।
समुद्रवचनाच्चैव मैनाकस्य च दर्शनम् ।।

28. The climbing of the mountain & the crossing over (flying over) the ocean (by Hanumaan); By the words (of advice) of the King of Oceans, the sighting of Mainika mountain (by Hanumaan).

❍ ❍ ❍

२९. राक्षसीतर्जनं चैव छायाग्राहस्य दर्शनम् ।
सिंहिकायाश्च निधनं लमामलयदर्शनम् ।।
रात्रौ लङ्काप्रवेशं च एकस्यापि विचिन्तनम् ।।

29. The threats of demoness; The seizure by the shadow (of demoness); The sight (of this demoness by Hanumaan), the killing of Simhika; The (first glimpse &) sight of Malaya mountain (by Hanumaan); His entry into Lanka at night; The perceptions of one, (of this Hanumaan), who was all by himself (at Lanka).

❍ ❍ ❍

३०. आपानभूमिगमनमवरोधस्य दर्शनम् ।
दर्शनं रावणस्यापि पुष्पकस्य च दर्शनम् ।।

30. (Hanumaan's) sight of Banquet hall (of Lanka palace); His seeing of the Inner apartments (of the palace); Seeing Pushpak (the Aircraft-Space Station) of Raavana.

❍ ❍ ❍

३१. अशोकवनिकायानं सीतायाश्चापि दर्शनम् ।
अभिज्ञानप्रदानं च रावणस्य च दर्शनम् ।।

31. (Hanumaan's) Visit to Asoka forest; His seeing (& meeting) of Seetha there; His handing over the (Signet Ring) the token of remembrance, (to Seetha); His seeing Raavana there.

❍ ❍ ❍

३२. राक्षसीतर्जनं चैव त्रिजटास्वप्नदर्शनम् ।
अभिज्ञानप्रदानं च सीतायाश्चाभिभाषणम् ।।

32. The threats of the demonesses; The Dream of Thrijaata; The bestowal of the ring of remembrance; Conversation with Seetha.

❍ ❍ ❍

३३. मणिप्रदानं सीताया वृक्षभङ्गं तथैव च ।
राक्षसीविद्रवं चैव किमराणां निबर्हणम् ।।

33. The handing over the Ornament (Choodaamani) by Seetha; (Hanumaan's) Destruction of big trees; The fleeing of demonesses (in fright); The destruction of attendants.

❍ ❍ ❍

३४. ग्रहणं वायूसूनोश्च लमादाहाभिगर्जनम् ।।

34. The Binding of (Hanumaan) the 'son' of Lord of Wind; The Burning up of (part of) Lanka (by Hanumaan); His roar.

❍ ❍ ❍

३५. प्रतिप्लवनमेवाथ मधूनां हरणं तथा ।
राघवाश्वासनं चैव बलनिर्यातनं तथा ।।

35. The Flying back (to India from Lanka by Hanumaan); The ravishing of Honeys (and honey bearing trees); The consoling of (Raama the) Raaghava; The march of the Army (of monkeys to make war with Lanka).

The Reaching of the Ocean (at the tip of India by the army) The construction of bridge (across ocean with the aid) of Nala The association with Vibheeshana; The efforts taken for destruction of demons (of Lanka: the planning of war).

❍ ❍ ❍

३६. सङ्गमं च समुद्रेण नलसेतोश्च बन्धनम् ।
विभीषणेन संसर्गं वधोपायनिवेदनम् ।।
प्रतारं च समुद्रस्य रात्रौ लमावरोधनम् ।।

36. The crossing over the ocean and the siege of Lanka at night.

❍ ❍ ❍

३७. कुम्भकर्णस्य निधनं मेघनादनिबर्हणम् ।।
रावणस्य विनाशं च सीतावाप्तिमरेः पुरे ।
३८. विभीषणाभिषेकं च पुष्पकारोहणं तथा ।।
अयोध्यायाश्च गमनं भरतेन समागमम् ।
३९. रामाभिषेकाभ्युदयं सर्वसैन्यविसर्जनम् ।।
स्वराष्ट्ररञ्जनं चैव वैदेह्याश्च विसर्जनम् ।।

37-39:

The killing of Kumbhakarna & killing of Meghanaadha; The destruction of Raavana; The retrieval of Seetha; The coronation of Vibheeshana; The riding of Pushpak Aircraft Space Station (to get back to Ayodhya from Lanka) The return to Ayodhya; The meeting (of Raama) with Bharatha: The grand coronation of Raama; The sending back of (the vast monkey army) The happiness in his kingdom; likewise (Seetha the) Vaidhehi's banishment (later on).

❍ ❍ ❍

४०. अनागतं च यत्किञ्चिद्रामस्य वसुधातले ।
तच्चकारोत्तरे काव्ये वाल्मीकिर्भगवानृषिः ।।

40. And the Lord Rishi Vaalmeeki (even) wrote about whatever was yet to happen in this world in Raama's history, in the Uthara Kaanda.

(Enlightened by Naaradha & blessed by God Bramma, Vaalmeeki is able to perceive the entire story of Raama. In the above chapter, some major events in the History which he "saw" through his spiritual power, is listed at random. The first four chapters are a prelude. The Epic, Vaalmeeki's Raamaayana, begins from 5th Chapter.).

❍ ❍ ❍

Chapter 4

The Arrival of Lava & Kuscha in Raama's Court (Council Hall)

(Lava & Kuscha, the two sons of Raama who grew up in hermitage of sages, sing Vaalmeeki Raamaayana: This was how Vaalmeeki's Raamaayana was popularised. Incidentally, Raama was not aware that these two boys were his children as his wife Seetha had given birth to them in a hermitage & not in Ayodhya, as she had been banished from Ayodhya owing to a misunderstanding because of Raama. He had been ruling Ayodhya for quite some time).

❍ ❍ ❍

१. प्राप्तराज्यस्य रामस्य वाल्मीकिर्भगवानृषिः ।
चकार चरितं कृत्स्नं विचित्रपदमात्मवान् ।।

1. The Lord, the sage Vaalmeeki the self reliant, did this entire Epic of Raama who had got his kingdom back (from his brother Bharatha), with wonderful words & expressions.

❍ ❍ ❍

२. चतुर्विंशत्सहस्राणि श्लोकानामुक्तवानृषिः ।
तथा सर्गशतान् पञ्च षट्काण्डानि तथोत्तरम् ।।

2. The sage (Vaalmeeki) narrated (the Epic) in 24,000 stanzas, covering them in 500 chapters (sargams) in 6 Volumes (Cantos); he also narrated Uthara Kaanda.

(The Uthara kaanda gives details of life after Raama was crowned king of Ayodhya: This work does not cover Uthara Kaanda).

❍ ❍ ❍

३. कृत्वाऽपि तन्महाप्राज्ञः सभविष्यं सहोत्तरम् ।
चिन्तयामास को न्वेतत् प्रयुञ्जीयादिति प्रभुः ।।

3. Having completed this (Epic) along with the great (work of) Uthara (kaanda) which (foresaw even) future events, the most intelligent (Vaalmeeki) began to worry; = Which able person can recite (all) this (work of mine)? =

(Vaalmeeki was worried as to who will popularise his work- Like finding a good publisher in modern times!).

❍ ❍ ❍

४. तस्य चिन्तयमानस्य महर्षेर्भावितात्मनः ।
अगृह्णीतां ततः पादौ मुनिवेषौ कुशीलवौ ।।

4. Then (at that place), Kuscha & Lava who were in ascetic robes, prostrated at the feet of this great sage Vaalmeeki who had realised 'The Soul' through meditation of The Supreme, and who was worrying about this (about popularising his Raamaayana).

❍ ❍ ❍

५. कुशीलवौ तु धर्मज्ञौ राजपुत्रौ यशस्विनौ ।
भ्रातरौ स्वरसंपन्नौ ददर्शाश्रमवासिनौ ।।

5. And he saw the brothers Lava & Kuscha, the two princes who were famous brothers, who knew Dharma, who

were endowed with good voice & who were living in a hermitage (nearby).

❍ ❍ ❍

६. स तु मेधाविनौ दृष्ट्वा वेदेषु परिनिष्ठितौ ।
वेदोपबृंहणार्थाय तावग्राहयत प्रभुः ॥

6. (Readers should know that the two boys did not know at that time that Raama was their father; of course Raama did not know either).

Seeing these two who were masters of Vedha and (highly) skilled, this lord (Vaalmeeki) went into meditation (& pondered over the) desirability of expounding this Vedha & its substance.

(Readers must remember—Indians consider Raamaayana a Vedha, not just history of a king).

❍ ❍ ❍

७. काव्यं रामायणं कृत्स्नं सीतायाश्चरितं महत् ।
पौलस्त्यवधमित्येव चकार चरितव्रतः ॥

7. The austere (Vaalmeeki), then did the work of the entire Epic in Poetic Form, the great story of Raama, the story of Seetha and the destruction of (Raavana) of the Pulasthya family.

❍ ❍ ❍

८. पाठ्ये गेये च मधुरं प्रमाणैस्त्रिभिरन्वितम् ।
जातिभिः सप्तभिर्बद्धं तन्त्रीलयसमन्वितम् ॥

8. (Lava & Kuscha learn the Epic from Vaalmeeki and they set it to Music).

Whether read or sung, the Epic from Vaalmeeki was sweet (& musical) like (the strains) from (Musical instrument the) Veena which has 7 strings fixed on it with three side strings, rhythm coming out from them.

❍ ❍ ❍

९. हास्यश्रृङ्गारकरुणवीररौद्रभयानकैः ।
बीभत्सादिरसैर्युक्तं काव्यमेतदगायताम् ।।

9. They sang the Epic that was endowed with qualities of: Schringaara (Pleasure & Romance); Karuna (Compassion); Veera (Valour); Roudhra (Wrath); Bhaayaanaka (Fear etc.); Haasya (Laughter, joy); Bheebhatsa (Revulsion, disgust).

(The 7 qualities poetically compared to 7 strings of Veena).

❍ ❍ ❍

१०. तौ तु गन्धर्वतत्त्वज्ञौ मूर्च्छनास्थानकोविदौ ।
भ्रातरो स्वरसंपन्नौ गन्धर्वाविव रूपिणौ ।।

10. These two were brothers; Further, they knew the (Science &) essence of Ghaandhrava Arts (like painting, music etc.). Well versed in various style of singing (with melody, tempo etc.); Endowed with fine voice; And like the Ghandharvas, they had divine, (lovely) form.

❍ ❍ ❍

११. रूपलक्षणसंपन्नौ मधुरस्वरभाषिणौ ।
बिम्बादिवोद्धृतौ बिम्बौ रामदेहात्तथाऽपरौ ।।

11. They were endowed with beauty and robust body; their speech, very sweet; Like mirror image from mirror, they were born out of the body of Raama (they resembled Raama, their father).

❍ ❍ ❍

१२. तौ राजपुत्रौ कात्स्न्र्येन धर्म्यमाख्यानमुत्तमम् ।
वाचो विधेयं तत्सर्वं कृत्वा काव्यमनिन्दितौ ।।

12. Adapting this foremost Epic that is full of Dharma & that is entirely in (the form of) Poetry for Vocal (musical Expression), the two stainless princes ..... .

❍ ❍ ❍

१३. ऋषीणां च द्विजातीनां साधूनां च समागमे ।
यथोपदेशं तत्त्वज्ञौ जगतुस्तौ कुशीलवौ ।।
महात्मानौ महाभागौ सर्वलक्षणलक्षितौ ।।

13. Lava & Kuscha who had knowledge of The (Ultimate) Reality, who were most eminent & illustrious, who were endowed with all (noble) qualities, sang this (Epic) before the assembly of Braamins, good folks, Rishi-s, just as they were taught (as per Text of Vaalmeeki).

❍ ❍ ❍

१४. तौ कदाचित्समेतानामृषीणां भावितात्मनाम् ।
आसीनानां समीपस्थाविदं काव्यमगायताम् ।।

14. Once, these two sang this Epic before the Rishi-s who were all 'purified' by their devotion to God, when they were sitting together.

❍ ❍ ❍

१५. तच्छ्रुत्वा मुनयः सर्वेबाष्पपर्याकुलेक्षणाः ।
साधु साध्विति तावूचुः परं विस्मयमागताः ।।

15. After listening to this (Musical rendering of Raamaayana by Lava & Kuscha) all the sages became wonder struck; copious tears made their eyes blurred. And they said: = Good, Good.=

❍ ❍ ❍

१६. ते प्रीतमनसः सर्वेमुनयो धर्मवत्सलाः ।
प्रशशंसुः प्रशस्तव्यौ गायमानौ कुशीलवौ ।।

16. These sages who were devotees of Dharma & who were pleased, extolled the praiseworthy Lava & Kuscha when they sang.

❍ ❍ ❍

१७. अहो गीतस्य माधुर्यं श्लोकानां च विशेषतः ।
चिरनिर्वृत्तमप्येतत् प्रत्यक्षमिव दर्शितम् ।।

17. The music and particularly the (substance of the)

verses were all sweet (to hear). Ah! (what a wonder). Although these events happened sometime back they appear vivid (they said).

❍ ❍ ❍

१८. प्रविश्य तावुभौ सुष्टु तदा भावमगायताम् ।
सहितौ मधुरं रक्तं संपन्नं स्वरसम्पदा ।।

18. Entering, these two sang in proper Musical Scale (format) & in sweet Raaga-s, delving deeply into the substance (of the verses).

❍ ❍ ❍

१९. एवं प्रशस्यमानौ तौ तपःश्लाघ्यैर्महात्मभिः ।
संरक्ततरमत्यर्थं मधुरं तावगायताम् ।।

19. These two sang in renowned (foremost)* Raaga-s and very melodiously; And they were extolled by the great soul (sages, Rishi-s there) who were foremost in (doing) penance.

(*Vaalmeeki uses word- Samraktha-).

❍ ❍ ❍

२०. प्रीतः कश्चिन्मुनिस्ताभ्यां संस्थितः कलशं ददौ ।
प्रसन्नो वल्कले कश्चिद्ददौ ताभ्यां महायशाः ।।

20. (These two present the entire Raamaayana as a musical; Thus it was popularised. Music has ever been an integral part of India.)

One happy sage, getting up, gave them water mugs (as presents); One very famous sage offered them dresses of Bark material, very pleased.

❍ ❍ ❍

२१. अन्यः कृष्णाजिनं प्रादाद्यज्ञसूत्रं तथाऽपरः ।
कश्चित् कमण्डलुं प्रादान्मौञ्जीमन्यो महामुनिः ।।

21. Another one gave deer skins; one sage gave vessels; another, Sacred thread (worn across the body); one

gave a seat made of grass cushion; one great sage gave a carpet.

❍ ❍ ❍

२२. बृसीं ददौ तदा चान्यः कुठारमपरो मुनिः ।।

22. Another one gave a seating dais; another, a sword.

❍ ❍ ❍

२३. काषायमपरो वस्त्रं चीरमन्यो ददौ मुनिः ।
जटाबन्धनमन्यस्तु काष्ठरज्जुं मुदाऽन्वितः ।।

23. One gave yellow (Kaashaaya) robes; another Muni gave Bark dresses; another who was very happy, gave strings for Hair locks and also ropes for tying wood sticks.

❍ ❍ ❍

२४. यज्ञभाण्डमृषिः कश्चित्काष्ठभारं तथाऽपरः ।
औदुम्बरीं बृसीमन्ये स्वस्ति केचित्तदाऽवदन् ।।

24. One Rishi gave utensils for Rituals; Another a seat made from Audhumbara wood (Ficus Religiosa); some offered blessings of Swasthi some fire wood.

❍ ❍ ❍

२५. आयुष्यमपरे प्राहुर्मुदा तत्र महर्षयः ।
ददुश्चैव वरान् सर्वेमुनयः सामवादिनः ।।

25. There, some other sages, in great joy (blessed them &) said = May you Live Long* = And sages who recited the Saama Vedha, all of them offered Boons. (*Aayushyam blessings).

(Amongst the four main Vedha-s, the Saama Vedha is most musical; excellent voice is needed to recite this).

❍ ❍ ❍

२६. आश्चर्यमिदमाख्यानं मुनिना संप्रकीर्तितम् ।
परं कवीनामाधारं समाप्तं च यथाक्रमम् ।।

26. This extraordinary (Epic) which was well designated

& completed by sage (Vaalmeeki) properly and which was a 'Reservoir' and (inspiration) for poets ..... .

❍ ❍ ❍

२७. अभिगीतमिदं गीतं सर्वगीतेषु कोविदौ ।
आयुष्यं पुष्टिजनकं सर्वश्रुतिमनोहरम् ।।

27. .....and this music which was so well sung that it captivated the ears & hearts of all citizens, and which brought health & welfare (to all listeners): Sung by these experts who were well versed in all aspects (& forms) of music ....

❍ ❍ ❍

२८. प्रशस्यमानौ सर्वत्र कदाचित्तत्र गायकौ ।
रथ्यासु राजमार्गेषु ददर्श भरताग्रजः ।।

28. .... And once (Raama) the elder brother of Bharatha, saw these two singers (Lava & Kuscha) who were extolled (by citizens) in roads, royal boulevards, and everywhere.

❍ ❍ ❍

२९. स्ववेश्म चानीय ततो भ्रातरौ स कुशीलवौ ।
पूजयामास पूजार्हौ रामः शत्रुनिबर्हणः ।।

29. The destroyer of enemies, (king) Raama, invited these two brothers Lava & Kuscha who deserved honour, to his residence (to his palace), from there. And he honoured them.

(Raama of course was not aware that he was honouring his sons).

❍ ❍ ❍

३०. आसीनः काञ्चने दिव्ये स च सिंहासने प्रभुः ।
उपोपविष्टः राचिवैर्भ्रातृभिश्च परंतपः ।।

30. The tormentor of enemies (Raama) who was sitting in the divine golden throne surrounded by his brothers & ministers. . . . this Lord. . . . (this) disciplined.

❍ ❍ ❍

३१. दृष्ट्वा तु रूपसंपन्नौ तावुभौ नियतस्तदा ।
उवाच लक्ष्मणं रामः शत्रुघ्नं भरतं तदा ।।

31. ..... (Raama), seeing these two who were well endowed with form & beauty, addressed Lakshmana, Bharatha & Schathrugna.

❍ ❍ ❍

३२. श्रूयतामिदमाख्यानमनयोर्देववर्चसोः ।
इत्युक्त्वा सदृशौ तौ तु गायकौ तावुवाच ह ।।
विचित्रार्थपदं सम्यग्गायन्तौ समचोदयत् ।।

32. (Raama asks every one to listen to these two 'singers ').

May we all listen properly to this epic that is wonderfully constructed with substance & meter and (sung) by these two whose brilliance is comparable to (Celestial) Dheva-s. Saying thus, he talked to these singers who were alike; And he 'goaded' them, (cheered them to sing).

❍ ❍ ❍

३३. तौ चापि मधुरं रक्तं स्वञ्चितायतनिःस्वनम् ।
तन्त्रीलयवदत्यर्थं विश्रुतार्थमगायताम् ।।

33. There upon these two sang the Epic in melodious Raaga, like music & rhythm of Veena, in loud & clear voice, with words coming out very clearly with meaning.

❍ ❍ ❍

३४. ह्लादयत्सर्वगात्राणि मनांसि हृदयानि च ।
श्रोत्राश्रयसुखं गेयं तद्बभौ जनसंसदि ।।

34. Their music gave great solace to the listeners in the (Royal) hall; it gave happiness to body, heart & mind of every one.

❍ ❍ ❍

३५. इमौ मुनी पार्थिवलक्षणान्वितौ कुशीलवौ चैव महातपस्विनौ ।
ममापि तद्भूतिकरं प्रचक्ष्यते महानुभावं चरितं निबोधत ।।

35. (And Raama said): These two, Lava & Kuscha, although are (young) Muni-s with great penance behind them, are endowed with qualities of royalty. Further an Epic story that makes me lofty and makes me prosperous is being sung; May you listen.

(Raama has a lurking doubt! Perhaps these boys are princes).

❍ ❍ ❍

३६. ततस्तु तौ रामवचःप्रचोदितावगायतां मार्गविधानसंपदा ।
स चापि रामः परिषद्गतः शनैर्बुभूषया सक्तमना बभूव ह ।।

36. Then, encouraged by Raama's (cheering) words, these two sang in Maarga style of singing; And Raama who had reached council hall slowly, desirous of hearing (the concert), set his heart (on this).

❍ ❍ ❍

Chapter 5

Description of (the Capital of) Ayodhya

(Vaalmeeki's Raamaayana begins from this chapter: This is the Epic, Lava & Kuscha sang before vast audiences to popularise the work; And they sang before Raama, the principal character !)

❍ ❍ ❍

१. सर्वापूर्वमियं येषामासीत् कृत्स्ना वसुन्धरा ।
प्रजापतिमुपादाय नृपाणां जयशालिनाम् ।।

1. Once this entire Earth was unapproachable (& was obscure); From the Lord of Procreation (The Prajaapathi), came victorious kings, amongst whom .....

❍ ❍ ❍

२. येषां स सगरो नाम सागरो येन खानितः ।
षष्टिः पुत्रसहस्राणि यं यान्तं पर्यवारयन् ।।

2. .... was Sagara by name, by whom the Ocean itself was dug up, (dug up by this king Sagara) who was 'surrounded ' by his 60,000 sons , when he went out.....

❍ ❍ ❍

३. इक्ष्वाकूणामिदं तेषां राज्ञां महात्मनाम् ।
महदुत्पन्नमाख्यानं रामायणमिति श्रुतम् ।।

3. .... The great story renowned as The Raamaayana, originated from the lineage of the kings of the great & eminent Ikshwaaku-s.

❍ ❍ ❍

४. तदिदं वर्तयिष्यामि सर्वं निखिलमादितः ।
धर्मकामार्थसहितं श्रोतव्यमनसूयया ।।

4. This (such an Epic), I am expounding; The story which is embellished with Dharma (Moral code, norms); Artha (Substance, wealth etc.); and Kaama (Desires, mundane pleasures etc.). May you listen to the story in full, from the beginning (and listen) without (ill will or) jealousy.

❍ ❍ ❍

५. कोसलो नाम मुदितः स्फीतो जनपदो महान् ।
निविष्टः सरयूतीरे प्रभूतधनधान्यवान् ।।

5. The gay, prosperous & mighty kingdom of Kosala by name, with its abundance of wealth & grains, was established on the banks of Saraayu river.

❍ ❍ ❍

६. अयोध्या नाम नगरी तत्रासील्लोकविश्रुता ।
मनुना मानवेन्द्रेण या पूरी निर्मिता स्वयम् ।।

6. The world famous (capital) city of Ayodhya was there; This city was created by (no less a person than) Manu himself, the lord of human race...... .

❍ ❍ ❍

७. आयता दश च द्वे च योजनानि महापुरी ।
श्रीमती त्रीणि विस्तीर्णा सुविभक्तमहापथा ।।

7. Most affluent; Its length was 12 yojana-s; its width, 3 yojanas. in this mighty city, there were well laid out roads..... .

❍ ❍ ❍

८. राजमार्गेण महता सुविभक्तेन शोभिता ।
मुक्तपुष्पावकीर्णेन जलसिक्तेन नित्यशः ।।

8. .... (This city) shone brilliantly with its broad Royal boulevards that were well constructed and which were always cleansed with water & showered with flowers. (A Yojana is about 9 miles).

❍ ❍ ❍

९. तां तु राजा दशरथो महाराष्ट्रविवर्धनः ।
पुरीमावासयामास दिवं देवपतिर्यथा ।।

9. King Dhascharatha who increased the prosperity of the great kingdom, ruled like (Indhra), the lord of Dheva-s ruling the celestial kingdom.

❍ ❍ ❍

१०. कवाटतोरणवतीं सुविभक्तान्तरापणाम् ।
सर्वयन्त्रायुधवतीमुपेतां सर्वशिल्पिभिः ।।

10. (Vaalmeeki describes Ayodhya further; stanzas 10 to 24). There were Gates at the entrance (to the city). In the centre (of the city) well laid out shops; There were machineries, implements etc.; (City full) with Artisans & sculptors ..... .

❍ ❍ ❍

११. सूतमागधसंबाधां श्रीमतीमतुलप्रभाम् ।
उच्चाट्टालध्वजवतीं शतघ्नीशतसंवृताम् ।।

11. Full of Sootha-s & Magadha-s (Poets & singers); (air of) affluence (permeates); Prominent buildings carried

bright masts & banners of unequalled brilliance; There were hundreds of mortar guns (like) Schathaagni...... and huge Watch Towers.

❍ ❍ ❍

१२. वधूनाटकसङ्घैश्च संयुक्तां सर्वतः पुरीम् ।
उद्यानाम्रवणोपेतां महतीं सालमेखलाम् ।।

12. Many dance teachers teaching the girls (this fine art) found everywhere in the great city; Gardens & Mango groves (were there); There were Ramparts like golden belt (like ornament of Mekhala) ....

❍ ❍ ❍

१३. दुर्गगम्भीरपरिघां दुर्गामन्यैर्दुरासदाम् ।
वाजिवारणसंपूर्णां गोभिरुष्ट्रैः खरैस्तथा ।।

13. .... Big forts with wide moats with deep waters, impenetrable; city unapproachable by inimical outsiders; City full with horses, elephants, cows, camels & asses ....

❍ ❍ ❍

१४. सामन्तराजसङ्घैश्च बलिकर्मभिरावृताम् ।
नानादेशनिवासैश्च वणिग्भिरुपशोभिताम् ।।

14. ..... City was full of chieftains and dukes paying tutelage (to King Dhascharatha); Number of merchants coming to the city from many places (for doing business at Ayodhya) ....

❍ ❍ ❍

१५. प्रासादै रत्नविकृतैः पर्वतैरिव शोभिताम् ।
कूटागारैश्च संपूर्णामिन्द्रस्येवामरावतीम् ।।

15. .... Shining with buildings that are like mountains, done up with stones & gems; Multistorey houses there; it was like Lord Indhra's city of Amaraavathy ....

❍ ❍ ❍

१६. चित्रामष्टापदाकारां वरनारीगणैर्युताम् ।
सर्वरत्नसमाकीर्णां विमानगृहशोभिताम् ।।

16. ..... (City architecturally) Designed in the wonderful form of Ashtaapada (Like Chequer board); City with multitude of charming girls; Full of gems & stones; Full with mansions large like space craft.

❍ ❍ ❍

१७. गृहगाढामविच्छिद्रां समभूमौ निवेशिताम् ।
शालितण्डुलसंपूर्णामिक्षुकाण्डरसोदकाम् ।।

17. Full with (rows of) houses close together; Stainless; Constructed on flat surfaces; (City) full with red Rice/ paddy grains; The drinking water (Supply) like sweet sugar cane juice ....

❍ ❍ ❍

१८. दुन्दुभीभिर्मृदङ्गैश्च वीणाभिः पणवैस्तथा ।
नादितां भृशमत्यर्थं पृथिव्यां तामनुत्तमाम् ।।

18. ...... The city reverberated with sounds from Dhundhubi (Drums), Mridunga sounds (percussion instrument played with two hands on both faces); Veena strains (A seven stringed instrument); And likewise many other types of percussion instruments (reverberated the city) that was foremost on earth ....

❍ ❍ ❍

१९. विमानमिव सिद्धानां तपसाऽधिगतं दिवि ।
न कुबेरस्य चेन्द्रस्य यमस्य वरुणस्य वा ।।

19. ...... City foremost, like those of the Sidha-s (of heaven) who obtain (such) foremost (cities) through penance; Neither for Kubhaera, (the celestial lord of wealth), nor for Indhra (the lord of celestials), nor for Yama (the lord of Death), nor for Varuna (lord of Rain) ....

❍ ❍ ❍

२०. ब्रह्मणोऽपि पुरी रम्या नेदृशी च स्वयंभुवः ।
सुनिवेशितवेश्मान्तां नरेन्द्रोत्तमसेविताम् ।।

20. ..... such a city there was. Even the beautiful city of The Self Created God Bramma (is not like this Ayodhya); (There were rows of) Well constructed houses with lovely apartments lived in by foremost men (of Ayodhya) ....

❍ ❍ ❍

२१. ये च बाणैर्न विध्यन्ति विविक्तमपरापरम् ।
शब्दवेध्यं च विततं लघुहस्ता विशारदाः ।।

21. .... (The city of Ayodhya) where bows are never 'stretched' by experts in Archery with dexterous hands, (to discharge arrows) & hit those who are lonely (& helpless), or to hit those who are without progeny (& support), or to hit those who can 'see' only through sound (of hearing, men who are blind)...... .

❍ ❍ ❍

२२. सिंहव्याघ्रवराहाणां मत्तानां नदतां वने ।
हन्तारो निशितैः शस्त्रैर्बलाद्बाहुबलैरपि ।।

22. ...... (But) who kill with sharp weapons, with their strength & power of their arms, lions, tigers and roaring mad elephants of the forest...... .

❍ ❍ ❍

२३. तादृशानां सहस्रैस्तामभिपूर्णां महारथैः ।
पुरीमावासयामास राजा दशरथस्तदा ।।

23. ...... (City) Full of such great warriors (charioteers), in thousands; Such a city (& kingdom) Dhascharatha ruled at that time...... .

(The warriors although men of great valour, were men of Dharma).

❍ ❍ ❍

२४. तामग्निमद्भिर्गुणवद्भिरावृतां द्विजोत्तमैर्वेदषडङ्गपारगैः ।
सहस्रदैः सत्यरतैर्महात्मभिर्महर्षिकल्पैर्ऋषिभिश्च केवलैः ॥

24. ...... (This Ayodhya) Was full of foremost Braamins who were comparable to great sages; full of great soul Rishi-s who were distinguished and who were devoted to Truth, who perform Rituals, who have mastered the renowned Vedha-s & the Six Ancillary (parts of) Vedha-s & who offer gifts by thousands.

(Note: Ayodhya means = A - Yudh = Difficult to fight against).

❍ ❍ ❍

Chapter 6

King Dhascharatha's Rule described

१. तस्यां पुर्यामयोध्यायां सर्ववित्सर्वसंग्रहः ।
दीर्घदर्शी महातेजाः पौरजानपदप्रियः ॥

1. In the city (& kingdom) of Ayodhya, all citizens, from town & villages, endeared to him; he was most brilliant; a man with extensive knowledge (who knew all matters); a man of vision (who could foresee things); he was guardian of all...... .

❍ ❍ ❍

२. इक्ष्वाकूणामतिरथो यज्वा धर्मरतो वशी ।
महर्षिकल्पो राजर्षिस्त्रिषु लोकेषु विश्रुतः ॥

2. ...... Foremost warrior amongst Ikshwaaku-s, this man devoted to Dharma, performed many Yaaga-s (Sacrifices). He was a royal sage, comparable to very great sages; & (by love), every one 'surrendered 'to him; Renowned in all the three worlds...... .

❍ ❍ ❍

३. बलवान्निहतामित्रो मित्रवान् विजितेन्द्रियः ।
धनैश्च सञ्चयैश्चान्यैः शक्रवैश्रवणोपमः ।।

3. ...... Mightily strong, he destroyed enemies; had many friends; he controlled his passion & senses; he was comparable to Kubhaera & Lord Indhra, in wealth, in munificence & other things...... .

❍ ❍ ❍

४. यथा मनुर्महातेजा लोकस्य परिरक्षिता ।
तथा दशरथो राजा वसञ्जगदपालयत् ।।

4. ...... Like the most brilliant king Manu (his ancestor) who protected the worlds, this Dhascharatha the king, who lived here, protected the world.

❍ ❍ ❍

५. तेन सत्याभिसन्धेन त्रिवर्गमनुतिष्ठता ।
पालिता सा पुरी श्रेष्ठा शक्रेणेवामरावती ।।

5. Wedded to Truth, he followed the path of the three Dharma-s; Like Lord Indhra ruling over (celestial city) Amaraavathy, this foremost city (kingdom) was ruled by him.

❍ ❍ ❍

६. तस्मिन् पुरवरे हृष्टा धर्मात्मानो बहुश्रुताः ।
नरास्तुष्टा धनैः स्वैः स्वैरलुब्धाः सत्यवादिनः ।।

6. The citizens were happy in this foremost city; Men of Dharma; They knew Dharma; They were happy & content with their own assets; They did not covet; They ever spoke Truth.

❍ ❍ ❍

७. नाल्पसन्निचयः कश्चिदासीत्तस्मिन् पुरोत्तमे ।
कुटुम्बी यो ह्यसिद्धार्थोऽगवाश्वधनधान्यवान् ।।

7. In this great city, there was no family which possessed cheap stuffs; which did not have cows, horses, wealth & grain; nor was there one whose wishes were not met.

❍ ❍ ❍

८. कामी वा न कदर्योवा नृशंसः पुरुषः क्वचित् ।
द्रष्टुं शक्यमयोध्यायां नाविद्वान्न च नास्तिकः ।।

8. You could not see any one in the kingdom of Ayodhya who was avaricious, petty minded nor mischievous; nor any one not learned; nor one who was an Atheist.

❍ ❍ ❍

९. सर्वेनराश्च नार्यश्च धर्मशीलाः सुसंवृताः ।
उदिताः शीलवृत्ताभ्यां महर्षय इवामलाः ।।

9. All the men and women were followers of Dharma (Moral code); well behaved & united and were like great sages who were born with good conduct, (sinless & pure) stainless.

❍ ❍ ❍

१०. नाकुण्डली नामकुटी नास्रग्वी नाल्पभोगवान् ।
नामृष्टो नानुलिप्ताङ्गो नासुगन्धश्च विद्यते ।।

10. None who did not sport ear rings; none who was not wearing crests & (gold) chains; none who did not enjoy pleasures; none impure; none whose body was not besmeared (with sandal paste etc.) and none who emanated bad smell (from breath & body).

❍ ❍ ❍

११. नामृष्टभोजी नादाता नाप्यनङ्गदनिष्कधृक् ।
नाहस्ताभरणो वाऽपि दृश्यते नाप्यनात्मवान् ।।

11. None who did not eat well; none who did not give (charities); None who did not wear arm bracelets & ornaments; none who did not wear bangles; none who did not control his senses & passion

None were seen (without these qualities).

❍ ❍ ❍

१२. नानाहिताग्निर्नायज्वा न क्षुद्रो वा न तस्करः ।
कश्चिदासीदयोध्यायां न च निर्वृत्तसमरः ।।

12. In Ayodhya there was none who did not perform daily rituals; nor Yaaga-s (Sacrificial ceremonies); No one was mean; no thief; none married against (norms of) caste.

❍ ❍ ❍

१३. स्वकर्मनिरता नित्यं ब्राह्मणा विजितेन्द्रियाः ।
दानाध्ययनशीलाश्च संयताश्च प्रतिग्रहे ।।

13. The Braamins who had control over passion & senses, were always devoted to their own daily rituals & duties; Were of charitable disposition, devoted to meditation (of the Supreme): were eager to learn (& study).

❍ ❍ ❍

१४. न नास्तिको नानृतको न कश्चिदबहुश्रुतः ।
नासूयको न चाशक्तो नाविद्वान् विद्यते तदा ।।

14. At that time no one was an atheist there; none spoke a lie; none who did not study Shaasthra-s; none who was jealous; none who was incapable; none not learned.

❍ ❍ ❍

१५. नाषडङ्गविदत्रासीन्नाव्रतो नासहस्रदः ।
न दीनः क्षिप्तचित्तो वा व्यथितो नाऽपि कश्चन ।।

15. Here there was none who did not know the 6 parts of the Vedha; none who did not practice (religious) Vows; none who did not give in thousands; none feeble; none (crest fallen) with depression; none agitated.

❍ ❍ ❍

१६. कश्चिन्नरो वा नारी वा नाश्रीमान्नाप्यरूपवान् ।
द्रष्टुं शक्यमयोध्यायां नापि राजन्यभक्तिमान् ।।

16. You could not find any man or woman who was not resplendent; none without personality; nor any one who was not devoted to the king.

❍ ❍ ❍

१७. वर्णेष्वग्र्यचतुर्थेषु देवतातिथिपूजकाः ।
कृतज्ञाश्च वदान्याश्च शूरा विक्रमसंयुताः ॥

17. In (all the) foremost towns, all men from all the four great castes worshipped Deities and honoured (guests); they were all men of gratitude; very liberal & brave; .... Endowed with valour...... .

❍ ❍ ❍

१८. दीर्घायुषो नराः सर्वेधर्मं सत्यं च संश्रिताः ।
सहिताः पुत्रपौत्रैश्च नित्यं स्त्रीभिः पुरोत्तमे ॥

18. ...... Devoted to Truth & Dharma; (They abided by them); They enjoyed long life; They were well served by their wives, children & grand children.

❍ ❍ ❍

१९. क्षत्रं ब्रह्ममुखं चासीद्वैश्याः क्षत्रमनुव्रताः ।
शूद्राः स्वकर्मनिरतास्त्रीन् वर्णानुपचारिणः ॥

19. The Kshathriyas looked up to the Braamins; The Vysyas followed the Kshathriyas; The Schoodras served all the three castes. Every one was devoted to his own vocation.

❍ ❍ ❍

२०. सा तेनेक्ष्वाकुनाथेन पुरी सुपरिरक्षिता ।
यथा पुरस्तान्मनुना मानवेन्द्रेण धीमता ॥

20. Like by Manu the wise lord of men before, this city was well protected by (Dhascharatha) the (present) lord of Ikshwaaku-s.

❍ ❍ ❍

२१. योधानामग्निकल्पानां पेशलानां मनस्विनाम् ।
संपूर्णा कृतविद्यानां गुहा केसरिणामिव ॥

21. Like the caves (inhabited) by lions, so was the kingdom full, (with and protected by) warriors (army men) who were comparable to 'Fire', who were most learned (in

war science), who were high spirited (but) who were tender (& kind to citizens).

❍ ❍ ❍

२२. काम्भोजविषये जातैर्बाह्लीकैश्च हयोत्तमैः ।
वनायुजैर्नदीजैश्च पूर्णा हरिहयोत्तमैः ।।

22. (The kingdom boasted of and was) Full with foremost horses bred from Kaambhoja territory (Cambodia,Thailand), Bahli, Vanaayu, Sindhu (territories); they were like (Lord Indhra's) foremost horse (called Uchaisrawas).

❍ ❍ ❍

२३. विन्ध्यपर्वतजैर्मत्तैः पूर्णा हैमवतैरपि ।
मदान्वितैरतिबलैर्मातङ्गैः पर्वतोपमैः ।।

23. The kingdom was full of mightily strong elephants that were like mountains, very exhilarated; Tough; Bred in Vindhya ranges & from Himaalaya region.

❍ ❍ ❍

२४. ऐरावतकुलीनैश्च महापद्मकुलैस्तथा ।
अञ्जनादपि निष्पन्नैर्वामनादपि च द्विपैः ।।

24. (The lineage of these described: In those days, horses & elephants were indeed very important for Defence etc.).

❍ ❍ ❍

२५. भद्रैर्मन्द्रैर्मृगैश्चैव भद्रमन्द्रमृगैस्तथा ।
भद्रमन्द्रैभर्द्रमृगमन्द्रश्च सा पूरी ।।
नित्यमत्तैः सदा पूर्णा नागैरचलसन्निभैः ।।

25. ...... from Bhadhra, Mandhara, Mriga, and the cross breeds between Mriga & Bhandhra and the cross breeds Bhadhra & Mandhara-Mriga and likewise, Bhadhra-Mandhara and Mriga-Mandhara (cross breeds); They were all well bodied and were like mountains; kingdom was full of these elephants, very exhilarated.

❍ ❍ ❍

२६. सा योजने च द्वे भूयः सत्यनामा प्रकाशते ।
यस्यां दशरथो राजा वसञ्जगदपालयत् ॥

26. This, where king Dhascharatha lived and protected the world; It was full 2 Yojana-s (about 18 miles); True to its name, it shone bright (Dhascharatha was indeed an emperor to all this).

❍ ❍ ❍

२७. तां पुरीं स महातेजा राजा दशरथो महान् ।
शशास शमितामित्रो नक्षत्राणीव चन्द्रमाः ॥

27. This most brilliant & great king Dhascharatha ruled this city (& kingdom) with his enemies under check; He was like moon over stars.

❍ ❍ ❍

२८. तां सत्यनामां दृढतोरणार्गलां गृहैर्विचित्रैरुपशोभितां शिवाम् ।
पुरीमयोध्यां नृसहस्रसंकुलां शशास वै शक्रसमो महीपतिः ॥

28. This Lord of Earth (Dhascharatha) who was equal to (Schakra) Lord Indhra, ruled this Ayodhya which was true to its name; This city shone with wonderful houses, was auspicious, was full with thousands of citizens and was well served with Arches & (Big) Gates, well bolted.

❍ ❍ ❍

Chapter 7

(Vaalmeeki's) Description of Dhascharatha's Ministers

१. तस्यामात्या गुणैरासन्निक्ष्वाकोस्तु महात्मनः ।
मन्त्रज्ञाश्चेङ्गितज्ञाश्च नित्यं प्रियहिते रताः ॥

1. To the great soul Ikshwaaku (king Dhascharatha), there were ministers endowed with character who were devoted to his welfare, who ever appreciated other's (feelings and) views who were capable of

understanding other's feelings by their gesture and who were (experts in) tendering ministerial advice (to the king).

❍ ❍ ❍

२. अष्टौ बभूवुर्वीरस्य तस्यामात्या यशस्विनः ।
शुचयश्चानुरक्ताश्च राजकृत्येषु नित्यशः ।।

2. To the most famous & brave (king), were 8 ministers who were 'Clean' men & were committed to Royal duties (welfare of State).

❍ ❍ ❍

३. धृष्टिर्जयन्तो विजयः सिद्धार्थोह्यर्थसाधकः ।
अशोको मन्त्रपालश्च सुमन्त्रश्चाष्टमोऽभवत् ।।

3. (Council of Ministers)
Dhrishti; Jayantha; Vijaya; Sidhaartha; Ardhasaadhaka; Aschoka; Manthrapaul; Sumanthra who was the eighth. (Sumanthra was also minister in waiting, charioteer & his friend).

❍ ❍ ❍

४. ऋत्विजौ द्वावभिमतौ तस्यास्तामृषिसत्तमौ ।
वसिष्ठो वामदेवश्च मन्त्रिणश्च तथाऽपरे ।।

4. Likewise he had two other (special) ministers: Vasishta & Vaamadheva. These foremost Rishi-s were foremost Rithviks (High priests).

❍ ❍ ❍

५. विद्याविनीता ह्रीमन्तः कुशला नियतेन्द्रियाः ।
श्रीमन्तश्च महात्मानः शास्त्रज्ञा दृढविक्रमाः ।।

5. Men of great scholarship; Men of honour; and modesty Resplendent; Very competent; Men with self control; Most eminent (great soul); Had deep knowledge of Shaasthra-s; Resolute in valour.

❍ ❍ ❍

६. कीर्तिमन्तः प्रणिहिता यथावचनकारिणः ।
तेजःक्षमायशःप्राप्ताः स्मितपूर्वाभिभाषिणः ।।

6. Very renowned; Men of commitment (in affairs of State); Kept their word (did what they said): Brilliant; Famous; They had (enormous) patience; Always spoke with a smile.

❍ ❍ ❍

७. क्रोधात् कामार्थहेतोर्वा न ब्रूयुरनृतं वचः ।।

7. Never uttered a word of untruth either out of anger, passion or for any pecuniary benefits.

❍ ❍ ❍

८. तेषामविदितं किञ्चित् स्वेषु नास्ति परेषु वा ।
क्रियमाणं कृतं चापि चारेणापि चिकीर्षितम् ।।

8. There was nothing that was not known (to them) through their spies (& ambassadors); About what had happened, or what was happening or what was (being planned) to happen, either in their own (affairs of State) or elsewhere.

❍ ❍ ❍

९. कुशला व्यवहारेषु सौहृदेषु परीक्षिताः ।
प्राप्तकाले यथादण्डं धारयेयुः सुतेष्वपि ।।

9. Very skilled in settling disputes; Tested men in matters of (heart &) friendship; If such a moment arose, they would offer punishment even to their own sons.

❍ ❍ ❍

१०. कोशसंग्रहणे युक्ता बलस्य च परिग्रहे ।
अहितं चापि पुरुषं न विहिंस्युरदूषकम् ।।

10. They were devoted in the protection of the Treasury; And in safeguarding Army; They never harassed a sinless person even if he was inimical to them.

❍ ❍ ❍

११. वीराश्च नियतोत्साहा राजशास्त्रमनुष्ठिताः ।
शुचीनां रक्षितारश्च नित्यं विषयवासिनाम् ।।

11. These brave men were very energetic; They followed royal edict (State code); They were protectors of good & pious men living in the kingdom.

१२. ब्रह्म क्षत्रमहिंसन्तस्ते कोशं समपूरयन् ।
सुतीक्ष्णदण्डाः संप्रेक्ष्य पुरुषस्य बलाबलम् ।।

12. The ministers who were terribly zealous in protecting the Treasury, filled up (the office) with men after assessing their strength (merit & demerit) and (making sure) that they did no harm to poor Braamins & (various) Kshathriya-s.

❍ ❍ ❍

१३. शुचीनामेकबुद्धीनां सर्वेषां सम्प्रजानताम् ।
नासीत् पुरे वा राष्ट्रे वा मृषावादी नरः क्वचित् ।।

13. These ministers were clean; had one mind (the same objectives); moved as equals; Neither amongst them nor (even) from amongst men in towns nor in (entire) kingdom, they spoke falsehood.

❍ ❍ ❍

१४. कश्चिन्न दुष्टस्तत्रासीत् परदाररतिर्नरः ।
प्रशान्तं सर्वमेवासीद्राष्ट्रं पुरवरं च तत् ।।

14. Here there was not a single wicked man who coveted another's wife; There was peace in the kingdom and in foremost towns.

❍ ❍ ❍

१५. सुवाससः सुवेषाश्च ते च सर्वेसुशीलिनः ।
हितार्थं च नरेन्द्रस्य जाग्रतो नयचक्षुषा ।।

15. All of them were well dressed; wore jewellery: well behaved; For the sake of welfare of the king (& country), ever wide 'awake' with eye of prudence. (Very vigilant).

❍ ❍ ❍

१६. गुरौ गुणगृहीताश्च प्रख्याताश्च पराक्रमे ।
विदेशेष्वपि विज्ञाताः सर्वतो बुद्धिनिश्चयात् ।।
अभिज्ञा गुणवन्तश्च न चासन् गुणगर्विताः ।।

16. It was character they imbibed from their teachers; Renowned in bravery; By their steadfastness in thinking (having firm & unwavering mind) they were renowned in even in other kingdoms; Men of vision; Men of virtuous qualities but they were never arrogant because of their great qualities (and status).

१७. सन्धिविग्रहतत्त्वज्ञाः सर्वशास्त्रविशारदाः ।
मन्त्रसंवरणे युक्ताः शक्ताः सूक्ष्मासु बुद्धिषु ।।

17. They knew the art of making Treaties & breaking (the treaties); well versed in Shaasthra-s; they kept the Oath of Secrecy in ministerial matters; Very clever in intricate matters.

❍ ❍ ❍

१८. नीतिशास्त्रविशेषज्ञाः सततं प्रियवादिनः ।
ईदृशैस्तैरमात्यैश्च राजा दशरथोऽनघः ।।
उपपन्नगुणोपेतैरन्वशासद्वसुन्धराम् ।।

18. Masters in intricacies of Law; Ever spoke sweetly; With such ministers endowed with good qualities, the sinless king Dhascharatha ruled the Earth.

❍ ❍ ❍

१९. अवेक्षमाणश्चारेण प्रजा धर्मेण रञ्जयन् ।
प्रजानां पालनं कुर्वन्नधर्मं परिवर्जयन् ।।

19. (The king) had fine ambassadors through whom he 'saw' (affairs in other states); Delighted his subjects by (ruling through) Dharma; Ruling (the kingdom &) over the citizens, abandoning Non Dharma...... .

❍ ❍ ❍

२०. विश्रुतस्त्रिषु लोकेषु वदान्यः सत्यसङ्गरः ।
स तत्र पुरुषव्याघ्रः शशास पृथिवीमिमाम् ।।

20. ...... this 'tiger' amongst men (this Dhascharatha), ruled over this earth; This munificent (king) who was true to a promise, was renowned in all the three worlds.

❍ ❍ ❍

२१. नाध्यगच्छद्विशिष्टं वा तुल्यं वा शत्रुमात्मनः ।
मित्रवान्नतसामन्तः प्रतापहतकण्टकः ।।

21. (This king) Never allowed his enemies to be his equal or grow in strength; He was amongst friends; The feudal princes were obedient to him; By his power, he was a 'Thorn" to the enemy of...... .

❍ ❍ ❍

२२. स शशास जगद्राजा दिवं देवपतिर्यथा ।।

22. ...... state; This king ruled the earth like Lord Indhra ruling the celestial world.

❍ ❍ ❍

२३. तैर्मन्त्रिभिर्मन्त्रहिते निविष्टैर्वृतोऽनुरक्तैः कुशलैः समर्थैः ।
स पार्थिवो दीप्तिमवाप युक्तस्तेजोमयैर्गोभिरिवोदितोऽर्कः ।।

23. Surrounded by (such) ministers who were clever, able devoted and who bestowed sound ministerial advice that was salutary, this King (Dhascharatha) became endowed with brilliancy like the rising sun which is endowed with brilliant rays.

(Note: Poet Vaalmeeki has listed some of the qualities that are attributes of a good minister; Modern ministers / politicians should read all this).

❍ ❍ ❍

Chapter 8

(Dhascharatha) Decides to Perform Aschwamedha (Horse Sacrifice)

(This Sacrifice is considered the most difficult one: Only mighty kings can undertake this).

❍ ❍ ❍

१. तस्य त्वेवंप्रभावस्य धर्मज्ञस्य महात्मनः ।
सुतार्थं तप्यमानस्य नासीद्वंशकरः सुतः ।।

1. (But) this (King Dhascharatha) who possessed such splendor, who knew Dharma, who was a great soul, was in torment for (obtaining) a son; he had no son to propagate his lineage.

❍ ❍ ❍

२. चिन्तयानस्य तस्येयं बुद्धिरासीन्महात्मनः ।
सुतार्थं वाजिमेधेन किमर्थं न यजाम्यहम् ।।

2. To this great soul who was worrying for (obtaining) a son, a thought crossed (his mind): . . . = Why have I not performed The Aschwamedha Yaaga = (Why should I not do this for begetting a son).

❍ ❍ ❍

३. सुनिश्चितां मतिं कृत्वा यष्टव्यमिति बुद्धिमान् ।
मन्त्रिभिः सह धर्मात्मा सर्वैरेव कृतात्मभिः ।।

3. The wise & great soul king resolved this idea in his mind that he should perform Yaaga. (He wanted) all his accomplished ministers...... .

❍ ❍ ❍

४. ततोऽब्रवीदिदं राजा सुमन्त्रं मन्त्रिसत्तमम् ।
शीघ्रमानय मे सर्वान् गुरुंस्तान् सपुरोहितान् ।।

4. ......then the King (called &) told the following to the

foremost minister Sumanthra = Bring soon my Guru-s (teachers), Purohiths (Priests).= ......

❍ ❍ ❍

५. सुयज्ञं वामदेवं च जाबालिमथ काश्यपम् ।
पुरोहितं वसिष्ठं ये चान्ये द्विजसत्तमाः ।।

5. ...... = (and bring) Suyagnya, Vaamadheva, Jaabaali, Kaaschyapa, (chief) priest Vasishta and other Braamins.=

❍ ❍ ❍

६. ततः सुमन्त्रस्त्वरितं गत्वा त्वरितविक्रमः ।
समानयत् स तान् विप्रान् समस्तान् वेदपारगान् ।।

6. By this (command of the king), the man of fast strides, Sumanthra, went out fast and fetched these men of wisdom who were together, who were masters in Vedha-s.

❍ ❍ ❍

७. तान् पूजयित्वा धर्मात्मा राजा दशरथस्तदा ।
इदं धर्मार्थसहितं श्लक्ष्णं वचनमब्रवीत् ।।

7. King Dhascharatha who was man of Dharma, honoured them & then addressed them these sweet words full with content of Dharma.

❍ ❍ ❍

८. मम लालप्यमानस्य पुत्रार्थं नास्ति वै सुखम् ।
तदर्थं हयमेधेन यक्ष्यामीति मतिर्मम ।।

8. To me who is grieving for the sake of (obtaining) a son, there is no happiness. Therefore it is my intention to perform Aschwamedha Yaaga.

❍ ❍ ❍

९. तदहं यष्टुमिच्छामि शास्त्रदृष्टेन कर्मणा ।
कथं प्राप्स्याम्यहं कामं बुद्धिरत्र विचार्यताम् ।।

9. ......Therefore I desire to perform Yaaga as 'seen' (& based on) norms of Shaasthra-s; May your mind deliberate upon this so that my wish will be satisfied.

❍ ❍ ❍

१०. साधु साध्विति तद्वाक्यं ब्राह्मणाः प्रत्यपूजयन् ।
वसिष्ठप्रमुखाः सर्वेपार्थिवस्य मुखेरितम् ।।
ऊचुश्च परमप्रीताः सर्वेदशरथं वचः ।।

10. (Hearing) these words that were uttered from the mouth of the king, all the Braamins led by Vasishta said: "Good, Good " and they honoured (extolled) him...... .

❍ ❍ ❍

११. संभाराः संभ्रियन्तां ते तुरङ्गश्च विमुच्यताम् ।
सरय्वाश्चोत्तरे तीरे यज्ञभूमिर्विधीयताम् ।।

11. ...... All of them very pleased with Dhascharatha, said = Let materials be collected; Let (Sacrificial) Horse be released; Let the site for Yaaga ceremony be on the northern banks of Saraayu river.

❍ ❍ ❍

१२. सर्वथा प्राप्स्यसे पुत्रानभिप्रेतांश्च पार्थिव ।
यस्य ते धार्मिकी बुद्धिरियं पुत्रार्थमागता ।।

12. ...... Oh King: As this noble thought has struck you for the sake of progeny, you are sure to obtain (your wish of getting) beloved sons in every way –

❍ ❍ ❍

१३. ततः प्रीतोऽभवद्राजा श्रुत्वैतद् द्विजभाषितम् ।
अमात्यांश्चाब्रवीद्राजा हर्षपर्याकुलेक्षणः ।।

13. Hearing these words spoken by Braamins, the king became pleased; With tears in his eyes due to happiness, he addressed his ministers (again).

❍ ❍ ❍

१४. संभाराः संभ्रियन्तां मे गुरूणां वचनादिह ।
समर्थाधिष्ठितश्चाश्वः सोपाध्यायो विमुच्यताम् ।।

14. By the words (of command) of my teachers, let materials be procured; Let the (Sacrificial) Horse which is well protected (& groomed) by capable men along with priests, be released.

❍ ❍ ❍

१५. सरय्वाश्चोत्तरे तीरे यज्ञभूमिर्विधीयताम् ।
शान्तयश्चाभिवर्धन्तां यथाकल्पं यथाविधि ।।

15. Let Yaaga site be on north banks of Saraayu river; As per norms of Shaasthra-s let (preliminary) peace ritual also be performed (to augment the Yaaga- The house warming ceremony).

❍ ❍ ❍

१६. शक्यः प्राप्तुमयं यज्ञः सर्वेणापि महीक्षिता ।
नापराधो भवेत् कष्टो यद्यस्मिन् क्रतुसत्तमे ।।

16. This mighty Yaaga (if not properly done), grievous transgression will take place; Otherwise, (had it been a simple ceremony) this could be done by any (ordinary) king.

❍ ❍ ❍

१७. छिद्रं हि मृगयन्तेऽत्र विद्वांसो ब्रह्मराक्षसाः ।
विघ्नितस्य च यज्ञस्य सद्यः कर्ता विनश्यति ।।

17. (Even) The clever Bramma-Raakshasa-s 'chase', (look out, for) faults in this; Therefore (if there is any impediments to this Yaaga) the Doer of an obstructed (& wrongly done) Yaaga will soon perish.

(Readers may note that Aschwamedha Yaaga- The Horse Sacrifice ceremony is very elaborate & demanding; Only Emperors do this).

❍ ❍ ❍

१८. तद्यथा विधिपूर्वं मे क्रतुरेष समाप्यते ।
तथा विधानं क्रियतां समर्थाः करणेष्विह ।।

18. Therefore may my Yaaga be done in such a way that it can be completed as per norms; Such efforts may be taken; You are all capable in these tasks.

❍ ❍ ❍

१९. तथेति चाब्रुवन्सर्वेमन्त्रिणः प्रत्यपूजयन् ।
पार्थिवेन्द्रस्य तद्वाक्यं यथाज्ञप्तं निशम्य ते ।।

19. Hearing these words of (Dhascharatha, the) lord of earth, all his ministers said: = As commanded, we shall do.= And they extolled him (honoured him).

❍ ❍ ❍

२०. तथा द्विजास्ते धर्मज्ञा वर्धयन्तो नृपोत्तमम् ।
अनुज्ञातास्ततः सर्वेपुनर्जग्मुर्यथागतम् ।।

20. The learned Braamins who knew Dharma, after extolling the foremost king, took leave and went away as they came.

❍ ❍ ❍

२१. विसर्जयित्वा तान् विप्रान् सचिवानिदमब्रवीत् ।
ऋत्विग्भिरुपदिष्टोऽयं यथावत्क्रतुराप्यताम् ।।

21. After sending the Braamins away, he addressed his ministers thus: Let the (Goal of) Yaaga as per the 'Directives' of The Rithviks (High priests) be accomplished as per norms (of Shaasthra).

❍ ❍ ❍

२२. इत्युक्त्वा नृपशार्दूलः सचिवान् समुपस्थितान् ।
विसर्जयित्वा स्वं वेश्म प्रविवेश महाद्युतिः ।।

22. Saying thus, after giving leave to the ministers gathered there, the most radiant & foremost king (this 'lion' amongst kings, Dhascharatha) went back to his abode.

❍ ❍ ❍

२३. ततः स गत्वा ताः पत्नीर्नरेन्द्रो हृदयप्रियाः ।
उवाच दीक्षां विशत यक्ष्येऽहं सुतकारणात् ।।

23. This lord of men, (this Dhascharatha), going there, addressed his most beloved wives (who pleased his heart), thus = For the sake of progeny, I am performing Yaaga; May you observe Vows.=

❍ ❍ ❍

२४. तासां तेनातिकान्तेन वचनेन सुवर्चसाम् ।
मुखपद्मान्यशोभन्त पद्मानीव हिमात्यये ।।

24. By these most endearing words, the gleaming lotus like faces of the wives shone like lotuses at the end of the cold season (Early Spring).

❍ ❍ ❍

Chapter 9

Sumanthra Narrates a Story told by Old Sanathkumaara

(Sumanthra, who was king Dhascharatha's minister, charioteer & a dear friend as well, narrates a story he had heard from the very old Sanathkumaara long ago, which has a bearing on the Yaaga being undertaken by Dhascharatha for his progeny & welfare).

❍ ❍ ❍

१. एतच्छ्रुत्वा रहः सूतो राजानमिदमब्रवीत् ।
श्रूयतां यत्पुरावृत्तं पुराणेन मया श्रुतम् ।।
ऋत्विग्भिरुपदिष्टोऽयं पुरावृत्तो मया श्रुतः ।।

1. Hearing all this (Sumanthra the) charioteer told the king when he was alone: = This old story mentioned by the Rithviks was heard by me; You may (please) listen to this old story that was heard by me, an old man, long, (long) ago.

❍ ❍ ❍

२. सनत्कुमारो भगवान् पूर्वं कथितवान् कथाम् ।
ऋषीणां सन्निधौ राजन् तव पुत्रागमं प्रति ।।

2. Oh King! The Lord Sanathkumaar narrated this story long ago in front of holy men, pertaining to progeny for you.

❍ ❍ ❍

३. काश्यपस्य तु पुत्रोऽस्ति विभण्डक इति श्रुतः ।
ऋश्यश्रृङ्ग इति ख्यातस्तस्य पुत्रो भविष्यति ।।

3. (Sumanthra narrates the story of Rischyaschringa to King Dhascharatha. This was heard by him long, long ago from Sanathkumaara)

There is a renowned son named Vibhandaka for Kaaschyapa. He will beget a famous son Rischyaschringa by name.

❍ ❍ ❍

४. स वने नित्यसंवृद्धो मुनिर्वनचरस्तदा ।
नान्यं जानाति विप्रेन्द्रो नित्यं पित्रनुवर्तनात् ।।

4. This noble braamin sage (Rischyaschringa) who was growing up entirely in forest, did not know any other (life) having ever served his father (Vibhandaka) as a forest dweller.

❍ ❍ ❍

५. द्वैविध्यं ब्रह्मचर्यस्य भविष्यति महात्मनः ।
लोकेषु प्रथितं राजन् विप्रैश्च कथितं सदा ।।

5. There is going to be a great change to this great soul (Rischyaschringa) in respect of his absolute bachelorhood, which is ever spoken of highly by Braamins of the world. Oh (my) King!

(Rischyaschringa was so isolated by his father that he was not even aware of the existence of the other sex!)

❍ ❍ ❍

६. तस्यैवं वर्तमानस्य कालः समभिवर्तत ।
अग्निं शुश्रूषमाणस्य पितरं च यशस्विनम् ।।

6. Time passed away for this (Rischyaschringa) who was in this (state of bachelorhood), performing Fire Rituals etc. and who was serving his famous father.

❍ ❍ ❍

७. एतस्मिन्नेव काले तु रोमपादः प्रतापवान् ।
अङ्गेषु प्रथितो राजा भविष्यति महाबलः ।।

7. At that time, in the territory of Anga, there will be a renowned king named Romapaadha who will be majestic & mightily strong.

❍ ❍ ❍

८. तस्य व्यतिक्रमाद्राज्ञो भविष्यति सुदारुणा ।
अनावृष्टिः सुघोरा वै सर्वभूतभयावहा ।।

8. (But) Owing to this king's neglect & transgressions, a miserable & gruesome drought (famine etc) will occur which will cause fear to all living beings there (in his kingdom).

❍ ❍ ❍

९. अनावृष्ट्यां तु वृत्तायां राजा दुःखसमन्वितः ।
ब्राह्मणान् श्रुतवृद्धांश्च समानीय प्रवक्ष्यति ।।

9. Due to lack of rain (Draught & famine), when this occurs, the king (Romapaadha) will be in grief and will invite learned & elderly Braamins & tell them (thus).

❍ ❍ ❍

१०. भवन्तः श्रुतधर्माणो लोकचारित्रवेदिनः ।
समादिशन्तु नियमं प्रायश्चित्तं यथा भवेत् ।।

10. (This is what King Romapaadha will say)

Ye men who are all well versed in Dharma and know the ways of the world must suggest remedial measures (to me) so that there will be atonement (for my sins and relief from draught in my kingdom of Anga).

❍ ❍ ❍

११. वक्ष्यन्ति ते महीपालं ब्राह्मणा वेदपारगाः ।
विभण्डकसुतं राजन् सर्वोपायैरिहानय ।।

11. These scholars of Vedha-s (who have crossed the 'shores of the ocean of Vedha-s'), these braamins, will tell:= Oh king (Romapaadha)! By every means (at your disposal), try to bring here (to our Anga territory), (Rischyaschringa) the son of Vibhandaka.

❍ ❍ ❍

१२. आनाय्य च महीपाल ऋश्यश्रृङ्गं सुसत्कृतम् ।
प्रयच्छ कन्यां शान्तां वै विधिना सुसमाहितः ।।

12. Oh king (Romapaadha): Receive this Rischyaschringa with due honours; offer your daughter Shaantha (in marriage to him) in proper manner & without any reservations.

❍ ❍ ❍

१३. तेषां तु वचनं श्रुत्वा राजा चिन्तां प्रपत्स्यते ।
केनोपायेन वै शक्यमिहानेतुं स वीर्यवान् ।।

13. Hearing these words from them, this brave king (Romapaadha) will begin to worry about (as to how to bring Rischyaschringa here) & by what means (& strategy) he can possibly be brought.

❍ ❍ ❍

१४. ततो राजा विनिश्चित्य सह मन्त्रिभिरात्मवान् ।
पुरोहितममात्यांश्च प्रेषयिष्यति सत्कृतान् ।।

14. The self reliant king will decide upon sending Purohiths (priests) along with ministers and with (other) honoured ministers from there.

१५. ते तु राज्ञो वचः श्रुत्वा व्यथिता विनताननाः ।
न गच्छेम ऋषेर्भीता अनुनेष्यन्ति तं नृपम् ।।

15. (But) these men hearing their king's words, will plead and tell their king: = We Will Not Go= with a down trodden face, out of their fear of the sage (Vibhandaka, the father of Rischyaschringa) much perturbed.

❍ ❍ ❍

१६. वक्ष्यन्ति चिन्तयित्वा ते तस्योपायांश्च तत्क्षमान् ।
आनेष्यामो वयं विप्रं न च दोषो भविष्यति ।।

16. (But later) After thinking about effective steps to be taken to avoid evil (consequences), they are going to tell him: =We Will Bring The Braamin (Rischyaschringa)=

❍ ❍ ❍

१७. एवमङ्गाधिपेनैव गणिकाभिर्ऋषेः सुतः ।
आनीतोऽवर्षयद्देवः शान्ता चास्मै प्रदीयते ।।

17. Thus, the Muni 's son (Rischyaschringa) will be brought by the king of Anga through (the services of) courtesans. And at once Lord (of Rain) Varuna will shower. And Shaantha will be offered to him (in marriage).

१८. ऋश्यश्रृङ्गस्तु जामाता पुत्रांस्तव विधास्यति ।
सनत्कुमारकथितं यथा ते व्याहृतं मया ।।

18. (Sumanthra concludes this story of Rischyaschringa he had heard from Sanathkumaara long ago; and Sumanthra advises Dhascharatha).

Your relative, (nephew) Rischyaschringa will (bless you) & offer sons to you. (All) this was told to me by Sanathkumaara and (all) this is being told by me to you (now).

❍ ❍ ❍

१९. अथ हृष्टो दशरथः सुमन्त्रं प्रत्यभाषत ।
यथर्श्यश्रृङ्गस्त्वानीतो विस्तरेण त्वयोच्यताम् ।।

19. (Dhascharatha 's interest in Rischyaschringa is kindled; wants to hear more about him from his friend and minister Sumanthra.)

The king Dhascharatha who was pleased, replied to Sumanthra; = In great length (this story) of how Rischyaschringa was brought (to Anga long long ago), may please be told by you in detail =.

(Note: Sumanthra is a very old man; has seen lot of life. He is more than a minister to Dhascharatha. He recalls the story told to him by the Seer, the very old Sanathkumaara. And, he advises Dhascharatha that somehow Rischyaschringa must be brought to Ayodhya for the successful completion of The Yaaga and for obtaining progeny for him. And, of course, Dhascharatha accepts his suggestion, but wants to know more about the story of Rischyaschringa as narrated by Sanathkumaara to Sumanthra).

❍ ❍ ❍

Chapter 10

Decision to Invite Rischyaschringa

(Sumanthra continues the story told to him by Sanathkumaara).

❍ ❍ ❍

१. सुमन्त्रश्चोदितो राज्ञा प्रोवाचेदं वचस्तथा ।
यथर्श्यशृङ्गस्त्वानीतः श्रृणु मे मन्त्रिभिः स ह ।।

1. Goaded thus by the king, Sumanthra said the following: May you listen from me as to how Rischyaschringa was brought by ministers (to Anga).

❍ ❍ ❍

२. रोमपादमुवाचेदं सहामात्यं पुरोहितः ।
उपायो निरापायोऽयमस्माभिरभिचिन्तितः ।।

2. The (chief) Purohith addressed Romapaadha who was

with his ministers thus: The Means (& strategy) which are not harmful has been thought out by us...... .

❍ ❍ ❍

३. ऋश्यश्रृङ्गो वनचरस्तपस्स्वाध्यायने रतः ।
अनभिज्ञः स नारीणां विषयाणां सुखस्य च ।।

3. ...... this Rischyaschringa is devoted to penance & meditation; Being a forest dweller (ever since his birth) is ignorant about women; and earthly mundane pleasures.

❍ ❍ ❍

४. इन्द्रियार्थैरभिमतैर्नरचित्तप्रमाथिभिः ।
पुरमानाययिष्यामः क्षिप्रं चाध्यवसीयताम् ।।

4. ...... We shall bring him to our city, soon, by such temptations & desirables that would soften a man's heart; Let it be so resolved...... .

❍ ❍ ❍

५. गणिकास्तत्र गच्छन्तु रूपवत्यः स्वलंकृताः ।
प्रलोभ्य विविधोपायैरानेष्यन्तीह सत्कृताः ।।

5. ...... Let pretty courtesans dressed up well go there (to Rischyaschringa's abode); By various methods, let them entice (& seduce) him, entertain him & they will (surely) bring him over here.

❍ ❍ ❍

६. श्रुत्वा तथेति राजा च प्रत्युवाच पुरोहितम् ।
पुरोहितो मन्त्रिणश्च तथा चक्रुश्च ते तदा ।।
वारमुख्यास्तु तच्छ्रुत्वा वनं प्रविविशुर्महत् ।।

6. Listening to this, the king (Romapaadha) said to the Purohith = So Be it =. Then the ministers & purohiths did likewise (as suggested). Foremost courtesans, hearing this (command), entered the big forest (to entice Rischyaschringa as per the strategy).

❍ ❍ ❍

७. आश्रमस्याविदूरेऽस्मिन् यत्नं कुर्वन्ति दर्शने ।
ऋषिपुत्रस्य धीरस्य नित्यमाश्रमवासिनः ॥

7. Reaching the outskirts of the hermitage, they attempted to 'see ' the (most) composed (Rischyaschringa), who was the son of Rishi (Vibhandaka), and who ever lived in the hermitage (in the forest, who knew nothing else than forest life).

❍ ❍ ❍

८. पतुः स नित्यसन्तुष्टो नातिचक्राम चाश्रमात् ॥

8. And he (this Rischyaschringa), who was ever in service of his father, did not come out of his hermitage.

❍ ❍ ❍

९. न तेन जन्मप्रभृति दृष्टपूर्वं तपस्विना ।
स्त्री वा पुमान् वा यच्चान्यत् सत्त्वं नगरराष्ट्रजम् ॥

9. Right from his birth, nothing had been seen before by this man of penance; No woman, no man (other than his father), neither town nor village, nor any material things (other than forest products).

❍ ❍ ❍

१०. ततः कदाचित्तं देशमाजगाम यदृच्छया ।
विभण्डकसुतस्तत्र ताश्चापश्यद्वराङ्गनाः ॥

10. Then, one day, (Rischyaschringa) the son of Vibhandaka, by sheer accident came to the place (in the forest); And he saw the lovely damsels.

❍ ❍ ❍

११. ताश्चित्रवेषः प्रमदा गायन्त्यो मधुरस्वरैः ।
ऋषिपुत्रमुपागम्य सर्वा वचनमब्रुवन् ॥

11. The beautiful maidens who were bedecked in fine jewellery and dresses, all of them approached (this Rischyaschringa), the son of the Rishi, singing melodiously; They addressed him these words.

❍ ❍ ❍

१२. करत्वं किं वर्तसे ब्रह्मन् ज्ञातुमिच्छामहे वयम् ।
एकस्त्वं विजने घोरे वने चरसि शंस नः ।।

12. Oh Braamin! Who are you ? Why are you roaming in this unpopulated, gruesome forest ? Why are you here? We wish to know; Please tell us.

❍ ❍ ❍

१३. अदृष्टरूपास्तास्तेन काम्यरूपा वने स्त्रियः ।
हार्दात्तस्य मतिर्जाता आख्यातुं पितरं स्वकम् ।।

13. Having never seen such "creatures" with such pretty 'forms' in his forest, a thought occurred to him that he should tell these damsels about his father, out of his 'affection' (to these lovelies!).

❍ ❍ ❍

१४. पिता विभण्डकोऽस्माकं तस्याहं सुत औरसः ।
ऋश्यश्रृङ्ग इति ख्यातं नाम कर्म च मे भुवि ।।

14. (Risyaschringa tells them)= My father is Vibhandaka; I am his own son; Rishyaschringa is my name; My service is known in the world. (My service to my father and religious vows).

❍ ❍ ❍

१५. इहाश्रमपदोऽस्माकं समीपे शुभदर्शनाः ।
करिष्ये वोऽत्र पूजां वै सर्वासां विधिपूर्वकम् ।।

15. Nearby is our Hermitage; Oh pleasant looking beings! There, I will honour you all as per norms (of hospitality).

❍ ❍ ❍

१६. ऋषिपुत्रवचः श्रुत्वा सर्वासां मतिरास वै ।
तदाश्रमपदं द्रष्टुं जग्मुः सर्वाश्च तेन ताः ।।

16. Hearing the words of the Rishi (Rischyaschringa), the idea (to go with him was most welcome) to these damsels; They all went with him to 'see' his Hermitage.

❍ ❍ ❍

१७. गतानां तु ततः पूजामृषिपुत्रश्चकार ह ।
इदमर्घ्यमिदं पाद्यमिदं मूलमिदं फलम् ॥

17. (Rischyaschringa) the son of the Rishi honoured them who had come there (with him), saying = Here is Arghya; This is Paadhya; This is Tuber; This is fruit = (all for you).

❍ ❍ ❍

१८. प्रतिगृह्य च तां पूजां सर्वा एव समुत्सुकाः ।
ऋषेर्भीताश्च शीघ्रं ता गमनाय मतिं दधुः ॥

18. Greatly elated they all accepted the hospitality; Yet, as they were scared of the Rishi (Vibhandaka, the father of Rischyaschringa), they decided to go back soon (before he came).

❍ ❍ ❍

१९. अस्माकमपि मुख्यानि फलानीमानि वै द्विज ।
गृहाण प्रति भद्रं ते भक्षयस्व च मा चिरम् ॥

19. Oh Braamin (Rischyschringa)! Please accept from us these foremost fruits; welfare to you. Eat them; Don't delay. (The damsels are very clever; As return of his hospitality they offer him things he had never seen before in his life).

❍ ❍ ❍

२०. ततस्तास्तं समालिङ्ग्य सर्वा हर्षसमन्विताः ।
मोदकान् प्रददुस्तस्मै भक्ष्यांश्च विविधान् शुभान् ॥

20. (And the damsels 'work' upon this innocent Rischyschringa). The Damsels happily hugged him; they gave various 'cakes' & 'Eats', most delicious (not tasted by him, ever before).

❍ ❍ ❍

२१. तानि चास्वाद्य तेजस्वी फलानीति स्म मन्यते ।
अनास्वादितपूर्वाणि वने नित्यनिवासिना ॥

21. The brilliant (Rischyaschringa) who was ever a resident of forest & who had never tasted these before, when he ate them, thought that these were 'fruits'!

❍ ❍ ❍

२२. आपृच्छ्य च तदा विप्रं व्रतचर्यां निवेद्य च ।
गच्छन्ति स्मापदेशात्ता भीतास्तस्य पितुः स्त्रियः ।।

22. Then these damsels, being scared of his father (who might return to hermitage any moment), took his leave and went away under a pretext, telling him about some 'vows' (they had to perform immediately at their abode!).

❍ ❍ ❍

२३. गतासु तासु सर्वासु काश्यपस्यात्मजो द्विजः ।
अस्वस्थहृदयश्चासीद्दुःखात् संपरिवर्तते ।।

23. When they all had left, this Braamin (Vibhandaka) the son of Kaaschyapa was very sad & down hearted; he went hither & thither.

❍ ❍ ❍

२४. ततोऽपरेद्युस्तं देशमाजगाम स वीर्यवान् ।
मनोज्ञा यत्र ता दृष्टा वारमुख्याः स्वलमृताः ।।

24. (But) The next day, the courageous (Rischyaschringa) came to the same place where these captivating and well dressed up foremost damsels were seen (by him the previous day).

❍ ❍ ❍

२५. दृष्ट्वैव च तदा विप्रमायान्तं हृष्टमानसाः ।
उपसृत्य ततः सर्वास्तास्तमूचुरिदं वचः ।।

25. Then seeing the Braamin (Rischyaschringa) approaching them, (these damsels) approached him with a happy heart and said these words.

❍ ❍ ❍

२६. एह्याश्रमपदं सौम्य अस्माकमिति चाब्रुवन् ।
विचित्राणि बहूनि स्युर्मूलानि च फलानि च ।।
तत्राप्येष विधिः श्रीमान् विशेषेण भविष्यति ।।

26. (Now damsels really entice him).

Oh Pleasant one! Come to our 'Hermitage'; There are wonderful & numerous 'fruits' & 'tubers' there; further, this, (our) glorious hospitality (to you), will be very special. So they told him.

❍ ❍ ❍

२७. श्रुत्वा तु वचनं तासां सर्वासां हृदयङ्गमम् ।
गमनाय मतिं चक्रे तं च निन्युस्तदा स्त्रियः ।।

27. Hearing these words from them all which 'touched' his heart, he decided to go at once (with them); the damsels then led him along.

❍ ❍ ❍

२८. तत्र चानीयमाने तु विप्रे तस्मिन् महात्मनि ।
ववर्ष सहसा देवो जगत् प्रह्लादयंस्तदा ।।

28. The moment this great soul braamin was brought (to Anga by damsels), Lord (of Rain Varuna), showered, making earth happy.

❍ ❍ ❍

२९. वर्षेणैवागतं विप्रं विषयं स नराधिपः ।
प्रत्युद्गम्य मुनिं प्रह्वः शिरसा च महीं गतः ।।

29. The Braamin sage (Rischyaschringa) reached the city along with rain. (Even as he entered, rain was pouring): The king going towards him (to receive him) bowed to the Braamin respectfully, with his head touching the earth.

❍ ❍ ❍

३०. अर्घ्यं च प्रददौ तस्मै न्यायतः सुसमाहितः ।
वव्रे प्रसादं विप्रेन्द्रान्मा विप्रं मन्युराविशेत् ।।

30. With all his heart he offered Arghya to him as per norms (of hospitality); He sought the favour of this foremost Braamin (Rischyaschringa in such a way) that he would not get angry (with him because he was enticed by damsels).

❍ ❍ ❍

३१. अन्तःपुरं प्रविश्यास्मै कन्यां दत्त्वा यथाविधि ।
शान्तां शान्तेन मनसा राजा हर्षमवाप सः ॥

31. This king (Romapaadha) entering the inner apartments of his palace, offered his girl Shaantha (in marriage to Rischyaschringa) as per norms, and with peace of mind. He obtained happiness.

❍ ❍ ❍

३२. एवं स न्यवसत्तत्र सर्वकामैः सुपूजितः ।
ऋश्यश्रृङ्गो महातेजाः शान्तया सह भार्यया ॥

32. Thus, this most brilliant Rischyaschringa lived there (in Anga) along with his wife Shaantha, with all comforts, well honoured.

(Note: Having heard the full life story of Rischyaschringa from his minister & friend Sumanthra, King Dhascharatha realises that his prosperity rests with Rischyaschringa & his presence at Ayodhya is very vital for his Yaaga which he is about to perform for his progeny).

❍ ❍ ❍

Chapter 11

The Bringing of Rischyaschringa by Dhascharatha (to Ayodhya)

(And Sumanthra narrates the story of Sanathkumaara further which has a bearing on the proposed Yaaga by Dhascharatha).

❍ ❍ ❍

१. भूय एव च राजेन्द्र श्रृणु मे वचनं हितम् ।
यथा स देवप्रवरः कथायामेवब्रवीत् ।।

1. Oh Supreme king (Dhascharatha)! The divine sage (Seer Sanathkumaara) told me even more of this story; May you listen the following words from me that are salutary.

❍ ❍ ❍

२. इक्ष्वाकूणां कुले जातो भविष्यति सुधार्मिकः ।
नाम्ना दशरथो राजा श्रीमान् सत्यप्रतिश्रवः ।।

2. In the family of Ikshwaaku-s, a king by name of Dhascharatha will be born; he will be a man of Dharma, resplendent & who will abide by Truth.

(Readers may note that in those days, some very great sages could foresee the future & the very old Sanathkumaara was one such).

३. अङ्गराजेन सख्यं च तस्य राज्ञो भविष्यति ।
कन्या चास्य महाभागा शान्ता नाम भविष्यति ।।

3. There will be friendship for this king with the king of Anga; And there will be (born) an illustrious daughter Shaantha......

❍ ❍ ❍

४. पुत्रस्त्वङ्गाधिराजस्य रोमपाद इति श्रुतः ।
तं स राजा दशरथो गमिष्यति महायशाः ।।

4. ...... To Anga king, there will be a renowned son Romapaadha; And king Dhascharatha, the most famous, will go (& approach Anga king)...... .

❍ ❍ ❍

५. अनपत्योऽस्मि धर्मात्मन् शान्ताभर्ता मम क्रतुम् ।
आरभेत त्वयाऽऽज्ञप्तः सन्तानार्थं कुलस्य च ।।

5. . . . . . (and Dhascharatha will request his friend, the king of Anga like this).

= Oh noble soul! I am without son. For the sake of progeny in my family, commanded by you, may (your daughter) Shaantha's husband (Rischyschringa) perform my Yaaga.=

❍ ❍ ❍

६. श्रुत्वा राज्ञोऽथ तद्वाक्यं मनसा च विचिन्त्य च ।
प्रदास्यते पुत्रवन्तं शान्ताभर्तारमात्मवान् ।।

6. Hearing the words of king (Dhascharatha), the composed (Anga king) will then consider this (request) in his mind, and will offer (the services of) Shaantha's husband (Rischyaschringa) for the sake of sons (for Dhascharatha).

❍ ❍ ❍

७. तं च राजा दशरथो यशस्कामः कृताञ्जलिः ।
ऋश्यशृङ्गं द्विजश्रेष्ठं वरयिष्यति धर्मवित् ।।

7. This king (Dhascharatha) accepting (the services of) the Braamin (Rischyaschringa), will perform this Yaaga happily, with all his heart and free from worries.

❍ ❍ ❍

८. तं च राजा दशरथो यशस्कामः कृताञ्जलिः ।
ऋश्यशृङ्गं द्विजश्रेष्ठं वरयिष्यति धर्मवित् ।।

8. For the sake of fame, the king Dhascharatha the knower of Dharma, with folded arms, (will request &) bring the foremost Braamin Rischyaschringa (to Ayodhya)...... .

❍ ❍ ❍

९. यज्ञार्थं प्रसवार्थं च स्वर्गार्थं च नरेश्वरः ।
लभते च स तं कामं द्विजमुख्याद्विशां पतिः ॥

9. . . . . for the sake of his Yaaga, for the sake of progeny, and for obtaining Swarga, (heaven after death) And this foremost of men, this lord of men (Dhascharatha) will obtain his wishes from*the Braamin (Rischyschringa): (A Braamin is caled Dvija-twice 'born':

He is born when he comes out of womb: Again 'born' when he is initiated into study of Holy Vedhic Texts).

१0. पुत्राश्चास्य भविष्यन्ति चत्वारोऽमितविक्रमाः ।
वंशप्रतिष्ठानकराः सर्वलोकेषु विश्रुताः ॥

10. To (Dhascharatha) four sons will be born who will be famous in all the worlds, who will have immense valour & who will bring stability to his race.

❍ ❍ ❍

११. एवं स देवप्रवरः पूर्वं कथितवान् कथाम् ।
सनत्कुमारो भगवान् पुरा देवयुगे प्रभुः ॥

11. Long long ago in the Krithi Yuga, the old lord, the foremost of the Dheva-s, Lord Sanathkumaar told the story thus, (which I am now telling you, Oh king Dhascharatha).

१२. स त्वं पुरुषशार्दूल तमानय सुसत्कृतम् ।
स्वयमेव महाराज गत्वा सबलवाहनः ॥

12. Oh 'Tiger' amongst men! Oh great king (Dhascharatha)! You personally go there and fetch him, duly honouring him. Go with your full Army, chariots etc. (as mark of respect for Rischyaschringa).

❍ ❍ ❍

१३. अनुमान्य वसिष्ठं च सूतवाक्यं निशम्य च ।
सान्तःपुरः सहामात्यः प्रययौ यत्र स द्विजः ॥

13. (Dhascharatha accepts the advice, goes to fetch Rishyschringa).

Listening to the words (of advice) of his charioteer (Sumanthra) and getting approval of Vasishta, (Dhascharatha) went along with his wives to where this Braamin (Rischyaschringa) was.

❍ ❍ ❍

१४. वनानि सरितश्चैव व्यतिक्रम्य शनैः शनैः ।
अभिचक्राम तं देशं यत्र वै मुनिपुङ्गवः ।।

14. Crossing forests & rivers stage by stage, (Dhascharatha) reached the kingdom where the foremost muni (Rischyaschringa) lived.

❍ ❍ ❍

१५. आसाद्य तं द्विजश्रेष्ठं रोमपादसमीपगम् ।
ऋषिपुत्रं ददर्शादौ दीप्यमानमिवानलम् ।।

15. Reaching Romapaadha's place, he first saw the foremost Braamin (Rischyaschringa) the son of the Rishi (Vibhandaka) who was 'glowing like Fire'.

❍ ❍ ❍

१६. ततो राजा यथान्यायं पूजां चक्रे विशेषतः ।
सखित्त्वात्तस्य वै राज्ञः प्रहृष्टेनान्तरात्मना ।।

16. The king (of Anga), because of his friendship with the king (Dhascharatha), extended great hospitality with all his heart, very pleased, and as per norms.

❍ ❍ ❍

१७. रोमपादेन चाख्यातमृषिपुत्राय धीमते ।
सख्यं संबन्धकं चैव तदा तं प्रत्यपूजयत् ।।

17. By this Romapaadha, his friendship & relationship (with Dhascharatha) was told to (Rischyaschringa), the wise son of Rishi. (Vibhandaka): Then he honoured him.

❍ ❍ ❍

१८. एवं सुसत्कृतस्तेन सहोषित्वा नरर्षभः ।
सप्ताष्टदिवसान् राजा राजानमिदमब्रवीत् ।।

18. Well honoured thus, 'the bull' amongst men, king (Dhascharatha), spent 7 or 8 days with him & he addressed the king (of Anga) thus:

❍ ❍ ❍

१९. शान्ता तव सुता राजन् सह भर्त्रा विशां पते ।
मदीयं नगरं यातु कार्यं हि महदुद्यतम् ।।

19. Oh lord of the people! Oh king (of Anga)! May your daughter Shaantha, accompanied by her husband (Rischyaschringa) come to my capital; A great work (of Yaaga) has begun (at Ayodhya).

❍ ❍ ❍

२०. तथेति राजा संश्रुत्य गमनं तस्य धीमतः ।
उवाच वचनं विप्रं गच्छ त्वं सह भार्यया ।।

20. The king (of Anga) said, (in respect of) the very wise man (Rischyaschringa's) leaving (for Ayodhya with Dhascharatha) = So Be It = And he further said to the Braamin (Rischyaschringa): = You go, accompanied by your wife (Shaantha). =

❍ ❍ ❍

२१. ऋषिपुत्रः प्रतिश्रुत्य तथेत्याह नृपं तदा ।
स नृपेणाभ्यनुज्ञातः प्रययौ सह भार्यया ।।

21. Hearing this, (Rischyaschringa) the son of the Rishi, said = So Be It = Taking leave of the king (of Anga) he went along with his wife. (Shaantha).

❍ ❍ ❍

२२. तावन्योन्याञ्जलिं कृत्वा स्नेहात् संश्लिष्य चोरसा ।
ननन्दतुर्दशरथो रोमपादश्च वीर्यवान् ।।

22. These two, Dhascharatha & the brave Romapaadha, greeted each other (respectfully) with folded arms of Anjali, hugged, (drawing their) chests close in affection & they rejoiced.

❍ ❍ ❍

२३. ततः सुहृदमापृच्छ्य प्रस्थितो रघुनन्दनः ।
पौरेभ्यः प्रेषयामास दूतान् वै शीघ्रगामिनः ।।

23. (Dhascharatha the) darling of Raghu-s took leave of his friend (the king of Anga &) started out (after) sending (in advance) messengers who could go fast, to the well populated (city of Ayodhya).

❍ ❍ ❍

२४. क्रियतां नगरं सर्वं क्षिप्रमेव स्वलंकृतम् ।
धूपितं सिक्तसंमृष्टं पताकाभिरलंकृतम् ।।

24. (And Dhascharatha commands his messengers).

At once, everywhere in (our) city (of Ayodhya), may it be decorated with banners, (streets) cleaned with waters sprinkled, well decorated, with Incenses (making 'Air' sweet).

❍ ❍ ❍

२५. ततः प्रहृष्टाः पौरास्ते श्रुत्वा राजानमागतम् ।
तथा प्रचक्रुस्तत्सर्वं राज्ञा यत् प्रेषितं तदा ।।

25. (The messengers arrive at Ayodhya earlier for receiving the chief guest Rischyschringa well, with the city beautified).

Hearing of the king's arrival (soon), the citizens who were all happy, did all these with great enthusiasm as per the order of their king. (Dhascharatha).

❍ ❍ ❍

२६. ततः स्वलमृतं राजा नगरं प्रविवेश ह ।
शफ्ङ्खुन्दुभिनिर्घोषैः पुरस्कृत्य द्विजोत्तमम् ।।

26. The King (Dhascharatha) then entered the capital that was well decorated, followed by the noble braamin (Rischyaschringa), to the accompaniment of music, dhundhubi drums & conch blows.

❍ ❍ ❍

२७. ततः प्रमुदिताः सर्वेदृष्ट्वा तं नागरा द्विजम् ।
प्रवेश्यमानं सत्कृत्य नरेन्द्रेणेन्द्रकर्मणा ।।

27. On seeing this braamin (Rischyaschringa) who was duly honoured by their king (Dhascharatha) who was like Lord Indhra in valour & deeds, all the citizens were jubilant, as he was being led (into the city).

❍ ❍ ❍

२८. अन्तःपुरं प्रवेश्यैनं पूजां कृत्वा च शास्त्रतः ।
कृतकृत्यं तदाऽऽत्मानं मेने तस्योपवाहनात् ।।

28. Leading him to the inner apartments (of his palace), and honouring him with due hospitality, (Dhascharatha) considered himself as though his job (of Yaaga) was (already) accomplished (successfully) by (& because of) the arrival (of Rischyaschringa).

❍ ❍ ❍

२९. अन्तःपुराणि सर्वाणि शान्तां दृष्ट्वा तथाऽऽगताम् ।
सह भर्त्रा विशालाक्षीं प्रीत्याऽऽनन्दमुपागमन् ।।

29. The ladies of the household, all of them, were delightfully happy at seeing this wide eyed Shaantha who had come there with her husband (Rischyaschringa).

❍ ❍ ❍

३०. पूज्यमाना च ताभिः सा राज्ञा चैव विशेषतः ।
उवास तत्र सुखिता कंचित् कालं सभर्तृका ।।

30. And she, (Shaantha), also, being specially honoured by them all & by the king, lived in comfort there for sometime along with her husband.

(Note: The Great Yaaga is to be done with the patronage of the great Rischyaschringa. Dhascharatha's minister Sumanthra knew that Rischyaschringa's presence at Ayodhya will bring prosperity to the kingdom and also satisfy the wishes of Dhascharatha in the matter of progeny to him. Just as Rischschringa had brought Rain and prosperity to Anga kingdom long, long ago, so will he bring joy to Ayodhya kingdom. And the very old "Seer" and Sage, Sanathkumaar had even predicted that under the patronage of Rischyaschringa, when Dhascharatha completes the Yaaga, he will beget four noble sons).

❍ ❍ ❍

Chapter 12

Procurement of Yaaga Materials

(Under the patronage of Rischyaschringa, before lords & kings from other places & before multitude, The Great Yaaga is to begin).

❍ ❍ ❍

१. ततः काले बहुतिथौ कस्मिंश्चित् सुमनोहरे ।
वसन्ते समनुप्राप्ते राज्ञो यष्टुं मनोऽभवत् ।।

1. Then, when the captivating spring season which contains many Thithi-s (lunar days) started, the idea of commencing the yaaga arose in the king.

❍ ❍ ❍

२. ततः प्रणम्य शिरसा तं विप्रं देववर्णिनम् ।
यज्ञाय वरयामास सन्तानार्थं कुलस्य च ।।

2. Bowing before the celestial looking Braamin (Rischyaschringa) with his head bowed, king (Dhascharatha) solicited him for performing The Yaaga for the sake of progeny for his family.

❍ ❍ ❍

३. तथेति च स राजानमुवाच च सुसत्कृतः ।
संभाराः संभ्रियन्तां ते तुरगश्च विमुच्यताम् ।।

3. (Rischyaschringa) who was well honoured, said to the

king: =So Be It: May the materials be procured; Let (the Sacred) Horse be released.=

❍ ❍ ❍

४. ततो राजाऽब्रवीद्वाक्यं सुमन्त्रं मन्त्रिसत्तमम् ।
सुमन्त्रावाहय क्षिप्रमृत्विजो ब्रह्मवादिनः ॥

4. Then the king addressed the foremost minister (Sumanthra): Oh Sumanthra! Fetch at once the Rithviks who are expounders of the Vedha. (Brammam)...... .

❍ ❍ ❍

५. सुयज्ञं वामदेवं च जाबालिमथ काश्यपम् ।
पुरोहितं वसिष्ठं च ये चाप्यन्ये द्विजोत्तमाः ॥

5. ...... (fetch) Suyagnya, Vaamadheva, Jaabaali, Kaaschyapa, and the Purohith (chief priest) Vasishta and other foremost braamins.

❍ ❍ ❍

६. ततः सुमन्त्रस्त्वरितं गत्वा त्वरितविक्रमः ।
समानयत् स तान् विप्रान् समस्तान् वेदपारगान् ॥

6. Then Sumanthra who always acted quickly, (a man of quick action), went out fast and fetched all these braamins who had mastered the Vedha, (who had "crossed the shore of Vedha").

❍ ❍ ❍

७. तान् पूजयित्वा धर्मात्मा राजा दशरथस्तदा ।
धर्मार्थसहितं युक्तं श्लक्ष्णं वचनमब्रवीत् ॥

7. Noble soul man of Dharma, this Dhascharatha the king, honoured them: He addressed them with sweet, proper words, embellished in Dharma.

❍ ❍ ❍

८. मम लालप्यमानस्य पुत्रार्थं नास्ति सुखम् ।
तदर्थं हयमेधेन यक्ष्यामीति मतिर्मम ॥

8. There is no happiness for me who is in lament for

the sake of son (progeny); therefore it is my wish to perform The Yaaga through The Aschwamedha (The Horse Sacrifice- Yaaga).

❍ ❍ ❍

९. तदहं यष्टुमिच्छामि शास्त्रदृष्टेन कर्मणा ।
ऋषिपुत्रप्रभावेन कामान् प्राप्स्यामि चाप्यहम् ।।

9. Therefore I desire to perform The Yaaga as 'Seen' in the Shaasthra-s (as per norms); And further by the (grace &) power of (Rischyaschringa) the son of Rishi, I will (surely) obtain my wish.

❍ ❍ ❍

१०. ततः साध्विति तद्वाक्यं ब्राह्मणाः प्रत्यपूजयन् ।
वसिष्ठप्रमुखाः सर्वेपार्थिवस्य मुखेरितम् ।।

10. Hearing these words from the 'face' of the king, all the braamins including Vasishta extolled him, saying: = Good =

❍ ❍ ❍

११. ऋश्यशृङ्गपुरोगाश्च प्रत्यूचुर्नृपतिं तदा ।
संभाराः संभ्रियन्तां ते तुरगश्च विमुच्यताम् ।।

11. In the presence of Rischyaschringa, they spoke: = May the Yaaga materials be procured; May The Horse be released.=

❍ ❍ ❍

१२. सर्वथा प्राप्स्यसे पुत्रांश्चतुरोऽमितविक्रमान् ।
यस्य ते धार्मिकी बुद्धिरियं पुत्रार्थमागता ।।

12. (And said further): For the sake of progeny this thought associated with Dharma entered you; Four sons of incomparable valour, you will obtain totally (surely).

❍ ❍ ❍

१३. ततः प्रीतोऽभवद्राजा श्रुत्वैतद् द्विजभाषितम् ।
अमात्यांश्चाब्रवीद्राजा हर्षणदं शुभाक्षरम् ।।

14. As per the advice of my Guru-s (Teachers, priests), let materials for Yaaga be procured quickly; let The Horse that is well (groomed &) protected by capable men and which is with Upaadhyaaya-s (Teachers), be released.

❍ ❍ ❍

१५. सरय्वाश्चोत्तरे तीरे यज्ञभूमिर्विधीयताम् ।
शान्तयश्च प्रवर्तन्तां यथाकल्पं यथाविधि ।।

15. Further, let The Yaaga Center be established on the northern banks of Saraayu river; Let the preliminary (house warming) ceremonies be done as per Shaasthra-s.

❍ ❍ ❍

१६. शक्यः कर्तुमयं यज्ञः सर्वेणापि महीक्षिता ।
नापराधो भवेत् कष्टो यद्यस्मिन् क्रतुसत्तमे ।।

16. In this foremost Yaaga, there will be grievous harm (if not performed properly); Otherwise, (had it been a simple one), this Yaaga is capable of being performed by all, (by any) king.

❍ ❍ ❍

१७. छिद्रं हि मृगयन्तेऽत्र विद्वांसो ब्रह्मराक्षसाः ।
विघ्नितस्य तु यज्ञस्य सद्यः कर्ता विनश्यति ।।

17. (Even) the skilful Brammaraakshasa-s search for loopholes & faults in this; The Doer of this Yaaga which is done with impediments (& done wrongly), gets destroyed; indeed! very soon.

❍ ❍ ❍

१८. तद्यथा विधिपूर्वं मे क्रतुरेष समाप्यते ।
तथा विधानं क्रियतां समर्थाः करणेष्विह ।।

18. Therefore, may efforts be taken by you who are all most capable in such ceremonies, in such a way that this Yaaga of mine will be completed as per norms of Shaasthras.

❍ ❍ ❍

१९. तथेति च ततः सर्वेमन्त्रिणः प्रत्यपूजयन् ।
पार्थिवेन्द्रस्य तद्वाक्यं यथाऽऽज्ञप्तमकुर्वत ।।

19. Then, hearing the great king's words, all the ministers honoured him (by saying) = It will be done like this = And they acted as per king's orders.

❍ ❍ ❍

२०. ततो द्विजास्ते धर्मज्ञमस्तुवन् पार्थिवर्षभम् ।
अनुज्ञातास्ततः सर्वेपुनर्जग्मुर्यथागतम् ।।

20. Then the Braamins praised (Dhascharatha) 'the bull' amongst kings who knew Dharma: Taking leave, they went back again as they came.

❍ ❍ ❍

२१. गतेषु तेषु विप्रेषु मन्त्रिणस्तान्नराधिपः ।
विसर्जयित्वा स्वं वेश्म प्रविवेश महाद्युतिः ।।

21. After the Braamins left, the king went to his abode in splendor after sending away his ministers.

(Note: The Aschwamedha Yaaga- The Horse sacrifice is a celebrated ceremony performed only by men of immense strength & power & wealth. It is supposed to have its origin in Pre-Vedhic times. Hundred Aschwamedha ceremonies properly done can make a person rule all the Three worlds of Heaven, Earth & Underworlds. The Horse is trained & groomed by Upaadhyaya-s (Teachers). The Sacred horse, when let lose will roam about freely at will, over all the territories. None dares to stop it. And the king who releases the Sacred Horse, in effect extends his authority over the territories this horse roams about. If any one seizes the horse, it is obligatory on the part of the king who had released the Horse, to destroy the ruler of his territory).

❍ ❍ ❍

Chapter 13

The Ceremonial Yaaga Center: Entry into This Yaaga Center

१. पुनः प्राप्ते वसन्ते तु पूर्णः संवत्सरोऽभवत् ।
प्रसवार्थं ततो यष्टुं हयमेधेन वीर्यवान् ॥

1. When spring arrived again, (the old year) was over, the brave (king Dhascharatha) for the sake of begetting progeny, through Yaaga of Aschwamedha......

❍ ❍ ❍

२. अभिवाद्य वसिष्ठं च न्यायतः प्रतिपूज्य च ।
अब्रवीत् प्रश्रितं वाक्यं प्रसवार्थं द्विजोत्तमम् ॥
यज्ञो मे क्रियतामद्य यथोक्तं मुनिपुङ्गव ॥

2. ...... bowing before the foremost Braamin Vasishta & worshipping him with due respects, said these respectful words: =Oh (Vasishta), 'the tiger' amongst Muni-s! For the sake of progeny may my Yaaga be performed as per Shaasthra. =

(Readers may note that in India the new year starts in April, when spring ends & summer begins).

❍ ❍ ❍

३. यथा न विघ्नः क्रियते यज्ञाङ्गेषु विधीयताम् ॥

3. May (my Yaaga) be done (properly) in such a way that there are no obstacles in the (actual) details of the Yaaga.

❍ ❍ ❍

४. भवान् स्निग्धः सुहृन्मह्यं गुरुश्च परमो महान् ।
वोढव्यो भवता चैव भारो यज्ञस्य चोद्यतः ॥

4. You are my close friend; And you are (also) my foremost teacher; The load & (responsibility of) the Yaaga that is being started must be borne by you only.

❍ ❍ ❍

५. तथेति च स राजानब्रवीद् द्विजसत्तमः ।
करिष्ये सर्वमेवैतद्भवता यत् समर्थितम् ॥

5. The foremost braamin (Vasishta) said to the king = Let it be so; I will do all this as resolved by you.=

❍ ❍ ❍

६. ततोऽब्रवीद् द्विजान् वृद्धान् यज्ञकर्मसु निष्ठितान् ।
स्थापत्ये निष्ठितांश्चैव वृद्धान् परमाधार्मिकान् ॥

6. (Vasishta, the chief priest of Ikshwaaku kings takes over the responsibility; Stanzas 6 to 27; Vasishta gives orders) Then he said: The elderly braamins who are well versed in Yaagas, experts in construction work, elders who are foremost men of Dharma...... .

❍ ❍ ❍

७. कर्मान्तिकाञ्छिल्पकरान् वर्धकीन् खनकानपि ।
गणकाञ्छिल्पिनश्चैव तथैव नटनर्तकान् ॥
ततोऽब्रवीच्छास्त्रविदः पुरुषान् सुबहुश्रुतान् ॥

7. ...... Accountants, dancers & singers, carpenters, well diggers, decorators, sculptors, likewise other workers.

❍ ❍ ❍

८. यज्ञकर्म समीहन्तां भवन्तो राजशासनात् ।
इष्टका बहुसाहस्त्री शीघ्रमानीयतामिति ॥

8. ...... then he addressed men who were well versed in many Shaasthra-s...... .

❍ ❍ ❍

९. औपकार्याः क्रियन्तां च राज्ञां बहुगुणान्विताः ।
ब्राह्मणावसथाश्चैव कर्तव्याः शतशः शुभाः ॥

9. May royal cottages with all the *Guna-s' (of comfort & beauty) be constructed for kings And auspicious houses in hundreds must be constructed for Braamins. (*Guna- features).

❍ ❍ ❍

१०. भक्ष्यान्नपानैर्बहुभिः समुपेताः सुनिष्ठिताः ।
तथा पौरजनस्यापि कर्तव्या बहुविस्तराः ।।

10. Likewise, for the citizens let there be extensive (wide) range of foodstuffs, like eats, foods & drinks, well prepared; must be done.

❍ ❍ ❍

११. आवासा बहुभक्षाश्च सर्वकामैरुपस्थिताः ।
तथा जानपदस्यापि जनस्य बहु शोभनम् ।।

11. All the abodes must be well provided with plenty of eats with all desirable. And for folks from villages, many delightful...... .

१२. दातव्यमन्नं विधिवत् सत्कृत्य न तु लीलया ।।

12. . . . . dishes of Anna-s (Rice -grain preparations) must be offered with *respect, and as per norms (This) Not (to be. treated) lightly. (Indian hospitality-treat guests with honour).

❍ ❍ ❍

१३. सर्ववर्णा यथा पूजां प्राप्नुवन्ति सुसत्कृताः ।
न चावज्ञा प्रयोक्तव्या कामक्रोधवशादपि ।।

13. Men of all caste-s should be treated to (great) hospitality and (like as I have said), must receive due honours. Either out of anger or passion, no insult (or disrespect) should be shown (to any of them). (There were Castes, but no Casteism in those days).

❍ ❍ ❍

१४. यज्ञकर्मसु ये व्यग्राः पुरुषाः शिल्पिनस्तथा ।
तेषामपि विशेषेण पूजा कार्या यथाक्रमम् ।।
ते च स्युः संभृताः सर्वैर्वसुभिर्भोजनेन च ।।

14. These workers in the Yaaga work & (preparation), sculptors & the like who are engrossed in work, to all of these men particularly, due respect must be shown

as befitting them; they must all be satisfied by our (offerings of) money & foods.

❍ ❍ ❍

१५. यथा सर्वं सुविहितं न किञ्चित् परिहीयते ।
तथा भवन्तः कुर्वन्तु प्रीतिस्निग्धेन चेतसा ॥

15. With a mind (& heart) full of endearment & affection, you should do all (this) work in such a way it will be perfect, without any neglect.

❍ ❍ ❍

१६. ततः सर्वेसमागम्य वसिष्ठमिदमब्रुवन् ।
यथोक्तं तत्सुविहितं न किञ्चित् परिहीयते ॥
यथोक्तं तत् करिष्यामो न किञ्चित् परिहास्यते ॥

16. Then all of them came and said this to Vasishta.= All that has been told by you, must (and will be) be carried out; There should be no neglect; there will be no wanting in (our duties); We shall do exactly as you have said =

❍ ❍ ❍

१७. ततः सुमन्त्रमानीय वसिष्ठो वाक्यमब्रवीत् ।
निमन्त्रयस्व नृपतीन् पृथिव्यां ये च धार्मिकाः ॥

17. Then inviting Sumanthra, Vasishta said = You invite all those kings in the world who are men of Dharma.=

❍ ❍ ❍

१८. ब्राह्मणान् क्षत्रियान् वैश्यान् शूद्रांश्चैव सहस्रशः ।
समानयस्व सत्कृत्य सर्वदेशेषु मानवान् ॥

18. Extending hospitality you bring here men from all the kingdoms, the Braamins, Kshathriya-s, Vysya-s & Schoodhra-s, in thousands. (Citizens from all castes were invited for Yaaga- And honoured. No Discrimination those days although Caste existed).

❍ ❍ ❍

१९. मिथिलाधिपतिं वीरं जनकं सत्यविक्रमम् ।
निष्ठितं सर्वशास्त्रेषु तथा वेदेषु निष्ठितम् ।।

19. The king of Mithila, the brave Janaka is well versed in all Shaasthra-s and learned in Vedha-s and truly most valiant...... .

❍ ❍ ❍

२०. तमानय महाभागं स्वयमेव सुसत्कृतम् ।
पूर्वसंबन्धिनं ज्ञात्वा ततः पूर्वं ब्रवीमि ते ।।

20. ...... this illustrious (king), you fetch yourself (personally), honouring him. As I know, he is going to be the First *Sambandhi. Therefore I am telling you first.

(*When a boy & girl marry, their parents are called Sambandhi-s. Vasishta is a great Seer: knows that when Dhascharatha begets sons, his sons are going to marry the daughters of King Janaka. Hence this special invitation & Sumanthra, the first one to hear this: Dhascharatha and Janaka are going to be Sambhandhis).

❍ ❍ ❍

२१. तथा काशीपतिं स्निग्धं सततं प्रियवादिनम् ।
सद्वृत्तं देवसमाशं स्वयमेवानयस्व ह ।।

21. Likewise, our dear friend, the sweet tongued Ruler of Kaashi who is like a celestial on earth and who is of good conduct, must be personally invited by you.

❍ ❍ ❍

२२. तथा केकयराजानं वृद्धं परमधार्मिकम् ।
श्वशुरं राजसिंहस्य सपुत्रं त्वमिहानय ।।

22. Likewise you may invite the father.in.law of our old and Dharmic king, the king of Kekeya kingdom, along with his son.

❍ ❍ ❍

२३. अङ्गेश्वरं महाभागं रोमपादं सुसत्कृतम् ।
वयस्यं राजसिंहस्य तमानय यशस्विनम् ।।

23. You must (invite) with full honours & bring the illustrious & most famous king of Anga, Romapaadha who is a comrade of (our king Dhascharatha who is) 'lion' amongst kings.

❍ ❍ ❍

२४. प्राचीनान् सिन्धुसौवीरान् सौराष्ट्रेयांश्च पार्थिवान् ।
दाक्षिणात्यान्नरेन्द्रांश्च समस्तानानयस्व ह ।।

24. You must also invite kings from South, East, Sauraashtra, Sindhu & Sowveera territories, all of them.

❍ ❍ ❍

२५. सन्ति स्निग्धाश्च ये चान्ये राजानः पृथिवीतले ।
तानानय यथाक्षिप्रं सानुगान् सहबान्धवान् ।।

25. Kings from other parts of the world who are our friends should also be invited and brought along with their folks & relatives soon.=

❍ ❍ ❍

२६. वसिष्ठवाक्यं तच्छ्रुत्वा सुमन्त्रस्त्वरितस्तदा ।
व्यादिशत् पुरुषांस्तत्र राज्ञामानयने शुभान् ।।

26. Hearing Vasishta's words, Sumanthra then sent out immediately good men to fetch these kings. (& others).

❍ ❍ ❍

२७. स्वयमेव हि धर्मात्मा प्रययौ मुनिशासनात् ।
सुमन्त्रस्त्वरितो गत्वा समानेतुं महीक्षितः ।।

27. And the man of Dharma Sumanthra, under orders from Vasishta, went out on journey himself in great speed, to fetch the kings.

❍ ❍ ❍

२८. ते च कर्मान्तिकाः सर्वेवसिष्ठाय च धीमते ।
सर्वं निवेदयन्ति स्म यज्ञे यदुपकल्पितम् ।।

28. All the workmen informed the wise Vasishta (of the progress &) about all the (work) completed for the Yaaga.

❍ ❍ ❍

२९. ततः प्रीतो द्विजश्रेष्ठस्तान् सवानिदमब्रवीत् ।।

29. Then the foremost braamin (Vasishta), being very pleased, told all of them the following.

३०. अवज्ञया न दातव्यं कस्यचिल्लीलयाऽपि वा ।
अवज्ञया कृतं हन्याद्दातारं नात्र संशयः ।।

30. (Words of advice from Vasishta)

With disrespect & without grace, nothing is to be given to any one: Anything done with contempt (or given casually) will destroy the Giver. There is no doubt about this.

❍ ❍ ❍

३१. ततः कैश्चिदहोरात्रैरुपयाता महीक्षितः ।
बहूनि रत्नान्यादाय राज्ञो दशरथस्य च ।।

31. Thereafter (there was regular stream of) kings who came by day & night with many gems & stones (as presents) to king Dhascharatha.

❍ ❍ ❍

३२. ततो वसिष्ठः सुप्रीतो राजानमिदमब्रवीत् ।
उपयाता नरव्याघ्र राजानस्तव शासनात् ।।

32. Vasishta pleased (at the response), addressed the king thus= Oh (Dhascharatha the) 'Tiger' of men! As per your command, the kings have come.

❍ ❍ ❍

३३. मया च सत्कृताः सर्वेयथार्हं राजसत्तमाः ।
यज्ञियं च कृतं राजन् पुरुषैः सुसमाहितैः ।।

33. All the noble kings have been duly honoured by me with hospitality. Oh king! The work on Yaaga have also been completed by men well versed in this.

❍ ❍ ❍

३४. निर्यातु च भवान् यष्टुं यज्ञायतनमन्तिकात् ।
सर्वकामैरुपहृतैरुपेतं वै समन्ततः ।।

34. You may also go (now) to The Yaaga Center, to perform The Yaaga, where on all sides (you will find) all the necessary materials brought recently as per our wish.

❍ ❍ ❍

३५. द्रष्टुमर्हसि राजेन्द्र मनसेव विनिर्मितम् ।।

35. Oh Lord of kings! You will see (everything there exactly) as conceived by our mind. =

❍ ❍ ❍

३६. तथा वसिष्ठवचनादृश्यश्रृङ्गस्य चोभयोः ।
शुभे दिवसनक्षत्रे निर्यातो जगतीपतिः ।।

36. Then by the words of command of these two, Vasishta & Rischyaschringa, on an auspicious day & of stars, (King Dhascharatha) the lord of earth, started (for the Yaaga center).

❍ ❍ ❍

३७. ततो वसिष्ठप्रमुखाः सर्व एव द्विजोत्तमाः ।
ऋश्यश्रृङ्गं पुरस्कृत्य यज्ञकर्मारिभंस्तदा ।।
यज्ञवाटगताः सर्वेयथाशास्त्रं यथाविधि ।।

37. There, all those who reached the Yaaga Center, these foremost Braamins headed by Vasishta, began to perform The Yaaga as per norms & as per Shaasthra, in front of, (in the immediate presence of), Rischyaschringa.

❍ ❍ ❍

Chapter 14

(King Dhascharatha) Performs The Aschwamedha Yaaga

१. अथ संवत्सरे पूर्णेतस्मिन् प्राप्ते तुरङ्गमे ।
सरय्वाश्चोत्तरे तीरे राज्ञो यज्ञोऽभ्यवर्तत ।।

1. Then, with the arrival of The (Sacred) Horse at the end of the year, the king's Yaaga was performed on the northern banks of river Saraayu.

❍ ❍ ❍

२. ऋश्यश्रृङ्गं पुरस्कृत्य कर्म चक्रुर्द्विजर्षभाः ।
अश्वमेधे महायज्ञे राज्ञोऽस्य सुमहात्मनः ।।

2. Headed by (& in the august presence of) Rischyaschringa, the foremost braamins began the great Yaaga of Aschwamedha of this very great soul, king (Dhascharatha).

३. कर्म कुर्वन्ति विधिवद्याजका वेदपारगाः ।
यथाविधि यथान्यायं परिक्रामन्ति शास्त्रतः ।।

3. The Rithviks (Purohiths & priests) who were well versed in Vedha (who had crossed "the shores of the ocean of Vedha"), performed the yaaga as per norms, properly, as per the Code and Shaasthra-s.

❍ ❍ ❍

४. प्रवर्ग्यं शास्त्रतः कृत्वा तथैवोपसदं द्विजाः ।
चक्रुश्च विधिवत् सर्वमधिकं कर्म शास्त्रतः ।।

4. As per Shaasthra, these braamins did the (ceremony of) Pravarghya, Upasadh, and likewise, as per Shaasthra, they did further, other ceremonies, as per code.

❍ ❍ ❍

५. अभिपूज्य ततो हृष्टाः सर्वेचक्रुर्यथाविधि ।
प्रातःसवनपूर्णानि कर्माणि मुनिपुङ्गवाः ।।

5. In great happiness, all the foremost Muni-s (these sages who were 'tigers' amongst muni-s) worshipped and then did ceremonies like 'Praathas-savana', as per norms.

❍ ❍ ❍

६. ऐन्द्रश्च विधिवद्दत्तो राजा चाभिष्टुतोऽनघः ।
माध्यन्दिनं च सवनं प्रावर्तत यथाक्रमम् ।।

6. The Share (of oblations due) to Lord Indhra was given as per custom; and the sinless king (Sun) was extolled. And ceremonies to be done at noon, took place as per norms.

❍ ❍ ❍

७. तृतीयसवनं चैव राज्ञोऽस्य सुमहात्मनः ।
चक्रुस्ते शास्त्रतो दृष्ट्वा यथा ब्राह्मणपुङ्गवाः ।।

7. Noble Braamins (these 'tigers' of braamins) performed the third Savana ceremonies, (the evening ceremony) as 'Seen' in the Shaasthra, during the Yaaga of this great soul (Dhascharatha).

❍ ❍ ❍

८. न चाहुतमभूत्तत्र स्खलितं वाऽपि किञ्चन ।
दृश्यते ब्रह्मवत् सर्वं क्षेमयुक्तं हि चक्रिरे ।।

8. (During the Yaaga) there was no blunder whatsoever, nor in The Offerings (Oblations); (The Holy) Fire was burning all the time at the Vedhi-fire (mound) Everything appeared as per divine order; they did (all this) to bring tranquillity. (for mankind at large).

❍ ❍ ❍

९. न तेष्वहस्सु श्रान्तो वा क्षुधितो वाऽपि दृश्यते ।
नाविद्धान् ब्राह्मणस्तत्र नाशतानुचरस्तथा ।।

9. During the daytime, none was seen who was tired nor hungry; there was no braamin who was not learned; likewise none was there without retinue of disciples.

❍ ❍ ❍

१०. ब्राह्मणा भुञ्जते नित्यं नाथवन्तश्च भुञ्जते ।
तापसा भुञ्जते वाऽपि श्रमणा भुञ्जते तथा ।।

10. The braamins ate daily; the Schoodra-s ate well; men of penance ate well (too); likewise even the sages ate well.

❍ ❍ ❍

११. वृद्धाश्च व्याधिताश्चैव स्त्रियो बालास्तथैव च ।
अनिशं भुञ्जमानानां च तृप्तिरुपलभ्यते ।।

11. The elderly folks, the women, the kids and (even) sickly persons ate. Although they ate incessantly, they were still not 'satisfied'.

(So much food was there; so tasty that there was desire to eat more).

❍ ❍ ❍

१२. दीयतां दीयतामन्नं वासांसि विविधानि च ।
इति संचोदितास्तत्र तथा चक्रुरनेकशः ।।

12. (The staff) was directed repeatedly thus = May foods be offered (ever); May various dresses be offered =. (These men) were goaded to serve (the multitude) and they did likewise.

❍ ❍ ❍

१३. अन्नकूटाश्च बहवो दृश्यन्ते पर्वतोपमाः ।
दिवसे दिवसे तत्र सिद्धस्य विधिवत्तदा ।।

13. Everyday heaps of food of various (grains like) Rice, well cooked as per custom were seen there, looking like mountain (when they were stacked up).

❍ ❍ ❍

१४. नानादेशादनुप्राप्ताः पुरुषाः स्त्रीगणास्तथा ।
अन्नपानैः सुविहितास्तस्मिन् यज्ञे महात्मनः ।।

14. In this great (King's) Yaaga, men & women from various territories were satisfied with food & drink.

❍ ❍ ❍

१५. अन्नं हि विधिवत् स्वादु प्रशंसन्ति द्विजर्षभाः ।
अहो तृप्ताः स्म भद्रं ते इति शुश्राव राघवः ॥

15. = The Food is very tasty; properly (cooked & served); We are satisfied; welfare to you = Thus, the foremost braamins extolled. And (Dhascharatha) the Raaghava heard (all this during the yaaga).

❍ ❍ ❍

१६. स्वलंकृताश्च पुरुषा ब्राह्मणान् पर्यवेषयन् ।
उपासते च तानन्ये सुमृष्टमणिकुण्डलाः ॥

16. Well groomed (well dressed up) men served the braamins; And others who were wearing bright (ornament) of ear drops, studded with gems, served them.

❍ ❍ ❍

१७, कर्मान्तरे तदा विप्रा हेतुवादान् बहूनपि ।
प्राहुः सुवाग्मिनो धीराः परस्परजिगीषया ॥

17. In the Yaaga Center, the energetic & eloquent Braamins, entered into discussions, desirous of 'scoring' over the other, using diverse arguments.

❍ ❍ ❍

१८. दिवसे दिवसे तत्र संस्तरे कुशला द्विजाः ।
सर्वकर्माणि चक्रुस्ते यथाशास्त्रं प्रचोदिताः ॥

18. Every day these braamin experts, goaded by (high priests), performed all the rituals in this yaaga as per shaasthra-s.

❍ ❍ ❍

१९. नाषडङ्गविदत्रासीन्नाव्रतो नाबहुश्रुतः ।
सदस्यास्तस्य वै राज्ञो नावादकुशला द्विजाः ॥

19. There was none there who did not know 6 Vedha-s; none who did not practise Vows (austerities); none who did not know scriptures; In the assembly of the

king, no one who was not clever in discussion amongst the braamins.

❍ ❍ ❍

२०. प्राप्ते यूपोच्छ्रये तस्मिन् षड् बैल्वाः खादिरास्तथा ।
तावन्तो बिल्वसहिताः पर्णिनश्च तथाऽपरे ॥

20. (The Yaaga Center described)

When the time of fixing Pillars (Masts) arrived, 6 masts made of Bilva tree (Aegle Marmelosa-the wood apple tree), likewise the same (number of) masts made of Kadhira (Acacia Catechu) along with Bilva wood, and likewise same (number of masts made from) Parnin (Butea Frontosa) ....

❍ ❍ ❍

२१. श्लेष्मातकमयो दिष्टो देवदारुमयस्तथा ।
द्वावेव तत्र विहितौ बाहुव्यस्तपरिग्रहौ ॥

21. ...... And likewise, as per norms, Two (masts made from) Sleshma (Pandarus Odaratismus) and Dhevadhaaru (Avaria Longifolia) wood which were cut up to a height reachable by hand, were all erected.

❍ ❍ ❍

२२. कारिताः सर्व एवैते शास्त्रज्ञैर्यज्ञकोविदैः ।
शोभार्थं तस्य यज्ञस्य काञ्चनालंकृता भवन् ॥

22. All these were done up by men well versed in Yaaga rituals. By men who knew Shaasthra. For the sake of giving brightness to the Yaaga hall, they were decorated with (shining) gold.

❍ ❍ ❍

२३. एकविंशतियूपास्त एकविंशत्यरत्नयः ।
वासोभिरेकविंशद्भिरेकैकं समलंकृताः ॥

23. All these 21 Masts were beautifully draped with 21 metre-s (of cloth) individually.

❍ ❍ ❍

२४. विन्यस्ता विधिवत् सर्वैशिल्पिभिः सुकृता दृढाः ।
अष्टाश्रयः सर्व एव श्लक्ष्णरूपसमन्विताः ।।

24. All of them were decorated with artistic ornamentation; These masts were rigid, (well grounded); erected as per norms. There were 8 'Faces' with lovely shining figures.

❍ ❍ ❍

२५. आच्छादितास्ते वासोभिः पुष्पैर्गन्धैश्च भूषिताः ।
सप्तर्षयो दीप्तिमन्तो विराजन्ते यथा दिवि ।।

25. They were covered with cloth; decorated with flowers & besmeared with sandal paste; they shone like (Saptha Rishi-s), the seven Rishi-s of the celestial world.

❍ ❍ ❍

२६. आह्वयांचक्रिरे तत्र शक्रादीन् विबुधोत्तमान् ।
ऋश्यश्रृङ्गादयो मन्त्रैः शीक्षाक्षरसमन्वितैः ।।

26. Rischyaschringa & others invited the foremost Dheva-s (the celestials) like Lord Indhra, invoking with chants from Vedha-s, with correct pronunciation (& Intonation) in the Scheeksha (Style).

❍ ❍ ❍

२७. नीतिभिर्मधुरैः स्निग्धैर्मन्त्राह्वानैर्यथार्हतः ।
होतारो ददुराभाष्य हविर्भागान् दिवौकसाम् ।।

27. The Hotha-s (Holy priests) with beautiful gait, distributed portions of oblations to the Dheva-s with recitations, inviting them with endearment, with Chants & Invocations.

❍ ❍ ❍

२८. इष्टकाश्च यथान्यायं कारिताश्च प्रमाणतः ।
चित्योऽग्निर्ब्राह्मणैस्तत्र कुशलैः शिल्पकर्मणि ।।

28. In the Yaaga work, measured quantities of bricks were laid properly by clever braamins; Fire Mound was set up.

❍ ❍ ❍

२९. स चित्यो राजसिंहस्य सञ्चितः कुशलैर्द्विजैः ।
गरुडो रुक्मपक्षो वै त्रिगुणोऽष्टादशात्मकः ।।

29. At the foremost king's (Yaaga), at the Altar, Three sets of Eighteen parts of Garuda Bird with bright red wings were done up by proficient braamins.

❍ ❍ ❍

३०. नियुक्तास्तत्र पशवस्तत्तदुद्दिश्य दैवतम् ।
उरगाः पक्षिणश्चैव यथाशास्त्रं प्रचोदिताः ।।

30. As enjoined in Shaashtra-s, cows, reptiles, birds, were all tied up there for propitiating respective lords (celestials).

(All these to be sacrificed during Homa for pleasing various lords).

❍ ❍ ❍

३१. शामित्रे तु हयस्तत्र तथा जलचराश्च ये ।
ऋषिभिः सर्वमेवैतन्नियुक्तं शास्त्रतस्तथा ।।

31. Likewise, those marine creatures & Horse for Sacrificial ceremony were all tied there by Rishi-s as per Shaasthra.

❍ ❍ ❍

३२. पशूनां त्रिशतं तत्र यूपेषु नियतं तदा ।
अश्वरत्नोत्तमं तत्र राज्ञो दशरथस्य च ।।

32. There 300 cows were secured on the masts; And king Dhascharatha's foremost horse, a gem of a horse, (was also tied up).

❍ ❍ ❍

३३. कौसल्या तं हयं तत्र परिचर्यासमन्विता ।
कृपाणैर्विशशासैनं त्रिभिः परमया मुदा ।।

33. (And Dhascharatha's eldest wife) Kowsalya, with great devotion & care smote (& killed) with great joy, this horse, in 3 strokes.

❍ ❍ ❍

३४. पतत्रिणा तदा सार्धं सुस्थितेन च चेतसा ।
अवसद्रजनीमेकां कौसल्या धर्मकाम्यया ।।

34. Bound by Dharma, Kowsalya spent the night (& kept vigil) with the (Slaughtered) horse, with a resolute mind.

❍ ❍ ❍

३५. होताऽध्वर्युस्तथोद्गाता हयेन समयोजयन् ।
महिष्या परिवृत्त्या च वावातां च तथाऽपराम् ।।

35. (The priests) The Hotha, Adhwaryu & Udhgaatha, "enjoined" the first queen (Kowsalya), the (second) younger queen (Sumithra) & the (third) beloved queen, (Kaikeyi) with the Horse.

❍ ❍ ❍

३६. पतत्रिणस्तस्य वपामुद्धृत्य नियतेन्द्रियः ।
ऋत्विक् परमसंपन्नः श्रपयामास शास्त्रतः ।।

36. Taking the flesh of the Horse, an Adhwaryu who was greatly endowed (with qualities) & who had controlled his senses (& passion), apportioned the (oblation on fire) as per Shaasthra.

❍ ❍ ❍

३७. धूमगन्धं वपायास्तु जिघ्रन्ति स्म नराधिपाः ।
यथाकालं यथान्यायं निर्णुदन् पापमात्मनः ।।

37. Without wasting time, the kings (gathered there) smelt the fumes of Vedhi Fire from the flesh of (the sacrificed horse), in order to get rid of their sins, as per custom.

❍ ❍ ❍

३८. हयस्य यानि चाङ्गानि तानि सर्वाणि ब्राह्मणाः ।
अग्नौ प्रास्यन्ति विधिवत् समस्ताः षोडशर्त्विजः ।।

38. All the various parts of the body of the (Sacrificed) Horse, The 16 Priests who were all Braamins, made oblations to the (Holy) Fire as per custom.

❍ ❍ ❍

३९. प्लक्षशाखासु यज्ञानामन्येषां क्रियते हविः ।
अश्वमेधस्य चैकस्य वैतसो भाग इष्यते ।।

39. The Fire oblations for various other Yaaga-s is done with branches from Fig tree; but for Aschwamedha Yaaga the portions of oblations are kept in Reeds (Rumex Vesicarius).

❍ ❍ ❍

४०. त्र्यहोऽश्वमेधः संख्यातः कल्पसूत्रेण ब्राह्मणैः ।
अग्निष्टोममहस्यतस्य प्रथमं परिकल्पितम् ।।
उवथ्यं द्वितीयं संख्यातमतिरात्रं तथोत्तरम् ।।

40. As per Kalpa Soothra, (Manual for Sacrifices & Conduct) and as per The Brahmanaas (Doctrines), it is reckoned that the (period for) Aschwamedha Yaaga is (of) three days (duration). In this, the first day is fixed for Agnishtoma. The second is reckoned as day of Uvathyam; Likewise Athiraathra is next.

❍ ❍ ❍

४१. कारितास्तत्र बहवो विहिताः शास्त्रदर्शनात् ।।

41. Keeping an eye on Shaasthra, the many rituals that are prescribed, (all of them) were done.

❍ ❍ ❍

४२. ज्योतिष्टोमायुषी चैवमतिरात्रौ विनिर्मितौ ।
अभिजिद्विश्वजिच्चैवमप्तोर्यामो महाक्रतुः ।
अयजद्वाजिमेधेन दिशस्स्वकुलवर्धनः ।।

42. (The Twosome) Athiraathra- were done. Rituals of Jyothishta & Aayush (Homa): likewise Abhijith & Vischwajith, Mahaa (Yaaga): Aapthoryaama were (all done). The Entire directions (all regions) (this king Dhascharatha) who was seeking prosperity for his family, performed all this through the Ashwamedha Yaaga.

❍ ❍ ❍

४३. प्राचीं होत्रे ददौ राजा दिशं स्वकुलवर्धनः ।
अध्वर्यवे प्रतीचीं तु ब्रह्मणे दक्षिणां दिशम् ।।

43. The King who was seeking prosperity for his family, offered easterly direction (regions) to The Hotha-s: For Adhwaryu-s, the westerly (region) for God Bramma, the southerly direction (Region). And for Udhgaatha, the northern......

❍ ❍ ❍

४४. उद्गात्रे तु तथोदीचीं दक्षिणैषा विनिर्मिता ।
अश्वमेधे महायज्ञे स्वयंभुविहिते पुरा ।।

44. ...... Direction (Region). Long long ago, (as per old custom & tradition), in The Great Aschwamedha Sacrifice initiated by God Bramma (The self born), such gifts were offered (then).

❍ ❍ ❍

४५. क्रतुं समाप्य तु तदा न्यायतः पुरुषर्षभः ।
ऋत्विग्भ्यो हि ददौ राजा धरां तां कुलवर्धनः ।।

45. This king (Dhascharatha), the 'Bull' amongst men who was increasing (the prosperity) of his family, completed The Yaaga as per norms & then offered this Earth to the Rithviks......

❍ ❍ ❍

४६. ऋत्विजश्चाब्रुवन् सर्वेराजानं गतकल्मषम् ।
भवानेव महीं कृत्स्नामेको रक्षितुमर्हति ।।

46. (But) all the Rithviks told the king whose sins (if any) had gone away = Oh the lord of Earth! You alone are capable of protecting the entire earth.! . . . .

❍ ❍ ❍

४७. न भूम्या कार्यमस्माकं न हि शक्ताः स्म पालने ।
रताः स्वाध्यायकरणे वयं नित्यं हि भूमिप ।।
निष्क्रयं किञ्चिदेवेह प्रयच्छतु भवान् हि नः ।।

47. ...... We have no use with (your gift of) Earth; Nor are we capable of ruling it; we are ever devoted to doing meditation (& study). Oh lord of earth! Give us something equivalent in value (in kind)......

❍ ❍ ❍

४८. मणिरत्नं सुवर्णं वा गावो यद्वा समुद्यतम् ।
तत् प्रयच्छ नरश्रेष्ठ धरण्या न प्रयोजनम् ।।

48. ...... Oh foremost of men! Give us something, whatever, either ornaments, or gold or cows.=

❍ ❍ ❍

४९. एवमुक्तो नरपतिर्ब्राह्मणैर्वेदपारगैः ।
गवां शतसहस्राणि दश तेभ्यो ददौ नृपः ।।

49. When told thus by Braamins who were well versed in Vedhas, this lord of men, this king (Dhascharatha) gave them cows in millions & gold in hundred million (ten crores), four times of this.

❍ ❍ ❍

५०. दश कोटीस्सुवर्णस्य रजतस्य चतुर्गुणम् ।।

50. Ten crores of Silver, four times of this he gave: (Ten million = a crore; and hundred thousand = a lakh).

❍ ❍ ❍

५१. ऋत्विजश्च ततः सर्वेप्रददुः सहिता वसु ।
ऋश्यश्रृङ्गाय मुनये वसिष्ठाय च धीमते ।।

51. Then all the Rithviks got together and gave to Sage Rischyaschringa & to the wise Vasishta, excellent things.

❍ ❍ ❍

५२. ततस्ते न्यायतः कृत्वा प्रविभागं द्विजोत्तमाः ।
सुप्रीतमनसः सर्वेप्रत्यूचुर्मुदिता भृशम् ।।

52. Then these foremost Braamins, after taking their

(respective) due share, went back (to their places), fully satisfied & in joy.

❍ ❍ ❍

५३. ततः प्रसर्पकेभ्यस्तु हिरण्यं सुसमाहितः ।
जाम्बूनदं कोटिसंख्यं ब्राह्मणेभ्यो ददौ तदा ।।

53. Then the (king), well composed, (free from worries), gave gold from Jambu river (beds) in millions to all the braamins who were all (sitting) in the enclosures (of the Yaaga hall).

❍ ❍ ❍

५४. दरिद्राय द्विजायाथ हस्ताभरणमुत्तमम् ।
कस्मैचिद्याचमानाय ददौ राघवनन्दनः ।।

54. The darling of the Raghu-s (king Dhascharatha) then gave foremost bangle to some poor Braamin who had begged him.

५५. ततः प्रीतेषु विद्वत्सु द्विजेषु द्विजवत्सलः ।
प्रणाममकरोत्तेषां हर्षपर्याकुलेक्षणः ।।

55. Then, as the learned Braamins were all happy, this benefactor of the Braamins, (this Dhascharatha), bowed to them with tears in his eyes due to happiness.

❍ ❍ ❍

५६. तस्याशिषोऽथ विविधा ब्राह्मणैः समुदाहृताः ।
उदारस्य नृवीरस्य धरण्यां प्रणतस्य च ।।

56. When (Dhascharatha) was prostrating on the floor before them, to this foremost amongst the brave & most noble king, many blessings were offered, (well uttered) by these braamins.

❍ ❍ ❍

५७. ततः प्रीतमना राजा प्राप्य यज्ञमनुत्तमम् ।
पापापहं स्वर्नयनं दुस्तरं पार्थिवर्षभैः ।।

57. The king became pleased when he completed this

foremost Yaaga which is very difficult to perform (even) by foremost kings, (even by 'Bulls' amongst kings- None else can perform this Aschwamedha Yaaga) that will destroy sin & lead one to heaven.

❍ ❍ ❍

५८. ततोऽब्रवीदृश्यश्रृङ्गं राजा दशरथस्तदा ।
कुलस्य वर्धनं तन्तुं कर्तुमर्हसि सुव्रत ।।

58. The king Dhascharatha addressed Rischyaschringa thus = Oh man of Vows! For family's lineage, you must (bless me) with progeny =

❍ ❍ ❍

५९. तथेति च स राजानमुवाच द्विजसत्तमः ।
भविष्यन्ति सुता राजंश्चत्वारस्ते कुलोद्वहाः ।।

59. Rischyaschringa the noble braamin said = So Be It! Oh king, Four sons will be born to you, to establish lineage in your family =

❍ ❍ ❍

६०. स तस्य वाक्यं मधुरं निशम्य प्रणम्य तस्मै प्रयतो नृपेन्द्रः ।
जगाम हर्षं परमं महात्मा तमृश्यश्रृङ्गः पुनरप्युवाच ।।

60. This king of kings (Dhascharatha), hearing these sweet words, bowed before him with great respect; And he obtained great happiness; And this great soul Rischyaschringa once again addressed him.

❍ ❍ ❍

Chapter 15

Performance of Rituals for Progeny; The Vow to Kill Raavana

१. मेधावी तु ततो ध्यात्वा स किञ्चिदिदमुत्तरम् ।
लब्धसंज्ञस्तस्तं तु वेदज्ञो नृपमब्रवीत् ।।

1. Then the intelligent (Rischyaschringa) who knew Vedha-s, meditated for a while, addressed the king further thus after regaining his (normal state of) consciousness. (He was in a trance for a while).

❍ ❍ ❍

२. इष्टिं तेऽहं करिष्यामि पुत्रीयां पुत्रकारणात् ।
अथर्वशिरसि प्रोक्तैर्मन्त्रैः सिद्धां विधानतः ।।

2. I am going to perform (another) Yaaga ceremony for the sake of progeny to you, as 'told' in Atharvana Vedha which contains prayers and which contains appropriate rituals for the sake of progeny.

❍ ❍ ❍

३. ततः प्राक्रामदिष्टिं तां पुत्रीयां पुत्रकारणात् ।
जुहाव चाग्नौ तेजस्वी मन्त्रदृष्टेन कर्मणा ।।

3. Then the brilliant (Rischyaschringa) began this Yaaga pertaining to progeny (to the king); he performed oblations in Fire with rituals contained in Holy Texts.

❍ ❍ ❍

४. ततो देवाः सगन्धर्वाः सिद्धाश्च परमर्षयः ।
भागप्रतिग्रहार्थं वै समवेता यथाविधि ।।

4. Then the celestials who were with Ghandharva-s, along with Sidha-s & great sages, gathered there to take their share of oblations as per norms.

❍ ❍ ❍

५. ताः समेत्य यथान्यायं तस्मिन् सदसि देवताः ।
अब्रुवंल्लोककर्तारं ब्रह्माणं वचनं महत् ।।

5. All the celestials, assembled in the Hall in due course, & addressed these great words to God Bramma, the creator of World.

❍ ❍ ❍

६. भगवंस्त्वत्प्रसादेन रावणो नाम राक्षसः ।
सर्वान्नो बाधते वीर्याच्छासितुं तं न शक्नुमः ।।

6. Oh God (Bramma)! By Your Grace (& favour) Raavana the demon, is harassing us all with his might; We are unable to suppress him.

❍ ❍ ❍

७. त्वया तस्मै वरो दत्तः प्रीतेन भगवन् पुरा ।
मानयन्तश्च तं नित्यं सर्वं तस्य क्षमामहे ।।

7. Oh God (Bramma)! Pleased (as you were with him) a boon was given to him by you (long, long ago). And we are ever enduring all this (evil actions upon us from him) out of consideration & respect (for you and because of your boon to this evil Raavana).

❍ ❍ ❍

८. उद्वेजयति लोकांस्त्रीनुच्छ्रितान् द्वेष्टि दुर्मतिः ।
शक्रं त्रिदशराजानं प्रधर्षयितुमिच्छति ।।

8. This evil minded (Raavana) terrorises all the three Worlds: He hates elders; And he desires to embrocate (& crush) the lord of Dheva-s, Schakra, (Indhra, the wielder of Disc).

❍ ❍ ❍

९. ऋषीन् यक्षान् सगन्धर्वानसुरान् ब्राह्मणांस्तथा ।
अतिक्रामति दुर्धर्षोवरदानेन मोहितः ।।

9. Because of your offer of boon (to Raavana) who is uncrushable, who is mad (with passion and arrogance), he attacks the Rishi-s, Yaksha-s and Ghandharva-s, Asura-s and likewise, braamins.

❍ ❍ ❍

१०. नैनं सूर्यः प्रतपति पार्श्वेवाति न मारुतः ।
चलोर्मिमाली तं दृष्ट्वा समुद्रोऽपि न कम्पते ।।

10. Sun does not burn him up (nor torment him); Wind

does not go near him; and (even) the Ocean which shakes up with turbulent waves, does not shake when it sees him!

❍ ❍ ❍

११. तन्महन्नो भयं तस्माद्राक्षसाद्घोरदर्शनात् ।
वधार्थं तस्य भगवन्नुपायं कर्तुमर्हसि ।।

11. Thus, there is great fear for us from this gruesome looking demon; Oh God! May you (therefore) find a remedy for destroying him.

❍ ❍ ❍

१२. एवमुक्तः सुरैः सर्वैश्चिन्तयित्वा ततोऽब्रवीत् ।
हन्तायं विहितस्तस्य वधोपायो दुरात्मनः ।।

12. When all this was told by all the Dheva-s, (God Bramma) thought (for a while) and said = Well; As a means to kill this evil minded (Raavana), this must be observed, (this Yaaga being done by Rishyaschringa).

❍ ❍ ❍

१३. तेन गन्धर्वयक्षाणां देवदानवरक्षसाम् ।
अवध्योऽस्मीति वागुक्ता तथेत्युक्तं च तन्मया ।।

13. These words, "I am not to be killed by Ghandharva-s, Yaksha-Dheva-s, Dhaanava-s & Raakshasa-s", were told (by Raavana); "And So Be It", was told by me (as boon to Raavana).

(Readers should know that the great demon king Raavana of Lanka had obtained this boon from God Bramma by rigorous penance. He was so arrogant that he did not seek protection from ordinary human beings whom he considered no match for him, whom he treated with contempt. So he got this boon by which no harm will come to him from Celestials etc. And armed with this boon, he terrorised the whole world. And so when celestials approach God Bramma for relief, HE suggests the following: God Vishnu will be born as son of king

Dhascharatha who is childless, after Dhascharatha successfully completes The Ashwamedha yaaga under the patronage of Rishyaschringa who does a Yaaga for progeny for Dhascharatha. And of course in due course God Vishnu as son of Dhascharatha, will kill him, kill this Raavana).

❍ ❍ ❍

१४. नाकीर्तयदवज्ञानात्तद्रक्षो मानुषान् प्रति ।
तस्मात् स मानुषाद्वध्यो मृत्युर्नान्योऽस्य विद्यते ।।

14. (God Bramma continues). This Demon (Raavana), out of contempt, did not mention about (protection for him from) human beings. Therefore he will be killed by man only (eventually). He has no other death. (Will die only at the hands of a man, because my boon to Raavana does not cover men).

❍ ❍ ❍

१५. एतच्छ्रुत्वा प्रियं वाक्यं ब्रह्मणा समुदाहृतम् ।
सर्वेमहर्षयो देवाः प्रहृष्टास्तेऽभवंस्तदा ।।

15. Hearing such pleasing words, well spoken words, from God Bramma, the great Sages & Dheva-s were all very pleased.

❍ ❍ ❍

१६. एतस्मिन्नन्तरे विष्णुरुपयातो महाद्युतिः ।
शङ्खचक्रगदापाणिः पीतवासा जगत्पतिः ।।

16. At that moment, The Lord of the World, God Vishnu who was in great splendor, came there, dressed up in Peethaambara, (Golden, silken) dress, wielding Conch, Disc, & Mace in His hands. (God Vishnu is normally seen with Four Hands).

❍ ❍ ❍

१७. वैनतेयं समारुह्य भास्करस्तोयदं यथा ।
तप्तहाटककेयूरः पूज्यमानः सुरोत्तमैः ।।

17. Like Sun 'stepping out' of clouds, (God Vishnu) who was riding on Garuda (sacred big bird) and who was wearing shining golden armlets, and who was honoured by foremost celestials.

❍ ❍ ❍

१८. ब्रह्मणा च समागम्य तत्र तस्थौ समाहितः ।
तमब्रुवन् सुराः सर्वेसमभिष्टूय संनताः ॥

18. ...... (came) and met with God Bramma and stood there composed (& intent upon serving the cause of Dheva-s); All the Dheva-s extolled Him. And prostrating before Him, said:

❍ ❍ ❍

१९. त्वां नियोक्ष्यामहे विष्णो लोकानां हितकाम्यया ॥

19. Oh Vishnu! For welfare of the Worlds, we are beseeching you.

❍ ❍ ❍

२०. राज्ञो दशरथस्य त्वमयोध्याधिपतेः प्रभो ।
धर्मज्ञस्य वदान्यस्य महर्षिसमतेजसः ॥

20. Oh lord! The king of Ayodhya is a man of Dharma; a knower of Dharma; has the brilliancy comparable to great sages; he is munificent..... (To) this Dhascharatha...

❍ ❍ ❍

२१. तस्य भार्यासु तिसृषु ह्रीश्रीकीर्त्युपमासु च ।
विष्णो पुत्रत्वमागच्छ कृत्वाऽऽत्मानं चतुर्विधम् ॥

21. ...... Dividing yourself into four parts, you become sons (in the womb of) the three wives (of this Dhascharatha) who are renowned in character, fame & wealth.

(The celestials beg God Vishnu to be born on earth as sons of Dhascharatha who was doing Yaaga. His birth will serve. humanity. Only as a human being God Vishnu can kill Raavana).

❍ ❍ ❍

२२. तत्र त्वं मानुषो भूत्वा प्रवृद्धं लोककण्टकम् ।
अवध्यं दैवतैर्विष्णो समरे जहि रावणम् ।।

22. Oh Vishnu! There, (in the world), becoming a human being, you should conquer in war, this Raavana, the prosperous (Demon king of Lanka) who cannot be killed (even) by Dheva-s.

❍ ❍ ❍

२३. स हि देवान् सगन्धर्वान् सिद्धांश्च ऋषिसत्तमान् ।
रावणो राक्षसो मूर्खोवीर्योत्सेकेन बाधते ।।

23. This crooked demon Raavana, out of his arrogance of his valour, is harassing Dheva-s & Ghandharva-s, The Sidha-s & foremost Rishi-s.

❍ ❍ ❍

२४. ऋषयस्तु ततः सर्वेगन्धर्वाप्सरसस्तथा ।
क्रीडन्तो नन्दनवने रौद्रेण किल हिंसिताः ।।

24. Further, in the (Celestial) garden of Nandana, the Ghandharvas and Apsara maidens who are 'sporting' there and all the Rishi-s, are being tormented by this cruel (Raavana); Ah!

❍ ❍ ❍

२५. वधार्थं वयमायातास्तस्य वै मुनिभिः सह ।
सिद्धगन्धर्वयक्षाश्च ततस्त्वां शरणं गताः ।।

25. Therefore, we, the Sidha-s, Ghandhara-s, Yaksha-s, have come here to seek refuge under you along with Muni-s, for the sake of getting him killed. (by you).

❍ ❍ ❍

२६. त्वं गतिः परमा देव सर्वेषां नः परन्तप ।
वधाय देवशत्रूणां नृणां लोके मनः कुरु ।।

26. Oh Lord! Oh Tormentor of enemies! (Oh Vishnu)! To all of us you are The Salvation, the foremost (Refuge): Please direct your mind (to be born) in the world of

human beings for the destruction of (Raavana), the enemy of Dheva-s.

❍ ❍ ❍

२७. एवमुक्तस्तु देवेशो विष्णुस्त्रिदशपुङ्गवः ।
पितामहपुरोगांस्तान् सर्वलोकनमस्कृतः ।।
अब्रवीत्त्रिदशान् सर्वान् समेतान्धर्मसंहितान् ।।

27. When told thus, this lord of lords, the 'tiger' of Dheva-s, this God Vishnu who is worshipped by all the worlds, addressed all the celestial Dheva-s who had assembled there along with God Bramma and who were all 'endowed' with Dharma.

❍ ❍ ❍

२८. भयं त्यजत भद्रं वो हितार्थं युधि रावणम् ।
सपुत्रपौत्रं सामात्यं समित्रज्ञातिबान्धवम् ।।

28. Give up fear: Peace be with you; For your welfare, (will wage) war with Raavana and his sons, grandsons, ministers, folks, relatives.

❍ ❍ ❍

२९. हत्वा क्रूरं दुरात्मानं देवर्षीणां भयावहम् ।
दश वर्षसहस्राणि दश वर्षशतानि च ।।

29. ...... and kill this cruel, evil minded (demon) who causes fear (even) to Dheva-s; And 10, 000 years plus another 1,000 years.....

३०. वत्स्यामि मानुषे लोके पालयन् पृथिवीमिमाम् ।।

30. ...... I will live in this world of human beings, ruling over the earth. (Thus God Vishnu assures that he will annihilate Raavana soon being born as a man in the world).

❍ ❍ ❍

३१. एवं दत्त्वा वरं देवो देवानां विष्णुरात्मवान् ।
मानुषे चिन्तयामास जन्मभूमिमथात्मनः ।।

31. The Self reliant God Vishnu gave this assurance (Boon) to the Dheva-s.; Then he began to think about the place of his birth in human form (The incarnation).

❍ ❍ ❍

३२. ततः पद्मपलाशाक्षः कृत्वाऽऽत्मानं चतुर्विधम् ।
पितरं रोचयामास तदा दशरथं नृपम् ॥

32. Then the lotus eyed (God Vishnu) desired to have king Dhascharatha as his father by making himself into 'Four Parts' (to be born to the three wives of Dhascharatha as four sons).

❍ ❍ ❍

३३. तदा देवर्षिगन्धर्वाः सरुद्रा साप्सरोगणाः ।
स्तुतिभिर्दिव्यरूपाभिस्तुष्टुवुर्मधुसूदनम् ॥

33. At that moment, The Dheva-s, Ghandharva-s, Rishi-s, who were with multitude of Apsara maidens, extolled (Vishnu) the Madhusoodhana, with wonderfully composed recitations (praises).

❍ ❍ ❍

३४. त्वमुद्धतं रावणमुग्रतेजसं प्रवृद्धदर्पं त्रिदशेश्वरद्विषम् ।
विरावणं साधु तपस्विकण्टकं तपस्विनामुद्धर तं भयावहम् ॥

34. = You totally destroy this Raavana who causes fear to men of penance, who is a 'thorn' to all men of penance, who makes every one cry (in fear), who is enemy of Indhra, who is arrogant of his fierce prowess.

❍ ❍ ❍

३५. तमेव हत्वा सबलं सबान्धवं विरावणं रावणमुग्रपौरुषम् ।
स्वर्लोकमागच्छ गतज्वरश्चिरं सुरेन्द्र गुप्तं गतदोषकल्मषम् ॥

35. Oh foremost Lord (God Vishnu)! Killing the terribly (violent and) cruel Raavana who makes (every one) cry; (You kill him) along with his friends, folks, army, and then you may go (back) to your (heavenly) World, the eternal, impenetrable (world) which is stainless and bereft of sins, freed from worries.=

(Note: Indians believe that Gods have their purpose; you will find the hand of God in everything, good or bad. From time to time God descends on earth in various forms to destroy evil. Here God Vishnu decides to be born as a man to destroy Raavana, an evil. So He decides to be born as Raama, the son of Dhascharatha, who in fact is doing Yaaga for begetting sons).

❍ ❍ ❍

Chapter 16

The Offer of 'Paayasa'- Sacred Milk

१. ततो नारायणो विष्णुर्नियुक्तः सुरसत्तमैः ।
जानन्नपि सुरांश्चैवं श्लक्ष्णं वचनमब्रवीत् ।।

1. When beseeched by the foremost Dheva-s thus, Naaraayana God Vishnu, in spite of knowing (everything), addressed following sweet words to the Dheva-s.

❍ ❍ ❍

२. उपायः को वधे तस्य राक्षसाधिपतेः सुराः ।
यमहं तं समास्थाय निहन्यामृषिकण्टकम् ।।

2. Oh Dheva-s! What means (are there for me) in the killing of the demon king; with what steps, will I kill this (Raavana), the 'thorn' of Rishi-s.

(Readers may note that already This All Knowing God Vishnu of immense power behaves like a mortal in seeking advice!).

❍ ❍ ❍

३. एवमुक्ताः सुराः सर्वेप्रत्यूचुर्विष्णुमव्ययम् ।
मानुषं रूपमास्थाय रावणं जहि संयुगे ।।

3. When told thus (by God Vishnu), all the Dheva-s

replied to the eternal Vishnu: Taking on human form, you kill Raavana in war.

❍ ❍ ❍

४. स हि तेपे तपस्तीव्रं दीर्घकालमरिंदम ।
येन तुष्टोऽभवद्ब्रह्मा लोककृल्लोकपूर्वजः ।।

4. Oh destroyer of enemies (Oh Vishnu): Indeed (this Raavana) has performed rigorous penances for a long time; By this, (because of this), God Bramma, the Creator of The World who was 'born' before the world, had become pleased (with him).

❍ ❍ ❍

५. सन्तुष्टः प्रददौ तस्मै राक्षसाय वरं प्रभुः ।
नानाविधेभ्यो भूतेभ्यो भयं नान्यत्र मानुषात् ।।

5. This Lord (Bramma) who was pleased, had offered a boon to the Demon (Raavana by which) he has no fear (or danger to his life from) various beings other than man.

❍ ❍ ❍

६. अवज्ञाताः पुरा तेन वरदाने हि मानवाः ।।

6. Indeed, men have been insulted (& treated with contempt) by him, because of the boon (offered by Bramma to him) before.

❍ ❍ ❍

७. एवं पितामहात्तस्माद्वरं प्राप्य स दर्पितः ।
उत्सादयति लोकांस्त्रीन् स्त्रियश्चाप्यपकर्षति ।।
तस्मात्तस्य वधो दृष्टो मानुषेभ्यः परन्तप ।।

7. Having obtained such a boon from Bramma, in arrogance he ruins all the three worlds; he molests women; Therefore, Oh tormentor of enemies! His killing can come only through a man (his death is 'seen' at the hands of a man & you are that man).

❍ ❍ ❍

८. इत्येतद्वचनं श्रुत्वा सुराणां विष्णुरात्मवान् ।
पितरं रोचयामास तदा दशरथं नृपम् ।।

8. Hearing these words of Dheva-s thus (spoken), the self reliant God Vishnu then decided upon King Dhascharatha as his father.

❍ ❍ ❍

९. स चाप्यपुत्रो नृपतिस्तस्मिन् काले महाद्युतिः ।
अयजत् पुत्रियामिष्टिं पुत्रेप्सुररिसूदनः ।।

9. (The timing was appropriate Dhascharatha performs Yaaga for progeny; God Vishnu is to be 'born' on earth. Becomes his son).

Further, at this time, this king (Dhascharatha) the destroyer of enemies, who is most majestic, who is seeking a son being childless, did (the great) Yaaga for begetting a son.

❍ ❍ ❍

१०. स कृत्वा निश्चयं विष्णुरामन्त्र्य च पितामहम् ।
अन्तर्धानं गतो देवैः पूज्यमानो महात्मभिः ।।

10. Taking decision in his mind, God Vishnu took leave of Bramma & disappeared from there after being honoured by Dhevas & great men.

❍ ❍ ❍

११. ततो वै यजमानस्य पावकादतुलप्रभम् ।
प्रादुर्भूतं महद्भूतं महावीर्यं महाबलम् ।।

11. (Scene & action shifts back to The Yaaga Stanzas 11 to 18) There arose from Patron's (Dhascharatha's) Fire Mound, a mightily strong, mightily brave, dazzling with incomparable brilliance......

❍ ❍ ❍

१२. कृष्णं रक्ताम्बरधरं रक्तास्यं दुन्दुभिस्वनम् ।
स्निग्धहर्यक्षतनुजश्मश्रुप्रवरमूर्धजम् ।।

12. ...... A great ghost; It was wearing dark red clothes, its mouth was red, its voice like those from Dhundhubi drums, its skin & hair like those of a lion-soft & glossy, with plenty of hair on head, with side burns. . (mustache).

❍ ❍ ❍

१३. शुभलक्षणसम्पन्नं दिव्याभरणभूषितम् ।
शैलशृङ्गसमुत्सेधं दृप्तशार्दूलविक्रमम् ।।

13. ...... Endowed with good features, was wearing wonderful jewelleries, tall like a mountain peak; valiant like a proud tiger......

❍ ❍ ❍

१४. दिवाकरसमाकारं दीप्तानलशिखोपमम् ।
सिंहस्कन्धं महाबाहुमङ्गदद्धयशोभितम् ।।

14. ...... Its body radiant like the Sun; brilliant like flaming fire; its shoulders like those of a lion; long hands; it was wearing two forearm bracelets, shining (with ornaments)......

❍ ❍ ❍

१५. ताराधिपतिकल्पेन हारेणोरसि राजितम् ।
ताराधिपतिकल्पैश्च दन्तैः परमशोभितत् ।।

15. ...... On its chest there was a shining garland like (the lord of stars the) Moon; Its teeth (white & lovely) like the moon.; shining brilliantly......

❍ ❍ ❍

१६. ज्वलन्निव च तेजोभिर्दीपयन्निव च श्रिया ।
तप्तजाम्बूनदमयीं राजतान्तपरिच्छदाम् ।।

16. ...... As though making everything bright with the brilliance of its replendency; And made of pure (burnt & purified) gold with a lid made of silver......

❍ ❍ ❍

१७. दिव्यपायससम्पूर्णां पात्रीं पत्नीमिव प्रियाम् ।
प्रगृह्य विपुलां दोर्भ्यां स्वयं मायामयीमिवा ।।

17. ...... was a very large Pot which was full with wonderful Holy Milk (the Paayasa) which appeared as though it was an illusion created by magic, and which (this Holy Ghost) was carrying on its shoulders, as if it was a beloved wife......

❍ ❍ ❍

१८. समवेक्ष्याब्रवीद्वाक्यमिदं दशरथं नृपम् ।
प्राजापत्यं नरं विद्धि मामिहाभ्यागतं नृप ।।

18. ...... And looking at King Dhascharatha, this (holy ghost) said the following = Know me as (God) Bramma's Man (& representative) Who Has Come Here (to your Yaaga). =

❍ ❍ ❍

१९. ततः परं तदा राजा प्रत्युवाच कृताञ्जलिः ।
भगवन् स्वागतं तेऽस्तु किमहं करवाणि ते ।।

19. Then at that moment, king (Dhascharatha), with folded arms of Anjali, replied (to this Holy ghost) = Oh lord! Welcome to you; What must I do for you? =

❍ ❍ ❍

२०. अथो पुनरिदं वाक्यं प्राजापत्यो नरोऽब्रवीत् ।
राजन्नर्चयता देवानद्य प्राप्तमिदं त्वया ।।

20. Then (the Ghost who was) Prajaapathi (Bramma's) representative, once again said the following: Oh king! Ever worshipping the celestials as you are, this is now obtained by you.

❍ ❍ ❍

२१. इदं तु नृपशार्दूल पायसं देवनिर्मितम् ।
प्रजाकरं गृहाण त्वं धन्यमारोग्यवर्धनम् ।।

21. Oh Dhascharatha (the 'tiger' of men)! You receive this Holy Milk (Paayasa) now, which has been 'created' by Dheva-s, which will beget sons, which is auspicious, which will increase your health & prosperity.

❍ ❍ ❍

२२. भार्याणामनुरूपाणामश्नीतेति प्रयच्छ वै ।
तासु त्वं प्राप्स्यसे पुत्रान् यदर्थं यजसे नृप ।।

22. Give this to your devoted wives (telling them to) partake (this Paayasa) Oh king! For what purpose you are doing this (great) Yaaga, (that purpose will now be served as) you will now obtain sons (from your three queens when they drink this Paayasa).

❍ ❍ ❍

२३. तथेति नृपतिः प्रीतः शिरसा प्रतिगृह्य ताम् ।
पात्रीं देवान्नसंपूर्णां देवदत्तां हिरण्मयीम् ।।

23. The King then said=So Will It Be=And in great happiness, took this golden Pot (full with divine milk) offered by the Lord, on to his head.

❍ ❍ ❍

२४. अभिवाद्य च तद्भूतमद्भुतं प्रियदर्शनम् ।
मुदा परमया युक्तश्चकाराभिप्रदक्षिणम् ।।

24. ...... then bowed to this pleasant looking wonderful ghost; In great joy he circumbumbulated over (this holy ghost) on all sides.

❍ ❍ ❍

२५. ततो दशरथः प्राप्य पायसं देवनिर्मितम् ।
बभूव परमप्रीतः प्राप्य वित्तमिवाधनः ।।

25. Then Dhascharatha received The Holy Milk created by The Dheva (God Bramma) and he was greatly pleased, like a poor man obtaining a treasure.

❍ ❍ ❍

२६. ततस्तदद्भुतप्रख्यं भूतं परमभास्वरम् ।
संवर्तयित्वा तत्कर्म तत्रैवान्तरधीयत ।।

26. The (wonderful) Ghost of great radiance that appeared marvelous, after fulfilling its task, disappeared then after.

❍ ❍ ❍

२७. हर्षरश्मिभिरुद्योतं तस्यान्तःपुरमाबभौ ।
शारदस्याभिरामस्य चन्द्रस्येव नवांशुभिः ।।

27. The inner apartments (of Dhascharatha's palace) shone brilliantly by 'Rays of happiness', just like rays of the autumn moon which delights (all) as it rises.

❍ ❍ ❍

२८. सोऽन्तःपुरं प्रविश्यैव कौसल्यामिदमब्रवीत् ।
पायसं प्रतिगृह्णीष्व पुत्रीयं त्विदमात्मनः ।।

28. And (Dhascharatha) entered his palace and at once told Kowsalya (his eldest wife & queen) = Accept (& drink) this (holy) milk that will bring forth our son. =

❍ ❍ ❍

२९. कौसल्यायै नरपतिः पायसार्धं ददौ तदा ।
अर्धादर्धं ददौ चापि सुमित्रायै नराधिपः ।।
कैकेय्यै चावशिष्टार्धं ददौ पुत्रार्थकारणात् ।।

29. The lord of men (Dhascharatha) gave half portion of this milk to Kowsalya; Further he gave half of (remaining) half portion to Sumithra (his second wife). And to Kaikeyi he gave half portion; (all) for begetting sons (through these wives of his).

❍ ❍ ❍

३०. प्रददौ चावशिष्टार्धं पायसस्यामृतोपमम् ।
अनुचिन्त्य सुमित्रायै पुनरेव महीपतिः ।।

30. After thinking it over for sometime, (Dhascharatha the) Lord of earth, gave the balance half portion

(that remained) of this milk which was like nectar, to Sumithra again.

(In effect he gave one portion to Kowsalya, one portion to Kaikeyi & two portions to Sumithra).

❍ ❍ ❍

३१. एवं तासां ददौ राजा भार्याणां पायसं पृथक् ॥

31. Thus the king gave, (distributed) the milk to wives separately.

❍ ❍ ❍

३२. तास्त्वेतत्पायसं प्राप्य नरेन्द्रस्योत्तमाः स्त्रियः ।
सम्मानं मेनिरे सर्वाः प्रहर्षोदितचेतसः ॥

32. Receiving this milk, all these foremost wives of the king considered themselves greatly honoured and their mind & heart rejoiced.

❍ ❍ ❍

३३. ततस्तु ताः प्राश्य तदुत्तमस्त्रियो महीपतेरुत्तमपायसं पृथक् ।
हुताशनादित्यसमानतेजसोऽचिरेण गर्भान् प्रतिपेदिरे तदा ॥

33. Thus, the foremost wives of the king who had consumed the foremost milk separately, became pregnant soon, & they appeared like fire and sun in brilliance.

❍ ❍ ❍

३४. ततस्तु राजा प्रसमीक्ष्य ताः स्त्रियः प्ररूढगर्भाः प्रतिलब्धमानसः।
बभूव हृष्टस्त्रिदिवे यथा हरिः सुरेन्द्रसिद्धर्षिगणाभिपूजितः ॥

34. At that moment, seeing that these ladies had become pregnant, the king got back into his normal state of mind (of joy & happiness) and he became very happy like Lord Indhra who is honoured in heaven by foremost Dheva-s, Rishi-s, Sidha-s in multitude.

(Note: It is customary in India that Gifts must be offered to The Gods; The Prasaadha, the Propitiatory offerings; The remnants of the offering is to be received by the Doer with devotion & reverence. Here, the Prasaadha of The Holy Milk is the Gift of God Bramma Himself. No wonder The king accepts this in great joy: And his wives who were barren for long, conceive).

❍ ❍ ❍

Chapter 17

The creation of bears, monkeys & other animals on Earth (For strengthening God Vishnu's hands when he is born as Raama to wage war against Raavana & his vast army and to annihilate them).

❍ ❍ ❍

१. पुत्रत्वं तु गते विष्णौ राज्ञोऽस्य सुमहात्मनः ।
उवाच देवताः सर्वाः स्वयंभूर्भगवानिदम् ।।

1. When God Vishnu became, (decided to become), son to this great soul king (Dhascharatha), the Lord God Bramma told this to all the Dheva-s.

❍ ❍ ❍

२. सत्यसन्धस्य वीरस्य सर्वेषां नो हितैषिणः ।
विष्णोः सहायान् बलिनः सृजध्वं कामरूपिणः ।।

2. To our brave God Vishnu who is most truthful and who ever desires our welfare, we should create (on earth) strong (creatures) who can take on any form as they please, as His helpers (to assist Him when he is born as Raama to wage war with Raavana).

❍ ❍ ❍

३. मायाविदश्च शूरांश्च वायुवेगसमाञ्जवे ।
नयज्ञान् बुद्धिसंपन्नान् विष्णोस्तुल्यपराक्रमान् ।।

3. (The Creation of these 'Creatures' described: stanzas 3 to 33).

Creatures knowing art of magic; Brave; Having speed

of wind; Knowing Law & Code of conduct; Endowed with intelligence; Comparable to Vishnu in valour......

❍ ❍ ❍

४. असंहार्यानुपायज्ञान् दिव्यसंहनानान्वितान् ।
सर्वास्त्रगुणसंपन्नानमृतप्राशनानिव ।।

4. ...... knowing ways of self protection; powerful like Dheva-s; endowed with qualities drawn from all Asthra-s (Knowledge of all weapons); appearing like one who has consumed Nectar.

❍ ❍ ❍

५. अप्सरस्सु च मुख्यासु गन्धर्वीणां तनूषु च ।
यक्षपन्नगकन्यासु ऋक्षविद्याधरीषु च ।।

5. ...... (Born) From the body (womb) of foremost Apsara maidens, Ghandharva ladies, Yaksha & Pannaga women, Rikshividhyaadhara women ......

❍ ❍ ❍

६. किन्नरीणां च गात्रेषु वानरीणां तनूषु च ।
सृजध्वं हरिरूपेण पुत्रांस्तुल्यपराक्रमान् ।।

6. ...... and from the bodies (womb) of Kinnara females and from the bodies of monkey women, create 'sons' with incomparable (brilliance &) valour who will have the form of monkeys.

❍ ❍ ❍

७. पूर्वमेव मया सृष्टो जाम्बवानृक्षपुङ्गवः ।
जृम्भमाणस्य सहसा मम वक्त्रादजायत ।।

7. Long ago, even before, the king of Bears Jaambavaan was born, created by me at an instant by the yawn (let out) from my breath.

❍ ❍ ❍

८. ते तथोक्ता भगवता तत्प्रतिश्रुत्य शासनम् ।
जनयामासुरेवं ते पुत्रान् वानररूपिणः ।।

8. When told thus by the lord (Bramma), they accepted this command and created these sons with the form of monkeys as follows:

❍ ❍ ❍

९. ऋषयश्च महात्मानः सिद्धविद्याधरोरगाः ।
चारणाश्च सुतान् वीरान् ससृजुर्वनचारिणः ।।

9. The great soul Rishi-s, Sidha-s, Vidhyaadhara-s, Nagara-s, Chaarna-s, created brave sons (monkeys who roamed about the forest).

❍ ❍ ❍

१०. वानरेन्द्रं महाभागमिन्द्रो वालिनमूर्जितम् ।
सुग्रीवं जनयामास तपनस्तपतां वरः ।।

10. The great soul Rishi-s, Sidha-s, Vidhyaadhara-s, Nagara-s, Chaarna-s, created brave sons (monkeys who roamed about the forest).

❍ ❍ ❍

११. बृहस्पतिस्त्वजनयत्तारं नाम महाकपिम् ।
धनदस्य सुतः श्रीमान् वानरो गन्धमादनः ।।

11. Lord Brihaspathi created big monkey Thaara & Kubhaera's son was the resplendent monkey Gandhamaadhana. (Readers to note this Thaara is not to be confused with Thaara, the wife of Vaali).

❍ ❍ ❍

१२. सर्ववानरमुख्यानां बुद्धिमन्तमनुत्तमम् ।
विश्वकर्मा त्वजनयन्नलं नाम महाहरिम् ।।

12. And Vischwakarma created the great monkey Nala who was very intelligent & foremost amongst noble monkeys.

❍ ❍ ❍

१३. पावकस्य सुतः श्रीमन्नीलोऽग्निसदृशप्रभः ।
तेजसा यशसा वीर्यादत्यरिच्यत वानरान् ।।

13. And the resplendent son of Lord of Fire who was shining like Fire, was Neela, who surpassed monkeys by his fame, brilliance & valour.

❍ ❍ ❍

१४. रूपद्रविणसम्पन्नावश्विनौ रूपसंमतौ ।
मैन्दं च द्विविदं चैव जनयामासतुः स्वयम् ।।

14. The Ashwini-s endowed with beautiful form & famous for their beauty, created Maindha & Dvividha, themselves.

१५. वरुणो जनयामास सुषेणां नाम वानरम् ।
शरभं जनयामास पर्जन्यस्तु महाबलम् ।।

15. (Lord) Varuna created monkey Sushena: Lord of Rain created the mightily strong Scharabha (as well).

❍ ❍ ❍

१६. मारुतस्यात्मजः श्रीमान् हनुमान्नाम वानरः ।
सर्ववानरमुख्येषु बुद्धिमान् बलवानपि ।।

16. And the resplendent monkey, the strong Hanumaan who was foremost amongst noble monkeys in wisdom & intelligence, was son of Lord of Wind.

❍ ❍ ❍

१७. वज्रसंहननोपेतो वैनतेयसमो जवे ।
रुद्रस्य पुत्रो बलवान् हरिः सूर्याननः प्रभोः ।।

17. His body powerful like Vajra (thunderbolt), in speed comparable to Garuda bird, this strong monkey Sooryaanan was Lord Rudhra's son. (Lord Rudhra, a 'Manifestation'of God Shiva).

❍ ❍ ❍

१८. ते सृष्टा बहुसाहस्रा दशग्रीववधे धृताः ।
अप्रमेयबला वीरा विक्रान्ताः कामरूपिणः ।।

18. In thousands they were created who were all resolved in the destruction of Raavana, who were very brave

with incomparable strength, very valiant, and who could take on any form they pleased.

❍ ❍ ❍

१९. ते गजाचलसमाशा वपुष्मन्तो महाबलाः ।
ऋक्षवानरगोपुच्छाः क्षिप्रमेवाभिजज्ञिरे ।।

19. And soon bears, monkeys, Gopucha-s (a species of monkeys) were born who had mighty body like elephants & mountains and who were mightily strong.

❍ ❍ ❍

२०. यस्य देवस्य यद्रूपं वेषो यश्च पराक्रमः ।
अजायत समस्तेन तस्य तस्य सुतः पृथक् ।।

20. What form, what appearance, what (sort of) valour was distinct in a celestial, to him, (to that celestial), was born a 'son' equal to him, (inheriting all his characteristic features & qualities).

❍ ❍ ❍

२१. गोलाङ्गूलीषु चोत्पन्नाः केचित् संमतविक्रमाः ।
ऋक्षीषु च तथा जाता वानराः किन्नरीषु च ।।

21. Some monkeys famous for their valour were born (in the womb of) Golaankula women; likewise they were born in Riksha & Kinnara- (wombs).

❍ ❍ ❍

२२. देवा महर्षिगन्धर्वास्ताक्ष्र्यर्यक्षा यशस्विनः ।
नागाः किंपुरुषाश्चैव सिद्धविद्याधरोरगाः ।।

22. The famous great sages, many Dheva-s, Yakshas, Garuda-s, Naagaa-s, Kimpurusha-s, Sidha-s, Vidhyaadhara-s......

❍ ❍ ❍

२३. बहवो जनयामासुर्हृष्टास्तत्र सहस्रशः ।
वानरान् सुमहाकायान् सर्वान् वै वनचारिणः ।।

23. ...... Many of them, happily created big bodied monkeys in thousands, all these monkeys who roamed about in forest......

❍ ❍ ❍

२४. अप्सरस्सु च मुख्यासु तथा विद्याधरीषु च ।
नागकन्यासु च तथा गन्धर्वीणां तनूषु च ।।

24. ...... in the (wombs of) Apsara women, foremost Vidhyaadhara ladies, Naagakanya-s & Ghandharva ladies.

❍ ❍ ❍

२५. कामरूपबलोपेता यथाकामविचारिणः ।
सिंहशार्दूलसदृशा दर्पेण च बलेन च ।।

25. They had power to change their form at will; they roamed at their pleasure; In pride & strength they were like lions & tigers.

❍ ❍ ❍

२६. शिलाप्रहरणाः सर्वेसर्वेपादपयोधिनः ।
नखदंष्ट्रायुधाः सर्वेसर्वेसर्वास्त्रकोविदाः ।।

26. All of them could lift up mountains; all of them could wield trees as weapons; all of them could use their claws & teeth as weapons; all of them masters of all weapons.

❍ ❍ ❍

२७. विचालयेयुः शैलेन्द्रान् भेदयेयुः स्थितान्द्रुमान् ।
क्षोभयेयुश्च वेगेन समुद्रं सरितां पतिम् ।।

27. They could shake the mountains; they could uproot the well rooted (firm) trees (& split them up); By their force, could shake up the lord of rivers, the ocean itself.

❍ ❍ ❍

२८. दारयेयुः क्षितिं पद्भ्यामाप्लवेयुर्महार्णवम् ।
नभःस्थलं विशेयुश्च गृह्णीयुरपि तोयदान् ।।

28. They could split (make cleavages upon) Earth with their feet; they can jump over ocean; they can enter all regions; they can (even) seize clouds.

❍ ❍ ❍

२९. गृह्णीयुरपि मातङ्गान् मत्तान् प्रव्रजितान् वने ।
नर्दमानाश्च नादेन पातयेयुर्विहङ्गमान् ।।

29. They could catch mad elephants roaming about in forest; By their very roar, they could bring down the birds by their (terrible) sound.

❍ ❍ ❍

३०, ईदृशानां प्रसूतानि हरीणां कामरूपिणाम् ।
शतं शतसहस्राणि यूथपानां महात्मनाम् ।।

30. Hundred thousand of eminent monkeys with such (power) who could take on any form at pleasure & a hundred monkey chiefs were born: (100 monkey Commanders of The Army).

❍ ❍ ❍

३१. ते प्रधानेषु यूथेषु हरीणां हरियूथपाः ।
बभूवुर्यूथपश्रेष्ठा वीरांश्चाजनयन् हरीन् ।।

31. These army chiefs became foremost army chiefs of eminent monkeys; They created brave monkeys (in their turn).

❍ ❍ ❍

३२. अन्ये ऋक्षवतः प्रस्थानुपतस्थुः सहस्रशः ।
अन्ये नानाविधाञ्छैलान् काननानि च भेजिरे ।।

32. Some, in thousands, reached (& lived in) mountain slopes of Rikshavan; some others entered various forests & mountains.

❍ ❍ ❍

३३. सूर्यपुत्रं च सुग्रीवं शक्रपुत्रं च वालिनम् ।
भ्रातरावुपतस्थुस्ते सर्व एव हरीश्वराः ।।
नलं नीलं हनूमन्तमन्यांश्च हरियूथपान् ।।

33. All the monkey chiefs stood by the brothers, Sugreeva, the son of the Sun & Vaali, the son of Lord Indhra; And they stood by Nala, Neela, Hanumaan & other army chiefs.

३४. ते तार्क्ष्यबलसम्पन्नाः सर्वेयुद्धविशारदाः ।
विचरन्तोऽर्दयन्दर्पात् सिंहव्याघ्रमहोरगान् ।।

34. Endowed with strength of Garuda, all these (monkeys) who were masters in warfare & who were roaming about, crushed lions, tigers, big serpents in sheer arrogance.

❍ ❍ ❍

३५. तांश्च सर्वान् महाबाहुर्वाली विपुलविक्रमः ।
जुगोप भुजवीर्येण ऋक्षगोपुच्छवानरान् ।।

35. The mighty limbed Vaali who possessed immense valour, protected all the bears, Gopucha-s and monkeys, by the power of his arm.

❍ ❍ ❍

३६. तैरियं पृथिवी शूरैः सपर्वतवनार्णवा ।
कीर्णा विविधसंस्थानैर्नानाव्यञ्जनलक्षणैः ।।

36. This entire Earth consisting of mountains, forests, oceans, were full with these brave (animals) who had many forms & shapes and who had diverse characteristics.

❍ ❍ ❍

३७. तैर्मेघवृन्दाचलकूटकल्पैर्महाबलैर्वानरयूथपालैः ।
बभूव भूर्भीमशरीररूपैः समावृता रामसहायहेतोः ।।

37. The earth became (full) surrounded by the terrible bodied monkey leaders who were mightily strong, who were comparable to 'cluster' of clouds & mountain peaks, all for the sake of helping Raama (when Vishnu is born as Raama to destroy Raavana)

(Note: All these 'Creations' were done by celestials

at the command of & with blessings of God Bramma, the creator. Even the All powerful & Eternal God, God Vishnu, needs assistance, when He Incarnates himself as a man, Raama, who is to kill Raavana. Millions of these are 'foster sons of celestials).

❍ ❍ ❍

Chapter 18

Birth of Raama (The Scene shifts to Ayodhya)

१. नर्वृत्ते तु क्रतौ तस्मिन् हयमेधे महात्मनः ।
प्रतिगृह्य सुरा भागान् प्रतिजग्मुर्यथागतम् ।।

1. When the Aschwamedha Yaaga of this great soul (Dhascharatha) was over, the Dheva-s went back as they came, after taking their share of oblations.

❍ ❍ ❍

२. समाप्तदीक्षानियमः पत्नीगणसमन्वितः ।
प्रविवेश पुरीं राजा सभृत्यबलवाहनः ।।

2. The king having completed rituals, ceremonies & vows, entered, (went back to) the city (of Ayodhya) with his wives, folks & his army.

❍ ❍ ❍

३. यथार्हं पूजितास्तेन राज्ञा वै पृथिवीश्वराः ।
मुदिताः प्रययुर्देशान् प्रणम्य मुनिपुङ्गवम् ।।

3. Duly honoured by this king, various rulers of (various) territories went back to their kingdoms happily, after they bowed to (Rischyaschringa), the 'tiger' of Muni-s.

❍ ❍ ❍

४. श्रीमतां गच्छतां तेषां स्वपुराणि पुरात्ततः ।
बलानि राज्ञां शुभ्राणि प्रहृष्टानि चकाशिरे ।।

4. At that time, the armies of the kings which were well endowed & which were going to their own cities, shone very beautiful & exhilarated.

❍ ❍ ❍

५. गतेषु पृथिवीशेषु राजा दशरथः पुनः ।
प्रविवेश पुरीं श्रीमान् पुरस्कृत्य द्विजोत्तमम् ।।

5. When the kings had left, the resplendent king Dhascharatha once again entered his city followed by foremost braamins.

❍ ❍ ❍

६. शान्तया प्रययौ सार्धमृश्यश्रृङ्गः सुपूजितः ।
अन्वीयमानो राज्ञाऽथ सानुयात्रेण धीमता ।।

6. Likewise, after being well honoured by the wise king (Dhascharatha), Rischyaschringa, accompanied by (his wife) Schaantha, went along, with the retinue following them.

❍ ❍ ❍

७. एवं विसृज्य तान् सर्वान् राजा संपूर्णमानसः ।
उवास सुखितस्तत्र पुत्रोत्पत्तिं विचिन्तयन् ।।

7. Thus, having sent back all of them, the king, with his wishes fulfilled, lived there in comfort, thinking about progeny.

❍ ❍ ❍

८. ततो यज्ञे समाप्ते तु ऋतूनां षट् समत्ययुः ।।

8. Six Rithu (seasons) were over since completion of The Yaaga.

❍ ❍ ❍

९. ततश्च द्वादशे मासे चैत्रे नावमिके तिथौ ।
नक्षत्रेऽदितिदैवत्ये स्वोच्चसंस्थेषु पञ्चसु ।।

9. Then, in the 12th month, in the month of Chithra (Mid April), on the 9th day (of the ascendancy of the Moon)

when Star Punarvasu, along with 5 constellations were in ascendancy......

❍ ❍ ❍

१०. ग्रहेषु कर्कटे लग्ने वाक्पताविन्दुना सह ।
प्रोद्यमाने जगन्नाथं सर्वलोकनमस्कृतम् ।।

10. ...... In the house of Kataka, (lagna in Kataka), with star Jupiter & Moon in early ascendancy, this Lord of Earth, this man who was worshipped by all the worlds. . .

❍ ❍ ❍

११. कौसल्याऽजनयद्रामं दिव्यलक्षणसंयुतम् ।
विष्णोरर्धं महाभागं पुत्रमिक्ष्वाकुनन्दनम् ।।

11. ...... this Raama, the darling of Ikshwaaku-s & most illustrious, this son, Kowsalya gave birth to: (Raama) was the half portion of God Vishnu, endowed with divine qualities.

❍ ❍ ❍

१२. कौसल्या शुशुभे तेन पुत्रेणामिततेजसा ।
यथा वरेण देवानामदितिर्वज्रपाणिना ।।

12. By this son (Raama) of incomparable brilliance (born to her), Kowsalya shone like Adhithi, (the mother) of Lord Indhra, the wielder of Vajra, and who was foremost amongst the Dheva-s.

❍ ❍ ❍

१३. भरतो नाम कैकेय्यां जज्ञे सत्यपराक्रमः ।
साक्षाद्विष्णोश्चतुर्भागः सर्वैः समुदितो गुणैः ।।

13. As the fourth part of God Vishnu, this Bharatha endowed with all (noble) qualities, who was truly most valiant, was born to Kaikeyi.

❍ ❍ ❍

१४. अथ लक्ष्मणशत्रुघ्नौ सुमित्राऽजनयत् सुतौ ।
वीरौ सर्वास्त्रकुशलौ विष्णोरर्धसमन्वितौ ।।

14. As the fourth part of God Vishnu, this Bharatha endowed with all (noble) qualities, who was truly most valiant, was born to Kaikeyi.

❍ ❍ ❍

१५. पुष्ये जातस्तु भरतो मीनलग्ने प्रसन्नधीः ।
सार्पेजातौ च सौमित्री कुलीरेऽभ्युदिते रवौ ।।

15. Clear headed Bharatha, was born in Meena lagna with star Pushya; And the two sons of Sumithra were born in Saarpa (Aayilya) star in the kataka lagna when Sun was in ascendancy.

(Readers may note that according to Indian astrology, the horoscope of every one is based on Lagna (of birth) in one of the 12 'Houses': There are 9 constellations, namely Sun (Sunday), Moon (Monday); Mars (Tuesday); Mercury (Wednesday), Jupiter (Thursday), Venus (Friday), Saturn (Saturday) & Raahu- Kethu, are ethereal planets. As per Indian calendar New year begins in Chithra, Mid April. There are 7 days in a week, 12 months & 27 stars, with Moon having ascendancy & descendency).

❍ ❍ ❍

१६. राज्ञः पुत्रा महात्मनश्चत्वारो जज्ञिरे पृथक् ।
गुणवन्तोऽनुरूपाश्च रुच्या प्रोष्ठपदोपमाः ।।

16. Shining like twin stars of Proshta-pada (Nakshathra Poorattaadhi, Utharattaadhi) the four sons who were most eminent and endowed with qualities, were born to the king, every one equal to the other; (they were all born) in succession.

❍ ❍ ❍

१७. जगुः कलं च गन्धर्वा ननृतुश्चाप्सरोगणाः ।
देवदुन्दुभयो नेदुः पुष्पवृष्टिश्च खाच्च्युता ।।

17. The Ghandharva-s sang sweetly; The Apsara maidens

danced; Celestial Dhundhubi drums reverberated; there was shower of flowers from sky.

❍ ❍ ❍

१८. उत्सवश्च महानासीदयोध्यायां जनाकुलः ।।

18. In Ayodhya, there was festivities & multitudes gathered.

❍ ❍ ❍

१९. रथ्याश्च जनसंबाधा नटनर्तकसंकुलाः ।
गायकैश्च विराविण्यो वादकैश्च तथाऽपरैः ।।

19. The streets were crowded with people; Artists & Dancers performed; (Entire city) reverberated with sounds (of music) from singers, (orchestra-s) and instrumentalists & others.

❍ ❍ ❍

२०. प्रदेयांश्च ददौ राजा सूतमागधवन्दिनाम् ।
ब्राह्मणेभ्यो ददौ वित्तं गोधनानि सहस्रशः ।।
अतीत्यैकादशाहं तु नामकर्म तथाऽकरोत् ।।

20. The king offered gifts to Sootha-s, Maagadha-s & Vandhithas (poets, & others who sing praises, who extol the king & his family) And he gave moneys to Braamins; and a wealth of cows in thousands; And after the 11th day, he did the naming ceremony.

❍ ❍ ❍

२१. ज्येष्ठं रामं महात्मानं भरतं कैकयीसुतम् ।
सौमित्रिं लक्ष्मणमिति शत्रुघ्नमपरं तथा ।।
वसिष्ठः परमप्रीतो नामानि कृतवांस्तदा ।।

21. In great happiness (his chief priest) Vasishta, named the eldest, the great soul, as Raama: Kaikeyi's son he named as Bharatha; And Sumithra's son as Lakshmana & her other one as Schathrugna.

❍ ❍ ❍

२२. ब्राह्मणान् भोजयामास पौरजानपदानपि ।
अददाद्ब्राह्मणानां च रत्नौघममितं बहु ॥
तेषां जन्मक्रियादीनि सर्वकर्माण्यकारयत् ॥

22. He fed Braamins from villages & cities; And further he offered limitless quantities of various gems to braamins; he performed their birthday Rituals & Ceremonies.

❍ ❍ ❍

२३. तेषां केतुरिव ज्येष्ठो रामो रतिकरः पितुः ।
बभूव भूयो भूतानां स्वयंभूरिव संमतः ॥

23. And Raama who was the eldest amongst them all and who was like a pillar (of strength) to his father, who gave immense pleasure, endeared to him most, like God Braama to living beings.

❍ ❍ ❍

२४. सर्वेवेदविदः शूराः सर्वेलोकहिते रताः ।
सर्वेज्ञानोपपन्नाश्च सर्वेसमुदिता गुणैः ॥

24. All knew The Vedha-s; Were very brave; all devoted to do good to the world; all endowed with wisdom; all of them with noble qualities.

❍ ❍ ❍

२५. तेषामपि महातेजा रामः सत्यपराक्रमः ।
इष्टः सर्वस्य लोकस्य शशाम इव निर्मलः ॥

25. And yet, amongst them, the truly valiant most brilliant Raama who was like the spotless moon, was the beloved of all the world.

❍ ❍ ❍

२६. गजस्कन्धोऽश्वपृष्ठे च रथचर्यासु संमतः ।
धनुर्वेदे च निरतः पितृशुश्रूषणे रतः ॥

26. (Raama) was most competent in riding elephants, horses, and driving chariots; And in the science of

weapons, most devoted, (expert in arms); He delighted in doing service to his father.

❍ ❍ ❍

२७. बाल्यात् प्रभृति सुस्निग्धो लक्ष्मणो लक्ष्मिवर्धनः ।
रामस्य लोकरामस्य भ्रातुर्ज्येष्ठस्य नित्यशः ॥

27. And ever since his childhood, Lakshmana who increased (every one's) happiness (& prosperity), was ever most attached to his eldest brother Raama, who delights the world.

❍ ❍ ❍

२८. सर्वप्रियकरस्तस्य रामस्यापि शरीरतः ।
लक्ष्मणो लक्ष्मिसंपन्नो बहिःप्राण इवापरः ॥

28. Endowed with beauty (& charm) Lakshmana, without even caring for his body, (for his own comfort), did good service to Raama and pleased Raama in every way as though (Raama) was another 'breath' of his. (albeit in another body).

❍ ❍ ❍

२९. न च तेन विना निद्रां लभते पुरुषोत्तमः ।
मृष्टमन्नमुपानीतमश्नाति न हि तं विना ॥

29. Without (Raama) this foremost of men (Lakshmana), did not obtain any sleep; without him, he did not eat (even) foremost foods brought up to him.

(Lakshmana 's attachment to Raama was so intense excepting for his body that was separate, he was one with Raama.).

❍ ❍ ❍

३०. यदा हि हयमारूढो मृगयां याति राघवः ।
अथैनं पृष्ठतो याति सधनुः परिपालयन् ॥

30. When (Raama the) Raaghava, riding on a horse, goes hunting, (Lakshmana), armed with bow as protection, goes along behind him.

❍ ❍ ❍

३१. भरतस्यापि शत्रुघ्नो लक्ष्मणावरजो हितः ।
प्राणैः प्रियतरो नित्यं तस्य चासीत्तथा प्रियः ।।

31. And Lakshmana's brother Schathrugna loved Bharatha more than his life; And he was his beloved, doing good to him ever.

❍ ❍ ❍

३२. स चतुर्भिर्महाभागैः पुत्रैर्दशरथः प्रियैः ।
बभूव परमप्रीतो देवैरिव पितामहः ।।

32. This Dhascharatha with his beloved and most illustrious four sons, was very happy like God Bramma with his Dheva-s.

❍ ❍ ❍

३३. ते यदा ज्ञानसम्पन्नाः सर्वेसमुदिता गुणैः ।
ह्रीमन्तः कीर्तिमन्तश्च सर्वज्ञा दीर्घदर्शिनः ।।

33. They were all endowed with wisdom; endowed with noble qualities; they were ashamed (if they did anything mean); very renowned; they knew all, had vision (to foresee things)......

❍ ❍ ❍

३४. तेषामेवंप्रभावानां सर्वेषां दीप्ततेजसाम् ।
पिता दशरथो हृष्टो ब्रह्मा लोकाधिपो यथा ।।

34. ...... all of them had such a glory & shining with brilliance, that from the time he became their father, Dhascharatha was always in a state of exhilaration like the lord of the world, God Bramma

❍ ❍ ❍

३५. ते चापि मनुजव्याघ्रा वैदिकाध्ययने रताः ।
गुरुशुश्रूषणपरा धनुर्वेदे च निष्ठिताः ।।

35. And yet, these four brothers who were 'tigers' amongst men, were devoted to the study of Vedha- &

Shaasthra-s; they loved serving elders & teachers and they were skilled in archery (DhanurVedha).

❍ ❍ ❍

३६. अथ राजा दशरथस्तेषां दारक्रियां प्रति ।
चिन्तयामास धर्मात्मा सोपाध्यायः सबान्धवः ।।

36. Then, the noble soul king Dhascharatha who was with the Upaadhyaa-s (teachers) and relatives, began to think about marriage for them.

❍ ❍ ❍

३७ तस्य चिन्तयमानस्य मन्त्रिमध्ये महात्मनः ।
अभ्यागच्छन्महातेजा विश्वामित्रो महामुनिः ।।

37. This great soul was thinking along with his ministers, when the most brilliant & very great Muni Vischwaamithra came there.

❍ ❍ ❍

३८. स राज्ञो दर्शनाकाङ्क्षी द्वाराध्यक्षानुवाच ह ।
शीघ्रमाख्यात मां प्राप्तं कौशिकं गाधिनन्दनम् ।।

38. Desirous of meeting the king, (Vischwaamithra) told the (Palace) guards = Inform Immediately That Son of Gaadhi of Kuschika Family Has Come; (announce) Me.=

❍ ❍ ❍

३९. तच्छ्रुत्वा वचनं तस्य राज्ञो वेश्म प्रदुद्रुवुः ।
संभ्रान्तमनसः सर्वेतेन वाक्येन चोदिताः ।।

39. Hearing these words, all of them commanded by these words, rushed to king's palace; with their minds in a state of agitation (Readers to note that Vischwaamithra is not to be kept waiting; His request to see the king is a command for audience).

❍ ❍ ❍

४०. ते गत्वा राजभवनं विश्वामित्रमृषिं तदा ।
प्राप्तमावेदयामासुर्नृपायैक्ष्वाकवे तदा ।।

40. Reaching king's palace, they then informed (Dhascharatha the) Ikshwaaku king about the arrival of Rishi Vischwaamithra there.

❍ ❍ ❍

४१. तेषां तद्वचनं श्रुत्वा सपुरोधाः समाहितः ।
प्रत्युज्जगाम तं हृष्टो ब्रह्माणमिव वासवः ।।

41. Hearing their words, he happily went towards him with devotion, along with his purohiths, like Lord Indhra before God Bramma.

❍ ❍ ❍

४२. स दृष्ट्वा ज्वलितं दीप्त्या तापसं संशितव्रतम् ।
प्रहृष्टवदनो राजा ततोऽर्घ्यं समुपाहरत् ।।

42. Seeing (& meeting) this Muni who was resolute in his Vows and who was shining like flame, the king then offered Arghya, his face beaming with joy.

❍ ❍ ❍

४३. स राज्ञः प्रतिगृह्यार्घ्यं शास्त्रदृष्टेन कर्मणा ।
कुशलं चाव्ययं चैव पर्यपृच्छन्नराधिपम् ।।

43. Receiving the king's (hospitality of) Arghya as 'seen' in norms of Shaasthra-s, he then enquired the king about his welfare & about his imperishable (kingdom of Ayodhya).

❍ ❍ ❍

४४. पुरे कोशे जनपदे बान्धवेषु सुहृत्सु च ।
कुशलं कौशिको राज्ञः पर्यपृच्छत् सुधार्मिकः ।।

44. Endowed with foremost qualities of Dharma this (Vischwaamithra) of Kuschika family, then enquired about king's welfare, about his city, the state of finance, about his relatives, friends etc.

❍ ❍ ❍

४५. अपि ते सन्नताः सर्वेसामन्ता रिपवो जिताः ।
दैवं च मानुषं चापि कर्म ते साध्वनुष्ठितम् ।।

45. (Vischwaamithra observes protocol; asks the king): Are the feudal lords & kings loyal to you? (& obedient), all of them? Are your enemies conquered by you? Are your mundane & spiritual activities being properly observed?

❍ ❍ ❍

४६. वसिष्ठं च समागम्य कुशलं मुनिपुङ्गवः ।
ऋषींश्चान्यान् यथान्यायं महाभागानुवाच ह ।।

46. And this 'tiger' of Muni-s, approached Vasishta & enquired about his welfare and also about other most illustrious Rishi-s there as per norms (of protocol).

❍ ❍ ❍

४७. ते सर्वेहृष्टमनसस्ततो राज्ञो निवेशनम् ।
विविशुः पूजितास्तत्र निषेदुश्च यथार्हतः ।।

47. With a happy mind & well honoured, all of them then entered the King's Hall; They then sat at their respective places.

❍ ❍ ❍

४८. अथ हृष्टमना राजा विश्वामित्रं महामुनिम् ।
उवाच परमोदारो हृष्टः समभिपूजयन् ।।

48. Then with a happy heart (& mind), the most generous king who was exhilarated, addressed this great Muni Vischwaamithra, well honoured (by his visit).

❍ ❍ ❍

४९. यथाऽमृतस्य संप्राप्तिर्यथा वर्षमनूदके ।
यथा सदृशदारेषु पुत्रजन्म प्रशस्यते ।।

49. (Dhascharatha was so honoured by his visit he addresses him thus): Like obtaining nectar, like rainfall

in waterless places, like being highly commended (& praised) by the birth of a son in one's worthy wife......

❍ ❍ ❍

५०. प्रनष्टस्य यथा लाभो यथा हर्षोमहोदये ।
तथैवागमनं मन्ये स्वागतं ते महामुने ।।

50. ...... like profit for one who has lost, like joy in great festivities. . . . Your coming here, I consider most welcome, Oh great Muni (Vischwaamithra)!

❍ ❍ ❍

५१. कं च ते परमं कामं करोमि किमु हर्षितः ।
पात्रभूतोऽसि मे विप्र दिष्ट्या प्राप्तोऽसि धार्मिक ।।

51. Oh Braamin (Vischwaamithra)! Rejoicing as I am, I will do whatever foremost you desire, in every way. (I will fulfill whatever you order me to do). You are fit to receive gifts (from me). Oh man of Dharma! By divine grace, you have come here (as honour to me).

❍ ❍ ❍

५२. अद्य मे सफलं जन्म जीवितं च सुजीवितम् ।।

52. (Only) Now my life is fruitful; My existence is worthwhile.

❍ ❍ ❍

५३. पूर्वं राजर्षिशब्देन तपसा द्योतितप्रभः ।
ब्रह्मर्षित्वमनुप्राप्तः पूज्योऽसि बहुधा मया ।।

53. Once you were spoken of as a royal sage but (later on) by penance, you obtained the state of Bramma Rishi, glowing with brilliance; You are to be honoured by me in many ways.

❍ ❍ ❍

५४. तदद्भुतमिदं विप्र पवित्रं परमं मम ।
शुभक्षेत्रगतश्चाहं तव संदर्शनात् प्रभो ।।

54. Oh Lord! By your (presence &) sight, I have obtained auspicious status: Oh Braamin. This, (your visit), is foremost purification for me.

❍ ❍ ❍

५५. ब्रूहि यत्प्रार्थितं तुभ्यं कार्यमागमनं प्रति ।
इच्छाम्यनुगृहीतोऽहं त्वदर्थपरिवृद्धये ।।

55. Please tell me as to what work (job) is solicited (by you) by your coming here. Obliged as I am, I desire to serve your cause.

❍ ❍ ❍

५६. कार्यस्य न विमर्शं च गन्तुमर्हसि कौशिक ।
कर्ता चाहमशेषेण दैवतं हि भवान् मम ।।

56. Oh Kowschik (Vischwaamithra)! Do not have any misgivings in the work (and my service to you): I will do (everything) without leaving (out anything); Indeed you are my God!

❍ ❍ ❍

५७. मम चायमनुप्राप्तो महानभ्युदयो द्विज ।
तवागमनजः कृत्स्नो धर्मश्चानुत्तमो मम ।।

57. d!

57: Oh Braamin! For me, this great prosperity & elevation has come about (by your visit). The Dharma by your coming (over to me) here, is totally foremost to me.

❍ ❍ ❍

५८, इति हृदयसुखं निशम्य वाक्यं श्रुतिसुखमात्मवता विनीतमुक्तम् ।
प्रथितगुणयशा गुणैर्विशिष्टिः परम ऋषिः परमं जगाम हर्षम् ।।

58. Hearing (the words) that were sweet to hear and pleasing to the heart, uttered with great reverence & modesty by the wise & noble soul (Dhascharatha), the great Rishi (Vischwaamithra) who was endowed with

good qualities and who possessed renowned fame, became very happy.

(Note: This visit of Vischwaamithra to Dhascharatha's court is a very significant event in the life of Prince Raama; Readers may also note the protocol observed).

❍ ❍ ❍

Chapter 19

Raama's Assistance Sought by Vischwaamithra

(The great sage Vischwaamithra tells king Dhascharatha the purpose of his visit; He wants the services of young Raama during the Yaaga he is performing. He wants Raama to accompany him).

❍ ❍ ❍

१. तच्छ्रुत्वा राजसिंहस्य वाक्यमद्भुतविस्तरम् ।
हृष्टरोमा महातेजा विश्वामित्रोऽभ्यभाषत ॥

1. Hearing such a marvelous & detailed speech from (Dhascharatha) the 'lion' amongst kings, the most brilliant Vischwaamithra who was in raptures, spoke (thus).

❍ ❍ ❍

२. सदृशं राजशार्दूल तवैव भुवि नान्यतः ।
महावंशप्रसूतस्य वसिष्ठव्यपदेशिनः ॥

2. Oh 'Tiger' amongst kings! It is befitting you (to speak like this), born as you are in a great family in this world, with Vasishta as your adviser; It cannot be otherwise!

❍ ❍ ❍

३. यत्तु मे हृद्गतं वाक्यं तस्य कार्यस्य निश्चयम् ।
कुरुष्व राजशार्दूल भव सत्यप्रतिश्रवः ॥

3. Oh 'tiger' amongst kings! What is in my heart, is now

expressed (by me to you). You must make this task (of mine) certain. You must be true to your promise. (I am going to ask you something you should not refuse under any circumstances as per your assurance).

❍ ❍ ❍

४. अहं नियममातिष्ठे सिद्ध्यर्थं पुरुषर्षभ ।
तस्य विघ्नकरौ द्वौ तु राक्षसौ कामरूपिणौ ।।

4. Oh 'bull' amongst men! For the sake of tranquillity & peace, I have started on a Yaaga (of Restraint): There are two demons who can take on any form, who are now creating obstacles for this (Yaaga of mine in my hermitage).

❍ ❍ ❍

५. मारीचश्च सुबाहुश्च वीर्यवन्तौ सुशिक्षितौ ।
तौ मांसरुधिरौघेण वेदिं तामभ्यवर्षताम् ।।

६. व्रते मे बहुशश्चीर्णेसमाप्त्यां राक्षसाविमौ ।।

5. & 6.

When my Vow & Austerities was being observed and in progress, and was nearing completion, these demons Maareecha & Subhaahu who are brave & well trained, shower the (Sacred) Altar, with blood, along with flesh & meat.

❍ ❍ ❍

७. अवधूते तथाभूते तस्मिन्नियमनिश्चये ।
कृतश्रमो निरुत्साहस्तस्माद्देशादपाक्रमम् ।।

7. When that happened like that & when fulfillment of austerities was shaken up (& obstacles were put in my way) I came away from that place without any zeal, my effort in vain.

❍ ❍ ❍

८. न च मे क्रोधमुत्स्रष्टुं बुद्धिर्भवति पार्थिव ।
तथाभूता हि सा चर्या न शापस्तत्र मुच्यते ।।

8. Oh Ruler of Earth! My mind is not in deploying my wrath (on these two); Because the observance of this (Yaaga) is such; Therefore my curse (on them) was not to be released (& was not released).

❍ ❍ ❍

९. स्वपुत्रं राजशार्दूल रामं सत्यपराक्रमम् ।
काकपक्षधरं वीरं ज्येष्ठं मे दातुमर्हसि ।।

9. Oh 'Tiger' of kings! (Therefore) You should give me your brave eldest son who is truly valiant & who sports hair* style of side burns. (* a sort of tuft on head as well).

❍ ❍ ❍

१०. शक्तो ह्येष मया गुप्तो दिव्येन स्वेन तेजसा ।
राक्षसा येऽपकर्तारस्तेषामपि विनाशने ।।

10. Protected by me, this (Raama) is capable of the destruction of these demons who are oppressors, by his divine brilliance (prowess).

❍ ❍ ❍

११. श्रेयश्चास्मै प्रदास्यामि बहुरूपं न संशयः ।
त्रयाणामपि लोकानां येन ख्यातिं गमिष्यति ।।

11. I will bestow him with various distinctions: No doubt about it; He will obtain fame in all the three worlds.

❍ ❍ ❍

१२. न च तौ राममासाद्य शक्तौ स्थातुं कथञ्चन ।
न च तौ राघवादन्यो हन्तुमुत्सहते पुमान् ।।

12. These two (demons), when they approach (and confront) Raama, are not capable of standing up before him at all. And no other man than (Raama) the Raaghava is capable of killing these two.

❍ ❍ ❍

१३. वीर्योत्सिक्तौ हि तौ पापौ कालपाशवशं गतौ ।
रामस्य राजशार्दूल न पर्याप्तौ महात्मनः ।।
न च पुत्रकृतं स्नेहं कर्तुमर्हसि पार्थिव ।।

13. These two sinful (demons) who are arrogant of their valour & who are bound by Yama's rope (of imminent death), are no match or equal to the great soul Raama: Further, Oh king, you should not (fail to send your son along with me) on account of (a natural) attachment (of a father) towards a son.

❍ ❍ ❍

१४. दशरात्रस्तु यज्ञश्च तस्मिन् रामेण राक्षसौ ।
हन्तव्यौ विघ्नकर्तारौ मम यज्ञस्य वैरिणौ ।।

14. And the Yaaga (my Vows & Austerities) is only for 10 days (& nights). During this time, the two enemy demons who are creators of disturbance to my yaaga, must be killed by Raama.

❍ ❍ ❍

१५. अहं ते प्रतिजानामि हतौ तौ विद्धि राक्षसौ ।।

15. I affirm this to you; Know ye that these two demons are (as good as) killed (if Raama is with me.)

❍ ❍ ❍

१६. अहं वेद्मि महात्मानं रामं सत्यपराक्रमम् ।
वसिष्ठोऽपि महातेजा ये चेमे तपसि स्थिताः ।।

16. I know Raama as a man of great soul; truly valiant; And the most brilliant Vasishta also (knows this). And also those who are steadfast in doing penance.

❍ ❍ ❍

१७. यदि ते धर्मलाभं च यशश्च परमं भुवि ।
हितमिच्छसि राजेन्द्र रामं मे दातुमर्हसि ।।

17. Oh lord of kings! If you desire fruits of Dharma in this world, & great salutary fame, then you should give Raama to me.

❍ ❍ ❍

१८. यद्यभ्यनुज्ञां काकुत्स्थ ददते तव मन्त्रिणः ।
वसिष्ठप्रमुखाः सर्वेततो रामं विसर्जय ।।

18. Oh (Dhascharatha the) Kaakuthsa! Vasishta, and all your ministers are giving their consent; As such you should give leave to Raama.

❍ ❍ ❍

१९. अभिप्रेतमसंसक्तमात्मजं दातुमर्हसि ।
दशरात्रं हि यज्ञस्य रामं राजीवलोचनम् ।।

19. For the sake of Yaaga (& austerities), you should give this lotus eyed most beloved son Raama and be without his company for 10 days.

❍ ❍ ❍

२०. नात्येति कालो यज्ञस्य यथाऽयं मम राघव ।
तथा कुरुष्व भद्रं ते मा च शोके मनः कृथाः ।।

20. Oh (Dhascharatha the) Raaghava! You must do (this for me) in such a way that this period (of 10 days) of my Yaaga passes through (without hindrance); Welfare to you. Do not let your mind (get submerged) in grief. (due to separation from Raama).

❍ ❍ ❍

२१. इत्येवमुक्त्वा धर्मात्मा धर्मार्थसहितं वचः ।
विरराम महातेजा विश्वामित्रो महामुनिः ।।

21. Saying thus these words enjoined with Dharma, the man of Dharma, this most brilliant great sage Vischwaamithra 'rested'.

❍ ❍ ❍

२२. स तन्निशम्य राजेन्द्रो विश्वामित्रवचः शुभम् ।
शोकमभ्यगमत्तीव्रं व्यषीदत भयान्वितः ।।

22. Hearing these auspicious words of Vischwaamithra, this lord of kings, (Dhascharatha) obtained terrible sorrow; he was terribly scared and became despondent.

❍ ❍ ❍

२३. इति हृदयमनोविदारणं मुनिवचनं तदतीव शुश्रुवान् ।
नरपतिरभवन्महान् महात्मा व्यथितमनाः प्रचचाल चासनात् ।।

23. This great lord of men, the great soul (Dhascharatha), hearing such words of the Muni which split the vitals of his heart, became terribly depressed. And he trembled in his throne.

(Note: Sage Vishwaamithra could easily kill these demons who were disturbing his austerities. But being a man of penance, he wishes this job to be done by this soldier-prince. And the great seer he is, Vischwamithra has a purpose in taking Raama away with him. He is going to teach Raama during his stay with him. Of course Dhascharatha could not see it in this light; he loved his son so much: He felt his son was too young to take on responsibility).

❍ ❍ ❍

Chapter 20

And Dhascharatha Refuses (to Send his Son)

१. तच्छ्रुत्वा राजशार्दूलो विश्वामित्रस्य भाषितम् ।
मुहूर्तमिव निस्संज्ञः संज्ञावानिदमब्रवीत् ।।

1. For one full Muhoortha (about 48 minutes), (Dhascharatha), the 'tiger' amongst kings, lost his consciousness after hearing Vischwaamithra's words; Recovering (Regaining) consciousness, he said this.

❍ ❍ ❍

२. ऊनषोडशवर्षोमे रामो राजीवलोचनः ।
न युद्धयोग्यतामस्य पश्यामि सह राक्षसैः ।।

2. My lotus eyed Raama is hardly 16; I cannot possibly see in him the capacity to fight with demons.

❍ ❍ ❍

३. इयमक्षौहिणी पूर्णा यस्याहं पतिरीश्वरः ।
अनया संवृतो गत्वा योद्धाऽहं तैर्निशाचरैः ।।

3. To (the kingdom) to which I am the lord & sovereign, this (kingdom) is full with an army (formation) of Akshowhini: (Therefore) Surrounded by this (my vast army), I will (myself) go (with you) & fight these demons.

❍ ❍ ❍

४. इमे शूराश्च विक्रान्त भृत्या मेऽस्त्रविशारदाः ।
योग्या रक्षोगणैर्योद्धुं न रामं नेतुमर्हसि ।।

4. These my (soldiers and) dependents who are all brave, most valiant, well versed in weaponry, are all capable of fighting with a multitude of demons; (So please) do not take away Raama.

❍ ❍ ❍

५. अहमेको धनुष्पाणिर्गोप्ता समरमूर्धनि ।
यावत् प्राणान् धरिष्यामि तावद्योत्स्ये निशाचरैः ।।

5. Single handedly, with bow in my arm in battlefield, as protector, I will fight these demons, (these night prowlers), till I bear life (in my body).

❍ ❍ ❍

६. निर्विघ्ना व्रतचर्या सा भविष्यति सुरक्षिता ।
अहं तत्र गमिष्यामि न रामं नेतुमर्हसि ।।

6. This, (your observance of) Vow and Austerities, will become well protected (by me & my army); I will go there (with you); (but please) do not take away Raama.

❍ ❍ ❍

७. बालो ह्यकृतविद्यश्च न च वेत्ति बलाबलम् ।
न चास्त्रबलसंयुक्तो न च युद्धविशारदः ।।
न चासौ रक्षसां योग्यः कूटयुद्धा हि ते ध्रुवम् ।।

7. He is but a boy! Inexperienced; Does not know (about

relative) strength & weakness; Does not possess (sufficient) strength in weaponry; has no proficiency in war; is no match for the demons; And they, (these demons), surely fight by magic (and sorcery).

❍ ❍ ❍

८. विप्रयुक्तो हि रामेण मुहूर्तमपि नोत्सहे ।
जीवितुं मुनिशार्दूलं न रामं नेतुमर्हसि ।।

8. Oh (Vischwaamithra the) 'tiger' amongst sages! Separated from Raama even for a muhoortha, I cannot bear to live on; Therefore dont take away Raama.

❍ ❍ ❍

९. यदि वा राघवं ब्रह्मन्नेतुमिच्छसि सुव्रत ।
चतुरङ्गसमायुक्तं मया च सहितं नय ।।

9. Oh (Vischwaamithra the) Braamin of great vows & austerities! If you desire to take away (with you, Raama the) Raaghava, then take me also (with you) along with my Foursome Army (Readers to note. The Akshowhini foursome army consists of 21,870 elephants, 21,870 chariots, 65,000 horses, & 109,350 foot soldiers).

❍ ❍ ❍

१०. षष्टिर्वर्षसहस्राणि जातस्य मम कौशिक ।
दुःखेनोत्पादितश्चायं न रामं नेतुमर्हसि ।।

10. Oh (Vischwaamithra the) Kowschik! To me for whom 60,000 years (of life) has passed away (without sons), this (Raama) was born with great difficulty (through Yaaga): Dont take away Raama.

❍ ❍ ❍

११. चतुर्णामात्मजानां हि प्रीतिः पारमिका मम ।
ज्येष्ठं धर्मप्रधानं च न रामं नेतुमर्हसि ।।

11. Amongst my four sons, I have more (& a special) attachment towards this eldest (son Raama) who is

foremost in Dharma; Therefore do not take away Raama.

❍ ❍ ❍

१२. किंवीर्या राक्षसास्ते च कस्य पुत्राश्च के च ते ।
कथंप्रमाणाः के चैतान् रक्षन्ति मुनिपुङ्गव ।।

12. These demons: What kind of valour do they possess? Whose sons are they? Who are they? What sort of figure they possess? Oh 'tiger' amongst sages! Further, who protects them all. (Readers may note this: A king should 'investigate' the enemy before he fights. No wonder, Dhascharatha puts these questions).

❍ ❍ ❍

१३. कथं च प्रतिकर्तव्यं तेषां रामेण रक्षसाम् ।
मामकैर्वा बलैर्ब्रह्मन् मया वा कूटयोधिनाम् ।।

13. Oh (Vischwaamithra, the) Braamin! How should attack be done against these demons who fight through (art of) magical warfare, by me, by my Raama & by my army?

❍ ❍ ❍

१४. सर्वं मे शंस भगवन् कथं तेषां मया रणे ।
स्थातव्यं दुष्टभावानां वीर्योत्सिक्ता हि राक्षसाः ।।

14. Oh Lord! In battle with these evil minded (demons), how should they be confronted by me? These demons are arrogant of their prowess, indeed. Tell me all.

❍ ❍ ❍

१५. तस्य तद्वचनं श्रुत्वा विश्वामित्रोऽभ्यभाषत ।।

15. And hearing his words, Vischwaamithra replied.

❍ ❍ ❍

१६. पुलस्त्यवंशप्रभवो रावणो नाम राक्षसः ।।

16. There is a demon called Raavana, born in Pulasthya family.

❍ ❍ ❍

१७. स ब्रह्मणा दत्तवरस्त्रैलोक्यं बाधते भृशम् ।
महाबलो महावीर्योराक्षसैर्बहुभिर्वृतः ।।

17. (This Raavana) having obtained a boon from God Bramma and being mightily strong, mightily brave, and surrounded by many demons, oppresses greatly the Three Worlds.

❍ ❍ ❍

१८. श्रूयते हि महावीर्योरावणो राक्षसाधिपः ।
साक्षाद्वैश्रवणभ्राता पुत्रो विश्रवसो मुनेः ।।

18. This, the own brother of Kubhaera, this son of Muni Vischrawas, is Raavana, the lord of all demons & is renowned as mightily brave.

❍ ❍ ❍

१९. सदा न खलु यज्ञस्य विघ्नकर्ता महाबलः ।
तेन संचोदितौ तौ तु राक्षसौ कामरूपिणौ ।।
मारीचश्च सुबाहुश्च यज्ञविघ्नं करिष्यतः ।।

19. Mightily strong; Will always put obstacles in Yaaga-s; When (he does) not, goaded by him, the demons Maareecha & Subhaahu who can take on any form, will cause harm to Yaaga.

❍ ❍ ❍

२०. इत्युक्तो मुनिना तेन राजोवाच मुनिं तदा ।
न हि शक्तोऽस्मि संग्रामे स्थातुं तस्य दुरात्मनः ।।

20. (Dhascharatha is even more scared now to send Raama). . When he was told thus by the Muni, the king addressed the Muni (Vischwaamithra): I myself have no capacity to stand before (& face) this evil minded demon in war.

❍ ❍ ❍

२१. स त्वं प्रसादं धर्मज्ञ कुरुष्व मम पुत्रके ।
मम चैवाल्पभाग्यस्य दैवतं हि भवान् गुरुः ।।

21. Oh knower of Dharma! Most unfortunate I am: To me you are my Teacher & God. You must show your grace (& mercy) on my son.

❍ ❍ ❍

२२. देवदानवगन्धर्वा यक्षाः पतगपन्नगाः ।
न शक्ता रावणं सोढुं किं पुनर्मानवा युधि ।।

22. Even Dheva-s, Asura-s, Ghandharva-s, Yaksha-s, Birds, Reptiles cannot bear Raavana in war; How can then (ordinary) men?

❍ ❍ ❍

२३. स हि वीर्यवतां वीर्यमादत्ते युधि राक्षसः ।
तेनाहं नैव शक्तोऽस्मि संयोद्धुं तस्य वा बलैः ।।
सबलो वा मुनिश्रेष्ठ सहितो वा ममात्मजैः ।।

23. This demon snatches away the bravery from the brave; Therefore, Oh foremost Muni, I, along with my army, or with my sons, am incapable to fight with him or with his army.

❍ ❍ ❍

२४. कथमप्यमरप्रख्यं संग्रामाणामकोविदम् ।
बालं मे तनयं ब्रह्मन्नैव दास्यामि पुत्रकम् ।।

24. Oh Braamin! I Will Never Give My Son (Raama to you) whatsoever. (As he is) a mere boy, is progenitor of my family, is ignorant of wars, that are like wars of the celestials.

❍ ❍ ❍

२५. अथ कालोपमौ युद्धे सुतौ सुन्दोपसुन्दयोः ।
यज्ञविघ्नकरौ तेन नैव दास्यामि पुत्रकम् ।।

25. Further, these two who cause disruption (& harm) to the Yaaga-s are sons of Sundha & Upasundha; In war they are like lord of Death. Therefore I will never give my beloved son.

❍ ❍ ❍

२६. तौ तु राक्षसकन्यायां जातौ दैत्यकुलोद्वहौ ।
मारीचश्च सुबाहुश्च वीर्यवन्तौ सुशिक्षितौ ।।

26. Maareecha & Subhaahu are born in (wombs of) Demonesses to elevate (& foster) the race of demons. Endowed with bravery; Further, very well trained.

❍ ❍ ❍

२७. तयोरन्यतरेणाहं योद्धा स्यां ससुहृद्गणः ।
अन्यथा त्वनुनेष्यामि भवन्तं सहबान्धवः ।।

27. Even against any one of them, I cannot fight (although) I may be accompanied by multitude of my folks & friends. I beseech you with my friends (here). : (Please dont ask for my son).

❍ ❍ ❍

२८. इति नरपतिजल्पनाद् द्विजेन्द्रं कुशिकसुतं सुमहान् विवेश मन्युः ।
सुहुत इव मखेऽग्निराज्यसिक्तः समभवदुज्ज्वलितो महर्षिवह्नि ।।

28. Hearing the king (Dhascharatha's) 'chatter' like this, great wrath seized (entered) this foremost Braamin, the son of Kuschika, (this Vischwaamithra): Like Fire in a Yaaga well fed with oblations of melted butter (Ghee), the Fire that was this great sage (Vischwaamithra) was 'Burning'

(Note: Vischwaamithra is in rage because of two reasons. After giving assurance to do whatever he asked for, Dhascharatha backs out. Refuses to send Raama with him. Secondly, Dhascharatha refuses to send Raama with him even though Vischwaamithra had given assurance that he would protect Raama. And Vishwaamithra is not an ordinary Rishi-Sage. He was once a mighty king, even shook Lord Indhra's world).

❍ ❍ ❍

Chapter 21

Under Assurance of Vasishta, Raama is Sent (along with Vischwaamithra)

१. तच्छ्रुत्वा वचनं तस्य स्नेहपर्याकुलाक्षरम् ।
समन्युः कौशिको वाक्यं प्रत्युवाच महीपतिम् ।।

1. Hearing these words spoken by (Dhascharatha) with confusion & bewilderment caused by his attachment (to his son Raama), (Vischwaamithra) the Kowschik, replied the following words to this lord of earth (Dhascharatha), in great wrath.

❍ ❍ ❍

२. पूर्वमेव प्रतिश्रुत्य प्रतिज्ञां हातुमिच्छसि ।
राघवाणामयुक्तोऽयं कुलस्यास्य विपर्ययः ।।

2. (Vischwaamithra is known for his wrath; he gives vent to his feelings). Having at first given the assurance (that you will do anything for me), you now desire to utterly disregard your promise; This is not befitting to this family of Raghu-s, this perversion (of going back on word).

❍ ❍ ❍

३. यदीदं ते क्षमं राजन् गमिष्यामि यथाऽऽगतम् ।
मिथ्याप्रतिज्ञः काकुत्स्थ सुखीं भत सबान्धवः ।।

3. If this is proper for you, then I am going back as I came. Oh (Dhascharatha the) Kaakuthsa! You live happily with your folks (with stigma of a man) breaking a promise.

❍ ❍ ❍

४. तस्य रोषपरीतस्य विश्वामित्रस्य धीमतः ।
चचाल वसुधा कृत्स्ना विवेश च भयं सुरान् ।।

4. The entire Earth shook before this wise Vischwaamithra

who was overcome by wrath. Fear seized even celestials (in heaven).

❍ ❍ ❍

५. त्रस्तरूपं तु विज्ञाय जगत्सर्वं महानृषिः ।
नृपतिं सुव्रतो धीरो वसिष्ठो वाक्यमब्रवीत् ।।

5. Realising that all the world was scared, the serene great Rishi Vasishta of many austerities & vows, then addressed the king.

❍ ❍ ❍

६. इक्ष्वाकूणां कुले जातः साक्षाद्धर्म इवापरः ।
धृतिमान् सुव्रतः श्रीमान्न धर्मं हातुमर्हसि ।।

6. Born in the family of Ikshwaaku-s as another Dharma itself, you (the Dharma personified), are a man of steadfastness, man of vows; most resplendent. (As such) you should not desert Dharma.

❍ ❍ ❍

७. त्रिषु लोकेषु विख्यातो धर्मात्मा इति राघवः ।
स्वधर्मं प्रतिपद्यस्व नाधर्मं वोढुमर्हसि ।।

7. You are a Raaghava; In three worlds you are known as a man of Dharma. Abide by your Dharma; You should not follow Adharma (Non Dharma).

❍ ❍ ❍

८. आश्रुत्यैवं करिष्यामीत्युक्त्वा वाक्यमकुर्वतः ।
इष्टापूर्तक्षयो भूयात्तस्माद्रामं विसर्जय ।।

8. = I Will Do Like (what you say) = :Having told thus & resolved, if word (of commitment) is not honoured (as promised) there will be no fulfilment (fruits) for all your previous Rites & Rituals.Therefore give leave for Raama to go (with Vischwaamithra).

❍ ❍ ❍

९. कृतास्त्रमकृतास्त्रं वा नैनं शक्ष्यन्ति राक्षसाः ।
गुप्तं कुशिकपुत्रेण ज्वलनेनामृतं यथा ।।

9. Like Nectar (that cannot be touched) by Fire, demons cannot harm this (Raama) whether (Raama) is proficient in weapons or not proficient, when he is protected by (Vischwaamithra), the son of Kuschika.

❍ ❍ ❍

१०. एष विग्रहवान्धर्म एष वीर्यवतां वरः ।
एष बुध्याऽधिको लोकें तपसश्च परायणम् ।।

10. This (Vischwaamithra) is (living) embodiment of Dharma: He is foremost amongst the brave; he is foremost in the world in wisdom; And he is the last resort in penance.

❍ ❍ ❍

११. एषोऽस्त्रान् विविधान् वेत्ति त्रैलोक्ये सचराचरे ।
नैनमन्यः पुमान् वेत्ति न च वेत्स्यन्ति केचन ।।

11. (Vishwaamithra) has knowledge of diverse weapons; In all the three worlds of moving & non moving things, no other man can really 'know' him; And no one will ever 'know' him.

❍ ❍ ❍

१२. न देवा ऋषयः केचिन्नासुरा न च राक्षसाः ।
गन्धर्वयक्षप्रवराः सकिन्नरमहोरगाः ।।

12. Celestials & Rishi-s know him not; Nor Asura-s, nor demons, None, neither Ghandharva-s, nor foremost Yaksha-s, nor Mahaa-Uraga-s & Kinnara-s.

❍ ❍ ❍

१३. सर्वास्त्राणि भृशाश्वस्य पुत्राः परमधार्मिकाः ।
कौशिकाय पुरा दत्ता यदा राज्यं प्रशासति ।।

13. All the weapons are 'Sons' of Brischaaschwa; (The weapons) are foremost 'Persons' of Dharma: When

long ago Kowschik (Vishwaamithra) was ruling the kingdom, they were given to him.

❍ ❍ ❍

१४. तेऽपि पुत्रा भृशाश्वस्य प्रजापतिसुतास्तु ये ।
नैकरूपा महावीर्या दीप्तिमन्तो जयावहाः ॥

14. The sons of Brischaaswas & sons of Prajaapathi, all these have diverse forms; mightily brave; they glow brilliantly; They bring victories, ("Sons" take shape and form of celestial weapons).

❍ ❍ ❍

१५. जया च सुप्रभा चैव दक्षकन्ये सुमध्यमे ।
ते सुवातेऽस्त्रशस्त्राणि शतं परमभास्वरम् ॥

15. Jaya & Suprabha are Dhaksha's daughters; Are slender waist; and these two obtained hundreds of weapons that are most brilliant.

❍ ❍ ❍

१६. पञ्चाशतं सुतांल्लेभे जया लब्धवरा पुरा ।
वधायासुरसैन्यानामक्षयान् कामरूपिणः ॥

16. Long ago, having obtained boons, Jaya begot 500 sons for the sake of the destruction of Asura army; they are all-imperishable & can take on any form.

❍ ❍ ❍

१७. सुप्रभाऽजनयच्चापि पुत्रान् पञ्चाशतं पुनः ।
संहारान्नाम दुर्धर्षान्दुराक्रामान् बलीयसः ॥

17. And further, Suprabha begot 500 'sons' named Samhaara; they are very strong, uncrushable, unconquerable. (Readers to note that these 'Sons' are Divine weapons).

❍ ❍ ❍

१८. तानि चास्त्राणि वेत्त्येष यथावत् कुशिकात्मजः ।
अपूर्वाणां च जनने शक्तो भूयश्च धर्मवित् ॥

18. This knower of Dharma (this Vischwaamithra the) son of Kuschika knows all about these weapons; And he has the capability to create new, even better weapons.

❍ ❍ ❍

१९. एवंवीर्योमहातेजा विश्वामित्रो महायशाः ।
तेनास्य मुनिमुख्यस्य धर्मज्ञस्य महात्मनः ।।
२०. न किञ्चिदप्यविदितं भूतं भव्यं च राघव ।
न रामगमने राजन् संशयं गन्तुमर्हसि ।।

19. & 20.

Vischwaamithra has such a valour; most famous; most brilliant; He is knower of Dharma. This foremost amongst Muni-s, this great soul. . . . . To him, nothing is not known; What is past, what is to happen and even what is not known (he can foresee). Therefore, Oh King (Dhascharatha)! Let there be no (doubt and) misgivings in sending Raama (with Vischwaamithra).

❍ ❍ ❍

२१. तेषां निग्रहणे शक्तः स्वयं च कुशिकात्मजः ।
तव पुत्रहितार्थाय त्वामुपेत्याभियाचते ।।

21. (As for) The destruction of these (Demons) this (Vishwaamithra the) son of Kuschika, is capable of doing himself, (without assistance of Raama or any one else) Yet for the sake of (doing good to) your son, he has come to you & 'begs' you (requests you).

❍ ❍ ❍

२२. इति मुनिवचनात् प्रसन्नचित्तो रघुवृषभश्च मुमोद भास्वराङ्गः ।
गमनमभिरुरोच राघवस्य प्रथितयशाः कुशिकात्मजाय बुद्ध्या ।।

22. (Listening to and) By these words of Muni (Vasishta), the 'Bull' amongst kings (Dhascharatha), regained his composure, became bright, and rejoiced. For the sake of the renowned (Vischwaamithra) the son Kuschika, he approved, (consented Raama) the Raaghava's going with him.

(Note: Dhascharatha is very fortunate he has a fine set of Ministers, teachers & advisers. A King should never 'wriggle out' of a promise or commitment. Vasishta reminds his king: And Dhascharatha being a great king accepts Vasishta's advice & sends Raama. And Vasishta reminds his king that single handedly Vischwaamithra could destroy any one; but then the great Vischwaamithra is no longer a man of violence but a great spiritual man & that is why he wanted Raama by his side when he was going to do Austerities & Yaaga. The killing is to be done by Raama).

❍ ❍ ❍

Chapter 22

Vischwaamithra Leaves (with Raama)

१. तथा वसिष्ठे ब्रुवति राजा दशरथस्तदा ।
प्रहृष्टवदनो राममाजुहाव सलक्ष्मणम् ।।

1. When Vasishta told him thus, king Dhascharatha, then summoned Raama who was (ever) with Lakshmana, his face beaming with joy.

❍ ❍ ❍

२. कृतस्वस्त्ययनं मात्रा पित्रा दशरथेन च ।
पुरोधसा वसिष्ठेन मङ्गलैरभिमन्त्रितम् ।।

३. स पुत्रं मूर्ध्न्युपाघ्राय राजा दशरथः प्रियम् ।
ददौ कुशिकपुत्राय सुप्रीतेनान्तरात्मना ।।

2. & 3.

Blessed by his father (Dhascharatha) & by his mother (Kowsalya), and blessed with auspicious chants by their family teacher Vasishta ...... (Such a) Beloved son this king Dhascharatha kissed on his forehead

& 'handed' him over to (Vischwaamithra) the son of Kuschika, with joy & with all his heart.

❍ ❍ ❍

४. ततो वायुः सुखस्पर्शोनीरजस्को ववौ तदा ।
विश्वामित्रगतं रामं दृष्ट्वा राजीवलोचनम् ।।

4. At that moment, (lord of) Wind seeing the lotus eyed Raama going with Vischwaamithra (as his ward), blew air, soft & pure.

❍ ❍ ❍

५. पुष्पवृष्टिर्महत्यासीद्देवदुन्दुभिनिस्वनः ।
शङ्खदुन्दुभिनिर्घोषः प्रयाते तु महात्मनि ।।

5. When the great soul (Vischwaamithra) started (out of Ayodhya with his ward Raama) a great shower of flowers (fell) and sounds from Dhundhubi drums of celestials & conch blows with drum beats were (heard).

❍ ❍ ❍

६. विश्वामित्रो ययावग्रे ततो रामो महायशाः ।
काकपक्षधरो धन्वी तं च सौमित्रिरन्वगात् ।।

6. Vischwaamithra went first; then the most famous Raama with his Kaapaksha Hair style (Side burns & hair locks) & wielding bow, followed him. Then (the son of Sumitra), Lakshmana followed.

❍ ❍ ❍

७. कलापिनौ धनुष्पाणी शोभयानौ दिशो दश ।
विश्वामित्रं महात्मानं पञ्चशीर्षाविवोरगौ ।।

7. With quivers, wielding bow in their hands, radiating their brilliance in all directions, and shining like five headed cobra, (accompanying) the great soul Vischwaamithra ......

❍ ❍ ❍

८. तदा कुशिकपुत्रं तु धनुष्पाणी स्वलमृतौ ।
बद्धगोधाङ्गलित्राणौ खड्गवन्तौ महाद्युती ।।

8. ...... well decorated, (their) hands gripping (firmly) the bow, in great splendor, (& armed) with sword, wearing gloves made of leather, (they followed) this (Vischwaamithra) the son of Kuschika ......

❍ ❍ ❍

९. कुमारौ चारुवपुषौ भ्रातरौ रामलक्ष्मणौ ।
अनुजग्मतुरक्षुद्रौ पितामहमिवाश्विनौ ।।
स्थाणुं देवमिवाचिन्त्यं कुमाराविव पावकी ।।

9. ...... these young brothers, Raama & Lakshmana who had beautiful bodies followed him like the two sons of Fire following the unimaginable Sthaanu (Rudhra-Schiva), like the lovely Ashwin (brothers) following God Bramma.

❍ ❍ ❍

१०. अध्यर्धयोजनं गत्वा सरय्वा दक्षिणे तटे ।
रामेति मधुरां वाणीं विश्वामित्रोऽभ्यभाषत ।।

10. Reaching the southern bank of the river Saraayu, and after going 1 1/2 Yojana-s (about 13 miles), Vischwaamithra called Raama (by name) and spoke to him sweet words (thus).

❍ ❍ ❍

११. गृहाण वत्स सलिलं मा भूत्कालविपर्ययः ।
मन्त्रग्रामं गृहाण त्वं बलामतिबलां तथा ।।

11. Oh 'Son'! Take 'waters': Let not time be wasted (Dont delay): You (shall) receive the Manthra- of

Manthra-s, Bhala & Athibhala. (The Sacred hymns & prayers).

❍ ❍ ❍

१२. न श्रमो वा ज्वरो वा ते न रूपस्य विपर्ययः ।
न च सुप्तं प्रमत्तं वा धर्षयिष्यन्ति नैर्ऋताः ।।

12. There will be no weariness in you; no sickness; No change in (body's normal) Form; These (night prowling) demons will not embrocate you when you are sleepy or not on guard (or careless).

❍ ❍ ❍

१३. न बाह्वोः सदृशो वीर्ये पृथिव्यामस्ति कश्चन ।
त्रिषु लोकेषु वा राम न भवेत्सदृशस्तव ।।

13. In this world none is equal to you in power of your arms; Oh Raama! And none will be there equal to you in all the three worlds.

❍ ❍ ❍

१४. न सौभाग्ये न दाक्षिण्ये न ज्ञाने बुद्धिनिश्चये ।
नोत्तरे प्रतिवक्तव्ये समो लोके तवानघ ।।

14. Oh sinless (Raama)! In this world, none is a match for you in grace (& beauty); nor in dexterity; In wisdom & firmness of mind, none (to equal you); In rejoinder (Repartee during discussion) and in speech, none (can score over you in debates, conversation).

❍ ❍ ❍

१५. एतद्विद्याद्वये लब्धे भविता नास्ति ते समः ।
बला चातिबला चैव सर्वज्ञानस्य मातरौ ।।

15. The Mother of All Knowledge is The Bhala & Athibhala; When you 'obtain' these two (disciplines) knowledge, no one will be equal to you. (And none will be born who will be equal to you).

❍ ❍ ❍

१६. क्षुत्पिपासे न ते राम भविष्येते नरोत्तम ।
बलामतिबलां चैव पठतः पथि राघव ।।

16. Oh noble (Raama the) Raaghava! When you 'recite' Bhala & Athibhala, there will be no hunger or thirst for you on your way & (during tiring journeys)

❍ ❍ ❍

१७. अर्हणां सर्वलोकस्य प्राप्स्यसे रघुनन्दन ।
विद्याद्वयमधीयानो यशस्वी च भवेद्भुवि ।।

17. (Oh Raama the) darling of Raghu-s! When you study (& master) these two 'Knowledge' you will command the respect of the world; will become famous in the world.

❍ ❍ ❍

१८. पितामहसुते ह्येते विद्ये तेजस्समन्विते ।
प्रदात्तुं तव काकुत्स्थ सदृशस्त्वं हि धार्मिक ।।

18. These two 'Knowledge' are God Braama's daughters; Endowed with brilliance; Oh man of Dharma (Raama the) Kaakuthsa! You alone are fit to be given such (knowledge) ......

❍ ❍ ❍

१९. कामं बहुगुणाः सर्वेत्वय्येते नात्र संशयः ।
तपसा संभृते चैते बहुरूपे भविष्यतः ।।

19. ...... There is no doubt about it ... That all the various (noble) qualities are in you ... These have been obtained by my penance And these, will take on many forms (at your hands). surely.

❍ ❍ ❍

२०. ततो रामो जलं स्पृष्ट्वा प्रहृष्टवदनः शुचिः ।
प्रतिजग्राह ते विद्ये महर्षेर्भावितात्मनः ।।

20. With a happy face & pure (mind) Raama 'touched' (Ritual) waters & he received these two Teachings (Bhala/Athibhala) from the great Rishi (Vischwaamithra) who had realised "Self" (& whose soul was purified by meditation of The Supreme).

❍ ❍ ❍

२१. विद्यासमुदितो रामः शुशुभे भूरिविक्रमः ।
सहस्ररश्मिर्भगवाञ्छरदीव दिवाकरः ।।

21. With knowledge (of these two) duly acquired, Raama shone like lord Sun of 1,000 rays during autumn; He obtained immense valour.

❍ ❍ ❍

२२. गुरुकार्याणि सर्वाणि नियुज्य कुशिकात्मजे ।
उषुस्तां रजनीं तत्र सरय्वां सुसुखं त्रयः ।।

22. After serving (Vischwaamithra) the son of Kuschika with all that is due to a teacher, all the three, (Raama, Lakshmana, Vischwaamithra) then spent the night pleasantly on the banks of Sarayu river.

❍ ❍ ❍

२३. दशरथनृपसूनुसत्तमाभ्यां तृणशयनेऽनुचिते सहोषिताभ्याम् ।
कुशिकसुतवचोऽनुललिताभ्यां सुखमिव सा विबभौ विभावरी च ।।

23. Delighted in hearing the talks from (Vischwaamithra) the son of Kuschika and lying down in the *strange bed of grass, this night was spent away pleasantly by these (two) foremost sons of king Dhascharatha (*These Princes have never slept in a bed of grass!)

❍ ❍ ❍

Chapter 23

(Continuing their journey)
They Reach Kaama Hermitage

१. प्रभातायां तु शर्वर्यां विश्वामित्रो महामुनिः ।
अभ्यभाषत काकुत्स्थं शयानं पर्णसंस्तरे ।।

1. When darkness became bright, (at day break), the great Muni Vischwaamithra addressed (Raama) the Kaakuthsa who was sleeping on a bed of grass.

❍ ❍ ❍

२. कौसल्यासुप्रजा राम पूर्वा सन्ध्या प्रवर्तते ।
उत्तिष्ठ नरशार्दूल कर्तव्यं दैवमाह्निकम् ।।

2. Oh Raama, the beloved son of Kowsalya! Oh 'Tiger' of men! Early morning of Sandhya is approaching. Get Up. The holy daily (Morning) Rituals are to be done.

❍ ❍ ❍

३. महर्षेः परमोदारं वचः श्रुत्वा नरोत्तमौ ।
स्नात्वा कृतोदकौ वीरौ जेपतुः परमं जपम् ।।

3. Hearing the vibrant (voice &) words of this great Rishi, the foremost men, these two brave (Raama & Lakshmana), took their baths, offered ritual waters, & recited foremost chants (& prayers).

❍ ❍ ❍

४. कृताह्निकौ महावीर्यौ विश्वामित्रं तपोधनम् ।
अभिवाद्याभिसंहृष्टौ गमनायोपतस्थतुः ।।

4. After doing morning Rituals, these two great warriors bowed before Vischwaamithra whose wealth was in penance; and they stood there before him, ready to leave, and in great joy.

❍ ❍ ❍

५. तौ प्रयातौ महावीर्यौ पुण्यां त्रिपथगां नदीम् ।
ददृशाते ततस्तत्र सरय्वाः सङ्गमे शुभे ।।

६. तत्राश्रमपदं पुण्यमृषीणामुग्रतेजसाम् ।
बहुवर्षसहस्राणि तप्यतां परमं तपः ।।

5. & 6.

Then commencing (their journey), these two mighty warriors saw the holy river of Thripadhaga (Ganges) at the confluence with the pure Sarayu river ...... and they saw there the holy hermitage of the fiercely brilliant Rishi-s who had been doing rigorous penance for many thousand years.

❍ ❍ ❍

७. तं दृष्ट्वा परमप्रीतौ राघवौ पुण्यमाश्रमम् ।
ऊचतुस्तं महात्मानं विश्वामित्रमिदं वचः ।।

7. Seeing this holy hermitage they were very happy; And these two Raaghava-s (Raama & Lakshmana) then addressed the great soul Vischwaamithra.

❍ ❍ ❍

८. कस्यायमाश्रमः पुण्यः को न्वस्मिन् वसते पुमान् ।
भगवञ्छ्रोतुमिच्छावः परं कौतूहलं हि नौ ।।

8. Oh Lord! Whose is this hermitage? Which persons live here? We desire to hear this: Our curiosity is foremost, indeed.

❍ ❍ ❍

९. तयोस्तद्वचनं श्रुत्वा प्रहस्य मुनिपुङ्गवः ।
अब्रवीच्छ्रूयतां राम यस्यायं पूर्व आश्रमः ।।

9. Hearing the words of these two, (Vischwaamithra) the 'tiger' of muni-s, said with a smile: = Oh Raama! Whose hermitage it was before, (This I will tell): May you hear =

❍ ❍ ❍

१०. कन्दर्पोमूर्तिमानासीत काम इत्युच्यते बुधैः ।।

10. By the learned he was called Kaama (The Inflamer of passion & love). This lord of love (Manmatha) was (there) in human form.

❍ ❍ ❍

११. तपस्यन्तमिह स्थाणुं नियमेन समाहितम् ।
कृतोद्वाहन्तु देवेशं गच्छन्तं समरुद्गणम् ।।
धर्षयामास दुर्मेधा हुंकृतश्च महात्मना ।।

11. At this place, this fool (this Inflamer) tried (to tempt &) embrocate that lord of Dheva-s, Sthaanu (Schiva) who was (in trance) doing penance, with his senses fully under control, totally involved (in penance),

(living there) as a married person along with multitude of Dheva-s. And by this great soul (Sthaanu- Schiva) he, (this Inflamer), was 'done for', by His mere breath "Hum".

❍ ❍ ❍

१२. निर्दग्धस्तस्य रौद्रेण चक्षुषा रघुनन्दन ।
व्यशीर्यन्त शरीरात् स्वात् सर्वगात्राणि दुर्मतेः ।।

12. Oh (Raama) the darling of Raghu-s! By (the power of the rays of) Rudhra, (God Schiva- The Sthaanu's) Eyes, (this Inflamer of passions) was burnt. And from the body of this stupid minded (Lord of Love), all parts scattered.

❍ ❍ ❍

१३. तस्य गात्रं हतं तत्र निर्दग्धस्य महात्मनः ।
अशरीरः कृतः कामः क्रोधाद्देवेश्वरेण हि ।।

13. His body that was burnt up by the great soul (God Schiva-Rudhra - Sthaanu) was destroyed there itself; (and thus) the lord of love became formless (and made body less) by the wrath of the lord of lords, (Schiva). Indeed.!! (Readers may note- we can jocularly say- that is why love has no barrier, no figure, form, it is ethereal & perhaps love is blind as saying goes.)

❍ ❍ ❍

१४. अनङ्ग इति विख्यातस्तदाप्रभृति राघव ।
स चाङ्गविषयः श्रीमान् यत्राङ्गं स मुमोच च ।।

14. Oh (Raama the) Raaghava! From that time he became known as Ananga (the formless); And where he lost his form, this is that resplendent Anga Kingdom.

❍ ❍ ❍

१५. तस्यायमाश्रमः पुण्यस्तस्येमे मुनयः पुरा ।
शिष्या धर्मपरा वीर तेषां पापं न विद्यते ।।

15. This holy hermitage was his; all these sages were his disciples; Oh brave (Raama). They were men of Dharma: No sin ever accrues to them.

❍ ❍ ❍

१६. इहाद्य रजनीं राम वसेम शुभदर्शन ।
पुण्ययोः सरितोर्मध्ये श्वस्तरिष्यामहे वयम् ।।

16. Oh pleasant looking Raama! We shall spend this night here in the middle of the two great rivers that are holy; we shall cross over tomorrow.

❍ ❍ ❍

१७. अभिगच्छामहे सर्वेशुचयः पुण्यमाश्रमम् ।
स्नाताश्च कृतजप्याश्च हुतहव्या नरोत्तम ।।

१८. इह वासः परो राम सुखं वत्स्यामहे वयम् ।।

17. & 18.

Oh foremost of men (Oh Raama)! We will enter the holy hermitage as pure persons, having (first) taken baths; we will perform Homa (Fire rituals) and chant prayers...... and living in this place is exceedingly (delightful); We will live here pleasantly.

❍ ❍ ❍

१९. तेषां संवदतां तत्र तपोदीर्घेण चक्षुषा ।
विज्ञाय परमप्रीता मुनयो हर्षमागमन् ।।

19. While they were conversing there thus, the Rishi-s there saw them with their eyes that were 'deep', (sunken), due to (constant) penance; And they, who were all greatly pleased, obtained joy.

❍ ❍ ❍

२०. अर्घ्यं पाद्यं तथाऽऽतिथ्यं निवेद्य कुशिकात्मजे ।
रामलक्ष्मणयोः पश्चादकुर्वन्नतिथिक्रियाम् ।।

20. They all offered Arghya, Paadhya and extended hospitality (first) to the son of Kuschika

(Vischwaamithra) & then offered hospitality to Raama-Lakshmana.

❍ ❍ ❍

२१. सत्कारं समनुप्राप्य कथाभिरभिरञ्जयन् ।
यथार्हमजपन् सन्ध्यामृषयस्ते समाहिताः ॥

21. After the hospitality was completed, they delighted them with stories (& anecdotes); Together, they (all) performed the evening Sandhya Rituals as per norms.

❍ ❍ ❍

२२. तत्र वासिभिरानीता मुनिभिः सुव्रतैः सह ।
न्यवसन् सुसुखं तत्र कामाश्रमपदे तदा ॥

22. Led by these sages living there who were all men of vows & austerities, (Vischwaamithra & the princes) stayed in comfort there, at Kaama hermitage.

❍ ❍ ❍

२३. कथाभिरभिरामाभिरभिरामौ नृपात्मजौ ।
रमयामास धर्मात्मा कौशिको मुनिपुङ्गवः ॥

23. This noble soul man of Dharma, this (Vischwamithra) the Kowschik who was a 'tiger' amongst muni-s, delighted the two royal princes who were most delightful, with lovely stories.

❍ ❍ ❍

Chapter 24

(Continuing their Journey) They Go to Thaataka (forest).

१. ततः प्रभाते विमले कृत्वाऽह्निकमरिन्दमौ ।
विश्वामित्रं पुरस्कृत्य नद्यास्तीरमुपागतौ ॥

1. At the bright morning, these two, (Raama & Lakshmana) the destroyers of enemies, did their

morning rituals and reached the banks of the river, following Vischwaamithra.

❍ ❍ ❍

२. ते च सर्वेमहात्मानो मुनयः संशितव्रताः ।
उपस्थाप्य शुभां नावं विश्वामित्रमथाब्रुवन् ।।

2. These great soul Muni-s for whom vows & austerities never ceased, brought a good boat and then addressed Vischwaamithra.

❍ ❍ ❍

३. आरोहतु भवान्नावं राजपुत्रपुरस्कृतः ।
अरिष्ट गच्छ पन्थानं मा भूत् कालविपर्ययः ।।

3. Going in front of these two royal princes, you please get into this boat. (Please) Take this easy way; Do not delay.

❍ ❍ ❍

४. विश्वामित्रस्तथेत्युक्त्वा तानृषीनभिपूज्य च ।
ततार सहितस्ताभ्यां सरितं सागरङ्गमाम् ।।

4. And Vischwaamithra said = So Be It = And after honouring these sages, he, along with these two (princes), crossed the river that was flowing towards the sea.

❍ ❍ ❍

५. ततः शुश्राव तां शब्दमतिसंरंभवर्धितम् ।
मध्यमागम्य तोयस्य सह रामः कनीयसा ।।

5. Accompanied by his younger (brother), Raama, when he reached the middle (of the river, the boat being half way), heard a sound, a furious (sound of) intensity (emanating from under).

❍ ❍ ❍

६. अथ रामः सरिन्मध्ये पप्रछ मुनिपुङ्गवम् ।
वारिणो भिद्यमानस्य किमयं तुमुलो ध्वनिः ।।

6. Then Raama asked the 'tiger' of muni-s, (standing in the boat while) in the middle of the river:= What is this tumultuous sound (as though emanating) by the 'cleavage' of the water (bed)? =

❍ ❍ ❍

७. रामस्य वचनं श्रुत्वा कौतूहलसमन्वितम् ।
कथयामास धर्मात्मा तस्य शब्दस्य निश्चयम् ।।

7. Hearing Raama the Raaghava's words asked with curiosity, the noble soul man of Dharma (Vischwaamithra), narrated the truth about this sound.

❍ ❍ ❍

८. कैलासपर्वते राम मनसा निर्मितं सरः ।
ब्रह्मणा नरशार्दूल तेनेदं मानसं सरः ।।

8. Oh 'tiger' of men! Oh Raama! Conceived in his mind, a lake was created by God Bramma in mountain Kailaash (in Himaalayas); thus it is known as Manas (The Mind-Manasarovar).

❍ ❍ ❍

९. तस्मात् सुस्राव सरसः साऽयोध्यामुपगूहते ।
सरःप्रवृत्ता सरयूः पुण्या ब्रह्मसरश्च्युता ।।

9. River Sarayu that originates from Saras gets swollen from Bramma Saras; Very Holy; Then this flows around Ayodhya.

❍ ❍ ❍

१०. तस्यायमतुलः शब्दो जाह्नवीमभिवर्तते ।
वारिसंक्षोभजो राम प्रणामं नियतः कुरु ।।

10. It then joins Jaahnavi (Ganges); this incomparable sound is caused by the violent confluence (of these two rivers). Oh Raama! Make obeisance with devotion.

❍ ❍ ❍

११. ताभ्यां तु तावुभौ कृत्वा प्रणाममतिधार्मिकौ ।
तीरं दक्षिणमासाद्य जग्मतुर्लघुविक्रमो ।।

11. These two who were foremost men of Dharma, bowed to these two (rivers), then they reached the Southern banks; They then walked along with light strides.

❍ ❍ ❍

१२. स वनं घोरसमाशं दृष्ट्वा नरवरात्मजः ।
अविप्रहतमैक्ष्वाकः पप्रच्छ मुनिपुङ्गवम् ।।

12. Seeing the desolate gruesome looking forest, the prince of Ikshwaaka race who was son (of Dhascharatha) the foremost of men asked the 'tiger' of men, (Vischwaamithra).

❍ ❍ ❍

१३. अहो वनमिदं दुर्गं झिल्लिकागणनादितम् ।
भैरवैः श्वापदैः पूर्णं शकुन्तैर्दारुणस्वनैः ।।
१४. नानाप्रकारैः शकुनैर्वाश्यद्भिर्भैरवैः स्वनैः ।
सिंहव्याघ्रवराहैश्च वारणैश्चोपशोभितम् ।।
१५. धवाश्वकर्णखदिरैर्बिल्वतिन्दुकपाटलैः ।
समीर्णं बदरीभिश्च किमिदं दारुणं वनम् ।।

13, 14 & 15.

Ah! This forest is impenetrable; it is humming with sounds from beetles; Inhabited by beasts of prey; terrible animals; full with gruesome sounds from birds (of prey). . . . . . . (inhabited) by various types of birds that shriek with gruesome sounds; inhabited by lions, tigers, wild boars, elephants ..... What forest is this which is gruesome, which is clustered with trees of Dhava (Grislen Tormentosa), Ashwakarma (Vatica Robusta), Kadhira, Bhilva (Agele Mormelosa) Bhadharia (Ziziphus jujuba)?

❍ ❍ ❍

१६. तमुवाच महातेजा विश्वामित्रो महामुनिः ।
श्रूयतां वत्स काकुत्स्थ यथैतद्दारुणं वनम् ।।

16. The most brilliant Vischwaamithra, the great Muni,

said to him = Oh 'son'! Oh (Raama) the Kaakuthsa! May you listen as to how this forest became cruel. = (The story of this forest)

❍ ❍ ❍

१७. एतौ जनपदौ स्फीतौ पूर्वमास्तां नरोत्तम ।
मलदाश्च करूशाश्च देवंनिर्माणनिर्मितौ ॥

17. Oh noble man! These two were once prosperous; Created by Dheva-s; they were the territories (called) Maladha & Karusha.

❍ ❍ ❍

१८. पुरा वृत्रवधे राम मलेन समभिप्लुतम् ।
क्षुधा चैव सहस्राक्षं ब्रह्महत्या यदाऽऽविशत् ॥
१९. तमिन्द्रं स्नापयन्देवा ऋषयश्च तपोधनाः ।
कलशैः स्नापयामासुर्मलश्चास्य प्रमोचयन् ॥

18 & 19.

Oh Raama! Long ago, after the killing of Vrithra, the thousand eyed (Indhra) who was afflicted by sickness & hunger, the crime of killing a Braamin seized him ...... The Dheva-s & men of penance, the Rishi-s, bathed this Indhra; they bathed him in (holy waters from) pots; (and) thus they released his Dirt (Sin).

❍ ❍ ❍

२०. इह भूम्यां मलं दत्त्वा कारूशमेव च ।
शरीरजं महेन्द्रस्य ततो हर्षं प्रपेदिरे ॥

20. In this Earth (territory), they removed the 'Dirt' (the sin) from the body of Indhra and they also removed his hunger (& thirst) & thus became happy.

❍ ❍ ❍

२१. निर्मलो निष्करूशश्च शुचिरिन्द्रो यदाऽभवत् ।
ददौ देशस्य सुप्रीतो वरं प्रभुरनुत्तमम् ॥

21. When Indhra became sinless, freed from hunger, &

became pure, he became so pleased, that this lord gave foremost boon to this territory.

❍ ❍ ❍

२२. इमौ जनपदौ स्फीतौ ख्यातिं लोके गमिष्यतः ।
मलदाश्च करूशाश्च ममाङ्गमलधारिणौ ॥

22. (Indhra's boon); These two prosperous territories Maladha & Karusha that will bear the 'features from my limbs', are going to attain fame & renown in the world.

❍ ❍ ❍

२३. साधु साध्विति तं देवाः पाकशासनमब्रुवन् ।
देशस्य पूजां तां दृष्ट्वा कृतां शक्रेण धीमता ॥

23. Seeing the honour bestowed upon these two territories by the wise Schakra (Indhra), the Dheva-s told (Indhra) the destroyer of Paaka; = Good , Good =

❍ ❍ ❍

२४. एतौ जनपदौ स्फीतौ दीर्घकालमरिन्दम ।
मलदाश्च करूशाश्च मुदितौ धनधान्यतः ॥

24. (Listen further) Oh Raama the destroyer of enemies! These two prosperous territories, known as Maladha & Karusha, were abundant with riches & grains for a very long time.

❍ ❍ ❍

२५. कस्यचित्त्वथ कालस्य यक्षी वै कामरूपिणी ।
बलं नागसहस्रस्य धारयन्ती तदा ह्यभूत् ॥
ताटका नाम भद्रं ते भार्या सुन्दस्य धीमतः ॥

२६. मारीचो राक्षसः पुत्रो यस्याः शक्रपराक्रमः ॥

२७. वृत्तबाहुर्महाशीर्षोविपुलास्यतनुर्महान् ।
राक्षसो भैरवाकारो नित्यं त्रासयते प्रजाः ॥

25, 26 & 27.

After sometime was born a woman, a Yakshi, by the

name of Thaataka who could take on any form she pleased, who bore the strength of 1,000 elephants ...... who was the wife of the wise Sundha ...... whose son was Maareecha, the demon whose valour was like that of Lord Indhra (the mighty powerful lord) ...... (This demon) has concealed hands; has a mighty head; is very huge; has large face & body; demon of gruesome countenance, always terrorises men ...... Welfare to you (Oh Raama & listen further).

❍ ❍ ❍

२८. इमौ जनपदौ नित्यं विनाशयति राघव ।
मलदांश्च करूशांश्च ताटका दुष्टचारिणी ।।

28. Oh (Raama) the Raaghava! This Thaataka is of evil conduct; always ravishes these two territories of Maladha & Karusha.

❍ ❍ ❍

२९. सेयं पन्थानमावार्य वसत्यत्यर्धयोजने ।
अत एव च गन्तव्यं ताटकाया वनं यतः ।।

29. Blocking the way, she lives 1 1/2 Yojana-s (about 14 miles) from here; We should now go to where Thaataka forest is.

❍ ❍ ❍

३०. स्वबाहुबलमाश्रित्य जहीमां दुष्टचारिणीम् ।
मन्नियोगादिमं देशं कुरु निष्कण्टकं पुनः ।।

30. By my command, you should conquer this woman of evil conduct with power of your arms; Make this territory free from the 'thorn' (of Thaataka); once again (may there be peace here).

❍ ❍ ❍

३१. न हि कश्चिदिमं देशं शक्तोऽन्यो गन्तुमीदृशम् ।
यक्षिण्या घोरया राम उत्सादितमसह्यया ।।

31. Oh Raama! No one else has the ability to go to this

territory that is ruined like this by this gruesome Yakshi, who is unbearable. Indeed (You alone can fight her & kill her).

❍ ❍ ❍

३२. एतत्ते सर्वमाख्यातं यथैतद्दारुणं वनम् ।
यक्ष्या चोत्सादितं सर्वमद्यापि न निवर्तते ।।

32. This entire forest was ruined like this by this Yakshi (Thaataka). yet she does not stop; All this, (the story about this place), has been narrated to you (Oh Raama).

❍ ❍ ❍

Chapter 25

(Vischwaamithra) Goads (Raama) to Kill Thaataka

१. अथ तस्याप्रमेयस्य मुनिर्वचनमुत्तमम् ।
श्रुत्वा पुरुषशार्दूलः प्रत्युवाच शुभां गिरम् ।।

1. After listening to the foremost words of the Muni (Vischwaamithra) who was incomparable, then (Raama), the 'tiger' of men, replied with following utterance.

❍ ❍ ❍

२. अल्पवीर्या यदा यक्षाः श्रूयन्ते मुनिपुङ्गव ।
कथं नागसहस्रस्य धारयत्यबला बलम् ।।

2. (Oh Vischwaamithra) the 'tiger' amongst sages! It is said (& heard) that Yaksha-s possess feeble valour. Yet, how is it this woman bears the strength of 1,000 elephants?

❍ ❍ ❍

३. तस्य तद्वचनं श्रुत्वा रामस्य विदितात्मनः ।
हर्षयञ्श्लक्ष्णया वाचा सलक्ष्मणमरिन्दमम् ।।

४. विश्वामित्रोऽब्रवीद्वाक्यं श्रुणु येन बलोत्तरा ।
वरदानकृतं वीर्यं धारयत्यबला बलम् ।।

3 & 4.

Hearing these words of Raama, (Vischwaamithra) who knew & had "realised the Soul", gladdening (this Raama) the destroyer of enemies who was (ever) with Lakshmana, with sweet words..... this Vischwaamithra addressed him the following words = This woman is foremost in strength; She is bearing such a strength & valour through offer of a boon (to her); May you listen as to how (she got all this). (Vischwaamithra narrates-Thaataka).

❍ ❍ ❍

५. पूर्वमासीन्महायक्षः सुकेतुर्नाम वीर्यवान् ।
अनपत्यः शुभाचारः स च तेपे महत्तपः ।।

5. Long ago there was a great Yaksha named Sukethu who was very brave. Being without a son, he did great penance with austere conduct (to get progeny).

❍ ❍ ❍

६. पितामहस्तु सुप्रीतस्तस्य यक्षपतेस्तदा ।
कन्यारत्नं ददौ राम ताटकां नाम नामतः ।।

6. Oh Raama (Listen)! And being pleased with this, God Bramma offered this Yaksha lord, only a 'gem' of a girl named Thaataka.

❍ ❍ ❍

७. ददौ नागसहस्रस्य बलं चास्याः पितामहः ।
न त्वेव पुत्रं यक्षाय ददौ ब्रह्मा महायशाः ।।

7. And God Bramma gave her, the strength of 1,000 elephants; But the most famous God Bramma did not give this Yaksha any son.

❍ ❍ ❍

८. तां तु जातां विवर्धन्तीं रूपयौवनशालिनीम् ।
जम्भपुत्राय सुन्दाय ददौ भार्यां यशस्विनीम् ।।

8. After birth and as she grew up, this famous (Thaataka) who was endowed with youth & beauty, was given to Sundha, the son of Jarjha, as his wife.

❍ ❍ ❍

९. कस्यचित्त्वथ कालस्य यक्षी पुत्रं व्यजायत ।
मारीचं नाम दुर्धर्षं यः शापाद्राक्षसोऽभवत् ।।

9. After sometime, this Yakshi (Thaataka) begot a 'uncrushable' son called Maareecha: By a curse, (Maareecha) became a demon.

❍ ❍ ❍

१०. सुन्दे तु निहते राम साऽगस्त्यमृषिसत्तमम् ।
ताटका सह पुत्रेण प्रधर्षयितुमिच्छति ।।

10. (and listen) Oh Raama! When Sundha passed away, this Thaataka along with her son desired (& began to) embrocate the foremost Muni, Agasthya.

❍ ❍ ❍

११. ताडिता कामबाणौघैर्युवती सा दिगम्बरा ।
रत्यर्थं कृतसंरम्भा गायन्ती साऽभ्यधावत ।।

11. Young and (almost) naked, she was 'hit' by a multitude of 'arrows' of passion: With zeal to have sexual pleasures, she ran towards him, singing along.

❍ ❍ ❍

१२. आपतन्तीं तु तां दृष्ट्वा पुनस्तस्यास्तदा भृशम् ।
क्रुद्धः कृशानुसमाश अगस्त्यो भगवानभूत् ।।

12. Seeing her approaching him again & again and seeing her fierceness (& determination to have affair with him), this lord (sage Agasthya) who was comparable to Fire, became very angry.

❍ ❍ ❍

१३. राक्षसत्वं भजस्वेति मारीचं व्याजहार सः ॥

13. He cursed (first, her son) Maareecha thus:= You Abide In a State of Demonhood.=

❍ ❍ ❍

१४. अगस्त्यः परमक्रुद्धस्ताटकामपि शप्तवान् ।
पुरुषादी महायक्षी विरूपा विकृतानना ॥
१५. इदं रूपमपाहाय दारुणं रूपमस्तु ते ॥

14 & 15.

In great wrath, Agasthya cursed Thaataka also thus = Oh ye great Yakshee! With a deformed face, as a cannibal and with an ugly form . . . . may you have the dreadful appearance (from now on), abandoning this (present) form (which is lovely) =

❍ ❍ ❍

१६. सैषा शापकृतामर्षा ताटका क्रोधमूर्च्छिता ।
देशमुत्सादयत्येनमगस्त्यचरितं शुभम् ॥

16. This Thaataka, stupefied by wrath, humiliated thus by the curse, is ruining this great auspicious place which is treaded by Agasthya.

❍ ❍ ❍

१७. एनां राघव दुर्वृत्तां यक्षीं परमदारुणाम् ।
गोब्राह्मणहितार्थाय जहि दुष्टपराक्रमाम् ॥

17. Oh (Raama the) Raaghava, (listen)! For the welfare of Braamins, cows, you destroy this Yakshee (Thaataka) who is of evil conduct, who is most cruel and whose valour is malignant.

❍ ❍ ❍

१८. न ह्येनां शापसंसृष्टां कश्चिदुत्सहते पुमान् ।
निहन्तुं त्रिषु लोकेषु त्वामृते रघुनन्दन ॥

18. Oh (Raama) the darling of Raghu-s! To kill this (Thaataka) who is afflicted by curse, there is no man

in all the three worlds who has adequate power to kill other than you.

❍ ❍ ❍

१९. न हि ते स्त्रीवधकृते घृणा कार्या नरोत्तम ।
चातुर्वर्ण्यहितार्थाय कर्तव्यं राजसूनुना ।।

19. Let there be no aversion in you in killing a woman; Because, for the sake of welfare of all the four Caste-s, this (deed) is to be done by (you who are after all) the son of a king.

❍ ❍ ❍

२०. नृशंसमनृशंसं वा प्रजारक्षणकारणात् ।
पातकं वा सदोषं वा कर्तव्यं रक्षता सताम् ।।

20. Whether cruel or not cruel, whether proper or sinful, for the sake of protection of subjects, protection of the good must (always) be undertaken by you.

❍ ❍ ❍

२१. राज्यभारनियुक्तानामेष धर्मः सनातनः ।
अधर्म्यां जहि काकुत्स्थ धर्मोह्यस्या न विद्यते ।।

21. For those who are ever devoted in taking on the load of (ruling) the kingdom (& protecting it), this is the eternal Dharma: Oh (Raama) the Kaakuthsa! She has no Dharma: You destroy this (woman) of Adharma (Non Dharma).

❍ ❍ ❍

२२. श्रूयते हि पुरा शक्रो विरोचनसुतां नृप ।
पृथिवीं हन्तुमिच्छन्तीं मन्थरामभ्यसूदयत् ।।

22. Oh (Raama) the 'king'! (Listen)! It was heard indeed; Long ago, Indhra killed Virochana's daughter Mandhara when she desired to destroy the earth.

❍ ❍ ❍

२३. विष्णुना च पुरा राम भृगुपत्नी दृढव्रता ।
अनिन्द्रं लोकमिच्छन्ती काव्यमाता निषूदिता ।।

23. Oh Raama! Long ago the mother of Kaavya, who was resolute in vows & austerities, who was Bhrigu's wife, was killed by God Vishnu when she desired that the World should be without Lord Indhra.

❍ ❍ ❍

२४. एतैश्चान्यैश्च बहुभी राजपुत्र महात्मभिः ।
अधर्मसहिता नार्योहताः पुरुषसत्तमैः ।।
तस्मादेनां घृणां त्यक्त्वा जहि मच्छासनान्नृप ।।

24. (Oh Raama) the son of king (Dhascharatha)! By these many men of great 'Soul' and by other noble men, women of Adharma have been killed. Therefore, by my command, abandon this aversion (in you, of killing a woman): Kill her.

(Note: Readers may note this; In those days great men followed precedents. They observed norms. Vischwamithra cites precedents. Raama is a chivalrous prince, would not like to take away the life of a woman. But his 'Teacher' presses him. And Raama has precedents. Even 'Gods' have taken away the lives of women.)

❍ ❍ ❍

Chapter 26

The Killing of Thaataka (by Raama)

१. मुनेर्वचनमक्लीबं श्रुत्वा नरवरात्मजः ।
राघवः प्राञ्जलिर्भूत्वा प्रत्युवाच दृढव्रतः ।।

1. After listening to the stainless words of Muni (Vischwaamithra), (Raama) the Raaghava, the son of

a noble man and a man who was resolute in vows & austerities, folded his arms (respectfully) in Anjali and replied.

❍ ❍ ❍

२. पितुर्वचननिर्देशात् पितुर्वचनगौरवात् ।
वचनं कौशिकस्येति कर्तव्यमविशमया ।।

३. अनुशिष्टोऽस्म्ययोध्यायां गुरुमध्ये महात्मना ।
पित्रा दशरथेनाहं नावज्ञेयं च तद्वचः ।।

2 & 3.

By the words (of command) of my father and out of respect to my father's words, (Vischwaamithra the) Kowshik's words (of command) must be done without any hesitation . . . . I am commanded thus by the great 'soul', my father Dhascharatha at Ayodhya, in the midst of teachers; and so these words (of Vischwaamithra) are not to be disregarded (by me at any cost).

(Readers may know: The Six Commandments: Obey Father; Obey The Teacher, etc.)

❍ ❍ ❍

४. सोऽहं पितुर्वचः श्रुत्वा शासनाद्ब्रह्मवादिनः ।
करिष्यामि न सन्देहस्ताटकावधमुत्तमम् ।।

4. Such as I am, having heard words (of command) of my father & by the command of (Vischwaamithra) who is expounder of the Holy Texts (The Brammam), I will do this killing of Thaataka, No doubt (about this) great killing.

❍ ❍ ❍

५. गोब्राह्मणहितार्थाय देशस्यास्य हिताय च ।
तव चैवाप्रमेयस्य वचनं कर्तुमुद्यतः ।।

5. For welfare of cows & braamins, and for the good of this region, I will at once undertake (to honour) the words (of command) from you who are 'unfathomable'.

❍ ❍ ❍

६. एवमुक्त्वा धनुर्मध्ये बध्वा मुष्टिमरिन्दमः ।
ज्याघोषमकरोत्तीव्रं दिशः शब्देन पूरयन् ।।

6. (Raama) The destroyer of enemies having said thus, gripped his bow in the middle with his fist, filling all the directions with sound, fiercely stringing up the bow.

❍ ❍ ❍

७. तेन शब्देन वित्रस्तास्ताटकावनवासिनः ।
ताटका च सुसङ्क्रुद्धा तेन शब्देन मोहिता ।।

7. By the sound (emanating from his bow), the residents of Thaataka forest became scared; And Thaataka was 'stupefied' with great wrath by the sound.

❍ ❍ ❍

८. तं शब्दमभिनिध्याय राक्षसी क्रोधमूर्च्छिता ।
श्रुत्वा चाभ्यद्रवत क्रुद्धा यतः शब्दो विनिःसृतः ।।

8. Hearing the sound, becoming angry, stupefied by wrath and pondering for a while, this demoness (Thaataaka) ran towards (the place) from where sound emanated.

❍ ❍ ❍

९. तां दृष्ट्वा राघवः क्रुद्धां विकृतां विकृताननाम् ।
प्रमाणेनातिवृद्धां च लक्ष्मणं सोऽभ्यभाषत ।।

9. And (Raama the) Raaghava, seeing this wrathful, disfigured and gruesome faced (Thaataka) who had 'grown' in height, said to Lakshmana.

❍ ❍ ❍

१०. पश्य लक्ष्मण यक्षिण्या भैरवं दारुणं वपुः ।
भिद्येरन्दर्शनादस्या भीरूणां हृदयानि च ।।

10. Oh Lakshmana! See the cruel terrible body of this Yakshee: By her very sight, the heart of the timid will burst.

❍ ❍ ❍

११, एनां पश्य दुराधर्षां मायाबलसमन्विताम् ।
विनिवृत्तां करोम्यद्य हृतकर्णाग्रनासिकाम् ।।

11. See this. I am now going to make this uncrushable (Thaataka) who possesses magical strength, lose her nose & ear lobe. (And I will scare her away, making her) go back (for good).

❍ ❍ ❍

१२. न ह्येनामुत्सहे हन्तुं स्त्रीस्वभावेन रक्षिताम् ।
वीर्यं चास्या गतिं चापि हनिष्यामीति मे मतिः ।।

12. By nature, (by norms), a woman is to be protected and so I have no zeal to kill her. Therefore I am going to 'destroy' her (arrogance of her) bravery & her mobility. This is (on) my mind.

(Note: Poor Raama: Chivalry does not leave him; he still feels that peace can be achieved by merely scaring her away: No killing!)

❍ ❍ ❍

१३. एवं ब्रुवाणे रामे तु ताटका क्रोधमूर्च्छिता ।
उद्यम्य बाहू गर्जन्ती राममेवाभ्यधावत ।।

13. When Raama was saying this, Thaataka who was stupefied by wrath, lifted her hands, rushed towards Raama, roaring.

❍ ❍ ❍

१४. विश्वामित्रस्तु ब्रह्मर्षिहुंकारेणाभिभर्त्स्य ताम् ।
स्वस्ति राघवोरस्तु जयं चैवाभ्यभाषत ।।

14. Threatening her at once with (sound of) 'Hum', 'Hum', (from his breath) the Braamin sage Vischwaamithra said to (Raama & Lakshmana), the two Raaghava-s = May there be welfare of Swasthi. Likewise victory to you.=

❍ ❍ ❍

१५. उद्धून्वाना रजो घोरं ताटका राघवावुभौ ।
रजोमेघेन महता मुहूर्तं सा त्वमोहयत् ।।

15. Raising huge amount of dust, this Thaataka stupefied these two Raagava-s (Raama & Lakshmana) for sometime, by the cloud of dust engulfing them. (She was invisible to them).

❍ ❍ ❍

१६. ततो मायां समास्थाय शिलावर्षेण राघवौ ।
अवाकिरत् सुमहता ततश्चुक्रोध राघवः ।।

16. Taking on her magical prowess, she showered these two Raaghava-s with a 'Rain' of rocks. And by this, (Raama) the Raaghava became angry.

❍ ❍ ❍

१७. शिलावर्षं महत्तस्याः शरवर्षेण राघवः ।
प्रतिहत्योपधावन्त्याः करौ चिच्छेद पत्रिभिः ।।

17. And by a shower of arrows, (Raama) the Raaghava repelled her great shower of rocks, (pulverised the stones), and (even) as she was rushing, he cut off her two hands with arrows.

❍ ❍ ❍

१८. ततश्छिन्नभुजां श्रान्तामभ्याशे परिगर्जतीम् ।
सौमित्रिरकरोत् क्रोधाद्धृतकर्णाग्रनासिकाम् ।।

18. And (Lakshmana) the son of Sumithra, in great wrath, made her, whose hands had been cut off, and who was tired, lose her ears & tip of her nose, even as she was roaring & assailing him.

❍ ❍ ❍

१९. कामरूपधरा सद्यः कृत्वा रूपाण्यनेकशः ।
अन्तर्धानं गता यक्षी मोहयन्ती च मायया ।।
अश्मवर्षं विमुञ्चन्ती भैरवं विननाद सा ।।

19. This Yakshee (Thaataka) who could take on any form,

at once took on various forms, went into hiding; Stupefying them with her magic, she roared and discharged a terrible shower of stones.

❍ ❍ ❍

२०. ज्यास्वनं चक्रतुर्वीरौ वज्राशनिसमं तदा ।
मोहिता तेन शब्देन लब्धसंज्ञा चिरात्तदा ।।

20. The two warriors, (tightening the bow), let out sounds from the bow strings that was like Vajra (thunder bolt of Indhra). By this sound, she became stupefied (but) regained her consciousness after sometime.

❍ ❍ ❍

२१. ततस्तावश्मवर्षेण ववर्ष क्रोधमूर्च्छिता ।
पुरा नमुचितनया यथा विष्णुपुरन्दरौ ।।

21. Like long ago, when daughter of Namuchi (attacked) Lord Indhra and God Vishnu, (Thaataka), who was stupefied by wrath, rained a shower of rocks on these two.

❍ ❍ ❍

२२. ततस्तावश्मवर्षेण कीर्यमाणौ समन्ततः ।
दृष्ट्वा गाधिसुतः श्रीमानिदं वचनमब्रवीत् ।।

22. (All this Vischwaamithra was watching and he was dissatisfied with 'proceedings'; He felt Raama was not putting in his best efforts. Readers may know that Raama had still some misgivings in killing a woman. He just wanted to scare her away by maiming her).

Seeing these two strewn by a shower of rocks on all sides, the resplendent (Vischwaamithra), the son of Gaadhi, then said this.

❍ ❍ ❍

२३. अलं ते घृणया राम पापैषा दुष्टचारिणी ।
यज्ञविघ्नकरी यक्षी पुरा वर्धेत मायया ।।

23. Oh Raama! Enough of this aversion (to kill) and compassion (for her). This Yakshee is of evil conduct; sinful; causes harm to Yaaga-s; And by magic, will grow again (& gain strength).

❍ ❍ ❍

२४ वध्यतां तावदेवैषा पुरा सन्ध्या प्रवर्तते ।
रक्षांसि सन्ध्याकालेषु दुर्धर्षाणि भवन्ति हि ।।

24. Evening is fast approaching; Let her be killed before (sunset); Because, during period of sunset (Sandhya), demons become uncrushable. (Demons are called night prowlers).

❍ ❍ ❍

२५. इत्युक्तस्तु तदा यक्षीमश्मवृष्ट्याऽभिवर्षतीम् ।
दर्शयञ्छब्दवेधित्वं तां रुरोध स सायकैः ।।

25. When told thus, (Raama), exhibiting his ability of knowing ('seeing' the enemy) by mere sound, then stopped the Yakshee with his weapons, even as she was showering stones on him.

❍ ❍ ❍

२६. सा रुद्धा शरजालेन मायाबलसमन्विता ।
अभिदुद्राव काकुत्स्थं लक्ष्मणं च विनेदुषी ।।

26. Stilled by shower of arrows, this Yakshee who possessed power of magic rushed towards (Raama) the Kaakuthsa & Lakshmana, roaring.

❍ ❍ ❍

२७. तामापतन्तीं वेगेन विक्रान्तामशनीमिव ।
शरेणोरसि विव्याध सा पपात ममार च ।।

27. With just one Arrow he pierced her chest as she was falling upon him in great speed & attacking him like a thunderbolt; She fell down on earth and died.

❍ ❍ ❍

२८. तां हतां भीमसमाशां दृष्ट्वा सुरपतिस्तदा ।
साधु साध्विति काकुत्स्थं सुराश्च समपूजयन् ।।

28. When they saw the terrible looking (Thaataka) killed, all the Dheva-s, and the Lord of Dheva-s (Lord Indhra), extolled (Raama) the Kaakuthsa (saying): = Well (Done), Well (Done). =

❍ ❍ ❍

२९. उवाच परमप्रीतः सहस्राक्षः पुरन्दरः ।
सुराश्च सर्वेसंहृष्टा विश्वामित्रमथाब्रुवन् ।।

29. The thousand eyed Indhra, in great joy said; And so did all the Dheva-s, all of them, in great happiness said to Vischwaamithra (these words).

❍ ❍ ❍

३०. मुने कौशिक भद्रं ते सेन्द्राः सर्वेमरुद्गणाः ।

30. Oh Muni. Oh Kowschik! Welfare to you. By this deed the multitude of Maruth-s (Dheva-s) along with Indhra are all pleased. Show your deep attachment to (Raama) the Raaghava: (Bless him).

❍ ❍ ❍

३१. प्रजापतेर्भृशाश्वस्य पुत्रान् सत्यपराक्रमान् ।
तपोबलभृतान् ब्रह्मन् राघवाय निवेदय ।।

३२. पात्रभूतश्च ते ब्रह्मंस्तवानुगमने धृतः ।
सुराणां च महत् कर्म कर्तव्यं राजसूनुना ।।

31 & 32.

(The Celestials request Vischwaamithra to teach Raama the divine weapons, as by this deed Raama is worthy enough to receive them. The Brischaaswas 'sons'- the divine weapons; And Raama is going to need them when he fights Raavana later on).

Oh Braamin (Vischwaamithra)! (This Raama) is resolute in following you, (devoted to you in service); He is worthy of you (to receive 'Knowledge' from you).

And further, the great task for the Dheva-s is to be done by (Raama), the king's son ...... Oh Braamin! You (enlighten &) communicate to Raama about Prajaapathi Bhrishaaswas's 'sons', who are truly most valiant and who are reared by power of penance.

❍ ❍ ❍

३३. एवमुक्त्वा सुराः सर्वेजग्मुर्हृष्टा यथागतम् ।
विश्वामित्रं पूजयित्वा ततः सन्ध्या प्रवर्तते ।।

33. Saying thus, all the Dheva-s honoured Vischwaamithra and went back as they came, in great joy; Then the evening time (of Sandhya) fell.

❍ ❍ ❍

३४. ततो मुनिवरः प्रीतस्ताटकावधतोषितः ।
मूर्ध्नि राममुपाघ्राय इदं वचनमब्रवीत् ।।

34. Extremely happy at the killing of Thaataka, the foremost Muni Vischwaamithra) kissed Raama on his forehead very pleased and said the following words.

❍ ❍ ❍

३५. इहाद्य रजनीं राम वसेम शुभदर्शन ।
श्वः प्रभाते गमिष्यामस्तदाश्रमपदं मम ।।

35. Oh Raama of pleasing looks! We will spend the night here: Tomorrow morning we will go to my hermitage.

❍ ❍ ❍

३६. विश्वामित्रवचः श्रुत्वा हृष्टो दशरथात्मजः ।
उवास रजनीं तत्र ताटकाया वने सुखम् ।।

36. Hearing Vischwaamithra's words, (Raama) the son of Dhascharatha who was happy, spent the night in comfort in this forest of Thaataka.

❍ ❍ ❍

३७. मुक्तशापं वनं तच्च तस्मिन्नेव तदाऽहनि ।।

३८. चम्पकाशोकपुन्नागमल्लिकाद्यैः सुशोभितम् ।।

३९. चूतैश्च पनसैः पूगैर्नारिकेलैश्च शोभितम् ।
वापीकूपतटाकैश्च दीर्घिकाभिरलंकृतम् ॥

37, 38 & 39.

Released from curse (now that Thaataka was dead), this forest, from that day ...... shone (bright) with Champaka (Michelia Champaka), Asoka (Jonesia Asoka), Punnage (Rottleria), Mallika (Jasminum Zambus) trees ...... and shone with Chootha (Mango), Panasa (Bread fruit), Poonga, (Areca Catechu), Naarikkala (Coconut) trees; And was 'Decorated' with ponds, tanks & wells and even big lakes......

❍ ❍ ❍

४०. मल्लिकाहेमकूटैश्च मण्टपैरुपशोभितम् ।
रमणीयं हि बभ्राज वनं चैत्ररथं यथा ॥

40. Golden hued peaks, full of Jasmine flowers and with Bowers, (this region now) shone. It appeared lovely like Kubhaera's forest of Chaithyaratha.

❍ ❍ ❍

४१. निहत्य तां यक्षसुतां स रामः प्रशस्यमानः सुरसिद्धसङ्घैः ।
उवास तस्मिन् मुनिना सहैव प्रभातवेलां प्रतिबोध्यमानः ॥

41. Having killed this (Thaataka) the daughter of a Yaksha, this Raama was extolled by Sura-s, Sidha-s, in multitude. He stayed there with Muni (Vischwaamithra & brother Lakshmana) and was woken up early morning (next day).

❍ ❍ ❍

Chapter 27

The Teaching of Divine Weapons (to Raama)

१. अथ तां रजनीमुष्य विश्वामित्रो महायशाः ।
प्रशस्य राघवं वाक्यमुवाच मधुरस्वरम् ।।

1. The most famous Vischwaamithra, having spent the night, then addressed (Raama) the Raaghava with following words in sweet voice, extolling him.

❍ ❍ ❍

२. परितुष्टोऽस्मि भद्रं ते राजपुत्र महायशः ।
प्रीत्या परमया युक्तो ददाम्यस्त्राणि सर्वशः ।।

2. Oh famous (Raama) the son of king! Welfare to you! I am very pleased. In great joy I am (now) 'offering' you all (Divine) Weapons.

❍ ❍ ❍

३. देवासुरगणान्वाऽपि सगन्धर्वोरगानपि ।
यैरमित्रान् प्रसह्याजौ वशीकृत्य जयिष्यसि ।।

3. (Vishwaamithra teaches Raama use of various divine weapons). By these (weapons), you will, with great force, subdue Ghandharva-s, Uraga-s, Dheva-s, Asura-s, multitudes of them, and (other) enemies, and will win wars.

❍ ❍ ❍

४. तानि दिव्यानि भद्रं ते ददाम्यस्त्रीणि सर्वशः ।
दण्डचक्रं महद्दिव्यं दास्यामि तव राघव ।।

4. Oh Raaghava! Welfare to you! I am 'giving' you (teaching you) the Divine weapons, totally. I am giving you the mighty divine Dhanda Discus.

❍ ❍ ❍

५. धर्मचक्रं ततो वीर कालचक्रं तथैव च ।
विष्णुचक्रं तथाऽत्युग्रमैन्द्रमस्त्रं तथैव च ।।

६. वज्रमस्त्रं नरश्रेष्ठ शैवं पाशुपतं तथा ।
अस्त्रं ब्रह्मशिरश्चैव ऐषीकमपि राघव ।।
७. देवचक्रं महद्दिव्यं तव दास्यामि राघव ।
ददामि ते महाबाहो ब्राह्ममस्त्रमनुत्तमम् ।।
८. गदे द्वे चैव काकुत्स्थ मोदकी शिखरी उभे ।
प्रदीप्ते नरशार्दूल प्रयच्छामि नृपात्मज ।।
९. धर्मपाशं महद्धाम कालपाशं तथैव च ।
वारुणं पाशमस्त्रं च ददाम्यहमनुत्तमम् ।।
१०. अशनी द्वे प्रयच्छामि शुष्कार्द्रेरघुनन्दन ।
ददामि चास्त्रं पैनाकमस्त्रं नारायणं तथा ।।
११. आग्नेयमस्त्रं दयितं शिखरं नाम नामतः ।
वायव्यं प्रथनं राम ददामि तव चानघ ।।
१२. अस्त्रं हयशिरो नाम क्रौञ्चमस्त्रं तथैव च ।
शक्तिद्वयं च काकुत्स्थ ददामि तव राघव ।।
वधार्थं रक्षसां यानि ददाम्येतानि सर्वशः ।।
१३. कमालं मुसलं घोरं कापालमथ कमणम् ।
धारयन्त्यसुरा यानि ददाम्येतानि सर्वशः ।।
१४. वैद्याधरं महास्त्रं च नन्दनं नाम नामतः ।
असिरत्नं महाबाहो ददामि नृवरात्मज ।।
१५. गान्धर्वमस्त्रं दयितं मानवं नाम नामतः ।
प्रस्वापनप्रशमने दद्यां सौर्यं च राघव ।।
१६. दर्पणं शोषणं चैव सन्तापनविलापने ।
मदनं चैव दुर्धर्षं कन्दर्पदयितं तथा ।।
१७. पैशाचमस्त्रं दयितं मोहनं नाम नामतः ।
प्रतीच्छ नरशार्दूल राजपुत्र महायशः ।।
१८. तामसं नरशार्दूल सौमनं च महाबल ।
संवर्तं चैव दुर्धर्षं मौसलं च नृपात्मज ।।
१९. सत्यमस्त्रं महाबाहो तथा मायाधरं परम् ।
सौरं तेजःप्रभं नाम परतेजोऽपकर्षणाम् ।।

२०. सोमास्त्रं शिशिरं नाम त्वाष्ट्रमस्त्रं सुदारुणम् ।
दारुणं च भगस्यापि शीतेषुमथ मानवम् ॥
२१. एतान् राम महाबाहो कामरूपान् महाबलान् ।
गृहाण परमोदारान् क्षिप्रमेव नृपात्मज ॥

5 to 21.

(All the divine weapons 'given' - taught by Vischwaamithra; Stanza 4 to 21)

Oh Brave (Raama)! Further, the Dharma Chakra; likewise Kaala Chakra; most fierce Vishnu Chakra; likewise, Indhra weapon ...... Oh foremost of men! The Vajra; likewise, weapon Paaschupathy (of Schiva); weapon Brammaschiras; likewise Eyesheeka ...... (These I am offering) Oh (Raama)the Raaghava! ...... Oh the mighty limbed one!.

I am giving you the mighty divine weapon, Dhevachakra; the foremost Bramma weapon; ...... Oh (Raama)! the Kaakuthsa! Oh the son of king (Dhascharatha)! I am giving two clubs, Modhaki & Schikari, these 'burning' & fierce (clubs) ...... Oh Raama! I am giving Dharmapaascha, likewise, Kaalapaascha & foremost Varuna Paascha weapons ...... Oh (Raama) the darling of Raghu-s! I am likewise giving you the two thunderbolts- Schushka & Ardhra; the Pinaaka weapon; Naaraayana weapon ...... Oh sinless Raama I am giving weapon named Schikara, the fire weapon and most cherished; And Vaayava weapon Prathana by name, as well ...... Oh Raama, the Raaghava! Oh Kaakuthsa! Weapon of Hayaschiras; likewise weapon Krauncha; Two Schakthi weapons of Vishnu & Rudhra, I am giving you; For the sake of destruction of demons, all this ...... The terrible Musala, Kangkana, Kaapaala; All these that are used by Asura-s, I am giving you ...... Oh mighty limbed (Raama) the son of foremost of men! I am giving the great (weapon) named Nandhana, the Vidhyaadhara weapon; And also, a gem of a Sword ......

Oh (Raama) the Raaghava: I am giving The Ghandharva weapon, a most cherished weapon called Maanava; And weapons of Prasva paana, Prasmana & Sowrya ...... Oh (Raama the) Raaghava! Dharpana, Schoshana, Santhaapana, Vilaapana, the weapon cherished by Kandharpa, the uncrushable Madhana ...... Receive these: The Paischaacha weapon; the most cherished Mohana by name ...... I give you Oh famous (Raama) the son of king, Oh (Raama) who is a 'lion'amongst men! ...... Thaamsa, Sowmana, uncrushable Samvartha, the Mowsala, Sathya weapons, likewise Oh mighty limbed (Raama), The foremost weapon, Maayaadhara, and The Sun's Thejaprabha by name which will 'drag' the enemy's briiliance ...... (I offer these) Oh 'tiger' of men!, Oh the mightily strong (Raama) the son of king! ...... The Soma weapon called Schischira, the cruel Thwashtra weapon, and Bhaga's most cruel Maanava weapon, Scheetheshu ...... Receive these at once which are mightily strong, which can take on any form, which are very 'lofty', Oh mighty limbed Raama, the son of king (Dhascharatha).

❍ ❍ ❍

२२. स्थितस्तु प्रायुखो भूत्वा शुचिर्मुनिवरस्तदा ।
दद‍ौ रामाय सुप्रीतो मन्त्रग्राममनुत्तमम् ।।

22. Then, the foremost muni (Vishwaamithra) standing & facing east, joyfully & gleamingly "offered" Raama these foremost weapons, The 'Collection' of mystical (Weapons that are discharged with chants & prayers).

❍ ❍ ❍

२३. सर्वसंग्रहणं येषां दैवतैरपि दुर्लभम् ।
तान्यस्त्राणि तदा विप्रो राघवाय न्यवेदयत् ।।

23. All these (celestial weapons) which are difficult to obtain even for the Dheva-s, this Braamin (Vischwaamithra) offered at that time. These weapons (he taught) Raama the Raaghava.

❍ ❍ ❍

२४. जपतस्तु मुनेस्तस्य विश्वामित्रस्य धीमतः ।
उपतस्थुर्महार्हाणि सर्वाण्यस्त्राणि राघवम् ।।

24. These most precious weapons of the wise Muni Vischwaamithra who was chanting (Prayers), appeared before (Raama) the Raghava, all these (divine ones, in human form).

❍ ❍ ❍

२५. ऊचुश्च मुदिता रामं सर्वेप्राञ्जलयस्तदा ।
इमे स्म परमोदाराः किमरास्तव राघव ।।

25. Then all of them, with joy, and with folded arms of Anjali said to Raama: = Oh (Raama) the Raaghava! We are indeed your lofty servants. (We are ever at your service) =

❍ ❍ ❍

२६. प्रतिगृह्य च काकुत्स्थः समालभ्य च पाणिना ।
मानसा मे भविष्यध्वमिति तानभ्यचोदयत् ।।

26. And (Raama) the Kaakuthsa, holding them with his hands, accepted them. (And he said &) Commanded them = May you be dear to my heart.=

❍ ❍ ❍

२७. ततः प्रीतमना रामो विश्वामित्रं महामुनिम् ।
अभिवाद्य महातेजा गमनायोपचक्रमे ।।

27. Then with a happy mind, the most brilliant Raama bowed before the great Muni Vischwaamithra and began to leave at the command of Vischwaamithra (accompanied by his brother Lakshmana)

(Note: Readers may note, that one of the purposes of 'drawing away' young Raama to forest was to teach Raama Divine weaponry & give him experience. This is an ideal situation- The great Teacher Vischwaamithra has a great disciple in Raama. A second thought appears; Raama is going to need them in future when he is going to fight Demon Raavana, Yet another thought may appear to us; After all Raama is God Vishnu on earth; These must necessarily get back to the Almighty lord!)

❍ ❍ ❍

Chapter 28

The Teaching of the Art of Control of (Divine) Weapons

१. प्रतिगृह्य ततोऽस्त्राणि प्रहृष्टवदनः शुचिः ।
गच्छन्नेव च काकुत्स्थो विश्वामित्रमथाब्रवीत् ।।

1. Having 'received' the Asthra-s, (celestial weapons), (Raama) the Kaakuthsa, whose face was bright with joy and who was pure (& radiant), addressed Vischwaamithra as he was walking along.

❍ ❍ ❍

२. गृहीतास्त्रोऽस्मि भगवन्दुराधर्षः सुरैरपि ।
अस्त्राणां त्वहमिच्छामि संहारं मुनिपुङ्गव ।।

2. Oh my lord! Oh (Vischwaamithra) the 'tiger' of muni-s! Having obtained weapons, I am uncrushable even by Dheva-s: (But) I desire to know (& be enlightened) about the *retrieval (& control of these weapons). (Poet uses word =* Samhaara =)

❍ ❍ ❍

३. एवं ब्रुवति काकुत्स्थे विश्वामित्रो महातपाः ।
संहारं व्याजहाराथ धृतिमान् सुव्रतः शुचिः ।।

3. When (Raama) the Kaakuthsa was saying thus, the man of penance, the man of vows and austerities, the pure Vischwaamithra, who was resolute in Dharma, then taught The Samhaara of weapons (The retrieval & control).

❍ ❍ ❍

(Vishwaamithra teaches Raama: stanzas 4 to 10: The Samhaara)

४. सत्यवन्तं सत्यकीर्तिं धृष्टं रभसमेव च ।
प्रतिहारतरं नाम परायुखमवायुखम् ।।

५. लक्षाक्षविक्रमौ चैव दृढनाभसुनाभकौ ।
दशाक्षशतवक्त्रौ च दशशीर्षशतोदरौ ।।

६. पद्मनाभमहानाभौ दुन्दुनाभसुनाभकौ ।
ज्योतिषं क्रथनं चैव नैराश्यविमलावुभौ ।।

७. योगन्धरविनिद्रौ च दैत्यप्रशमनौ तथा ।
शुचिर्बाहुर्महाबाहुर्निष्कुलिर्विरुचिस्तथा ।।
सार्चिमाली धृतिर्माली वृत्तिमान् रुचिरस्तथा ।।

८. पितृसौमनसं चैव विधूतमकरावुभौ ।
करवीरकरं चैव धनधान्यौ च राघव ।।

९. कामरूपं कामरुचिं मोहनं मारणं तथा ।
जृंभकं सर्वनाभं च सन्धानवरुणावुभौ ।।

१०. भृशाश्वतनयान् राम भास्वरान् कामरूपिणः ।
प्रतीच्छ मम भद्रं ते पात्रभूतोऽसि राघव ।।

4 to 10.

(Knowledge of) Sathyavath, Sathyakeerthi, Dhrishta, Rabhasa; Prathihaara; And (knowledge) known as Paraangmukh & Avangmukh ...... Laksha & Aksha Vikram; Dhridanaabha & Sunaabhaka, Dhaschaaksha & Schathaaksha; Dhascha-scheersha & Schathodhara; ...... Padmanaabha & Mahaanaabha; Dhundhunaabha, Jyothishta, Kathana, Nairaaschya, Vimala ...... the two which teach Samhara of asura weapons, Yogandhara, & Vinidhra, ... Suchi, Bhaahu, MahaaBhaahu, Nishkuli, Viruchi, likewise Saarchimaali, Dhrithimaali, Vrithimaana, Ruchira ...... And these two Vidhootha & Makra, Pithrusowmansa, Karaveerakara, Dhana & Dhaanya (oh Raaghava, I offer to you) ...... Kaamaroopa, Kaamaruchi, Mohana, Maarana, likewise Jrimbhuka, Sarvanaabha, the two Sandhana & Varuna ...... Oh

Raama, Oh Raaghava! Receive these bright 'Sons' of Brishaaswas from me which can take on any form; You are indeed fit to receive these (this divine knowledge) Welfare to you.

❍ ❍ ❍

११. बाढमित्येव काकुत्स्थः प्रहृष्टेनान्तरात्मना ।।

11. And (Raama) the Kaakuthsa, with a happy & contented mind said = I Affirm. = (I am devoted to this "Discipline").

❍ ❍ ❍

१२. दिव्यभास्वरदेहाश्च मूर्तिमन्तः सुखप्रदाः ।
केचिदङ्गारसदृशाः केचिद्धूमोपमास्तथा ।।

१३. चन्द्रार्कसदृशाः केचित् प्रह्वाञ्जलिपुटास्तथा ।
रामं प्राञ्जलयो भूत्वाऽब्रुवन् मधुरभाषिणः ।।
इमे स्म नरशार्दूल शाधि किं करवाम ते ।।

12 & 13.

(Some) whose body was shining luminous; some having human body; some who offered comfort and some were comparable to Fire; some comparable to Sun and Moon; some with folded arms of Anjali. . . . . . all these in Anjali addressed Raama, speaking sweetly: Oh (Raama) the 'tiger' of men = All of us are here (at your service): What should be done (by us) for you Command us.=

❍ ❍ ❍

१४. गम्यतामिति तानाह यथेष्टं रघुनन्दनः ।
मानसाः कार्यकालेषु साहाय्यं मे करिष्यथ ।।

14. And (Raama) the darling of Raghu-s told them = You may do service to me at opportune moment (when I need you), with all your heart & mind. You may (now) go as you please. =

(Note: All these weapons appear in human form before

Raama; Like in Alladin's Lamp story, they will come when Raama beckons).

❍ ❍ ❍

१५. अथ ते राममान्त्र्य कृत्वा चापि प्रदक्षिणम् ।
एवमस्त्विति काकुत्स्थमुक्त्वा जग्मुर्यथागतम् ।।
प्रणम्य शिरसा रामं सर्वेसम्मतविक्रमाः ।।

15. After telling (Raama) the Kaakuthsa- "It Will Be So", they, who were recognised as truly valiant, all went round Raama in circumbambulation, bowed before him with their hands down (respectfully), took leave & left as they came.

❍ ❍ ❍

१६. ततस्तु रामः काकुत्स्थः शासनाद्ब्रह्मवादिनः ।
लक्ष्मणाय च तान् सर्वान् वरास्त्रान् रघुनन्दनः ।।
संहारान् स च संहृष्टः श्रीमांस्तस्मै न्यवेदयत् ।।

16. Then this Kaakuthsa the darling of Raghu-s, this resplendent Raama, by the command of (Vischwaamithra) the expounder of Brammam (Spiritual Texts), taught all the foremost weapons and their comprehensive usage, to Lakshmana, happily. (Readers may note that it is Raama who teaches Lakshmana, not Vischwaamithra).

❍ ❍ ❍

१७. स च तान् राघवो ज्ञात्वा विश्वामित्रं महामुनिम् ।
गच्छन्नेवाथ मधुरं श्लक्ष्णं वचनमब्रवीत् ।।

17. Having learnt these (celestial weapons), this (Raama), the Raaghava then said to the great Muni Vischwaamithra these sweet, 'polished' words, even as he was walking along (with him).

❍ ❍ ❍

१८. किञ्चैतन्मेघसमाशं पर्वतस्याविदूरतः ।
वृक्षषण्डमितो भाति परं कौतूहलं हि मे ।।

१९. दर्शनीयं मृगाकीर्णं मनोहरमतीव च ।
नानाप्रकारैः शकुनैः वल्गुभाषैरलमृतम् ।।

18 & 19.

What is this! Not far from this mountain, a cluster of trees is shining like clouds; My curiosity is great ...... (to know about this place) ...... It is full of deers; Is well 'decorated' by various types of birds that have captivating voice (& the place) is delightful to look at

❍ ❍ ❍

२०. निःसृताः स्म मुनिश्रेष्ठ कान्ताराद्रोमहर्षणात् ।।

20. Oh Muni (Vischwaamithra)! We have come out of hair raising wilderness.

❍ ❍ ❍

२१. अनया त्ववगच्छामि देशस्य सुखवत्तया ।
सर्वं मे शंस भगवन् कस्याश्रमपदं त्विदम् ।।

21. Oh Lord (Vischwaamithra) By the 'comfort' & beauty of this place, I recognise all (that it is like paradise): Whose hermitage is this? (Please) tell me.

❍ ❍ ❍

२२. संप्राप्ता यत्र ते पापा ब्रह्मघ्ना दुष्टचारिणः ।
तव यज्ञस्य विघ्नाय दुरात्मानो महामुने ।।

२३. भगवंस्तत्र को देशः सा यत्र तव याज्ञिकी ।
रक्षितव्या क्रिया ब्रह्मन् मया वध्याश्च राक्षसाः ।।

22 & 23.

Oh great Muni! Where are the sinful (demons) who are evil minded, who are of evil conduct and who kill braamins and cause harm to your Yaaga. . . . . . . Oh my lord! Oh Braamin (Vischwaamithra)! This, your yaaga, where should it be protected by me? Which is the place where the demons are to be killed by me?

❍ ❍ ❍

२४. एतत्सर्वं मुनिश्रेष्ठ श्रोतुमिच्छाम्यहं प्रभो ।।

24. Oh foremost Muni! Oh Lord! I desire to hear all this.

(Note: Raama being devoted in duty, asks his Guru. He is keen to shoulder responsibility to offer protection to Vischwaamithra's yaaga.. And readers may have observed that this very great sage Vischwaamithra is not only a great teacher of Warfare, but a great historian as well. He enlightens these two princes about the History & Geography of these places. Infact in the whole of Baala Kaanda, the First Book of Vaalmeeki, it is Vischwaamithra who 'moulds' the two princes.)

❍ ❍ ❍

Chapter 29

(Vischwaamithra & the Two Princes) Go to Sidhdha Hermitage

१. अथ तस्याप्रमेयस्य तद्वनं परिपृच्छतः ।
विश्वामित्रो महातेजा व्याख्यातुमुपचक्रमे ।।

1. The most brilliant Vischwaamithra then began to describe about this forest to (Raama) of limitless valour who had asked him.

❍ ❍ ❍

२. इह राम महाबाहो विष्णुर्देववरः प्रभुः ।
अदृश्यः सर्वभूतानां सर्वात्मा सर्वलोकभृत् ।।
मोहनार्थं तु लोकस्य सर्वेषां जगतः प्रभुः ।।

३. वर्षाणि सुबहूनीह तथा युगशतानि च ।
तपश्चरणयोगार्थमुवास स महातपाः ।।

2 & 3.

(The story of King Bali narrated by Vischwaamithra to the princes).

Oh the mighty limbed Raama! The Lord, (God) Vishnu, the foremost of Dheva-s, who is lord of all the worlds and beings, who is unseen and who is protector of all the worlds, who is the Soul (of Universe), to cause bewilderment to all ...... lived here (long ago) as lord of great penance, doing penance & Yoga for many years & hundreds of Yuga-s (millennium).

❍ ❍ ❍

४. एष पूर्वाश्रमो राम वामनस्य महात्मनः ।
सिद्धाश्रम इति ख्यातः सिद्धो ह्यत्र महातपाः ।।

4. Oh Raama! This was previously the great soul Vaamana's hermitage (God Vishnu's hermitage). Here the man of great penance (Vaamana, The Vishnu) attained Sidhdhi. (Total beatitude & bliss): Thus it is known as Sidhdha hermitage.

❍ ❍ ❍

५. एतस्मिन्नेव काले तु राजा वैरोचनो बलिः ।
निर्जित्य दैवतगणान् सेन्द्रांश्च समरुद्गणान् ।।
कारयामास तद्राज्यं त्रिषु लोकेषु विश्रुतः ।।
६. यज्ञं चकार बलवानसुरेन्द्रो महाबलिः ।।

5 & 6.

At that time, there was a king called Bali, the mighty Bali who was the son of Virochana: Having conquered multitude of Dheva-s & Maruth-s including Lord Indhra ...... he began to rule this kingdom renowned in all the worlds ...... this mighty Bali, the strong Bali who was lord of all Asura-s did a Yaaga.

❍ ❍ ❍

७. बलेस्तु यजमानस्य देवाः साग्निपुरोगमाः ।
समागम्य स्वयं चैव विष्णुमूचुरिहाश्रमे ।।

7. While Bali was doing Yaaga, the Dheva-s, following Lord Agni (Fire), approached God Vishnu in this hermitage, and said:

❍ ❍ ❍

८. बलिर्वैरोचनो विष्णो यजते यज्ञमुत्तमम् ।
असमाप्ते क्रतौ तस्मिन् स्वकार्यमभिपद्यताम् ।।

8. Oh God Vishnu! Virochana's son Bali is doing a great Yaaga; Before he completes the Yaaga, your "Work" must be undertaken (Readers may note: The Dheva-s who are traditional enemies of Asura-s are scared. If this lord of Asura-s completes this Yaaga, he may wield so much power that he can shake up the world. So Dheva-s seek God Vishnu's help).

❍ ❍ ❍

९. ये चैनमभिवर्तन्ते याचितार इतस्ततः ।
यच्च यत्र यथावच्च सर्वं तेभ्यः प्रयच्छति ।।

9. Those, from any where, when (& if) they 'seek.' him, to all of them (this Bali) gives all, gives whatever they want (Exactly as per their wish; so munificent is Bali).

❍ ❍ ❍

१०. स त्वं सुरहितार्थाय मायायोमुपाश्रितः ।
वामनत्वं गतो विष्णो कुरु कल्याणमुत्तमम् ।।

10. Oh Vishnu! You are such a (Lord); for the sake of welfare of Dheva-s; using your magical prowess and taking on the form of a *midget, please do us foremost good. (*Vaamana-Midget).

❍ ❍ ❍

११. एतस्मिन्नन्तरे राम कश्यपोऽग्निसमप्रभः ।
अदित्या सहितो राम दीप्यमान इवौजसा ।।

१२. देवीसहायो भगवान् दिव्यं वर्षसहस्रकम् ।
व्रतं समाप्य वरदं तुष्टाव मधुसूदनम् ।।

11 & 12.

Oh (Raama the) Delighter! (Listen further) Oh Raama! At this time, the great soul sage Kaschyapa, who was shining like burning fire in brilliance, along with Adhithi ...... along with his wife (Adhithi) began to (pray &) please this (Vishnu), the Madhusoodhana who had completed thousand divine years in penance.

❍ ❍ ❍

१३. तपोमयं तपोराशिं तपोमूर्तिं तपात्मकम् ।
तपसा त्वां सुतप्तेन पश्यामि पुरुषोत्तमम् ।।

13. (Kaschyapa to Vishnu): Oh (Vishnu)! Through my penance 'See', (know) you, as a foremost of beings (as Purushothama), as embodiment of penance, as creator of penance, as a store house of penance.

❍ ❍ ❍

१४. शरीरे तव पश्यामि जगत्सर्वमिदं प्रभो ।
त्वमनादिरनिर्देश्यस्त्वामहं शरणं गतः ।।

14. Oh Lord! I see the whole Universe in your body. You are not created (but self born); You cannot be described. I have surrendered to you (have sought refuge in you).

❍ ❍ ❍

१५. तमुवाच हरिः प्रीतः कश्यपं धूतकल्मषम् ।
वरं वरय भद्रं ते वरार्होऽसि मतो मम ।।

15. And Hari (Vishnu), in great joy, addressed this Kaschyapa who had shaken off his sins (totally); = Welfare to you; As you have endeared to me, you are fit to receive boon from me.=

❍ ❍ ❍

१६. तच्छ्रुत्वा वचनं तस्य मारीचः कश्यपोऽब्रवीत् ।।

16. Hearing (Vishnu's) words, Kaschyapa, the son of Mareech said.

❍ ❍ ❍

१७. अदित्या देवतानां च मम चैवानुयाचतः ।
वरं वरद सुप्रीतो दातुमर्हसि सुव्रत ।।

17. Oh (God Vishnu of) Good vows & austerities! Oh (Lord) the giver of boons! For Adhithi, for Dheva-s, and for me who is beseeching you, you must give boon happily.

❍ ❍ ❍

१८. पुत्रत्वं गच्छ भगवन्नदित्यां मम चानघ ।
भ्राता भव यवीयांस्त्वं शक्रस्यासुरसूदन ।।
शोकार्तानां तु देवानां साहाय्यं कर्तुमर्हसि ।।

18. Oh sinless (Vishnu) the destroyer of asura-s! Oh Lord! You should become 'son' to me & Adhithi: And (by this) you become Lord Indhra's younger brother; You should offer help to Dheva-s who are suffering in grief...... (Lord Indhra is the son of Adhithi & Kaschyapa, readers may note).

❍ ❍ ❍

१९. अयं सिद्धाश्रमो नाम प्रसादात्ते भविष्यति ।
सिद्धे कर्मणि देवेश उत्तिष्ठ भगवन्नितः ।।

19. Oh Lord of Dheva-s, Oh God (Vishnu)! By your grace, when the yaaga is completed, this (region) is going to be named Sidhdha Hermitage. Arise now from here.

❍ ❍ ❍

२०. एवमुक्तो हृषीकेशः पीतवासा जनार्दनः ।
सर्वज्ञस्तत्तथेत्युक्त्वा कश्यपस्य तपस्यतः ।।
२१. अथ विष्णुर्महातेजा अदित्यां समजायत ।
छत्री भिक्षुकरूपेण कमण्डलुशिखोज्ज्वलः ।।

20 & 21.

When told thus, (Vishnu) the knower of all, the Janaardhana, the Hrisheekesa, the lord who sports Peethaambara dress (Yellow silken), told the man of penance Kaschyapa:= So Be It.= ... then the most brilliant God Vishnu was born to Adhithi; Taking the form of a mendicant, carrying an umbrella, a vessel & a begging bowl ...... and taking the form of a midget, approached (Bali) the son of Virochana.

❍ ❍ ❍

२२. वामनं रूपमास्थाय वैरोचनमुपागमत् ॥

(Readers may note that God Vishnu has 1,000 names; Janaardhana, the exciter of men; Hrisheekesa, bristles with joy & makes one bristle with joy. The incarnation of God Vishnu as a midget Vaamana, as son of Kaschyapa to humble the mighty Asura lord Bali, is being narrated by Vischwaamithra to Raama/Lakshmana.)

❍ ❍ ❍

२३. आसाद्य यजमानं तमुवाच भगवान् हरिः ।
स्वस्ति तेऽस्तु महाराज यज्ञश्चातीव शोभते ॥

23. Lord Hari (Vishnu), approaching this (Bali) who was doing Yaaga, said: = May there be welfare to you of Swasthi! Oh great king! This Yaaga (of yours) shines, surpasses (every yaaga).

❍ ❍ ❍

२४. वयं दानार्थिनो राजन् श्रुत्वा यज्ञमनुत्तमम् ।
त्वां दृष्ट्वा तव यागेषु किञ्चिल्लब्धुमिहागताः ॥

24. Oh King (Bali)! Hearing about your foremost Yaaga, seeking Gifts, *'we' have come here to meet you to obtain something from you (& your) Yaaga.= (* use of 'we' for 'I').

❍ ❍ ❍

२५. वामनेनैवमुक्ते तु मुदा राजा तमब्रवीत् ।
अद्य मे सफलं जन्म अद्य मे शफलं तपः ॥

25. When told thus by God Vishnu who was in the form of a midget, king (Bali) said, in joy: = (only) Now my life has become fruitful; (only) Now my penance has become fruitful =

(Readers may note: This Asura Lord Bali, was the most munificent of men. And God Vishnu, as a Beggar on earth, humbles this great Asura king Bali, knowing fully well that Bali never denies any request for gifts, assistance, or help.)

❍ ❍ ❍

२६. अद्य मे सफलं राज्यमद्य मे सुकृतं कृतम् ।
अद्य मे सफलो यज्ञः कृतार्थः कृतवानहम् ।।

26. (Only) Now my rule of kingdom has obtained fruits (of prosperity) (Only) Now my deed has been well done; (Only) Now my Yaaga has become fruitful. (Only now) I have become accomplished by my work (Yaaga).

❍ ❍ ❍

२७. त्वदर्थं कल्पितं चैव मम सर्वस्वमेव हि ।
धनौघं रत्नराशिं च भूषणं धान्यसञ्चयम् ।।

२८. ग्रामं वा नगरं वाऽपि राष्ट्रं वा यानमेव वा ।
हस्त्यश्वरथपत्तीनां संग्रहश्चान्यदेव वा ।।

27 & 28.

(Bali of course did not know this Midget as the All Powerful God Vishnu: And the munificent king offers gifts to Vishnu!) ...... All this are 'made' for you: My heaps of wealth, heaps of gems, ornaments, granaries, Villages, cities, kingdoms, my vehicles, elephants, horses, chariots. . . . All other accumulations of mine. (Chose any of these, says the munificent king Bali).

❍ ❍ ❍

२९. किमिच्छसि महाबाहो तद्ददामि तवानघ ।।

29. Oh sinless one! Oh *mighty limbed! What you desire, I will give. that. (*Readers may note that king Bali addresses this Midget as mighty limbed; Poet Vaalmeeki uses this expression. Did Bali have a suspicion that this person with a begging bowl was really no midget, but a mighty limbed God Vishnu in disguise).

❍ ❍ ❍

३०. एवमुक्तस्तदा राज्ञा भगवान् पुरुषोत्तमः ।
उवाचैनं स्मितं कृत्वा युजमानं महाबलिम् ।।

30. At that moment, the lord (Vishnu who came there in the form of midget), this foremost Being, (The Purusha), when told thus by the king, smiled and then said to this great Bali who was doing this Yaaga, thus:

❍ ❍ ❍

३१. एतैः किं मम राजेन्द्र तैस्तु नास्ति प्रयोजनम् ।
अस्मत्पादत्रयाक्रान्तां देहि भूमिं विभो मम ।।

31. (This "Midget" 'plays a game' with this Bali, the munificent) Oh King! of what (use) are these to me; There is no benefit for me with these; Oh Lord! (But) You give me (as much) Land (as I can cover) with my Three Strides!

❍ ❍ ❍

३२. श्रुत्वा तद्वामनेनोक्तं स्मितं कृत्वाऽसुरोत्तमः ।
येनेष्टं पूर्यते ब्रह्मन् तत् कुर्मेति ततोऽब्रवीत् ।।

32. When he was told thus by the midget, (King Bali) the foremost Asura, smiled, and said: = Oh Braamin! (Anything) By which your desire may be satisfied, that I will do. (I will gladly give you the Land as requested by you) =

❍ ❍ ❍

३३. वामनाय महीं दातुं निश्चितेऽसुरसत्तमे ।
तं निवार्य महाराजं प्राह शुक्रो द्विजोत्तमः ।।

33. When this foremost Asura (Bali) decided to give land to the midget, the foremost of Braamins, (Sage) Schukra, (who was Adviser to Asuras & to king Bali), restrained this great king by saying:

❍ ❍ ❍

३४. विरिञ्चिभवशक्राद्या योगिनश्च सुरासुराः ।
यं न जानन्ति देवाश्च स देवो विष्णुरव्ययः ।।

34. (Schukra warns his king; dont offer this midget). . . . (This midget) is indeed He, the Imperishable Lord Vishnu, whom neither Braamma, nor Schiva, nor Indhra, nor Dheva-s, nor Yogi-s, nor Sura-s nor Asura-s (really) know!

❍ ❍ ❍

३५. दानारक्ते ततः शुक्रे शुक्रं राजपुरोहितम् ।
गृहीत्वा ताडयामास वैनतेयो महाबलः ।।

35. When Schukra tried to stop this offer (of land to the midget), the mightily strong Garuda (the lord of birds), seized this Schukra, the royal priest (of king Bali) and hit him.

❍ ❍ ❍

३६. पत्नया सह विनिश्चित्य यजमानो महाबलिः ।
मायारूपेण देवेशो मम यज्ञं गतो यदि ।।

३७. तदैतद्यज्ञसाफल्यमेवमस्त्विवति चाब्रवीत् ।।

३८. इति मत्वोदकं दत्तं वामनाय महात्मने ।
तव पादत्रयाक्रान्तां गृहणाद्य महीं प्रभो ।।

36, 37 & 38.

Taking (firm) decision along with his wife, the mighty Bali who was doing the Yaaga (thought): If the Lord of all lords, (God Vishnu) Himself has come to me. . . to my Yaaga in the magical form (of a midget), this only (means) that my Yaaga is fruitful ...... And he said: ...... =. Oh lord: With your feet, take Land now with Three Steps:= And deciding thus, he offered (Ritual) waters to the great soul Midget, (thus honouring his commitment).

❍ ❍ ❍

३९. उदके स्पृष्टमात्रे तु विश्वरूपधतो हरिः ।
तत्रस्थ एव ववृधे येन पूर्णं जगत्त्रयम् ।।

39. The moment (Midget) Vishnu touched the (Ritual)

waters, He "Rose up" (and grew & grew), standing there, assuming Vischwaroopa (The All Pervasive Form Engulfing the Universe).

❍ ❍ ❍

४०. सायुधैर्बाहुभिः पूर्णं दिग्विदिक् सर्वमेव हि ॥

40. With His hands wielding weapons, He engulfed the entire area of Earth & Regions.

❍ ❍ ❍

४१. तं दृष्ट्वाऽसुरराजेन्द्रो वामनत्वाच्च विस्मितः ।
माधवोऽयमिति ज्ञात्वा पूजयामास धर्मतः ॥
पूजितस्तेन धर्मात्मा सर्वलोकहिताय वै ॥
४२. त्रीन् क्रमानथ भिक्षित्वा प्रतिगृह्य च वामनः ।
आक्रम्य लोकान् लोकात्मा सर्वलोकहिते रतः ॥
४३. महेन्द्राय पुनः प्रादान्नियम्य बलिमोजसा ।
त्रैलोक्यं स महातेजाश्चक्रे शंक्रवशं पुनः ॥

41, 42 & 43.

Seeing him (Growing in size) from Midget form, the lord of Asura-s, (king Bali) became wonder struck and realised that this (midget) was none other than Maadhava (God Vishnu) and he prayed to Him as per Dharma ...... Worshipped thus by him, (God Vishnu) whose soul is Dharma, who is the "Soul of the Universe", who is devoted to the welfare of the world, and who had, as a midget, begged 'Three steps' of Land, for the welfare of the world, engulfed The Worlds and had seized (Bali's world) by his Three steps ...... (This God Vishnu) the most brilliant, subdued thus King Bali by His power, and He offered the three worlds to lord Indhra (thus), and made (the worlds) come under the control of Schakra (Indhra) once again.

❍ ❍ ❍

४४. तेनैष पूर्वमाक्रान्त आश्रमः श्रमनाशनः ।
मयाऽपि भक्त्या तस्यैव वामनस्योपभुज्यते ॥

44. (Vischwaamithra concludes the story of king Bali that occurred long, long ago, thus) ...... This invigorating hermitage (that destroys weariness) was first lived in by (God Vishnu): And in devotion to the midget (God Vishnu, the Vaamana), it is now lived in by me also & enjoyed.

❍ ❍ ❍

४५. एतमाश्रममायान्ति राक्षसा विघ्नकारिणः ।
अत्र ते पुरुषव्याघ्र हन्तव्या दुष्टचारिणः ।।

45. Oh (Raama) the 'tiger' of men! The demons of evil conduct who create harm come to this hermitage; and so they must be killed here (by you).

❍ ❍ ❍

४६. अद्य गच्छामहे राम सिद्धाश्रममनुत्तमम् ।
तदाश्रमपदं तात तवाप्येतद्यथा मम ।।

46. With His hands wielding weapons, He engulfed the entire area of Earth & Regions.

❍ ❍ ❍

४७. इत्युक्त्वा परमप्रीतो गृह्य रामं सलक्ष्मणम् ।
प्रविशन्नाश्रमपदं व्यरोचत महामुनिः ।।
शशीव गतनीहारः पुनर्वसुसमन्वितः ।।

47. Saying thus, the great Muni, taking along Raama who was (ever) with Lakshmana, entered the abode in the hermitage in great joy. And he appeared like Moon along with star Punarvasu when the cold season is gone. ..... (Poet Vaalmeeki is poetic-Punarvasu happens to be Raama's Birth star!).

❍ ❍ ❍

४८. तं दृष्ट्वा मुनयः सर्वेसिद्धाश्रमनिवासिनः ।
उत्पत्योत्पत्य सहसा विश्वामित्रमपूजयन् ।।

48. Seeing him, all the sages residing in Sidhdha Hermitage,

honoured Vischwaamithra with great cheer, going up to him again & again.

❍ ❍ ❍

४९. यथार्हं चक्रिरे पूजां विश्वामित्राय धीमते ।
तथैव राजपुत्राभ्यामकुर्वन्नतिथिक्रियाम् ।।

49. They did 'honours' to Vischwaamithra, the wise sage, as befitting him; And likewise they extended hospitality to the two princes (Raama/Lakshmana).

❍ ❍ ❍

५०. मुहूर्तमथ विश्रान्तौ राजपुत्रावरिन्दमौ ।
प्राञ्जली मुनिशार्दूलमूचतू रघुनन्दनौ ।।

50. After resting for a while, the destroyers of enemies, these two princes (Raama/Lakshmana) who were darlings of Raghu-s, then addressed (Vischwaamithra), the 'tiger' amongst Muni-s, with their hands cupped in Anjali (exhibiting their reverence).

❍ ❍ ❍

५१. अद्यैव दीक्षां प्रविश भद्रं ते मुनिपुङ्गव ।
सिद्धाश्रमोऽयं सिद्धः स्यात्सत्यमस्तु वचस्तव ।।

51. Oh 'tiger' amongst Muni-s! (Oh Vischwaamithra)! May you take to Dheeksha now itself: Welfare to you; This, The Sidha Hermitage will bring you fulfillment: May your words be true.

(Readers may note: Sidhdha in Sanskrit means Fulfillment: And Dheeksha is consecration for rituals, vows, austerities etc. Total control of breath, total control of senses etc. Total devotion to The Supreme Soul).

❍ ❍ ❍

५२. एवमुक्तो महातेजा विश्वामित्रो महामुनिः ।
प्रविवेश तदा दीक्षां नियतो नियतेन्द्रियः ।।

52. When told thus, the most brilliant great Muni

Vischwaamithra, then entered (into a state of) Dheeksha, steadfast, controlling his senses.

❍ ❍ ❍

५३. कुमारावपि तां रात्रिमुषित्वा सुसमाहितौ ।
प्रभातकाले चोत्थाय पूर्वां सन्ध्यामुपास्य च ।।

५४. स्पृष्टोदकौ शुची जप्यं समाप्य नियमेन च ।
हुताग्निहोत्रमासीनं विश्वामित्रमवन्दताम् ।।

53 & 54.

The two princes spent the night in peace of mind, with devotion; And when it was morning time, got up, performed early morning Rituals ...... (like) water oblations, chanted prayers with devotion, performed Fire rituals after purifying themselves (taking baths etc.): They then bowed to Vischwaamithra who was seated there having performed Fire rituals. (earlier)

❍ ❍ ❍

Chapter 30

The Protection of the Yaaga (of Sage Vischwaamithra)

१. अथ तौ देशकालज्ञौ राजपुत्रावरिन्दमौ ।
देशे काले च वाक्यज्ञावब्रूतां कौशिकं वचः ।।

1. The destroyers of enemy, these two princes (Raama/ Lakshmana) who were masters of speech, who knew proper time & place (for doing things), then addressed the following words to (Vischwaamithra) the son of Kuschika, at the right time & place.

❍ ❍ ❍

२. भगवञ्छ्रोतुमिच्छावो यस्मिन् काले निशाचरौ ।
संरक्षणीयौ तौ ब्रह्मन्नातिवर्तेत तत्क्षणम् ।।

2. Oh lord, Oh Braamin (Vischwaamithra)! We desire to

hear at what time the two demons must be protected against, (& restrained), so that, that time may not be 'violated' (by us in negligence).

❍ ❍ ❍

३. एवं ब्रुवाणौ काकुत्स्थौ त्वरमाणौ युयुत्सया ।
सर्वेते मुनयः प्रीताः प्रशशंसुर्नृपात्मजौ ।।

3. Hearing the words spoken by the two sons of (king Dhascharatha), (words of) the two Kaakuthsa-s (Raama Lakshmana) who were in great haste desirous of fighting (with demons), all the Muni-s there (at the hermitage) said this happily.

❍ ❍ ❍

४. अद्यप्रभृति षड्रात्रं रक्षेतां राघवावुभौ ।
दीक्षां गतो ह्येष मुनिर्मौनित्वं च गमिष्यति ।।

4. This Muni Vischwaamithra is going to obtain Dheeksha: He is in vow (of total) silence; therefore the two Raaghava-s (Raama-Lakshmana) must protect (the Yaaga) for 6 days and nights from today

❍ ❍ ❍

५. तौ तु तद्वचनं श्रुत्वा राजपुत्रौ यशस्विनौ ।
अनिद्रौ षडहोरात्रं तपोवनमरक्षताम् ।।

5. Hearing their words, these two foremost princes protected (the Hermitage), this forest of penance, for 6 days & nights without sleep.

❍ ❍ ❍

६. उपासाञ्चक्रतुवीरौ यत्तौ परमधन्विनौ ।
ररक्षतुर्मुनिवरं विश्वामित्रमरिन्दमौ ।।

6. Very watchful, these brave (warriors) who were destroyers of enemies, stood guard as great wielders of bow; they protected the foremost Muni Vischwaamithra.

❍ ❍ ❍

७. अथ काले गते तस्मिन् षष्ठेऽहनि समागते ।
सौमित्रिमब्रवीद्रामो यत्तो भव समाहितः ।।

7. As time passed away & when the 6th day arrived, Raama addressed (Lakshmana) the son of Sumithra:= Be Watchful; Be Dedicated (in duty).=

❍ ❍ ❍

८. रामस्यैवं ब्रुवाणस्य त्वरितस्य युयुत्सया ।
प्रजज्वाल ततो वेदिः सोपाध्यायपुरोहिता ।।

8. When Raama who was in great (eagerness &) haste in doing battle was saying thus, The Sacrificial Fire Altar, surrounded by The Rithviks & Upaadhyaa-s (Priests etc), was burning bright.

❍ ❍ ❍

९. सदर्भचमसस्रुक्का ससमित्कुसुमोच्चया ।
विश्वामित्रेण सहिता वेदिर्जज्वाल सर्त्विजा ।।

9. The Fire mound burnt brilliantly; With Samith-s (Twigs), flowers in multitude and with Dharbha grass, vessels, drinking cups, & with Vischwaamithra & the Rithviks (surrounding the altar).

❍ ❍ ❍

१०. मन्त्रवच्च यथान्यायं यज्ञोऽसौ संप्रवर्तते ।
आकाशे च महाञ्छब्दः प्रादुरासीद्भयानकः ।।

10. This Yaaga 'is' being* done as per norms and with chants; And in the sky, a terrifying sound arose. (* Note use of present tense- ofcourse to read - was done-)

❍ ❍ ❍

११. आवार्य गगनं मेघो यथा प्रावृषि निर्गतः ।
तथा मायां विकुर्वाणौ राक्षसावभ्यधावताम् ।।

11. Like in the Rainy season when clouds that come out after covering the sky, the two demons who practised magic, ran across.

❍ ❍ ❍

१२. मारीचश्च सुबाहुश्च तयोरनुचरास्तथा ।
आगम्य भीमसमाशान् रुधिरौघानवासृजन् ।।

12. Maareecha & Subaahu and likewise, the followers of these two, came and showered loathsome & fearsome bath of blood.

❍ ❍ ❍

१३. सा तेन रुधिरोघेण वेदिर्जज्वाल मण्डिता ।
दृष्ट्वा वेदिं तथाभूतां राघवः क्रोधसंयुतः ।।
सहसाऽभिद्रुतो रामस्तावपश्यत्ततो दिवि ।।

13. Mixed with blood bath, this Fire mound shone (glowed); Seeing the Fire mound like this, (Raama) the Raaghava who was seized by wrath, rushed at once & saw these two (demons standing) in the sky.

❍ ❍ ❍

१४. तावापतन्तौ सहसा दृष्ट्वा राजीवलोचनः ।
लक्ष्मणं चाथ संप्रेक्ष्य रामो वचनमब्रवीत् ।।

14. The lotus eyed Raama, saw them falling down quickly (upon earth) and (Raama) looking at Lakshmana said these words:

❍ ❍ ❍

१५. पश्य लक्ष्मण दुर्वृत्तान् राक्षसान् पिशिताशनान् ।
मानवास्त्रसमाधूताननिलेन यथा घनान् ।।

15. Oh Lakshmana! You (are about to) See these demons of bad conduct, who eat flesh, 'Blown' away like clouds, with The Maanava weapon (discharged by me).

❍ ❍ ❍

१६. मानवं परमोदारमस्त्रं परमभास्वरम् ।
चिक्षेप परमक्रुद्धो मारीचोरसि राघवः ।।

16. (Raama now puts to good use the Divine weapons he was taught by Vischwaamithra) ...... In terrible wrath, (Raama) the Raaghava, discharged on Maareecha's

body, the Maanava Asthra (weapon) that was most lofty & which had great brilliance.

❍ ❍ ❍

१७, स तेन परमास्त्रेण मानवेन समाहतः ।
संपूर्णं योजनशतं क्षिप्तः सागरसंप्लवे ॥

17. Hit by this foremost weapon of Maanava, this (Maareecha) was hurled full 100 yojana-s (about 900 miles) away into the waters of the ocean.

❍ ❍ ❍

१८. विचेतनं विघूर्णन्तं शीतेषुमुखताडितम् ।
निरस्तं दृश्य मारीचं रामो लक्ष्मणमब्रवीत् ॥

18. Seeing that Maareecha was numbed by the hit from the tip of Maanava weapon & tossed (into the ocean) and cast away, Raama said to Lakshmana:

❍ ❍ ❍

१९. पश्य लक्ष्मण शीतेषुं मानवं धर्मसंहितम् ।
मोहयित्वा नयत्येनं न च प्राणैर्वियुज्यते ॥

19. Oh Lakshmana! See this 'Dhaarmic' Maanava weapon, this 'frigid' (weapon): It is 'leading him away', stupefying him; but is not taking lives (does not kill him).

❍ ❍ ❍

२०. इमानपि वधिष्यामि निर्घृणान्दुष्टचारिणः ।
राक्षसान् पापकर्मस्थान् यज्ञघ्नान् रुधिराशनान् ॥

20. I am going to destroy also, these blood drinking demons who are of evil conduct, who do evil deeds, who cause harm to Yaaga-s and who lack compassion.

❍ ❍ ❍

२१. इत्युक्त्वा लक्ष्मणं चाशु लाघवं दर्शयन्निव ।
संगृह्यास्त्रं ततो रामो दिव्यमाग्नेयमद्भुतम् ॥
सुबाहूरसि चिक्षेप स विद्धः प्रापतद्भुवि ॥

२२. शेषान् वायव्यमादाय निजघान महायशाः ।
राघवः परमोदारो मुनीनां मुदमावहन् ।।

21 & 22.

Saying thus to Lakshmana, then Raama exhibiting his dexterity, quickly took on the wonderful, divine, Agni (Fire) weapon and discharged it on the chest of Subaahu: Hit by this, he fell down on earth...... This most famous & lofty (Raama) the Raaghava bringing joy to the Muni-s, then took on Vaayavya Asthra & killed all other remaining demons.

❍ ❍ ❍

२३. स हत्वा राक्षसान्सर्वान् यज्ञघ्नान् रघुनन्दनः ।
ऋषिभिः पूजितस्तत्र यथेन्द्रो विजये पुरा ।।

23. (This Raama) the darling of Raghu-s, after killing all the demons who were causing harm to the Yaaga, was honoured there by the Muni-s, like Lord Indhra (being honoured) in victory in olden times.

❍ ❍ ❍

२४. अथ यज्ञे समाप्ते तु विश्वामित्रो महामुनिः ।
निरीतिका दिशो दृष्ट्वा काकुत्स्थमिदमब्रवीत् ।।

24. When the Yaaga was (successfully) completed, the great Muni Vischwaamithra, seeing the entire region freed (from demons) said this to (Raama) the Kaakuthsa:

❍ ❍ ❍

२५. कृतार्थोऽस्मि महाबाहो कृतं गुरुवचस्त्वया ।
सिद्धाश्रममिदं सत्यं कृतं राम महायशः ।।

25. Oh Raama of mighty limbs! Oh famous one! I Am Now Accomplished: Guru's (teacher's) words (of command) were honoured by you. This Sidhdha hermitage has been made pure.

❍ ❍ ❍

२६. स हि रामं प्रशस्यैवं ताभ्यां सन्ध्यामुपागमत् ।।

26. Extolling (Raama) the Raaghava thus, he performed Sandhya rituals along with these two (along with Raama & Lakshmana).

(Readers may note that Raama did not kill Maareecha but hurled him away 900 miles, putting terror into him for good).

❍ ❍ ❍

Chapter 31

Visit to Mithila (Dhascharatha is pleased. But before getting back to Ayodhya they visit Mithila)

१. अथ तां रजनीं पुत्र कृतार्थौ रामलक्ष्मणौ ।
ऊषतुर्मुदितौ वीरौ प्रहृष्टेनान्तरात्मना ।।

1. The brave Raama & Lakshmana who were pleased (by their service at Sidhdha hermitage) having accomplished their tasks, spent the night there happily with pleasant feelings.

❍ ❍ ❍

२. प्रभातायां तु शर्वर्यां कृतपौर्वाह्निकक्रियौ ।
विश्वामित्रमृषींश्चान्यान् सहितावभिजग्मतुः ।।

2. When night became bright, (in the morning), after completing morning rituals, (these two) together, approached Vischwaamithra and other Rishi-s there. (They presented themselves).

❍ ❍ ❍

३. अभिवाद्य मुनिश्रेष्ठं ज्वलन्तमिव पावकम् ।
ऊचतुर्मधुरोदारं वाक्यं मधुरभाषिणौ ।।

3. They bowed before the foremost Muni (Vischwaamithra)

who was luminescent like flame: They, who (ever) spoke sweetly, said the following sweet & lofty words.

❍ ❍ ❍

४. इमौ स्म मुनिशार्दूल किमरौ समुपस्थितौ ।
आज्ञापय यथेष्टं वै शासनं करवाव किम् ।।

4. Oh (Vischwamithra) the 'tiger' of Muni-s! We two who are standing (before you) are your 'servants'. (We are at our service); Command us as you please: What command (you give), we will do (accordingly).

❍ ❍ ❍

५. एवमुक्तास्ततस्ताभ्यां सर्व एव महर्षयः ।
विश्वामित्रं पुरस्कृत्य रामं वचनमब्रुवन् ।।

5. When told thus by these two (Princes), all the sages there with Vischwaamithra before them, then told these words to Raama:

❍ ❍ ❍

६. मैथिलस्य नरश्रेष्ठ जनकस्य भविष्यति ।
यज्ञः परमधर्मिष्ठस्तत्र यास्यामहे वयम् ।।

6. Oh foremost of men: (Oh Raama)! There is going to be a Yaaga of great Dharma (done by &) of Janaka, the king of Mithila: We are going there (to Mithila).

❍ ❍ ❍

७. त्वं चैव नरशार्दूल सहास्माभिर्गमिष्यसि ।
अद्भुतं च धनूरत्नं तत्र त्वं द्रष्टुमर्हसि ।।

7. Oh 'tiger' of men ! (Oh Raama)! You should also come with us: (Because) You alone are fit to 'See' a wonderful gem of a bow there.

❍ ❍ ❍

८. तद्धि पूर्वं नरश्रेष्ठ दत्तं सदसि दैवतैः ।
अप्रमेयबलं घोरं मखे परमभास्वरम् ।।

8. Oh foremost of men (Oh Raama)! (This bow) was

long ago given by the Deities in a Yaaga assembly: It is gruesome, its strength incomparable and it has immense brilliance (& power).

❍ ❍ ❍

९. नास्य देवा न गन्धर्वा नासुरा न च राक्षसाः ।
कर्तुमारोपणं शक्ता न कथश्चन मानुषाः ।।

9. No one, not even Dheva-s are capable of stringing this up; Nor Asura-s, nor demons, nor men, nor Ghandharva-s: However much (they try).

❍ ❍ ❍

१०. धनुषस्तस्य वीर्यं हि जिज्ञासन्तो महीक्षितः ।
न शेकुरारोपयितुं राजपुत्रा महाबलाः ।।

10. The mightily strong kings & princes who are desirous of 'Knowing' about the power of this bow, are unable even to (lift it up) and string it up.

❍ ❍ ❍

११. तद्धनुर्नरशार्दूल मैथिलस्य महात्मनः ।
तत्र द्रक्ष्यसि काकुत्स्थ यज्ञं चाद्भुतदर्शनम् ।।

11. Oh (Raama) the Kaakuthsa, the 'tiger' of men! You will see the Yaaga of the great soul king of Mithila and thus (see also) this bow of wonderful appearance (there).

❍ ❍ ❍

१२. तद्धि यज्ञफलं तेन मैथिलेनोत्तमं धनुः ।
याचितं नरशार्दूल सुनाभं सर्वदैवतैः ।।

12. Oh (Raama) 'the tiger' of men! This foremost bow which has lovely grip, was sought (& obtained) by the king of Mithila along with the Dheva-s there, as 'fruit' of a Yaaga (done long ago).

❍ ❍ ❍

१३. आयागभूतं नृपतेस्तस्य वेश्मनि राघव ।
अर्चितं विविधैर्गन्धैर्धूपैश्चागरुगन्धिभिः ।।

13. Oh (Raama) the Raaghava! In the king's palace (this bow) is (kept &) honoured: It is worshipped with various perfumes & scents, Agara & other incenses.

❍ ❍ ❍

१४. एवमुक्त्वा मुनिवरः प्रस्थानमकरोत्तदा ।
सर्षिसङ्घः सकाकुत्स्थ आमन्त्र्य वनदेवताः ।।

१५. स्वस्ति वोऽस्तु गमिष्यामि सिद्धः सिद्धाश्रमादहम् ।
उत्तरे जाह्नवीतीरे हिमवन्तं शिलोच्चयम् ।।

14 & 15.

(Although residents of Sidhdha hermitage tell Raama, it is Vischwaamithra who decides Raama's itinerary) ...... When told thus, this foremost Muni (Vischwaamithra) then worshipped the forest deities (fairies) & began journey along with multitude of Rishi-s and the (two) Kaakuthsa-s (Raama & Lakshmana)...... (And Vischwaamithra) said: Having obtained Sidhdhi (fulfillment), I am now going to the north of Sidhdha hermitage towards mountains of Himaalayas near (Jahnavi) Ganges river: May there be welfare of Swasthi to you all.

❍ ❍ ❍

१६. प्रदक्षिणं ततः कृत्वा सिद्धाश्रममनुत्तमम् ।
उत्तरां दिशमुद्दिश्य प्रस्थातुमुचक्रमे ।।

16. Then going round the incomparable Sidhdha hermitage in circumbumbulation, (Vischwaamithra) began to leave towards northerly direction.

❍ ❍ ❍

१७. तं व्रजन्तं मुनिवरमन्वयादनुसारिणाम् ।
शकटीशतमात्रं तु प्रयाणे ब्रह्मवादिनाम् ।।

१८. मृगपक्षिगणाश्चैव सिद्धाश्रमनिवासिनः ।
अनुजग्मुर्महात्मानं विश्वामित्रं महामुनिम् ।।
निवर्तयामास ततः पक्षिसङ्घान् मृगानपि ।।

17 & 18.

Hundreds of carriages carrying priests who were reciting Brammam (holy texts), followed this foremost Muni in his journey. . . (even) the multitude of birds & animals living in Sidhdha hermitage, followed this great soul Muni Vischwaamithra: (but) he sent them back, these flocks of birds, animals etc. there itself.

(Readers may note: Indians worship & honour Nature. Ecology was an integral part of life those days. Even birds & animals obeyed Dharma).

❍ ❍ ❍

१९. ते गत्वा दूरमध्वानं लम्बमाने दिवाकरे ।
वासं चक्रुर्मुनिगणाः शोणाकूले समाहिताः ।।

19. Going a long way, these, the multitude of Muni-s, (reached), camped there together, on the banks of Shona river when Sun set.

❍ ❍ ❍

२०. तेऽस्तं गते दिनकरे स्नात्वा हुतहुताशनाः ।
विश्वामित्रं पुरस्कृत्य निषेदुरमितौजसः ।।

20. When Sunset, they bathed, did Fire Rituals; And they who had incomparable brilliance, sat before Vischwaamithra.

❍ ❍ ❍

२१. रामोऽपि सहसौमित्रिर्मुनींस्तानभिपूज्य च ।
अग्रतो निषसादाथ विश्वामित्रस्य धीमतः ।।

21. And Raama who was (ever) with Lakshmana, honoured these Muni-s and then sat before the wise Vischwaamithra.

❍ ❍ ❍

२२. अथ रामो महातेजा विश्वामित्रं महामुनिम् ।
पप्रच्छ मुनिशार्दूलं कौतूहलसमन्वितः ।।

22. The most brilliant Raama, with great curiosity, asked the great Muni Vischwaamithra, the 'tiger' of munis.

❍ ❍ ❍

२३. भगवन् को न्वयं देशः समृद्धवनशोभितः ।
श्रोतुमिच्छामि भद्रं ते वक्तुमर्हसि तत्त्वतः ।।

23. Oh Lord! Whose place is this which shines with lush forests: I desire to hear: Welfare to you! You should tell me exactly.

❍ ❍ ❍

२४. चोदितो रामवाक्येन कथयामास सुव्रतः ।
तस्य देशस्य निखिलमृषिमध्ये महातपाः ।।

24. Goaded by these words of Raama, (this Vischwaamithra) the man of great penance, began to describe everything about this region.

(Note: Raama is ever keen to know all about history & geography of the regions. And of course, in Sage Vischwaamithra, he has a very great teacher to enlighten him).

Chapter 32

Description of the Family of Kowschik

१. ब्रह्मयोनिर्महानासीत् कुशो नाम महातपाः ।
अक्लिष्टव्रतधर्मश्च सज्जनप्रतिपूजकः ।।

1. (Vischwaamithra narrates another story-The history of Kowschiks) There was one Kuscha by name, son of Bramma; He was a great man of penance, unwearied in vows and observance of Dharma; He respected & honoured good men.

❍ ❍ ❍

२. स महात्मा कुलीनायां युक्तायां रघुनन्दन ।
वैदेह्यां जनयामास चतुरस्सदृशान् सुतान् ।।
कुशाम्बं कुशनाभं च अधूर्तरजसं वसुम् ।।

2. Oh (Raama) the darling of Raghu-s! This great man begot four sons like him (in character) through (his wife) Vaidhehi, who came from a befitting & good family. (The sons were) Kuschaamba, Kuschanaabha, Adhoortharajas & Vasu.

❍ ❍ ❍

३. दीप्तियुक्तान् महोत्साहान् क्षत्रधर्मचिकीर्षया ।
तानुवाच कुशः पुत्रान्धर्मिष्ठान् सत्यवादिनः ।।
क्रियतां पालनं पुत्रा धर्मं प्राप्स्यथ पुष्कलम् ।।

3. Desirous of protecting Kshathriya Dharma (Royal duty), he told these sons who were endowed with radiance, great zeal, and who were men of Dharma, & who (ever) were speaking Truth; =Oh (my) Sons! May you offer protection (to people); And (thus) obtain extensive (fruits) of Dharma. =

❍ ❍ ❍

४. कुशस्य वचनं श्रुत्वा चत्वारो लोकसंमताः ।
निवेशांश्चक्रिरे सर्वेपुराणि नृवरास्तदा ।।

4. Hearing Kuscha's words, the four noble sons who were endeared by the world, established cities (Kingdoms), all of them.

❍ ❍ ❍

५. कुशाम्बस्तु महातेजाः कौशाम्बीमकरोत्पुरीम् ।
कुशनाभस्तु धर्मात्मा पुरं चक्रे महोदयम् ।।

६. अधूर्तरजसो राम धर्मारण्यं महीपतिः ।
चक्रे पुरवरं राजा वसुश्चक्रे गिरिव्रजम् ।।

5 & 6.

The most brilliant Kuschaamba established city of

Kowschaambi; the man of Dharma Kuschanaabha established city of Mahodhaya. . . . . The 'lord' of earth, Adhoortharajas established fine city of Dharmaaranya; King Vasu established city of Girivraja.

❍ ❍ ❍

७. एषा वसुमती राम वसोस्तस्य महात्मनः ।
एते शैलवराः पञ्च प्रकाशन्ते समन्ततः ।।

7. Oh Raama! This Vasumathi (territory) is this great man Vasu's These five mountains encircle them & shines (beautifully).

❍ ❍ ❍

८. सुमागधी नदी राम मागधान् विश्रुताऽऽययौ ।
पञ्चानां शैलमुख्यानां मध्ये मालेव शोभते ।।

8. Oh Raama! (Listen): The renowned river originating in Magadha kingdom flows around the Magadha kingdom; It shines like a garland amidst the mountains.

❍ ❍ ❍

९. सैषा हि मागधी राम वसोस्तस्य महात्मनः ।
पूर्वाभिचरिता राम सुक्षेत्रा सस्यमालिनी ।।

9. Oh Raama! This originates in Magadha territory; It is that great man Vasu's; Flows from east to west; The land is fertile with excellent crops, Oh Raama.

(This region perhaps comprises Southern Nepal, Eastern end of Vindhya range mountains; Certain areas of Bihar, Madhya Pradesh).

❍ ❍ ❍

१०. कुशनाभस्तु राजर्षिः कन्याशतमनुत्तमम् ।
जनयामास धर्मात्मा घृताच्यां रघुनन्दन ।।

10. Oh Raama the darling of Raghu-s! The man of Dharma, the royal sage Kuschanaabha begot 100.

❍ ❍ ❍

११. तास्तु यौवनशालिन्यो रूपवत्यः स्वलंकृताः ।
उद्यानभूमिमागम्या प्रावृषीव शतह्रदाः ॥
१२. गायन्त्यो नृत्यमानाश्च वादयन्त्यश्च राघव ।
आमोदं परमं जग्मुर्वराभरणभूषिताः ॥

11 & 12.

Growing into lovely maidens, beautiful, well decorated, appearing like lightning during rainy season, going to (sport in) Royal garden..... Singing & dancing there, playing musical instruments, they all obtained great happiness. (Listen further) Oh Raama!...

❍ ❍ ❍

१३. अथ ताश्चारुसर्वाङ्ग्यो रूपेणाप्रतिमा भुवि ।
उद्यानभूमिमागम्य तारा इव घनान्तरे ॥

13. With every part of their bodies beautiful, these who were of incomparable beauty, went to the royal gardens (regularly) and shone like stars around the clouds.

❍ ❍ ❍

१४. ताः सर्वगुणसंपन्ना रुपयौवनसंयुताः ।
दृष्ट्वा सर्वात्मको वायुरिदं वचनमब्रवीत् ॥

14. The sustainer of life, of all life, (the lord of) Wind, seeing them who were all endowed with good qualities of youth & beauty, said these words to them:

❍ ❍ ❍

१५. अहं वः कामये सर्वा भार्या मम भविष्यथ ।
मानुषस्त्यज्यतां भावो दीर्घमायुरवाप्स्यथ ॥

15. I desire you all! Become wives to me. Give up this human form. Obtain long life.

❍ ❍ ❍

१६. चलं हि यौवनं नित्यं मानुषेषु विशेषतः ।
अक्षयं यौवनं प्राप्ता अमर्यश्च भविष्यथ ॥

16. In human life particularly, youth will always (finally & soon) pass away. Therefore you become celestials obtaining eternal youth.

❍ ❍ ❍

१७. तस्य तद्वचनं श्रुत्वा वायोरक्लिष्टकर्मणः ।
अपहास्य ततो वाक्यं कन्याशतमभाषत ।।

17. Hearing these words (of lord) Wind who is never wearied in action, these 100 maidens laughed, & then said these words:

❍ ❍ ❍

१८. अन्तश्चरसि भूतानां सर्वेषां त्वं सुरोत्तम ।
प्रभावज्ञास्तु ते सर्वाः किमस्मानवमन्यसे ।।

18. Oh foremost Dheva! You are 'found' in everyone's body (You are the free air of every living being); All know your prowess. Why are you teasing us!

❍ ❍ ❍

१९. कुशनाभसुताः सर्वाः समर्थास्त्वां सुरोत्तम ।
स्थानाच्च्यावयितुं देवं रक्षामस्तु तपः वयम् ।।

19. Oh the foremost Dheva! We who are all Kuschanaabha's daughters are capable of throwing you out of your status although you are a Dheva. Yet we protect penance (and avoid violence).

❍ ❍ ❍

२०. मा भूत् स कालो दुर्मेधः पितरं सत्यवादिनम् ।
नावमन्यस्व धर्मेण स्वयं वरमुपास्महे ।।

20. Oh fool! Do not disrespect our father who ever speaks Truth. Let him not become your (lord of) Death. As per Dharma, we shall chose our own (husbands).

❍ ❍ ❍

२१. पिता हि प्रभुरस्माकं दैवतं परमं हि सः ।
यस्य नो दास्यति पिता स नो भर्ता भविष्यति ।।

21. Our father indeed is our lord; He is our foremost 'God': Therefore to whom our father offers, they alone will become husbands (to us).

❍ ❍ ❍

२२. तासां तद्वचनं श्रुत्वा वायुः परमकोपनः ।
प्रविश्य सर्वगात्राणि बभञ्ज भगवान् प्रभुः ।।

22. Hearing such words, the lord of Wind, this lord became terribly angry and he "entered" into all parts of their body and destroyed (their virginity- a sort of celestial rape!).

❍ ❍ ❍

२३. ताः कन्या वायुना भग्ना विविशुर्नृपतेर्गृहम् ।
प्रापतन् भुवि संभ्रान्ताः सलज्जाः साश्रुलोचनाः ।।

23. Dishonoured by (Lord of) Wind, these maidens who were bewildered and felt ashamed, entered king's palace with tears in their eyes: And they fell down on earth (before their father).

❍ ❍ ❍

२४. स च ता दयिता दीनाः कन्याः परमशोभनाः ।
दृष्ट्वा भग्नास्तदा राजा संभ्रान्त इदमब्रवीत् ।।

24. Seeing these dear & most beautiful maidens miserable & 'broken' down the king then said this, bewildered.

❍ ❍ ❍

२५. किमिदं कथ्यतां पुत्र्यः को धर्ममवन्यते ।
कुब्जाः केन कृताः सर्वा चेष्टन्त्यो नाभिभाषथ ।।

२६. श्रोतुमिच्छामि तं पुत्र्यः कस्येदं कर्म गर्हितम् ।।

25 & 26.

Oh daughters: What is this? Tell (me): By whom is Dharma dishonoured? By whom have you all been made to be (like) hunchback & shrunken (women)? Why are you all not speaking? ...... Oh daughters! This condemnable act, whose is it? Why are you all not speaking? I desire to hear this.

❍ ❍ ❍

२७. एवं राजा विनिश्वास्य समाधिं सन्दधे ततः ॥

27. The king breathing hard & deep, went into 'contemplation'.

❍ ❍ ❍

Chapter 33

Brammadhatta Marries Kuschanaabha's Daughters (Vishwaamithra Continues Narration to Raama)

१. तस्य तद्वचनं श्रुत्वा कुशनाभस्य धीमतः ।
शिरोभिश्चरणौ स्पृष्ट्वा कन्याशतमभाषत ॥

1. Hearing the words of the wise Kuschanaabha, these hundred maidens touched his feet with their head (respectfully), & said.

❍ ❍ ❍

२. वायुः सर्वात्मको राजन् प्रधर्षयितुमिच्छति ।
अशुभं मार्गमास्थाय न धर्मं प्रत्यवेक्षते ॥
सोऽस्माभिरुक्तः सर्वाभिर्वायुः कामवशं गतः ॥

2. Oh king! (Oh dear father)! The lord of Air who is in every body's 'soul' did not follow Dharma. Taking to the wrong path, desires to embrocate us: Although told (& warned) by all of us, this (Lord of) Wind went into a state of passion.

❍ ❍ ❍

३. पितृमत्यः स्म भद्रं ते स्वच्छन्दे न वयं स्थिताः ।
पितरं नो वृणीष्व त्वं यदि नो दास्यते तव ॥

3. (oh father, we told him): We have father; we are not

independent; you may please ask our father; And if he gives us to you (in marriage) then welfare to you, (good luck to you).

❍ ❍ ❍

४. तेन पापानुबन्धेन वचनं न प्रतीच्छता ।
एवं ब्रुवन्त्यः सर्वाः स्मो वायुना निहता भृशम् ।।

4. Ignoring (& not accepting) our words spoken by all of us, we have become afflicted by (the action of this lord of) Wind who is 'bound' by sin. (A case of celestial 'rape', Readers may call it!)

❍ ❍ ❍

५. तासां तु वचनं श्रुत्वा राजा परमधार्मिकः ।
प्रत्युवाच महातेजाः कन्याशतमनुत्तमम् ।।

5. Hearing these words of these foremost damsels, the foremost man of Dharma, the most brilliant king addressed them all.

❍ ❍ ❍

६. क्षान्तं क्षमावतां पुत्र्यः कर्तव्यं सुमहत् कृतम् ।
ऐकमत्यमुपागम्य कुलश्चावेक्षितं मम ।।

6. Oh my daughters! Patience & forbearance, as befitting a person of restraint & endurance, was well exhibited by you (all). My family which is united (& well knit) is honoured (by your restraint).

❍ ❍ ❍

७. अलमारो हि नारीणां क्षमा हि पुरुषस्य वा ।।

7. Tolerance is the embodiment (the ornament) for men & women. Indeed.

❍ ❍ ❍

८. दुष्करं तच्च वः क्षान्तं त्रिदशेषु विशेषतः ।
यादृशी वः क्षमा पुत्र्यः सर्वासामविशेषतः ।।

8. The* Endurance (& the 'Bearing') of yours, particularly

towards celestials, is indeed arduous (and calls for tremendous self control); Oh daughters! How can I compare your endurance, particularly this unanimity (in Endurance inspite of such a violation). (Readers may note that Poet Vaalmeeki uses the word *Kshama).

❍ ❍ ❍

९. क्षमा दानं क्षमा सत्यं क्षमा यज्ञश्च पुत्रिकाः ।
क्षमा यशः क्षमा धर्मः क्षमायां विष्ठितं जगत् ।।
१०. विसृज्य कन्याः काकुत्स्थ राजा त्रिदशविक्रमः ।
मन्त्रज्ञो मन्त्रयामास प्रदानं सह मन्त्रिभिः ।।
देशे काले प्रदानस्य सदृशे प्रतिपादनम् ।।

9 & 10.

Oh daughters! Patience & Forbearance is wealth; Patience & Forbearance is Truth; Patience & Forbearance is Fame; Patience & Forbearance is Yaaga: Patience & Forbearance is Dharma; Indeed Patience & Forbearance sustains the world ..... ; Oh (Raama) the Kaakuthsa, (Listen)! After sending away the girls, the king (Kuschanaabha) whose valour was like those of Dheva-s and who had knowledge of, (who knew the value of), ministerial advice, consulted his ministers regarding the offer (of marriage of his daughters) and about the performance of marriage at proper time, place etc.

❍ ❍ ❍

११. एतस्मिन्नेव काले तु चूली नाम महामुनिः ।
ऊर्ध्वरेताः शुभाचारो ब्राह्मं तप उपागमत् ।।

11. At about this time, living in total chastity, a great Muni named Chooli of noble conduct performed penance of Brammam.

❍ ❍ ❍

१२. तप्यन्तं तमृषिं तत्र गन्धर्वी पर्युपासते ।
सोमदा नाम भद्रं ते ऊर्मिलातनया तदा ।।

12. There, while Rishi (Chooli) was doing penance, Oormila's daughter Somadha by name, a ghandharva lady, was serving (him): Welfare to you (Oh Raama listen further).

❍ ❍ ❍

१३. सा च तं प्रणता भूत्वा शुश्रूषणपरायणा ।
उवास काले धर्मिष्ठा तस्यास्तुष्टोऽभवद्गुरुः ॥

13. This woman Somadha, a woman of Dharma, bowing before him (ever), lived there, devoted in doing service to him. At one time, the Guru (Chooli) became pleased with her (taking note of her service to him).

❍ ❍ ❍

१४. स च तां कालयोगेन प्रोवाच रघुनन्दन ।
परितुष्टोऽस्मि भद्रं ते किं करोमि तव प्रियम् ॥

14. Oh Raama, the darling of Raghu-s (Listen); In due course of time, he spoke to her. = I am very pleased with you; Welfare to you; What do you desire? I will do this (& fulfill your wish)=

❍ ❍ ❍

१५. परितुष्टं मुनिं ज्ञात्वा गन्धर्वी मधुरस्वरा ।
उवाच परमप्रीता वाक्यज्ञा वाक्यकोविदम् ॥

15. Realising that this Muni (Chooli) who was well versed in speech, was pleased (with her), this Ghandharava lady, who was greatly pleased & who knew (the art of) speech, & who had sweet voice, said:

❍ ❍ ❍

१६. लक्ष्म्या समुदितो ब्राह्म्या ब्रह्मभूतो महातपाः ।
ब्राह्मेण तपसा युक्तं पुत्रमिच्छामि धार्मिकम् ॥

16. You are lofty with the power of Brammam: You are fully absorbed in Brammam; You are a man of mighty penance; I desire a son endowed with Dharma

& adorned with power (drawn from) penance of Brammam.

❍ ❍ ❍

१७. अपतिश्चास्मि भद्रं ते भार्या चास्मि न कस्य चित् ।
ब्राह्मणोपगतायाश्च दातुमर्हसि मे सुतम् ॥

17. Welfare to you! I am without a husband; I am not a wife to anybody; (Yet) You must give me who is seeking (you), the Braamin, a son.

❍ ❍ ❍

१८. तस्याः प्रसन्नो ब्रह्मर्षिर्ददौ पुत्रमनुत्तमम् ।
ब्रह्मदत्तमिति ख्यातं मानसं चूलिनः सुतम् ॥

18. Kindly disposed towards her, this Bramma Rishi (Chooli) 'offered' a son, a renowned son named Brammadatta created by Chooli with his mind. (Readers may note, that through his spiritual power, this son was 'created', there was no 10 month waiting period for this Ghandharva lady).

❍ ❍ ❍

१९. स राजा सोमदेयस्तु पुरमध्यावसत्तदा ।
कांपिल्यां परया लक्ष्म्या देवराजो यथा दिवम् ॥

19. Yet, being son of Somadha, he was a Kshathriya (although Chooli who 'created him' was a braamin). He ruled in prosperity like Lord Indhra (ruling) over celestial world. He ruled this Kaampilya.

❍ ❍ ❍

२०. स बुद्धिं कृतवान्राजा कुशनाभः सुधार्मिकः ।
ब्रह्मदत्ताय काकुत्स्थ दातुं कन्याशतं तदा ॥

20. Oh (Raama) the Kaakuthsa (listen)! At that time, king Kuschanaabha who was foremost man of Dharma, decided in his mind to offer (in marriage) his 100 daughters to Brammadatta.

❍ ❍ ❍

२१. तमाहूय महातेजा ब्रह्मदत्तं महीपतिम् ।
दददौ कन्याशतं राजा सुप्रीतेनान्तरात्मना ।।

21. The most brilliant king invited this 'lord of earth' Brammadatta; In great happiness and fullness of heart, offered these 100 girls.

❍ ❍ ❍

२२. यथाक्रमं ततः पाणीञ्जग्राह रघुनन्दन ।
ब्रह्मदत्तो महीपालस्तासां देवपतिर्यथा ।।

22. Oh (Raama) the darling of Raghu-s! Like lord of Dhevas, this 'lord of earth' Brammadatta, clasped their hands in succession.

❍ ❍ ❍

२३. स्पृष्टमात्रे ततः पाणौ विकुब्जा विगतज्वराः ।
युक्तं परमया लक्ष्म्या बभौ कन्याशतं तदा ।।

23. The moment the hands were (clasped &) touched, their 'deformity' was gone; And they became freed from worries; the 100 damsels were greatly endowed with resplendency. (Readers may remember that when Lord of Wind molested them, their bodies shriveled, they lost their charm, all due to this shame, due to their natural modesty; now they got back their natural beauty, charm etc.),

❍ ❍ ❍

२४. स दृष्ट्वा वायुना मुक्ताः कुशनाभो महीपतिः ।
बभूव परमप्रीतो हर्षं लेभे पुनः पुनः ।।

24. The 'Lord of earth' Kuschanaabha seeing them released (from the stain of molestation by Lord) of Wind, became very pleased: And his happiness increased further & further (more & more).

❍ ❍ ❍

२५. कृतोद्वाहं तु राजानं ब्रह्मदत्तं महीपतिम् ।
सदारं प्रेषयामास सोपाध्यायगणं तदा ।।

25. This 'lord of earth' (Kuschanaabha) then sent away (the newly) married King Brammadatta along with his wives, accompanied by braamins.

❍ ❍ ❍

२६. सोमदाऽपि सुसंहृष्टा पुत्रस्य सदृशीं क्रियाम् ।
यथान्यायं च गन्धर्वी स्नुषास्ताः प्रत्यनन्दत ।।
दृष्ट्वा स्पृष्ट्वा च ताः कन्याः कुशनाभं प्रशस्य च ।।

26. This Ghandharva lady Somadha, bristling with joy, seeing these girls, (touched) & hugged (& stroked) them: She extolled these daughters In-law, and Kuschanaabha, and her son's foremost deed (of marrying them), befittingly. She rejoiced greatly.

❍ ❍ ❍

Chapter 34

The Birth of Vischwaamithra

१. कृतोद्वाहे गते तस्मिन् ब्रह्मदत्ते च राघव ।
अपुत्रः पुत्रलाभाय पौत्रीमिष्टिमकल्पयत् ।।

1. (Vishwaamithra continues narration; Tells Raama about his forefathers). After the newly wed Brammadatta had left (with his 100 daughters), this (Kuschanaabha) who had no son, started the Yaaga of Puthra Kaama for obtaining a son.

❍ ❍ ❍

२. इष्ट्यां तु वर्तमानायां कुशनाभं महीपतिम् ।
उवाच परमोदारः कुशो ब्रह्मसुतस्तदा ।।

2. When Yaaga was going on, at that time, Bramma's son, the lofty Kuscha said to the lord of earth Kuschanaabha.

❍ ❍ ❍

३. पुत्रस्ते सदृशः पुत्र भविष्यति सुधार्मिकः ।
गाधिं प्राप्स्यसि येन त्वं कीर्तिं लोके च शाश्वतीम् ।।

3. (Readers may note that Kuscha comes down from Heaven to bless his son). Oh my son! You will have a son, very worthy, a man of Dharma: By this (son of yours by the name of) Gaadhi, you will obtain eternal fame & renown in the world.

❍ ❍ ❍

४. एवमुक्त्वा कुशो राम कुशनाभं महीपतिम् ।
जगामाकाशमाविश्य ब्रह्मलोकं सनातनम् ।।

4. Saying thus to the lord of earth Kuschanaabha, Kuscha entered the sky and went over to the eternal Bramma world. Oh Raama (Listen further).

❍ ❍ ❍

५. कस्यचित्त्वथ कालस्य कुशनाभस्य धीमतः ।
जज्ञे परमधर्मिष्टो गाधिरित्येव नामतः ।।

5. After sometime, to this wise Kuschanaabha, a great man of Dharma, Gaadhi by name, was born.

❍ ❍ ❍

६. स पिता मम काकुत्स्थ गाधिः परमधार्मिकः ।
कुशवंशप्रसूतोऽस्मि कौशिको रघुनन्दन ।।

6. Oh (Raama the) Kaakuthsa! (Listen)! This foremost man of Dharma, this Gaadhi is my father: Oh (Raama) the darling of Raghu-s! He was born in the family of Kuscha & (thus) I became a Kowschik.

❍ ❍ ❍

७. पूर्वजा भगिनी चापि मम राघव सुव्रता ।
नाम्ना सत्यवती नाम ऋचीके प्रतिपादिता ।।

7. My renowned (sister) Sathyavathi by name, who is a woman of vows, was born before me as sister to me. She was offered in marriage to Rishi Richika.

❍ ❍ ❍

८. सशरीरा गता स्वर्गं भर्तारमनुवर्तिनी ।
कौशिकी परमोदारा प्रवृत्ता च महानदी ।।

8. She was devoted to (& followed) her husband; And she went to heaven in her own body! And she (eventually) became a great, lofty river Kowschiki.

❍ ❍ ❍

९. दिव्या पुण्योदका रम्या हिमवन्तमुपाश्रिता ।
लोकस्य हितकामार्थं प्रवृत्ता भगिनी मम ।।

9. With wonderful divine waters and (looking) most delightful, this sister who had reached Himaalayas has come forth (to earth) desirous of doing good to the world.

❍ ❍ ❍

१०. ततोऽहं हिमवत्पार्श्वेवसामि निरतः सुखम् ।
भगिन्यां स्नेहसंयुक्तः कौशिक्यां रघुनन्दन ।।

10. Oh (Raama) the darling of Raghu-s! (Listen): Out of affection to my sister Kowschiki, I am always living happily in the slopes of Himaalayas. (at the origin of river).

❍ ❍ ❍

११. सा तु सत्यवती पुण्या सत्ये धर्मेप्रतिष्ठिता ।
पतिव्रता महाभागा कौशिकी सरितां वरा ।।

11. Amongst rivers, this woman of chastity, this illustrious Sathyavathi who is holy and steadfast in Dharma and Truth, is foremost. (Sathyavathi the woman & Kowschiki river are the same).

❍ ❍ ❍

१२. अहं हि नियमाद्राम हित्वा तां समुपागतः ।
सिद्धाश्रममनुप्राप्य सिद्धोऽस्मि तव तेजसा ।।

12. For observance of vows (of restraint), leaving her, I came here; I reached Sidhdha hermitage and (thanks to

you &) by your brilliancy, I am accomplished (& have fulfilled my Vows), Oh Raama!

❍ ❍ ❍

१३. एषा राम ममोत्पत्तिः स्वस्य वंशस्य कीर्तिता ।
देशस्य च महाबाहो यन्मां त्वं परिपृच्छसि ।।

13. Oh Raama of mighty limbs! What you asked me, all this (about) my family & my kingdom's origin have been described (to you).

❍ ❍ ❍

१४. गतोऽर्धरात्रः काकुत्स्थ कथाः कथयतो मम ।
निद्रामभ्येहि भद्रं ते मा भूद्विघ्नोऽध्वनीह नः ।।

14. Oh (Raama) the Kaakuthsa! As I was narrating stories, half the night is gone away. Get (some) sleep. Welfare to you. Let there be no impediments in our (return) journey.

❍ ❍ ❍

१५. निष्पन्दास्तरवः सर्वेनिलीना मृगपक्षिणः ।
नैशेन तमसा व्याप्ता दिशश्च रघुनन्दन ।।

15. Oh (Raama) the darling of Raghu-s! All the trees are motionless; the birds & beasts are 'clinging' together; And the 'Directions' are engulfed in darkness.of night.

❍ ❍ ❍

१६. शनैर्वियुज्यते सन्ध्या नभो नेत्रैरिवावृतम् ।
नक्षत्रतारागहनं ज्योतिर्भिरवभासते ।।

16. The early part of the night is slowly going away (it is past midnight); With stars & constellations, the sky shines as though with bright eyes 'revolving' over it.

❍ ❍ ❍

१७. उत्तिष्ठति च शीतांशुः शशी लोकतमोनुदः ।
ह्लादयन् प्राणिनां लोके मनांसि प्रभया विभो ।।

17. Oh king (Raama)! And the moon, with his cool rays,

destroying darkness of the world, rises, bringing joy to the hearts of the people with his luminescence.

❍ ❍ ❍

१८. नैशानि सर्वभूतानि प्रचरन्ति ततस्ततः ।
यक्षराक्षससङ्घाश्च रौद्राश्च पिशिताशनाः ।।

18. (But) All the night prowling living beings, the Yaksha-s & the demons and the cruel beings who devour flesh, are roaming about, hither & thither.

❍ ❍ ❍

१९. एवमुक्त्वा महातेजा विरराम महामुनिः ।
साधु साध्विति तं सर्व ऋषयो ह्यभ्यपूजयन् ।।

19. Saying thus, the most brilliant great Muni (Vischwaamithra) rested (became silent); And the Rishi-s, all of them, said= Good, Good = & they extolled him.

❍ ❍ ❍

२०. कुशिकानामयं वंशो महान्धर्मपरः सदा ।
ब्रह्मोपमा महात्मानः कुशवंश्या नरोत्तमाः ।।

20. (The Rishi-s & Muni-s praise Vischwaamithra): The family of this Kuschanaabha (the family of Vischwaamithra) is ever great; they are keen followers of Dharma: The members of Kuscha family are foremost men. Comparable to God Bramma, great souls.

❍ ❍ ❍

२१. निशेषेण भवानेव विश्वामित्रो महायशाः ।
कौशिकी च सरिच्छ्रेष्ठा कुलोद्योतकरी तव ।।

21. And you Vischwaamithra, are the most renowned: And particularly, the foremost of rivers, Kowschiki, (your sister), brings glory to your family.

❍ ❍ ❍

२२. इति तैर्मुनिशार्दूलैः प्रशस्तः कुशिकात्मजः ।
निद्रामुपागमच्छ्रीमानस्तङ्गर इवांशुमान् ।।

22. After being praised by all these noble Muni-s (these 'tigers' of Muni-s), the most honoured, resplendent, Vischwaamithra obtained (some) sleep, like the Sun obtaining sunset!

❍ ❍ ❍

२३. रामोऽपि सहसौमित्रिः किञ्चिदागतविस्मयः ।
प्रशस्य मुनिशार्दूलं निद्रां समुपसेवते ।।

23. And Raama who was (ever) with Lakshmana the son of Sumithra, after praising the foremost Muni (Vischwaamithra), then obtained sleep, wonderstruck.

❍ ❍ ❍

Chapter 35

(Vischwaamithra) Narrates about Ganges & Goddess Paarvathy)

१. उपास्य रात्रिशेषं तु शोणाकूले समाहितः ।
निशायां सुप्रभातायां विश्वामित्रोऽभ्यभाषत ।।

1. After spending the balance of night at the banks of Schona river, the composed Vischwaamithra spoke when night had ended.

❍ ❍ ❍

२. सुप्रभाता निशा राम पूर्वा सन्ध्या प्रवर्तते ।
उत्तिष्ठोत्तिष्ठ भद्रं ते गमनायाभिरोचय ।।

2. Oh Raama! Night is over with day break; Early morning Sandhya appears; Get up, get up; Welfare to you; Be pleased (& prepare) to leave (on our journey).

❍ ❍ ❍

३. तच्छ्रुत्वा वचनं तस्य कृत्वा पौर्वाह्णिकीं क्रियाम् ।
गमनं रोचयामास वाक्यं चेदमुवाच ह ॥

3. Hearing his words, he desired to leave after completing rituals; And he said the following:

❍ ❍ ❍

४. अयं शोणः शुभजलो गाधः पुलिनमण्डितः ।
कतरेण पथा ब्रह्मन् सन्तरिष्यामहे वयम् ॥

4. The waters of the good Schona river are shallow; full of sand banks: Oh Braamin! By which route shall we cross the river?

❍ ❍ ❍

५. एवमुक्तस्तु रामेण विश्वामित्रोऽब्रवीदिदम् ।
एष पन्था मयोद्दिष्टो येन यान्ति महर्षयः ॥

5. When told thus by Raama, Vischwaamithra said the following; = By which (route) the great Rishi-s go, that route is considered by me. (as proper for our journey) =

❍ ❍ ❍

६. ते गत्वा दूरमध्वानं गतेऽर्धदिवसे तदा ।
जाह्नवीं सरितां श्रेष्ठां ददृशुर्मुनिसेविताम् ॥

6. After travelling for quite a distance, when it was past mid-day, they saw the foremost river Ganges which is worshipped by Muni-s.

❍ ❍ ❍

७. तां दृष्ट्वा पुण्यसलिलां हंससारससेविताम् ।
बभूवुर्मुनयः सर्वेमुदिताः सहराघवाः ॥
तस्यास्तीरे ततश्चक्रुस्तत्रावासपरिग्रहम् ॥

7. Seeing this (Ganges) whose waters are holy and which was full with swans & cranes, the Muni-s & the two Raaghava-s, all of them became happy. Then, there, on the banks (of Ganges), they prepared their camp.

❍ ❍ ❍

८. ततः स्नात्वा यथान्यायं सन्तर्प्य पितृदेवताः ।
हुत्वा चैवाग्निहोत्राणि प्राश्य चामृवद्धविः ॥

8 & 9.

Taking baths, after performing water rituals for pleasing their forefathers and the deities as per norms, after performing Fire rituals and partaking nectar like oblations. .....they sat down on the banks of the pure river Ganges with a happy heart, surrounding the great soul Vischwaamithra on all sides.

❍ ❍ ❍

१०. संप्रहृष्टमना रामो विश्वामित्रमथाब्रवीत् ।
भगवञ्छ्रोतुमिच्छामि गङ्गां त्रिपथगां नदीम् ॥
११. त्रैलोक्यं कथमाक्रम्य गता नदनदीपतिम् ॥

10 & 11.

With an elated mind, Raama then said to Vischwaamithra:= Oh Lord! I desire to know about river Ganges which flows in Three Ways...... How did it reach the (ocean which is) the lord of all rivers, after permeating all the three worlds.? =

❍ ❍ ❍

१२. चोदितो रामवाक्येन विश्वामित्रो महामुनिः ।
वृद्धिं जन्म च गङ्गाया वक्तुमेवोपचक्रमे ॥

12. Goaded thus by Raama, the great Muni Vischwaamithra began to tell about Ganges: Its origin & its expanse.

❍ ❍ ❍

१३. शैलेन्द्रो हिमवान्नाम धातूनामाकरो महान् ।
तस्य कन्याद्वयं राम रूपेणाप्रतिमं भुवि ॥

13. (Vischwaamithra narrates another story: Origin of Ganges) ...... Oh Raama! Himavaan is the mighty lord of mountains (Lord of Himaalyas), which is the 'Creator' of all Elements: To him were two daughters, incomparable in the world for their form (beauty).

(There is strong belief that Himaalayas is the repository of all Elements of the world; Not only that, many of the medicinal plants too.

❍ ❍ ❍

१४. या मेरुदुहिता राम तयोर्माता सुमध्यमा ।
नाम्ना तु मेनका नाम पत्नी हिमवतः प्रिया ॥

14. Oh Raama! Meru's daughter, is Himavaan's beloved wife; Named Menaka, renowned; this woman of slender waist was the mother of these two (Uma & Ganga).

❍ ❍ ❍

१५. तस्यां गङ्गा समभवज्ज्येष्ठा हिमवतः सुता ।
उमा नाम द्वितीयाऽभून्नाम्ना तस्यैव राघव ॥

15. Oh (Raama) the Raaghava! (Listen); And through her, Ganga (Ganges) was the elder daughter to Himavaan; And his second (younger daughter) was the famous Uma by name.

❍ ❍ ❍

१६. अथ ज्येष्ठां सुराः सर्वे देवतार्थचिकीर्षया ।
शैलेन्द्रं वरयामासुर्गङ्गां त्रिपथगां नदीम् ॥

16. Then, all the Dheva-s, who were desirous of fulfilling the work of Dheva-s, requested this Lord of mountain (Himavaan) for (services of) the eldest, river Ganga, that flows in Three ways.

❍ ❍ ❍

१७. ददौ धर्मेण हिमवांस्तनयां लोकपावनीम् ।
स्वच्छन्दपथगां गङ्गां त्रैलोक्यहितकाम्यया ॥

17. For sake of Dharma & desirous of doing good to the three worlds, Himavaan, offered his daughter Ganga who flowed as per her wish, purifying the world.

❍ ❍ ❍

१८. प्रतिगृह्य त्रिलोकार्थं त्रिलोकहितकारिणः ।
गङ्गामादाय तेऽगच्छन् कृतार्थेनान्तरात्मना ॥

18. And these (Dheva-s) who were doing good to the three worlds, accepting Ganga and taking her along, went with a contented mind having accomplished their task, for the sake of three worlds.

❍ ❍ ❍

१९. या चान्या शैलदुहिता कन्याऽऽसीद्रघुनन्दन ।
उग्रं सा व्रतमास्थाय तपस्तेपे तपोधना ॥

19. Oh (Raama) the darling of Raghu-s (Listen): And she who was the other daughter of (Himavaan) the lord of Mountains, began to do penance, taking on rigorous vows, (considering that) wealth is penance.

❍ ❍ ❍

२०. उग्रेण तपसा युक्तां ददौ शैलवरः सुताम् ।
रुद्रायाप्रतिरूपाय उमां लोकनमस्कृताम् ॥

20. And this foremost of mountains (Himavaan) gave his daughter Uma, who was associated with many rigorous penance, & who was worshipped by all the world, to Lord Rudhra (God Schiva) of incomparable form.

❍ ❍ ❍

२१. एते ते शैलराजस्य सुते लोकनमस्कृते ।
गङ्गा च सरितां श्रेष्ठा उमा देवी च राघव ॥

21. These two daughters, Oh Raama the Raaghava, are worshipped by all the world; These two, the foremost Ganga, (River Ganges) which is foremost amongst all rivers, and Uma are daughters of the king of Mountains, (Himavaan).

❍ ❍ ❍

२२. एतत्ते सर्वमाख्यातं यथा त्रिपथगा नदी ।
खं गता प्रथमं तात गतिं गतिमतां वर ॥

22. Oh lad (Oh Raama) who is foremost amongst those who have lovely strides! How this Thripadhaga (Ganges) river first flowed in the sky, all this has been told to you. (How Ganga obtained movement as river Ganges in the sky).

❍ ❍ ❍

२३. सैषा सुरनदी रम्या शैलेन्द्रस्य सुता तदा ।
सुरलोकं समारूढा विपापा जलवाहिनी ॥

23. This beautiful daughter of (Himavaan) the lord of mountains, bereft of sin, carrying flood of waters, as a celestial river, 'climbed' (flowed) into the celestial world at that time.

(Note: This is introductory story of Ganges: The flow of Ganges as a mighty river on earth is well narrated by Vischwaamithra in following chapters.)

❍ ❍ ❍

Chapter 36

(Vischwaamithra) Narrates Uma's Glory & Majesty

१. उक्तवाक्ये मुनौ तस्मिन्नुभौ राघवलक्ष्मणौ ।
अभिनन्द्य कथां वीरावू चतुर्मुनिपुङ्गवम् ॥

1. When this Muni (Vischwaamithra) had told these words, these two brave Raghava-s, Raama & Lakshmana, rejoicing in the story, then said to (Vischwaamithra) the 'tiger' of Muni-s.

❍ ❍ ❍

२. धर्मयुक्तमिदं ब्रह्मन् कथितं परमं त्वया ।
दुहितुः शैलराजस्य ज्येष्ठाया वक्तुमर्हसि ॥
विस्तरं विस्तरज्ञोऽसि दिव्यमानुषसंभवम् ॥

2. Oh braamin! This (Story about Uma & Ganga) which is very holy, was narrated by you; You should tell in detail about the elder daughter of the king of mountains, her origin in the celestial world, her entry into the world of human beings. (Indeed) You have extensive knowledge.

❍ ❍ ❍

३. त्रीन् पथो हेतुना केन प्लावयेल्लोकपावनी ॥

3. For what reason this (Ganga) who purifies the worlds, flows in three ways?

❍ ❍ ❍

४. कथं गङ्गा त्रिपथगा विश्रुता सरिदुत्तमा ।
त्रिषु लोकेषु धर्मज्ञ कर्मभिः कैः समन्विता ॥

4. Oh knower of Dharma! What deeds are associated with Ganges that flows in three ways? How is she so renowned in the world amongst rivers?

❍ ❍ ❍

५. तथा ब्रुवति काकुत्स्थे विश्वामित्रस्तपोधनः ।
निखिलेन कथां सर्वामृषिमध्ये न्यवेदयत् ॥

5. When (Raama) the Kaakuthsa was saying this, Vischwaamithra whose wealth was penance s, then narrated the entire story fully, in front of the Rishi-s (gathered there).

❍ ❍ ❍

६. पुरा राम कृतोद्वाहो नीलकण्ठो महातपाः ।
दृष्ट्वा च स्पृहया देवीं मैथुनायोपचक्रमे ॥

6. Oh Raama (Listen)! Long ago, the (Lord) of great penance, (God Schiva the) Neelakanta who was then married, viewing (his consort) Dhevi-Uma (with passion), began to enjoy carnal pleasures in love.

❍ ❍ ❍

७. नीलकण्ठस्य देवस्य दिव्यं वर्षशतं गतम् ।
न चापि तनयो राम तस्यामासीत् परन्तप ।।

7. Oh (Raama the) tormentor of enemies! Hundred celestial years passed by to this Lord Neelakanta (God Schiva); Yet he did not get a son through her.

❍ ❍ ❍

८. ततो देवाः समुद्विग्नाः पितामहपुरोगमाः ।
यदिहोत्पद्यते भूतं कस्तत् प्रतिसहिष्यते ।।

8. The Dheva-s who were accompanied & led by God Bramma, 'trembled' (as they said). .= When a son is born (to Him), who can 'bear' & 'sustain' him? =

❍ ❍ ❍

९. अभिगम्य सुराः सर्वेप्रणिपत्येदमब्रुवन् ।।

9. All the Sura-s & Dheva-s approached (God Schiva): Bowed before Him; and said the following:

❍ ❍ ❍

१०. देवदेव महादेव लोकस्यास्य हिते रत ।
सुराणां प्रणिपातेन प्रसादं कर्तुमर्हसि ।।

10. Oh Lord of lords! Oh Mahaadheva (the great Lord Schiva) who is devoted in the welfare of this world! You must grace us even as all the Dheva-s bow to you.

❍ ❍ ❍

११. न लोका धारयिष्यन्ति तव तेजः सुरोत्तम ।
ब्राह्मेण तपसा युक्तो देव्या सह तपश्चर ।।

11. Oh foremost Dheva! The worlds cannot 'Bear' your power (& brilliance); (So we beg you); To do penance of highest Brammanical order, along with (your consort) Dhevi-Uma.

❍ ❍ ❍

१२. त्रैलोक्यहितकामार्थं तेजस्तेजसि धारय ।
रक्ष सर्वानिमान् लोकान्नालोकं कर्तुमर्हसि ।।

12. For the sake of welfare of the three worlds, (Restrain) and 'Bear' the power (in your own) body; Protect the entire world; You should not make it worldless.

(God Schiva-The Neelakanta is so powerful, even his breath may cause harm to the world; He has the Third Eye as well; The Dheva-s know that God Schiva is The Rudhra, the terrible).

❍ ❍ ❍

१३. देवतानां वचः श्रुत्वा सर्वलोकमहेश्वरः ।
बाढमित्यब्रवीत् सर्वान् पुनश्चेदमुवाच ह ॥
१४. धारयिष्याम्यहं तेजस्तेजस्येव सहोमया ।
त्रिदशाः पृथिवी चैव निर्वाणमधिगच्छतु ॥

13 & 14.

Hearing the words of the celestials, the great God of all the worlds (Schiva), addressed all of them = So Be It.= And he said further thus . . . (God Schiva said). . =. With Uma, I will Bear All My Power Within My Own Powerful (Body) Oh Dheva-s! May The Entire Earth Obtain Tranquillity. =

❍ ❍ ❍

१५. यदिदं क्षुभितं स्थानान्मम तेजो ह्यनुत्तमम् ।
धारयिष्यति कस्तन्मे ब्रुवन्तु सुरसत्तमाः ॥

15. When this, my foremost power, is 'tossed' up from this place (from my body), tell me, Oh foremost Dheva-s, who is going to 'Bear' this?

❍ ❍ ❍

१६. एवमुक्तास्ततो देवाः प्रत्यूचुर्वृषभध्वजम् ।
यत्तेजः क्षुभितं ह्येतत्तद्धरा धारयिष्यति ॥

16. When asked thus (by Schiva), the Dheva-s replied to him who has bull as His mast = That Power That Is Tossed Up, Earth Will Bear That =

❍ ❍ ❍

१७. एवमुक्तः सुरपतिः प्रमुमोच महीतले ।
तेजसा पृथिवी येन व्याप्ता सगिरिकानना ।।

17. When told thus, the lord of Dheva-s (God Schiva) shed (His power) on Earth; By this power, the earth was filled with mountains, forests etc.

❍ ❍ ❍

१८. ततो देवाः पुनरिदमूचुश्चाथ हुताशनम् ।
आविश त्वं महातेजो रौद्रं वायुसमन्वितः ।।

18. Then the Dheva-s told Agni (the lord of Fire) the following: You 'combine' with 'Vaayu' (Air, the vital breath) and Enter (the body of the) most brilliant Rudhra, (God Schiva), somehow.

❍ ❍ ❍

१९. तदग्निना पुनर्व्याप्तं संजातः श्वेतपर्वतः ।
दिव्यं शरवणं चैव पावकादित्यसन्निभम् ।।
यत्र जातो महातेजाः कार्तिकेयोऽग्निसंभवः ।।

19. Then, pervaded by Agni (Fire), this became a Snow white mountain: (and so) was born Kaarthikeya, born out of Agni, in the thicket of forests, as most powerful (son), comparable to Fire & Sun.

❍ ❍ ❍

२०. अथोमां च शिवं चैव देवाः सर्षिगणास्तदा ।
पूजयामासुरत्यर्थं सुप्रीतमनसस्ततः ।।

20. And the Dheva-s who were with Rishi-s, became very pleased at heart & worshipped Uma & Schiva greatly.

❍ ❍ ❍

२१. अथ शैलसुता राम त्रिदशानिदमब्रवीत् ।
अप्रियस्य कृतस्याद्य फलं प्राप्स्यथ मे सुराः ।।

21. Oh Raama (listen)! This daughter of mountain king, (this Uma), said the following; = Oh Dheva-s! You shall (reap) obtain the fruits of your unkindly act done upon me, now (itself).=

(Readers may note: Uma-Paarvathy is very sad that Dheva-s wanted a son from God Schiva without her being its mother; So she curses them all. Kaarthikeya was not born through her womb.)

❍ ❍ ❍

२२. इत्युक्त्वा सलिलं गृह्य पार्वती भास्करप्रभा ।
समन्युरशपत् सर्वान् क्रोधसंरक्तलोचना ॥

22. Saying thus Paarvathy (Uma), who was radiant like the Sun, took waters (as ritual) and she cursed them all in wrath, her eyes turning red due to anger (thus).

❍ ❍ ❍

२३. यस्मान्निवारिता चाहं सङ्गता पुत्रकाम्यया ।
अपत्यं स्वेषु दारेषु नोत्पादयितुमर्हथ ॥

23. Fond as I am & intent on having a son, as I was 'discarded' (by you all), you will all have no capability to beget children through your wives.

❍ ❍ ❍

२४. अद्यप्रभृति युष्माकंप्रजाः सन्तु पत्नयः ।
एवमुक्त्वा सुरान् सर्वाञ्छशाप पृथिवीमपि ॥
२५. अवने नैकरूपा त्वं बहुभार्या भविष्यसि ।
न च पुत्रकृतां प्रीतिं मत्क्रोधकलुषीकृता ॥

24 & 25.

From today, may your wives be without children; Saying thus to all the Dheva-s, she cursed The Earth as well....... Oh Earth! You Will Take On Many Forms (will be ugly as well); Will Be Wife To Many; Oh Wicked One! As You Did Not Desire That I Should Have A Son, By My Wrath, You Will Never Obtain Joy associated with Sons. You Will Be Impure!....

❍ ❍ ❍

२६. प्राप्स्यसि त्वं सुदुर्मेधे मम पुत्रमनिच्छती ॥

26. Then the Lord of Dheva-s (Schiva) seeing these Dheva-s ashamed (thus by Uma), started to go out towards the (westerly) direction that is 'protected' by Lord Varuna.

❍ ❍ ❍

२७. तान् सर्वान् व्रीडितान्दृष्ट्वा सुरान् सुरपतिस्तदा ।
गमनायोपचक्राम दिशं वरुणपालिताम् ।।

27. Then this Maheshwara (Schiva) going along, went to the peaks of the Himaalya-s on the northern side of the mountain & did penance there with Uma.

❍ ❍ ❍

२८. स गत्वा तप आतिष्ठत्पार्श्वेतस्योत्तरे गिरेः ।
हिमवत्प्रभवे श्रृङ्गे सह देव्या महेश्वरः ।।

२९. एष ते विस्तरो राम शैलपुत्र्या निवेदितः ।
गङ्गायाः प्रभवं चैव श्रृणु मे सहलक्ष्मणः ।।

28 & 29.

Oh Raama! The story of Uma, the daughter of Himavaan (the Mountain king) has been narrated to you; Likewise you & Lakshmana, may hear from me about the origin & greatness of Ganga.

(Note: Religious Indians believe that this world is cursed: Cursed by the greatest Goddess of penance, Uma-Paarvathy. The other name of Paarvathy is Aparna, one who did not even eat dried leaves that fall off from trees during the long drawn penance. No wonder this earth is full of suffering, in spite of being blessed by other Gods from time to time).

❍ ❍ ❍

Chapter 37

(Vischwaamithra Narrates) The Birth of Skandha

१. तप्यमाने तपो देवे देवाः सर्षिगणाः पुरा ।
सेनापतिमभीप्सन्तः पितामहमुपागमन् ।।

1. When the lord (God Schiva) was performing penance, the Dhevas along with multitude of Rishi-s, approached first, God Bramma, desirous of having a Senaapathi (a Commander-in-chief).

❍ ❍ ❍

२. ततोऽब्रुवन् सुराः सर्वेभगवन्तं पितामहम् ।
प्रणिपत्य सुराः सर्वेसेन्द्राः साग्निपुरोगमाः ।।

2. Then all the Dheva-s bowed before God Bramma: And these Dheva-s who were following Lord Indhra & lord of Fire, said this.

❍ ❍ ❍

३. यो नः सेनापतिर्देव दत्तो भगवता पुरा ।।

3. Oh lord! He who was 'offered' before by God (Schiva), is our Commander-in-chief. (God Shiva had promised to offer the Dheva army, a commander-in-chief to protect Dhevas).

❍ ❍ ❍

४. स तपः परमास्थाय तप्यते स्म सहोमया ।।

4. And He (God Schiva) has taken to foremost penance & is doing penance with Uma.

❍ ❍ ❍

५. यदत्रानन्तरं कार्यं लोकानां हितकाम्यया ।
संविधत्स्व विधानज्ञ त्वं हि नः परमा गतिः ।।

5. (And Dheva-s tell God Bramma further thus); Oh knower of rules & laws! For the sake of welfare of the worlds, you must think about further work that is to be done in this matter. You are indeed our foremost Refuge!

❍ ❍ ❍

६. देवतानां वचः श्रुत्वा सर्वलोकपितामहः ।
सान्त्वयन् मधुरैर्वाक्यैस्त्रिदशानिदमब्रवीत् ।।

6. Hearing these words of the Dheva-s, (God Bramma) the Godfather of all the worlds, addressed these words that were sweet, that gave comfort to the Dheva-s.

❍ ❍ ❍

७. शैलपुत्र्या यदुक्तं तदप्रजाः स्वासु पत्निषु ।
तस्या वचनमक्लिष्टं सत्यमेव न संशयः ॥

7. (Bramma tells them not to worry) What was told by the daughter of mountain king, (by this Uma), that you will not have sons through your wives, these, her words (of curse) cannot be 'shaken'. They are true (will be as she has cursed you all). No doubt about it at all.

(Dheva-s are worried that Schiva may not after all give them a 'Son' who alone will be a competent Commander-in-chief for Dhevas.)

❍ ❍ ❍

८. इयमाकाशगा गङ्गा यस्यां पुत्रं हुताशनः ।
जनयिष्यति देवानां सेनापतिमरिन्दमम् ॥

९. ज्येष्ठा शैलेन्द्रदुहिता मानयिष्यति तं सुतम् ।
उमायास्तद्बहुमतं भविष्यति न संशयः ॥

8 & 9.

(Bramma says) ...... When Lord of Fire Agni, through Ganga (Ganges) who has (now) gone to the sky region, 'Creates' a Son who will be (your) Commander-in-chief who will destroy the enemies of Dheva-s, ... this Ganga, the eldest daughter of (Himavaan) the king of mountains, will venerate this son (& bear him); And this (the birth of such a son) will be highly 'esteemed' by (her sister) Uma also. No doubt about it.

❍ ❍ ❍

१०. तच्छ्रुत्वा वचनं तस्य कृतार्था रघुनन्दन ।
प्रणिपत्य सुराः सर्वेपितामहमपूजयन् ॥

10. Oh (Raama) the darling of Raghus (Listen)! Hearing his

words, all the Dheva-s having achieved their objective, bowed before God Bramma & honoured him.

❍ ❍ ❍

११, ते गत्वा पर्वतं राम कैलासं धातुमण्डितम् ।
अग्निं नियोजयामासुः पुत्रार्थं सर्वदेवताः ।।

11. Oh Raama! (Listen)! Then all the Dheva-s went over to Kailaash, (top of Himaalayas), that is 'decorated' with various 'Elements' and they beseeched Lord of Fire, for sake of a son (who is to be their Commander-in-chief & protector).

❍ ❍ ❍

१२. कार्यमिदं देव साधयस्व हुताशन ।
शैलपुत्र्यां महातेजो गङ्गायां तेज उत्सृज ।।

12. (Dheva-s pray to Lord Agni); Oh lord of Fire (Agni)! You must fulfill this celestial work; Oh most brilliant lord! Release your power in Ganga, the daughter of mountain (king Himavaan).

❍ ❍ ❍

१३. देवतानां प्रतिज्ञाय गङ्गामभ्येत्य पावकः ।
गर्भं धारय वै देवि देवतानामिदं प्रियम् ।।

13. The lord of Fire resolved before these Dheva-s; Then went to Ganga (and said); Oh Lady! Bear this in your womb; This is the wish of Dheva-s. (Will be greatly gratified, if you bear a son.)

❍ ❍ ❍

१४. इत्येतद्वचनं श्रुत्वा दिव्यं रूपमधारयत् ।
सा तस्य महिमां दृष्ट्वा समन्तादवकीर्यत ।।

14. Hearing these words in this matter, she took on Celestial Form: "Seeing" (& thinking about) his virility, she spread herself out on all sides.

❍ ❍ ❍

१५. समन्ततस्तदा देवीमभ्यषिञ्चत पावकः ।
सर्वस्रोतांसि पूर्णानि गङ्गाया रघुनन्दन ॥

15. And the (Lord of) Fire 'wetted' this Dhevi (Ganga) everywhere: Oh Raama the darling of Raghu-s (Listen)! All the parts of Ganga's (celestial) body became full. (pregnant)

(A Divine conception: She conceived through (the sperm), the power of God Schiva, carried & impregnated by Lord of Agni.)

❍ ❍ ❍

१६. तमुवाच ततो गङ्गा सर्वदेवपुरोगमम् ।
अशक्ता धारणे देव तव तेजः समुद्धतम् ॥
दह्यमानाऽग्निना तेन संप्रव्यथितचेतना ॥

16. Then Ganga addressed him who was leader of all Dheva-; Your 'Power' (your creation) is growing (increasing beyond measure); I am unable to bear this, being 'burnt' by this (Power from) Agni I am terribly depressed in my mind.

❍ ❍ ❍

१७. अथाब्रवीदिदं गङ्गां पावको हिमवत्सुताम् ।
इह हैमवते पादे गर्भोऽयं संनिवेश्यताम् ॥

17. And Lord Agni then told Ganga the daughter of Himavaan = In that case, may this Foetus be kept in the slopes of Himaalyas= (Being conceived by Fire power of God Schiva, Ganga was unable to bear this child the full 10 months in her body: And This was growing up fast!)

❍ ❍ ❍

१८. श्रुत्वाऽग्नेर्वचनं गङ्गा तं गर्भमतिभास्वरम् ।
उत्ससर्ज महातेजः स्रोतोभ्यो रघनन्दन ॥

18. Oh most brilliant Raama! The darling of Raghu-s! (Listen further)! . . Hearing Lord Agni's words, Ganga

then released the Foetus, (gave birth to the creation in her), that shone brilliantly, from the part of her body.

❍ ❍ ❍

१९. यदस्या निर्गतं तस्मात्तप्तजाम्बूनदप्रभम् ।
काञ्चनं धरणीं प्राप्तं हिरण्यमतुलप्रभम् ।।

२०. ताम्रं कार्ष्णायसं चैव तैक्ष्ण्यादेवाभ्यजायत ।
मलं तस्याभवत्तत्र त्रपु सीसकमेव च ।
तदेतद्धरणीं प्राप्य नानाधातुरवर्धत ।।

19 & 20.

(Elements created by the Power of this Creation of Shiva). When this (foetus) that came out of her, reached the earth (& was dropped at the foothills of Himaalyas), because of this (touch) (it created), Gold, (pure) like Jambu river gold, glittering, and (also) incomparable Silver ...... Fiery Copper, Steel, were created. From its secretion, was created Tin, Lead etc.; And when this reached the earth (touched the foothills), many elements were created.

❍ ❍ ❍

२१. निक्षिप्तमात्रे गर्भेतु तेजोभिरभिरञ्जितम् ।
सर्वं पर्वतसन्नद्धं सौवर्णमभवद्वनम् ।।

21. When the foetus was 'kept' there, the entire forests found in the mountain became golden, even as the mountain was 'permeated' by brilliancy.

❍ ❍ ❍

२२. तं देशं तु ततो ब्रह्मा संप्राप्यैनमभाषत ।
जातरस्य रूपं यत्तस्माज्जातरूपं भविष्यति ।।

22. Then God Bramma who came down to this place, told him: Being created thus, this material element is going to be called Jaatharoopa.

❍ ❍ ❍

२३. जातरूपमिति ख्यातं तदाप्रभृति राघव ।
सुवर्णं पुरुषव्याघ्र हुताशनसमप्रभम् ।।
तृणवृक्षलतागुल्मं सर्वं भवति काञ्चनम् ।।

23. Oh Raama the Raaghava, the tiger of men! (Listen further); Even dust, trees, reefs, bushes became gold; From that time, gold that shines with brilliancy of fire is famously known as Jaatharoopa.

❍ ❍ ❍

२४. तं कुमारं ततो जातं सेन्द्राः साग्निमरुद्गणाः ।
क्षीरसंभावनार्थाय कृत्तिकाः समयोजयन् ।।

24. Lord Indhra, Lord Agni & the multitude of Dheva-s, commissioned Nymphs to act as Foster Mothers to this child who was born out of this Foetus, with a view to nurse it with (Breast) milk & make this strong.

❍ ❍ ❍

२५. ताः क्षीरं जातमात्रस्य कृत्वा समयमुत्तमम् ।
ददुः पुत्रोऽयमस्माकं सर्वासामिति निश्चिताः ।।

25. These (Nymphs) said: This (Child) is son to all of us; After making an agreement, (a schedule of feeding), they decided to give their milk to the child born, (prematurely).

❍ ❍ ❍

२६. ततस्तु देवताः सर्वाः कार्तिकेय इति ब्रुवन् ।
पुत्रस्त्रैलोक्यविख्यातो भविष्यति न संशयः ।।

26. All the Dheva-s said: This son will be renowned in all the three worlds as Kaarthikeya. (As one born through nursing of Krithika nymphs) No doubt about it.

❍ ❍ ❍

२७. तेषां तद्वचनं श्रुत्वा स्कन्नं गर्भपरिस्रवे ।
स्नापयन् परया लक्ष्म्या दीप्यमानमिवानलम् ।।

27. Hearing these words from them, they bathed this child,

who, like Fire, was glowing with foremost resplendency and who had 'slipped' out of the foetus.

❍ ❍ ❍

२८. स्कन्द इत्यब्रुवन् देवारस्कन्नं गर्भपरिस्रवात् ।
कार्तिकेयं महाभागं काकुत्स्थ ज्वलनोपमम् ।।

28. Oh Raama the Kaakuthsa! As this (child) came out of the womb leaping forth, 'slipping forth', the Dheva-s called this most illustrious Kaarthikeya who was comparable to Fire, Skandha. (Skandh in Sanskrit means, leaps forth, jumps, hops etc.)

❍ ❍ ❍

२९. प्रादुर्भूतं ततः क्षीरं कृत्तिकानामनुत्तमम् ।
षण्णां षडाननो भूत्वा जग्राह स्तनजं पयः ।।

29. At that time the 6 Nymphs (Krithika-s) had foremost milk (for this child); And 'Becoming' Six headed, (this child) received The Milk from their Breasts. (Another name for Kaarthikeya is Shanmugha - Six faced - six mouthed - God)

❍ ❍ ❍

३०. गृहीत्वा क्षीरमेकाम। सुकुमारवपुस्तदा ।
अजयत् स्वेन वीर्येण दैत्यसेनागणान् विभुः ।।

30. (Even as a child) One day, after receiving (Breast) Milk, this Lord with body of a (mere) child, conquered an Army of Daithya-s, by his own valour.

❍ ❍ ❍

३१. सुरसेनागणपतिं ततस्तमतुलद्युतिम् ।
अभ्यषिञ्चन् सुरगणास्समेत्याग्निपुरोगमाः ।।

31. The multitude of Dheva-s who were following (Lord of) Fire, got together and they crowned him who had incomparable power, as the Commander-in-chief of this Army of Celestials.

❍ ❍ ❍

३२. एष ते राम गङ्गाया विस्तरोऽभिहितो मया ।
कुमारसंभवश्चैव धन्यः पुण्यस्तथैव च ॥

32. (Vischwaamithra concludes narration of Birth of Skandha) Oh Raama! This origin of Ganges and likewise the birth of Kumaar, the holy, opulent (Kaarthikeya, the Skandha) has been told to you by me.

❍ ❍ ❍

३३. य इमं श्रृणुयाद्राम कार्तिकेयस्य संभवम् ।
सर्वपापविनिर्मुक्तो याति ब्रह्म सनातनम् ॥

33. Oh Raama! (In this world), this, the birth of Kaarthikeya, if one hears, (if one listens to the story), he attains eternal Brammam, released from all sins.

❍ ❍ ❍

३४. भक्तश्च यः कार्तिकेये काकुत्स्थ भुवि मानवः ।
आयुष्मान् पुत्रपौत्रैश्च स्कन्दसालोक्यमाप्नुयात् ॥

34. Oh (Raama) the Kaakuthsa! In the world, if a man is a devotee of Kaarthikeya, such a man will obtain long life along with sons & grandsons and will obtain Skandha's world (of happiness).

(Note: The birth of Skandha may appear strange to us. It is of course divine birth. The birth is Divine Conception. God Schiva's Power through Lord Agni (Fire) 'permeating' the Holy Ganga (Ganges) who 'conceives' but cannot 'Bear & hold' this 'Power' in her womb for long. This Kumaar, this Kaarthikeya, This Skandha, This Shanmugha, This Senaapathi. . . . . is one of the most revered Deities in India that is Bhaarath).

❍ ❍ ❍

Chapter 38

(Vischwaamithra Narrates)
Sagara's Aschwamedha Yaaga

१. तां कथां कौशिको रामे निवेद्य मधुराक्षराम् ।
पुनरेवापरं वाक्यं काकुत्स्थमिदमब्रवीत् ।।

1. After narrating this story with sweet words to Raama, then, (Vischwaamithra), the Kowschik said the following words; (yet) another (story) to (Raama) the Kaakuthsa.

❍ ❍ ❍

२. अयोध्याधिपतिः शूरः पूर्वमासीन्नराधिपः ।
सगरो नाम धर्मात्मा प्रजाकामः स चाप्रजाः ।।

2. Long long ago, there lived a brave, man of Dharma named Sagara as king of Ayodhya; This lord of men was desirous of having children, yet had no issues.

❍ ❍ ❍

३. वैदर्भदुहिता राम केशिनी नाम नामतः ।
ज्येष्ठा सगरपत्नी सा धर्मिष्ठा सत्यवादिनी ।।

3. Oh Raama! (Listen): And Sagara's wife, named Keschini, renowned, a woman of Dharma, was the daughter of Vidharbha king. Ever truth speaking, she was his eldest wife.

❍ ❍ ❍

४. अरिष्टनेमिदुहिता रूपेणाप्रतिमा भुवि ।
द्वितीया सगरस्यासीत्पत्नी सुमतिसंज्ञिता ।।

4. And Arishtanemi's (Kaaschyapa's) daughter named Sumathi who was incomparable in the world in beauty, was his second wife.

❍ ❍ ❍

५. ताभ्यां सह तथा राजा पत्नीभ्यां तप्तवांस्तपः ।
हिमवन्तं समाश्रित्य भृगुप्रस्रवणे गिरौ ॥

5. Then king (Sagara) along with his two wives, went to Himaalya-s & did penance in mountain Bhriguprasravana there.

❍ ❍ ❍

६. अथ वर्षशते पूर्णेतपसाऽऽराधितो मुनिः ।
सगरस्य वरं प्रादाद्भृगुः सत्यपराक्रमः ॥

6. After completing 100 years like this (in penance), the truly mighty Muni Bhrighu, who was solicited (by Sagara) through his penance, offered a boon to Sagara.

❍ ❍ ❍

७. अपत्यलाभः सुमहान् भविष्यति तवानघ ।
कीर्तिं चाप्रतिमां लोके प्राप्स्यसे पुरुषर्षभ ॥

7. (Bhrighu blesses Sagara): Oh sinless (Sagara) ! Great many sons are going to be obtained for you; Oh 'Bull' amongst men! You will also obtain fame in the world.

❍ ❍ ❍

८. एका जनयिता तात पुत्रं वंशकरं तव ।
षष्टिं पुत्रसहस्राणि अपरा जनयिष्यति ॥

8. Oh 'son'! One amongst (your wives) will beget one son who will propagate your family; The other (wife) will beget 60,000 sons.

❍ ❍ ❍

९. भाषाणां महात्मानं राजपुत्र्यौ प्रसाद्य तम् ।
ऊचतुः परमप्रीते कृताञ्जलिपुटे तदा ॥

9. The two queens who were very pleased, after honouring (this Muni) with their hands cupped in Anjali, said to this great soul (Bhrighu) who had spoken thus.

❍ ❍ ❍

१०. एकः कस्यास्सुतो ब्रह्मन् का बहून् जनयिष्यति ।
श्रोतुमिच्छावहे ब्रह्मन् सत्यमस्तु वचस्तव ।।

10. Oh Braamin (Bhrigu)! Who (from amongst us) will have one son? And who will beget many? Oh Braamin, we desire to hear this; May your words come true.

❍ ❍ ❍

११. तयोस्तद्वचनं श्रुत्वा भृगुः परमधार्मिकः ।
उवाच परमां वाणीं स्वच्छन्दोऽत्र विधीयताम् ।।

11. Hearing their words, the foremost (sage of) Dharma, told these foremost words: = In this matter, your (choice) & desire may be fulfilled. (Bhrigu leaves the option to these two wives of king, as to who should have what)=

❍ ❍ ❍

१२. एको वंशकरो वाऽस्तु बहवो वा महाबलाः ।
कीर्तिमन्तो महोत्साहाः का वा कं वरमिच्छति ।।

12. (Raama's curiosity is kindled, asks Vischwaamithra) One alone will create lineage for family; The many (60,000 sons) will be mightily strong; very renowned; will possess great zeal; Who desired what boon? (I desire to know, Oh Vischwaamithra).

❍ ❍ ❍

१३. मुनेस्तद्वचनं श्रुत्वा केशिनी रघुनन्दन ।
पुत्रं वंशकरं राम जग्राह नृपसन्निधौ ।।

13. Oh the darling of Raghu-s Oh Raama (Listen); Hearing Muni (Bhrighu's) words, Keschini who was by the side of the king (& husband) asked for one son to propagate the family.

❍ ❍ ❍

१४. षष्ठिं पुत्रसहस्राणि सुपर्णभगिनी तदा ।
महोत्साहान् कीर्तिमतो जग्राह सुमतिः सुतान् ।।

14. Likewise, the lady Sumathi who was born along with Garuda, (the King of Birds), asked for 60,000 sons of great renown and zeal.

❍ ❍ ❍

१५. प्रदक्षिणमृषिं कृत्वा शिरसाऽभिप्रणम्य तम् ।
जगाम स्वपुरं राजा सभार्योरघुनन्दन ॥

15. Oh (Raama the) darling of Raghu-s (Listen); The king along with his wives went round this Rishi (Bhrighu) in circumbumbulation, bowed to him with his head, and then left for his capital (Ayodhya).

❍ ❍ ❍

१६. अथ काले गते तस्मिञ्ज्येष्ठा पुत्रं व्यजायत ।
असमञ्ज इति ख्यातं केशिनी सगरात्मजम् ॥

16. In due course of time, the eldest Keschini begot a notorious son Asamanja, as son of Sagara.

❍ ❍ ❍

१७. सुमतिस्तु नरव्याघ्र गर्भतुम्बं व्यजायत ।
षष्टिः पुत्रसहस्राणि तुम्बभेदाद्विनिस्सृताः ॥

17. Oh (Raama), 'tiger' of men. (Listen)! And Sumathi (the other wife of Sagara) begot a 'Flesh' (a big Foetus); From this Flesh, 60,000 sons came out.

❍ ❍ ❍

१८. घृतपूर्णेषु कुम्भेषु धात्र्यस्तान् समवर्धयन् ।
कालेन महता सर्वेयौवनं प्रतिपेदिरे ॥

18. Nurses, nursed these (60,000 babies) in pots filled with oil (filled with Herbals etc.). In due course of time they all grew up to become youths.

❍ ❍ ❍

१९. अथ दीर्घेण कालेन रूपयौवनशालिनः ।
षष्टिः पुत्रसहस्राणि सगरस्याभवंस्तदा ॥

19. Sagara's 60,000 sons, in due course of time, became endowed with Youth & Beauty.

❍ ❍ ❍

२०. स च ज्येष्ठो नरश्रेष्ठः सगरस्यात्मसंभवः ।
बालान् गृहीत्वा तु जले सरय्वा रघुनन्दन ।।
प्रक्षिप्य प्रहसन्नित्यं मज्जतस्तान्निरीक्ष्य वै ।।

20. Oh Raama, the darling of Raghu-s! Although he was the eldest son of Sagara & foremost, this (Asamanja) was always catching young children and dumping them in waters of Sarayu and was 'laughing' at them while they drowned (He was a sadist).

❍ ❍ ❍

२१. एवं पापसमाचारः सज्जनप्रतिबाधकः ।
पौराणामहिते युक्तः पित्रा निर्वासितः पुरात् ।।

21. This (Asamanja) of evil behaviour who was tormenting good folks & who was keen to do harm to the citizens, was driven away from the capital by the king (his father Sagara).

❍ ❍ ❍

२२. तस्य पुत्रोंऽशुमान्नाम असमञ्जस्य वीर्यवान् ।
संमतः सर्वलोकस्य सर्वस्यापि प्रियंवदः ।।

22. This Asamanja had a son named Amschumaan: Was very brave; To everyone he spoke kindly (sweetly); He was loved by all the citizens.

❍ ❍ ❍

२३. ततः कालेन महता मतिः समभिजायत ।
सगरस्य नरश्रेष्ठ यजेयमिति निश्चिता ।।

23. Oh foremost of men (Oh Raama, listen)! After some time, a firm thought entered his mind-; = Will Do Yaaga?=(Why not!)

❍ ❍ ❍

२४. स कृत्वा निश्चयं राजा सोपाध्यायगणस्तदा ।
यज्ञकर्मणि वेदज्ञो यष्टुं समुपचक्रमे ॥

24. This king (Sagara) who knew Vedha-s, took a decision along with his group of Purohith-s to do Yaaga and so began (Aschwamedha) Yaaga.

❍ ❍ ❍

Chapter 39

Sagara's Sons' Search of The Yaaga Horse

१. विश्वामित्रवचः श्रुत्वा कथान्ते रघुनन्दनः ।
उवाच परमप्रीतो मुनिं दीप्तमिवानलम् ॥

1. (Vischwaamithra continues his story of king Sagara to Raama) Hearing Vischwaamithra's words (about Sagara), the darling of Raghu-s, (this Raama), said the following to the Muni who was radiant like fire, at the end of the (previous) narration.

❍ ❍ ❍

२. श्रोतुमिच्छामि भद्रं ते विस्तरेण कथामिमाम् ।
पूर्वको मे कथं ब्रह्मन् यज्ञं वै समुपाहरत् ॥

2. Oh Braamin (Vischwaamithra): Welfare to you. How did my forefather (Sagara) perform his Yaaga? I desire to hear the story in detail.

❍ ❍ ❍

३. तस्य तद्वचनं श्रुत्वा कौतूहलसमन्वितम् ।
विश्वामित्रस्तु काकुत्स्थमुवाच प्रहसन्निव ।
श्रूयतां विस्तरो राम सगरस्य महात्मनः ॥

3. Hearing his words, Vischwaamithra then smiled and said to (Raama) the Kaakuthsa who was seized with curiosity. Oh Raama! May you hear the great soul Sagara's (story) in detail.

❍ ❍ ❍

४. शमरश्वशुरो नाम हिमवानचलोत्तमः ।
इन्द्रदत्तवरः श्रीमानद्रिराजोऽभिषेचितः ।।
विन्ध्यपर्वतमासाद्य निरीक्षेते परस्परम् ।।

4. (Vischwaamithra continues story of Sagara to Raama).... The resplendent Himavaan by name who was (blessed with &) offered boon by Lord Indhra & who was crowned king of mountains, and who was the father-in-law of Schankara (God Schiva), extended (his reach) upto Vindhya (Ranges), (so close he got to Vindhya-s) that they could 'See' each other. (You may say that eastern part of Vindhya range was touching the South East parts of Himaalayas.)

❍ ❍ ❍

५. तयोर्मध्ये प्रवृत्तोऽभूद्यज्ञः स पुरुषोत्तम ।
स हि देशो नरव्याघ्र प्रशस्तो यज्ञकर्मणि ।।

5. Oh (Raama) the foremost of men (Listen)! The yaaga took place in between these two (mountains); Because (Oh Raama the) 'tiger' of men, that place was foremost for doing Yaaga-s.

❍ ❍ ❍

६. तस्याश्वचर्यां काकुत्स्थ दृढधन्वा महारथः ।
अंशुमानकरोत्तात सगरस्य मते स्थितः ।।

6. Oh lad, Oh Kaakuthsa! The great charioteer, great bowman, this Amschumaan, standing firm on the orders of (his grandfather) Sagara, followed the (Sacred) Horse (during the Aschwamedha).

❍ ❍ ❍

७. तस्य पर्वणि तं यज्ञं यजमानस्य वासवः ।
राक्षसीं तनुमास्थाय याज्ञीयाश्वमपाहरत् ।।

7. At the day of a parvaan (at an opportune moment), Lord Indhra, taking on the form of a demon, stole this

sacrificial Horse of the Yaaga of this (Sagara) who was doing Yaaga.

❍ ❍ ❍

८. ह्रियमाणे तुरङ्गे तु तस्मिन् यज्ञे महात्मनः ।
उपाध्यायगणाः सर्वेयजमानमथाब्रवन् ।।

8. When the Horse was snatched away in the Yaaga of this great soul (Sagara), all the multitude of Upaadhyaaya-s (Holy priests), told the Doer (of this Yaaga, Sagara) thus:

❍ ❍ ❍

९. अयं पर्वणि वेगेन याज्ञीयाश्वोऽपनीयते ।
हर्तारं जहि काकुत्स्थ हयश्चैवोपनीयताम् ।।

9. Oh (Raama) The Kaakuthsa (Listen)! = At the day of Parvan (at an opportune moment), this Yaaga Horse has been taken away by force; Conquer the abductor & may the horse be retrieved =.

❍ ❍ ❍

१०. यज्ञच्छिद्रं भवत्येतत्सर्वेषामशिवाय नः ।
तत्तथा क्रियतां राजन्यथाऽच्छिद्रः क्रतुर्भवेत् ।।

10. (They said further); = Oh King (Sagara)! This impediment to our Yaaga will become very harmful to all of us. Therefore, let it be done in such a way that this Yaaga proceeds without any loopholes. (Without the Sacred Horse, there is no Aschwamedha Yaaga).=

❍ ❍ ❍

११. उपाध्यायवचः श्रुत्वा तस्मिन् सदसि पार्थिवः ।
षष्टिं पुत्रसहस्राणि वाक्यमेतदुवाच ह ।।

11. Hearing the words of the priests, the king addressed his 60,000 sons before an assembly, the following words:

❍ ❍ ❍

१२. गतिं पुत्रा न पश्यामि रक्षसां पुरुषर्षभाः ।
मन्त्रपूतैर्महाभागैरास्थितो हि महाक्रतुः ।।

12. Oh noble sons! (Oh Ye 'Bulls' amongst men)! I cannot see the entry of demons here; Because, this great Yaaga is performed by illustrious (priests) with pure chants of prayers.

❍ ❍ ❍

१३. तद्गच्छत विचिन्वध्वं पुत्रका भद्रमस्तु वः ।
समुद्रमालिनीं सर्वां पृथिवीमनुगच्छत ।।

13. Therefore, Oh my sons! Go! Search! Welfare to you; Search the entire earth which is 'garlanded' by oceans.

❍ ❍ ❍

१४. एकैकं योजनं पुत्रा विस्तारमधिगच्छत ।।

14. Oh my sons! You 'reach' (& search) every Yojana (9 square miles) area. (Search thoroughly, like 'inch by inch'.)

❍ ❍ ❍

१५. यावत्तुरगसंदर्शस्तावत् खनत मेदिनीम् ।
नागलोकं समासाद्य विचिन्वध्वं विशेषतः ।।

१६. दिशागजानहीन्द्रं च वैनतेयं च मातुलम् ।
आमन्त्र्य सुरलोकं वै विचिन्वध्वं विशेषतः ।।

१७. उदयाचलमारभ्य निवृत्तास्तमयं गिरिम् ।
निवर्तध्वं सतुरगा आलोक्य ब्रह्मणो गृहम् ।।
तं चैव हयहर्तारं मार्गमाणा ममाज्ञया ।।

15, 16 & 17.

(Sagara gives orders to his sons); You should search till you see (& find) the Horse; Digging the Earth (if necessary); (Search) thoroughly, going to the world of reptiles...... You should search thoroughly, with permission of Dhik Gaja-s (the mythical Elephants who are supposed to 'support' the earth), Aheendhra,

Garuda (the king of birds), Maathula (the lord of reptiles), the regions of the Sura-s, ... And by my command, from sunrise to sunset (When Sun rises in Udhaya & sets in Astha), you make search, looking over Bramma's place (also); you should come back with Horse and the person who stole the Horse.

❍ ❍ ❍

१८. दीक्षितः पौत्रसहितस्सोपाध्यायगणो ह्यहम् ।
इह स्थास्यामि भद्रं वो यावत्तुरगदर्शनम् ।।

18. I am in Dheeksha (In vow): Along with my grandson (Amschumaan) and the multitude of Upaadhyaa-s, I will stay here till I see the (Sacred) Horse; Welfare to you.

❍ ❍ ❍

१९. इत्युक्ता हृष्टमनसो राजपुत्रा महाबलाः ।
प्रणम्य शिरसा तस्मै कृत्वा चापि प्रदक्षिणम् ।।
२०. जग्मुर्महीतलं राम पितुर्वचनयन्त्रिताः ।।

19 & 20.

Oh Raama (Listen further)! When told thus, the mightily strong royal princes (the 60,000 sons), who were bristling with joy did circumbambulation to him, bowed to him with their heads, ... and reached the 'earth', bound by the command of their father (Sagara).

❍ ❍ ❍

२१. योजनायामविस्तारमेकैको धरणीतलम् ।
बिभिदुः पुरुषव्याघ्र वज्रस्पर्शसमैर्भुजैः ।।

21. Oh (Raama) the 'tiger' of men! (Listen). Every one of them split open the surface of Earth with hands that were like 'The Touch of Vajra'- (Lord Indhra's thunderbolt), yojana by yojana.

❍ ❍ ❍

२२. शूलैरशनिकल्पैश्च हलैश्चापि सुदारुणैः ।
भिद्यमाना वसुमती ननाद रघुनन्दन ॥

22. Oh (Raama) the darling of Raghu-s (Listen)! The Earth, which was ripped open by Spears that were like thunderbolts, and by gruesome spades, wailed (in great agony).

❍ ❍ ❍

२३. नागानां वध्यमानानामसुराणां च राघव ।
राक्षसानां च दुर्धर्षः सत्त्वानां निनदोऽभवत् ॥

23. Oh (Raama the) Raaghava! The wailing of the living beings (of Earth) that were tortured (thus), the (suffering) of Naaga-s, of Asura-s and of the demons, became unbearable.

❍ ❍ ❍

२४. योजनानां सहस्राणि षष्टिं तु रघुनन्दन ।
बिभिदुर्धरणीं वीरा रसातलमनुत्तमम् ॥

24. Oh (Raama) the darling of Raghu-s! These warriors (60,000 of them) ripped open the Earth and the foremost Underworld, in 60,000 Yojana-s (area, of 500,000 miles square).

❍ ❍ ❍

२५. एवं पर्वतसंबाधं जम्बूद्वीपं नृपात्मजाः ।
खनन्तो नरशार्दूल सर्वतः परिचक्रमुः ॥

25. Oh (Raama) the 'lion' amongst men! (Listen)! Digging Jamboodveepa which is full of mountains, they roamed all over, these Royal princes; (The Jamboodveepa—the seven continents, around Meru India is part of this.)

❍ ❍ ❍

२६. ततो देवाः सगन्धर्वाः सासुरास्सहपन्नगाः ।
सम्भ्रान्तमनसः सर्वेपितामहमुपागमन् ॥

26. The Dheva-s who were with Ghandharva-s, Asura-s

& Pannaga-s, all of them who were terribly agitated in mind approached God Bramma.

❍ ❍ ❍

२७. ते प्रसाद्य महात्मानं विषण्णवदनास्तदा ।
ऊचुः परमसंत्रस्ताः पितामहमिदं वचः ॥

27. Paying respects to (God Bramma), the great soul who was Forefather (to all), they, who were all scared, said the following words with a down trodden face:

❍ ❍ ❍

२८. भगवन् पृथिवी सर्वा खन्यते सगरात्मजैः ।
बहवश्च महात्मानो वध्यन्ते तलवासिनः ॥

28. Oh Lord! The entire Earth is being dug up by sons of Sagara; And many great souls, many living beings in the Underworlds, are being killed thereby.

❍ ❍ ❍

२९. अयं यज्ञहरोऽस्माकमनेनाश्वोऽपनीयते ।
इति ते सर्वभूतानि हिंसन्ति सगरात्मजाः ॥

29. (The Dheva-s complain; How the 60,000 sons who are on search, deal with innocent beings)= This one has spoiled our Yaaga; By this one our horse is stolen = Saying like this, all living beings are being harassed by sons of Sagara.

❍ ❍ ❍

Chapter 40

Sagara's Sons Reduced to Ashes

१. देवतानां वचः श्रुत्वा भगवान् वै पितामहः ।
प्रत्युवाच सुसन्त्रस्तान् कृतान्तबलमोहितान् ॥

1. (Vischwaamithra continues narration to Raama: the

Sagara story) Hearing the words of Dheva-s, God Bramma the forefather of all, replied to them who were all scared & who were stupefied by the might of these (sons of Sagara) who were causing harm.

❍ ❍ ❍

२. यस्येयं वसुधा कृत्स्ना वासुदेवस्य धीमतः ।
महिषी माधवस्यैषा स एव भगवान् प्रभुः ।।
३. कापिलं रूपमास्थाय धारयत्यनिशं धराम् ।
तस्य कोपाग्निना दग्धा भविष्यन्ति नृपात्मजाः ।।

2 & 3.

(God Bramma assures): This entire Earth is Maadhava's consort, the wise Lord, God Vaasudheva's ...... Which is constantly sustained, (nourished by Him); And when (this lord) takes recourse through (Sage) Kapila (by 'entering' his) body, these (60, 000) sons of the king will be burnt to death by the fire of His wrath.

❍ ❍ ❍

४. पृथिव्याश्चापि निर्भेदो दृष्ट एव सनातनः ।
सगरस्य च पुत्राणां विनाशोऽदीर्घजीविनाम् ।।

4. (Do not worry, says Bramma; God Vishnu's spirit will enter Sage Kapila's body & this will destroy Sagara's sons who cause havoc) Further, it was ordained, this cutting up of the eternal earth and the destruction of the short lived sons of Sagara.

❍ ❍ ❍

५. पितामहवचः श्रुत्वा त्रयस्त्रिंशदरिंदम ।
देवाः परमसंहृष्टाः पुनर्जग्मुर्यथागतम् ।।

5. (God Bramma says there is divine purpose behind all this) . . . . Oh (Raama) the destroyer of enemies! (Listen); The 33 Dheva-s, when they heard the words of God Bramma, became very happy & went back as they came.

❍ ❍ ❍

६. सगरस्य च पुत्राणां प्रादुरासीन्महात्मनाम् ।
पृथिव्यां भिद्यमानायां निर्घातसमनिःस्वनः ॥

6. And when Earth was being ripped open, a mighty sound like fall of thunderbolt became audible to these eminent sons of Sagara.

❍ ❍ ❍

७. ततो भित्त्वा महीं सर्वां कृत्वा चापि प्रदक्षिणम् ।
सहिताः सागराः सर्वेपितरं वाक्यमब्रुवन् ॥

7. Then having ripped open the entire Earth, all the sons of Sagara together went back and after doing circumbambulation to their father (Sagara), they said to him;

❍ ❍ ❍

८. परिक्रान्ता मही सर्वा सत्त्ववन्तश्च सूदिताः ।
देवदानवरक्षांसि पिशाचोरगपन्नगाः ॥

8. The Earth, all of it has been gone around; The energetic Pischaacha-s, The Uraga-s, Pannaga-s have been destroyed: And so also the Dheva-s, Asura-s & Raakshasa-s.

❍ ❍ ❍

९. न च पश्यामहेऽश्वं तमश्वहर्तारमेव च ।
किं करिष्याम भद्रं ते बुद्धिरत्र विचार्यताम् ॥

9. (But) Neither the horse nor the thief of the Horse, we could see (& find). What shall we do (now)? Welfare to you. In this matter may you deliberate with your mind (the future course of action).

❍ ❍ ❍

१०. तेषां तद्वचनं श्रुत्वा पुत्राणां राजसत्तमः ।
समन्युरब्रवीद्वाक्यं सगरो रघुनन्दन ॥

10. Oh (Raama) the darling of Raghu-s! (Listen)! Hearing

the words of these sons, the foremost king Sagara became angry & said

❍ ❍ ❍

११. भूयः खनत भद्रं वो निर्भिद्य वसुधातलम् ।
अश्वहर्तारमासाद्य कृतार्थाश्च निवर्तथ ॥

11. (Sagara wants to intensify search): = Split up the earth once again and dig it up (& search thoroughly); Welfare to you all; Confronting the thief who stole the horse, you return with your mission accomplished. =

❍ ❍ ❍

१२. पितुर्वचनमास्थाय सगरस्य महात्मनः ।
षष्टिः पुत्रसहस्राणि रसातलमभिद्रवन् ॥

12. Accepting the words (of command) of their most eminent father, the 60,000 sons rushed to The Underworlds.

❍ ❍ ❍

१३. खन्यमाने ततस्तस्मिन्ददृशुः पर्वतोपमम् ।
दिशागजं विरूपाक्षं धारयन्तं महीतलम् ॥

13. When this was being dug up, they saw a (mighty form) like a mountain; the Dhischagaja named Viroopaaksha, that was supporting the earth (Mythology says Earth is supported thus!).

❍ ❍ ❍

१४, सपर्वतवनां कृत्स्नां पृथिवीं रघुनन्दन ।
धारयामास शिरसा विरूपाक्षो महागजः ॥

14. The great Gaja (pillar), this Viroopaaksha, was supporting the entire Earth along with its mountains, forests (oceans) on its head.

❍ ❍ ❍

१५. यदा पर्वणि काकुत्स्थ विश्रमार्थं महागजः ।
स्वेदाच्चालयते शीर्षं भूमिकम्पस्तदा भवेत् ॥

15. Oh (Raama) the Kaakuthsa! (Listen)! At the Parva (season), when the great Gaja, out of tiresomeness, shakes its head to seek relief & rest, there will then be earthquake!

❍ ❍ ❍

१६. तं ते प्रदक्षिणं कृत्वा दिशापालं महागजम् ।
मानयन्तो हि ते राम जग्मुर्भित्त्वा रसातलम् ।।

16. Oh Raama! They did circumbambulation to this great Gaja, and after honouring this Dhikpaala (Guardian of earth), they went along, ripping the Paathaala (Underworlds).

(The world is supposed to be supported by Mighty Mystical Forms- Various 'Directions' protected by Dhikpaala-s.)

❍ ❍ ❍

१७. ततः पूर्वां दिशं भित्त्वा दक्षिणां बिभिदुः पुनः ।
दक्षिणस्यामपि दिशि ददृशुस्ते महागजम् ।।

१८. महापद्मं महात्मानं सुमहत्पर्वतोपमम् ।
शिरसा धारयन्तं ते विस्मयं जग्मुरुत्तमम् ।।

17 & 18.

After splitting the eastern region, they split up the southern side; And again another mighty, most eminent form they saw in the southern region. . . . It was foremost, the most eminent, Mahaapadhma, which was comparable to a mountain & which was 'Bearing' the Earth on its head. They, (the 60,000 sons), were astonished.

❍ ❍ ❍

१९. ततः प्रदक्षिणं कृत्वा सगरस्य महात्मनः ।
षष्टिः पुत्रसहस्राणि पश्चिमां बिभिदुर्दिशम् ।।

19. The most eminent sons, the 60,000 sons of Sagara, did circumbambulation to it & then started digging the western region.

❍ ❍ ❍

२०. पश्चिमायामपि दिशि महान्तमचलोपमम् ।
दिशागजं सोमनसं ददृशुस्ते महाबलाः ।।

20. These mightily strong (sons of Sagara) saw a mighty Dhischagaja called Sowmanasa that was comparable to mountain, in the western direction.

❍ ❍ ❍

२१. तं ते प्रदक्षिणं कृत्वा पृष्ट्वा चापि निरामयम् ।
खनितुं समुपाक्रान्त दिशं सोमवतीं ततः ।।
उत्तरस्यामपि दिशि ददृशुर्हिमपाण्डुरम् ।

21. After doing circumbambulation to it and after enquiring about its welfare, they then began to dig up northern direction.

❍ ❍ ❍

२२. भद्रं भद्रेण वपुषा धारयन्तं महीमिमाम् ।।
समालभ्य च तं सर्वेकृत्वा चापि प्रदक्षिणम् ।

22. In the northern direction they saw (a form) called Bhadhra which was supporting the Earth with its excellent (& auspicious) body that was white like snow.

❍ ❍ ❍

२३. षष्टिः पुत्रसहस्राणि बिभिदुर्वसुधातलम् ।।
ततः प्रागुत्तरां गत्वा सागराः प्रथितां दिशम् ।

23. After enquiring about its welfare and after going round in circumbambulation, the 60,000 sons dug up the earth there.

❍ ❍ ❍

२४. रोषादभ्यखनन्सर्वेपृथिवीं सगरात्मजाः ।।
ते तु सर्वेमहात्मानो भीमवेगा महाबलाः ।

24. All the sons of Sagara went up the famous north-east direction and then, there the Sagara sons dug up well, the earth, in wrath.

❍ ❍ ❍

२५. ददृशुः कपिलं तत्र वासुदेवं सनातनम् ।।
हयं च तस्य देवस्य चरन्तमविदूरतः ।
२६. प्रहर्षमतुलं प्राप्ताः सर्वेते रघुनन्दन ।।
ते तं हयहरं ज्ञात्वा क्रोधपर्याकुलेक्षणाः ।

25 & 26.

These mightily strong, fast moving, most eminent (sons of Sagara), saw there the eternal Vaasudheva (in the form of) Sage Kapila ...... and not far, they saw the Horse roaming about near the lord (Kapila) All of them obtained immense joy (Oh Raama) the darling of Raghu's, (Listen to what happened next).

❍ ❍ ❍

२७. खनित्रलाङ्गलधरा नानावृक्षशिलाधराः ।।
अभ्यधावन्तं संक्रुद्धास्तिष्ठ तिष्ठेति चाब्रुवन् ।।

27. Thinking that he was the Horse thief, they, whose eyes were rolling in anger, rushed towards him in wrath, wielding various trees & rocks (as weapons) and carrying crowbars & pickaxes. And they said= Stop, Stop! (Meaning, Dont run away, you thief)=

❍ ❍ ❍

२८. अस्माकं त्वं हि तुरगं याज्ञीयं हृतवानसि ।
दुर्मेधस्त्वं हि संप्राप्तान् विद्धि नः सगरात्मजान् ।।

28. (These sons charge him with offense of stealing,) Oh (Raama) the darling of Raghu-s! (Listen to the story): = Oh evil one; You are the one who 'becomes' the thief of Our Yaaga Horse. You should know us who have come here, as Sagara's sons.

❍ ❍ ❍

२९. श्रुत्वा तद्वचनं तेषां कपिलो रघुनन्दन ।
रोषेण महताऽऽविष्टो हुमाऽरमकरोत्तदा ।।

29. Oh (Raama the) darling of Raghu-s! (Listen to their fate now): Hearing their words, at once Kapila who was

seized with terrible wrath, (emitted from his breath), A 'Hum' (Sound).

❍ ❍ ❍

ड३०. ततस्तेनाप्रमेयेन कपिलेन महात्मना ।
भस्मराशीकृताः सर्वेकाकुत्स्थ सगरात्मजाः ।।

30. Oh (Raama) the Kaakuthsa! By this great soul Kapila of immeasurable (prowess) all the (60,000) sons of Sagara were reduced to ashes.

(This was the fate of 60,000 sons of Sagara who perished because (a) they caused havoc on Earth & on the entire population (b) they charged an innocent man with robbery.)

❍ ❍ ❍

Chapter 41

Completion of Sagara's Yaaga

१. पुत्रांश्चिरगतान् ज्ञात्वा सगरो रघुनन्दन ।
नप्तारमब्रवीद्राजा दीप्यमानं स्वतेजसा ।।

1. (Vischwaamithra continues narration to Raama: Prelude to the story of the descent of Ganges on earth). . . . Oh (Raama) the darling of Raghu-s (Listen)! Observing that his sons had gone away for a long time, King Sagara addressed his grandson (Amschumaan) who was shining by his own brilliance.

❍ ❍ ❍

२. शूरश्च कृतविद्यश्च पूर्वैस्तुल्योऽसि तेजसा ।
पितॄणां गतिमन्विच्छ येन चाश्वोऽपवाहितः ।।

2. You are brave, well versed in knowledge, equal to your forefathers in brilliance; You find out about your

'fathers' (uncles) and also about the person by whom the horse was stolen.

❍ ❍ ❍

३. अन्तर्भौमानि भूतानि वीर्यवन्ति महान्ति च ।
तेषां त्वं प्रतिघातार्थं सासिं गृह्णीष्व कार्मुकम् ॥

3. The evil spirits (residing) in the Underworld of Earth, are very 'strong', mighty; Therefore you take along a sword with you & a Bow to counter them.

❍ ❍ ❍

४. अभिवाद्याभिवाद्यांस्त्वं हत्वा विघ्नकरानपि ।
सिद्धार्थस्सन्निवर्तस्व मम यज्ञस्य पारगः ॥

4. And bowing before all those who should be bowed to, and killing those who obstruct you, you come back as an accomplished man to complete my Yaaga.

❍ ❍ ❍

५. एवमुक्तोंशुमान् सम्यक् सगरेण महात्मना ।
धनुरादाय खड्गं च जगाम लघुविक्रमः ॥

5. When told thus by the most eminent Sagara precisely, Amschumaan went with fast strides, taking along sword & bow.

❍ ❍ ❍

६. स खातं पितृभिर्मार्गमन्तर्भौमं महात्मभिः ।
प्रापद्यत नरश्रेष्ठस्तेन राज्ञाऽभिचोदितः ॥

6. Commanded by the king (Sagara), this foremost (Amschumaan) reached the path under the Earth that had been dug up by the most eminent uncles (the 60,000 sons of his grandfather Sagara).

❍ ❍ ❍

७. दैत्यदानवरक्षोभिः पिशाचपतगोरगैः ।
पूज्यमानो महातेजा दिशागजमपश्यत ॥

7. And this most brilliant (Amschumaan) saw Dhischagaja

that is worshipped by Asura-s, Dhanava-s, Demons, Pischaacha-s, Birds, Reptiles.

❍ ❍ ❍

८. स तं प्रदक्षिणं कृत्वा पृष्ट्वा चैव निरामयम् ।
पितॄन् स परिपप्रच्छ वाजिहर्तारमेव च ॥

8. Making circumbambulation to it, and enquiring about its welfare, he asked about his 'Fathers' and also about the horse thief.

❍ ❍ ❍

९. दिशागजस्तु तच्छ्रुत्वा प्रीत्याऽऽहांशुमतो वचः ।
आसमञ्ज कृतार्थस्त्वं सहाश्वः शीघ्रमेष्यसि ॥

9. Hearing Amschumaan's words, this Dhischagaja replied affectionately; = Oh Amschumaan! You will soon return with your mission accomplished, along with (Yaaga) Horse. =

❍ ❍ ❍

१०. तस्य तद्वचनं श्रुत्वा सर्वानेव दिशागजान् ।
यथाक्रमं यथान्यायं प्रष्टुं समुपचक्रमे ॥

10. Hearing its words, he began to enquire (about their welfare) about all the Dhischagaja-s, properly and as per custom.

❍ ❍ ❍

११. तैश्च सर्वैर्दिशापालैर्वाक्यज्ञैर्वाक्यकोविदैः ।
पूजितः सहयश्चैव गन्तासीत्यभिचोदितः ॥

11. Blessed by these Dhischapaala-s who knew (art of) speech and who had command over speech, he was goaded thus: =You will go (back) with Horse.=

❍ ❍ ❍

१२. तेषां तद्वचनं श्रुत्वा जगाम लघुविक्रमः ।
भस्मराशीकृता यत्र पितरस्तत्र सागराः ॥

12. Hearing their words, (Amshumaan) who had fast (&

easy) strides, went to (the place) where his 'fathers' (the 60,000 sons) of Sagara, had been reduced to heap of ashes.

❍ ❍ ❍

१३. स दुःखवशमापन्नस्त्वसमञ्जसुतस्तदा ।
चुक्रोश परमार्तस्तु वधात्तेषां सुदुःखितः ।।

13. And this (Amschumaan) the son of Asamanja, was overwhelmed by grief by their destruction and he wailed in great sorrow, in great torment.

❍ ❍ ❍

१४. याज्ञीयं च हयं तत्र चरन्तमविदूरतः ।
ददर्श पुरुषव्याघ्रो दुःखशोकसमन्वितः ।।

14. Engulfed by grief, this 'tiger' of men (Amschumaan) saw the Yaaga horse not far from there, roaming about.

❍ ❍ ❍

१५. स तेषां राजपुत्राणां कर्तुकामो जलक्रियाम् ।
सलिलार्थी महातेजा न चापश्यज्जलाशयम् ।।

15. Desirous of doing 'Water Rituals' for them, for these (60,000) Royal princes (who were reduced to ashes), he could not find any place with water, even as he was searching for water.

❍ ❍ ❍

१६. विसार्य निपुणां दृष्टिं ततोऽपश्यत् खगाधिपम् ।
पितृणां मातुलं राम सुपर्णमनिलोपमम् ।।

16. (The king of Birds, Garuda, gives advice to Amschumaan) Oh Raama (Listen)! Casting his capable 'sight' all over (the place), he saw the king of birds, Suparna, who was uncle for his 'fathers' (As readers know, Suparna-The Garuda was born along with Amschuman's grandmother).

❍ ❍ ❍

१७. स चैनमब्रवीद्वाक्यं वैनतेयो महाबलः ।
मा शुचः पुरुषव्याघ्र वधोऽयं लोकसंमतः ।।

17. And this mightily strong Garuda said the following words to him; = Oh foremost of men! Do not grieve: This killing (of 60,000 sons of Sagara) is (going to be) good for the world. =

❍ ❍ ❍

१८. कपिलेनाप्रमेयेन दग्धा हीमे महाबलाः ।
सलिलं नार्हसि प्राज्ञ दातुमेषां हि लौकिकम् ।।

18. (Stanzas 18 to 23, this king of birds Garuda, a close relative of Amschumaan gives the reason why this killing is good for the world)

These mightily strong (60,000 sons of Sagara) were burnt by Kapila of immense power; Therefore Oh intelligent (Amschumaan)! You should not 'give' ordinary waters (as Water Rituals for the dead), Is it not!

❍ ❍ ❍

१९. गङ्गा हिमवतो ज्येष्ठा दुहिता पुरुषर्षभ ।
तस्यां कुरु महाभाग पितृणां तु जलक्रियाम् ।।

19. Oh noble (Amschumaan) the 'Bull' amongst men! Ganga is the eldest daughter of Himavaan; most illustrious; Perform Water Rituals with her (Waters-With the Ganges waters).

(A Note: Readers may note that Ganges was not flowing as river in the world long, long ago. It is Garuda who advises Amschumaan to bring the Ganges from heaven down to earth and to flow into the region where his 60,000 uncles had perished. Only Ganges waters can 'Resurrect them', says Garuda. Even today, Water Ritual is performed by Indians for their forefathers).

❍ ❍ ❍

२०. भस्मराशीकृतानेतान् प्लावयेल्लोकपावनी ।
तया क्लिन्नमिदं भस्म गङ्गया लोककान्तया ।।

२१. षष्टिं पुत्रसहस्राणि स्वर्गलोकं नयिष्यति ॥

20 & 21.

This Ganga, the purifier of the World must bathe these (60,000 dead sons of Sagara) who are reduced to ashes.; When these ashes are wetted by this (Ganga-Ganges) who is the beloved of the world ...... it will lead the 60,000 sons to heaven.

❍ ❍ ❍

२२. गङ्गामानय भद्रं ते देवलोकान्महीतलम् ।
क्रियतां यदि शक्तोऽसि गङ्गाया अवतारणम् ॥

22. Bring Ganga to Earth trom The World of Dheva-s (of heaven); If You are Capable, May The Descent of Ganga be Done; Welfare to You.

❍ ❍ ❍

२३. गच्छ चाश्वं महाभाग संगृह्य पुरुषर्षभ ।
यज्ञं पैतामहं वीर निर्वर्तयितुमर्हसि ॥

23. Oh most illustrious (Amschumaan)! Oh 'bull' amongst men (Now) You go, taking, the (Yaaga) Horse; You should complete the Yaaga of your grandfather (Sagara who is awaiting you at Ayodhya).

❍ ❍ ❍

२४. सुपर्णवचनं श्रुत्वा सोंऽशुमानतिवीर्यवान् ।
त्वरितं हयमादाय पुनरायान्महायशाः ॥

24. Hearing the words of Garuda Suparna, the very valiant Amshumaan, seized the (Yaaga) Horse, came back quickly (to Ayodhya) with great fame (having retrieved the horse).

❍ ❍ ❍

२५. ततो राजानमासाद्य दीक्षितं रघुनन्दन ।
न्यवेदयद्यथावृत्तं सुपर्णवचनं यथा ॥

25. (Listen, Oh Raama) the darling of Raghu-s! Approaching the king (Sagara) who was in Dheeksha (Vow), (Amschumaan) narrated the words of Garuda exactly as told by (Garuda) to him.

❍ ❍ ❍

२६. तच्छुत्वा घोरसमायां वाक्यमंशुमतो नृपः ।
यज्ञं निर्वर्तयामास यथातत्त्वं यथाविधि ॥

26. Hearing the gruesome words of Amschumaan (the destruction of the 60,000 son of Sagara) the king then completed the Yaaga exactly as per norms of Shaasthra-s.

❍ ❍ ❍

२७. स्वपुरं चागमच्छ्रीमानिष्टयज्ञो महीपतिः ।
गङ्गायाश्चागमे राजा निश्चयं नाभ्यगच्छत ॥

27. This resplendent King (Sagara) who had completed the Yaaga returned to his city: But he could not perceive any means to bring Ganga (to resurrect his 60,000 sons).

❍ ❍ ❍

२८, अगत्वा निश्चयं राजा कालेन महता महान् ।
त्रिशद्वर्षसहस्राणि राज्यं कृत्वा दिवं गतः ॥

28. The mighty king, unable to find means, ruled the kingdom for 30,000 years and after this long time went to heaven (died).

❍ ❍ ❍

Chapter 42

Bhageeratha's Effort in Bringing Ganges to Earth

(Vischwaamithra continues Story, tells Raama how his forefathers, the 60,000 sons were resurrected & how Bhageeratha brought Ganges down)

❍ ❍ ❍

१. कालधर्मं गते राम सगरे प्रकृतीजनाः ।
राजानं रोचयामासुरंशुमन्तं सुधार्मिकम् ।।

1. Oh Raama (Listen)! When Sagara passed away, the citizens of nobility appointed Amschumaan, the man of Dharma, as king.

❍ ❍ ❍

२. स राजा सुमहानासीदंशुमान् रघुनन्दन ।
तस्य पुत्रो महानासीद्दिलीप इति विश्रुतः ।।

2. Amschumaan was a great king: To him was a son, Dhileepa (by name), renowned & great.

❍ ❍ ❍

३. तस्मिन् राज्यं समावेश्य दिलीपे रघुनन्दन ।
हिमवच्छिखरे रम्ये तपस्तेपे सुदारुणम् ।।

3. Oh (Raama) the darling of Raghu-s! Entrusting the kingdom to Dhileepa, he did penance, a terrible penance in the beautiful peaks of Himaalaya-s.

❍ ❍ ❍

४. द्वात्रिंशच्च सहस्राणि वर्षाणि सुमहायशाः ।
तपोवनगतो राजा स्वर्गं लेभे तपोधनः ।।

4. This most famous king (Amschumaan) whose wealth was penance, having spent 32,000 years in forest of penance, reached heaven (died).

❍ ❍ ❍

५. दिलीपस्तु महातेजाः श्रुत्वा पैतामहं वधम् ।
दुःखोपहतया बुद्ध्या निश्चयं नाधिगच्छति ॥

5. And this most brilliant Dhileepa also, having heard about the destruction of his forefathers, could not perceive any solution, his mind seized by grief.

❍ ❍ ❍

६. कथं गङ्गावतरणं कथं तेषां जलक्रिया ।
तारयेयं कथं चैनानिति चिन्तापरोऽभवत् ॥

6. How to bring Ganga down? How to do water rituals for them? How can I resurrect them? . . . . Thus he became worried.

❍ ❍ ❍

७. तस्य चिन्तयतो नित्यं धर्मेण विदितात्मनः ।
पुत्रो भगीरथो नाम जज्ञे परमधार्मिकः ॥

7. To this man who was ever thinking about (& concerned with) Dharma, to this (Dhileepa) who had knowledge of 'The Self', a son was born named Bhageeratha who was foremost in Dharma.

❍ ❍ ❍

८. दिलीपस्तु महातेजा यज्ञैर्बहुभिरिष्टवान् ।
त्रिंशद्वर्षसहस्राणि राजा राज्यमकारयत् ॥

8. And this most brilliant Dhileepa, after performing many Yaaga-s spent 30,000 years as ruler of his kingdom.

❍ ❍ ❍

९. अगत्वा निश्चयं राजा तेषामुद्धरणं प्रति ।
व्याधिना नरशार्दूल कालधर्ममुपेयिवान् ॥

9. Oh (Raama) the 'lion' amongst men (Listen!) Unable to find the means to 'Uplift' them (to resurrect the 60,000 Sagara sons) this king (Dhileepa) obtained Death, (succumbed to the law of time) after illness.

❍ ❍ ❍

१०. इन्द्रलोकं गतो राजा स्वार्जितेनैव कर्मणा ।
राज्ये भगीरथं पुत्रमभ्यषिञ्चन्नरर्षभम् ।।

10. (Before dying) This noble king Dhileepa, the 'bull' amongst men, crowned his son Bhageeratha in the kingdom: By deeds done by him, (Dhileepa) went to the world of Lord Indhra (Heaven).

❍ ❍ ❍

११. भगीरथस्तु राजर्षिर्धार्मिको रघुनन्दन ।
अनपत्यो महातेजाः प्रजाकामः स चाप्रजः ।।

१२. मन्त्रिष्वाधाय तद्राज्यं गङ्गावतरणे रतः ।।

11 & 12.

(Oh Raama) The darling of Raghu-s! This man of Dharma, the most brilliant royal sage, this Bhageeratha, as he had no son, desired to have a son; He who was childless ...... entrusted his kingdom to his ministers, intent on bringing Ganga.

❍ ❍ ❍

१३. स तपो दीर्घमातिष्ठद्गोकर्णेरघुनन्दन ।
ऊर्ध्वबाहुः पञ्चतपा मासाहारो जितेन्द्रियः ।।

13. Oh (Raama) the darling of Raghu-s! (Listen)! Raising his hands high up, in the midst of Sacred Five Fires, eating only once a month, controlling his senses, he did rigorous penance in Gokarna.

❍ ❍ ❍

१४. तस्य वर्षसहस्राणि घोरे तपसि तिष्ठतः ।
अतीतानि महाबाहो तस्य राज्ञो महात्मनः ।।
सुप्रीतो भगवान् ब्रह्मा प्रजानां प्रभुरीश्वरः ।।

14. Oh (Raama of) Mighty limbs! Steadfast in (doing) this terrible penance, 1,000 years passed away for him; And the Lord of all living beings, God Bramma, was pleased with this great soul king (Bhageeratha).

❍ ❍ ❍

१५. ततः सुरगणैः सार्धमुपागम्य पितामहः ।
भगीरथं महात्मानं तप्यमानमथाब्रवीत् ।।

15. Then coming there along with multitude of Dheva-s, God Bramma the Forefather of all, addressed the great soul Bhageeratha who was in penance, thus:

❍ ❍ ❍

१६. भगीरथ महातेजः प्रीतस्तेऽहं जनेश्वर ।
तपसा च सुतप्तेन वरं वरय सुव्रत ।।

16. (God Bramma blesses Bhageeratha): Oh most brilliant Bhageeratha, the lord of men! By your well done penance, I am pleased. Oh man of good vows, ask boon.

❍ ❍ ❍

१७. तमुवाच महातेजाः सर्वलोकपितामहम् ।
भगीरथो महाभागः कृताञ्जलिरुपस्थितः ।।

17. Cupping his hands in Anjali, this most brilliant & most illustrious Bhageeratha, standing before him (in reverence), addressed him who was The Pithaamaha of all the worlds. (The Creator).

❍ ❍ ❍

१८. यदि मे भगवन् प्रीतो यद्यस्ति तपसः फलम् ।
सगरस्यात्मजाः सर्वेमत्तः सलिलमाप्नुयुः ।।

18. Oh God (Bramma)! If you are pleased with my penance and if there will be fruits (to my penance), all the sons of Sagara must receive waters from me. (The Ritual waters of Ganga).

❍ ❍ ❍

१९. गङ्गायाः सलिलक्लिन्ने भस्मन्येषां महात्मनाम् ।
स्वर्गं गच्छेयुरत्यन्तं सर्वेमे प्रपितामहाः ।।

19. And when the ashes of these eminent men are wetted with waters of Ganga, then these forefathers, all of them, (all the 60,000 sons of Sagara) should go to the

'endless' (the eternal) Heaven, (their curse by Kapila being 'lifted' by Ganges water).

❍ ❍ ❍

२०. देया च सन्ततिर्देव नावसीदेत् कुलं च नः ।
इक्ष्वाकूणां कुले देव एष मेऽस्तु वरः परः ।।

20. Oh Lord Dheva! (Oh Bramma)! And you should give me progeny for family of Ikshwaaku-s: And our race (of Ikshwaaku) should never come to an end: Oh Dheva! This is the foremost boon (I seek; may this boon be the foremost).

❍ ❍ ❍

२१. उक्तवाक्यं तु राजानं सर्वलोकपितामहः ।
प्रत्युवाच शुभां वाणीं मधुरां मधुराक्षराम् ।।

21. (God Bramma) The creator of all the world then replied to the king (Bhageeratha) who was speaking thus with auspicious sweet speech, full with sweet words.

❍ ❍ ❍

२२. तपोधन महाभाग भगीरथ महारथ ।
एवं भवतु भद्रं ते इक्ष्वाकुकुलवर्धन ।।

22. Oh most illustrious! Oh man with a wealth of penance! Oh Bhageeratha! Who fosters Ikshwaaku race Oh great charioteer (warrior)! Let It Be So: Welfare To You.

❍ ❍ ❍

२३. इयं हैमवती गङ्गा ज्येष्ठा हिमवतः सुता ।
तां वै धारयितुं राजन् हरस्तत्र नियुज्यताम् ।।
२४. गङ्गायाः पतनं राजन् पृथिवी न सहिष्यति ।
तां वै धारयितुं वीर नान्यं पश्यामि शूलिनः ।।

23 & 24.

This Ganga is Hemavathy, Himavaan's eldest daughter. May God Hara (Schiva) be worshipped in this matter of 'Bearing' her (bearing her fury)...... The Earth cannot bear the fall of this Ganga; Oh Bhageeratha, Oh brave King! I cannot possibly see any one other than Schooli (Schiva) who can bear her (fury) (Only God Schiva, can 'regulate' her through his power- Schiva can act as a dam!)

❍ ❍ ❍

२५. तमेवमुक्त्वा राजानं चाभाष्या लोककृत् ।
जगाम त्रिदिवं देवः सह सर्वैर्मरुद्गणैः ।।

25. After saying thus to the king and after extolling Ganga, the Creator of the world, (God Bramma the) Dheva, went to the celestial world along with Maruth-s.

(Note Indians believe that if a person does not 'wash away 'the sins of his forefathers, that will recoil on them & their progeny. And water rituals & Shraadha-s are performed even today for forefathers. As the sin committed by the 60,000 Sagara sons was indeed gruesome, they could be resurrected only through waters of the Holy Ganges. And in bringing Ganges down, a very great purpose is also served; World gets Ganges.)

❍ ❍ ❍

Chapter 43

The Descent of Ganges

१. देवदेवे गते तस्मिन् सोऽङ्गुष्ठाग्रनिपीडिताम् ।
कृत्वा वसुमतीं राम संवत्सरमुपासत ।।

1. (Vischwaamithra continues the Story of Ganges to Raama:.How she was brought down to earth by Bhageeratha) ...... After this lord of all lords (God Bramma) left, (Bhageeratha), for one full year, did penance, touching the earth only with the tips of his thumbs.......

❍ ❍ ❍

२. ऊर्ध्वबाहुर्निरालंबो वायुभक्षो निराश्रयः ।
अचलः स्थाणुवत् स्थित्वा रात्रिंदिवमतन्द्रितः ।।

2. ...... raising both his hands up, without any hold, 'eating' only air, without any support, standing like a pillar day & night (motionless), (ever) alert (unwearied)...... Oh Raama (this is how your forefather Bhageeratha did such a rigorous penance).

❍ ❍ ❍

३. अथ संवत्सरे पूर्णेसर्वलोकनमस्कृतः ।
उमापतिः पशुपती राजानमिदमब्रवीत् ।।

3. After one full year, (God Schiva) the lord of Uma, the Paschupathi, who is bowed by the entire world (came there &) addressed the king (Bhageeratha):

❍ ❍ ❍

४. प्रीतस्तेऽहं नरश्रेष्ठ करिष्यामि तव प्रियम् ।
शिरसा धारयिष्यामि शैलराजसुतामहम् ।।

4. (God Schiva blesses Bhageeratha): Oh foremost of men! I am pleased with you. I will fulfill your wish: I will 'Bear' (Ganga), the daughter of (Himavaan) the king of mountains, on my head.

❍ ❍ ❍

५. ततो हैमवती ज्येष्ठा सर्वलोकनमस्कृता ।
तदा सा तु महद्रूपं कृत्वा वेगं च दुस्सहम् ।।
आकाशादपतद्गङ्गा शिवे शिवशिरस्च्युत ।।

5. Then this (Ganga), the eldest daughter of Himavaan, who is worshipped by all the world, this Ganges, took on an expansive form and an unbearable Force & Fury and fell down from sky into the gracious head of God Schiva. Ah!

❍ ❍ ❍

६. अचिन्तयच्च सा देवी गङ्गा परमदुर्धरा ।
विशाम्यहं हि पातालं स्रोतसा गृह्य शमरम् ।।

6. This most unbearable lady Ganga (River) thought (arrogantly): = I Will Carry Off God Schankara (Schiva) with My Flood and Enter The Underworlds=

❍ ❍ ❍

७. तस्याऽबलेपनं ज्ञात्वा क्रुद्धस्तु भगवान् हरः ।
तिरोभावयितुं बुद्धिं चक्रे त्रिणयनस्तदा ॥

7. (but) The three eyed God (Schiva), this Hara, noticing her arrogance, became angry and got the idea, and decided to make her unseen, (disappear as though).

❍ ❍ ❍

८. सा तस्मिंन् पतिता पुण्या पुण्ये रुद्रस्य मूर्धनि ।
हिमवत्प्रतिमे राम जटामण्डलगह्वरे ॥

8. Oh Raama (Listen further)! This holy (Ganges) fell on (God Schiva the) Rudhra's head whose braided locks of hair was like holy mountain of Himaalya-s, ... cave like.

❍ ❍ ❍

९. सा कथञ्चिन्महीं गन्तुं नाशक्नोद्यत्नमास्थिता ।
नैव सा निर्गमं लेभे जटामण्डलमोहिता ॥

9. However much she tried to reach the earth, she could not: (Engulfed &) Stupefied in the hair locks (of Schiva), she did not obtain descent (on to earth).

❍ ❍ ❍

१०. तत्रैवाबभ्रमद्देवी संवत्सरगणान् बहून् ।
तामपश्यन् पुनस्तत्र तपः परममास्थितः ॥

10. And this Dhevi (Ganga) whirled around there itself for many years (Unseen by the worlds): And unable to 'see' her (& find her), (Bhageeratha) performed a foremost penance (once again).

❍ ❍ ❍

११. स तेन तोषितश्चासीत्यर्थं रघुनन्दन ।
विससर्ज ततो गङ्गां हरो बिन्दुसरः प्रति ॥

11. Oh (Raama) the darling of Raghu-s! (Listen): By this, (by Bhageeratha's penance), (God Schiva) the Hara, became pleased: and he then released Ganga (from His head) towards Bhindhu-Saras.

❍ ❍ ❍

१२. तस्यां विसृज्यमानायां सप्त स्रोतांसि जज्ञिरे ॥

12. Seven currents sprung up from her when she was discharged from the (locks of Schiva's Hair).

❍ ❍ ❍

१३. ह्लादिनी पावनी चैव नलिनी च तथाऽपरा ।
तिस्रः प्राचीं दिशं जग्मुर्गङ्गाश्शिवजलाश्शुभाः ॥

13. Hlaadhini, Paavani, likewise, the other, Nalini, the good holy waters of these three Ganga-s, went towards east.

❍ ❍ ❍

१४. सुचक्षुश्चैव सीता च सिन्धुश्चैव महानदी ।
तिस्रस्त्वेता दिशं जग्मुः प्रतीचीं तु शुभोदकाः ॥

14. The great rivers, Suchaakshu, Seetha, Sindhu, these three with good waters, went towards westerly direction.

❍ ❍ ❍

१५. सप्तमी चान्वगात्तासां भगीरथमथो नृपम् ॥

15. Then the seventh amongst them, followed king Bhageeratha.

❍ ❍ ❍

१६. भगीरथोऽपि राजर्षिर्दिव्यं स्यन्दनमास्थितः ।
प्रायादग्रे महातेजा गङ्गा तं चाप्यनुव्रजत् ॥

16. The most brilliant Royal Sage Bhageeratha, riding a wonderful chariot went first; And this Ganga followed him.

❍ ❍ ❍

१७. गगनाच्छमरशिरस्ततो धरणिमास्थिता ।
व्यसर्पत जलं तत्र तीव्रशब्दपुरस्कृतम् ।।

17. From heaven, through (Hara) Schiva's head, she reached the Earth:And there she spread her waters, making roaring sounds.

❍ ❍ ❍

१८. मत्स्यकच्छपसङ्घैश्च शिंशुमारगणैस्तथा ।
पतद्भिः पतितैश्चान्यैर्व्यरोचत वसुन्धरा ।।

18. The earth shone with the fall of multitude of fishes, tortoises, multitude of crocodiles and other species, falling down.

❍ ❍ ❍

१९. ततो देवर्षिगन्धर्वा यक्षसिद्धगणास्तथा ।
व्यलोकयन्त तां तत्र गगनाद्गां गतां तदा ।।

19. At that moment, the Dheva-s, Rishi-s, Ghandhrva-s, Yaksha-s, Sidhdha-s, in multitude, saw her, who had reached the earth like this from heaven.

❍ ❍ ❍

२०. विमानैर्नगराकारैर्हयैर्गजवरैस्तथा ।
पारिप्लवगतैश्चापि देवतास्तत्र विष्ठितः ।।

20. On horses that go energetically, on Aircrafts that were like cities in expanse, and likewise on foremost elephants, the Dheva-s (came) & stood there, particularly (these men amongst others).

❍ ❍ ❍

२१. तदद्भुततमं लोके गङ्गापतनमुत्तमम् ।
दिद्दक्षवो देवगणाः समेयुरमितौजसः ।।

21. Desirous of seeing this most wonderful & foremost descent of Ganga on earth, the multitude of Dheva-s of incomparable brilliance assembled together.

❍ ❍ ❍

२२. संपतद्भिः सुरगणैस्तेषां चाभरणौजसा ।
शतादित्यमिवाभाति गगनं गततोयदम् ॥

22. The cloudless sky appeared as though it was with 100 suns by the multitude of Dheva-s who had assembled there, by the glitter of their ornaments.

❍ ❍ ❍

२३. शिंशुमारोरगगणैर्मीनैरपि च चञ्चलैः ।
विद्युद्भिरिव नक्षत्रैराकाशमभवत्तदा ॥

23. At that time, the sky appeared like stars & lightning, by the multitude of jumping crocodiles, (River) snakes & fishes.

❍ ❍ ❍

२४. पाण्डुरैः सलिलोत्पीडैः कीर्यमाणैः समन्ततः ।
शारदाभ्रैरिवाकीर्णं गगनं हंससंप्लवैः ॥

24. Like the sky during autumn clouds when it is full & scattered with multitude of whitish yellow swans, (the sky) appeared by the vast surging waters spread everywhere.

❍ ❍ ❍

२५. क्वचिद्द्रुततरं याति कुटिलं क्वचिदायतम् ।
विततं क्वचिदुद्धूतं क्वचिद्याति शनैः शनैः ॥

25. At some places (River) went fast; at some places, it went straight; and in some places windingly; at some places it 'dropped' (as a waterfall): and in some place it rose (as though): In some places went slowly and slowly.

❍ ❍ ❍

२६. सलिलेनैव सलिलं क्वचिदभ्याहतं पुनः ।
मुहुरूर्ध्वपथं गत्वा पपात वसुधां पुनः ॥

26. At some place the waters rose up high, knocked about by surging (water waves) and then fell back on the bed (of river: like tidal waves of ocean).

❍ ❍ ❍

२७. विष्णुपादात् परिभ्रष्टं प्लावयित्वेन्दुमण्डलम् ।
तच्छम्भरशिरो भ्रष्टं भ्रष्टं भूमितले पुनः ।।
व्यरोचत तदा तोयं निर्मलं गतकल्मषम् ।।

27. Flowing out from the feet of God Vishnu, crossing over the region of Moon, entering through God Schankara's head and emerging out once again, jumping on to Earth, this Water (of Ganga) shone (bright) and clear, bereft of any stain.

❍ ❍ ❍

२८. तत्र देवर्षिगन्धर्वा वसुधातलवासिनः ।
भवाङ्गपतितं तोयं पवित्रमिति पस्पृशुः ।।

28. The living beings on earth, the Dheva-s, Rishi-s, Ghandharva-s, extolled this Water (of Ganga) that came out of the body of God, as (Holy &) Sacred.

❍ ❍ ❍

२९. शापात् प्रपतिता ये च गगनाद्वसुधातलम् ।
कृत्वा तत्राभिषेकं ते बभूवुर्गतकल्मषाः ।।

29. Whoever, by curse (was thrown out) from heaven and fell on earth, they all, after taking bath in this (Ganga), became sinless & stainless.

❍ ❍ ❍

३०. धूतपापाः पुनस्तेन तोयेनाथ सुभास्वता ।
पुनराकाशमाविश्य स्वान् लोकान् प्रतिपेदिरे ।।

30. By (taking baths in) the beautiful waters, they entered once again the Sky, being rid of their sins again, and they reached their worlds (of Heaven).

❍ ❍ ❍

३१. मुमुदे मुदितो लोकस्तेन तोयेन भास्वता ।
कृताभिषेको गङ्गायां बभूव विगतक्लमः ।।

31. By these splendid waters, the world rejoiced with

happiness; Having 'bathed' by Ganges, (the world) was relieved from pain & suffering.

❍ ❍ ❍

३२. भगीरथोऽपि राजर्षिर्दिव्यं स्यन्दनमास्थितः ।
प्रायादग्रे महातेजस्तं गङ्गा पृष्ठतोऽन्वगात् ।।

32. (Even the world was purified by Ganges: No wonder Ganges is very holy to Indians): . . . The most brilliant royal sage Bhageeratha, riding on a chariot, went first; And Ganga followed him.

❍ ❍ ❍

३३. देवाः सर्षिगणाः सर्वेदैत्यदानवराक्षसाः ।
गन्धर्वयक्षप्रवरः सकिन्नरमहोरगाः ।।

३४. सर्वाश्चाप्सरसो राम भगीरथरथानुगाः ।
गङ्गामन्वगमन् प्रीताः सर्वेजलचराश्च ये ।।

33 & 34.

Dheva-s, multitude of Rishi-s, Daithyas, Dhaanava-s, Demons, Kinnara-s, Ghandharva-s, Yasha-s, Maha-Uraga-s, Yaksha-s. . all of them. . . and all the Apsara (maidens) and all the marine species, following Bhageeratha, went along, following Ganga in joy.

❍ ❍ ❍

३५. यतो भगीरथो राजा ततो गङ्गा यशस्विनी ।
जगाम सरितां श्रेष्ठा सर्वपापप्रणाशिनी ।।

35. Where the king (Bhageeartha went), there this Ganga, the famous & foremost of rivers which destroyed all sins, went along.

❍ ❍ ❍

३६. ततो हि यजमानस्य जह्नोरद्भुतकर्मणः ।
गङ्गा संप्लावयागास यज्ञवाटं महात्मनः ।।

36. Then Ganga submerged The Yaaga region of the

great soul Sage Jahnu of wonderful deeds, the doer of (foremost) Yaaga-s.

❍ ❍ ❍

३७. तस्यावलेपनं ज्ञात्वा क्रुद्धो जह्नुश्च राघव ।
अपिबच्च जलं सर्वं गङ्गायाः परमाद्भुतम् ।।

37. Oh (Raama) the Raaghava (Listen)! Realising that Ganga had 'smeared' (& deluged his Yaaga place), the sage Jahnu became angry & miraculously drank up all of Ganga's waters. (Another instance of Ganga's arrogance: First with God Schiva, now with sage Jahnu).

❍ ❍ ❍

३८. ततो देवाः सगन्धर्वा ऋषयश्च सुविस्मिताः ।
पूजयन्ति महात्मानं जह्नुं पुरुषसत्तमम् ।।
गङ्गां चापि नयन्ति स्म दुहितृत्वे महात्मनः ।।

38. Then the Dheva-s along with Ghandharva-s & Rishi-s who were all perplexed (& amazed), worshipped the great soul (Sage Jahnu) who was foremost of men; They 'goaded' this great soul to accept this Ganga as his 'Daughter'.

❍ ❍ ❍

३९. ततस्तुष्टो महातेजाः श्रोत्राभ्यामसृजत् पुनः ।।
४०. तस्माज्जह्नुसुता गङ्गा प्रोच्यते जाह्नवीति च ।।

39 & 40.

(Treat her like your daughter, let Ganga come out from your body, beg all these Rishi-s & others).. Then the most brilliant (Sage) being pleased, once again discharged (this Ganges waters) through his Ears. . . . . . Therefore, as Jahnu's 'daughter' (having come out of his body), Ganges is called Jahnavi (as well).

❍ ❍ ❍

४१. जगाम च पुनर्गङ्गा भगीरथरथानुगा ।
विवेश सागरं चापि सा सरित्प्रवरा तदा ।।
रसातलमुपागच्छत् सिद्ध्यर्थं तस्य कर्मणः ।।

41. And Ganges once again followed, went along with Bhageeratha: This foremost of rivers reached the ocean: And for the sake of fulfilling his mission, she reached the Paathaala (Underworld).

❍ ❍ ❍

४२. भगीरथोऽपि राजर्षिर्गङ्गामादाय यत्नतः ।
पितामहान् भस्मकृतानपश्यद्दीनचेतनः ।।

42. And thus, the royal sage, this Bhageeratha, with great effort, brought Ganges and saw his forefathers (the 60,000 sons of Sagara) who had been reduced to ashes, with a dejected spirit.

❍ ❍ ❍

४३. अथ तद्भस्मनां राशिं गङ्गासलिलमुत्तमम् ।
प्लावयद्धूतपाप्मानः स्वर्गं प्राप्ता रघूत्तम ।।

43. Then the foremost waters of Ganga submerged the heaps of the Ashes (of 60,000 sons of Sagara): Oh (Raama) the foremost of Raghu-s! (Listen further): With their sins blown off, they (all) attained Heaven.

(Note: This was the story of Ganges, Vischwaamithra narrated to Raama: After all Sagara was a forefather of Raama; An Ikshwaaku king of Ayodhya. And Bhageeratha had not only resurrected Sagara sons, but did perhaps the greatest service for posterity. He brought Ganges to India).

❍ ❍ ❍

Chapter 44

Sagara's 60,000 Sons Resurrected: Go to Heaven

१. स गत्वा सागरं राजा गङ्गयाऽनुगतस्तदा ।
प्रविवेश तलं भूमेर्यत्र ते भस्मसात्कृताः ॥

1. (Vischwaamithra continues narration to Raama:)

This king (Bhageeratha) followed by Ganga, reached the ocean: And he entered the place in the earth where they were all reduced to ashes

❍ ❍ ❍

२. भस्मन्यथाप्लुते: राम गङ्गायाः सलिलेन वै ।
सर्वलोकप्रभुर्ब्रह्मा राजानमिदमब्रवीत् ॥

2. Oh Raama (Listen)! When the ashes were 'bathed' by the waters of Ganges, God Braamma, the lord of all the worlds, addressed king (Bhageeratha) thus

❍ ❍ ❍

३. तारिता नरशार्दूल दिवं याता हि देववत् ।
षष्टिः पुत्रसहस्राणि सगरस्य महात्मनः ॥

3. Oh 'Lion' amongst men (Bageeratha) The 60,000 sons of the great soul Sagara have been 'carried across', (have been resurrected), and have gone to the celestial world like the Dheva-s.

❍ ❍ ❍

४. सागरस्य जलं लोके यावत् स्थास्यति पार्थिव ।
सगरस्यात्मजास्तावत् स्वर्गेस्थास्यन्ति देबवत् ॥

4. Oh king (Bhageeratha)! As long as waters are there in the ocean, till that time, Sagara's sons will live in heaven like Dhevas.

❍ ❍ ❍

५. इयं च दुहिता ज्येष्ठा तव गङ्गा भविष्यति ।
त्वत्कृतेनैव नाम्नाऽथ लोके स्थास्यति विश्रुता ॥

5. And this Ganga, is (now) going to be your eldest 'Daughter': (From now on), in this world, by your deed and by your fame, she, (this Ganges), will stand renowned.

❍ ❍ ❍

६. गङ्गा त्रिपथगा राजन् दिव्या भागीरथीति च ।
त्रीन् पथो भावयन्तीति ततस्त्रिपथगा स्मृता ॥

6. (As Bhageeratha had 'brought her forth' to Earth, he becomes father to her): Oh king (Bhageeratha)! She flows in three ways. Therefore she is (also) called Thripathaga. And also, she who flows in three ways, is called Bhaageerathi (also, named after you!).

❍ ❍ ❍

७. पितामहानां सर्वेषां त्वमत्र मनुजाधिप ।
कुरुष्व सलिलं राजन् प्रतिज्ञामपवर्तय ॥

7. Oh lord of men (Bhageeratha)! In these waters, you do water rituals for your forefathers: Oh king! Fulfill your vow.

❍ ❍ ❍

८. पूर्वकेणापि ते राजंस्तेनातियशसा तदा ।
धर्मिणां प्रवरेणाथ नैष प्राप्तो मनोरथः ॥

8. Further, Oh King (Bhageeratha)! This heartfelt desire of those ancestors of yours who were famous & foremost men of Dharma, was not obtained then (by them all). (Readers may know that Amschumaan, Dhileepa had failed in bringing Ganga down & resurrecting the 60,000 sons of Sagara. Only Bhageeratha achieved this.)

❍ ❍ ❍

९. तथैवांशुमता वत्स लोकेऽप्रतिमतेजसा ।
गङ्गां प्रार्थयता नेतुं प्रतिज्ञा नापवर्जिता ॥

9. Oh Lad! Likewise, this vow to bring into this world the Ganges of incomparable brilliance, was abandoned by Amschumaan who longed for this. (he failed)

❍ ❍ ❍

१०. राजर्षिणा गुणवता महर्षिसमतेजसा ।
मत्तुल्यतपसा चैव क्षत्रधर्मस्थितेन च ॥

११. दिलीपेन महाभाग तव पित्रा यशस्विना ।
पुनर्न शकिता नेतुं गङ्गां प्रार्थयताऽनघ ॥

10 & 11.

By that Royal sage who was endowed with qualities, with brilliance comparable to that of great sages and who was equal to me in penance and who stood firm by the Kshathriya Dharma...... By that famous & most illustrious father of yours, by this Dhileepa who wished to bring Ganges down, (even by him) this was not accomplished.

❍ ❍ ❍

१२. सा त्वया समतिक्रान्ता प्रतिज्ञा पुरुषर्षभ ।
प्राप्तोऽसि परमं लोके यशः परमसम्मतम् ॥

12. Oh (Bhageeratha) the 'Bull' amongst men! This vow was well accomplished by you: You have obtained great renown, accepted as such by all in the world.

❍ ❍ ❍

१३. यच्च गङ्गावतरणं त्वया कृतमरिन्दम ।
अनेन च भवान् प्राप्तो धर्मस्यायतनं महत् ॥

13. Oh (Bhageeratha the) destroyer of enemies! This bringing down of Ganges was done by you, (only by you): Therefore you alone have obtained great sanctuary for Dharma.

❍ ❍ ❍

१४. प्लावयस्व त्वमात्मानं नरोत्तम सदोचिते ।
सलिले पुरुषव्याघ्र शुचिः पुण्यफलो भव ॥

14. Oh (Bhageeratha) the foremost of men, the 'tiger' of men! You bathe in the ever delightful waters; You will become pure & obtain fruits of meritorious deeds.

❍ ❍ ❍

१५. पितामहानां सर्वेषां कुरुष्व सलिलक्रियाम् ।
स्वस्ति तेऽस्तु गमिष्याति स्वं लोकं गम्यतां नृप ।।

15. Do water Rituals for all your forefathers: Welfare to you I am going back to my world; Oh king, may you leave, (get back).

❍ ❍ ❍

१६. इत्येवमुक्त्वा देवेशः सर्वलोकपितामहः ।
यथाऽऽगतं तथाऽऽगच्छद्देवलोकं महायशाः ।।

16. (Thus extolled God Bramma: The Flow of Ganges in the world is indeed very, very auspicious. And Bhageeratha had done it!) And saying thus, the Lord of Dheva-s, the most famous (God Bramma) who is The Creator (& forefather) of all in the world, went back as he came, to his Dheva world.

❍ ❍ ❍

१७. भगीरथोऽपि राजर्षिः कृत्वा सलिलमुत्तमम् ।
यथाक्रमं यथान्यायं सागराणां महायशाः ।।

१८. कृतोदकः शुची राजा स्वपुरं प्रविवेश ह ।
समृद्धार्थोनरश्रेष्ठ स्वराज्यं प्रशशास ह ।।

17 & 18.

And the Royal Sage Bhageeratha also, performed the foremost water rituals for the sons of Sagara as per norms & as per Shaasthra-s. . . . and this most famous & pure king entered his city: His mission accomplished, he ruled his kingdom. (Oh Raama) the foremost of men (listen).

❍ ❍ ❍

१९. प्रमुमोद च लोकस्तं नृपमासाद्य राघव ।
नष्टशोकः समृद्धार्थोबभूव विगतज्वरः ।।

19. Oh (Raama) the Raaghava! The world, having obtained this (Bhageeratha as) king, rejoiced, bereft of any suffering: It was full with wealth, free of diseases.

❍ ❍ ❍

२०. एष ते राम गङ्गाया विस्तरोऽभिहितो मया ।
स्वस्ति प्राप्नुहि भद्रं ते सन्ध्याकालोऽतिवर्तते ।।

20. Oh Raama! The description of (the Story of) Ganges has been told to you by me: Obtain Swasthi: Welfare to you: Sandhya time is approaching.

❍ ❍ ❍

२१. धन्यं यशस्यमायुष्यं पुत्र्यं स्वर्ग्यमथापि च ।
यः श्रावयति विप्रेषु क्षत्रियेष्वितरेषु च ।।
प्रीयन्ते पितरस्तस्य प्रीयन्ते दैवतानि च ।।

२२. इदमाख्यानमव्यग्रं गङ्गावतरणं शुभम् ।
यः श्रृणोति च काकुत्स्थ सर्वान् कामानवाप्नुयात् ।।
सर्वेपापाः प्रणश्यन्ति आयुः कीर्तिश्च वर्धते ।।

21 & 22.

(Vischwaamithra concludes by telling Raama this): Whoever listens (to this story of Ganges) which will bring wealth, long life, fame, children, heaven (after death), ... (whoever listens from) Braamins, or from Kshathriyas or even from others, his fore-fathers will become pleased...... So also the Gods...... And he who listens to this auspicious story of the origin of Ganga (in the world) with devotion, will obtain all desires. All his sins are destroyed; His life extends: And fame also increases.

(Vischwaamithra concluded this narration to Raama: Vischwaamithra moulds Raama. Not only has he taught him The Weapons. He was teaching him Geography & History as well. He virtually moulds Prince Raama.)

❍ ❍ ❍

Chapter 45

Visit to Vischaala Territory

१. विश्वामित्रवचः श्रुत्वा राघवः सहलक्ष्मणः ।
विस्मयं परमं गत्वा विश्वामित्रमथाब्रवीत् ।।

1. (Vischwaamithra narrates yet another story: The churning of Milky Ocean) Hearing the words of Vischwaamithra, (Raama) the Raaghaava who was (ever) with Lakshmana, became greatly wonder struck & he then addressed Vischwaamithra:

❍ ❍ ❍

२. अत्यद्भुतमिदं ब्रह्मन् कथितं परमं त्वया ।
गङ्गावतरणं पुण्यं सागरस्यापि पूरणम् ।।

2. Oh Braamin! This (story of) Descent of Ganga, its final entry into the ocean, told by you, is most wonderful, very sacred.

❍ ❍ ❍

३. क्षणभूतेव नौ रात्रिः संवृत्तेयं महामुने ।
इमां चिन्तयतोः सर्वां निखिलेन कथां तव ।।

3. Oh great Muni! To us who were thinking about this story of yours, all of it, in entirety, this night has passed away in a trice.

❍ ❍ ❍

४. तस्य सा शर्वरी सर्वा सह सौमित्रिणा तदा ।
जगाम चिन्तयानस्य विश्वामित्रकथां शुभाम् ।।

4. At that time, To this (Raama) who was thinking (& conversing) with Lakshmana about the auspicious story (narrated by) Vischwaamithra, the entire night passed away quickly.

❍ ❍ ❍

५. ततः प्रभाते विमले विश्वामित्रं महामुनिम् ।
उवाच राघवो वाक्यं कृताह्निकमरिन्दमः ।।

5. When it was clear daylight, (Raama) the Raaghava, the destroyer of enemies, addressed the great Muni Vischwaamithra who had finished his morning rituals, with (following) words......

❍ ❍ ❍

६. गता भगवती रात्रिः श्रोतव्यं परमं श्रुतम् ।।

6. What (surely is) foremost (in history that) must be heard, was (indeed) heard (by us two, this Ganges story) Night has passed away 'divinely'.

❍ ❍ ❍

७. तराम सरितां श्रेष्ठां पुण्यां त्रिपथगां नदीम् ।
नौरेषा हि सुखास्तीर्णा ऋषीणां पुण्यकर्मणाम् ।।
भगवन्तमिह प्राप्तं ज्ञात्वा त्वरितमागता ।।

7. Having heard of your arrival here, there is a boat here, quickly brought by the Rishi-s who ever do holy deeds; We shall cross the holy Ganges which is foremost of rivers, (by this boat) which has comfortable seats.

❍ ❍ ❍

८. तस्य तद्वचनं श्रुत्वा राघवस्य महात्मनः ।
सन्तारं कारयामास सर्षिसङ्घः सराघवः ।।

8. Hearing the words of the great soul (Raama) the Raaghava, (Vischwaamithra), accompanied by a group of Rishi-s, and along with the two Raaghava-s, made the crossing to the other bank.

❍ ❍ ❍

९. उत्तरं तीरमासाद्य संपूज्यर्षिगणांस्ततः ।
गङ्गाकूले निविष्टास्ते विशालां ददृशुः पुरीम् ।।

9. Reaching the northern bank, there, they honoured the

multitude of Rishi-s; and they sat down on the banks of river Ganges: They saw Vischaala city, thus.

❍ ❍ ❍

१०. ततो मुनिवरस्तूर्णं जगाम सहराघवः ।
विशालां नगरीं रम्यां दृष्ट्वा स्वर्गोपमां तदा ॥

10. Then seeing the beautiful city of Vischaala that was comparable to 'Heaven', the noble Muni (Vischwaamithra), accompanied by the two Raaghava-s (Raama/Lakshmana), went at once to that place.

❍ ❍ ❍

११. अथ रामो महाप्राज्ञो विश्वामित्रं महामुनिम् ।
पप्रच्छ प्राञ्जलिर्भूत्वा विशालामुत्तमां पुरीम् ॥

१२. कतरो राजवंशोऽयं विशालायां महामुने ।
श्रोतुमिच्छामि भद्रं ते परं कौतूहलं हि मे ॥

11 & 12.

And the most intelligent (Raama) asked the great Muni Vischwaamithra, with his arms folded in Anjali, about this foremost Vischaala city, thus: = Oh great muni! My curiosity is great, so I desire to hear about the royal family now (living in) the city of Vischaala: Welfare to you.=

❍ ❍ ❍

१३. तस्य तद्वचनं श्रुत्वा रामस्य मुनिपुङ्गवः ।
आख्यातुं तत् समारेभे विशालायाः पुरातनम् ॥

13. Hearing the words of Raama, (Vischwaamithra the) 'Tiger' of Muni-s began to narrate about the ancient story of Vischaala.

❍ ❍ ❍

१४. श्रूयतां राम शक्रस्य कथां कथयतः शुभाम् ।
अस्मिन् हि देशे यद् वृत्तं तत्त्वेन श्रृणु राघव ॥

14. Oh Raama, the Raaghava! May you Listen. You listen

to me as I narrate exactly about the holy story, about Schakra (Lord Indhra), and all that happened before in this place.

❍ ❍ ❍

१५. पूर्वं कृतयुगे राम दितेः पुत्रा महाबलाः ।
अदितेश्च महाभाग वीर्यवन्तः सुधार्मिकाः ।।

15. Oh most illustrious Raama: Long, long ago, in The Krithi Yuga, the sons of Dhithi were mightily strong: And Adhithi's (sons) were valiant & were men of Dharma.

❍ ❍ ❍

१६. ततस्तेषां नरव्याघ्र बुद्धिरासीन्महात्मनाम् ।
अमरा विज्वराश्चैव कथं स्याम निरामयाः ।।

16. Oh (Raama) 'the tiger' of men! At that time, to these most eminent men, a thought occurred, as to how they can be eternal, free from disease & worry.

❍ ❍ ❍

१७. तेषां चिन्तयतां राम बुद्धिरासीद्विपश्चिताम् ।
क्षीरोदमथनं कृत्वा रसं प्राप्स्याम तत्र वै ।।

17. Oh Raama (Listen)! To these distinguished men who were pondering thus, thought occurred: = We Shall Churn The Milky Ocean and Obtain From This, Nectar.=

❍ ❍ ❍

१८. ततो निश्चित्य मथनं योक्त्रं कृत्वा च वासुकिम् ।
मन्थानं मन्दरं कृत्वा ममन्थुरमितौजसः ।।

18. Endowed with boundless power, they decided to churn: Using Mandhara mountain as churning rod and (the king of serpents) Vasooki as rope, they churned (the milky ocean).

❍ ❍ ❍

१९. अथ दीर्घेण कालेन कालाग्निसदृशं विषम् ।
उदतिष्ठन्नरश्रेष्ठ हालाहलमिति श्रुतम् ।।

19. Oh (Raama) the foremost of men!: After a long time, a poison called Haalahala issued forth that was like Fire at Pralaya (at Deluge at the end of Universe).

❍ ❍ ❍

२०. सुरासुराश्च वित्रस्ता दग्धास्तेन विषाग्निना ।
शरण्यं शरणं जग्मुर्भगवन्तं महेश्वरम् ।।

20. Unable to bear the fire of this poison, the Dheva-s and Asuras who were scared, sought refuge under God Maheshwara (God Schiva) who is refuge (to all).

❍ ❍ ❍

२१. अथ देवा महादेवं शमरं शरणार्थिनः ।
नत्वा पशुपतिं रुद्रं त्राहि त्राहीति तुष्टुवुः ।।

21. Then the Dheva-s who had sought refuge under Mahaadheva (Schiva), went there, extolled Him & said this to Schankara, the Rudhra, this Paschupathi. (this God Schiva): = Save, Save (us)! =

❍ ❍ ❍

२२. एवमुक्तेषु देवेषु देवदेवेश्वरः प्रभुः ।
प्रादुरासीत्ततोऽत्रैव शङ्खचक्रधरो हरिः ।।

22. When the Dheva-s were telling thus, at that moment, the lord of lords, Lord Hari, (God Vishnu), appeared there wielding Conch & Disc. (Vishnu's divine weapons)

❍ ❍ ❍

२३. उवाचैनं स्मितं कृत्वा रुद्रं शूलधरं हरिः ।
दैवतैरत्वं प्राथ्यर्मानो यत्पूर्वं समुपागतम् ।।

२४. तत्त्वदीयं सुरश्रेष्ठ सुराणामग्रजो हि यत् ।
अग्रपूजामिति स्मृत्वा गृहाणेदं विषं प्रभो ।।

23 & 24.

And Hari (God Vishnu) addressed with a smile, Rudhra,

(God Schiva), the bearer of the Spear,: = In respect of this (poison) that came out first, You are being begged by the Dheva-s and others. ..... Oh Lord, the foremost of Dheva-s (Oh Schiva)! As this (poison) was the first to be 'Born' (the first to come out of The Churning), this belongs to You: Therefore, considering this as first & foremost honour, You accept (this poison) =

❍ ❍ ❍

२५. इत्युक्त्वा च सुरश्रेष्ठस्तत्रैवान्तरधीयत ।
देवतानां भयं दृष्ट्वा देवदेवो महेश्वरः ।।
२६. हालाहलं विषं सर्वं संजहारामृतोपमं ।
कृत्वाऽल्पपिण्डं पाणिस्थं तद्विषं भगवान् हरः ।।

25 & 26.

Saying thus about this Poison, the foremost Dheva (Vishnu), then disappeared: Then the lord of lords, Maheshwara (Schiva), seeing the fear in these Dheva-s..... this Hara (Schiva) made this poison Halaahala, all of it, a cupful in his palm and (drank it) as though it was Nectar and (thus) destroyed (its poisonous effect).

❍ ❍ ❍

२७. सर्वलोकहितार्थाय भगवान् परमेश्वरः ।
कण्ठस्थमकरोत् प्राश्य लीलयाऽमरपूजितः ।।

27. God Parameshwara (Schiva) who is honoured by all celestials, treating this like (child's) play, consumed this and made this (poison) remain in (the gullet of) his neck, all for the sake of the good of all the worlds.

❍ ❍ ❍

२८. ततो देवासुराः सर्वेप्रणम्य वृषभध्वजम् ।
मन्दरं पूर्ववत् कृत्वा ममन्थुरमितौजसः ।।

28. The Dhevas & Asura-s of immense power, all of them, bowed before (God Schiva) whose mast is Bull: And

then, like before, they started churning with Mandhara Mountain (as churning rod).

(God Schiva drunk up this terrific poison that could have destroyed the whole world, poisoning everything. And Schiva lodges this in his gullet: His neck became blue due to the Fire of this poison. And thus Schiva's other name is Neelakanta- God with blue neck.)

❍ ❍ ❍

२९. प्रविवेशाथ पातालं मन्थानो मन्दरोत्तमः ।
ततः पर्वतमूलं तु पाताले तु प्रवेशितम् ।।

29. Then the foremost Mandhara mountain which was the churning rod entered the Paathaala world from there: (The Churning rod, this mountain sunk deep): The roots of the mountain got stuck up in Paathaala (underworld).

❍ ❍ ❍

३०. सुरासुराश्च निश्चेष्टा बभूवुः क्लेशविह्वलाः ।
ततो देवास्सगन्धर्वास्तुष्टुवुर्मधुसूदनम् ।।

30. The Dheva-s and Asura-s whose mind was crestfallen, became immobile (unable to know what to do next): Then the Dheva-s along with Ghandharva-s (went) and extolled Madhusoodhana (God Vishnu) thus:

❍ ❍ ❍

३१. त्वं गतिस्सर्वभूतानां विशेषेण दिवौकसाम् ।
पालयास्मान् महायोगिन् गिरिमुद्धर्तुमर्हसि ।।

31. Oh great Yogi (Oh Vishnu)! You are indeed the last resort to all living beings, particularly to (us) Dheva-s. Protect us (Save us): You should pull up the Mountain (The Churning Rod):

❍ ❍ ❍

३२. इति श्रुत्वा हृषीकेशः कच्छपं रूपमास्थितः ।
पर्वतं पृष्ठतः कृत्वा ववृधे कूर्मरूपधृक् ।।

32. Hearing this, Hrisheekescha (Vishnu) took on the form of a Tortoise: Supported this mountain on His back and came up, assuming the form of tortoise (as an Incarnation).

❍ ❍ ❍

३३. सुरासुरैरनाक्रान्त उद्धतोऽथ नगोत्तमः ।
नगाग्रं पीडयामास वामहस्तेन माधवः ।।

33. This foremost mountain that could not be moved by Dheva-s & Asura-s, rose up! And then Maadhava (God Vishnu), pressed the peaks of the mountain with His left hand. (The mountain was well fixed as Churning Rod again.)

❍ ❍ ❍

३४. ममन्थ देवतानां च मध्ये नारायणो हरिः ।।

34. And Naaraayana, The Hari (God Vishnu) also churned, along with the Dheva-s.

❍ ❍ ❍

३५. अथ वर्षसहस्रेण ज्येष्ठा नाम वराङ्गना ।
उत्पपात वरारोहा साग्रजैरेव कल्पिता ।।

35. After 1,000 years (of churning), as first 'Born' (the first to come out), a handsome woman, created with lovely hips and body, came, Jyeshta by name.

❍ ❍ ❍

३६. अभवत् पारिजाताख्यो वृक्ष इन्द्राय कल्पितः ।
कामधुक सुरभिश्चाभूच्चतुर्दन्तो महागजः ।।

36. For Lord Indhra, a great elephant with four tusks was created (which came out): A tree was 'created' named Paarijaatha. (A cow) Surabhi that could offer anything desired, was (also) 'born'.

❍ ❍ ❍

३७. अथ वर्षसहस्रेण आयुर्वेदमयः पुमान् ।
उदतिष्ठत् स धर्मात्मा सदण्डः सकमण्डलुः ॥
तदा धन्वन्तरिर्नामाऽप्सरसश्च सुवर्चसः ॥

37. Then, after 1,000 years, Dhanvanthri by name, who was the embodiment of the science of Aayurvedha (Medicine), came up, holding a stick (in one hand) and a bowl (in another), a noble man of Dharma. And then (followed) the splendid and lustrous Apsara maidens (Literal meaning of Apsara- is: Ap means water, Sara is flow; Flowing from water, born from water).

❍ ❍ ❍

३८. अप्सु निर्मथनादेव रसात्तस्माद्वरस्त्रियः ।
उत्पेतुर्मनुजश्रेष्ठ तस्मादप्सरसोऽभवन् ॥

38. Oh (Raama) the foremost of men! (Listen further)! These foremost ladies came out from 'the juice' that came out of the churning of water (of milky ocean) Therefore they became Apsara.

❍ ❍ ❍

३९. षष्टिः कोट्योऽभवंस्तासामप्सराणां सुवर्चसाम् ।
असङ्ख्येयास्तु काकुत्स्थ यास्तासां परिचारिकाः ॥

४०. न ताः स्म प्रतिगृह्णन्ति सर्वेते देवदानवाः ।
अप्रतिग्रहणादेव ता वै साधारणाः स्मृताः ॥

39 & 40.

Oh (Raama) the Kaakuthsa! 600 million Apsara-s who were most radiant were 'born': And the servant maids for them, their number could not be reckoned...... The Dheva-s, the Dhaanava-s, all of them, never married them; Without being married, they were remembered as (maidens) "belonging" to all.

❍ ❍ ❍

४१. वरुणस्य ततः कन्या वारुणी रघुनन्दन ।
उत्पपात महाभागा मार्गमाणा परिग्रहम् ॥

41. Oh (Raama) the darling of Raghu-s: Then the daughter of Lord Varuna, the illustrious Vaaruni (by name), searching for a husband, came out:

❍ ❍ ❍

४२. दितेः पुत्रा न तां राम जगृहुर्वरुणात्मजाम् ।
अदितेस्तु सुता वीर जगृहुस्तामनिन्दिताम् ।।

42. (But) Dhithi-s sons did not accept this (Vaaruni), the daughter of Varuna: (But) Oh brave (Raama)!: Adheethi's sons accepted this irreproachable (Vaaruni).

❍ ❍ ❍

४३. असुरास्तेन दैतेया सुरास्तेनादितेः सुताः ।
हृष्टाः प्रमुदिताश्चासन् वारुणीग्रहणात् सुराः ।।

43. Dhithi's sons were known as Asura-s: And Adheethi's sons were known as Sura-s: These Sura-s, as they (married) and accepted Varuna's daughter (Vaaruni), rejoiced and became happy.

❍ ❍ ❍

४४. उच्चैः श्रवा हयश्रेष्ठो मणिरत्नं च कौस्तुभम् ।
उदतिष्ठन्नरश्रेष्ठ सोमदेवस्तथैव च ।।

44. Oh foremost of men, (Oh Raama)! The foremost of horses, Uchaishrawas and a gem amongst stones, Kousthubha, and likewise (lord) Moon appeared.

❍ ❍ ❍

४५. तुरगं देवराजाय कौस्तुभं केशवाय च ।
महादेवाय सोमं तु कल्पयामासुरीश्वराः ।।
धन्वन्तरिर्महातेजा लोकरक्षणतत्परः ।
आयुर्वेदमयो राम तथा साधारणः स्मृतः ।।

45. The deities settled (to give & so offered) The Horse to Lord Indhra: The Kowsthubha to Keschava (Vishnu), The Moon to Mahadheva (Schiva); Oh Raama! (Listen): Likewise, the most brilliant Dhanvanthari, the embodiment of Aayurvedha (Medicine), who was

totally devoted to protection (& welfare) of all in the world, was considered common to all. (Readers may consider Dhanvanthari as the first doctor of India.)

❍ ❍ ❍

४६. सुरासुराश्च गन्धर्वाः क्षोभयामासुरम्बुधिम् ॥

46. And the Sura-s and Asura-s and the Ghandharva-s churned The Ocean again.

❍ ❍ ❍

४७. ततो दीर्घेण कालेन चोत्पन्ना कमलालया ।
अतीव रूपसम्पन्ना प्रथमे वयसि स्थिता ॥

47. Then, after a long time, came a (maiden) endowed with great beauty, ever remaining young in years, reposing in Lotus.

❍ ❍ ❍

४८. सर्वाभरणपूर्णाङ्गी सर्वलक्षणलक्षिता ।
मकुटाङ्गदचित्राङ्गी नीलकुञ्चितमूर्धजा ॥

48. All parts of her body were bedecked in jewellery: She was distinguished by all (wonderful) qualities: She had a crown: wore forearm bracelets and had variegated ornaments; she had curly blue hair.

❍ ❍ ❍

४९. तप्तहाटकसमाशा मुक्ताभरणभूषिता ।
चतुर्भुजा महादेवी पद्महस्ता वरानना ॥

49. This great Dhevi had a complexion of pure molten gold; she had a necklace of pearls; she had four shoulders (& arms); And she held lotus in (one) hand: had a lovely face.

❍ ❍ ❍

५०. सा च देवी तथोत्पन्ना पद्मा श्रीर्लोकपूजिता ।
सा पद्मा पद्मनाभस्य ययौ वक्षस्थलं हरेः ॥

50. This Dhevi who appeared was (none other than) Schree

(Goddess Lakshmi), The Padhma, who is worshipped by all in the world. this (Goddess) Padhma reposed in the chest of Padhmanaabha (God Vishnu, as his consort).

❍ ❍ ❍

५१. उदतिष्ठन्नरश्रेष्ठ तथैवामृतमुत्तमम् ॥

51. Oh (Raama) the foremost of men! And then the foremost Nectar came (out from this great churning, at last).

❍ ❍ ❍

५२. अथ तस्य कृते राम महानासीत् कुलक्षयः ।
अदितेस्तु ततः पुत्रा दितेः पुत्रानसूदयन् ॥

52. Oh Raama! Then came a great (family feud) and the destruction of family, all because (& for the sake) of The Nectar (Amrutha). Adhithi's sons killed Thithi's sons....

❍ ❍ ❍

५३. एकतोऽभ्यागमन् सर्वेह्यसुरा राक्षसैस्सह ।
युद्धमासीन्महाघोरं वीर त्रैलोक्यमोहनम् ॥

53. Oh Brave (Raama)! (Listen): All the Asura-s, along with Raakshasa-s (Demons) came together on one side to attack: A most gruesome war ensued which stupefied the three worlds.

❍ ❍ ❍

५४. यदा क्षयं गतं सर्वं तदा विष्णुर्महाबलः ।
अमृतं सोऽहरत्तूर्णं मायामास्थाय मोहिनीम् ॥

54. When everything became destroyed (desolate), the mightily strong Vishnu, at once took on a form of a temptress, an Illusory woman, and seized this Amrutha (Nectar).

❍ ❍ ❍

५५. ये तदाऽभिमुखं विष्णुमक्षयं पुरुषोत्तमम् ।
संपिष्टास्ते तदा युद्धे विष्णुना प्रभविष्णुना ॥

55. All those who faced the imperishable (eternal) God Vishnu, the foremost Purusha, in order to attack Him, were killed in war by God Vishnu, the glorious All Pervader.

❍ ❍ ❍

५६. अदितेरात्मजा वीरा दितेः पुत्रान्निजघ्निरे ।
तस्मिन् घोरे महायुद्धे दैतेयादित्ययोर्भृशम् ॥

56. In this mighty gruesome war between Dhithi's sons and Adhithi's sons, the valiant Adhithi's sons killed Dhithi's sons greatly (in large numbers).

❍ ❍ ❍

५७. निहत्य दितिपुत्रांस्तु राज्यं प्राप्य पुरन्दरः ।
शशास मुदितो लोकान् सर्षिसङ्घान् सचारणान् ॥

57. And lord Indhra, destroying the sons of Dhithi, obtained his (Celestial) kingdom and ruled the world happily along with multitude of Rishi-s & Chaarana-s.

❍ ❍ ❍

Chapter 46

The Creation of Maruth-s

१. हतेषु तेषु पुत्रेषु दितिः परमदुःखिता ।
मारीचं काश्यपं राम भर्तारमिदमब्रवीत् ॥

1. (Vischwaamithra continues narration: about Dhithi-Maruth-s) Oh Raama (Listen): When her sons were killed, Dhithi became very sad & addressed her husband Kaaschyapa, the son of Mareechi, thus.

❍ ❍ ❍

२. हतपुत्राऽस्मि भगवंस्तव पुत्रैर्महाबलैः ।
शक्रहन्तारमिच्छामि पुत्रं दीर्घतपोऽर्जितम् ॥

2. Oh Lord! by your mightily strong sons (through your other wife Adhithi) my sons were killed: I desire to have a son who can kill Lord Indhra and who can be obtained through rigorous penance.

❍ ❍ ❍

३. साऽहं तपश्चरिष्यामि गर्भं मे दातुमर्हसि ।
बलवन्तं महेष्वासं स्थितिज्ञं समदर्शिनम् ।।
ईदृशं शक्रहन्तारं त्वमनुज्ञातुमर्हसि ।।

3. Such as I am, am doing penance: You should offer me pregnancy. As mightily strong, mighty wielder of bow, a man of composure who can look at things *impartially, such a (son) who can kill Indhra, you should offer me (*Sama Dharschin).

❍ ❍ ❍

४. तस्यास्तद्वचनं श्रुत्वा मारीचः काश्यपस्तदा ।
प्रत्युवाच महातेजा दितिं परमदुःखिताम् ।।

4. Hearing her words, the most brilliant Kaaschyapa the son of Mareechi, replied to Dhithi who was in great sorrow.

❍ ❍ ❍

५. एवं भवतु भद्रं ते शुचिर्भव तपोधने ।
जनयिष्यसि पुत्रं त्वं शक्रहन्तारमाहवे ।।

5. Oh lady for whom penance is wealth! So Be It: Welfare to you: You will beget a son from me who can kill Lord Indhra in battle: Be pure (& so be happy).

❍ ❍ ❍

६. पूर्णेवर्षसहस्रे तु शुचिर्यदि भविष्यसि ।
पुत्रं त्रैलोक्यभर्तारं मत्तस्त्वं जनयिष्यसि ।।

6. For 1,000 years if you remain pure (& steadfast in penance): you will beget a son from me who will be lord of the three worlds.

❍ ❍ ❍

७. एवमुक्त्वा महातेजाः पाणिना स ममार्ज ताम् ।
तामालभ्य ततः स्वस्तीत्युक्त्वा स तपसे ययौ ।।

7. This most brilliant (Kaaschyapa), after saying thus, stroked her with his hands; and he hugged her; and after (blessing her) with Swasthi, went away to do penance.

❍ ❍ ❍

८. गते तस्मिन्नरश्रेष्ठे दितिः परमहर्षिता ।
कुशप्लवनमासाद्य तपस्तेपे सुदारुणम् ।।

8. Oh (Raama) the foremost of men! (Listen): After he had left, Dhithi who was very happy, reached Kuschaplavana and did rigorous penance:

❍ ❍ ❍

९. तपस्तस्यां हि कुर्वन्त्यां परिचर्यां चकार ह ।
सहस्राक्षो नरश्रेष्ठ परया गुणसंपदा ।।

9. Oh (Raama) the foremost of men (Listen)! When she was doing penance, the thousand eyed (Lord Indhra) came there and served her with great merit, exceedingly. (Readers may note that Lord Indhra was scared; If she conceived by the boon of Kaaschyapa, her son will be his Death.)

❍ ❍ ❍

१०. अग्निं कुशान् काष्ठमपः फलं मूलं तथैव च ।
न्यवेदयत् सहस्राक्षो यच्चान्यदपि काङ्क्षितम् ।।

10. The thousand eyed (Indhra) brought up to her, ritual fire, Dharbha grass, sticks of wood (Samiths), water, fruits, tubers & other desirables.

❍ ❍ ❍

११. गात्रसंवहनैश्चैव श्रमापनयनैस्तथा ।
शक्रः सर्वेषु कालेषु दितिं परिचचार ह ।।

11. And this Schakra (Indhra) served this Dhithi at all

times, (even) giving her body massage, and tended to her comforts.

❍ ❍ ❍

१२. अथ वर्षसहस्रे तु दशोने रघुनन्दन ।
दितिः परमसंप्रीता सहस्राक्षमथाब्रवीत् ।।

12. Oh (Raama) the darling of Raghu-s! (Listen); When 10 years was short of 1,000 years, Dhithi, who was very pleased, addressed the thousand eyed (Indhra) the following:

❍ ❍ ❍

१३. याचितेन सुरश्रेष्ठ पित्रा तव महात्मना ।
वरो वर्षसहस्रान्ते मम दत्तः सुतं प्रति ।।

13. Oh Lord of Dheva-s (Indhra)! Begged by me for a son, a boon was offered to me by your father, the great soul (Kaaschyapa), of getting a son at the end of 1,000 years (of penance).

❍ ❍ ❍

१४. तपश्चरन्त्या वर्षाणि दश वीर्यवतां वर ।
अवशिष्टानि भद्रं ते भ्रातरं द्रक्ष्यसे ततः ।।

14. Oh foremost amongst the brave (Oh Indhra): Welfare to you: After the balance of 10 years, after doing penance, you will see 'your brother' (step brother, that is).

❍ ❍ ❍

१५. तमहं त्वत्कृते पुत्रं समाधास्ये जयोत्सुकम् ।
त्रैलोक्यविजयं पुत्रं सह भोक्ष्यसि विज्वरः ।।

15. I offer (& pledge) this son to you for your sake who will ever be seeking victory: Free from worries, you will enjoy, along with this son (of mine) who will conquer the three worlds.

(But lord Indhra has other ideas: he is not one who shares power.)

❍ ❍ ❍

१६. एवमुक्त्वा दितिः शक्रं प्राप्ते मध्यं दिवाकरे ।
निद्रयाऽपहृता देवी पादौ कृत्वाऽथ शीर्षतः ॥

16. Saying thus to Indhra, when the Sun was in mid (Sky), Lady Dhithi, (raised) and placed her (knee of her) legs on her head, seized by sleepiness (tiresomeness); (She crouched, her face resting on the raised knees, thereby exposing her inner parts).

❍ ❍ ❍

१७. दृष्ट्वा तामुशुचिं शक्रः पादयोः कृतमूर्धजाम् ।
शिरःस्थाने कृतौ पादौ जहास च मुमोद च ॥

17. When her feet was placed on her head (her head resting like this), when her hair was flowing on to her legs, she therefore became 'shameless' ('impure'); Seeing her (like this), Lord Indhra rejoiced; laughed derisively.

❍ ❍ ❍

१८. तस्याः शरीरविवरं प्रविवेश पुरन्दरः ।
गर्भं च सप्तधा राम चिच्छेद परमात्मवान् ॥

18. Oh Raama (Listen)! Lord Indhra who had great confidence in himself, 'entered' into her inner parts of body, then cut the Foetus (that was growing in her womb), into 7 parts.

(This is not the first time the so called lord Indhra has used dubious & vile means to hold on to power. Power was all he cared for. He commits the greatest crime: molesting a woman who is in the last stage of pregnancy.)

❍ ❍ ❍

१९. भिद्यमानस्ततो गर्भोवज्रेण शतपर्वणा ।
रुरोद सुस्वरं राम ततो दितिरबुध्यत ॥

19. Oh Raama! When (the child in her womb) was pierced by his Vajra of 100 spikes, this foetus cried with a 'nice' voice. And Dhithi woke up.

❍ ❍ ❍

२०. मा रुदो मा रुदश्चेति गर्भं शक्रोऽभ्यभाषत ।
बिभेद च महातेजा रुदन्तमपि वासवः ॥

20. And Lord Indhra 'told' the child in the womb: = Dont Cry, Dont Cry. = And this most powerful (Indhra) the Vaasava, split up the crying foetus – child.

❍ ❍ ❍

२१. न हन्तव्यो न हन्तव्य इत्येवं दितिरब्रवीत् ।
निष्पपात ततः शक्रो मातुर्वचनगौरवात् ॥

21. And Dhithi (beggingly) said: = Dont Kill, Dont Kill= Then Lord Indhra came out (of her body) respecting a mother's words (of anguish).

❍ ❍ ❍

२२. प्राञ्जलिर्वज्रसहितो दितिं शक्रोऽभ्यभाषत ।
अशुचिर्देवि सुप्ताऽसि पादयोः कृतमूर्धजा ॥

22. Lord Indhra, wielding his Vajra, then spoke thus to Dhithi, cupping his hands in Anjali: = Oh lady! You slept with your feet on your head with hair falling on it and you became 'impure' (immodest).

❍ ❍ ❍

२३. तदन्तरमहं लब्ध्वा शक्रहन्तारमाहवे ।
अभिन्दं सप्तधा देवि तन्मे त्वं क्षन्तुमर्हसि ॥

23. Having obtained (this opportunity), at that moment, Oh Lady (Dhithi), I cut off (this womb child of yours) into 7 parts, as he, (if he was born), was to kill me in war, You must therefore bear (condone) this (gruesome) deed of mine.

(If Hindoos condone such acts, particularly such acts by Lord Indhra the lord of Dheva-s, it is because they strongly believe even vilest acts have divine sanctions & purpose. Readers will know more about this power mad Indhra. Yet Hindoos offer prayers to him!).

❍ ❍ ❍

Chapter 47

The Story of Vischaala

१. सप्तधा तु कृते गर्भेदितिः परमदुःखिता ।
सहस्राक्षं दुराधर्षं वाक्यं सानुनयाऽब्रवीत् ॥

1. (Vischwaamithra continues narration to Raama:) When the child in her womb was cut up into 7 parts, Dhithi became terribly sad: (But) courteously addressed this thousand eyed (Indhra) who could not be crushed (easily).

❍ ❍ ❍

२. ममापराधाद्गर्भोऽयं सप्तधा विफलीकृतः ।
नापराधोऽस्ति देवेश तवात्र बलसूदन ॥

2. Oh Lord of Dheva-s (Oh Indhra) the destroyer of (demon) Bhala! By my (negligence &) transgression, this child in womb was cut up and this (conception) has ended in failure. In this, there is no fault in you. (I dont blame you, says Dhithi, surprisingly).

❍ ❍ ❍

३. प्रियं त्वत्कृतमिच्छामि मम गर्भविपर्यये ।
मरुतां सप्त सप्तानां स्थानपाला भवन्त्विमे ॥

3. I desire a good, a (favour), to be done by you even as this conception took a different turn. May these 7 parts become Seven Maruth-s and be Heavenly Bodies.

❍ ❍ ❍

४. वातस्कन्धा इमे सप्त चरन्तु दिवि पुत्रकाः ।
मारुता इति विख्याता दिव्यरूपा ममात्मजाः ॥

4. May these creations from my body, these 'sons', taking divine forms, roam about in ethereal regions, in the celestial worlds, renowned as The Seven Maruth-s.

❍ ❍ ❍

५. ब्रह्मलोकं चरत्वेक इन्द्रलोकं तथाऽपरः ।
दिवि वायुरिति ख्यातस्तृतीयोऽपि महायशाः ॥

5. Let one roam around Bramma world; another in world of Indhra; likewise, the third one in heaven. Renowned as Vaayu & most famous.

❍ ❍ ❍

६. चत्वारस्तु सुरश्रेष्ठ दिशो वै तव शासनात् ।
सञ्चरिष्यन्ति भद्रं ते देवभूता ममात्मजाः ॥
त्वत्कृतेनैव नाम्ना च मारुता इति विश्रुताः ॥

6. Oh foremost of Dheva-s (Oh Indhra): Welfare to you! And the four of my sons, by your command, (under your authority), roam about all the directions with divine forms, named by you as Maruths, & becoming renowned.

❍ ❍ ❍

७. तस्यास्तद्वचनं श्रुत्वा सहस्राक्षः पुरन्दरः ।
उवाच प्राञ्जलिर्वाक्यं दितिं बलनिषूदनः ॥

7. Hearing her words, the thousand eyed Purandhara (Indhra), the killer of Bhala, addressed Dhithi thus, with his hand cupped in Anjali (in reverence).

❍ ❍ ❍

८. सर्वमेतद्यथोक्तं ते भविष्यति न संशयः ।
विचरिष्यन्ति भद्रं ते देवभूतास्तवात्मजाः ॥

8. Welfare to you! All this spoken by you will take place: No doubt about it; Your sons will roam about in divine form.

❍ ❍ ❍

९. एवं तौ निश्चयं कृत्वा मातापुत्रौ तपोवने ।
जग्मतुस्त्रिदिवं राम कृतार्थाविति नः श्रुतम् ॥

9. Thus the (step) mother & her (step) son, taking such a decision, went together to the heavenly world,

accomplished. Oh Raama! This is what was heard by us. (Such was the story I had heard long ago, says Vischwaamithra to Raama).

❍ ❍ ❍

१०. एष देशः स काकुत्स्थ महेन्द्राध्युषितः पुरा ।
दितिं यत्र तपस्सिद्धामेवं परिचचार सः ।।

10. Oh (Raama)The Kaakuthsa! This is the place where Lord Indhra lived; and where long ago, in this very place, he served Dhithi who was in a state of penance.

❍ ❍ ❍

११. इक्ष्वाकोस्तु नरव्याघ्र पुत्रः परमधार्मिकः ।
अलम्बुसायामुत्पन्नो विशाल इति विश्रुतः ।।

11. Oh (Raama) 'the tiger' of men! Further, As son of Ikshwaaku, a man who was foremost in Dharma & renowned as Vischaala, was born in the (city of) Alambusa.

❍ ❍ ❍

१२. तेन चासीदिह स्थाने विशालेति पुरी कृता ।
विशालस्य सुतो राम हेमचन्द्रो महाबलः ।।

12. And by him, in this very place was the city of Vischaala established: (city named after him): Oh Raama! And Vischaala had a son (named) Hemchandhra, who was mightily strong.

❍ ❍ ❍

१३. सुचन्द्र इति विख्यातो हेमचन्द्रादनन्तरः ।
सुचन्द्रतनयो राम धूम्राश्व इति विश्रुतः ।।

13. And renowned as Suchandhra, followed this Hemchandhra: And Suchandhra's son was renowned as Dhoomraaschwa.

❍ ❍ ❍

१४. धूम्राश्वतनयश्चापि सृञ्जयः समपद्यत ।
सृञ्जयस्य सुतः श्रीमान् सहदेवः प्रतापवान् ।।

14. Then Srinjaya became Dhoomraashwa's son: And Srinjaya's son was the majestic & resplendent Sahadhev.

❍ ❍ ❍

१५. कुशाश्वः सहदेवस्य पुत्रः परमधार्मिकः ।
कुशाश्वस्य महातेजाः सोमदत्तः प्रतापवान् ।।

15. And Sahadhev's son was the foremost man of Dharma, Kuschaaschwa. And to Kuschaaschwa was (the son) Somadhaththa, most brilliant, most majestical.

❍ ❍ ❍

१६. सोमदत्तस्य पुत्रस्तु ककुत्स्थ इति विश्रुतः ।।

16. And Somadhaththa's son was known as Kakuthsa.

❍ ❍ ❍

१७. तस्य पुत्रो महातेजाः संप्रत्येष पुरीमिमाम् ।
आवसत्यमरप्रख्यः सुमतिर्नाम दुर्जयः ।।

१८. इक्ष्वाकोस्तु प्रसादेन सर्वेवैशालिका नृपाः ।
दीर्घायुषो महात्मानो वीर्यवन्तः सुधार्मिकाः ।।

17 & 18.

And his son named Sumathi is very brilliant, comparable to the celestials, is invincible ..... And he lives in the city now. By the blessings of Ikshwaaku-s, all the kings of Vischaala are long lived: Great men (most eminent): Very brave, good men of Dharma.

❍ ❍ ❍

१९. इहाद्य रजनीं राम सुखं वत्स्यामहे वयम् ।
श्वः प्रभाते नरश्रेष्ठ जनकं द्रष्टुमर्हसि ।।

19. Oh Raama! We shall stay here for the night comfortably: Oh (Raama) the foremost of men! Tomorrow morning, we will go to 'see', (Visit), Janaka (the Mithila king).

❍ ❍ ❍

२०. सुमतिस्तु महातेजा विश्वामित्रमुपागतम् ।
श्रुत्वा नरवरश्रेष्ठः प्रत्युद्गच्छन्महायशाः ।।
२१. पूजां च परमां कृत्वा सोपाध्यायः सबान्धवः ।
प्राञ्जलिः कुशलं पृष्ट्वा विश्वामित्रमथाब्रवीत् ।।

20 & 21.

Hearing that Vischwaamithra was around, the most brilliant & most famous and foremost of men, Sumathi came towards him...... along with Upaadhyaya-s (Priests & teachers) and along with his folks. He paid his respects to him, enquired about his welfare, and then with his arms in Anjali (in reverence) addressed Vischwaamithra.

❍ ❍ ❍

२२. धन्योऽस्म्यनुगृहीतोऽस्मि यस्य मे विषयं मुनिः ।
संप्राप्तो दर्शनं चैव नास्ति धन्यतरो मया ।।

22. Oh Muni (Vishwaamithra)! By your visit to my place and by your 'Dharshan' (sight before me), I am indeed fortunate; I am most blessed (& favoured); There is none who is more fortunate than I.

❍ ❍ ❍

Chapter 48

The Curse upon Ahalya

१. पृष्ट्वा तु कुशलं तत्र परस्परसमागमे ।
कथान्ते सुमतिर्वाक्यं व्याजहार महामुनिम् ।।

1. (Vischwaamithra along with Raama & Lakshmana at Vischaala) There, at their mutual meeting they exchanged greetings & asked about their (mutual) welfare: At the end of conversation, Sumathi uttered the following to the great Rishi (Vischwaamithra).

❍ ❍ ❍

२. इमौ कुमारौ भद्रं ते देवतुल्यपराक्रमौ ।
गजसिंहगती वीरौ शार्दूलवृषभोपमौ ॥
३. पद्मपत्रविशालाक्षौ खड्गतूणीधनुर्धरौ ।
अश्विनाविव रूपेण समुपस्थितयौवनौ ॥
४. यदृच्छयैव गां प्राप्तौ देवलोकादिवामरौ ।
कथं पद्भ्यामिह प्राप्तौ किमर्थं कस्य वा मुने ॥
५. भूषयन्ताविमं देशं चन्द्रसूर्याविवाम्बरम् ।
परस्परस्य सदृशौ प्रमाणेङ्गितचेष्टितैः ॥
६. किमर्थं च नरश्रेष्ठौ सम्प्राप्तौ दुर्गमे पथि ।
वरायुधधरौ वीरौ श्रोतुमिच्छामि तत्त्वतः ॥

2 to 6:

Welfare to you! These two young boys are valiant looking like Dheva-s, their gait is like those of a lion and elephant & bull; very brave..... their eyes are like those of lotus petal; large; And they are wielding sword, bow & quivers; By their beauty, they appear like The Ashwini-s; they have attained youthhood...... like Dheva-s descended upon earth, spontaneously from the Dheva world! Why have these two come on foot? Oh Muni (Vischwaamithra)! For what purpose? And for whose sake? ..... Like Moon and Sun brightening the sky, they 'decorate' this place! In stature, in walk, in dress and appearance, they resemble each other...... These foremost men are very brave; For what purpose have they come, treading the most difficult path (to travel), wielding foremost weapons:? I desire to hear (all this) exactly.

७. तस्य तद्वचनं श्रुत्वा यथावृत्तं न्यवेदयत् ।
अयोध्याधिपतेः पुत्रौ राज्ञो दशरथस्य हि ॥
मम यज्ञसमाप्त्यर्थमागतौ रामलक्ष्मणौ ॥
८. सिद्धाश्रममनुप्राप्य राक्षसानभिहत्य च ।
इमं देशमनुप्राप्तौ वीरौ दशरथात्मजौ ॥

7 & 8.

(Vischwaamithra tells Sumathi): Hearing such words, he informed him exactly as it (all) happened.= These (two) Raama & Lakshmana are the sons of Dhascharatha, the king of Ayodhya. They came (with me) to complete my Yaaga (They protected me!) These two sons of Dhascharatha came (with me) to my Sidha hermitage, destroyed demons & have come to this place =

❍ ❍ ❍

९. विश्वामित्रवचः श्रुत्वा राजा परमहर्षितः ।
अतिथी परमौ प्राप्तौ पुत्रौ दशरथस्य तौ ।।
पूजयामास विधिवत् सत्कारार्हौ महाबलौ ।।

9. Hearing Vischwaamithra's words, the king (Sumathi) who was very happy, honoured these two sons of Dhascharatha who were mightily strong and who deserved to be honoured and who had come there as foremost guests. (He honoured them) as per norms......

❍ ❍ ❍

१०. ततः परमसत्कारं सुमतेः प्राप्य राघवौ ।
उष्य तत्र निशामेकां जग्मतुर्मिथिलां ततः ।।

10. Accepting the foremost hospitality of Sumathi, Raama & Lakshmana spent the night there and then started for Mithila.

❍ ❍ ❍

११. तां दृष्ट्वा मुनयः सर्वेजनकस्य पुरीं शुभाम् ।
साधु साध्विति शंसन्तो मिथिलां समपूजयन् ।।

11. All the Rishi-s (who were accompanying Vischwaamithra), seeing this lovely Mithila city (from a distance), the city of King Janaka, extolled this Mithila (saying): = Well, Well! (How lovely)=.

❍ ❍ ❍

१२. मिथिलोपवने तत्र आश्रमं दृश्य राघवः ।
पुराणं निर्जनं रम्यं पप्रच्छ मुनिपुङ्गवम् ।।

12. And (Raama) the Raaghava, seeing the uninhabited beautiful, old (but dilapidated) lovely hermitage in the forest around Mithila, asked (Vischwaamithra), the 'Tiger' amongst Muni-s

❍ ❍ ❍

१३. श्रीमदाश्रमसमाशं किं न्विदं मुनिवर्जितम् ।
श्रोतुमिच्छामि भगवन् कस्यायं पूर्व आश्रमः ।।

13. Oh Lord (Vishwaamithra)! This resplendent hermitage, but uninhabited by Muni-s, What is this (Place)? Whose Hermitage was this before? I desire to hear.

❍ ❍ ❍

१४. तच्छ्रुत्वा राघवेणोक्तं वाक्यं वाक्यविशारदः ।
प्रत्युवाच महातेजा विश्वामित्रो महामुनिः ।।

14. Hearing the words told by (Raama) the Raaghava, the great Muni Vischwaamithra who was most brilliant & who was well versed in speech, replied.

❍ ❍ ❍

१५. हन्त ते कथयिष्यामि श्रृणु तत्त्वेन राघव ।
यस्यैतदाश्रमपदं शप्तं कोपान्महात्मना ।।

15. Well! (Raama the) Raaghava! I will narrate to you exactly: This hermitage, whose (it was); and how, by the wrath of a man of great soul, this was cursed.

❍ ❍ ❍

१६. गौतमस्य नरश्रेष्ठ पूर्वमासीन्महात्मनः ।
आश्रमो दिव्यसमाशः सुरैरपि सुपूजितः ।।

16. (Vischwaamithra narrates yet another story to Raama, Ahalya's) Oh (Raama) the foremost of men! (Listen)! Long ago, this was the hermitage of the great soul, Sage

Gauthama, which was looking like celestial world and which was honoured by Dheva-s as well.

❍ ❍ ❍

१७. स चेह तप आतिष्ठदहल्यासहितः पुरा ।
वर्षपूगाननेकांश्च राजपुत्र महायशः ॥

17. Oh most famous (Raama) the royal prince! Along with (his wife) Ahalya, he did many years of penance here, in succession.

❍ ❍ ❍

१८. कदाचिद्दिवसे राम ततो दूरं गते मुनौ ।
तस्यान्तरं विदित्वा तु सहस्राक्षः शचीपतिः ॥
मुनिवेषधरोऽहल्यामिदं वचनमब्रवीत् ॥

18. Oh Raama! One day, when the Muni (Gauthama) had gone far away from there, during this period, taking note (of Gauthama's absence), the thousand eyed Indhra, the husband of Sachi (came there) taking the form of sage (Gauthama, in disguise) and said this to Ahalya.

❍ ❍ ❍

१९. ऋतुकालं प्रतीक्षन्ते नार्थिनः सुसमाहिते ।
सङ्गमं त्वहमिच्छामि त्वया सह सुमध्यमे ॥

19. (As usual Lord Indhra is upto mischief: Here is an example of his debauchery); (This Indhra said to Ahalya when her husband was away). . . . Oh lady with well formed (figure)! Men of passion do not await proper time (& care for even woman's monthly periods, nor time & place). Oh lady with lovely waist! I desire carnal pleasure with you! (Readers may note that Poet Vaalmeeki uses the Sanskrit word- Rithu Kaala-which means proper season, and here refers to woman's periods. This Indhra of course cannot wait, must have an affair when the husband is away. In the

Hindu Dharma this is nothing but Rape, even if done willingly. And Sex is taboo in the early mornings.)

❍ ❍ ❍

२०. मुनिवेषं सहस्राक्षं विज्ञाय रघुनन्दन ।
मतिं चकार दुर्मेधा देवराजकुतूहलात् ।।

20. Oh (Raama) the darling of Raghu-s! (Listen)! Knowing fully well that this man (who came there in disguise) in the form of the Muni (her husband Gauthama) was the thousand eyed Lord Indhra, this stupid (woman Ahalya) lost her mind (& heart) to him because of her desire (towards him) as he was the 'king' of Dheva-s (Ahalya voluntarily submitted to him out of passion).

❍ ❍ ❍

२१. अथाब्रवीत् सुरश्रेष्ठं कृतार्थेनान्तरान्मना ।
कृतार्थाऽस्मि सुरश्रेष्ठ गच्छ शीघ्रमितः प्रभो ।।

21. With her desire fulfilled, with all her heart she addressed the Lord of Dheva-s: = Oh the foremost Dheva (Indhra)! I have fulfilled my wish. Oh Lord! Go away from here quickly =

❍ ❍ ❍

२२. आत्मानं मां च देवेश सर्वदा रक्ष मानद ।
इन्द्रस्तु प्रहसन् वाक्यमहल्यामिदमब्रवीत् ।।

22. Oh Lord of Dheva-s; Oh protector of honour, yours & mine, always! Protect (me & yourself: let not others know this); And Lord Indhra, too, said the following to Ahalya, (sporting a victory) smile.

❍ ❍ ❍

२३. परितुष्टोऽस्मि सुश्रोणि गमिष्यामि यथाऽऽगतम् ।।

23. Oh lady with beautiful hips! I am very pleased (with my affair with you): I will go back as I came.

❍ ❍ ❍

२४. एवं सङ्गम्य तु तया निश्चक्रामोटजात्ततः ।
स संभ्रमात्त्वरन् राम शमि तो गौतमं प्रति ।।

24. Oh Raama (Listen)! Having had an affair with her, then (Indhra) became apprehensive over Gauthama; and in a flurry began to leave (to make a quick 'Get Away', like a thief), quickly from the hermitage.

❍ ❍ ❍

२५. गौतमं स ददर्शाथ प्रविशन्तं महामुनिम् ।
देवदानवदुर्धर्षं तपोबलसमन्वितम् ।।

25. (But fate decides otherwise: the 'Thief' is caught)!. At once (at that very moment), he (this Indhra) saw the great Muni Gauthama who was endowed with enormous power of penance and who was 'uncrushable' by Dheva-s and Dhaanava-s, enter (his hermitage).

❍ ❍ ❍

२६. तीर्थोदकपरिक्लिन्नं दीप्यमानमिवानलम् ।
भस्मोद्धूलितसर्वाङ्गमुमापतिमिवापरम् ।।
२७. शिवभक्तं महात्मानं सर्वतत्त्वार्थवेदिनम् ।
गृहीतसमिधं राम सकुशं मुनिपुङ्गवम् ।।
२८. दृष्ट्वा सुरपतिस्त्रस्तो विषण्णवदनोऽभवत् ।।

26 to 28.

(Poet Vaalmeeki describes how Gauthama appeared before Indhra)..... He was wet after (early) bath in pure waters: He was 'glowing' like Fire; He was besmeared with sacred ash all over his body; he was like another Umaapathi (Rudhra-God Schiva)....... he was worshipper of Schiva: was a great soul; he knew the essence of all knowledge (Shaasthra-s)-- The Truth-s; he was carrying Samiths that he had gathered, (twigs for fire rituals); He had Dharbha grass (with him); Oh Raama! (Indhra saw such a man): The moment he saw, this lord of Sura-s (Indhra) became terribly scared with a downcast face.

❍ ❍ ❍

२९. अथ दृष्ट्वा सहस्राक्षं मुनिवेषधरं मुनिः ।
दुर्वृत्तं वृत्तसम्पन्नो रोषाद्वचनमब्रवीत् ।।

29. Endowed with (impeccable) conduct, this Rishi (Gauthama), when he saw this thousand eyed Indhra of immoral conduct, at once addressed him in wrath, (seeing him disguised) as a Muni.

❍ ❍ ❍

३०. मम रूपं समास्थाय कृतवानसि दुर्मते ।
अकर्तव्यमिदं तस्माद्विफलस्त्वं भविष्यसि ।।

30. (The great sage he was, Gauthama at once knew that this scoundrel Indhra had committed adultery with his wife). = Oh evil minded (Indhra)! Taking on my form, (impersonating me) you have done this deed that should never have been done. Therefore you shall become Impotent. =

❍ ❍ ❍

३१. गौतमेनैवमुक्ते तु सरोषेण महात्मना ।
पेततुर्वृषणौ भूमौ सहस्राक्षस्य तत्क्षणात् ।।

31. When told thus by the great soul Gauthama in wrath, at once, the two Testicles of the thousand eyed (Indhra) fell on earth.

❍ ❍ ❍

३२. अथ शप्त्वा च वै शक्रं भार्यामपि च शप्तवान् ।
इह वर्षसहस्राणि बहूनि त्वं निवत्स्यसि ।।

३३. वायुभक्षा शिला भूत्वा तप्यन्ती भस्मशायिनी ।
अदृश्या सर्वभूतानामाश्रमेऽस्मिन् भविष्यसि ।।

32 & 33.

Then, after cursing Indhra, he cursed his wife (Ahalya) thus: = You Shall Remain Here - 1,000 long years. . . . Becoming a Stone, 'Eating' Only Air: In Torment; Lying in Dust; Unseen By All The Living Beings, In This Very Hermitage.

❍ ❍ ❍

३४. यदा चैतद्वनं घोरं रामो दशरथात्मजः ।
आगमिष्यति दुर्धर्षस्तदा पूता भविष्यसि ॥

34. And when the uncrushable Raama, the son of Dhascharatha, comes to this gruesome forest (this desolate place), then you will be purified (and become a woman again).

❍ ❍ ❍

३५. तस्यातिथ्येन दुर्वृत्ते लोभमोहविवर्जिता ।
मत्सकाशं मुदा युक्ता स्वं वपुर्धारयिष्यसि ॥

35. Oh (Ahalya) of evil conduct! When you honour (Raama) as a guest, then you will become happy and (take your place again) by my side, and bear your own (normal) body, bereft of passion & avarice. =

❍ ❍ ❍

३६. एवमुक्त्वा महातेजा गौतमो दुष्टचारिणीम् ।
इममाश्रममुत्सृज्य सिद्धचारणसेविते ॥
हिमवच्छिखरे रम्ये तपस्तेपे महातपाः ॥

36. The most brilliant Gauthama, after telling her this, left this hermitage and this man of mighty penance did penance in the beautiful peaks of Himaalaya-s that is inhabited by Sidhdha-s & Chaarana-s.

(Note: Vischwaamithra is a very great personality: In bringing Raama to this desolate place, a great purpose is served. 1,000 years of curse upon Ahalya is over; When Raama places his feet on the 'The Stone', Ahalya's curse is over & she is bereft of sin.)

❍ ❍ ❍

Chapter 49

The resurrection of Ahalya

(Vischwaamithra brings Raama to where Ahalya is a stone by the curse on her by husband Gauthama: Raama resurrects her.)

❍ ❍ ❍

१. अफलस्तु ततः शक्रो देवानग्निपुरोगमान् ।
अब्रवीत्त्रस्तवदनः सर्षिसङ्घान् सचारणान् ।।

1. This impotent Indhra, with a trembling face addressed the Dheva-s, who were with a group of Rishi-s & Chaarana-s, and who were accompanied by Lord of Fire (Agni).

(Indhra does not waste time: He cannot be without Sex organs!)

❍ ❍ ❍

२. कुर्वता तपसो विघ्नं गौतमस्य महात्मनः ।
क्रोधमुत्पाद्य हि मया सुरकार्यमिदं कृतम् ।।

2. This Deed (of sex with Ahalya) which was done by me that caused harm to the penance of the great soul Gauthama & which brought wrath to him, is verily the work of Dheva-s.

(Indhra takes 'cover'; Justifies his ignominy as though his immoral act was a 'conspiracy' hatched by Dheva-s for good of the world.)

❍ ❍ ❍

३. अफलोऽस्मि कृतस्तेन क्रोधात् सा च निराकृता ।
शापमोक्षेण महता तपोऽस्यापहृतं मया ।।

3. By (Gauthama's) wrath, I have been made impotent: And she (Ahalya) was also cursed. By the release of the great curse (upon us), his penance, (fruits of his

penance) has been 'snatched' away from (Gauthama) by me."

(Readers may note: Penance is like a Bank account; Once you use the power of your penance, like throwing a curse, then you lose much of the 'fruits' of your penance & you must do penance again to 'build up' your account! Indhra cannot tolerate any threat to his position as Lord of Dheva-s & celestials. In this affair with Ahalya, Indhra gets a sadistic satisfaction that not only did he enjoy sex with Ahalya, he also made her husband lose the fruits of his penance by 'making him' curse him. Indhra feels that his 'subjects', the Dheva-s, must be grateful to him that he 'raped' Ahalya!!).

❍ ❍ ❍

४. तन्मां सुरवराः सर्वेसर्षिसङ्घाः सचारणाः ।
सुरकार्यकरं यूयं सफलं कर्तुमर्हथ ॥

4. Therefore, all of you, the foremost Dheva-s who are with multitude of Rishi-s & Chaarana-s, must make me, who has done this task for Dheva-s, (sexually) 'Potent' (once again).

❍ ❍ ❍

५. शतक्रतोर्वचः श्रुत्वा देवाः साग्निपुरोगमाः ।
पितृदेवानुपेत्याहुः सह सर्वैर्मरुद्गणैः ॥

5. After listening to the words of Indhra, Lord Agni and other Dheva-s, all of them together with congregation of Maruths, sought The Pithrudheva-s (Deities) & said;

❍ ❍ ❍

६. पुराऽविचार्य मोहेन ऋषिपत्नीं शतक्रतुः ।
धर्षयित्वा मुनेश्शापात्तत्रैव विफलः कृतः ॥

6. Without giving thought earlier, Lord Indhra, out of passion, *embrocated (Ahalya) the wife of Rishi (Gauthama) and (therefore) by the curse of Rishi (Gauthama), was made impotent there itself. (poet

Vaalmeeki uses word*Grish-Embrocate, grind, rub etc.; Here it of course means, what it means!)

❍ ❍ ❍

७. अयं मेषः सवृषणः शक्रो ह्यवृषणः कृतः ।
मेषस्य वृषणौ गृह्य शक्रायाशु प्रयच्छत ।।

7. This goat is virile: And Lord Indhra has no testicles: Taking out the two testicles (Sex organs) of the goat, you shall give these to Indhra quickly. (A case of sex organ transplantation!)

❍ ❍ ❍

८. अफलस्तु कृतो मेषः परां तुष्टिं प्रदास्यति ।।
९. भवतां हर्षणार्थं च ये च दास्यन्ति मानवाः ।।

8 & 9.

This goat that will be made impotent will give great satisfaction! Like such of those who offer gifts for your pleasure.

❍ ❍ ❍

१०. इत्येग्नेर्वचनं श्रुत्वा पितृदेवाः समागताः ।
उत्पाट्य मेषवृषणौ सहस्राक्षे न्यवेशयन् ।।

10. Hearing such words of Lord Agni, The Pithrudheva-s got together and pulled out the sex organs of the goat & 'placed' (transplanted) on the thousand eyed (Lord Indhra).

❍ ❍ ❍

११. तदाप्रभृति काकुत्स्थ पितृदेवाः समागताः ।
अफलान् भुञ्जते मेषान् फलैस्तेषामयोजयन् ।।

11. Oh (Raama) the Kaakuthsa (Listen)! From those times, The Pithrudheva-s eat goats without sex organs By their service, one obtains fruits for (such of those who render such services).

❍ ❍ ❍

१२. इन्द्रस्तु मेषवृषणस्तदाप्रभृति राघव ।
गौतमस्य प्रभावेण तपसश्च महात्मनः ।।

12. Oh (Raama) the Raaghava! And Lord Indhra also became a (MeshaVrishna) from that time, thanks to the power of the great soul Gauthama's penance. (Mesha-Goat: Vrishna-sex organ).

❍ ❍ ❍

१३. तदागच्छ महातेज आश्रमं पुण्यकर्मणः ।
तारयैनां महाभागामहल्यां देवरूपिणीम् ।।

13. (And Vishwaamithra 'invites' Raama to visit the dilapidated hermitage of sage Gauthama to resurrect Ahalya)..... Therefore Oh Raama the most brilliant! Come to the hermitage of the holy Rishi: Release the most illustrious, this Ahalya who has the form of a celestial (from the curse on her).

❍ ❍ ❍

१४. विश्वामित्रवचः श्रुत्वा राघवः सहलक्ष्मणः ।
विश्वामित्रं पुरस्कृत्य तमाश्रममथाविशत् ।।

14. Hearing Vischwaamithra's words, (Raama) the Raaghava, along with Lakshmana, at once entered this hermitage.

❍ ❍ ❍

१५. ददर्श च महाभागां तपसा द्योतितप्रभाम् ।
लोकैरपि समागम्य दुर्निरीक्षां सुरासुरैः ।।

१६. प्रयत्नान्निर्मितां धात्रा दिव्यां मायामयीमिव ।
सतुषारावृतां साभ्रां पूर्णचन्द्रप्रभामिव ।।

१७. धूमेनाभि परीताङ्गीं दीप्तामग्निशिखामिव ।
मध्येऽम्भसौ दुराधर्षां दीप्तां सूर्यप्रभामिव ।।

15 to 17.

(Stanzas 15 to 18 the scene at the dilapidated hermitage; Raama saw her: He alone could see her)...... He saw her; As most illustrious; radiating brilliance by (power of her) penance; she was unseen by men in the world, (even by) Sura-s & Asura-s (when they came there) together..... Was created by great effort by God Bramma; Was divinely; Was Invisible; like magic; like a full moon covered by snow & clouds. . ... like burning flame of fire although covered by smoke; she was like rays of the burning Sun that cannot be 'embrocated' even in the middle of waters.

❍ ❍ ❍

१८. सा हि गौतमवाक्येन दुर्निरीक्ष्या बभूव ह ।
त्रयाणामपि लोकानां यावद्रामस्य दर्शनम् ।।
शापस्यान्तमुपागम्य तेषां दर्शनमागता ।।

18. (Note: Raama alone could see her like this; others saw her only as stone: The 1,000 years have passed away & Raama has presented himself before her. This 1,000 years are considered penance for her, understandably. As a stone, she saw everything happening around; but could do nothing because she was a stone. She 'suffered' all the suffering of the world around her but had to remain silent; That was her penance.)

And she (this Ahalya), because of Gauthama's words (of curse), was unseen by all the three worlds till she (obtained) Raama's (presence &) sight: When the curse had ended (after 1,000 years), she came to be seen by all in the worlds.

❍ ❍ ❍

१९. राघवौ तु ततस्तस्याः पादौ जगृहतुस्तदा ।
स्मरन्ती गौतमवचः प्रतिजग्राह सा च तौ ।।

19. Then the two Raaghava-s (Raama & Lakshmana), touched her feet: And (Ahalya) remembering (her husband) Gauthama's words, greeted them all.

❍ ❍ ❍

२०. पाद्यमर्घ्यं तथाऽऽतिथ्यं चकार सुसमाहिता ।
प्रतिजग्राह काकुत्स्थो विधिदृष्टेन कर्मणा ।।

20. With due regard & care, she extended hospitality, (offering) Arghya & Paadhya. And (Raama) the Kaakuthsa, accepted her (hospitality) that was done as per norms of Shaasthra-s.

❍ ❍ ❍

२१. पुष्पवृष्टिर्महत्यासीद्देवदुन्दुभिनिस्वनः ।
गन्धर्वाप्सरसां चापि महानासीत् समागमः ।।

21. Great blossoms of flowers appeared (at once): Sounds of Dhundhubi drums of celestials (reverberated): And the congregation of Ghandharva-s & Apsara-s became large.

❍ ❍ ❍

२२. साधु साध्विति देवास्तामहल्यां समपूजयन् ।
तपोबलविशुद्धाङ्गीं गौतमस्य वशानुगाम् ।।

22. The Dheva-s honoured this Ahalya as she had become 'obedient' to Gauthama with her body purified by the power of her penance: (They all said): Splendid, Splendid!

❍ ❍ ❍

२३. गौतमो हि महातेजा अहल्यासहितः सुखी ।
रामं सम्पूज्य विधिवत्तपस्तेपे महातपाः ।।

23. And the most brilliant Gauthama also, was enjoined with Ahalya & he honoured Raama well, being very happy; And he began to do penance (once again) desirous of doing penance.

❍ ❍ ❍

२४. रामोऽपि परमां पूजां गौतमस्य महामुनेः ।
सकाशाद्विधिवत् प्राप्य जगाम मिथिलां ततः ।।

24. Having obtained foremost honour from the great soul

Muni Gauthama, Raama then left for Mithila (along with Vischwaamithra).

(Note: Ahalya is resurrected & once again joins her husband Gauthama. Not only that; This great Hermitage & the forest around, gets back its 'Lustre' as before. Raama was such a man.)

Chapter 50

The Journey to Mithila

(Vischwaamithra takes the two princes to Mithila where King Janaka is performing a great Yaaga; But he has another reason, purpose.)

❍ ❍ ❍

१. ततः प्रागुत्तरां गत्वा रामः सौमित्रिणा सह ।
विश्वामित्रं पुरस्कृत्य यज्ञवाटमुपागमत् ॥

1. From there, Raama along with (Lakshmana) the son of Sumithra, following Vischwaamithra, reached The Yaaga centre, going in the north easterly direction.

❍ ❍ ❍

२. रामस्तु मुनिशार्दूलमुवाच सहलक्ष्मणः ।
साध्वी यज्ञसमृद्धिर्हि जनकस्य महात्मनः ॥

2. And Raama who was (ever) with Lakshmana, addressed (Vischwaamithra), the 'Lion' amongst Muni-s:= The most eminent (King) Janaka's Yaaga arrangements, are excellent. Indeed =.

❍ ❍ ❍

३. बहुनीह सहस्राणि नानादेशनिवासिनाम् ।
ब्राह्मणानां महाभाग वेदाध्ययनशालिनाम् ॥

3. Oh (Vischwaamithra) the most illustrious! Many

thousands of Braamins well versed in the study of Vedha-s residing in various places are here.

❍ ❍ ❍

४. ऋषिवाटाश्च दृश्यन्ते शकटीशतसंकुलाः ।
देशो विधीयतां ब्रह्मन् यत्र वत्स्यामहे वयम् ।।

4. The dwelling places of Rishi-s are 'seen' to be stacked up with cart loads of materials. Oh Braamin! Where shall we stay? That place may be decided upon by you.

❍ ❍ ❍

५. रामस्य वचनं श्रुत्वा विश्वामित्रो महामुनिः ।
निवेशमकरोद्देशे विविक्ते सलिलायुते ।।

5. Hearing Raama's words, the great soul Muni Vischwaamithra decided upon their stay in a place near waterfront, away from crowd. (isolated spot).

❍ ❍ ❍

६. विश्वामित्रमनुप्राप्तं श्रुत्वा स नृपतिस्तदा ।
शतानन्दं पुरस्कृत्य पुरोहितमनिन्दितम् ।।
प्रत्युज्जगाम सहसा विनयेन समन्वितः ।।

6. Hearing of the arrival of Vischwamithra, the king (Janaka) at once went towards him in all humility, accompanied by the irreproachable priest, Schathaanandh, going in front of him.

❍ ❍ ❍

७. ऋत्विजोऽपि महात्मानस्त्वर्घ्यमादाय सत्वरम् ।
विश्वामित्राय धर्मेण ददुर्मन्त्रपुरस्कृतम् ।।

7. The most eminent Rithviks soon took (with them) Arghya and offered this to Vischwaamithra with chants & as per Dharma.

❍ ❍ ❍

८. प्रतिगृह्य तु तां पूजां जनकस्य महात्मनः ।
पप्रच्छ कुशलं राज्ञो यज्ञस्य च निरामयम् ।।

8. Receiving the honour of the great soul Janaka, (Vischwaamithra) enquired the king about his welfare and about (the progress of the) Yaaga without stoppage (& hindrance).

❍ ❍ ❍

९. स तांश्चापि मुनीन् पृष्ट्वा सोपाध्यायपुरोधसः ।
यथान्यायं ततः सर्वैः समागच्छत्प्रहृष्टवत् ।।

9. (Vischwaamithra) then enquired (about the welfare of) these Muni-s who were with Purohiths & Upaadhyaya-s (Priests, teachers), successively. And he rejoiced with them all.

❍ ❍ ❍

१०. अथ राजा मुनिश्रेष्ठं कृताञ्जलिरभाषत ।
आसने भगवन्नास्तां सहैभिर्मुनिसत्तमैः ।।

10. Then the king (Janaka) who had cupped his hands in Anjali, spoke to (Vischwaamithra), the foremost of Muni-s: Oh Lord! May you be seated along with these foremost Muni-s here.

❍ ❍ ❍

११. जनकस्य वचः श्रुत्वा निषसाद महामुनिः ।
पुरोधा ऋत्विजश्चैव राजा च सह मन्त्रिभिः ।।

11. After hearing king Janaka's words, the great Muni (Vischwaamithra) sat down; Then the Purohith-s, Rithviks, along with his ministers, sat; likewise the King.

❍ ❍ ❍

१२. आसनेषु यथान्यायमुपविष्टान् समन्ततः ।
दृष्ट्वा स नृपतिस्तत्र विश्वामित्रमथाब्रवीत् ।।

12. Seeing that they were seated properly (as per protocol) on all sides, this king (Janaka) addressed Vischwaamithra.

❍ ❍ ❍

१३. अद्य यज्ञसमृद्धिर्मेसकला दैवतैः कृता ।
अद्य यज्ञफलं प्राप्तं भगवद्दर्शनान्मया ।।

13. The preparations of my Yaaga, all of this, was done by Dhevas: And by my lord's presence, (by your sight), the fruits of my Yaaga has been 'obtained' by me now.

❍ ❍ ❍

१४. धन्योऽस्म्यनुगृहीतोऽस्मि यस्य मे मुनिपुङ्गव ।
यज्ञोपसदनं ब्रह्मन् प्राप्तोऽसि मुनिभिः सह ।।

14. Oh (Vischwaamithra) the 'tiger' of Muni-s!, Oh Braamin! As you have come to my Yaaga center along with Muni-s, I have become blessed: Am (most) fortunate.

❍ ❍ ❍

१५. द्वादशाहं तु ब्रह्मर्षेशेषमाहुर्मनीषिणः ।
ततो भागार्थिनो देवान् द्रष्टुमर्हसि कौशिक ।।

15. Oh Bramma Rishi (Vischwaamithra)! The learned Pundits tell (me) that 12 days remain; Oh Vischwaamithra! Then you will see the Deities who will come for their share of oblations.

(As readers may know by now, various lords & deities come down to earth to personally receive The Oblations of any great Yaaga performed on earth; and they honour & bless The Doer of Yaaga.)

❍ ❍ ❍

१६. इत्युक्त्वा मुनिशार्दूलं प्रहृष्टवदनस्तदा ।
पुनस्तं परिपप्रच्छ प्राञ्जलिः प्रणतो नृपः ।।

16. Saying thus to (Vischwaamithra) the 'Lion' amongst Muni-s, the king whose face beamed with joy, bowed to him; And cupping his hands in Anjali asked once again:

❍ ❍ ❍

१७. इगौ कुगारौ भद्रं ते देवतुल्यपराक्रमौ ।
गजसिंहगती वीरौ शार्दूलवृषभोपमौ ।।

१८. पद्मपत्रविशालाक्षौ खड्गतूणीधनुर्धरौ ।
अश्विनाविव रूपेण समुपस्थितयौवनौ ।।

१९. यदृच्छयैव गां प्राप्तौ देवलोकादिवामरौ ।
पुण्डरीकविशालाक्षौ वरायुधधरावुभौ ।।

२०. बद्धगोधांगुलित्राणौ खड्गवन्तौ महाद्युती ।
काकपक्षधरौ वीरौ कुमाराविव पावकी ।।

२१. रूपौदार्यगुणैः पुंसां दृष्टिचित्तापहारिणौ ।।

२२. प्राकाश्यं कुलमस्माकं मामुद्धर्तुमिहागतौ ।
कथं पद्भ्यामिह प्राप्तौ किमर्थं कस्य वा मुने ।।

२३. वरायुधधरौ वीरौ कस्य पुत्रौ महात्मनः ।
भूषयन्ताविमं देशं चन्द्रसूर्याविवाम्बरम् ।।

२४. परस्परस्य सदृशौ प्रमाणेङ्गितचेष्टितैः ।
काकपक्षधरौ वीरौ श्रोतुमिच्छामि तत्त्वतः ।।

17 to 24.

(Janaka asks Vishwaamithra) Their strides are like those of elephants & lions; They wield bow, sword, (carry) quivers: In beauty like Ashwini-s...... Their eyes are wide & like lotus; they have 'reached' youth-hood...... (they appear) like Dheva-s descended on earth from heaven; by divine chance Like lotus flower eyes wide, and these two are wielding foremost weapons; (He asked about the two princes):...... Welfare to you These two youths; they appear to be equal to Dheva-s in valour; they are like lion & bull, very brave: In their fingers they are wearing gloves made of leather; they are wielding swords; they sport side burns & hairlocks (A hair style); They are like Paavaki, the sons of Fire (Kumaara-Skandha); these two youths....... By their beauty & graceful form of body, they capture the eyes & hearts of men....... Why have they come here on foot (as though for) raising the status of my family and me (as well)! Oh Rishi. What purpose & for whom (have they come with you) .... Whose great man's sons are these two brave (youths) who 'decorate' this place, like Sun

& Moon over sky....... These two warriors who wield foremost weapons resemble each other in appearance, gait-strides & in manners: I desire to hear (about them) exactly (in detail).

❍ ❍ ❍

२५. तस्य तद्वचनं श्रुत्वा जनकस्य महात्मनः ।
न्यवेदयन्महात्मानौ पुत्रौ दशरथस्य तौ ॥

25. Hearing the most eminent Janaka's words, (Vischwaamithra) informed him that these (two) eminent (youths) were sons of Dhascharatha.

❍ ❍ ❍

२६. सिद्धाश्रमनिवासं च राक्षसानां वधं तथा ।
तच्चागमनमव्यग्रं विशालायाश्च दर्शनम् ॥

२७. अहल्यादर्शनं चैव गौतमेन समागमम् ।
महाधनुषि जिज्ञासां कर्तुमागमनं तथा ॥

26 & 27.

(Vischwaamithra tells Janaka about Raama/ Lakshmana) Their stay in Sidhdha hermitage; the destruction of demons there; the sight of, (visit to), Vischaala: their safe journey (to this place)...... the sight of, (the meeting with), Ahalya: And (after her resurrection) her rejoining (her husband) Gauthama: And their coming here (to Mithila) desirous of finding out about a very great Bow.......

❍ ❍ ❍

२८. एतत्सर्वं महातेजा जनकाय महात्मने ।
निवेद्य विरराामाथ विश्वामित्रो महामुनिः ॥

28. After informing about all these to the most brilliant & most eminent Janaka, the great Muni Vishwaamithra rested (became silent).

❍ ❍ ❍

Chapter 51

Vischwaamithra's Life History

(Vischwaamithra is at Mithila with Raama & Lakshmana: Purpose of their visit already disclosed to King Janaka of Mithila: These two princes are to take a good look at the Mighty Divine Bow kept there by King Janaka in great 'reverence': King Janaka's minister & adviser, is the renowned sage, Schathaanandh who is the son of Ahalya & Gauthama. And Raama had just 'resurrected' his mother Ahalya. And naturally, Schathaanandh is very anxious to know about his mother Ahalya & his father Gauthama, who were separated for 1,000 years because of her transgression & the curse upon her by his father Gauthama. And in the following chapters, the next 14 chapters, readers will get a glimpse of this great man Vischwaamithra who was once a mighty king, but later gave up everything for becoming a Bramma Rishi- the highest title for a man of penance. It is this Schathaanandh who narrates the history of Vischwaamithra to Raama, telling him how fortunate Raama is that he has Vischwaamithra as his Guru- Teacher - in diverse ways. Chapters 51 to 65 it is all about the great Vischwaamithra: Raama is indeed privileged!)

❍ ❍ ❍

१. तस्य तद्वचनं श्रुत्वा विश्वामित्रस्य धीमतः ।
हृष्टरोमा महातेजाः शतानन्दो महातपाः ॥

1. Hearing the words of the wise Vischwaamithra, the most brilliant Schathaanandh of great penance, became thrilled with rapture.

❍ ❍ ❍

२. गौतमस्य सुतो ज्येष्ठस्तपसा द्योतितप्रभः ।
रामसन्दर्शनादेव परं विस्मयमागतः ॥

2. (This Schathaanandh), the eldest son of Gauthama,

was shining with lustre by (the power of his) penance; He was most wonder struck by the very presence of Raama.

❍ ❍ ❍

३. स तौ निषण्णौ संप्रेक्ष्य सुखासीनौ नृपात्मजौ ।
शतानन्दो मुनिश्रेष्ठं विश्वामित्रमथाब्रवीत् ।।

3. Seeing these two princes (Raama/Lakshmana) who were resting in comfort & reclining (in 'sofa'), this Schathaanandh then addressed the foremost Muni Vischwaamithra.

❍ ❍ ❍

४. अपि सा मुनिशार्दूल मम माता यशस्विनी ।
दर्शिता राजपुत्राय तपो दीर्घमुपागता ।।

4. (Oh Vischwaamithra) the 'Tiger' amongst Muni-s! Was my most famous mother (Ahalya) who had entered into a deep state of penance (of 1,000 years as a stone) introduced to Raama in forest?

❍ ❍ ❍

५. अपि रामे महातेजो मम माता यशस्विनी ।
वन्यैरुपाहरत् पूजां पूजार्हेसर्वदेहिनाम् ।।

5. Oh most brilliant (Vischwaamithra)! Did my famous mother honour Raama who deserves to be honoured by all beings, with (the hospitality of) forest products?........ (Readers may note: A son's love for mother never wanes: Although his mother Ahalya had committed a sin, a sin that was considered a very great sin for a woman of Dharma those days, Schathanandha still loves her)

❍ ❍ ❍

६. अपि रामाय कथितं यथावृत्तं पुरातनम् ।
मम मातुर्महातेजो दैवेन यदनुष्ठितम् ।।

6. Oh most brilliant (Vischwaamithra): Was Raama fully

told about all those events that happened before, all that happened to my mother (Ahalya) due to fate?

❍ ❍ ❍

७. अपि कौशिक भद्रं ते गुरुणा मम सङ्गता ।
माता मम मुनिश्रेष्ठ रामसन्दर्शनादितः ।।

7. Oh foremost Muni: Oh Kowschik (Oh Vischwaamithra)! Welfare to you: And, from the time of 'seeing' (and meeting) Raama, was my mother enjoined with my father (Gauthama).

(A good son never wants anything better for his parents than that they should live together in peace; No child likes divorce: This scene is heart rending; Schathaanandh's anxiety is understandable.)

❍ ❍ ❍

८. अपि मे गुरुणा रामः पूजितः कुशिकात्मज ।
इहागतो महातेजाः पूजां प्राप्तो महात्मनः ।।

8. Oh (Vischwaamithra) the son of Kuschika!: This most brilliant Raama who has come (here with you), was he honoured by my Guru, (my father, Gauthama)? And did he accept the great soul's (my father's) hospitality and honours?

❍ ❍ ❍

९. अपि शान्तेन मनसा गुरुर्मेकुशिकात्मज ।
इहागतेन रामेण पूजितेनाभिवादितः ।।

9. Oh (Vischwaamithra the) son of Kuschika! My Guru (my father Gauthama), was he addressed salutarily by the revered Raama who is here, with a tranquil mind? (Readers may appreciate Schathaanandh's anxiety: Perhaps Raama would have a contempt for my father because he had cursed my mother so cruelly!)

❍ ❍ ❍

१०. तच्छ्रुत्वा वचनं तस्य विश्वामित्रो महामुनिः ।
प्रत्युवाच शतानन्दं वाक्यज्ञो वाक्यकोविदम् ।।

10. (And Vischwaamithra sets Schathaanandh's mind at rest) Hearing these words of his, the great Muni Vischwaamithra who knew (the art of) speech, replied to Schathaanandh who was (also) well versed in speech.

❍ ❍ ❍

११. नातिक्रान्तं मुनिश्रेष्ठ यत् कर्तव्यं कृतं मया ।
सङ्गता मुनिना पत्नी भार्गवेणेव रेणुका ॥

11. Oh Foremost Muni (Schathaanandh)! Whatever Was To Be Done, (all that) Was Not Transgressed: It Was Well Completed (& done) By Me: ...... Like Renuka with Bhaarghava (Jamadhagni), the Wife, (your mother Ahalya), Was Enjoined With (your father Gauthama the) Muni.

(Poet Vaalmeeki, by the above stanza, tells us how Vischwaamithra saw to it that Raama visited the dilapidated hermitage where Ahalya was cursed as a stone for 1,000 years & how she was resurrected & how Schathaanandh's parents lived happily together.)

❍ ❍ ❍

१२. तच्छ्रुत्वा वचनं तस्य विश्वामित्रस्य धीमतः ।
शतानन्दो महातेजा रामं वचनमब्रवीत् ॥

12. Hearing the words of the wise Vischwaamithra, the most brilliant Schathaanandh, addressed the following to Raama:

❍ ❍ ❍

१३. स्वागतं ते नरश्रेष्ठ दिष्ट्या प्राप्तोऽसि राघव ।
विश्वामित्रं पुरस्कृत्य महर्षिमपराजितम् ॥

13. Oh (Raama) the foremost of men! Oh The Raaghava!. . Welcome to you! It is our good fortune that you have come accompanying the unconquerable great Rishi Vischwaamithra.

❍ ❍ ❍

१४. अचिन्त्यकर्मा तपसा ब्रह्मर्षिरतुलप्रभः ।
विश्वामित्रो महातेजा वेत्स्येनं परमां गतिम् ।।

14. (And Schathaanandh tells Raama what a very great man this Vishwaamithra is)...... This Vischwaamithra is (a man whose) deeds are unimaginable. By penance, he became a Bramma Rishi; He is most brilliant: And you should know (this): He is The Foremost Refuge.

❍ ❍ ❍

१५. नास्ति धन्यतरो राम त्वत्तोऽन्यो भुवि कश्चन ।
गोप्ता कुशिकपुत्रस्ते येन तप्तं महत्तपः ।।

15. Oh Raama! This son of Kuschika, (this Vischwaamithra) by whom many penance were done, is (indeed) protector to you; (I cannot possibly see) any one in this world more fortunate than you.

(And Schathaanandh begins narration of historical events connected with this very great sage Vischwaamithra: As indicated in introduction to this chapter, for the next 14 Chapters, Poet Vaalmeeki, through the mouth of Schathaanandh, takes us through the life of the great Vischwaamithra.) (Schathaanandh to Raama:)

❍ ❍ ❍

१६. श्रूयतामभिधास्यामि कौशिकस्य महात्मनः ।
यथाबलं यथातत्त्वं तन्मे निगदतः श्रृणु ।।

16. I will now describe what the power of this great soul (Vischwaamithra) the Kowschik is (really) like: May you hear (this): May you listen as I narrate (all this) exactly (as it all happened before).

❍ ❍ ❍

१७. राजाऽभूदेषु धर्मात्मा दीर्घकालमरिन्दमः ।
धर्मज्ञः कृतविद्यश्च प्रजानां च हिते रतः ।।

17. This man of Dharma, this knower of Dharma

(Vischwaamithra), was (long ago), a king for a long time: A destroyer of enemies; And having studied all the knowledge, was ever devoted in doing good to his subjects.

❍ ❍ ❍

१८. प्रजापतिसुतश्चासीत् कुशो नाम महीपतिः ।
कुशस्य पुत्रो बलवान् कुशनाभः सुधार्मिकः ।।

18. (Long ago) Bramma's son Kuscha lived as a king; Kuscha's son was Kuschanaabha who was mightily strong and a man of Dharma.

❍ ❍ ❍

१९. कुशनाभसुतस्त्वासीद्गाधिरित्येव विश्रुतः ।
गाधेः पुत्रो महातेजा विश्वामित्रो महामुनिः ।।

२०. विश्वामित्रो महातेजाः पालयामास मेदिनीम् ।
बहुवर्षसहस्राणि राजा राज्यमकारयत् ।।

19 & 20.

And Kuschanaabha's son was the celebrated Gaadhi: And Gaadhi's son is the most brilliant & great Muni, this Vischwaamithra. The most brilliant ischwaamithra ruled the earth as king; ruled the kingdom for many thousands of years.

❍ ❍ ❍

२१. कदाचित्तु महातेजा योजयित्वा वरूथिनीम् ।
अक्षौहिणीपरिवृत्तः परिचक्राम मेदिनीम् ।।

21. At one time the most brilliant (Vischwaamithra), commanding an Army of Akshowhini 'circled' the earth. (Readers may like to know that An Akshowhini consists of: 21,870 elephants, 21,870 chariots, 65,610 horses & 109, 350 Infantry.)

❍ ❍ ❍

२२. नगराणि च राष्ट्राणि सरितश्च तथा गिरीन् ।
आश्रमान् क्रमशो राम विचरन्नाजगाम ह ।।

२३. वसिष्ठस्याश्रमपदं नानापुष्पफलद्रुमम् ।
नानामृगगणाकीर्णं सिद्धचारणसेवितम् ॥

२४. देवदानवगन्धर्वैः किन्नरैरुपशोभितम् ।
प्रशान्तहरिणाकीर्णं द्विजसङ्घनिषेवितम् ॥

२५. ब्रह्मर्षिगणसमीर्णं देवर्षिगणसेवितम् ।
पुराणैस्तापसैः सिद्धैरग्निकल्पैर्महात्मभिः ॥

२६. अब्भक्षैर्वायुभक्षैश्च शीर्णपर्णाशनैस्तथा ।
फलमूलाशनैर्दान्तैर्जितरोषैर्जितेन्द्रियैः ॥

२७. ऋषिभिर्वालखिल्यैश्च जपहोमपरायणैः ।
अन्यैर्वैखानसैश्चैव समन्तादुपशोभितम् ॥

२८. ऊसिष्ठस्याश्रमपदं ब्रह्मलोकमिवापरम् ।
ददर्श जयतां श्रेष्ठो विश्वामित्रो महाबलः ॥

22 to 28.

(How during his wanderings all over the earth, he saw Sage Vasishta & his hermitage: And the beginning of enmity between him & Vasishta due to jealousy & his arrogance).

Oh Raama! (Listen)! One after the other, country by country, city by city, rivers, mountains, hermitages, he roamed about & travelled. (as a king with his Army)...... (He finally) reached Vasishta's hermitage that was full with various trees in full blossom of flowers & fruits, full with various types of animals in multitude,: His place was frequented by Sidhdha-s & Chaarana--s ...... Shining with (& inhabited by) Dheva-s, Dhaanava-s, & Ghandhravaa-s, Kinnara-s: Full with serene deers: Inhabited by group of braamins...... With a congregation of Bramma Rishi-s: And DhevaRishi-s, Inhabited by elders (old men) who were comparable to (Lord of) Fire...... and other (men of penance) who sustain themselves on mere water; some who live on mere air; some who live on dried leaves; some who live on fruits & tubers: All of them restrained (controlling their senses); Controlling their anger & sense organs.

Inhabited by Rishi-s who were ever doing prayers, and reciting chants; Others like Vaikanaasa: Everywhere shining brilliantly...... (Such was) Vasishta's Hermitage that looked like another world of God Bramma...... This foremost amongst the victorious, this mightily strong Vischwaamithra, saw......

❍ ❍ ❍

Chapter 52

Vasishta's hospitality to (king) Vischwaamithra

(Schathaanand continues narration to Raama about Vischwaamithra: About Vischwaamithra's meeting with sage Vasishta & his hostility.)

❍ ❍ ❍

१. स दृष्ट्वा परमप्रीतो विश्वामित्रो महाबलः ।
प्रणतो विनयाद्धीरो वसिष्ठं जपतां वरम् ।।

1. This brave mightily strong Vischwaamithra, seeing this Vasishta who was foremost amongst (men of) prayers & chants, became very happy & bowed to him in respect.

❍ ❍ ❍

२. स्वागतं तव चेत्युक्तो वसिष्ठेन महात्मना ।
आसनं चास्य भगवान् वसिष्ठो व्यादिदेश ह ।।

2. He was told by the great soul, Vasishta:= You are (most) welcome!= And lord (sage) Vasishta at once directed him to a seat.

❍ ❍ ❍

३. उपविष्टाय च तदा विश्वामित्राय धीमते ।
यथान्यायं ऋषिवरः फलमूलमुपाहरत् ।।

3. Then the foremost Rishi (Vasishta) offered fruits & tubers to the wise Vischwaamithra who was seated there, as per custom.

❍ ❍ ❍

४. प्रतिगृह्य च तां पूजां वसिष्ठाद्राजसत्तमः ।
तपोऽग्निहोत्रशिष्येषु कुशलं पर्यपृच्छत ।।
५. विश्वामित्रो महातेजा वनस्पतिगणे तदा ।
सर्वत्र कुशलं चाह वसिष्ठो राजसत्तमम् ।।

4 & 5.

Accepting the hospitality from Vasishta, the foremost of Kings (Vischwaamithra), asked him about the welfare of his disciples, his penance, his (daily) Fire Ritual..... And the most brilliant Vischwaamithra asked him about (the state of) the trees & plants (ecology): And Vasishta told this foremost king that all was well (with him and his hermitage).

❍ ❍ ❍

६. सुखोपविष्टं राजानं विश्वामित्रं महातपाः ।
पप्रच्छ जपतां श्रेष्ठो वसिष्ठो ब्रह्मणः सुतः ।।

6. The man of penance, this God Bramma's son Vasishta who was foremost amongst men of prayers & chants, asked king Vischwaamithra who was seated comfortably:

❍ ❍ ❍

७. कच्चिते कुशलं राजन् कच्चिद्धर्मेण रञ्जयन् ।
प्रजाः पालयसे राजन् राजवृत्तेन धार्मिक ।।

7. Oh king (Oh Vischwaamithra)! How is your welfare. Oh king who is a man of Dharma! Are you ruling over your subjects by proper royal conduct & delighting them all through Dharma?

❍ ❍ ❍

८. कच्चिते संभृता भृत्याः कच्चित्तिष्ठन्ति शासने ।

कच्चिते विजिताः सर्वेरिपवो रिपुसूदन ॥

8. Are your servants well provided for (& well treated): Do they stand by your command? Oh conqueror of enemies! Have your enemies been conquered? All of them?

❍ ❍ ❍

९. कच्चिद्बलेषु कोशेषु मित्रेषु च परंतप ।
कुशलं ते नरव्याघ्र पुत्रपौत्रे तथाऽनघ ॥

9. Oh 'Tiger' of men! Oh sinless (Vischwaamithra)! Oh tormentor of enemies! How is the welfare of your Army, your treasury, your friends, your sons, grandsons?

❍ ❍ ❍

१०. सर्वत्र कुशलं राजा वसिष्ठं प्रत्युदाहरत् ।
विश्वामित्रो महातेजा वसिष्ठं विनयान्वितः ॥

११. कृत्वोभौ सुचिरं कालं धर्मिष्ठौ ताः कथाः शुभाः ।
मुदा परमया युक्तौ प्रीयेतां तौ परस्परम् ॥

10 & 11.

The most brilliant, this king Vischwaamithra who had great respect for Vasishta, then replied to Vasishta that everything was well with him...... These two men of Dharma who rejoiced greatly together (& conversed) with pleasant stories (& anecdotes), for long moments became fond of each other:

❍ ❍ ❍

१२. ततो वसिष्ठो भगवान् कथान्ते रघुनन्दन ।
विश्वामित्रमिदं वाक्यमुवाच प्रहसन्निव ॥

12. Oh (Raama) the darling of Raghu-s! (Listen)! Then when conversation ended, the Lord (sage) Vasishta said the following words to Vischwaamithra with a smile.

❍ ❍ ❍

१३. आतिथ्यं कर्तुमिच्छामि बलस्यास्य महाबल ।
तव चैवाप्रमेयस्य यथार्हं सम्प्रतीच्छ मे ॥

13. Oh mightily strong (Vischwaamithra)! I Desire To Offer Proper Hospitality To Your Army, and To You of Incomparable (prowess): May You Accept This From Me.

❍ ❍ ❍

१४. सत्क्रियां हि भवानेतां प्रतीच्छतु मयोद्यताम् ।
राजा त्वमतिथिश्रेष्ठः पूजनीयः प्रयत्नतः ॥

14. You are a king: You are (my) foremost guest who should be honoured with great zeal & effort (& consideration). You should accept this hospitality that is extended by me.

❍ ❍ ❍

१५. एवमुक्तो वसिष्ठेन विश्वामित्रो महामतिः ।
कृतमित्यब्रवीद्राजा प्रियवाक्येन मे त्वया ॥

१६. फलमूलेन भगवन् विद्यते यत्तवाश्रमे ।
पाद्येनाचमनीयेन भगवद्दर्शनेन च ॥

१७. सर्वथा च महाप्राज्ञ पूजार्हेण सुपूजितः ।
गमिष्यामि नमस्तेऽस्तु मैत्रेणेक्षस्व चक्षुषा ॥

15 to 17.

When told thus by Vasishta, the most intelligent Vischwaamithra, the king, (told): (This hospitality) has been done to me by you (already) with your sweet words...... and with fruits & tubers and with all that is found in Hermitage, and with Arghya & Paadhya, and (most of all) by the very audience & sight of you.... Oh Lord (Vasishta).... In every way I have been honoured (with hospitality) by you who merits honour from every one (in the world): Therefore I am leaving (now): I bow to you: 'See' me ((bless me) with your friendly eyes, Oh most intelligent (Vasishta)!

(Vishwaamithra thanks Vasishta for his hospitality; but is baffled when Vasishta presses him to stay on to enjoy more hospitality. What more hospitality can this man of forest offer me, wonders Vischwaamithra, the king).

❍ ❍ ❍

१८. एवं ब्रुवन्तं राजानं वसिष्ठः पुनरेव हि ।
न्यमन्त्रयत धर्मात्मा पुनः पुनरुदारधीः ।।

18. The noble soul Vasishta who was very lofty, invited the king again and again and again even as the king (Vischwaamithra) was speaking thus;

❍ ❍ ❍

१९. बाढमित्येव गाधेयो वसिष्ठं प्रत्युवाच ह ।
यथा प्रियं भगवतस्तथाऽस्तु मुनिसत्तम ।।

19. And (Vischwaamithra) the son of Gaadhi replied to Vasishta:: = Oh foremost Muni (Vasishta)! Very well! Let it be as it pleases (you) =

❍ ❍ ❍

२०. एवमुक्तो महातेजा वसिष्ठो जपतां वरः ।
आजुहाव ततः प्रीतः कल्माषीं धूतकल्मषः ।।

20. The most brilliant Vasishta, who had 'blown off' all sins from himself, and who was foremost amongst men of prayers & chants, when told thus (by Vischwaamithra), became pleased and he called (invoked), Kalmaashi (Holy Cow Kaamadhenu).

(Readers may remember that this Kaamadhenu, the divine holy cow, was a 'Creation' during the Churning of the Milky Ocean.)

❍ ❍ ❍

२१. एह्येहि शबले क्षिप्रं श्रृणु चापि वचो मम ।
सबलस्यास्य राजर्षेः कर्तुं व्यवरितोऽस्म्यहम् ।।
भोजनेन महार्हेण सत्कारं संविधत्स्व मे ।।

21. Oh Schabala (Oh Kaamadhenu)! At once come, come! Listen to my words: I have decided to extend hospitality to the royal sage, (king Vischwaamithra) who is accompanied by his Army, with 'Great Dinner': Make preparations for me (for this hospitality I am extending to this king).

❍ ❍ ❍

२२. यस्य यस्य यथाकामं षड्रसेष्वभिपूजितम् ।
तत्सर्वं कामधुक् क्षिप्रमभिवर्ष कृते मम ॥

22. Oh Kaamadhenu! For my sake, (various foods) with *Six Tastes which will meet with approval (as per individual's taste), of one and all, ... all this as desired, you should 'Shower ' quickly.

❍ ❍ ❍

२३. रसेनान्नेन पानेन लेह्यचोष्येण संयुतम् ।
अन्नानां निचयं सर्वं सृजस्व शबले त्वर ॥

23. Oh Schabala! Prepare at once heaps of foods, all of them (all varieties); Foods with spices, cereal foods, Drinks, Sweet & syrupy foods etc.

(Note: The six tastes are: Chilly-hot, Sour; Salty: Sweetish; Bitter: Pungent: King Vishwaamithra is in for a surprise. Readers may note a few points. Firstly a sage or a Rishi must enquire about the welfare of a king, even though they may lead a spiritual life & a life of renunciation. Secondly, even a Sage living in forest must extend hospitality. Of course Vasishta is no ordinary sage; He is about to throw a fantastically great Party by his divine power to the king, with the help of The Divine Cow, Kaamadhenu.)

❍ ❍ ❍

Chapter 53

Vishwaamithra asks Vasishta to give him Schabala, the divine cow

(Schathaanandh continues narration to Raama: Vasishta's Great Feast to King Vischwaamithra:...... Vischwaamithra's enmity.)

❍ ❍ ❍

१. एवमुक्ता वसिष्ठेन सबला शत्रुसूदन ।
विदधे कामधुक्कामान् यस्य यस्य यथेप्सितम् ।।
२. इक्षून्मधुरसान् लाजान् मैरेयांश्च वरासवान् ।
पानानि च महार्हाणि भक्ष्यांश्चोच्चावचांस्तथा ।।
३. उष्णाढ्यस्यौदनस्यात्र राशयः पर्वतोपमाः ।
मृष्टान्नानि च सूपाश्च दधिकुल्यास्तथैव च ।।
४. नानास्वादुरसानां च षड्रसानां तथैव च ।
भाजनानि सुपूर्णानि गौडानि च सहस्रशः ।।

1 to 4:

Oh (Raama) the destroyer of enemies! (Listen)! When told thus by Vasishta, Schabala, the Kaamadhenu, gave whatever one desired...... Cane juices, Honey preparations, Parched grain Eats, Maireya Wines & liqours, fruit juices & drinks, variegated & foremost Eats...... Heaps of hot boiled food grains (Rice & the like), Foods sprinkled with condiments: (Heaps of food stacked up) like a mountain; Soups, & like wise milk products-like sourcream ...... (Readers may be interested to know the Sanskrit word for Soups is Soopa)...... Various types of sweet liquids, likewise foods with six different tastes: Vessels; Syrupy (molasses) foods......

❍ ❍ ❍

५. सर्वमासीत्सुसन्तुष्टं हृष्टपुष्टजनायुतम् ।
विश्वामित्रबलं सर्वं वसिष्ठेनातितर्पितम् ।।

5. The well fed & satisfied men of the army of Vischwaamithra, all of them, were very pleased and fully satisfied by (the hospitality of) Vasishta......

❍ ❍ ❍

६. विश्वामित्रोऽपि राजर्षिर्हृष्टः पुष्टस्तदाऽभवत् ।
सान्तःपुरवरो राजा सब्राह्मणपुरोहितः ।।

6. This Raaja Rishi, this king Vischwaamithra who had come along with the foremost ladies of his household (harem), and who was with Braamins, Purohiths (& priests), was happy, well fed.

❍ ❍ ❍

७. सामात्यो मन्त्रिसहितः सभृत्यः पूजितस्तदा ।
युक्तः परमहर्षेण वसिष्ठमिदमब्रवीत् ।।

7. (Vischwaamithra) who was with his ministers, his counselors & his attendants & servants, honoured (thus by Vasishta), then addressed Vasishta in a state of great joy, the following:

❍ ❍ ❍

८. पूजितोऽहं त्वया ब्रह्मन् पूजार्हेण सुसत्कृतः ।
श्रूयतामभिधास्यामि वाक्यं वाक्यविशारद ।।
गवां शतसहस्रेण दीयतां शबला मम ।।

8. Oh Braamin, (Oh Vasishta) who is well versed in speech! I have been honoured and extended great hospitality by you who deserves to be honoured (by all): (I wish to) Say the following words: May you listen: May Schabala (your holy cow) be given to me (in exchange for) 100,000 cows (from me).

❍ ❍ ❍

९. रत्नं हि भगवन्नेतद्रत्नहारी च पार्थिवः ।
तस्मान्मे शबलां देहि ममैषा धर्मतो द्विज ।।

9. Oh Lord (Vasishta): Oh Braamin! Only a king is possessor of Gem (of anything in the world: king alone

must have the best). This is the Dharma. And this is a 'Gem'. So it is mine. Therefore you give me Schabala (your divine cow Kaamadhenu), this gem.

(Vischwaamithra, although a king, abuses the hospitality of his host Vasishta: in making this request -proposition.)

❍ ❍ ❍

१०. एवमुक्तस्तु भगवान् वसिष्ठो मुनिसत्तमः ।
विश्वामित्रेण धर्मात्मा प्रत्युवाच महीपतिम् ।।

10. Having heard thus from Vischwaamithra, the foremost Muni, the man of Dharma, this Lord Sage Vasishta replied to the king thus:

❍ ❍ ❍

११. नाहं शतसहस्रेण नापि कोटिशतैर्गवाम् ।
राजन्दास्यामि शबलां राशिभी रजतस्य वा ।।

11. Oh King (Vischwaamithra)! (Whether you give me in exchange) Cows in 100,000 or even in 100 millions, or in heaps of silver, Never (will I part with my Kaamadhenu): I will not give Kaamadhenu (to you).

❍ ❍ ❍

१२. न परित्यागमर्हेयं मत्सकाशादरिन्दम ।
शाश्वती शबला मह्यं कीर्तिरात्मवतो यथा ।।

12. Oh destroyer of enemies (Vischwaamithra)! Just as for a self possessed (self reliant) man, fame is everything, likewise this Kaamadhenu is to me. And it is not proper (that this) be given up by me.

❍ ❍ ❍

१३. अस्यां हव्यं च कव्यं च प्राणायात्रा तथैव च ।
आयत्तमग्निहोत्रं च बलिर्होमस्तथैव च ।।

13. The celestial duties, The Oblations to forefathers, Fire Rituals, Propitiatory Oblations, The Homa-s, (The

very) support of Life-Breath, all these repose in this (my Kaamadhenu).

❍ ❍ ❍

१४. स्वाहाकारवषट्कारौ विद्याश्च विविधास्तथा ।
आयत्तमत्र राजर्षेसर्वमेतान्न संशयः ।।

14. Oh Raajarishi (Vischwaamithra)! The (renowned chants) Swaahaa, Vashat and the various Vedha-s rests in this (Cow): No doubt about it.

❍ ❍ ❍

१५. सर्वस्वमेतत्सत्येन मम तुष्टिकरी सदा ।
कारणैर्बहुभी राजन्न दास्ये शबलां तव ।।

15. Oh king! With various means (& various ways), this satisfies (me) at all times: This is truly everything for me: Surely I Will Never Give Schabala To You.

❍ ❍ ❍

१६. वसिष्ठेनैवमुक्तस्तु विश्वामित्रोऽब्रवीत्ततः ।
संरब्धतरमत्यर्थं वाक्यं वाक्यविशारदः ।।

16. When told thus by Vasishta, Vischwaamithra who was well versed in (the art of) speech, said the following words, greatly excited by anger.

❍ ❍ ❍

१७. हैरण्यकक्ष्याग्रैवेयान् सुवर्णाङ्कुशभूषितान् ।
ददामि कुञ्जराणां ते सहस्राणि चतुर्दश ।।

17. I will give you 14,000 elephants with gold waist bands, with golden chains & elephant driver hooks made of gold.

❍ ❍ ❍

१८. हैरण्यानां रथानां च श्वेताश्वानां चतुर्युजाम् ।
ददामि ते शतान्यष्टौ किङ्किणीशतभूषितान् ।।

18. And I will give you 800 golden chariots decorated with

hundreds of tinkling bells and drawn by four white horses & yoked with four horses.

❍ ❍ ❍

१९. हयानां देशजातानां कुलजानां महौजसाम् ।
सहस्रमेकं दश च ददामि तव सुव्रत ॥

19. Oh (Vasishta of) good vows & austerities! I will offer 11,000 horses of high pedigree (& breeding), bred in various lands, which possess tremendous power.

❍ ❍ ❍

२०. नानावर्णविभक्तानां सवत्सानां तथैव च ।
ददाम्येकां गवां कोटिं शबला दीयतां मम ॥

20. I will give you 10 million cows with calves of various breeds: But You Should Give Me Schabala.

❍ ❍ ❍

२१. यावदिच्छसि रत्नं वा हिरण्यं वा द्विजोत्तम ।
तावद्ददामि ते सर्वं शबला दीयतां मम ॥

21. Oh foremost Braamin (Vasishta)! Be it Gems; Be it Gold: Whatever, in whatever quantity that you desire, all that I will give to you: But Schabala. May Be (must be) Given To Me.

❍ ❍ ❍

२२. एवमुक्तस्तु भगवान्विश्वामित्रेण धीमता ।
न दास्यामीति शबलां प्राह राजन् कथञ्चन ॥

22. When told thus by the 'wise' Vischwaamithra, the Lord Sage Vasishta replied thus: Oh king! I Will Not Give Schabala: However Much (you may press me and tempt me with).

❍ ❍ ❍

२३. एतदेव हि मे रत्नमेतदेव हि मे धनम् ।
एतदेव हि सर्वस्वमेतदेव हि जीवितम् ॥

23. This indeed is my gem: This is my wealth: This is my everything: This is my very life.

❍ ❍ ❍

२४. दर्शश्च पूर्णमासश्च यज्ञाश्चैवाप्तदक्षिणाः ।
एतदेव हि मे राजन्विविधाश्च क्रियास्तथा ॥

24. Oh king! the ritual (pertaining to) New Moon: The ritual on Full Moon: The Yaaga-s done with many gifts and the many (other) rituals. This (Kaamadhenu) is indeed all these for me.

❍ ❍ ❍

२५. अतोमूलाः क्रियाः सर्वा मम राजन्न संशयः ।
बहुना किं प्रलापेन न दास्ये कामदोहिनीम् ॥

25. Oh king (Vischwaamithra)! All my (Spiritual) Sacrifices have their roots in this: No doubt at all; (But) Why All This Prattle...... I Will Not Give (Up) My Kaamadhenu.

(Note: Vasishta, in no uncertain terms, tells king Vischwaamithra that he will never give (or give up) this Divine Cow that is required for all his spiritual activities. And this refusal enrages Vishwaamithra so much, that his enmity towards Vasishta starts.)

❍ ❍ ❍

Chapter 54

The abduction of Kaamadhenu

(Schathaanand continues narration: Vischwaamithra's enmity):

❍ ❍ ❍

१. कामधेनुं वसिष्ठोऽपि यदा न त्यजते मुनिः ।
तदाऽस्य शबलां राम विश्वामित्रोऽन्वकर्षत ॥

1. Oh Raama (Listen)! When Muni Vasishta did not give up Kaamadhenu, Vischwaamithra dragged his Kaamadhenu by force.

❍ ❍ ❍

२. नीयमाना तु शबला राम राज्ञा महात्मना ।
दुःखिता चिन्तयामास रुदन्ती शोककर्शिता ।।

2. Oh Raama! And when it was being dragged away by the eminent king (Vischwaamithra), Schabala, (the Kaamadhenu), became very sad and overwhelmed by grief, began to cry, began to think (about its fate).

❍ ❍ ❍

३. परित्यक्ता वसिष्ठेन किमहं सुमहात्मना ।
याऽहं राजभटैर्दीना ह्रियेयं भृशदुःखिता ।।

3. (Kaamadhenu wailed): I am being dragged by the king's mercenaries: Miserable as I am, am suffering immense grief: Oh What! Am I being abandoned by the very great soul Vasishta?

❍ ❍ ❍

४. किं मयाऽपकृतं तस्य महर्षेर्भावितात्मनः ।
यन्मामनागसं भक्तामिष्टां त्यजति धार्मिकः ।।

4. What wrong has been committed by me upon that great Muni (Vasishta) whose soul is purified by meditation: Because, this man of Dharma (Vasishta) is abandoning me who is his beloved, who is blameless and who is his devotee.

❍ ❍ ❍

५. इति सञ्चिन्तयित्वा तु निःश्वस्य च पुनः पुनः ।
जगाम वेगेन तदा वसिष्ठं परमौजसम् ।।

5. Sighing (deeply) again & again and pondering (over its fate), then (this Cow) went to Vasishta of immense power, in great speed.

❍ ❍ ❍

६. निर्धूय तांस्तदा भृत्याञ्छतशः शत्रुसूदन ।
जगामानिलवेगेन पादमूलं महात्मनः ॥

6. Oh (Raama) the destroyer of enemies (Listen further)! Then 'shaking off' thousands of (King's) men with speed of Air, it reached the feet of the great soul Muni (Vasishta).

❍ ❍ ❍

७. शबला सा रुदन्ती च क्रोशन्ती चेदमब्रवीत् ।
वसिष्ठस्याग्रतः स्थित्वा मेघदुन्दुभिराविणी ॥

7. Standing before Vasishta, this Kaamadhenu wailed & cried with a voice like sounds from Dhundhubi & (thunder of) clouds; It said:

❍ ❍ ❍

८. भगवन् किं परित्यक्ता त्वयाऽहं ब्रह्मणः सुत ।
यस्माद्राजभटा मां हि नयन्ते त्वत्सकाशतः ॥

8. (Kaamadhenu asks Vasishta): The king's mercenaries are leading me (dragging me) away from your presence: Oh Lord! Oh Bramma's son! Am I being forsaken by you or What?

❍ ❍ ❍

९. एवमुक्तस्तु ब्रह्मर्षिरिदं वचनमब्रवीत् ।
शोकसन्तप्तहृदयां स्वसारमिव दुःखिताम् ॥

9. When told thus, the Bramma Rishi (Vasishta) said the following words (to Kaamadhenu) who was like his own sister and who was in sorrow and whose heart was tormented by (utter) grief.

❍ ❍ ❍

१०. न त्वां त्यजामि शबले नापि मेऽपकृतं त्वया ।
एष त्वां नयते राजा बलान्मत्तो महाबलः ॥

११. न हि तुल्यं बलं मह्यं राजा त्वद्य विशेषतः ।
बली राजा क्षत्रियश्च पृथिव्याः पतिरेव च ॥

१२. इयमक्षौहिणी पूर्णा सवाजिरथसंकुला ।
हस्तिध्वजसमाकीर्णा तेनासौ बलवत्तरः ।।

10 to 12.

Oh Schabala! I do not abandon you. There was no (never any) transgression done upon me by you. This king (Vischwaamithra) is taking you away from me by force (& he) is mightily strong..... Particularly because this strong Kshathriya king is lord of earth, there is no strength in me equal to his..... And his army is full with an Akshowhini; Full with horses and chariots: full with tough elephants: Therefore he is more powerful than I am.

❍ ❍ ❍

१३. एवमुक्ता वसिष्ठेन प्रत्युवाच विनीतवत् ।
वचनं वचनज्ञा सा ब्रह्मर्षिमतुलप्रभम् ।।

13. When told thus by Vasishta, this (Kaamadhenu) which had knowledge of speech, replied the Bramma Rishi (Vasishta) of incomparable brilliance, with following words, in great humility.

❍ ❍ ❍

१४. न बलं क्षत्रियस्याहुर्ब्राह्मणो बलवत्तरः ।
ब्रह्मन् ब्रह्मबलं दिव्यं क्षत्रात्तु बलवत्तरम् ।।

14. Oh Braamin (Vasishta)! No one talks about the power of a Kshathriya (as of any consequence): The Power of the Braamin is divine; it is more powerful than that of Kshathriya: It is Braamin who is more powerful.

❍ ❍ ❍

१५. अप्रमेयं बलं तुभ्यं न त्वसौ बलवत्तरः ।
विश्वामित्रो महावीर्यस्तेजस्तव दुरासदम् ।।

15. And your strength is immeasurable; Your brilliance is 'unapproachable' (No one dares to face you): Even this very brave (& powerful king) Vischwaamithra is not stronger than you.

❍ ❍ ❍

१६. नियुङ्क्ष्व मां महातेजस्त्वद्ब्रह्मबलसंभृताम् ।
तस्य दर्पं बलं यत्तन्नाशयामि दुरात्मनः ।।

16. Oh most brilliant (Vasishta): You commission me who has been nourished by your Braamin Power. And I will destroy that arrogance & power of the evil minded (Vischwaamithra).

❍ ❍ ❍

१७. इत्युक्तस्तु तया राम वसिष्ठस्तु महायशाः ।
सृजस्वेति तदोवाच बलं परबलार्दनम् ।।
तस्य तद्वचनं श्रुत्वा सुरभिः साऽसृजत्तदा ।।

17. Oh Raama (Listen further)! When told thus by this (Kaamadhenu), the most famous Vasishta said thus:= You create an Army that will crush enemy's forces.= And this (Kaamadhenu) Surabhi, hearing these words of his, created (an army etc.)......

❍ ❍ ❍

१८. तस्या हुमारवोत्सृष्टाः पह्लवाः शतशो नृप ।
नाशयन्ति बलं सर्वं विश्वामित्रस्य पश्यतः ।।

18. Oh King (Raama)! (Listen to what happened next): Even while Vischwaamithra was looking on, his entire Army was destroyed in hundreds by The Paplava-s who were created (by this divine cow) from the grunt, (from the sound), of Humkaara (released from its nostrils).

❍ ❍ ❍

१९. स राजा परमक्रुद्धः क्रोधविस्फारितेक्षणः ।
पह्लवान्नाशयामास शस्त्रैरुच्चावचैरपि ।।

19. And this king (Vischwaamithra) became very angry, with his eyes throbbing in wrath; and he destroyed these Paplava-s with his weapons, Big & Small (mighty and ordinary weapons).

❍ ❍ ❍

२०. विश्वामित्रार्दितान् दृष्ट्वा पह्लाञ्छतशस्तदा ।
भूय एवासृजत्कोपाच्छकान्यवनमिश्रितान् ॥

20. Seeing that Paplava-s were killed by Vischwaamithra in thousands, (Kaamadhenu) in great wrath, created once again The Schaaka-s of the Yaavana clan.

❍ ❍ ❍

२१. तैरासीत्संवृता भूमिः शकैर्यवनमिश्रितैः ।
प्रभावद्भिर्महावीर्यैर्हेमकिञ्जल्कसन्निभैः ॥

21. The Earth was filled with Schaaka-s along with Yaavana-s who had great brilliance, who were very valiant & who were like the stalks of Hemakunjalika flowers (Naagara flowers).

❍ ❍ ❍

२२. दीर्घासिपट्टिशधरैर्हेमवर्णाम्बरावृतैः ।
निर्दग्धं तद्बलं सर्वं प्रदीप्तैरिव पावकैः ॥

22. Like burning fire, (Vischwaamithra's) entire army was burnt up by these (Schaka-Yaavana brigade) who were wearing golden dresses & who were wielding long swords & Pattisa spears.

❍ ❍ ❍

२३. ततोऽस्त्राणि महातेजा विश्वामित्रो मुमोच ह ।
तैस्तैर्यवनकाम्भोजाः वर्वशश्चाकुलीकृताः ॥

23. Then the most brilliant Vischwaamithra released his arrows: By these, by such & such (arrows), the Yaavana-s, the Kaambhojas and the Paplava-s became confounded (& they were subdued).

❍ ❍ ❍

Chapter 55

Vischwaamithra obtains knowledge of Dhanur Vedha

(Schathaanandh continues the story about Vischwaamithra, the king: Raama listens in awe about his benefactor/ patron/teacher.)

❍ ❍ ❍

१. ततस्तानाकुलान् दृष्ट्वा विश्वामित्रास्त्रमोहितान् ।
वसिष्ठश्चोदयामास कामधुक् सृज योगतः ।।

1. Then seeing them stupefied & perplexed by Vischwaamithra's weapons, Vasishta goaded her: = Oh Kaamadhenu! Create by (power of) Yoga, =

❍ ❍ ❍

२. तस्या हुंकारतो जाताः काम्भोजा रविसन्निभाः ।
ऊधसस्त्वथ संजाताः वर्वराः शस्त्रपाणयः ।।

३. योनिदेशाच्च यवनाः शकृद्देशाच्छकास्तथा ।
रोमकूपेषु च म्लेच्छा हारीताः सकिरातकाः ।।

2 & 3.

And by its mere 'Hum' sound from its breath (by its grunt), the Kaambhoja-s who were like the Sun, were created; From its belly were created the Paplava-s with weapons in their hands. . . . from its navel region, the Yaavana-s, from the Anus, the Schaaka-s, from its hair, the Mlecha-s, Haareetha-s & Kiraathakas.

❍ ❍ ❍

४. तैस्तैर्निषूदितं सैन्यं विश्वामित्रस्य तत्क्षणात् ।
सपदातिगजं साश्वं सरथं रघुनन्दन ।।

4. Oh (Raama) the darling of Raghu-s (Listen)! Vischwaamithra's army, the Infantry with elephants,

horses, chariots, were all wiped out at once by these (created by Kaamadhenu).

❍ ❍ ❍

५. दृष्ट्वा निषूदितं सैन्यं वसिष्ठेन महात्मना ।
विश्वामित्रसुतानां तु शतं नानाविधायुधम् ।।
अभ्यधावत्सुसंक्रुद्धं वसिष्ठं जपतां वरम् ।।

5. Seeing this entire army wiped out by the great soul Vasishta, the 100 sons of Vischwaamithra became very angry & rushed towards Vasishta who was foremost amongst those who do prayers & chants, with various weapons.

❍ ❍ ❍

६. हुंकारेणैव तान् सर्वान्निर्ददाह महानृषिः ।।

6. The great Rishi (Vasishta) burnt them all by his (mere) breath, (emitting the sound of) 'Hum'!

❍ ❍ ❍

७. ते साश्वरथपादाता वसिष्ठेन महात्मना ।
भस्मीकृता मुहूर्तेन विश्वामित्रसुतास्तदा ।।

7. Along with horses, chariots, and infantry, the sons of Vischwaamithra were reduced to ashes in just a moment by the great soul Vasishta.

❍ ❍ ❍

८. दृष्ट्वा विनाशितान् पुत्रान्बलं च सुमहायशाः ।
सव्रीडश्चिन्तयाऽऽविष्टो विश्वामित्रोऽभवत्तदा ।।

8. Then seeing his entire army and his sons destroyed, this most famous Vischwaamithra became ashamed of himself, became seized with worry.

❍ ❍ ❍

९. समुद्र इव निर्वेगो भग्नदंष्ट्र इवोरगः ।
उपरक्त इवादित्यः सद्यो निष्प्रभतां गतः ।।

9. He at once attained (a state) bereft of (any) brilliance; He was like a still ocean, was like a cobra whose teeth had been pulled out, was like the Sun afflicted by Raahu (during eclipse).

❍ ❍ ❍

१०. हतपुत्रबलो दीनो लूनपक्ष इव द्विजः ।
हतदर्पोहतोत्साहो निर्वेदं समपद्यत ।।

10. Having lost sons, his arrogance gone, he was like a featherless bird; Feeling feeble, his zeal gone, he became despondent.

❍ ❍ ❍

११. स पुत्रमेकं राज्याय पालयेति नियुज्य च ।
पृथिवीं क्षत्रधर्मेण वनमेकोऽन्वपद्यत ।।

11. (Vischwaamithra is in wrath: Takes a decision: Must acquire more strength So decides to go to forest for doing penance). Appointing one son of his to rule his kingdom saying: =You rule the Earth as per Dharma of Kshathriya-s = he at once left for forest alone.

❍ ❍ ❍

१२. स गत्वा हिमवत्पार्श्वं किन्नरोरगसेवितम् ।
महादेवप्रसादार्थं तपस्तेपे महातपाः ।।

12. Going to the region of Himaalaya-s which is full of Kinnara-s & Uraga-s, he did a (mighty) penance as a man of penance, to obtain the (blessings) & favour of Mahaadheva (God Schiva).

❍ ❍ ❍

१३. केनचित्त्वथ कालेन देवेशो वृषभध्वजः ।
दर्शयामास वरदो विश्वामित्रं महाबलम् ।।

13. After sometime, the Lord of Dheva-s (God Schiva) whose mast is bull and who is giver of boons, gave

an audience to the mightily strong Vischwaamithra. (Schiva appears before him to give boons).

❍ ❍ ❍

१४. किमर्थं तप्यसे राजन् ब्रूहि यत्ते विवक्षितम् ।
वरदोऽस्मि वरो यस्ते काङ्क्षितः सोऽभिधीयताम् ।।

14. Oh King (Vischwaamithra)! For what purpose are you doing (this) penance? Whatever you wish (to seek from me), tell me that; Tell me what boon you seek. I am (here before you) as giver of boons.

❍ ❍ ❍

१५. एवमुक्तस्तु देवेन विश्वामित्रो महातपाः ।
प्रणिपत्य महादेवमिदं वचनमब्रवीत् ।।

15. When he was told thus by The Dheva (God Schiva), Vischwaamithra the man of great penance, bowed to Mahaadheva (Schiva) and then said these words:

❍ ❍ ❍

१६. यदि तुष्टो महादेव धनुर्वेदो ममानघ ।
साङ्गोपाङ्गोपनिषदः सरहस्यः प्रदीयताम् ।।

16. Oh the sinless! Oh Mahaadheva! If you are pleased (with me), may you (teach me &) offer me The Dhanur Vedha (The science of weaponry & war), its secrets, along with Upanishad-s & the limbs (of the Vedha).

❍ ❍ ❍

१७. यानि देवेषु चास्त्राणि दानवेषु महर्षिषु ।
गन्धर्वयक्षरक्षःसु प्रतिभान्तु ममानघ ।।
तव प्रसादाद्भवतु देवदेव ममेप्सितम् ।।

17. Oh the sinless (God Schiva) the Dheva of The Dheva-s! All those found with Dheva-s, Asura-s, great sages, Ghandharva-s, Yaksha-s an Demons, all these weapons, must manifest before me: By your grace, may this, my desire, be (fulfilled).

❍ ❍ ❍

१८. एवमस्त्विति देवेशो वाक्यमुक्त्वा दिवं गतः ।।

18. And the God of Dheva-s (Schiva) said: = So Be It:= And He left for heaven after saying this.

❍ ❍ ❍

१९. प्राप्य चास्त्राणि राजर्षिर्विश्वामित्रो महाबलः ।
दर्पेण महता युक्तो दर्पपूर्णोऽभवत्तदा ।।

19. This mightily strong RaajaRishi (king) Vischwaamithra who was seized with great arrogance, obtained these 'Weapons': By this, he became terribly insolent......

❍ ❍ ❍

२०. विवर्धमानो वीर्येण समुद्र इव पर्वणि ।
हतमेव तदा मेने वसिष्ठमृषिसत्तमम् ।।

20. (And armed with mystic weapons, Vischwaamithra wants revenge upon Vasishta): ...... Like ocean in monsoon season, (this Vischwaamithra) who was 'thriving' with his (newly acquired weapons and) bravery, thought that the foremost Rishi Vasishta was (already) killed (by him, a wishful thinking!)

❍ ❍ ❍

२१. ततो गत्वाऽऽश्रमपदं मुमोचास्त्राणि पार्थिवः ।
यैस्तत्तपोवनं सर्वं निर्दग्धं चास्त्रतेजसा ।।

21. Going to the hermitage, the king (Vischaamithra) discharged these (newly acquired) 'Weapons': By the power of these (Mystic) weapons this forest of penance was burnt up entirely.

❍ ❍ ❍

२२. उदीर्यमाणमस्त्रं तद्विश्वामित्रस्य धीमतः ।
दृष्ट्वा विप्रद्रुता भीता मुनयः शतशो दिशः ।।

२३. वसिष्ठस्य च ये शिष्यास्तथैव मृगपक्षिणः ।
विद्रवन्ति भयाद्भीता नानादिग्भ्यः सहस्रशः ।।

२४. वसिष्ठस्याश्रमपदं शून्यमासीन्महात्मनः ।
मुहूर्तमिव निश्शब्दमासीदिरिणसन्निभम् ।।

२५. वदतो वै वसिष्ठस्य मा भैष्टेति मुहुर्मुहुः ।
नाशयाम्यद्य गाधेयं नीहारमिव भास्करः ।।

22 to 25.

(Perhaps Vishwaamithra tries out these before confronting Vasishta!)...... Seeing these weapons of the 'wise' Vischwaamithra being discharged, the Muni-s there ran away in thousands in all directions in fear....... Vasishta's disciples, the animals & birds, ran away in all directions, in thousands, scared, by the (great) fear....... the great soul Vasishta's hermitage became desolate in just a Muhoortha (in less than an hour), with no sounds or inhabitation...... even as Vasishta was saying (& assuring them) again and again.= Like Sun (driving away) the cold, I will destroy this (Vischwaamithra), the son of Gaadhi; Dont fear=

❍ ❍ ❍

२६. एवमुक्त्वा महातेजा वसिष्ठो जपतां वरः ।
विश्वामित्रं तदा वाक्यं सरोषमिदमब्रवीत् ।।

26. Saying thus, the most brilliant Vasishta who was foremost amongst men of prayers & chants, at once addressed the following words to Vischwaamithra, that indicated his wrath.

❍ ❍ ❍

२७. आश्रमं चिरसंवृद्धं यद्विनाशितवानसि ।
दुराचारोऽसि यन्मूढ तस्मात्वं न भविष्यसि ।।

27. As you have destroyed this most cherished and long and well augmented hermitage, you will not live, Oh you fool! you are a man of evil conduct......

❍ ❍ ❍

२८. इत्युक्त्वा परमक्रुद्धो दण्डमुद्यम्य सत्वरः ।
विधूम इव कालाग्निर्यमदण्डमिवापरम् ।।
उपतस्थे महातेजा वसिष्ठः कौशिकस्य तु ।।

28. Saying thus, this most brilliant Vasishta who became terribly angry and was like smokeless fire, at once lifted up a Rod that was like another Yama Rod, (The Rod of Death) and stood before Vischwaamithra.

(Note: It is revenge that king Vischwaamithra seeks: And again Vasishta humbles him as we shall see in the next chapter.)

❍ ❍ ❍

Chapter 56

Vischwaamithra does penance again

(Schathaanandh continues before Raama: How Vasishta humbles Vischwaamithra again, who goes to forest to seek more power.)

❍ ❍ ❍

१. एवमुक्तो वसिष्ठेन विश्वामित्रो महाबलः ।
आग्नेयमस्त्रमुत्क्षिप्य तिष्ठेति चाब्रवीत् ।।

1. The mightily strong Vischwaamithra, when told by Vasishta, lifted up the Agni (fire) weapon and said: Stop, Stop (Dont run away!).

❍ ❍ ❍

२. ब्रह्मदण्डं समुत्क्षिप्य कालदण्डमिवापरम् ।
वसिष्ठो भगवान् क्रोधादिदं वचनमब्रवीत् ।।

2. And the Lord sage Vasishta, in great wrath, raising up high The Bramma Rod that was like another Kaala Dhanda, the Rod of Death, said the following:

❍ ❍ ❍

३. क्षत्रबन्धो स्थितोऽस्म्येष यद्बलं तद्विदर्शय ।
नाशयाम्यद्य ते दर्पं शस्त्रस्य तव गाधिज ।।

3. Oh (Vischwaamithra) You, a kshathriya kinsman! Here, I am standing (before you: & am not running away): Whatever your strength, exhibit that (before me): Oh son of Gadhi! I Will Now Destroy Your Arrogance & Your Weapons' Arrogance (as well).

❍ ❍ ❍

४. क्व च ते क्षत्रियबलं क्व च ब्रह्मबलं महत् ।
पश्य ब्रह्मबलं दिव्यं मम क्षत्रियपांसन ।।

4. Oh (Vishwaamithra) The corrupter of Kashathriya race! Where is Kshathriya power and where is the mighty Bramma Power: (You Shall) See my divine Bramma power.

❍ ❍ ❍

५. तस्यास्त्रं गाधिपुत्रस्य घोरमाग्नेयमुद्यतम् ।
ब्रह्मदण्डेन तच्छान्तमग्नेर्वेग इवाम्भसा ।।

5. Like Fire (being quenched) by water, this gruesome Agni weapon of Vischwamithra that was raised up, was (totally) subdued by The Bramma Rod (of Vasishta, the braamin).

❍ ❍ ❍

६. वारुणं चैव रौद्रं च ऐन्द्रं पाशुपतं तथा ।
ऐषीकं चापि चिक्षेप कुपितो गाधिनन्दनः ।।

6. And (Vischwaamithra) the son of Gaadhi who was in terrible wrath, discharged, Varuna, Roudhra, Indhra, Paaschupathy, Eyesheeka, weapons.

❍ ❍ ❍

७. मानवं मोहनं चैव गान्धर्वं स्वापनं तथा ।
जृम्भणं मादनं चैव सन्तापनविलापने ।।

८. शोषणं दारुणं चैव वज्रमस्त्रं सुदुर्जयम् ।
ब्रह्मपाशं कालपाशं वारुणं पाशमेव च ।।

९. पिनाकास्त्रं च दयितं शुष्कार्द्रेअशनी उभे ।
दण्डास्त्रमथ पैशाचं क्रौञ्चमस्त्रं तथैव च ।।
१०. धर्मचक्रं कालचक्रं विष्णुचक्रं तथैव च ।
वायव्यं मथनं चैव अस्त्रं हयशिरस्तथा ।।
११. शक्तिद्वयं च चिक्षेप कमालं मुसलं तथा ।
वैद्याधरं महास्त्रं च कालास्त्रमथ दारुणम् ।।
त्रिशूलमस्त्रं घोरं च कापालमथ कमणम् ।।

7 to 11.

(Readers may note that Vischwaamithra discharged many celestial weapons on Vasishta: But they had no effect before Vasishta & his Bramma Rod. Stanzas 7 to 11 describe the various weapons)...... Maanava, Mohana, Ghandharva, Sthaapana, Jrimmana, Maadhana, Santhaapa, Vilaapa...... Schoshana, Dhaaruna, Vajra weapon that is invincible, Brammapaascha, Kaala paascha, Varunapaascha,...... the cherished Pinaaka weapon, The wet & dry twin weapons of Ashani, Dhanda weapon, the Paischaacha, the krauncha...... Dhanda chakra, Kaala chakra, Vishnu chakra, like wise (Ethereal) Vaayu weapon, Mayana, Hayaschiras,...... likewise the twin weapons of Schakthi, Kangala, Musala, (Vischwaamithra) discharged: And the Vidhyaadhara, the great weapon; The most cruel Kaala weapon, gruesome Thrischool, Kapaala, and the Kangara. (This Kshathriya Vischwaamithra discharged on his enemy, the Braamin Vasishta).

❍ ❍ ❍

१२. एतान्यस्त्राणि चिक्षेप सर्वाणि रघुनन्दन ।
वसिष्ठे जपतां श्रेष्ठे तदद्भुतमिवाभवत् ।।

12. Oh (Raama) the darling of Raghu-s (Listen further)! All these weapons he discharged! It only ended up as a 'miracle' before Vasishta the foremost amongst men of chants & prayers. (The miracle of these weapons was that they became like ' feathers').

❍ ❍ ❍

१३. तानि सर्वाणि दण्डेन ग्रसते ब्रह्मणः सुतः ।
तेषु शान्तेषु ब्रह्मास्त्रं क्षिप्तवान् गाधिनन्दनः ।।

13. This (Vasishta) the son of Bramma, devoured all these (weapons) with his solitary Rod, (The Bramma Rod): And when (all) his (weapons) were subdued, (Vischwaamithra) the son of Gadhi discharged The Bramma Asthra (Readers may note that amongst the celestial weapons, this is one of the foremost weapon).

❍ ❍ ❍

१४. तदस्त्रमुद्यतं दृष्ट्वा देवाः साग्निपुरोगमाः ।
देवर्षयश्च सम्भ्रान्ता गन्धर्वाः समहोरगाः ।।

14. Seeing this Bramma weapon being discharged, the Dheva-s who were accompanied by Agni (the lord of Fire), the Rishi-s, the Ghandharvas, and the MahaUraga-s were all bewildered.

❍ ❍ ❍

१५. त्रैलोक्यमासीत् संत्रस्तं ब्रह्मास्त्रे समुदीरिते ।।

15. And the three worlds became scared when Bramma weapon was discharged.

(Each Asthra- celestial weapon is highly selective and has specific objective. The fire weapon can be quenched with water weapon for instance. The swaapana weapon will put the enemy to sleep And of course The Bramma Asthra is a very, very powerful weapon.)

❍ ❍ ❍

१६. तदप्यस्त्रं महाघोरं ब्राह्म ब्राह्मेण तेजसा ।
वसिष्ठो ग्रसते सर्वं ब्रह्मदण्डेन राघव ।।

16. Oh (Raama) the Raaghava, (Listen)! Even this Bramma Asthra, most gruesome in every way, sage Vasishta 'devoured' with his Bramma Rod, by his sheer brilliance.

❍ ❍ ❍

१७. ब्रह्मास्त्रं ग्रसमानस्य वसिष्ठस्य महात्मनः ।
त्रैलोक्यमोहनं रौद्रं रूपमासीत्सुदारुणम् ।।

17. (World is really scared watching all this: The Bramma Asthra). When Bramma weapon was devoured, the great soul Vasishta's Form (& countenance) became very dreadful, terrible, stunning all the three worlds......

❍ ❍ ❍

१८. रोमकूपेषु सर्वेषु वसिष्ठस्य महात्मनः ।
मरीच्य इव निष्पेतुरग्नेर्धूमाकुलार्चिषः ।।

18. From the hairs of the body of the great soul Vasishta, (from all his hairs), sparks of light with smoke & flame, came out as though from (burning) fire.

❍ ❍ ❍

१९. प्राज्वलद्ब्रह्मदण्डश्च वसिष्ठस्य करोद्यतः ।
विधूम इव कालाग्निर्यमदण्ड इवापरः ।।

19. And this Bramma Rod that was wielded by Vasishta in his hand, and which was like another Rod of Yama (Rod of death), shone like smokeless Pralaya Fire (at the annihilation of earth).

❍ ❍ ❍

२०. ततोऽस्तुवन्मुनिगणा वसिष्ठं जपतां वरम् ।
अमोघं ते बलं ब्रह्मंस्तेजो धारय तेजसि ।।

20. At that moment, the congregation of Muni-s extolled Vasishta who was foremost amongst men of prayers & chants, (They said): Oh Braamin! Your Strength Is Unfailing: Efficacious: (But please) Bear this (Bramma) power by your own power.

(Vasishta is in such a wrath that the power he had released to 'Devour' all the celestial weapons should not have any (side) effects: The world may be destroyed: Such a power he wielded at that moment: Like Nuclear Bombs!)

❍ ❍ ❍

२१. निगृहीतस्त्वया ब्रह्मन् विश्वामित्रो महाबलः ।
प्रसीद जपतां श्रेष्ठ लोकाः सन्तु गतव्यथाः ।।

21. (They pray): Oh Braamin who is foremost in prayers & chants! The mightily strong Vischwaamithra has been 'Bound' by you; Now be tranquil: May the Worlds be freed from pain (suffering).

❍ ❍ ❍

२२. एवमुक्तो महातेजाः शमं चक्रे महातपाः ।
विश्वामित्रोऽपि निकृतो विनिश्वस्येदमब्रवीत् ।।

22. When the most brilliant and most austere (Vasishta) was told thus, he attained, (regained) his composure (& equanimity): And Vischwaamithra who was (humiliated) & subdued, said the following, sighing deeply.

❍ ❍ ❍

२३. धिग्बलं क्षत्रियबलं ब्रह्मतेजोबलं बलम् ।
एकेन ब्रह्मदण्डेन सर्वास्त्राणि हतानि मे ।।

23. (Fie, Fie): Shame On The Power of Kshathriya Power; (Indeed) It Is The Bramma Power That is Power (The Real Power): (No wonder), That With One Bramma Rod All My Weapons Were Subdued (destroyed by the Braamin Vasishta.)

❍ ❍ ❍

२४. तदेतत्समवेक्ष्याहं प्रसन्नेन्द्रियमानसः ।
तपो महत् समास्थास्ये यद्वै ब्रह्मत्वकारकम् ।।

24. (And Vishwaamithra takes a Vow): As I acknowledge this (truth about Bramma power), I will undertake to perform that mighty penance which will beget me Brammanhood (The Brammam), by doing penance in tranquillity, controlling all my 'senses'.

(Note: Thus Schaathanandh narrated all this about Vischwaamithra-Vasishta confrontation. Vasishta was a Braamin, initiated into Brammam. And King Vischwaamithra is a Kshathriya, with knowledge of war & weapons. If analogy is not taken literally, how can conventional weapons stand before Nuclear weapons which are born out of 'Sages' like Einstein.)

❍ ❍ ❍

Chapter 57

Thrischanku begs (support) for his Yaaga

(Schathaanandh continues narration to Raama: How after being humbled by Vasishta, king Vischwaamithra decides to do more penance to acquire more power; The Episode of Thrischanku.)

❍ ❍ ❍

१. ततः संतप्तहृदयः स्मरन्निग्रहमात्मनः ।
विनिश्वस्य विनिश्वस्य कृतवैरो महात्मना ॥
२. स दक्षिणां दिशं गत्वा महिष्या सह राघव ।
तताप परमं घोरं विश्वामित्रो महातपाः ॥

1 & 2.

Oh (Raama the) Raaghava! (listen)! Sighing deeply again & again, totally down hearted, thinking over the humiliation done to him, he developed hatred towards the great soul (Vasishta)...... And this man of penance Vischwaamithra, went to southern region along with his wife (consort), and did great, gruesome (rigorous) penance.

❍ ❍ ❍

३. फलमूलाशनो दान्तश्चकार परमं तपः ।
अथास्य जज्ञिरे पुत्राः सत्यधर्मपरायणाः ॥
हविष्यन्दो मधुष्यन्दो दृढनेत्रो महारथः ॥

3. With great restraint, sustaining himself on tubers & fruits, he did a mighty penance.: (During this time) Sons were born to him, (named) Havishyandhan, Madhushyandha, Dhridanethra, & Mahaaratha, who were (all) steadfast in Truth & Dharma.

❍ ❍ ❍

४. पूर्णेवर्षसहस्रे तु ब्रह्मा लोकपितामहः ।
अब्रवीन्मधुरं वाक्यं विश्वामित्रं तपोधनम् ।।

4. After 1,000 years were over, the Father of all the Worlds, (God) Bramma addressed this Vischwaamithra who possessed (by now) wealth of penance, with these sweet words:

❍ ❍ ❍

५. जिता राजर्षिलोकास्ते तपसा कुशिकात्मज ।
अनेन तपसा त्वां हि राजर्षिरिति विद्महे ।।

5. Oh (Vischwaamithra the) son of Kuschika! By your penance, "The World of Royal sages" has been 'won'! By this penance, we recognise you as a Raaja rishi (Royal sage:, but not a Bramma Rishi which he wanted to be).

❍ ❍ ❍

६. एवमुक्त्वा महातेजा जगाम सह दैवतैः ।
त्रिविष्टपं ब्रह्मलोकं देवानां परमेश्वरः ।।

6. The most brilliant great God (Bramma), saying thus, went to Bramma world along with Dheva-s, via Thrivishtapa (region of Linga-s), for the sake of the Dheva-s.

❍ ❍ ❍

७. विश्वामित्रोऽपि तच्छ्रुत्वा ह्रिया किञ्चिदवाङ्मुखः ।
दुःखेन महताऽऽविष्टः समन्युरिदमब्रवीत् ।।

7. Hearing this (from God Bramma), Vischwaamithra whose face was down trodden, was seized with sorrow

and shame, and he talked (to himself) the following in anger.

❍ ❍ ❍

८. तपश्च सुमहत्तप्तं राजर्षिरिति मां विदुः ।
देवाः सर्षिगणाः सर्वेनास्ति मन्ये तपःफलम् ।।

8. Great penance was done by me: The multitude of Dheva-s & Rishi-s know me (and accept me now) as a RaajaRishi. I realise that 'Fruits' of my penance are not there (for me because I am not a Bramma Rishi, but just a RaajaRishi).

❍ ❍ ❍

९. एवं निश्चित्य मनसा भूय एव महातपाः ।
रोषेण महताऽऽविष्टस्त्रैलोक्यं व्यथयन्निव ।।
तपश्चकार धर्मात्मा काकुत्स्थ परमात्मवान् ।।

9. Oh (Raama) The Kaakuthsa (Listen further)! After (thinking) thus and deciding in his mind, this man of great penance who was seized with great fury, did another penance, a penance that made the three Worlds shudder, as a man of Dharma & as a man well (& totally) composed

(Readers may note that the world shudders whenever rigorous penance are done by men with evil intentions: We must remember that Vischwaamithra has not forgotten Vasishta!)

❍ ❍ ❍

१०. एतस्मिन्नेव काले तु सत्यवादी जितेन्द्रियः ।
त्रिशमु रिति विख्यात इक्ष्वाकुकुलनन्दनः ।।

10. (The Story of Thrischanku follows: Schathanandh narrates Vischwaamithra's part in this episode). . . . . At about this time, there lived Thrischanku, renowned, son of the Ikshwaaku clan, who ever spoke Truth and who had controlled his 'senses' (& passion.)

❍ ❍ ❍

११. तस्य बुद्धिः समुत्पन्ना यजेयमिति राघव ।
गच्छेयं सशरीरेण देवानां परमां गतिम् ।।

11. Oh (Raama) the Raaghava! (Listen): A thought entered his mind: = I Must Obtain The Foremost State Of The Dheva-s With My Own (mortal) Body: I Will Perform Yaaga. = (Readers know that none can go to heaven in this mortal body of ours.)

❍ ❍ ❍

१२. स वसिष्ठं समाहूय कथयामास चिन्तितम् ।
अशक्यमिति चाप्युक्तो वसिष्ठेन महात्मना ।।

12. He (Thrischanku) invited Vasishta and conveyed his thoughts: (But) he was told, that it was not possible, even by (the efforts of) the great soul Vasishta.

❍ ❍ ❍

१३. प्रत्याख्यातो वसिष्ठेन स ययौ दक्षिणां दिशम् ।
ततस्तत्कर्मसिद्ध्यर्थं पुत्रांस्तस्य गतो नृपः ।।
१४. वासिष्ठा दीर्घतपसस्तपो यत्र हि तेपिते ।।

13 & 14.

Refused by (Sage) Vasishta, (Thrischanku) went to Southern regions: This king, to achieve his object, went..... there, to where the sons of Vasishta who had been doing penance for a very long time, were doing penance (again).

❍ ❍ ❍

१५. त्रिशमुः सुमहातेजाः शतं परमभास्वरम् ।
वासिष्ठान् सन्ददर्शाथ तप्यमानान् यशस्विनः ।।

15. And this most brilliant Thrischanku saw the 100 sons of Vasishta who were all famous, who were doing penance, and who were shining with great brilliancy. (Having failed with Vasishta, Thrischanku foolishly seeks Vasishta's sons' help.)

❍ ❍ ❍

१६. सोऽभिगम्य महात्मानः सर्वानेव गुरोः सुतान् ।
अभिवाद्यानुपूर्व्येण ह्रिया किञ्चिदवायुखः ।।
१७. अब्रवीत् सुमहातेजाः सर्वानेव कृताञ्जलिः ।।

16 & 17.

Approaching all these most eminent sons of his Guru (Teacher Vasishta), this most brilliant (Thrischanku) bowed to every one successively; And with arms in Anjali, addressed them all, his head somewhat bent due to his bashfulness.

❍ ❍ ❍

१८. शरणं वः प्रपद्येऽहं शरण्याञ्छरणागतः ।
प्रत्याख्यातोऽस्मि भद्रं वो वसिष्ठेन महात्मना ।।

18. I was refused (discarded) by (your father) the great soul Vasishta: I am seeking refuge (before you); I have come here for refuge under you all who give refuge to those (who seek refuge) Welfare to you all.

❍ ❍ ❍

१९. यष्टुकामो महायज्ञं तदनुज्ञातुमर्हथ ।
गुरुपुत्रानहं सर्वान्नमस्कृत्य प्रसादये ।।

19. I am bowing to you all who are my Guru's (teacher's) sons; I am beseeching you. I am desirous of doing a great Yaaga: You must give me your consent to this (& do what all is necessary).

❍ ❍ ❍

२०. शिरसा प्रणतो याचे ब्रह्मणांस्तपसि स्थितान् ।
ते मां भवन्तः सिद्ध्यर्थं याजयन्तु समाहिताः ।।
सशरीरो यथाऽहं हि देवलोकमवाप्नुयाम् ।।

20. With my head bowed, I am begging you Braamins who are steadfast in penance: You must perform this Yaaga for me & devote (your attention) for fulfillment of my wish in such a way that I will go to (Heaven which is) Dheva-s' world, with my own (mortal) body!

❍ ❍ ❍

२१. प्रत्याख्यातो वसिष्ठेन गतिमन्यां तपोधनाः ।
गुरुपुत्रानृते सर्वान्नाहं पश्यामि काञ्चन ॥

21. Oh Ye men whose wealth is penance! As I am 'discarded' (refused) by Vasishta, I do not see any other salvation for me than through (you all who are) sons of my teacher (Vasishta).

❍ ❍ ❍

२२. इक्ष्वाकूणां हि सर्वेषां पुरोधाः परमा गतिः ।
पुरोधसस्तु विद्वांसस्तारयन्ति सदा नृपान् ॥

22. The learned priests (carry out &) protect kings at all times: Therefore, for the Ikshwaaku (kings), for all of them, the Purohith (Vasishta) alone is foremost in Refuge.

❍ ❍ ❍

२३. तस्मादनन्तरं सर्वेभवन्तो दैवतं मम ॥

23. But next to him, you, all of you (being his sons), are my Gods.

(Note: As Thrischanku is an Ikshwaaku king, he is Raama's ancestor: Secondly, traditionally, Vasishta is The Purohith for them all, for the Ikshwaaku clan)

❍ ❍ ❍

Chapter 58

The Curse on Thrischanku

(Schathaanandh continues narration to Raama: The Thrischanku episode in Vischwaamithra's life):

❍ ❍ ❍

१. ततस्त्रिशमोर्वचनं श्रुत्वा क्रोधसमन्वितम् ।
ऋषिपुत्रशतं राम राजानमिदमब्रवीत् ॥

1. Oh Raama! (Listen)! Hearing Thrischanku's words, the 100 sons of Rishi (Vasishta), became angry and told this king (Thrischanku):

❍ ❍ ❍

२. प्रत्याख्यातो हि दुर्बुद्धे गुरुणा सत्यवादिना ।
तं कथं समतिक्रम्य शाखान्तरमुपेयिवान् ।।

2. Oh Fool! Rejected by our father (Vasishta) who ever speaks Truth, how can you transgress him, (go against his advice), and approach another 'Branch of his tree' (How dare you approach us who are his sons?):

❍ ❍ ❍

३. इक्ष्वाकूणां हि सर्वेषां पुरोधाः परमा गतिः ।
न चातिक्रमितुं शक्यं वचनं सत्यवादिनः ।।

3. For all the Ikshwaaku-s, The Purohith (Vasishta) alone is the foremost Refuge: Indeed! (Therefore) it is not possible to transgress the words of the truth speaking man.

❍ ❍ ❍

४. अशक्यमिति चोवाच वसिष्ठो भगवानृषिः ।
तं वयं वै समाहर्तुं क्रतुं शक्ताः कथं तव ।।

4. The Rishi Vasishta has said this is not possible; (When that is so) How are we capable to complete this Yaaga for you?

❍ ❍ ❍

५. बालिशस्त्वं नरश्रेष्ठ गम्यतां स्वपुर पुनः ।
याजने भगवाञ्छक्तस्त्रैलोक्यस्यापि पार्थिव ।।
अवमानं वयं कर्तुं तस्य शक्ष्यामहे कथम् ।।

5. Oh King (Thrischanku)! Oh foremost of men! You are childish. May you go back to your city; This Lord (our father Vasishta) is capable of doing Yaaga for persons of all the Three worlds: How then are we competent (& dare) to show disrespect to such a man.

❍ ❍ ❍

६. तेषां तद्वचनं श्रुत्वा क्रोधपर्याकुलेक्षणः ।
स राजा पुनरेवैतानिदं वचनमब्रवीत् ।।

6. Hearing their words, the king addressed them all thus: once again with these words, his eyes blurred due to wrath.

❍ ❍ ❍

७. प्रत्याख्यातो वसिष्ठेन गुरुपुत्रैस्तथैव च ।
अन्यां गतिं गमिष्यामि स्वस्ति वोऽस्तु तपोधनाः ।।

7. I have been discarded by Vasishta: And discarded by (you) the sons of my Teacher (Vasishta) also; Oh Ye men (of penances) for whom wealth is penance! Welfare to you all: I Will Seek Another Resort. (I will get my wish of going to heaven in my mortal body through penance, with assistance of someone else.)

❍ ❍ ❍

८. ऋषिपुत्रास्तु तच्छ्रुत्वा वाक्यं घोराभिसंहितम् ।
शेपुः परमसंक्रुद्धाश्चण्डालत्वं गमिष्यसि ।।

8. When the sons of Rishi (Vasishta) heard such a 'Gruesome' (unbecoming) words from him, they became very angry and they cursed him thus: = You Will Obtain The State Of A Chandaala (You will become an untouchable). =

❍ ❍ ❍

९. एवमुक्त्वा महात्मानो विविशुस्ते स्वमाश्रमम् ।।

9. These eminent sons having said thus, went back to their hermitage.

❍ ❍ ❍

१०. अथ रात्र्यां व्यतीतायां राजा चण्डालतां गतः ।
नीलवस्त्रधरो नीलः परुषो ध्वस्तमूर्धजः ।।
चित्यमाल्याङ्गरागश्च आयसाभरणोऽभवत् ।।

10. When night passed away, the king became an

'Untouchable'! He became rugged, his body turning blue, his dress was bluish-black; All hair fallen from his head (He became bald): His body besmeared with ashes, (strewn & withered) flowers & garlands of the cremation ground; his ornaments turning to iron from gold.

❍ ❍ ❍

११. तं दृष्ट्वा मन्त्रिणः सर्वेत्यक्त्वा चण्डालरूपिणम् ।
प्राद्रवन् सहिता राम पौरा येऽस्यानुगामिनः ॥

11. Oh Raama (Listen)! Seeing him in this form of a Chandaala, all the citizens, his ministers who were with him, and his other followers, (all of them) abandoned him & ran away.

❍ ❍ ❍

१२. एको हि राजा काकुत्स्थ जगाम परमात्मवान् ।
दह्यमानो दिवारात्रं विश्वामित्रं तपोधनम् ॥

12. (And the 'Fun' starts: it is in this condition that Thrischanku approaches Vasishta's 'Enemy' Vischwaamithra, for redress) (Raama) the Kaakuthsa! (Listen) This king (who normally was) a man of great self reliance, (but who was then) being 'burnt up' (by his plight) day & night, went to Vischwaamithra, the man whose wealth was (now) in penance, all alone (by himself, as no one came near him any more, he being an untouchable, a chandaala).

❍ ❍ ❍

१३. विश्वामित्रस्तु तं दृष्ट्वा राजानं विफलीकृतम् ।
चण्डालरूपिणं राम मुनिः कारुण्यमागतः ॥

13. Oh Raama (Listen)! Seeing this king was in the form of a Chandaala and (terribly) frustrated, Muni Vischwaamithra became compassionate (towards him).

❍ ❍ ❍

१४. कारुण्यात् स महातेजा वाक्यं परमधार्मिकः ।
इदं जगाद भद्रं ते राजानं घोरदर्शनम् ।।

14. This most brilliant & foremost man of Dharma, (this Vischwaamithra) addressed this gruesome looking king with these words, out of compassion: Welfare to you (Oh Raama, and listen further).

❍ ❍ ❍

१५. किमागमनकार्यं ते राजपुत्र महायशः ।
अयोध्याधिपते वीर शापाच्चण्डालतां गतः ।।

15. Oh Royal son! Oh (Thrischanku) the famous & brave king of Ayodhya! By curse you have attained the state of Untouchability. (Tell me) What is the purpose of your coming here?

❍ ❍ ❍

१६. अथ तद्वाक्यमाकर्ण्य राजा चण्डालतां गतः ।
अब्रवीत् प्राञ्जलिर्वाक्यं वाक्यज्ञो वाक्यकोविदम् ।।

16. Hearing these words, the king (Thrischanku) who knew (the art of) speech and who had attained the state of untouchability, addressed (Vischwaamithra) who was well versed in speech, with following words, his hands cupped in Anjali (in reverence).

❍ ❍ ❍

१७. प्रत्याख्यातोऽस्मि गुरुणा गुरुपुत्रैस्तथैव च ।
अनवाप्यैव तं कामं मया प्राप्तो विपर्ययः ।।

17. By my Guru (Vasishta) and likewise by my Gurus's sons, I was discarded: And without obtaining my wish (of going to heaven in my mortal body), only the opposite, (this perversity of my body being transformed into a Chandaala-Untouchable) has been obtained by me.

❍ ❍ ❍

१८. सशरीरो दिवं यायामिति मे सौम्यदर्शन ।
मया चेष्टं क्रतुशतं तच्च नावाप्यते फलम् ।।

18. Oh pleasant looking (Vischwaamithra)! 100 Yaaga-s were performed by me so that I could go to heaven with my own body; But the 'fruits' of Yaaga, I have not obtained.

❍ ❍ ❍

१९. अनृतं नोक्तपूर्वं मे न च वक्ष्ये कदाचन ।
कृच्छ्रेष्वपि गतः सौम्य क्षत्रधर्मेण ते शपे ।।

19. Oh pleasant (Vischwaamithra)! I swear on my Kshathriya Dharma: Untruth Has Never Been Spoken By Me Before! Not Even When In Difficulty: And Never (in future also), Will I Speak (Untruth).

❍ ❍ ❍

२०. यज्ञैर्बहुविधैरिष्टं प्रजा धर्मेण पालिताः ।
गुरवश्च महात्मानः शीलवृत्तेन तोषिताः ।।

20. Various types of Yaaga-s were done by me: The citizens have been ruled by Dharma: And the most eminent Guru-s have (always) been pleased by my good conduct.

❍ ❍ ❍

२१. धर्मेप्रयतमानस्य यज्ञं चाहर्तुमिच्छतः ।
परितोषं न गच्छन्ति गुरवा मुनिपुङ्गव ।।

21. (Oh Vischwaamithra) the 'tiger' amongst Muni-s! (My) Teachers (including Vasishta) were not delighted over my desire to accomplish the Yaaga (done with) zeal & effort as per Dharma.

❍ ❍ ❍

२२. दैवमेव परं मन्ये पौरुषं तु निरर्थकम् ।
दैवेनाक्रम्यते सर्वं दैवं हि परमा गतिः ।।

22. Everything is caused by Fate: Fate is Supreme: Fate is Foremost Refuge: I Consider Man's Efforts Worthless (before Fate).

❍ ❍ ❍

२३. तस्य मे परमार्तस्य प्रसादमभिकांक्षतः ।
कर्तुमर्हसि भद्रं ते दैवोपहतकर्मणः ।।

२४. नान्यां गतिं गमिष्यामि नान्यः शरणमस्ति मे ।
दैवं पुरुषकारेण निवर्तयितुमर्हसि ।।

23 & 24.

You should bestow your grace upon me who is afflicted by the 'cause' of fate, who is in great distress, and who is longing for (doing) Yaaga...... No one else has given me refuge. I am not going to anyone else to seek refuge: By (your) human effort, you should change this (my state of Untouchability) caused by fate.

❍ ❍ ❍

Chapter 59

The Curse on Vasishta's sons

(Schathaanandh continues narration to Raama; Vischwaamithra takes up the challenge; "I will send Thrischanku to heaven by Yaaga: My 'enemy' Vasishta will know who I am"!)

❍ ❍ ❍

१. उक्तवाक्यं तु राजानं कृपया कुशिकात्मजः ।
अब्रवीन्मधुरं वाक्यं शापाच्चण्डालरूपिणम् ।।

1. When King (Thrischanku) who had become an Untouchable by curse, told these words, (Vischwaamithra) the son of Kuschika, addressed this king thc following words with compassion.

❍ ❍ ❍

२. ऐक्ष्वाक स्वागतं वत्स जानामि त्वां सुधार्मिकम् ।
शरणं ते भविष्यामि मा भैषीर्मनुजाधिप ।।

2. Oh 'son'! Oh Ikshwaaku! Oh King of men! (Oh Thrischanku): Do not fear: I know you as a man of Dharma: I will be your Refuge Welcome to you.

❍ ❍ ❍

३. अहमामन्त्रये सर्वान् महर्षीन् पुण्यकर्मणः ।
यज्ञसाह्यकरान् राजंस्ततो यक्ष्यसि निर्वृतः ।।

3. Oh king! I will invite all the great Rishi-s who are auspicious (merit worthy), who will assist us in this Yaaga (I will preside over): After that, you can perform Yaaga without restraint (& hindrance).

❍ ❍ ❍

४. गुरुशापकृतं रूपं यदिदं त्वयि वर्तते ।
अनेनैव हि रूपेण सशरीरो गमिष्यसि ।।

4. This form of yours which is caused by the curse by your Guru, with that very form and body you will go (to heaven).

❍ ❍ ❍

५. हस्तप्राप्तमहं मन्ये स्वर्गं तव नराधिप ।
यस्त्वं कौशिकमागम्य शरण्यं शरणागतः ।।

5. Oh (Thrischanku) the Lord of men! You approached (me) a Kowschik for seeking refuge & you have taken refuge (under me; I take you as my protégé): I think this Heaven is (now) in your hands!

❍ ❍ ❍

६. एवमुक्त्वा महातेजाः पुत्रान् परमधार्मिकान् ।
व्यादिदेश महाप्राज्ञान् यज्ञसम्भारकारणात् ।।
सर्वाञ्छिष्यान् समाहूय वाक्यमेतदुवाच ह ।।

6. Having said thus, the most brilliant (Vischwaamithra) appointed his sons who were foremost men of Dharma & most intelligent, for the preparations of The Yaaga: He called all his disciples and said the following words.

❍ ❍ ❍

७. सर्वानृषिगणान् वत्सा आनयध्वं ममाज्ञया ।
सशिष्यसुहृदश्चैव सर्त्विजः सुबहुश्रुतान् ।।

7. Oh Lads! By my command, you shall bring a congregation of Rishi-s along with Rithviks who are well versed in Shaasthra-s, and with them, their disciples & friends (as well).

❍ ❍ ❍

८. यदन्यो वचनं ब्रूयान्मद्वाक्यबलचोदितः ।
तत्सर्वमखिलेनोक्तं मामाख्येयमनादृतम् ।।

8. If any one who is commanded by my words of authority (shows disrespect) and speaks with disrespectful words, then you shall report to me about all of it spoken (by such persons), without leaving out (& hiding it from me).

❍ ❍ ❍

९. तस्य तद्वचनं श्रुत्वा दिशो जग्मुस्तदाज्ञया ।
आजग्मुरथ देशेभ्यः सर्वेभ्यो ब्रह्मवादिनः ।।

9. Hearing his words (of command), they went to (various) places: And from all regions, the expounders of Vedha-s came by his command.

❍ ❍ ❍

१०. ते च शिष्याः समागम्य मुनिं ज्वलिततेजसम् ।
ऊचुश्च वचनं सर्वं सर्वेषां ब्रह्मवादिनाम् ।।

10. Coming back to Muni (Vischwaamithra) who was 'burning' with brilliance, these disciples said about all the words (spoken) by all these expounders of Vedha-s, (about these invitees).

❍ ❍ ❍

११. श्रुत्वा ते वचनं सर्वेसमायान्ति द्विजातयः ।
सर्वदेशेषु चागच्छन् वर्जयित्वा महोदयम् ।।

11. (The disciples told Vischwaamithra): On hearing your

words (of command), Braamins from all the territories came together: Excepting Mahodhaya, all (who were invited by you have come).

❍ ❍ ❍

१२. वासिष्ठं तच्छतं सर्वं क्रोधपर्याकुलाक्षरम् ।
यदाह वचनं सर्वं श्रृणु त्वं मुनिपुङ्गव ॥

12. What words were spoken by all the 100 sons of Vasishta, the expressions filled with wrath, all this, Oh (Vischaamithra) the tiger amongst Muni-s, may you (please) listen (from us).

❍ ❍ ❍

१३. क्षत्रियो याजको यस्य चण्डालस्य विशेषतः ।
कथं सदसि भोक्तारो हविस्तस्य सुरर्षयः ॥

13. (the Disciples report back to Vischwaamithra about the response to his invitation for the Yaaga: The insults they received at the hands of Vasishta's sons, who had said) ...... = In an assembly of a Yaaga, how can (& will) the Dheva-s & Rishi-s partake The Oblations from this man (Thrischanku) for whom this Kshathriya (Vishwaamithra) is the Performer (& presiding officer of The Yaaga): And particularly when he (Vischwaamithra) is doing this (Yaaga) for (Thrischanku) who is a Chandaala (Untouchable) =

(Readers may note that normally a great Yaaga is performed by an eminent person under the patronage of a respected member of The Priest-Purohith (Braamin) community who are well versed in Shaasthra-s. Here Vischwaamithra is a Kshatriya & Thrischanku is an Untouchable now. So this Yaaga is unholy, against norms.)

❍ ❍ ❍

१४. ब्राह्मणा वा महात्मानो भुक्त्वा चण्डालभोजनम् ।
कथं स्वर्गं गमिष्यन्ति विश्वामित्रेण पालिताः ॥

14. Although the braamins are very eminent & protected by Vischwaamithra, how can they go back to heaven after partaking Chandaala's food (the oblations offered by him during Yaaga).

❍ ❍ ❍

१५. एतद्वचननैष्ठुर्यमूचुः संरक्तलोचनाः ।
वासिष्ठा मुनिशार्दूल सर्वेते समहोदयाः ।।

15. Oh 'Lion' amongst Muni-s (Oh Vischwamithra)! All these sons of Vasishta, along with Mahodhaya, spoke such harsh words, with their eyes red (in wrath).

❍ ❍ ❍

१६. तेषां तद्वचनं श्रुत्वा सर्वेषां मुनिपुङ्गवः ।
कोपसंरक्तनयनः सरोषमिदमब्रवीत् ।।

16. Hearing the words of all (the sons of his enemy, Vasishta) which were (spoken by them) in wrath, (Vischwaamithra) the 'tiger' of muni-s said this, his eyes turning red in anger.

❍ ❍ ❍

१७. ये दूषयन्त्यदुष्टं मां तप उग्रं समास्थितम् ।
भस्मीभूता दुरात्मानो भविष्यन्ति न संशयः ।।

17. These evil men, (these sons of Vasishta) who have insulted me who is innocent and who has undertaken this rigorous Yaaga, will (all) be reduced to ashes No doubt about it. (He cursed them.)

❍ ❍ ❍

१८. अद्य ते कालपाशेन नीता वैवस्वतक्षयम् ।
सप्तजातिशतान्येव मृतपाः सन्तु सर्वशः ।।

18. Today itself, they will go to the abode of Vaivaswatha (Death), by the Noose of 'Time'! And for 700 life spans they will live on meat of the dead. (A life span = 125 years.)

❍ ❍ ❍

१९. श्वमांसनियताहारा मुष्टिका नाम निर्घृणाः ।
विकृताश्च विरूपाश्च लोकाननुचरन्त्विमान् ।।

19. Named Mushtika, determined to eat only dog's meat for food, looking horrible, performing bad acts pitilessly, may they roam about the world.

❍ ❍ ❍

२०. महोदयश्च दुर्बुद्धिर्मामदूष्यं ह्यदूषयत् ।
दूषितः सर्वलोकेषु निषादत्वं गमिष्यति ।।

20. And this evil minded Mahodhaya insulted me who should never be insulted: Therefore, condemned by all the worlds, he will obtain the status of a hunter.

❍ ❍ ❍

२१. प्राणातिपातनिरतो निरनुक्रोशतां गतः ।
दीर्घकालं मम क्रोधाद्दुर्गतिं वर्तयिष्यति ।।

21. By (the curse of my) wrath, he will lead a life of misery for a long time: And 'devoted' to killing living beings without compassion: (Such a) Bad state (he will obtain).

❍ ❍ ❍

२२. एतावदुक्त्वा वचनं विश्वामित्रो महातपाः ।
विरराम महातेजा ऋषिमध्ये महामुनिः ।।

22. The most brilliant, this great Muni of mighty penance, this Vischwaamithra, after saying these words in the midst of Rishi-s, rested. (Readers may note: As though adding insult to injury, Vischwaamithra curses the sons of Vasishta: Total enmity now.)

❍ ❍ ❍

Chapter 60

Thrischanku goes to 'Heaven'

(Schathhanand continues narration to Raama: How Vischwaamithra sent Thrischanku to "heaven": He even created another world)...... :

❍ ❍ ❍

१. तपोबलहतान् कृत्वा वासिष्ठान् समहोदयान् ।
ऋषिमध्ये महातेजा विश्वामित्रोऽभ्यभाषत ।।

1. After (cursing &) crushing the sons of Vasishta including Mahodhaya by the power of his penance, the most brilliant Vischwaamithra spoke the following in the midst of the Rishi-s:

❍ ❍ ❍

२. अयमिक्ष्वाकुदायादस्त्रिशङ्कुरिति विश्रुतः ।
धर्मिष्ठश्च वदान्यश्च मां चैव शरणं गतः ।।
स्वेनानेन शरीरेण देवलोकजिगीषया ।।

2. This Thrischanku by name is renowned as a member of Ikshwaaku clan; a man of Dharma; and most munificent. He desires to go to Heaven with his own body. And he has come to me for Refuge (to seek his objective).

❍ ❍ ❍

३. यथाऽयं स्वशरीरेण स्वर्गलोकं गमिष्यति ।
तथा प्रवर्त्यतां यज्ञो भवद्भिश्च मया सह ।।

3. May Yaaga be performed by all of you along with me, in such a way that he will go to heaven with his body.

❍ ❍ ❍

४. विश्वामित्रवचः श्रुत्वा सर्व एव महर्षयः ।
ऊचुः समेत्य सहिता धर्मार्थसहितं वचः ।।

4. Hearing Vishwaamithra's words, all the great Muni-s, with great sufferance (& endurance), said together, these words of substance & duty.

❍ ❍ ❍

५. अयं कुशिकदायादो मुनिः परमकोपनः ।
यदाह वचनं सद्यः कर्तव्यं नात्र संशयः ।।

5. This Muni (Vischwaamithra) of Kuschika clan is a man of great temper: Whatever words (of command) is told, that must be done at once; No doubt about it.

❍ ❍ ❍

६. अग्निकल्पो हि भगवाञ्छापं दास्यति रोषितः ।
तस्मात् प्रवर्त्यतां यज्ञः सशरीरो यथा दिवम् ।।

७. गच्छेदिक्ष्वाकुदायादो विश्वामित्रस्य तेजसा ।
ततः प्रवर्त्यतां यज्ञः सर्वेसमधितिष्ठत ।।

6 & 7.

This lord (Vischwaamithra) is like Fire: In wrath he will curse: Therefore may Yaaga be started: In such a way that with his body...... this (Thrischanku) of Ikshwaaku family, will go to heaven by (the power &) brilliance of Vischwaamithra: May this Yaaga be done; Let us all perform (the Yaaga).

❍ ❍ ❍

८. एवमुक्त्वा महर्षयः संचक्रुस्ताः क्रियास्तदा ।
याजकश्च महातेजा विश्वामित्रोऽभवत् क्रतौ ।।

8. After saying thus, the great Rishi-s then commenced the work (of Yaaga): The most brilliant Vischwaamithra was the patron-in-chief (of the Yaaga).

❍ ❍ ❍

९. ऋत्विजश्चानुपूर्व्येण मन्त्रवन्मन्त्रकोविदाः ।
चक्रुः सर्वाणि कर्माणि यथाकल्पं यथाविधि ।।

9. The Rithviks who were well versed in chants, performed

all the Rituals from beginning to end, as per Kalpa Shaasthra & as per norms of Shaastra with chants.

❍ ❍ ❍

१०. ततः कालेन महता विश्वामित्रो महातपाः ।
चकारावाहनं तत्र भागार्थं सर्वदेवताः ।।

10. After a long time, Vischwaamithra of great penance, sent invitations to all the Deities to share the Oblations.

❍ ❍ ❍

११. नाभ्यागमंस्ततस्तत्र भागार्थं सर्वदेवताः ।।

11. Yet all the Deities did not come there to receive their due share.

❍ ❍ ❍

१२. ततः क्रोधसमाविष्टो विश्वामित्रो महामुनिः ।
स्रुवमुद्यम्य सक्रोधस्त्रिशङ्कुमिदमब्रवीत् ।।

12. Therefore the great Muni (Vischwaamithra) was seized with wrath: Lifting up the Sruva (the Ladle used as Pour-out), he said to Thrischanku:

❍ ❍ ❍

१३. पश्य मे तपसो वीर्यं स्वार्जितस्य नरेश्वर ।
एष त्वां सशरीरेण नयामि स्वर्गमोजसा ।।

13. Oh King! You (will) See The Power of Penance Earned By Me: Now I Will Send You To Heaven With Your Body.

❍ ❍ ❍

१४. दुष्प्रापं स्वशरीरेण दिवं गच्छ नराधिप ।।

14. Oh Ruler of men: With your own body go to heaven that is difficult to 'obtain'.

❍ ❍ ❍

१५. स्वार्जितं किञ्चिदप्यस्ति मया हि तपसः फलम् ।
राजंस्त्वं तेजसा तस्य सशरीरो दिवं व्रज ।।

15. Oh King (Thrischanku)! If fruits of my penance earned by me is worth anything at all, by that power, may you go to heaven with your body.

❍ ❍ ❍

१६. उक्तवाक्ये मुनौ तस्मिन् सशरीरो नराधिपः ।
दिवं जगाम काकुत्स्थ मुनीनां पश्यतां तदा ॥

16. Oh (Raama) the Kaakuthsa (Listen further)! ...... When the Muni (Vischwaamithra) spoke these words, (Thrischanku) went to heaven with his own body, even as all the Muni-s (there) were watching.

❍ ❍ ❍

१७. देवलोकगतं दृष्ट्वा त्रिशङ्कुं पाकशासनः ।
सह सर्वैः सुरगणैरिदं वचनमब्रवीत् ॥

17. When Thrischanku reached heaven, the destroyer of Paaka (this Lord Indhra), seeing all this (spectacle) along with the congregation of Sura-s, said the following words:

❍ ❍ ❍

१८. त्रिशङ्को गच्छ भूयस्त्वं नासि स्वर्गकृतालयः ।
गुरुशापहतो मूढ पत भूमिमवाक्छिराः ॥

18. Oh You Fool! Oh Thrischanku! Go back! You are afflicted by the curse of your Guru (Vasishta & his sons): You will never have abode in heaven. Fall down on earth headlong (upside down).

❍ ❍ ❍

१९. एवमुक्तो महेन्द्रेण त्रिशङ्कुरपतत्पुनः ।
विक्रोशमानस्त्राहीति विश्वामित्रं तपोधनम् ॥

19. When told thus by Lord Indhra, Thrischanku who was falling down towards earth, was wailing & crying aloud to Vishwaamithra, whose wealth was penance, (Saying) =Save me! =

❍ ❍ ❍

२०. तच्छ्रुत्वा वचनं तस्य क्रोशमानस्य कौशिकः ।
रोषमाहारयत्तीव्रं तिष्ठ तिष्ठेति चाब्रवीत् ।।

20. Hearing his wailing words, (Vischwaamithra the) Kowschik, took on fierce wrath. At once he said: = Stop, Stop (Stay there).=

❍ ❍ ❍

२१. ऋषिमध्ये स तेजस्वी प्रजापतिरिवापरः ।
सृजन्दक्षिणमार्गस्थान् सप्तर्षीनपरान् पुनः ।।

21. (Oh Raama, now you see Vischwaamithra in action when he is in wrath): . . .Standing up amidst the Rishi-s, looking like another God Bramma, this most brilliant (Vischwaamithra) created new, another set of Seven Rishi-s (Saptha Rishi-s) in the southern hemisphere of the sky.

❍ ❍ ❍

२२. नक्षत्रमालामपरामसृजत्क्रोधमूर्च्छितः ।
दक्षिणां दिशमास्थाय ऋषिमध्ये महातपाः ।।

22. And 'stupefied' by wrath, standing in the midst of the Rishis, this (Vishwaamithra) of great penance, created another 'Garland' of Stars to be 'stationed' in southern sky.

❍ ❍ ❍

२३. सृष्ट्वा नक्षत्रवंशं च क्रोधेन कलुषीकृतः ।
अन्यमिन्द्रं करिष्यामि लोको वा स्यादनिन्द्रकः ।।
दैवतान्यपि स क्रोधात्स्रष्टुं समुपचक्रमे ।।

23. After creating a family of Stars, (Vischwaamithra) who was 'shaken' by wrath (& more wrath) said: = Why! I Will (even) Create Another Indhra; or, Let This World Be Without Indhra (at all):= And in wrath, he began to 'create' (new) Dheva-s as well!

❍ ❍ ❍

२४. ततः परमसम्भ्रान्ताः सर्षिसङ्घाः सुरर्षभाः ।
सकिन्नरमहायक्षाः सहसिद्धाः सचारणाः ।।
विश्वामित्रं महात्मानमूचुः सानुनयं वचः ।।

24. Then, the foremost Sura-s, along with multitude of Rishi-s, and with kinnara-s, great Yaksha-s, and with Chaarana-s & Sidhas, addressed these words to the most eminent Vischwaamithra in humility, terribly bewildered (by his Creations & wrath).

❍ ❍ ❍

२५. अयं राजा महाभाग गुरुशापपरिक्षतः ।
सशरीरो दिवं यातुं नार्हत्येव तपोधन ।।

25. Oh most illustrious (Vischwaamithra) for whom penance is wealth! This king (Thrischanku) who is ruined by the curse of his Guru, cannot go to heaven with his body.

❍ ❍ ❍

२६. तेषां तद्वचनं श्रुत्वा देवानां मुनिपुङ्गवः ।
अब्रवीत्सुमहद्वाक्यं कौशिकः सर्वदेवताः ।।

26. Hearing these words of Dheva-s, (Vischwaamithra the) Kowshik who was, a 'tiger' amongst Muni-s, addressed all the Dheva-s with these great words.

❍ ❍ ❍

२७. सशरीरस्य भद्रं वस्त्रिशमोरस्य भूपतेः ।
आरोहणं प्रतिज्ञाय नानृतं कर्तुमुत्सहे ।।

27. Welfare to you all: Having (resolved &) promised to this king Thrischanku about his going to heaven in his body, I will never bear to 'cheat' him. (I will not be untrue to my word).

❍ ❍ ❍

२८. स्वर्गोऽस्तु सशरीरस्य त्रिशमोरस्य शाश्वतः ।
नक्षत्राणि च सर्वाणि मामकानि ध्रुवाण्यथ ।।

28. Let this "Heaven" of Thrischanku who is with his body, be eternal: And further, may all the stars of my creation be eternal.

❍ ❍ ❍

२९. यावल्लोका धरिष्यन्ति तिष्ठन्त्वेतानि सर्वशः ।
मत्कृतानि सुराः सर्वेतदनुज्ञातुमर्हथ ॥

29. As long as the worlds exist, let my creations, all these, remain in every way; Oh Dheva-s! You should all permit (& accept this situation).

❍ ❍ ❍

३०. एवमुक्ताः सुराः सर्वेप्रत्यूचुर्मुनिपुङ्गवम् ॥

30. Having heard thus, all the Dheva-s replied to this 'tiger' of Muni-s' (Vischwaamithra):

❍ ❍ ❍

३१. एवं भवतु भद्रं ते तिष्ठन्त्वेतानि सर्वशः ।
गगने तान्यनेकानि वैश्वानरपथाद्बहिः ॥

31. Welfare to you! Let it Be So! Let all these (creations) stay outside in the sky shining as many, in the path of Vaishwaanara (the path of the commons- in the path of moon).

❍ ❍ ❍

३२. नक्षत्राणि मुनिश्रेष्ठ तेषु ज्योतिषु जज्वलुः ।
अवाक्छिरास्त्रिशङ्कुश्च तिष्ठत्वमरसन्निभः ॥

32. Oh foremost Muni: Let stars shine in their (respective) 'Paths': Let Thrischanku stay there (Eternally) like a Dheva (although) upside down.

❍ ❍ ❍

३३. अनुयास्यन्ति चैतानि ज्योतींषि नृपसत्तमम् ।
कृतार्थं कीर्तिमन्तं च ब्रह्मलोकगतं यथा ॥

33. Like Heavenly bodies (attending upon) a person who is gone to The Bramma World, let these (your creations)

attend upon (& follow) this foremost & renowned king (Thrischanku) who has accomplished his desire.

❍ ❍ ❍

३४. विश्वामित्रस्तु धर्मात्मा सर्वदेवैरभिष्टुतः ।
ऋषिभिश्च महातेजा बाढमित्याह देवताः ॥

34. When extolled thus by all the Dheva-s & Rishi-s, this man of Dharma, this most brilliant Vischwaamithra said: = Let it be as it pleases Dheva-s! =

❍ ❍ ❍

३५. ततो देवा महात्मानो मुनयश्च तपोधनाः ।
जग्मुर्यथागतं सर्वेयज्ञस्यान्ते नरोत्तम ॥

35. Oh (Raama) the noble man! (Listen): Then at the end of (this) Yaaga) for Thrischanku, the most eminent Dheva-s, the Muni-s whose wealth lay in penance, all of them went back as they came.

(Note: Schathaandh tells Raama how fortunate he is that he has Vischwaamithra as his teacher, guardian & protégé. Vishwaamithra already is so powerful, like God Bramma the creator, he can even create a world, creates a Lord for this world as well; But Vischwaamithra's goal is to be a Bramma Rishi, like his enemy Vasishta: Because that is where real power lies: The Brammam. And therefore, he goes back to do even more rigorous penance: And he has not forgotten his 'enemy' Vasishta.)

❍ ❍ ❍

Chapter 61

The Story of Schunaschepa

(Schathaanandh narrates yet another story to Raama about this very great man, Vischwaamithra; Story of Ambareesha & Schunaschepa & Vischwaamithra's involvement.)

❍ ❍ ❍

१. विश्वामित्रो महात्माऽथ प्रस्थितान्प्रेक्ष्य तानृषीन् ।
अब्रवीन्नरशार्दूलः सर्वांस्तान्वनवासिनः ।।

1. Observing that these Rishi-s had departed, the most eminent Vischwaamithra, the 'tiger' of men, addressed all the inhabitants of the hermitage:

❍ ❍ ❍

२. महाविघ्नः प्रवृत्तोऽयं दक्षिणामास्थितो दिशम् ।
दिशमन्यां प्रपत्स्यामस्तत्र तप्स्यामहे तपः ।।

2. I came to stay at the southern region: (But) This great obstacle (to my penance) occurred. We will go to another place. We will (continue to do) our penance there.

❍ ❍ ❍

३. पश्चिमायां विशालायां पुष्करेषु महात्मनः ।
सुखं तपश्चरिष्यामः परं तद्धि तपोवनम् ।।

3. Oh, most eminent (Rishi-s)! We shall do penance in (peace) and comfort on the banks of river Vischaala in the west, at Pushkara: Because, this 'forest' for penance is foremost.

❍ ❍ ❍

४. एवमुक्त्वा महातेजाः पुष्करेषु महामुनिः ।
तप उग्रं दुराधर्षं तेपे मूलफलाशनः ।।

4. After saying this, the most brilliant & great Muni

(Vischwaamithra) did penance at Pushkara without hindrance, did a rigorous penance, sustaining himself on fruits & tubers.

❍ ❍ ❍

५. एतस्मिन्नेव काले तु अयोध्याधिपतिर्महान् ।
अम्बरीष इति ख्यातो यष्टुं समुपचक्रमे ॥

5. At about this time, a great, renowned king of Ayodhya named Ambareesha began a Yaaga.

❍ ❍ ❍

६. तस्य वै यजमानस्य पशुमिन्द्रो जहार ह ।
प्रनष्टे तु पशौ विप्रो राजानामिदमब्रवीत् ॥

6. (Once again this Indhra is upto some mischief): . . . While he was doing Yaaga, Lord Indhra snatched away the (Yaaga-Sacrificial) cow: When the cow was 'lost', the Braamins (The Priests) said these words to the king.

❍ ❍ ❍

७. पशुरद्याहृतो राजन्प्रनष्टस्तव दुर्नयात् ।
अरक्षितारं राजानं हन्ति दोषो नरेश्वर ॥

7. Oh King (Ambareesha)! Your Yaaga cow is now snatched away; It is lost because of your (sin & bad) conduct. Oh Lord of men! The sin of not offering protection, will destroy the king.

❍ ❍ ❍

८. प्रायश्चित्तं मखस्यैतन्नरं वा पुरुषर्षभ ।
आनयस्व पशुं शीघ्रं यावत्कर्म प्रवर्तते ॥

8. Oh (Ambaresha) the 'bull' amongst men!: You must bring at once to the 'Festival of Yaaga', a man, as Yaaga cow, as atonement, before we do (further) work (of your Yaaga).

❍ ❍ ❍

९. उपाध्यायवचः श्रुत्वा स राजा पुरुषर्षभ ।
अन्वियेष महाबुद्धिः पशुं गोभिः सहस्रशः ।।

9. (The Priests now want a human Sacrifice, Oh Raama, the 'Bull' amongst men, Listen): . . . Hearing the words of the priests, the most intelligent king (Ambareesha) searched for a man (as a) Yaaga cow, equal to 1,000 cows.

❍ ❍ ❍

१०. देशाञ्जनपदांस्तांस्तान्नगराणि वनानि च ।
आश्रमाणि च पुण्यानि मार्गमाणो महीपतिः ।।

10. This Lord of earth (Ambareesha) made enquiries in such and such lands, villages, cities and forests and in holy hermitages.

❍ ❍ ❍

११. स पुत्रसहितं तात सभार्यं रघुनन्दन ।
भृगुतुङ्गे समासीनमृचीकं संददर्श ह ।।

11. Oh dear (Lad) the darling of Raghu-s (Listen, Oh Raama)! And this king (Ambareesha) saw in (territory of) Bhrighuthunda, (Sage) Richeeka, who was seated comfortably with his wife, and was with his sons.

❍ ❍ ❍

१२. तमुवाच महातेजाः प्रणम्याभिप्रसाद्य च ।
ब्रह्मर्षिं तपसा दीप्तं राजर्षिरमितप्रभः ।।
पृष्ट्वा सर्वत्र कुशलमृचीकं तमिदं वचः ।।

12. This Royal sage (Ambareesha) who was most brilliant and of incomparable brilliance, bowed to the Bramma Rishi Richeeka who was 'burning' with (brilliancy) of penance. Enquiring about his welfare in all (of his matters), he addressed him thus, after making him well disposed towards him.

❍ ❍ ❍

१३. गवां शहसहस्रेण विक्रीणीषे सुतं यदि ।
पशोरर्थेमहाभाग कृतकृत्योऽस्मि भार्गव ॥

13. Oh most illustrious (Sage) of Bhrighu family If (as exchange) with 100,000 cows, you offer a son (of yours) for my yaaga as a Sacrificial Cow, then I will become accomplished (my visit to you will become most fruitful to me).

❍ ❍ ❍

१४. सर्वेपरिसृता देशा याज्ञीयं न लभे पशुम् ।
दातुमर्हसि मूल्येन सुतमेकं ततो मम ॥

14. All lands have been wandered around (by me in search of a human sacrifice); But I could not obtain a Yaaga 'Cow'. Therefore, you should offer me a son for a price.

❍ ❍ ❍

१५. एवमुक्तो महातेजा ऋचीकस्त्वब्रवीद्वचः ।
नाहं ज्येष्ठं नरश्रेष्ठ विक्रीणीयां कथञ्चन ॥

15. When told thus, the most brilliant sage Richeeka replied: = Oh foremost of men! I will never sell my eldest son, whatsoever. =

❍ ❍ ❍

१६. ऋचीकस्य वचः श्रुत्वा तेषां माता महात्मनाम् ।
उवाच नरशार्दूलमम्बरीषं तपस्विनी ॥

16. Hearing Richeeka's words, the mother of these most eminent (sons), this lady of penance, addressed Ambareesha who was a 'Lion' amongst men.

❍ ❍ ❍

१७. अविक्रेयं सुतं ज्येष्ठं भगवानाह भार्गवः ।
ममापि दयितं विद्धि कनिष्ठं शुनकं नृप ॥

१८. तस्मात्कनीयसं पुत्रं न दास्ये तव पार्थिव ॥

17 & 18.

Oh king! The lord of Bhrighu family, (my husband

Richeeka) has said that his eldest son is not to be sold: Likewise, know this: For me the last son Schunuka is my beloved. Therefore Oh king, I will not give you my last son.

❍ ❍ ❍

१९. प्रायेण हि नरश्रेष्ठ ज्येष्ठाः पितृषु बल्लभाः ।
मातॄणां च कनीयांसस्तस्मान्मोक्ष्ये कथं सुतम् ।।

19. Oh noble man! Generally, the eldest are the favourites of fathers; likewise the youngest are (favourites of) mothers: Therefore how can I give (this) son?

❍ ❍ ❍

२०. उक्तवाक्ये मुनौ तस्मिन्मुनिपत्न्यां तथैव च ।
शुनश्शेपः स्वयं राम मध्यमो वाक्यमब्रवीत् ।।

20. Oh Raama, (Listen)! When Muni Richeeka had said thus and likewise the Muni's wife, the middle son (the second of the three sons of Richeeka) Schunaschepa, himself (out of his own volition) spoke the following words.

❍ ❍ ❍

२१. पिता ज्येष्ठमविक्रेयं माता चाह कनीयसम् ।
विक्रेयं मध्यमं मन्ये राजन्पुत्रं नयस्व माम् ।।

21. Oh King (Ambareesha)! My father has said that his eldest son is not for sale; Mother likewise, that the youngest son is not for sale; I think you (should) take me, the middle son who is fit for sale.

❍ ❍ ❍

२२. गवां शहसहस्रेण शुनःशेपं नरेश्वरः ।
गृहीत्वा परमप्रीतो जगाम रघुनन्दन ।।

22. Oh Raama the darling of Raghu-s (Listen)! Giving 100,000 cows (as exchange price) this lord of men (Ambareesha) took Schunaschepa with him & left, mightily pleased.

❍ ❍ ❍

२३. अम्बरीषस्तु राजर्षी रथमारोप्य सत्वरम् ।
शुनःशेपं महातेजा जगामाशु महाबलः ।।

23. The mightily strong & most brilliant Royal sage Ambareesha, at once placed Schunaschepa in his chariot & drove away fast.

(Note: Sacrifices were the order of the day in Vedhic times: Goats, horses, cows and even humans were sacrificed in Yaaga-s.)

❍ ❍ ❍

Chapter 62

The Yaaga of Ambareesha

(Schathaanandh continues narration to Raama: Vischwaamithra's involvement in this Ambareesha-Schunaschepa Yaaga episode.)

❍ ❍ ❍

१. शनुःशेपं नरश्रेष्ठं गृहीत्वाऽथ महाबलः ।
व्यश्राम्यत्पुष्करे राजा मध्यो रघुनन्दन ।।

1. Oh (Raama) the darling of Raghu-s! (Listen)! Taking the noble man Schunaschepa with him, the mightily strong king (Ambareesha) rested at Pushkara at midday.

❍ ❍ ❍

२. तस्य विश्रममाणस्य शुनःशेपो महायशाः ।
पुष्करक्षेत्रमागम्य विश्वामित्रं ददर्श ह ।।
तप्यन्तमृषिभिः सार्धं मातुलं परमातुरः ।।

2. When (Ambaresha) reached the sacred place of Pushkar and was resting there, this most famous Schunaschepa who was in great distress, saw his maternal uncle Vishwaamithra who was doing penance along with

Rishi-s there. (Readers may note that Richeeka's wife was a cousin of Vischwaamithra).

❍ ❍ ❍

३. विषण्णवदनो दीनस्तृष्णया च श्रमेण च ।
पपाताङ्के मुने राम वाक्यं चेदमुवाच ह ॥

3. Oh Raama, (Listen)! With a dejected face, feeling feeble due to thirst & tiresomeness, he fell down at the lap of the Muni (Vischwaamithra): Then he said these words;

❍ ❍ ❍

४. नमेऽस्ति माता न पिता ज्ञातयो न च बान्धवाः ।
त्रातुमर्हसि मां सौम्य धर्मेण मुनिपुङ्गव ॥

4. Oh Raama, (Listen)! With a dejected face, feeling feeble due to thirst & tiresomeness, he fell down at the lap of the Muni (Vischwaamithra): Then he said these words; Dharma you must protect me (save me from this death as a sacrifice).

❍ ❍ ❍

५. त्राता त्वं हि नरश्रेष्ठ सर्वेषामपि कौशिक ॥

5. Oh (Vischwaamithra the) Kowschik! Oh foremost of men! Indeed you are the saviour for all.

❍ ❍ ❍

६. राजा च कृतकार्यः स्यादहं दीर्घायुरव्ययः ।
स्वर्गलोकमुपाश्नीयां तपस्तप्त्वा ह्यनुत्तमम् ॥

6. And this king (Ambareesha) also must fulfill his task (his Yaaga): And I also should live long without change; And after I do foremost penance, must enjoy the world of heaven.

(Schunaschepa is confident that Vischwaamithra can 'kill two birds with one stone'; That is, Ambareesha's Yaaga will be completed as per norms without sacrificing Schunaschepa at the Fire-Altar.)

❍ ❍ ❍

७. त्वं मे नाथो ह्यनाथस्य भव भव्येन चेतसा ।
पितेव पुत्रं धर्मात्मंस्त्रातुमर्हसि किल्बिषात् ।।

7. Indeed, with your pious mind, you should be the protector to me who has no protector: Oh man of Dharma! You should protect me like a father (protecting) his son from evil (predicaments).

❍ ❍ ❍

८. तस्य तद्वचनं श्रुत्वा विश्वामित्रो महातपाः ।
सान्त्वयित्वा बहुविधं पुत्रानिदमुवाच ह ।।

8. Hearing these words, Vischwaamithra the man of great penance, consoled him in many ways; Then he addressed his (own) sons.

❍ ❍ ❍

९. यत्कृते पितरः पुत्राञ्जनयन्ति शुभार्थिनः ।
परलोकहितार्थाय तस्य कालोऽयमागतः ।।

9. The purpose for which fathers beget sons who are desirous of (their parent's) welfare, is only for the sake of welfare in the Upper worlds. That time is here & now. (Oh my sons! It is time to obey me & do your duty for your father, says Vischwaamithra.)

❍ ❍ ❍

१०. अयं मुनिसुतो बालो मत्तः शरणमिच्छति ।
अस्य जीवितमात्रेण प्रियं कुरुत पुत्रकाः ।।

10. This muni's son, this boy, desires Refuge under me; Oh my sons: You should please him by merely 'making' him live on.

❍ ❍ ❍

११. सर्वेसुकृतकर्माणः सर्वेधर्मपरायणाः ।
पशुभूता नरेन्द्रस्य तृप्तिमग्नेः प्रयच्छथ ।।

11. All of you (my sons) have done all Rituals dutifully: You are all most virtuous men of Dharma: (So, offering

yourselves as &) becoming Sacrificial Cow for King (Ambareesha's) Yaaga, you please the Lord Agni ...... (You allow yourselves to be 'Offered' at The Fire-Altar- you immolate yourself at holy fire as substitute.)

❍ ❍ ❍

१२. नाथवांश्च शुनःशेपो यज्ञश्चाविघ्नितो भवेत् ।
देवतास्तर्पिताश्च स्युर्मम चापि कृतं वचः ।।

12. Schunaschepa (then) would have a true protector (in me): And Yaaga would be completed without hindrance; The Deities would be pleased (by your being fed into the Fire- altar & receiving oblations thereof) And my words (of command) would have been done (honoured by you, my sons).

❍ ❍ ❍

१३. मुनेस्तु वचनं श्रुत्वा मधुष्यन्दादयः सुताः ।
साभिमानं नरश्रेष्ठ सलीलमिदमब्रुवन् ।।

13. Oh (Raama) the noble man! (Listen further)! Hearing the Muni (Vischwaamithra's) words, his sons Madhyushyandha & others, said (haughty) words mockingly, that indicated their self interest. (No wonder!)

❍ ❍ ❍

१४. कथमात्मसुतान्हित्वा त्रायसेऽन्यसुतं विभो ।
अकार्यमिव पश्यामः श्वमांसमिव भोजने ।।

14. (The sons of Vischwaamithra refuse this gruesome command) Oh Lord (our father)! Sacrificing your own sons, how can you save another's son: Like dog's meat (served) in dinner, we see this & (view this) as highly improper (a command).

❍ ❍ ❍

१५. तेषां तद्वचनं श्रुत्वा पुत्राणां मुनिपुङ्गवः ।
क्रोधसंरक्तनयनो व्याहर्तुमुपचक्रमे ।।

15. Hearing these words from his sons, (Vischwaamithra) the 'tiger' of Muni-s, began to utter (Curse), his eyes turning red in wrath.

❍ ❍ ❍

१६. निःसाध्वसमिदं प्रोक्तं धर्मादपि विगर्हितम् ।
अतिक्रम्य तु मद्वाक्यं दारुणं रोमहर्षणम् ।।

16. (Vishwaamithra curses his own sons; Such a man is he!)...... My words (of command) were transgressed: Your reply indicates your consternation, straying from the path of Dharma: It causes 'hair raising' & it is very dreadful. (that you dare to disobey me)

❍ ❍ ❍

१७. श्वमांसभोजिनः सर्वेवासिष्ठा इव जातिषु ।
पूर्णं वर्षसहस्रं तु पृथिव्यामनुवत्स्यथ ।।

17. Like Vasishta's sons, all of you, in (various) births will live on earth for full 1,000 years, eating dog's meat.

❍ ❍ ❍

१८. कृत्वा शापसमायुक्तान् पुत्रान्मुनिवरस्तथा ।
शुनःशेपमुवाचार्तं कृत्वा रक्षां निरामयाम् ।।

18. After making his sons afflicted by his curse, the foremost Muni (Vischwaamithra) initiated the disturbed Schunaschepa with a Raksha Manthra (Prayer) that would protect him from danger & said.

❍ ❍ ❍

१९. पवित्रपाशैरासक्तो रक्तमाल्यानुलेपनः ।
वैष्णवं यूपमासाद्य वाग्भिरग्निमुदाहर ।।

19. Approaching the Yaaga mast which is sanctified by (Lord of Fire) Agni & God Vishnu, and wearing red garland and besmeared with scents & tying your wrist with Pavithra (the sacred thread), you recite (these) prayers.

❍ ❍ ❍

२०. इमे तु गाथे द्वे दिव्ये गायेथा मुनिपुत्रक ।
अम्बरीषस्य यज्ञेऽस्मिंस्ततः सिद्धिमवाप्स्यसि ॥

20. Oh son of Rishi (oh Schunaschepa)! In this Ambareesha's yaaga, these two divine Soothra-s, you recite; Thereby you will obtain Sidhdhi (Accomplishment of peace & life).

❍ ❍ ❍

२१. शुनश्शेपो गृहीत्वा ते द्वे गाथे सुसमाहितः ।
त्वरया राजसिंहं तमम्बरीषमुवाच ह ॥

21. With great steadfastness, this Schunaschepa learnt these two Soothra-s and then approached the foremost Ambareesha, the 'lion' amongst kings and said to him without wasting time.

❍ ❍ ❍

२२. राजसिंह महासत्त्व शीघ्रं गच्छावहे सदः ।
निर्वर्तयस्व राजेन्द्र दीक्षां च समुपाहर ॥

22. Oh most pure man! Oh 'Lion' amongst kings: Oh Lord of Kings! Let us go to yaaga center soon: Take vows & consecration; Complete the task (of Yaaga).

❍ ❍ ❍

२३. ऋषिपुत्रस्य तद्वाक्यं श्रुत्वा हर्षसमुत्सुकः ।
जगाम नृपतिः शीघ्रं यज्ञवाटमतन्द्रितः ॥

23. Hearing the words (of Schunaschepa) the son of Rishi (Richeeka), the king (Ambareesha) went at once to Yaaga center, greatly thrilled, and with great vigilance.

❍ ❍ ❍

२४. सदस्यानुमते राजा पवित्रकृतलक्षणम् ।
पशुं रक्ताम्बरं कृत्वा यूपे तं समयोजयत् ॥

24. With the permission of the (Priests) in the assembly (of Yaaga) the king tied (Schunaschepa) who had come as Sacrificial Cow, on to the mast, after dressing him up

with red dress and after tying on his hand the Pavithra (Sacred thread).

❍ ❍ ❍

२५. स बद्धो वाग्भिरग्र्याभिरभितुष्टाव वै सुरौ ।
इन्द्रमिन्द्रानुजं चैव यथावन्मुनिपुत्रकः ।।

25. Bound (to the Yaaga mast), this (Schunaschepa) the son of Muni, recited the foremost (Soothra-s) exactly (as taught by Vishwaamithra); and he extolled, the Sura-s, Indhra and his younger 'brother' (God Vishnu).

❍ ❍ ❍

२६. ततः प्रीतः सहस्राक्षो रहस्यस्तुतितर्पितः ।
दीर्घमायुस्ततः प्रादाच्छुनश्शेपाय वासवः ।।

26. Then being pleased by these mysterious (chants), the thousand eyed Indhra, became pleased and so he offered long life to Schunaschepa as a boon.

❍ ❍ ❍

२७. स च राजा नरश्रेष्ठ यज्ञस्य च समाप्तवान् ।
फलं बहुगुणं राम सहस्राक्षप्रसादजम् ।।

27. Oh noble man, Oh Raama (Listen!)!: And king Ambareesha also, obtained the fruits of his Yaaga and the blessings of the thousand eyed (Indhra) in large measure.

❍ ❍ ❍

२८. विश्वामित्रोऽपि धर्मात्मा तपस्तेपे महातपाः ।
पुष्करेषु नरश्रेष्ठ दश वर्षशतानि सः ।।

28. Oh (Raama) the foremost of men!: This (most eminent) man of Dharma of great penance, this Vischwaamithra too, did penance for 1,000 years at Pushkara (then, after saving Schunaschepa).

(Note: The point is that Vischwaamithra penance is hindered from time to time and he is wasting it: Readers may know that his goal is to become The Bramma Rishi, the highest amongst Rishi-s).

❍ ❍ ❍

Chapter 63

(Vischwaamithra's) Affair with Menaka

(Schathaanand narrates yet another episode to Raama about Vischwaamithra's life: Affair with lovely damsel Menaka; As usual lord Indhra plays mischief.)

❍ ❍ ❍

१. पूर्णे वर्षसहस्त्रे तु व्रतस्नातं महामुनिम् ।
अभ्यागच्छन्सुरा: सर्वे तप:फलचिकीर्षव: ।।

1. After completion of 1,000 years, all the Dheva-s came there to the great Muni (Vishwaamithra) who had completed his Vow (of penance), desirous of offering 'fruits' to him for his penance.

❍ ❍ ❍

२. अब्रवीत्सुमहातेजा ब्रह्मा सानुनयं वच: ।
ऋषिस्त्वमसि भद्रं ते स्वार्जितै: कर्मभि: शुभै: ।।

2. The most brilliant God Bramma, addressed these words most courteously: By your (hard) earned good deeds (of penance) you are now a Rishi; Welfare to you.

(But Vischwaamithra wants to be a Bramma Rishi, not just a Rishi.)

❍ ❍ ❍

३. तमेवमुक्त्वा देवेशस्त्रिदिवं पुनरभ्यगात् ।
विश्वामित्रो महातेजा भूयस्तेपे महत्तप: ।।

3. After saying this to him, the Lord of Dheva-s (Bramma) went back to the Dheva world. And this most brilliant Vischwaamithra did a mighty penance once again.

❍ ❍ ❍

४. तत: कालेन महता मेनका परमाप्सरा: ।
पुष्करेषु नरश्रेष्ट स्नातुं समुपचक्रमे ।।

4. After a long time, (as he was doing penance) the foremost Apsara damsel Menaka, went to Pushkara to take bath.

❍ ❍ ❍

५. तां ददर्श महातेजा मेनकां कुशिकात्मजः ।
रूपेणाप्रतिमां तत्र विद्युतं जलदे यथा ॥
दृष्ट्वा कन्दर्पवशगो मुनिस्तामिदमब्रवीत् ॥

5. And the most brilliant (Vischwaamithra) the son of Kuschika saw this Menaka who was like a lightning in cloud, and incomparable in beauty. As soon as he saw her, the Muni (Vischwaamithra) was seized by love & passion and he addressed her.

❍ ❍ ❍

६. अप्सरः स्वागतं तेऽस्तु वस चेह ममाश्रमे ।
अनुगृह्णीष्व भद्रं ते मदनेन सुमोहितम् ॥

6. Oh Apsara (Menaka)! Your (coming) here is most welcome! Welfare to you! Stay in my hermitage: You favour me who is 'stupefied' by passion (over you).

❍ ❍ ❍

७. इत्युक्ता सा वरारोहा तत्र वासमथाकरोत् ।
तपसो हि महाविघ्नो विश्वामित्रमुपागतः ॥

7. When told thus, (Menaka) who was most handsome with lovely hips, began to live there; Thus there was great hindrance (& break) to his penance.

❍ ❍ ❍

८. तस्यां वसन्त्यां वर्षाणि पञ्च पञ्च च राघव ।
विश्वामित्राश्रमे तस्मिन् सुखेन व्यतिचक्रमुः ॥

8. While she lived in Vischwaamithra's hermitage, 5 plus 5 (Ten) years passed away pleasantly.

❍ ❍ ❍

९. अथ काले गते तस्मिन्विश्वामित्रो महामुनिः ।
सव्रीड इव संवृत्तश्चिन्ताशोकपरायणः ॥

9. After this period of time went away, the great Muni Vischwaamithra became ashamed & was filled with worry, depression (& remorse).

❍ ❍ ❍

१०. बुद्धिर्मुनेः समुत्पन्ना सामर्षा रघुनन्दन ।
सर्वं सुराणां कर्मैतत्तपोऽपहरणं महत् ॥

10. Oh (Raama) the darling of Raghu-s (Listen)! And this thought occurred to the Muni: = All this that takes away my penance (all these hindrances), are the great work of the Dheva-s = He was enraged....... (and he pondered thus).

❍ ❍ ❍

११. अहोरात्रापदेशोन गताः संवत्सरा दश ।
काममोहाभिभूतस्य विघ्नोऽयं समुपस्थितः ॥

11. Engulfed in love & passion, 10 years passed away like a day and night (for me): (Thus) the hindrance to my penance came by.

❍ ❍ ❍

१२. विनिःश्वसन्मुनिवरः पश्चात्तापेन दुःखितः ।
भीतामप्सरसं दृष्ट्वा वेपन्तीं प्राञ्जलिं स्थिताम् ॥

१३. मेनकां मधुरैर्वाक्यैर्विसृज्य कुशिकात्मजः ।
उत्तरं पर्वतं राम विश्वामित्रो जगाम ह ॥

12 & 13.

The foremost Muni who was sighing & breathing hard, who was very sad feeling regret (over his infatuation with Menaka) saw this Apsara who was standing with her arms in Anjali, shivering with fear...... This Vischwaamithra, the son of Kuschika, gave her leave to go away with sweet words, and then he (also) left for (foremost) mountain in the north.

❍ ❍ ❍

१४. स कृत्वा नैष्टिकीं बुद्धिं तप्तुकामो महातपाः ।
कौशिकीतीरमासाद्य तपस्तेपे सुदारुणम् ।।

14. This great man of penance, reaching the banks of Kowshiki River, made up his mind to do penance without hindrance; and did a most rigorous penance, desirous of doing penance (steadfastly).

❍ ❍ ❍

१५. तस्य वर्षसहस्त्राणि घोरे तपसि तिष्टतः ।
उत्तरे पर्वते राम देवतानामभूद्भयम् ।।

15. Oh Raama! (Listen): When he was steadfast in doing gruesome penance for 1,000 years in the northern mountain (region), fear seized the Dheva-s.

❍ ❍ ❍

१६. आमन्त्रयन्समागम्य सर्वे सर्षिगणाः सुराः ।
महर्षिशब्दं लभतां साध्वयं कुशिकात्मजः ।।

16. (Fear & jealousy is found even amongst celestials: Lord Indhra can never tolerate threat to his power & position): . . . The Sura-s who were with congregation of Rishi-s, all of them got together, took counsel (and said) = Well! This Vischwaamithra, let him obtain the title of Maha Rishi = ...

❍ ❍ ❍

१७. देवतानां वचः श्रुत्वा सर्वलोकपितामहः ।
अब्रवीन्मधुरं वाक्यं विश्वामित्रं तपोधनम् ।।

१८. महर्षे स्वागतं तेऽस्तु तपसोग्रेण तोषितः ।
महत्त्वमृषिमुख्यत्वं ददामि तव कौशिक ।।

17 & 18.

God Bramma, listening to the words of the deities, addressed Vischwaamithra whose wealth was penance, with these sweet words...: Oh (Vischwaamithra the) Kowschik! I am pleased with your rigorous penance.

I am offering The State of MahaRishi, the high rank & position of a Rishi. Oh Ye MahaRishi! Welfare to you!

❍ ❍ ❍

१९. ब्रह्मणस्तु वचः श्रुत्वा विश्वामित्रस्तपोधनः ।
प्राञ्जलिः प्रणतो भूत्वा प्रत्युवाच महायशाः ॥

19. Hearing God Bramma's words, the most brilliant Vischwaamithra whose wealth: was penance, replied to him, with his (head) bowed and with his hands cupped in Anjali (in reverence).

❍ ❍ ❍

२०. ब्रह्मर्षिशब्दमतुलं स्वार्जितैः कर्मभिः शुभैः ।
यदि मे भगवानाह ततोऽहं विजितेन्द्रियः ॥

20. Only if my Lord (you, God Bramma) confers the incomparable title of Bramma Rishi on me because of my self earned virtues through my deeds, I would become one who has conquered (all) my senses (& passions).

❍ ❍ ❍

२१. तमुवाच ततो ब्रह्मा न तावत्त्वं जितेन्द्रियः ।
यतस्व मुनिशार्दूल इत्युक्त्वा त्रिदिवं गतः ॥

21. And God Bramma replied to this (request): = Oh 'Lion' amongst Muni-s! You Have Not (yet) Become One Who Has Conquered His Senses (& passion); = Endeavour (to reach that state).= Saying thus, he went back to the world of Dheva-s.

❍ ❍ ❍

२२. विप्रस्थितेषु देवेषु विश्वामित्रो महामुनिः ।
ऊर्ध्वबाहुर्निरालम्बो वायुभक्षस्तपश्चरन् ॥
२३. घर्मे पञ्चतपा भूत्वा वर्षास्वाकाशसंश्रयः ।
शिशिरे सलिलस्थायी रात्र्यहानि तपोधनः ॥
२४. एवं वर्षसहस्राणि तपो घोरमुपागमत् ॥

22 to 24.

(And Vischwaamithra started to do even more penance). When the Dheva-s (including Bramma) dispersed, the great Muni Vischwaamithra performed penance: Lifting up his hands, without any support (his body hanging in air so to speak), 'eating'only Air for food,.... staying in the middle of Five Fires in Summer and staying in cool waters in winters, staying under the sky (without roof) in rainy seasons, day & night, this man whose wealth was penance..... did most gruesome penance for thousands of years like this.

❍ ❍ ❍

२५. तस्मिन्संतप्यमाने तु विश्वामित्रे महामुनौ ।
संभ्रमः सुमहानासीत्सुराणां वासवस्य च ॥

25. When the great Muni Vischwaamithra was doing penance like this, great bewilderment seized the Dheva-s & (their chief) Lord Indhra.

❍ ❍ ❍

२६. रम्भामप्सरसं शक्रस्सर्वैस्सह मरुद्गणैः ।
उवाचात्महितं वाक्यमहितं कौशिकस्य च ॥

26. Schakra (Indhra), along with congregation of Maruth-s and all, addressed (another) Apsara damsel called Rambha, for the sake of (doing) harm on Kowschik, (all) for their own good.

(Note: Indhra is again at his usual game; = The age old trick; Get hold of a pretty girl & use her for your purpose: Destroy his penance and power.)

❍ ❍ ❍

Chapter 64

The Curse on Rambha (by Vischwaamithra)

(Schathanandh continues narration to Raama: The Rambha episode: How Indhra tries to spoil Vischwaamithra's penance again.)

❍ ❍ ❍

१. सुरकार्यमिदं रम्भे कर्तव्यं सुमहत्त्वया ।
लोभनं कौशिकस्येह काममोहसमन्वितम् ।।

1. (Indhra tells Rambha): Oh Rambha! At this moment, the enticement of (Vischwaamithra the) Kowschik by making him infatuated with passion & love, must be done by you: This work for Dheva-s is great (& most important for us all).

❍ ❍ ❍

२. तथोक्ता साऽप्सरा राम सहस्राक्षेण धीमता ।
व्रीडिता प्राञ्जलिर्भूत्वा प्रत्युवाच सुरेश्वरम् ।।

2. Oh Raama (Listen)! When told thus by the wise (Indhra of) thousand eyes, (Rambha) became embarrassed and replied to this lord of Dheva-s, with her hands cupped in Anjali.

❍ ❍ ❍

३. अयं सुरपते घोरो विश्वामित्रो महामुनिः ।
क्रोधमुत्स्रृजते घोरं देव न संशयः ।।
ततो हि मे भयं देव प्रसादं कर्तुमर्हसि ।।

3. Oh (Indhra) the lord of Sura-s: =Oh Dheva! Oh (my) Lord! This Vischwaamithra is a great Muni: Gruesome too; And he will discharge gruesome wrath on me: No doubt about it; Therefore there is fear in me; You must show me your favour (& grace): (please dont ask me to do this job, begs Rambha).

❍ ❍ ❍

४. तामुवाच सहस्राक्षो वेपमानां कृताञ्जलिम् ।
मा भैषि रम्भे भद्रं ते कुरुष्व मम शासनम् ।।

4. Then the thousand eyed (Indhra) addressed her who was shivering (with fear), whose hands were cupped in Anjali:= You should act as per my command: Do not fear: Welfare to you. =

❍ ❍ ❍

५. कोकिलो हृदयग्राही माधवे रुचिरद्रुमे ।
अहं कन्दर्पसहितः स्थास्यामि तव पार्श्वतः ।।

5. In the spring season when trees are lustrous, along with Kandharpa (lord of love), I will stand by your side in the form of a Kokila Bird which would captivate (any) one's heart.

❍ ❍ ❍

६. त्वं हि रूपं बहुगुणं कृत्वा परमभास्वरम् ।
तमृषिं कौशिकं रम्भे भेदयस्व तपस्विनम् ।।

6. Oh Rambha! And you, taking on a form endowed with all qualities (of beauty & form) and shining most radiant, 'Disturb' (the mind) & heart of (Vischwaamithra the) Rishi Kowschika who is doing penance.

❍ ❍ ❍

७. सा श्रुत्वा वचनं तस्य कृत्वा रूपमनुत्तमम् ।
लोभयामास ललिता विश्वामित्रं शुचिस्मिता ।।

7. Hearing Indhra's words, (Rambha) took on an incomparable form, became amorous and began to make overtures to (entice) Vischwaamithra, sporting a (enchanting) smile.

❍ ❍ ❍

८. कोकिलस्य तु शुश्राव वल्गु व्याहरतः स्वनम् ।
संप्रहृष्टेन मनसा तत एनामुदैक्षत ।।

8. (And Vischwaamithra) heard the sweet cooing emitted by the cuckoo bird, (with great pleasure) & exhilarated heart. At the same time he also saw (this Rambha).

❍ ❍ ❍

९. अथ तस्य च शब्देन गीतेनाप्रतिमेन च ।
दर्शनेन च रम्भाया मुनिः सन्देहमागतः ॥

9. By the cooing sounds (of the cuckoo) and by the sight of this Rambha of incomparable (beauty) and by the music, this Muni (Vischwaamithra) entertained 'doubts.' (about all this).

❍ ❍ ❍

१०. सहस्राक्षस्य तत्कर्म विज्ञाय मुनिपुङ्गवः ।
रम्भां कोपसमाविष्टः शशाप कुशिकात्मजः ॥

10. The noble Muni Vischwaamithra, the 'tiger' of Muni-s, realised that all this was the work of the thousand eyed (Indhra) and he cursed this Rambha, seized by wrath.

❍ ❍ ❍

११. यन्मां लोभयसे रम्भे कामक्रोधजयैपिणम् ।
दश वर्षसहस्राणि शैली स्थास्यसि दुर्भगे ॥

11. (Vischwaamithra does not fall into a trap like last time with Menaka & so says:) Oh Rambha! You are (trying to) entice me who is desirous of (controlling &) conquering anger and passion; Oh disgusting (woman)! You Shall Become A Stone for 10,000 Years.

❍ ❍ ❍

१२. ब्राह्मणः सुमहातेजास्तपोबलसमन्वितः ।
उद्धरिष्यति रम्भे त्वां मत्क्रोधकलुषीकृताम् ॥

12. Oh Rambha! The most brilliant God Bramma who is endowed with power of penance, will resurrect you from the evil that has befallen on you by my wrath.

❍ ❍ ❍

१३. एवमुक्त्वा महातेजा विश्वामित्रो महामुनिः ।
अशक्नुवन्धारयितुं कोपसन्तापमात्मनः ।।

13. (Readers may now note the change in Vischwaamithra) ..... Having said thus, the most brilliant Vischwaamithra the great Muni, could not bear the anguish caused by his own wrath (on her).

❍ ❍ ❍

१४. तस्य शापेन महता रम्भा शैली तदाऽभवत् ।
वचः श्रुत्वा च कन्दर्पोमहर्षेः स च निर्गतः ।।

14. By this great curse of the great Rishi (Vischwaamithra), at once Rambha became a 'Stone': And when he heard the words (of his curse), this cupid Kandharpa (lord of love), went back.

❍ ❍ ❍

१५. कोपेन सुमहातेजास्तपोऽपहरणे कृते ।
इन्द्रियैरजितै राम न लेभे शान्तिमात्मनः ।।

15. Oh Raama (Listen)! This most brilliant (Vischwaamithra) did not obtain any tranquillity when harm was caused to his penance because he was unable to conquer his senses due to his wrath.

❍ ❍ ❍

१६. बभूवास्य मनश्चिन्ता तपोऽपहरणे कृते ।।

16. A thought occurred to him then in this matter of hindrance to his penance.

❍ ❍ ❍

१७. नैव क्रोधं गमिष्यामि न च वक्ष्ये कथञ्चन ।
अथवा नोच्छ्वसिष्यामि संवत्सरशतान्यपि ।।

१८. अहं विशोषयिष्यामि ह्यात्मानं विजितेन्द्रियः ।
तावद्यावद्धि मे प्राप्तं ब्राह्मण्यं स्वतपोऽर्जितम् ।।
अनुच्छ्वसन्नभुञ्जानस्तिष्ठेयं शाश्वतीः समाः ।।

१९. न हि मे तप्यमानस्य क्षयं यास्यन्ति मूर्तयः ॥

17 to 19.

(Vischwaamithra resolves): Never will I give way to wrath, whatever (be the provocation), even for hundreds of thousand years: Nor will I speak: Not only that: I will also hold on to my breath (will control my breathing)..... And till such a time I become Bramma Rishi (the state of Brammam) earned through my penance, I will remain for a long time without breathing, without eating, subjecting myself to hardships & controlling my senses...... When I am in (such a) penance (I pray) let not my body 'wither' away (and decay).

❍ ❍ ❍

२०. एवं वर्षसहस्रस्य दीक्षां स मुनिपुङ्गवः ।
चकाराप्रतिमां लोके प्रतिज्ञां रघुनन्दन ॥

20. Oh (Raama) the darling of Raghus! (Listen): Consecrating himself, this (Vishwaamithra) the 'tiger' of Muni-s, took on this Vow of 1,000 years, which was unparalleled in the world.

(Note: Schathanadh narrates all this about Vischwaamithra to Raama who is indeed most fortunate that he has this very great man Vischwaamithra as a patron, tutor, guide, philosopher. Schathanandh tells Raama what all went into the making of this Bramma Rishi. Being a great king he was a Royal Rishi; Then became a Rishi: Then a Maha Rishi. And as we shall see, in the next chapter, he finally becomes a Bramma Rishi, the highest spiritual state (of Brammam).

❍ ❍ ❍

Chapter 65

Vischwaamithra becomes Bramma Rishi

(Schathaanandh finally concludes narration: He tells Raama how this very great sage Vischwaamithra, became a Bramma Rishi.)

❍ ❍ ❍

१. अथ हैमवतीं राम दिशं त्यक्त्वा महामुनिः ।
पूर्वां दिशमनुप्राप्य तपस्तेपे सुदारुणम् ।।

1. Oh Raama (Listen)! Leaving the northern region (around Himaalayas), the great Muni (Vischwaamithra) reached the eastern region and did rigorous penance.

❍ ❍ ❍

२. मौनं वर्षसहस्रस्य कृत्वा व्रतमनुत्तमम् ।
चकाराप्रतिमं राम तपः परमदुष्करम् ।।

2. Oh Raama! Observing the foremost Vow of Silence for 1,000 years, he did a most difficult and incomparable penance.

❍ ❍ ❍

३. पूर्णे वर्षसहस्रे तु काष्ठभूतं महामुनिम् ।
विघ्नैर्बहुभिराधूतं क्रोधो नान्तरमाविशत् ।।

3. In spite of being shaken up by many obstacles, till the completion of 1,000 years, anger never entered his mind: This great Muni was like a log of wood!

❍ ❍ ❍

४. स कृत्वा निश्चयं राम तप आतिष्ठदव्ययम् ।।

4. Oh Raama (Listen)! Making a firm resolve, this (Vischwaamithra) completed this penance, 'Unchanged' (without any change in his resolve).

❍ ❍ ❍

५. तस्य वर्षसहस्रस्य व्रते पूर्णेमहाव्रतः ।
भोक्तुमारब्धवानन्नं तस्मिन् काले रघूत्तम ।।
इन्द्रो द्विजातिर्भूत्वा तं सिद्धमन्नमयाचत ।।

5. Oh (Raama) the foremost of Raghu-s! (Listen): After 1,000 years, after the vow of this (Vischwaamithra) of great vows was completed, he began to eat Anna (Grain food): At that time Lord Indhra, taking the form of a Braamin, begged for this Anna (food) that was prepared (& served) for him.

❍ ❍ ❍

६. तस्मै दत्त्वा तदा सिद्धं सर्वं विप्राय निश्चितः ।
निःशेषितेऽन्ने भगवानभुक्त्वैव महातपाः ।।
न किञ्चिदवदद्विप्रं मौनव्रतमथास्थितः ।।

6. This Lord (Vischwaamithra) of great penances, gave all this (food that was meant to be) served for him, to the Braamin. When nothing was left over, this resolute (Vischwaamithra) who was observing the vow of silence, did not speak at all to this Braamin (Indhra), although he had not eaten anything (at all).

❍ ❍ ❍

७. तथैवासीत् पुनर्मौनमनुच्छ्वासं चकार ह ।
अथ वर्षसहस्रं वै नोच्छ्वसन्मुनिपुङ्गवः ।।

7. And likewise, once again, for 1,000 years, he observed Vow of Silence without even breathing; (Vischwaamithra) the 'tiger' of Muni-s , did not stand up (was sitting motionless).

❍ ❍ ❍

८. तस्यानुच्छ्वसमानस्य मूर्ध्नि धूमो व्यजायत ।
त्रैलोक्यं येन संभ्रान्तमादीपितमिवाभवत् ।।

8. (As he was doing penance thus) Without (even) breathing, (Holy) smoke came out from his head:

Because of this, the three Worlds became bewildered (and felt) burnt up as though.

❍ ❍ ❍

९. ततो देवर्षिगन्धर्वाः पन्नगोरगराक्षसाः ।
मोहितास्तेजसा तस्य तपसा मन्दरश्मयः ।।

9. Stupefied by the brilliancy of his penance, at that time, the Dheva-s, Rishi-s, Ghandarva-s, Pannaga-s, Uraga-s, Demons, became dull.

❍ ❍ ❍

१०. कश्मलोपहताः सर्वेपितामहमथाब्रुवन् ।।

10. Seized by despair, all of them told God Bramma (the Pithaamaha- The God Father of all).

❍ ❍ ❍

११. बहुभिः कारणैर्देव विश्वामित्रो महामुनिः ।
लोभितः क्रोधितश्चैव तपसा चाभिवर्धते ।।

11. Oh (Bramma) The Dheva! In spite of making him angry, in spite of being seduced in many ways, by his many deeds, this Vischwaamithra thrives by penance! (So resolute in penance).

❍ ❍ ❍

१२. न ह्यस्य वृजिनं किञ्चिद्दृश्यते सूक्ष्ममप्यथ ।।

12. Further, No wickedness is seen in him, not even a trifle.

❍ ❍ ❍

१३. न दीयते यदि त्वस्य मनसा यदभीप्सितम् ।
विनाशयति त्रैलोक्यं तपसा सचराचरम् ।।

13. Therefore, if what he desires in his mind is not given to him, he may destroy the three worlds along with its living and non living beings, by the (power of his) penance.

❍ ❍ ❍

१४. त्रयाकुलाश्च दिशः सर्वा न च किञ्चित्प्रकाशते ।
सागराः क्षुभिताः सर्वेविशीर्यन्ते च पर्वताः ।।

14. There is agitation in all the directions (of Universe)! Nothing shines: All the oceans are turbulent: The mountains are cracking up.

❍ ❍ ❍

१५. प्रकम्पते च पृथिवी वायुर्वाति भृशाकुलः ।
ब्रह्मन्न प्रतिजानीमो नास्तिको जायते जनः ।।

15. The earth trembles; Air blows violently: Oh God Bramma! We do not know what to do; People will become Naasthikas (Atheists),

❍ ❍ ❍

१६. सम्मूढमिव त्रैलोक्यं संप्रक्षुभितमानसम् ।
भास्करो निष्प्रभश्चैव महर्षेस्तस्य तेजसा ।।

16. By the power of the penance of this great Rishi, the three Worlds have become agitated in mind, shaken up, stupefied. Sun also has lost its brilliance.

❍ ❍ ❍

१७. बुद्धिं न कुरुते यावन्नाशे देव महामुनिः ।
तावत्प्रसाद्यो भगवानग्निरूपों महाद्युतिः ।।

17. Oh The Dheva (Bramma)! Before this Lord, this great Muni (Vischwaamithra) who is like (Lord of fire) Agni with its great brilliance, directs his mind to the destruction (of the worlds), He Must Be Propitiated.

❍ ❍ ❍

१८. कालाग्निना यथा पूर्वं त्रैलोक्यं दह्यतेऽखिलम् ।
देवराज्यं चिकीर्षेत दीयतामस्य यन्मतम् ।।

18. Like the Pralaya Fire long ago, the three worlds will be burnt up entirely; (Why!) He may even desire Lord Indhra's position as king of Dheva-s: Whatever Is On His Mind, That Must Be Given.

❍ ❍ ❍

१९. ततः सुरगणाः सर्वेपितामहपुरोगमाः ।
विश्वामित्रं महात्मानं वाक्यं मधुरमब्रुवन् ।।

19. Then all the celestials led by God Bramma, all of them addressed this great soul Vischwaamithra with these sweet words.

❍ ❍ ❍

२०. ब्रह्मर्षेस्वागतं तेऽस्तु तपसा स्म सुतोषिताः ।।

20. Oh Bramma Rishi! Welfare to you! We are pleased by your penance! (Readers may note that God Bramma addresses Vischwaamithra as Bramma Rishi for the first time).

❍ ❍ ❍

२१. ब्राह्मण्यं तपसोग्रेण प्राप्तवानसि कौशिक ।
दीर्घमायुश्च ते ब्रह्मन्ददामि समरुद्गणः ।।
स्वस्ति प्राप्नुहि भद्रं ते गच्छ सौम्य यथासुखम् ।।

21. Oh (Vischwaamithra) the Kowschik! By your fierce penance you have attained the state of Brammam: Oh Braamin! Along with Maruth-s here with me, I am offering you long life: Welfare to you. You will obtain Swasthy (tranquillity): Oh pleasant (Vischwaamithra)! You may go as you please (in all the worlds).

❍ ❍ ❍

२२. पितामहवचः श्रुत्वा सर्वेषां च दिवौकसाम् ।
कृत्वा प्रणामं मुदितो व्याजहार महामुनिः ।।

22. Hearing the words of Pithaamaha (Bramma), the great Muni (Vischwaamithra) became exhilarated and bowed to all the deities there: Then he uttered thus.

❍ ❍ ❍

२३. ब्राह्मण्यं यदि मे प्राप्तं दीर्घमायुस्तथैव च ।
ओंकारोऽथ वषट्कारो वेदाश्च वरयन्तु माम् ।।

23. If long life & likewise "The State of Brammam" has

been obtained by me, then let the sacred "Om Kaara" (the vital breath), "The Vashat Kaara" (various Saama chants) and The Vedha-s Cover Me. (May all these "permeate" me; let me be blessed by these).

❍ ❍ ❍

२४. क्षत्रवेदविदां श्रेष्ठो ब्रह्मवेदविदामपि ।
ब्रह्मपुत्रो वसिष्ठो मामेवं वदतु देवताः ।।
यद्ययं परमः कामः कृतो यान्तु सुरर्षभाः ।।

24. Oh Deities! The son of God Bramma, this Vasishta who is foremost amongst those well versed in The Kshathriya Vedha, (this Vasishta who is foremost amongst those well versed) in Bramma Vedha as well, should speak of me thus: (That I Am Bramma Rishi). If this foremost wish of mine is fulfilled, then only (you), the foremost Dheva-s, may go (from here).

(Vishwaamithra wants recognition from his old adversary, Vasishta: Vasishta must emphatically say that he is Bramma Rishi.)

❍ ❍ ❍

२५. ततः प्रसादितो देवैर्वसिष्ठो जपतां वरः ।
सख्यं चकार ब्रह्मर्षिरेवमस्त्विति चाब्रवीत् ।।

25. And Vasishta who was foremost amongst men of chants & prayers, and who was (himself) a Bramma Rishi and who was honoured by all Dheva-s said: = So Be It. = (From that time onwards) he, (Vischwaamithra), made friendship with (Vasishta).

❍ ❍ ❍

२६. ब्रह्मर्षिस्त्वं न सन्देहः सर्वं संपत्स्यते तव ।
इत्युक्त्वा देवताश्चापि सर्वा जग्मुर्यथागतम् ।।

26. You Are A Bramma Rishi: No Doubt!: You will obtain everything. Saying thus, all the Dheva-s went away as they came.

❍ ❍ ❍

२७. विश्वामित्रोऽपि धर्मात्मा लब्ध्वा ब्राह्मण्यमुत्तमम् ।
पूजयामास ब्रह्मर्षिं वसिष्ठं जपतां वरम् ।।
कृतकामो महीं सर्वां चचार तपसि स्थितः ।।

27. Having obtained the foremost State of Brammam, the noble soul Vischwaamithra, the man of Dharma, honoured Bramma Rishi Vasishta who was foremost amongst men of prayers & chants. Having obtained his wish (Vischwaamithra) roamed about all over the earth, ever steadfast in penance.

❍ ❍ ❍

२८. एवं त्वनेन ब्राह्मण्यं प्राप्तं राम महात्मना ।
एष राम मुनिश्रेष्ठ एष विग्रहवांस्तपः ।।
एष धर्मपरो नित्यं वीर्यस्यैष परायणम् ।।

28. (Schathaanandh thus narrated the stories connected with the great Vischwaamithra to Raama: and concluded his narration thus.)

Oh Raama! The State of Brammam Was Obtained By This Great Soul Thus: Oh Raama! He Is The Foremost of Rishi-s: Oh Raama! He Is The Embodiment Of Penance: (Oh Raama!) He Ever Practises Dharma: (Oh Raama!) He Is The Foremost Refuge In Bravery.

(Schathanandh thus enlightened Raama about Vischwaamithra before Janaka and others: Raama had not really 'known' him.)

❍ ❍ ❍

२९. शतानन्दवचः श्रुत्वा रामलक्ष्मणसन्निधौ ।
जनकः प्राञ्जलिर्वाक्यमुवाच कुशिकात्मजम् ।।

29. Hearing the words of Schathaanandh (hearing the great story & history of Vischwaamithra) told before Raama & Lakshmana, king Janaka addressed (Vischwaamithra) the son of Kuschika, cupping his hands in Anjali:

❍ ❍ ❍

३०. धन्योऽस्म्यनुगृहीतोऽस्मि यस्य मे मुनिपुङ्गव ।
यज्ञं काकुत्स्थसहितः प्राप्तवानसि कौशिक ॥

30. Oh (Vischwaamithra the) Kowshik! Oh 'Tiger' amongst Muni-s! Blessed as I am, as you have come to my Yaaga accompanied by the two Kaakuthsa-s. I am honoured.

❍ ❍ ❍

३१. पावितोऽहं त्वया ब्रह्मन्दर्शनेन महामुने ।
विश्वामित्र महाभाग ब्रह्मर्षिणां वरोत्तम ॥
गुणा बहुविधाः प्राप्तास्तव सन्दर्शनान्मया ॥

31. Oh Braamin! Oh most brilliant (Vischwaamithra)! Oh most illustrious! Oh foremost amongst Bramma Rishi-s Oh foremost amongst foremost! By your very sight (presence) I am purified. By your presence various Guna-s (Merit) has been obtained by me.

❍ ❍ ❍

३२. विस्तरेण च ते ब्रह्मन् कीर्त्यमानं महत्तपः ।
श्रुतं मया महातेजो रामेण च महात्मना ॥

32. Oh Braamin! Oh most brilliant (Vischwaamithra)! Your great (story, your history) and your penance which has been narrated in detail (by my minister-adviser Schathaanandh) was heard by me and by the great soul Raama.

❍ ❍ ❍

३३. सदस्यैः प्राप्य च सदः श्रुतास्ते बहवो गुणाः ॥

33. The Congregation that has gathered in the Assembly have also heard about your various (Great) Qualities.

❍ ❍ ❍

३४. अप्रमेयं तपस्तुभ्यमप्रमेयं च ते बलम् ।
अप्रमेया गुणाश्चैव नित्यं ते कुशिकात्मज ॥

34. Your penance is unparalleled; your power incomparable; Oh the son of Kuschika! Your qualities (Virtues) are ever incomparable.

❍ ❍ ❍

३५. तृप्तिराश्चर्यभूतानां कथानां नास्ति मे विभो ।
कर्मकालो मुनिश्रेष्ठ लम्बते रविमण्डलम् ।।

35. Oh Lord! (Vischwaamithra)! There is never full satisfaction for me in listening to the most wonderful stories (about you and your achievements) Oh foremost Muni! This is the time for evening rituals. Sun's rays are hanging down (Sun is setting).

❍ ❍ ❍

३६. श्वः प्रभाते महातेजो द्रष्टुमर्हसि मां पुनः ।
स्वागतं तपतां श्रेष्ठ मामनुज्ञातुमर्हसि ।।

36. Oh most brilliant (Vischwaamithra)! Oh foremost man of penance! Welcome! You must allow me to see you tomorrow: again You should give me leave to go (now).

❍ ❍ ❍

३७. एवमुक्तो मुनिवरः प्रशस्य पुरुषर्षभम् ।
विससर्जाशु जनकं प्रीतं प्रीतमनास्तदा ।।

37. When told thus, the foremost Muni (Vischwaamithra) who was pleased at heart, then extolled the dear (King) Janaka, the 'Bull' amongst men. Then he gave him leave to go.

❍ ❍ ❍

३८. एवमुक्त्वा मुनिश्रेष्ठं वैदेहो मिथिलाधिपः ।
प्रदक्षिणं चकाराशु सोपाध्यायः सबान्धवः ।।

38. The king of Vidheha, the Mithila king, saying thus, quickly went round in circumbambulation over the foremost Muni along with his Upaadhyaaya-s and with his folks.

❍ ❍ ❍

३९. विश्वामित्रोऽपि धर्मात्मा सरामः सहलक्ष्मणः ।
स्ववाटमभिचक्राम पूज्यमानो महर्षिभिः ।।

39. And Vischwaamithra, the man of Dharma, also,

honoured by the great Rishi-s there, then went to his own cottage along with Raama and Lakshmana.

(Note: Schathaanandh, the son of Gauthama-Ahalya is Minister-Adviser to King Janaka of Mithila: Thanks to Schathaanandh Raama gets to know the real Vischwaamithra. This Vischwaamithra, once, was a mighty king of Kanya-Kubja. He was a Kshathriya (Warrior class) by birth. Was arrogant of his might & power till Vasishta humbled him. But by constant penance, by penance unparalleled, he became a truly great Sage. He became a Royal Rishi, then a Rishi, then Maha Rishi & finally The Bramma Rishi. He was master of Dhanurvedha (Science of war & weapons) He taught Raama all the weapons, the conventional & the divine weapons. Raama is very fortunate indeed to have him as his guru, patron, and a well wisher.)

❍ ❍ ❍

Chapter 66

Raama sees The Divine Bow

(At Mithila, at the court of king Janaka, Vischwaamithra requests him to exhibit the divine bow: Raama who was with Lakshmana takes a good look at The Bow.)

❍ ❍ ❍

१. ततः प्रभाते विमले कृतकर्मा नराधिपः ।
विश्वामित्रं महात्मानमाजुहाव सराघवम् ।।

1. When it was morning, at daylight, after doing the morning rituals, king (Janaka) called on the great soul Vischwaamithra who was with the (two) Raaghava-s (Raama/Lakshmana).

❍ ❍ ❍

२. तमर्चयित्वा धर्मात्मा शास्त्रदृष्टेन कर्मणा ।
राघवौ च महात्मानौ तदा वाक्यमुवाच ह ॥

2. After duly honouring him and the two great soul Raaghava-s as per norms of Shaasthra-s, this noble soul man of Dharma (Janaka) then addressed these words:

❍ ❍ ❍

३. भगवन् स्वागतं तेऽस्तु किं करोमि तवानघ ।
भवानाज्ञापयतु मामाज्ञाप्यो भवता ह्यहम् ॥

3. Oh sinless (Vischwaamithra)! Oh Lord! Welcome to you. I am at your command (& to be commanded by you). Therefore command me. What is it that I should do for you?

❍ ❍ ❍

४. एवमुक्तस्तु धर्मात्मा जनकेन महात्मना ।
प्रत्युवाच मुनिश्रेष्ठो वाक्यं वाक्यविशारदः ॥

4. When told thus by the great soul Janaka, the foremost Muni (Vischwaamithra) the man of Dharma who was well versed in speech, replied with these words.

❍ ❍ ❍

५. पुत्रौ दशरथस्येमौ क्षत्रियौ लोकविश्रुतौ ।
धनुर्वेदविशेषज्ञौ कुशलौ रामलक्ष्मणौ ॥
द्रष्टुकामौ धनुःश्रेष्ठं यदेतत्त्वयि तिष्ठति ॥

5. These two who are Kshathriya-s are sons of Dhascharatha: (named) Raama & Lakshmana: Renowned in the world as distinguished in the knowledge of Dhanurvedha (Science of war, armaments). They are very competent and are desirous of 'Seeing' that foremost Bow that is with you.

❍ ❍ ❍

६. एतद्दर्शय भद्रं ते कृतकामौ नृपात्मजौ ।
दर्शनादस्य धनुषो यथेष्टं प्रतियास्यतः ॥

6. By the exhibition of The Bow there will be welfare for you: Exhibit this (Bow)! The two sons of king (Dhascharatha) would have then fulfilled their desire, if it pleases you to comply (with their request).

❍ ❍ ❍

७. एवमुक्तस्तु जनकः प्रत्युवाच महामुनिम् ।
श्रूयतामस्य धनुषो यदर्थमिह तिष्ठति ।।

7. When told thus, Janaka replied to the noble Muni (Vischwaamithra): May you listen about this Bow (as to how &) why it is here (with me now).

❍ ❍ ❍

८. देवरात इति ख्यातो निमेः षष्ठो महीपतिः ।
न्यासोऽयं तस्य भगवन् हस्ते दत्तो महात्मना ।।

8. (King Janaka narrates to Vishwaamithra about history of the Divine Bow)... As the sixth to the king Nimi, there was a renowned king Dhevaraatha: Oh Lord (Vischwaamithra)! This was entrusted in his hands; given by the great soul (God Schiva).

❍ ❍ ❍

९. दक्षयज्ञवधे पूर्वं धनुरायम्य वीर्यवान् ।
रुद्रस्तु त्रिदशान् रोषात् सलीलमिदमब्रवीत् ।।

9. Long, long ago, the brave (most powerful) Rudhra (God Schiva), while he was destroying the Yaaga of Dhaksha, in great wrath, taking on this Bow, addressed the Dheva-s mockingly, (there, at Dhaksha's Yaaga).

❍ ❍ ❍

१०. यस्माद्भागार्थिनो भागान्नाकल्पयत मे सुराः ।
वराङ्गाणि महार्हाणि धनुषा शातयामि वः ।।

10. Oh Dheva-s! The due share of oblations desired by me was not offered: Therefore I will cut off your precious heads with my Bow.

❍ ❍ ❍

११. ततो विमनसः सर्वेदेवा वै मुनिपुङ्गव ।
प्रसादयन्ति देवेशं तेषां प्रीतोऽभवद्भवः ।।

11. Oh (Vischwaamithra) the 'tiger' of Muni-s (Please listen)! Then all the Dheva-s who were down hearted, propitiated The Dheva of Dheva-s (Schiva): And Schiva became pleased.

❍ ❍ ❍

१२. प्रीतियुक्तः स सर्वेषां ददौ तेषां महात्मनाम् ।।

12. And (Schiva) who was dear to all these most eminent (Dhevas) gave (The Bow).

❍ ❍ ❍

१३. तदेतद्देवदेवस्य धनूरत्नं महात्मनः ।
न्यासभूतं तदा न्यस्तमस्माकं पूर्वके विभो ।।

13. Oh Lord (Vischwaamithra)! This is The Gem of a Bow, (Bow) of the great soul (Schiva), the Dheva of Dheva-s. This was entrusted with my forefathers as custody.

❍ ❍ ❍

१४. अथ मे कृषतः क्षेत्रं लाङ्गलादुत्थिता पुरा ।
क्षेत्रं शोधयता लब्धा नाम्ना सीतेति विश्रुता ।।

14. (And king Janaka narrates the 'Birth' of his 'adopted' daughter Seetha). Once, (a few years back), while I was ploughing the Earth for a Yaaga (center), there arose (a girl) from (the ground under the) plough: She was (thus) obtained by me as I was preparing the (Yaaga) ground: From then on, she was known Seetha by name.

❍ ❍ ❍

१५. भूतलादुत्थिता सा तु व्यवर्धत ममात्मजा ।
वीर्यशुल्केति मे कन्या स्थापितेयमयोनिजा ।।

15. Not born through womb, she came up from earth to me; She, this girl, is growing up as my own daughter. Because of this, it was decided (by me) that she should be (offered in marriage only) as prize for valour.

❍ ❍ ❍

१६. भूतलादुत्थितां तां तु वर्धमानां ममात्मजाम् ।
वरयामासुरागम्य राजानो मुनिपुङ्गव ।।

16. Oh (Vishwaamithra) the 'tiger' of Muni-s! (Many) Kings have come here and have sought her who is growing up as my daughter & who had arisen from the earth. (They have sought her hand in marriage).

❍ ❍ ❍

१७. तेषां वरयतां कन्यां सर्वेषां पृथिवीक्षिताम् ।
वीर्यशुल्केति भगवन्न ददामि सुतामहम् ।।

17. Oh (my) Lord (Vischwaamithra)! To all these lords of earth, to all of them who were seeking the (hand of this) girl (in marriage), I did not give my daughter to (any one of them) as she was (to be offered only as) prize for valour.

❍ ❍ ❍

१८. ततः सर्वेनृपतयः समेत्य मुनिपुङ्गव ।
मिथिलामभ्युपागम्य वीर्यजिज्ञासवस्तदा ।।

18. Oh (Vischwaamithra) the 'Tiger' of Muni-s! Then, because of this, all the kings came together, to Mithila, and prayed to know about (the test of such a) valour.

❍ ❍ ❍

१९. तेषां जिज्ञासमानानां वीर्यं धनुरुपाहृतम् ।
न शेकुर्ग्रहणे तस्य धनुषस्तोलनेऽपि वा ।।

19. To put to test their bravery, The Bow was brought for them: (but) they had no capability of even lifting up this Bow; nor holding it (in their hands).

❍ ❍ ❍

२०. तेषां वीर्यवतां वीर्यमल्पं ज्ञात्वा महामुने ।
प्रत्याख्याता नृपतयस्तन्निबोध तपोधन ।।

20. Oh (Vischwaamithra) whose wealth is penance! Oh great Muni, (kindly) understand (me)! Realising that

the power of these brave men was (really) very scant, these lords of men were all refused (as suitors to the hand of Seetha).

❍ ❍ ❍

२१. ततः परमकोपेन राजानो मुनिपुङ्गव ।
अरुन्धन्मिथिलां सर्वेवीर्यसंदेहमागताः ।।

21. Oh Vischwaamithra! 'The 'tiger' of Muni-s! Because (I had) entertained doubt about their bravery (& prowess) all these kings besieged Mithila in great wrath (they considered the Test as insult to them all).

❍ ❍ ❍

२२. आत्मानमवधूतं ते विज्ञाय नृपपुङ्गवाः ।
रोषेण महताऽऽविष्टाः पीडयन्मिथिलां पुरीम् ।।

22. These 'Tigers' amongst kings, considering their rejection (as an insult) became terribly furious and tormented Mithila city.

❍ ❍ ❍

२३. ततः संवत्सरे पूर्णेक्षयं यातानि सर्वशः ।
साधनानि मुनिश्रेष्ठ ततोऽहं भृशदुःखितः ।।

23. Oh Muni! Before one year was completed, my Army, all of it, obtained total destruction: Because of this I became terribly sad.

❍ ❍ ❍

२४. ततो देवगणान् सर्वांस्पसाऽहं प्रसादयम् ।
ददुश्च परमप्रीताश्चतुरङ्गबलं सुराः ।।

24. Then I propitiated all the Dheva-s through penance: The Dheva-s became very pleased and gave me an Army of Four Services (Regiment of infantry, horses, chariots & elephants).

❍ ❍ ❍

२५. ततो भग्ना नृपतयो हन्यमाना दिशो ययुः ।
अवीर्या वीर्यसन्दिग्धाः सामात्याः पापकारिणः ।।

25. These evil mongers, these kings, from then on ran away in all directions, along with their ministers, completely broken, losing their bravery, with danger to their (reduced) strength, attacked & hit (by my forces).

❍ ❍ ❍

२६. तदेतन्मुनिशार्दूल धनुः परमभास्वरम् ।
रामलक्ष्मणयोश्चापि दर्शयिष्यामि सुव्रत ।।

26. Oh (Vischwaamithra) of rigid vows! Oh 'Lion' amongst Muni-s! This most (brilliant) & radiant, such a Bow I will (now) exhibit before Raama, & (before) Lakshmana also.

❍ ❍ ❍

२७. यद्यस्य धनुषो रामः कुर्यादारोपणं मुने ।
सुतामयोनिजां सीतां दद्यां दाशरथेरहम् ।।

27. Oh Muni! If Raama does the stringing up of The Bow, I will give my daughter Seetha who has no birth through womb, to (Raama), the son of Dhascharatha.

❍ ❍ ❍

Chapter 67

The Breaking of (the Divine) Bow (by Rama)

(At Mithila, at king Janaka's court, Raama, before his mentor Vischwaamithra & the multitude, 'conquers' The Divine Bow.)

❍ ❍ ❍

१. जनकस्य वचः श्रुत्वा विश्वामित्रो महामुनिः ।
धनुर्दर्शय रामाय इति होवाच पार्थिवम् ।।

1. Hearing Janaka's words, the great Muni Vischwaamithra addressed the king thus: = Exhibit The Bow To Raama.=

❍ ❍ ❍

२. ततः स राजा जनकः सचिवान्व्यादिदेश ह ।
धनुरानीयतां दिव्यं गन्धमाल्यविभूषितम् ।।

2. The king Janaka commanded his ministers thus: = May this divine Bow be brought here, decorated with flowers & scented pastes. =

❍ ❍ ❍

३. जनकेन समादिष्टाः सचिवाः प्राविशन् पुरम् ।
तद्धनुः पुरतः कृत्वा निर्जग्मुः पार्थिवाज्ञया ।।

3. The ministers who were commanded by Janaka went out: Being commanded by their king they entered the (inner precincts of the) palace, looking & paying respects to The Bow.

❍ ❍ ❍

४. नृणां शतानिश्चाशूद्धचायतानां महात्मनाम् ।
मञ्जूषामष्टचक्रां तां समूहुस्ते कथंचन ।।

4. Five thousand eminent men who were capable of great effort, somehow brought The Chest kept in a cart of 8 wheels.

❍ ❍ ❍

५. तामादाय तु मञ्जूषामायसीं यत्र तद्धनुः ।
सुरोपमं ते जनकमूचुर्नृपतिमन्त्रिणः ।।

5. Bringing this Iron Chest from where this Bow was kept, these ministers addressed Janaka who was like a celestial.

❍ ❍ ❍

६. इदं धनुर्वरं राजन् पूजितं सर्वराजभिः ।
मिथिलाधिप राजेन्द्र दर्शनीयं यदिच्छसि ।।

6. Oh King of Mithila; Oh (the 'Indhra') of kings! Oh King

(Janaka)! Here Is The Foremost Bow That You Wished to Be Exhibited and Which Is Honoured By All Kings.

❍ ❍ ❍

७. तेषां नृपो वचः श्रुत्वा कृताञ्जलिरभाषत ।
विश्वामित्रं महात्मानं तौ चोभौ रामलक्ष्मणौ ।।

7. Hearing their words, king (Janaka) (looked at these) two, Raama & Lakshmana, and then addressed the great soul Vischwaamithra, with his hands cupped in Anjali (in reverence).

❍ ❍ ❍

८. इदं धनुर्वरं ब्रह्मञ्जनकैरभिपूजितम् ।
राजभिश्च महावीर्यैरशक्तैः पूरितुं पुरा ।।

8. Oh Braamin: This is the foremost Bow, honoured by the forefathers of Janaka & by mightily brave kings who could not bend this before.

❍ ❍ ❍

९. नैतत्सुरगणाः सर्वे नासुरा न च राक्षसाः ।
गन्धर्वयक्षप्रवराः सकिन्नरमहोरगाः ।।

१०. क्व गतिर्मानुषाणां च धनुषोऽस्य प्रपूरणे ।
आरोपणे समायोगे वेपने तोलनेऽपि वा ।।

9 & 10.

Not by multitude of Dheva-s, nor by Asura-s, nor by demons, nor by Ghandharva-s, nor by Yaksha-s, and the like, nor by Kinnara-s, nor by MahaUraga-s, ... (None of them had the capability) to bend the Bow, nor stringing it up, nor fixing arrows, nor stretching (for discharging arrows), nor even lifting up: When that is so, what is (ordinary) men's fate (before this Bow).

❍ ❍ ❍

११. तदेतद्धनुषां श्रेष्टगानीतं मुनिपुङ्गव ।
दर्शयैतन्महाभाग अनयो राजपुत्रयोः ।।

11. Oh illustrious great Muni (Vischwaamithra) who is 'tiger' amongst Muni-s! The foremost of Bows, this is brought: You may please 'show' this (Bow) to these two Royal princes.

❍ ❍ ❍

१२. विश्वामित्रस्तु धर्मात्मा श्रुत्वा जनकभाषितम् ।
वत्स राम धनुः पश्य इति राघवमब्रवीत् ॥

12. Having heard thus from Janaka, the man of Dharma, the noble soul Vischwaamithra addressed (Raama) the Raaghava, thus: = Oh Lad! Oh Raama! 'See' This Bow.=

❍ ❍ ❍

१३. महर्षेर्वचनाद्रामो यत्र तिष्टति तद्धनुः ।
मञ्जूषां तामपावृत्य दृष्ट्वा धनुरथाब्रवीत् ॥

13. By the words (of command) of the great Rishi (Vischwaamithra), Raama opened The Chest in which was this Bow: And he said: (after) seeing this Bow.

❍ ❍ ❍

१४. इदं धनुर्वरं ब्रह्मन् संस्पृशामीह पाणिना ।
यत्नवांश्च भविष्यामि तोलने पूरणेऽपि वा ॥
बाढमित्येव तं राजा मुनिश्च समभाषत ॥

14. Oh Braamin (Vischwaamithra)! I shall grip this mighty Bow with my hands now; I will make effort in lifting this up and bending it: Then King (Janaka) and the Muni (Vischwaamithra) said: = Okay.=

❍ ❍ ❍

१५. लीलया स धनुर्मध्ये जग्राह वचनान्मुनेः ।
पश्यतां नृसहस्त्राणां बहूनां रघुनन्दनः ॥

15. Even as many thousands of men were watching, this (Raama) the darling of Raghu-s, by the word (of assent given) by the Muni (Vischwaamithra), playfully seized (& gripped) the Bow in the middle.

(Readers may note that Raama like a devoted disciple of his mentor, addresses Vischwaamithra first before taking up the challenge.)

❍ ❍ ❍

१६. आरोपयत् स धर्मात्मा सलीलमिव तद्धनुः ।
तद्बभञ्ज धनुर्मध्ये नरश्रेष्ठो महायशाः ।।

16. This most famous man of Dharma (this Raama) the foremost of men, strung up this Bow playfully, and broke this Bow in the middle (by his power).

❍ ❍ ❍

१७. तस्य शब्दो महानासीन्निर्घातसमनिस्वनः ।
भूमिकम्पश्च सुमहान् पर्वतस्येव दीर्यतः ।।

17. (As it broke): The Sound of this Bow was mighty like the sound of thunder. The quaking of the Earth was mighty, like a mountain bursting up.

❍ ❍ ❍

१८. निपेतुश्च नराः सर्वे तेन शब्देन मोहिताः ।
वर्जयित्वा मुनिवरं राजानं तौ च राघवौ ।।

18. Excepting the foremost Muni (Vischwaamithra) and king (Janaka) and the two Raaghava-s (Raama/ Lakshmana), all the men there were stupefied, (made semiconscious), by the sound & they fell down.

❍ ❍ ❍

१९. प्रत्याश्वस्ते जने तस्मिन् राजा विगतसाध्वसः ।
उवाच प्राञ्जलिर्वाक्यं वाक्यज्ञो मुनिपुङ्गवम् ।।

19. When the multitude of men regained their 'Breath' (& consciousness), king (Janaka) the knower of speech, addressed (Vischwaamithra) the 'tiger' of Muni-s, cupping his hands in Anjali, greatly relieved of fear (and worry that there may not be any one in the world to 'Touch' this Bow & thus marry his daughter Seetha).

❍ ❍ ❍

२०. भगवन् दृष्टवीर्यो मे रामो दशरथात्मजः ।
अत्यद्भुतमचिन्त्यं च न तर्कितमिदं मया ।।

20. Oh Lord (Vischwaamithra)! This is most wonderful that surpasses anything; (unimaginable, unthinkable); Not comprehended by me: This Raama the son of Dhascharatha, is (indeed a man of) Tested Bravery. (Raama's valour is too obvious).

❍ ❍ ❍

२१. जनकानां कुले कीर्तिमाहरिष्यति मे सुता ।
सीता भर्तारमासाद्य रामं दशरथात्मजम् ।।

21. This Seetha, my daughter of Janaka family will obtain as her husband, Raama, the son of Dhascharatha, and will obtain fame & glory.

❍ ❍ ❍

२२. मम सत्या प्रतिज्ञा च वीर्यशुल्केति कौशिक ।
सीता प्राणैर्बहुमता देया रामाय मे सुता ।।

22. Oh (Vischwaamithra the) Kowschik! My resolution has come true (fulfilled) Therefore as prize for valour this Seetha who is dearer to me than my life, this (Seetha) my daughter, must be given to Raama.

❍ ❍ ❍

२३. भवतोऽनुमते ब्रह्मन् शीघ्रं गच्छन्तु मन्त्रिणः ।
मम कौशिक भद्रं ते अयोध्यां त्वरिता रथैः ।।

23. Oh Kowschik! Oh Braamin! With your permission, may my ministers who (ever) act fast, go to Ayodhya at once on chariots. Welfare to you.

❍ ❍ ❍

२४. राजानं प्रश्रितैर्वाक्यैरानयन्तु पुरं मम ।
प्रदानं वीर्यशुल्कायाः कथयन्तु च सर्वशः ।।

24. May (my ministers) tell everything to king (Dhascharatha) about my offer (of Seetha in marriage

to Raama) as prize for valour: With courteous words, let them bring (Dhascharatha) to my city.

❍ ❍ ❍

२५. मुनिगुप्तौ च काकुत्स्थौ कथयन्तु नृपाय वै ।
प्रीयमाणं तु राजानमानयन्तु सुशीघ्रगा: ।।

25. And let them say to the king that the two Kaakuthsa-s (Raama/Lakshmana) are under the guardianship (protection) of the Muni (Vischwaamithra): Let them bring the king (to Mithila) soon as a happy man.

❍ ❍ ❍

२६. कौशिकश्च तथेत्याह राजा चाभाष्य मन्त्रिण: ।
अयोध्यां प्रेषयामास धर्मात्मा कृतशासनान् ।।

26. (Vischwaamithra) the Kowschik then said: = So Be It: = Then the noble soul king Janaka invited his ministers and sent them to Ayodhya with proper instructions.....

❍ ❍ ❍

Chapter 68

King Dhascharatha Leaves for Mithila

(With the consent of Vischwaamithra, king Janaka sends ministers to inform King Dhacharatha, obtain his approval for marriage of his son Raama to Seetha, and fetch him to Mithila. The Protocol is observed as per custom: And the happy Dhascharatha leaves for Mithila for the celebration of marriage of his son Raama.)

❍ ❍ ❍

१. जनकेन समादिष्टा दूतास्ते क्लान्तवाहना: ।
त्रिरात्रमुषिता मार्गेतेऽयोध्यां प्राविशन् पुरीम् ।।

1. The emissaries (the ministers) commissioned by king Janaka were fatigued (by travel) and they spent three

nights on their way (to Ayodhya from Mithila): And they reached Ayodhya city.

❍ ❍ ❍

२. राज्ञो भवनमासाद्य द्वारस्थानिदमब्रुवन् ।
शीघ्रं निवेद्यतां राज्ञे दूताञ्नो जनकस्य च ॥
इत्युक्ता द्वारपालास्ते राघवाय न्यवेदयन् ॥

2. Approaching the king's palace, they said the following to the Guards (of the palace): = May you announce quickly that we are King Janaka's emissaries = When told thus, the guards informed Dhascharatha.

❍ ❍ ❍

३. ते राजवचनाद्दूता राजवेश्म प्रवेशिता: ।
ददृशुर्देवसमाशं वृद्धं दशरथं नृपम् ॥

3. By words (of command) of King (Dhascharatha), the guards allowed them to enter; And they saw Dhascharatha as an old man (but) looking like a celestial.

❍ ❍ ❍

४. बद्धाञ्जलिपुटा: सर्वे दूता विगतसाध्वसा: ।
राजानं प्रणता वाक्यमब्रुवन् मधुराक्षरम् ॥

4. Bowing before the king, the emissaries, all of them, addressed the king with sweet words, without any perturbation, with their hands cupped in Anjali (in reverence).

❍ ❍ ❍

५. राजसिंह महासत्त्व रघुश्रेष्ठ परन्तप ।
मैथिलो जनको राजा साग्निहोत्रपुरस्कृतम् ॥
कुशलं चाव्ययं चैव सोपाध्यायपुरोहितम् ॥

5. Oh 'lion' amongst kings! Oh Tormentor of enemies! Oh foremost Raghu! Oh most pure (Dhascharatha)! The King of Mithila, Janaka, (wishes to convey to you greetings and asked) about you who are ever with

Upaadhyaya-s and Purohith-s and who are (ever) performing Agnihothra (Fire rituals), (and he asked about) your imperishable welfare.

❍ ❍ ❍

६. मुहुर्मुहुर्मधुरया स्नेहसंयुक्तया गिरा ।
जनकस्त्वां महाराजाऽऽपृच्छते सपुरःसरम् ।।

6. King Janaka asked us to enquire about you who are ever served by good men, about your welfare, repeatedly, with sweet words of affection & friendship.

❍ ❍ ❍

७. पृष्ट्वा कुशलमव्यग्रं वैदेहो मिथिलाधिपः ।
कौशिकानुमते वाक्यं भवन्तमिदमब्रवीत् ।।

7. After enquiring about your welfare, the king of Mithila (king Janaka) of Vidheha, with the permission of (Vischwaamithra) the Kowschik who is steadfast (in vows), said these words (to be conveyed by us) to you.

❍ ❍ ❍

८. पूर्वं प्रतिज्ञा विहिता वीर्यशुल्का ममात्मजा ।
राजानश्च कृतामर्षा निर्वीर्या विमुखीकृताः ।।

8. Long ago, a resolution was made by me that my daughter (Seetha) should be offered as Prize for valour; Many kings who were turned away because they were not brave (enough), became terribly embittered (and angry).

❍ ❍ ❍

९. सेयं मम सुता राजन् विश्वामित्रपुरः सरैः ।
यदृच्छयाऽऽगतैर्वीरैर्निर्जिता तव पुत्रकैः ।।

9. Oh King (Dhascharatha): (But) This, my daughter was won by your brave son (Raama) who, by my good fortune, was brought (to Mithila) by Vischwaamithra.

❍ ❍ ❍

१०. तच्च राजन्धनुर्दिव्यं मध्ये भग्नं महात्मना ।
रामेण हि महातेजो महत्यां जनसंसदि ॥

10. Oh most brilliant king (Dhascharatha): In front of a great assembly of men, by this great soul Raama, The Divine Bow was broken in the middle:

❍ ❍ ❍

११. अस्मै देया मया सीता वीर्यशुल्का महात्मने ।
प्रतिज्ञां कर्तुमिच्छामि तदनुज्ञातुमर्हसि ॥

11. As prize for (this) valour, this Seetha must be given in marriage to this great soul (Raama, your son). I desire to fulfill my resolve: You should (please) consent to this.

❍ ❍ ❍

१२. सोपाध्यायो महाराज पुरोहितपुरस्कृतः ।
शीघ्रमागच्छ भद्रं ते द्रष्टुमर्हसि राघवौ ॥

12. Oh great King (Dhascharatha)! You should come to see (& meet) the Raaghava-s (your sons): You should come soon (to Mithila) along with your Upaadhyaya-s and with purohith-s. Welfare to you.

❍ ❍ ❍

१३. प्रतिज्ञां मम राजेन्द्र निर्वर्तयितुमर्हसि ।
पुत्रयोरुभयोः प्रीतिं लप्स्यसे वीर्यनिर्जिताम् ॥

13. Oh Emperor! You should fulfill this resolution (of mine) which is victory for valour & bravery. You will obtain the affection (& gratitude) of myself and my two sons.

❍ ❍ ❍

१४. एवं विदेहाधिपतिर्मधुरं वाक्यमब्रवीत् ।
विश्वामित्राभ्यनुज्ञातः शतानन्दमते स्थितः ॥

❍ ❍ ❍

१५. राजन्नागच्छसि यदि न चेद्वा रघुनन्दन ।
आज्ञापयोत्तरं देव जनकाय नरेश्वर ॥

14 & 15.

The Vidheha king (Janaka) who has got the consent of Vischwaamithra and who stands by the opinion of (his Minister & Adviser) Schathaanandh, has sent these sweet words to you (to be conveyed by us) ...... : Oh noble Lord of men! Oh the darling of Raghu-s! Oh king (Dhascharatha)! You may come (with us): Or give a reply (through us) to Janaka, if not.

❍ ❍ ❍

१६. इत्युक्त्वा विरता दूता राजगौरवशमिता: ।।

16. After saying thus, the emissaries became silent, with some apprehension (in regard) to the King's (consideration in this matter of acceptance of alliance with Janaka).

❍ ❍ ❍

१७. दूतवाक्यं तु तच्छ्रुत्वा राजा परमहर्षित: ।
वसिष्ठं वामदेवं च मन्त्रिणोऽन्यांश्च सोऽब्रवीत् ।।

17. Hearing the words of the emissaries, this king (Dhascharatha) became greatly pleased and addressed Vasishta, Vaamadheva & other ministers (of his).

❍ ❍ ❍

१८. गुप्त: कुशिकपुत्रेण कौसल्यानन्दवर्धन: ।
लक्ष्मणेन सह भ्रात्रा विदेहेषु वसत्यसौ ।।

18. This (my son Raama) who increases the joy of (his mother) Kowsalya, along with his brother Lakshmana, is staying in the Vidheha kingdom (under the guardianship &) protected by, (Vischwaamithra) the son of Kuschika.

❍ ❍ ❍

१९. दृष्टवीर्यस्तु काकुत्स्थो जनकेन महात्मना ।
संप्रदानं सुतायास्तु राघवे कर्तुमिच्छति ।।

19. (Raama) the Kaakuthsa has been found by the great

soul Janaka as truly brave; (his bravery having been put to test at Mithila) And now he desires to offer his daughter in marriage to Raama.

❍ ❍ ❍

२०. यदि वो रोचते वृत्तं जनकस्य महात्मनः ।
पुरीं गच्छामहे शीघ्रं मा भूत्कालस्य पर्ययः ॥

20. If this news pleases you, then we shall go to the great soul Janaka's city (of Mithila): (But) There should be no lapse of time.

(It is to be noted that Dhascharatha was so democratic, he seeks approval of his ministers; After all Raama's wife is to be the future queen of Ayodhya: And Dhascharatha wants a quick decision.)

❍ ❍ ❍

२१. मन्त्रिणो बाढमित्याहुः सह सर्वैर्महर्षिभिः ।
सुप्रीतश्चाब्रवीद्राजा श्वो यात्रेति स मन्त्रिणः ॥

21. And the ministers & the great Rishi-s, all of them together said: = 'Baadam' (okay).= Very pleased, king (Dhascharatha) then told the ministers: = Journey Tomorrow =

❍ ❍ ❍

२२. मन्त्रिणस्तु नरेन्द्रेण रात्रिं परमसत्कृताः ।
ऊषुः प्रमुदिताः सर्वे गुणैः सर्वैः समन्विताः ॥

22. All the ministers (the emissaries of Janaka) were (honoured) with great hospitality by the king, with all kinds (of foods, drinks etc.). They spent the night greatly pleased.

(Note: There is no evidence that Dhascharatha consulted his wives before taking his decision of accepting Seetha as daughter-in-Law.)

❍ ❍ ❍

Chapter 69

(Dhascharatha's) Arrival at Mithila

१. ततो रात्र्यां व्यतीतायां सोपाध्याय: सबान्धव: ।
राजा दशरथो हृष्ट: सुमन्त्रमिदमब्रवीत् ।।

1. (King Dhascharatha prepares to leave for Mithila): When night had passed away, the happy king Dhascharatha, who was with Upaadhyaya-s & with relatives, addressed Sumanthra (his Minister, charioteer & adviser) thus.

❍ ❍ ❍

२. अद्य सर्वे धनाध्यक्षा धनमादाय पुष्कलम् ।
व्रजन्त्वग्रे सुविहिता नानारत्नसमन्विता: ।।

2. Let officers of my treasury, all of them, taking various ornaments and plenty of cash (gold), go first, (go to Mithila) after making proper arrangements.

❍ ❍ ❍

३. चतुरङ्गबलं चापि शीघ्रं निर्यातु सर्वश: ।
ममाज्ञासमकालं च यानयुग्यमनुत्तमम् ।।

3. My foursome Army, along with foremost transport (like horses & chariots), should all (be ready to) leave at my command, soon, all of them.

❍ ❍ ❍

४. वसिष्ठो वामदेवश्च जाबालिरथ काश्यप: ।
मार्कण्डेय: सुदीर्घायुर्ऋषि: कात्यायनस्तथा ।।

५ एते द्विजा: प्रयान्त्वग्रे स्यन्दनं योजयस्व मे ।
यथा कालात्ययो न स्याद्दूता हि त्वरयन्ति माम् ।।

4 & 5.

Vasishta, Vaamdheva, Jaabaali, Kaaschyapa, Maarkandeya who has seen long years, Rishi

Kaathyaayana..... all these braamins should go first. The Emissaries (of king Janaka) are hurrying me; So without wasting time, make ready my chariot.

❍ ❍ ❍

६. इत्युक्त्वा स महातेजा राजा दशरथो रथम् ।
आरुरोह यथा भानुर्भगवान्त्रघुनन्दनः ॥

6. Shining like the Sun, this most brilliant king Dhascharatha of the Raghu dynasty, after saying thus, got into his chariot.

❍ ❍ ❍

७. वचनात्तु नरेन्द्रस्य सा सेना चतुरङ्गिणी ।
राजानमृषिभिः सार्धं व्रजन्तं पृष्ठतोऽन्वगात् ॥

7. The Foursome Army, as per the command of the king, followed king (Dhascharatha) who was going along with Rishi-s.

❍ ❍ ❍

८. गत्वा चतुरहं मार्गं विदेहानभ्युपेयिवान् ।
राजा तु जनकः श्रीमाञ्छ्रुत्वा पूजामकल्पयत् ॥

8. Going along the route for 4 days, he reached the Vidheha (kingdom): On hearing (of his arrival), the resplendent king Janaka prepared a reception.

❍ ❍ ❍

९. ततो राजानमासाद्य वृद्धं दशरथं नृपम् ।
जनको मुदितो राजा इर्षं च परमं ययौ ॥
उवाच च नरश्रेष्टो नरश्रेष्ठं मुदाऽन्वितम् ॥

9. Then, the happy king Janaka, approached (& received) the very old king Dhascharatha & became exhilarated. The foremost of men (Janaka) addressed the foremost of men (Dhascharatha) who was very happy, thus:

❍ ❍ ❍

१०. स्वागतं ते महाराज दिष्ट्या प्राप्तोऽसि राघव ।
पुत्रयोरुभयो: प्रीतिं लप्स्यसे वीर्यनिर्जिताम् ।।

10. Oh Raaghava! Oh Emperor (Dhascharatha)! Your arrival is very auspicious; Welcome to you! You must offer (your)*grace upon these two children, which they have 'won' through valour.

(It is through valour my daughter is going to be enjoined with your son Raama, says Janaka: * Word used is 'Preethi' - affection.)

❍ ❍ ❍

११. दिष्ट्या प्राप्तो महातेजा वसिष्ठो भगवानृषि: ।
सह सर्वैर्द्विजश्रेष्ठैर्देवैरिव शतक्रतु: ।।

11. Like Schathakrathu (Lord Indhra) before all the Dheva-s, the coming of this most brilliant Lord Rishi Vasishta, accompanied by foremost braamins, is (indeed) my good fortune.

❍ ❍ ❍

१२. दिष्ट्या मे निर्जिता विघ्ना दिष्ट्या मे पूजितं कुलम् ।
राघवै: सह संबन्धाद्वीर्यश्लाघ्यैर्महात्मभि: ।।

12. (All) my troubles are over: It is my good fortune: My family becomes honoured by alliance with the most eminent Raghu-s who are renowned in valour. By our good fortune!

❍ ❍ ❍

१३. श्व: प्रभाते नरश्रेष्ठ निर्वर्तयितुमर्हसि ।
यज्ञस्यान्ते नरश्रेष्ठ विवाहमृषिसत्तमै: ।।

13. Oh foremost of men (Dhascharatha) ! Tomorrow morning, at the completion of my Yaaga along with Muni-s, you should (join me) to perform marriage, Oh foremost man!

❍ ❍ ❍

१४. तस्य तद्वचनं श्रुत्वा ऋषिमध्ये नराधिप: ।
वाक्यं वाक्यविदां श्रेष्ठ: प्रत्युवाच महीपतिम् ।।

14. (And Dhascharatha formally accepts the proposal): ...... Hearing the words of his (spoken) before the Rishi-s, the foremost amongst men of good speech, king (Dhascharatha), replied to (King Janaka) the lord of Earth, with these words.

❍ ❍ ❍

१५. प्रतिग्रहो दातृवश: श्रुतमेतन्मया पुरा ।
यथा वक्ष्यसि धर्मज्ञ तत्करिष्यामहे वयम् ।।

15. That the acceptance (of gifts,daughter etc.) depends on the desire and the will of the Donor, is known to me for a long time; Oh knower of Dharma (Janaka)! Whatever you say, we shall abide by (Janaka is The Donor-Dhascharatha formally accepts her, as his daughter-in-law is a most precious gift from Janaka.)

❍ ❍ ❍

१६. धर्मिष्ठं च यशस्यं च वचनं सत्यवादिन: ।
श्रुत्वा विदेहाधिपति: परं विस्मयमागत: ।।

16. Hearing the words of the famous man of Dharma who ever spoke Truth, this Vidheha king (Janaka), became amazed.

❍ ❍ ❍

१७. तत: सर्वे मुनिगणा: परस्परसमागमे ।
हर्षेण महता युक्तास्तां निशामवसन्सुखम् ।।

17. At that time, the congregation of Muni-s who obtained great satisfaction by their mutual meeting (of old friends), spent the night comfortably.

❍ ❍ ❍

१८. राजा च राघवौ पुत्रौ निशाम्य परिहर्षित: ।
उवास परमप्रीतो जनकेनाभिपूजित: ।।

18. Seeing the two sons, the Raaghava-s (Raama & Lakshmana), king (Dhascharatha) who was exhilarated

with joy, was well honoured by Janaka (with great hospitality) & he stayed there, extemely pleased.

❍ ❍ ❍

१९. जनकोऽपि महातेजा: क्रियां धर्मेण तत्त्ववित् ।
यज्ञस्य च सुताभ्यां च कृत्वा रात्रिमुवास ह ॥

19. The most brilliant Janaka who knew Thathva (the essence) of Shaasthra-s, spent the night doing (& completing the) Rituals for his daughters & for the Yaaga, as per norms of Dharma.

❍ ❍ ❍

२०. ततो मुनीनां च नराधिपानां विसृज्य संघाञ्जनको महात्मनाम् ।
तद्यज्ञवाटं विधिवत्प्रविश्य उवास रात्रिं बलसूदनप्रिय: ॥

20. Then Janaka who was dear to (Indhra), the killer of Madhu, sent away the most eminent Muni-s & a large number of chiefs of territories (who had come) and then entered the Yaaga Hall & spent the night there as per norms.

(Note: It is interesting to note that Janaka was really amazed at the immediate acceptance of his daughter Seetha for his son Raama. Secondly, King Janaka performs Rituals for his two daughters, not just for his first daughter Seetha. Obviously, as events turned out, Janaka knew that there would be more than just one wedding. In fact all the four sons of Dhascharatha are wed on the same day Raama weds.)

❍ ❍ ❍

Chapter 70

The Lineage of King Dhascharatha

१. तत: प्रभाते जनक: कृतकर्मा महर्षिभि: ।
उवाच वाक्यं वाक्यज्ञ: शतानन्दं पुरोहितम् ॥

1. Then, in the morning, after finishing Rituals along with the great sages, the master of speech, Janaka, addressed Purohith Schathaandh (who was his Minister, adviser, charioteer & close friend), the following words:

❍ ❍ ❍

२. भ्राता मम महातेजा वीर्यवानतिधार्मिक: ।
कुशध्वज इति रव्यात: पुरीमध्यवसच्छुभाम् ।।
३. वार्यामलकपर्यन्ताम पिबन्निक्षुमतीं नदीम् ।
सामाश्यां पुण्यसमाशां विमानमिव पुष्पकम् ।।

2 & 3.

My brother who is most brilliant, brave, foremost in Dharma, renowned as Kuschadhwaja lives in the holy city..... Saankaascha, which is (large) like Pushpaka aircraft, which is embodiment of all that is holy, which is surrounded by cluster of Amala trees (Embellica Officinalis), drinking (enjoying the) waters of Ikshumathi (river) that flows around it.

❍ ❍ ❍

४. तमहं द्रष्टुमिच्छामि यज्ञगोप्ता स मे मत: ।
प्रीतिं सोऽपि महातेजा इमां भोक्ता मया सह ।।

4. This most brilliant (brother of mine) who is praiseworthy (& fit to be) protector of this Yaaga (of mine), will enjoy (& share) the happiness with me. I desire to see him. (I want him here now).

❍ ❍ ❍

५. एवमुक्ते तु वचने शतानन्दस्य सन्निधौ ।
आगता: केचिदव्यग्रा जनकस्तान्समादिशत् ।।

5. When these words were told in front of Schathaandh, the unoccupied* men, some of them, came there (at once): And Janaka commanded them. (*Word used is -Avyagra)

❍ ❍ ❍

६. शासनात्तु नरेन्द्रस्य प्रययुः शीघ्रवाजिभिः ।
समानेतुं नरव्याघ्रं विष्णुमिन्द्राज्ञया यथा ।।

6. Like God Vishnu (being served) by the orders of Indhra, by the king's command, they started to bring the 'tiger' of men (Janaka's brother Kuschadhwaja), getting on to fast moving horses.

❍ ❍ ❍

७. सामाश्यां ते समागत्य ददृशुश्च कुशध्वजम् ।
न्यवेदयन्यथावृत्तं जनकस्य च चिन्तितम् ।।
तद्वृत्तं नृपतिः श्रुत्वा दूतश्रेष्ठैर्महाबलैः ।
८. आज्ञयाऽथ नरेन्द्रस्य आजगाम कुशध्वजः ।
स ददर्श महातेजा जनकं धर्मवत्सलम् ।।

7 & 8.

They came to Sankaascha and saw Kuschadhwaja: And they announced all the happenings to the most brilliant king Kuschadhwaja: About (king) Janaka's intentions: Hearing the mightily strong foremost emissaries..... he came (to Mithila) as per the command of (his brother Janaka) the lord of men. And at once he (met &) saw Janaka, the man who was (ever) attached to Dharma.

❍ ❍ ❍

९. सोऽभिवाद्य शतानन्दं राजानं चापि धार्मिकम् ।
राजार्हं परमं दिव्यमासनं चाध्यरोहत ।।

9. After paying his respects to Schathaanandh & to (his brother) king (Janaka) the man of Dharma, he sat down in a great wonderful seat worthy of a king.

❍ ❍ ❍

१०. उपविष्टावुभौ तौ तु भ्रातरावमितौजसौ ।
प्रेषयामासतुर्वीरौ मन्त्रिश्रेष्ठं सुदामनम् ।।

10. These two brave brothers (Janaka & Kuschadhwaja) of incomparable brilliance, who were sitting and were engaged (in conversation) about this matter (of

forthcoming marriage), then sent out the foremost minister Sudhaaman (with following message).

❍ ❍ ❍

११. गच्छ मन्त्रिपते शीघ्रमैक्ष्वाकममितौजसम् ।
आत्मजैः सह दुर्धर्षमानयस्व समन्त्रिणम् ।।

11. Oh Chief Minister (Sudhaaman)! Go soon: Bring the Ikshwaaku king (Dhascharatha) who cannot be 'Bruised' (by any one in the universe), and who is of incomparable power, along with his sons & ministers.

❍ ❍ ❍

१२. औपकार्यं स गत्वा तु रघूणां कुलवर्धनम् ।
ददर्श शिरसा चैनमभिवाद्येदमब्रवीत् ।।

12. Then (Sudhaaman) went to the **Royal 'Tent' & saw (Dhascharatha) who increased the prosperity of The Raghu family: Bowing before him with his head down, he said this: (** Word used-Aupakaaryam-)

❍ ❍ ❍

१३. अयोध्याधिपते वीर वैदेहो मिथिलाधिपः ।
स त्वां द्रष्टुं व्यवसितः सोपाध्यायपुरोहितम् ।।

13. (Protocol observed: Chief minister personally extends invitation to the visiting dignitary). . . Oh king of Ayodhya! Oh brave (Dhascharatha)! The king of Mithila, this Vidheha King Janaka, is staying (& awaiting) to see you along with your Upaadhyaya-s & Purohiths.

❍ ❍ ❍

१४. मन्त्रिश्रेष्ठवचः श्रुत्वा राजा सर्षिगणस्तदा ।
सबन्धुरगमत्तत्र जनको यत्र वर्तते ।।

14. Hearing the words of this foremost minister, the king (Dhascharatha) then, accompanied by the congregation of Rishi-s & his folks, came to where Janaka was.

❍ ❍ ❍

१५. राजा च जनकः श्रीमान् राजराजं सहानुजः ।
प्रत्युद्गम्य प्रहृष्टात्मा प्रवेश्य गृहमर्हयत् ॥

15. The resplendent king Janaka whose heart was exhilarated with joy, along with his brother, went forth and received the king of kings (Dhascharatha). Then entering his palace along with (Dhascharatha), honoured him.

❍ ❍ ❍

१६. स राजा मन्त्रिसहितः सोपाध्यायः सबान्धवः ।
वाक्यं वाक्यविदां श्रेष्ठो वैदेहमिदमब्रवीत् ॥

16. And then the king (Dhascharatha) who was with his ministers & Upaadhyaya-s and his folks, and who was foremost amongst those well versed in speech, addressed the Vidheha king (Janaka) with following words.

❍ ❍ ❍

१७. विदितं ते महाराज इक्ष्वाकुकुलदैवतम् ।
वक्ता सर्वेषु कृत्येषु वसिष्ठो भगवानृषिः ॥

17. Oh great king (Janaka): ! The Lord Rishi, this Vasishta, is a 'God' to the Ikshwaaku family: It should be known to you that in all (our) matters, He Is The (First) One To Speak.

❍ ❍ ❍

१८. विश्वामित्राभ्यनुज्ञातः सह सर्वैर्महर्षिभिः ।
एष वक्ष्यति धर्मात्मा वसिष्ठो मे यथाक्रमम् ॥

18. The man of Dharma, this Vasishta who is here with all the great Rishi-s, will now tell, (describe), about my Lineage, with the (kind) permission of Vischwaamithra.

(Readers may note what a regard & respect Dhascharatha has for Vischwaamithra, although he had no official position.)

❍ ❍ ❍

१९. एवमुक्त्वा नरश्रेष्ठे राज्ञां मध्ये महात्मनाम् ।
तूष्णींभूते दशरथे वसिष्ठो भगवानृषिः ।।
उवाच वाक्यं वाक्यज्ञो वैदेहं सपुरोधसम् ।।

19. After saying thus before the kings (assembled there from various places) and before eminent men, the foremost of men Dhascharatha became silent: Then the knower of speech, Rishi Vasishta, addressed the following words to Vidheha king (Janaka) who was with his Purohiths.

❍ ❍ ❍

२०. अव्यक्तप्रभवो ब्रह्मा शाश्वतो नित्य अव्ययः ।
तस्मान्मरीचिः संजज्ञे मरीचेः काश्यपः सुतः ।।

20. (Vasishta Narrates The Lineage of The Ikshwaaku-s)........ God Bramma is Eternal: Innate: Imperishable (unchanged): Evolver of All Things: From Him, Mareechi was born; And Mareechi's son was Kaaschyapa.

❍ ❍ ❍

२१. विवस्वान् काश्यपाज्जज्ञे मनुर्वैवस्वतः स्मृतः ।
मनुः प्रजापतिः पूर्वमिक्ष्वाकुस्तु मनोः सुतः ।।

21. From Kaaschyapa was born the Sun (Vivaswaan): And Vivaswaan's son is known as Manu (Man), the first father of all human beings. Manu's son was Ikshwaaku.

❍ ❍ ❍

२२. तमिक्ष्वाकुमयोध्यायां राजानं विद्धि पूर्वकम् ।
इक्ष्वाकोस्तु सुतः श्रीमान्कुक्षिरित्येव विश्रुतः ।।

22. You should know he was the first king of Ayodhya - this Ikshwaaku. Renowned & resplendent; Kukshi was Ikshwaaku's son.

❍ ❍ ❍

२३. कुक्षेरथात्मजः श्रीमान् विकुक्षिरुदपद्यत ।
विकुक्षेस्तु महातेजा बाणः पुत्रः प्रतापवान् ।।

23. Then came Vikukshi as resplendent son of Kukshi: And Vikukshi's son was Bhaana, the most brilliant, most majestical.

❍ ❍ ❍

२४. बाणस्य तु महातेजा अनरण्यः प्रतापवान् ।
अनरण्यात् पृथुर्जज्ञे त्रिशङ्कुस्तु पृथोः सुतः ॥

24. The brilliant Anaranya & most glorious was son of Bhaana: And from Anaranya came Prithu: And Thrischanku was son of Prithu.

❍ ❍ ❍

२५. त्रिशङ्कोरभवत् पुत्रो धुन्धुमारो महायशाः ।
धुन्धुमारान्महातेजा युवनाश्वो महारथः ॥
युवनाश्वसुतः श्रीमान् मान्धाता पृथिवीपतिः ॥

25. And the most famous Dhundhumaara was born as son to Thrischanku: From Dhundhumaara, (was born) the most brilliant great warrior (Charioteer) Yuvanaascha: And Yuvanaascha's son was Maandhaatha, who was resplendent & lord of earth.

❍ ❍ ❍

२६. मान्धातुस्तु सुतः श्रीमान् सुसन्धिरुदपद्यत ।
सुसन्धेरपि पुत्रौ द्वौ ध्रुवसन्धिः प्रसेनजित् ॥

26. And resplendent Susandhi was born as son of Maandhaatha: And Dhruvaandhi & Prasenajith were the two sons of Susandhi.

❍ ❍ ❍

२७. यशस्वी ध्रुवसन्धेस्तु भरतो नाम नामतः ।
भरतात्तु महातेजा असितो नाम जातवान् ॥

27. And the renowned & famous Bharatha by name was Dhruvasandha's son. And the most brilliant Asitha by name was born to Bharatha (Bharatha not to be confused as Raama's brother).

❍ ❍ ❍

२८. यस्यैते प्रतिराजान उदपद्यन्त शत्रवः ।
हैहयास्तालजङ्घाश्च शूराश्च शशिबिन्दवः ॥
२९. तांस्तु संप्रतियुध्यन् हि युद्धे राजा प्रवासितः ॥

28 & 29.

(And to Asitha) to whom these brave Haihaiya-s & Thaalajanga-s, Schaschibindhu-s and other kings became enemies..... it is this king (Asitha) who fought against these in war (but) he was driven out (of Ayodhya).

(A temporary set back to the fortunes of Ayodhya & its kings.)

❍ ❍ ❍

३०. हिमवन्तमुपागम्य भार्याभ्यां सहितोऽवसत् ।
असितोऽल्पबलो राजा कालधर्ममुपेयिवान् ॥

30. Reduced in strength, this king Asitha, along with his two wives, went to Himaalya-s and lived there and died (there).

❍ ❍ ❍

३१. द्वे चास्य भार्येगर्भिण्यौ बभूवतुरिति श्रुतिः ।
एका गर्भविनाशाय सपत्न्यै तु गरं ददौ ॥

31. At that time both his wives were pregnant; so it was heard; One of them, with a view to abort, gave poison to her co-wife.

❍ ❍ ❍

३२. ततः शैलवरे रम्ये बभूवाभिरतो मुनिः ।
भार्गवश्च्यवनो नाम हिमवन्तमुपाश्रितः ॥

32. At that time, a Muni named Chyavana of Bhrighu clan, who was residing in Himaalayas, was delighting himself (in penance) in a beautiful mountain peak there.

❍ ❍ ❍

३३. तत्र चैका महाभागा भार्गवं देववर्चसम् ।
ववन्दे पद्मपत्राक्षी कांक्षन्ती सुतमुत्तमम् ।।

33. The most illustrious one (of the two wives of late Asitha), whose eyes were like lotus, desirous of obtaining a noble son, bowed before this (Chyavana) of Bhrighu clan whose brilliance was like that of a celestial.

❍ ❍ ❍

३४. तमृषिं साऽभ्युपागम्य कालिन्दी चाभ्यवादयत् ।
स तामभ्यवदद्विप्रः पुत्रेप्सुं पुत्रजन्मनि ।।

34. This lady Kaalindhi, approaching this Rishi, bowed to him: And this braamin spoke to her & blessed her in the matter of progeny to her who was desirous of having a son, thus:

❍ ❍ ❍

३५. तव कुक्षौ महाभागे सुपुत्रः सुमहाबलः ।
महावीर्यो महातेजा अचिरात् सञ्जनिष्यति ।।
गरेण सहितः श्रीमान् मा शुचः कमलेक्षणे ।।

35. (This Kaalindhi was the one poisoned by the co-wife)...... Oh Lady, whose eyes are like Lotus! Oh most illustrious (Kaalindhi)! You will soon conceive in your womb a mightily strong & mightily brave and most brilliant, resplendent son (although) engulfed in poison (in body). Do not grieve (& worry).

❍ ❍ ❍

३६. एवमुक्ता महाभागा असिते स्वर्गते सति ।
निधाय चेतो नृपतौ विद्युल्लेखेव सुप्रभा ।।
३७. च्यवनं तु नमस्कृत्य राजपुत्री पतिव्रता ।
पतिशोकातुरा तस्मात् पुत्रं देवी व्यजायत ।।

36 & 37.

When told thus, she who was bright like lightning, who was most illustrious and who had given her heart & mind to the (late) king Asitha, although he was (dead

&) gone to heaven...... this Royal princess who was a woman of chastity, who was ever in grief over loss of her husband (Asitha), bowed to Chyavana. Thereafter she got a son.

❍ ❍ ❍

३८. सपत्न्या तु गरस्तस्यै दत्तो गर्भजिघांसया ।
सह तेन गरेणैव जात: स सगरोऽभवत् ।।

38. By the Co-wife, Poison had been given to her to abort the child (in her womb): And he was born with the same poison (that had been administered to her). Therefore he became (and was named as), Sagara. (Sa= with; Gara = Poison. . . Born with poison!).

❍ ❍ ❍

३९. सगरस्यासमञ्जस्तु असमञ्जात्तथांऽशुमान् ।
दिलीपोंऽशुमत: पुत्रो दिलीपस्य भगीरथ: ।।
भगीरथात् ककुत्स्थस्तु रघुस्तस्मादजायत ।।

39. And Asamanja was Sagara's son. Then from Asamanja was born Amschumaan: And Dhileepa was Amschumaan's son. And Bhageeratha was Dhileepa's son. And from Bhageeratha came Kaakuthsa, and from him Raghu.

❍ ❍ ❍

४०. रघोस्तु पुत्रस्तेजस्वी प्रवृद्ध: पुरुषादक: ।
कल्माषपादोऽप्यभवत्तस्माज्जातस्तु शमण: ।।

40. Although brilliant, to Raghu was born a son named Pravridha whose legs were black and who was a cannibal. From him was born Schankana.

❍ ❍ ❍

४१. सुदर्शन: शमणस्य अग्निवर्ण: सुदर्शनात् ।
शीघ्रगस्त्वग्निवर्णस्य शीघ्रगस्य मरु: सुत: ।।
मरो: प्रशुश्रुकस्त्वासीदम्बरीष: प्रशुश्रुकात् ।।

41. Sudharshana was Schankana's son: Agnivarna was

Sudhana's Scheegratha was Agnivarna's son; Maru was Scheegratha's (son): Praaschruka was Maru's son. And Ambareesha was born to Praaschruka.

❍ ❍ ❍

४२. अम्बरीषस्य पुत्रोऽभून्नहुषः पृथिवीपतिः ।
नहुषस्य ययातिस्तु नाभागस्तु ययातिजः ॥

42. Ambareesha's son was Nahusha: He ruled as lord of earth and Nahusha's son was Yayaathi and Naabhaaga was son of Yayaathi.

❍ ❍ ❍

४३. नाभागस्य बभूवाजो अजाद्दशरथोऽभवत् ।
अस्माद्दशरथाज्जातौ भ्रातरौ रामलक्ष्मणौ ॥

43. Aja was born to Naabhaga from Aja was born Dhascharatha: And from Dhascharatha was born these brothers Raama & Lakshmana.

❍ ❍ ❍

४४. आदिवंशविशुद्धानां राज्ञां परमधर्मिणाम् ।
इक्ष्वाकुकुलजातानां वीराणां सत्यवादिनाम् ॥

४५. रामलक्ष्मणयोरर्थे त्वत्सुते वरये नृप ।
सदृशाभ्यां नरश्रेष्ठ सदृशे दातुमर्हसि ॥

44 & 45.

As kings of pure lineage, they were (all) great men of Dharma; Brave, ever truthful, born in this Ikshwaaku race and associated (with such a lineage), he is king of Raama & Lakshmana, this (King Dhascharatha): I Am Asking You To Give Your Daughters (in marriage) Oh foremost of men (Janaka)! You should give such worthy (daughters) to such worthy (sons, Raama & Lakslunana).

❍ ❍ ❍

Chapter 71

(Janaka) Affirms to offer his daughters in marriage

१. एवं ब्रुवाणं जनकः प्रत्युवाच कृताञ्जलिः ।
श्रोतुमर्हसि भद्रं ते कुलं नः परिकीर्तितम् ।।

1. When told thus, Janaka cupped his hands in Anjali & then replied: =You should listen to the description about our family: Welfare to you (It is Janaka's turn to describe his lineage)=

❍ ❍ ❍

२. प्रदाने हि मुनिश्रेष्ठ कुलं निरवशेषतः ।
वक्तव्यं कुलजातेन तन्निबोध महामुने ।।

2. (It is interesting to note that Janaka addresses Vasishta) Oh Foremost Muni (Vasishta)! Born (as I am) in a noble family, it is proper to be told about my family, without leaving out anything, at this time of presentation (of my daughters in marriage): Therefore, Oh great Muni! (Please) be enlightened by me.

❍ ❍ ❍

३. राजाऽभूत्त्रिषु लोकेषु बिश्रुतः स्वेन कर्मणा ।
निमिः परमधर्मात्मा सर्वसत्त्ववतां वरः ।।

3. There was a king called Nimi who was renowned in all the three worlds, & who was a great man of Dharma and who, by his deeds, was foremost amongst all good men.

❍ ❍ ❍

४. तस्य पुत्रो मिथिर्नाम मिथिला येन निर्मिता ।
प्रथमो जनको नाम जनकादप्युदावसुः ।।

4. Mithi was his son: He was the first of the Janaka-s, and by him Mithila was established: And from this Janaka (Mithi), was born Udhaavasu.

❍ ❍ ❍

५. उदावसोस्तु धर्मात्मा राजा वै नन्दिवर्धनः ।
नन्दिवर्धनपुत्रस्तु सुकेतुर्नाम नामतः ।।

5. The noble soul man of Dharma Nandhivardhana, the king, was Udhaavasu's son: Renowned Sukethu by name was Nandhivardhaman's son.

❍ ❍ ❍

६. सुकेतोरपि धर्मात्मा देवरातो महाबलः ।
देवरातस्य राजर्षेर्बृहद्रथ इति स्मृतः ।।

6. The mightily strong man of Dharma, Dhevaraatha, was Sukethu's son and Brihadhratha by name was son of Royal Rishi Dhevaratha.

❍ ❍ ❍

७. बृहद्रथस्य शूरोऽभून्महावीरः प्रतापवान् ।
महावीरस्य धृतिमान्सुधृतिः सत्यविक्रमः ।।

7. To Brihadhratha was born the famous & brave son Mahaaveera; The truly valiant and courageous Sudhrithi was Mahaaveera's son.

❍ ❍ ❍

८. सुधृतेरपि धर्मात्मा दृष्टकेतुः सुधार्मिकः ।
दृष्टकेतोस्तु राजर्षेर्हर्यश्व इति विश्रुतः ।।

8. The noble man of Dharma, noble soul Dhrishtakethu was Sudhrithi's son The renowned Hayaschwar by name was son of Royal Rishi Dhrishtakethu.

❍ ❍ ❍

९. हर्यश्वस्य मरुः पुत्रो मरोः पुत्रः प्रतिन्धकः ।
प्रतिन्धकस्य धर्मात्मा राजा कीर्तिरथः सुतः ।।

9. Maru was Haryaschwa's son; And Prathindhaka was Maru's son The noble soul king named Keerthiratha, was Prathindhaka's son.

❍ ❍ ❍

१०. पुत्रः कीर्तिरथस्याथ देवमीढ इति स्मृतः ।
देवमीढस्य विबुधो विबुधस्य महीध्रकः ॥

10. And called by name Dhevameeda, was son of Keerthiratha; Vibhudha was Dhevameeda's son; And Maheedhraka was Vibhuda's son.

❍ ❍ ❍

११. महीध्रकसुतो राजा कीर्तिरातो महाबलः ।
कीर्तिरातस्य राजर्षेर्महारोमा व्यजायत ॥

11. And Maheedhraka's son was the mightily strong King Keerthi Raatha; And Mahaaroma was born to Royal sage Keerthiratha.

❍ ❍ ❍

१२. महारोम्णस्तु धर्मात्मा स्वर्णरोमा व्यजायत ।
स्वर्णरोम्णस्तु राजर्षेर्ह्रस्वरोमा व्यजायत ॥

12. Man of Dharma, Swarnaroma was born to Mahaaroma; And Haswaroma was born to royal sage Swarnaroma.

❍ ❍ ❍

१३. तस्य पुत्रद्वयं राज्ञो धर्मज्ञस्य महात्मनः ।
ज्येष्ठोऽहमनुजो भ्राता मम वीरः कुशध्वजः ॥

13. And to this great soul knower of Dharma, to this king (Haswaroma), were born two sons: And I am the eldest: Born after me is my brave brother Kuschadhwaja.

❍ ❍ ❍

१४. मां तु ज्येष्ठं पिता राज्ये सोऽभिषिच्य नराधिपः ।
कुशध्वजं समावेश्य भारं मयि वनं गतः ॥

14. He, my father & king, crowned me who was his eldest (son) and entrusted (my brother) Kuschsadhwaja under my care & went away to forest.

❍ ❍ ❍

१५. वृद्धे पितरि स्वर्याते धर्मेण धुरमावहम् ।
भ्रातरं देवसमाशं स्नेहात्पश्यन्कुशध्वजम् ॥

15. When my old father went away to heaven, I took on the burden (of ruling the kingdom), with Dharma, looking (& treating) my brother Kuchadhwaja with affection.

❍ ❍ ❍

१६. कस्यचित्त्वथ कालस्य सांकाश्यादागतः पुरात् ।
सुधन्वा वीर्यवान् राजा मिथिलामवरोधकः ॥

16. Then, at one time the brave king Sudhanva, coming from the city of Saankaasa, came & besieged Mithila.

❍ ❍ ❍

१७. स च मे प्रेषयामास शैवं धनुरनुत्तमम् ।
सीता कन्या च पद्माक्षी मह्यं वै दीयतामिति ॥

17. He applied pressure on me saying: = You give me Schiva's foremost Bow & also the lotus eyed Seetha (my darling) girl =

❍ ❍ ❍

१८. तस्याऽप्रदानाद्ब्रह्मर्षेयुद्धमासीन्मया सह ।
स हतोऽभिमुखो राजा सुधन्वा तु मया रणे ॥

18. Oh Bramma Rishi (Vasishta, please listen further)! As he was refused, a war ensued between us (But at close range) when he faced me, this Sudhanva was killed by me in battle.

❍ ❍ ❍

१९. निहत्य तं मुनिश्रेष्ठ सुधन्वानं नराधिपम् ।
सामाश्ये भ्रातरं वीरमभ्यषिञ्चं कुशध्वजम् ॥

19. Oh noble Muni (Vaishta)! Having killed the king Sudhanva, I crowned my brave brother Kuschadhwaja at Saankaasa.

❍ ❍ ❍

२०. कनीयानेष मे भ्राता अहं ज्येष्ठो महामुने ॥

२१. ददामि परमप्रीता वध्वौ ते मुनिपुङ्गव ।
सीतां रामाय भद्रं ते ऊर्मिलां लक्ष्मणाय च ॥

20 & 21.

(King Janaka offers his own daughter Oormila also in marriage, apart from his adopted daughter Seetha, who was won by Raama). Oh great Muni (Vasishta)! He is my younger brother and I am his elder Oh 'tiger of Muni-s: With joy I am offering as brides Seetha for Raama & Oormila for Lakshmana Welfare to you.

❍ ❍ ❍

२२. वीर्यशुल्कां मम सुतां सीतां सुरसुतोपमाम् ।
द्विितीयाभूर्मिलां चैव त्रिर्ददामि न संशयः ॥

22. This Seetha, my daughter is comparable to celestial maiden and was (offered as) prize for valour, and my second (daughter) Oormila, I am offering (as brides & am affirming it by repeating it) thrice No doubt about (my decision).

❍ ❍ ❍

२३. रामलक्ष्मणयो राजन् गोदानं कारयस्व ह ।
पितृकार्यं च भद्रं ते ततो वैवाहिकं कुरु ॥

23. (And now King Janaka addresses King Dhascharatha) Oh king (Dhascharatha)! (Please) do the (pre-marriage Rituals) of "Godhaana", for Raama/Laakshmana & Oblations to their forefathers Then please do the marriage ceremony Welfare to you.

❍ ❍ ❍

२४. मघा ह्यद्य महाबाहो तृतीये दिवसे विभो ।
फल्गुन्यामुत्तरे राजंस्तस्मिन्वैवाहिकं कुरु ॥
रामलक्ष्मणयोरर्थे दानं कार्यं सुखोदयम् ॥

24. Oh man of strong limbs! Oh Lord (Dhascharatha)! Today is Star Maka (in ascendant): Then three days from now will be Phalguni and on this day, oh King, do the marriage ceremony on the Uthara star (Phalgun) And for the sake of (& welfare of) your sons Raama/

Lakshmana, gifts must be offered for 'growing' prosperity.

(Note: It is customary to describe one's lineage during a marriage ceremony in India; Today, due to paucity of time, the Bride's father & bridegroom's father (through their priests) tell the congregation about their parents & grandparents. There is no question or doubt about who is marrying whom! And readers may note: Protocol is observed at all times in as much as Dhascharatha has said that it is Vasishta who is The First to speak & speak on behalf of his family, King Janaka addresses Vasishta & not king Dhascharatha when he speaks about his lineage.)

❍ ❍ ❍

Chapter 72

The Performance of Godhaana Rituals etc.

(Vischwaamithra suggests that along with the marriages of Seetha with Raama & Oormila with Lakshmana, Bharatha & Schathrugna, the other two sons of Dhascharatha should also wed the two daughters of Kuschadhwaja, the brother of King Janaka.)

❍ ❍ ❍

१. तमुक्तवन्तं वैदेहं विश्वामित्रो महामुनिः ।
उवाच वचनं वीरं वसिष्ठसहितो नृपम् ।।

1. And the great Muni Vischwaamithra who was with Vasishta, addressed these words to the brave Vidheha king (Janaka) when he had spoken thus.

❍ ❍ ❍

२. अचिन्त्यान्यप्रमेयानि कुलानि कुलनन्दन ।
इक्ष्वाकूणां विदेहानां नैषां तुल्योऽस्ति कश्चन ।।

2. Oh delighter of your race! (Oh Janaka)! The families of Ikshwaaku-s & Vidheha-s, are most wonderful (unimaginable): Incomparable: There is nothing equal to these (two families).

❍ ❍ ❍

३. सदृशो धर्मसंबन्धः सदृशो रूपसंपदा ।
रामलक्ष्मणयो राजन्सीता चोर्मिलया सह ॥

3. Oh king (Janaka)! This alliance of Dharma between Raama/Lakshmana and Seetha/Oormila, is most appropriate, by beauty and status.

❍ ❍ ❍

४. वक्तव्यं च नरश्रेष्ठ श्रूयतां वचनं मम ॥

4. Oh foremost of men! My words which are proper to be told (now), may you (please) listen to.

❍ ❍ ❍

५. भ्राता यवीयान्धर्मज्ञ एष राजा कुशध्वजः ।
अस्य धर्मात्मनो राजन् रूपेणाप्रतिमं भुवि ॥
सुताद्वयं नरश्रेष्ठ पत्न्यर्थं वरयामहे ॥

5. Oh King (Janaka)!Oh foremost of men ! This king Kuschadhwaja is your younger brother; "We" are seeking the marriage of the two daughters of this noble soul who are both incomparable in beauty in the world.

❍ ❍ ❍

६. भरतस्य कुमारस्य शत्रुघ्नस्य च धीमतः ।
वरयेम सुते राजंस्तयोरर्थेमहात्मनोः ॥

6. Oh king! For the sake of this two most eminent (sons of Dhascharatha), the young Bharatha & the wise Schathrugna, we are asking for the two daughters (of your brother Kuschadhwaja).

❍ ❍ ❍

७. पुत्रा दशरथस्येमे रूपयौवनशालिनः ।
लोकपालोपमाः सर्वे देवतुल्यपराक्रमाः ॥

7. These sons of Dhascharatha are all endowed with beauty & youth: They are like protectors (& guardians) of the world (like Lokpaals); Their valour is comparable to those of celestials.

❍ ❍ ❍

८. उभयोरपि राजेन्द्र संबन्धेनानुबध्यताम् ।
इक्ष्वाकुकुलमव्यग्रं भवतः पुण्यकर्मणः ॥

8. Oh Lord of kings (Janaka)! By these (marriage) alliance, may the two families of the steady & steadfast Ikshwaaku-s & yours of holy deeds, be bound firmly.

❍ ❍ ❍

९. विश्वामित्रवचः श्रुत्वा वसिष्ठस्य मते तदा ।
जनकः प्राञ्जलिर्वाक्यमुवाच मुनिपुङ्गवौ ॥

१०. कुलं धन्यमिदं मन्ये येषां नो मुनिपुङ्गवौ ।
सदृशं कुलसंबन्धं यदाज्ञापयथः स्वयम् ॥

9 & 10.

(Janaka accepts the proposal of Vischwaamithra on behalf of his brother Kuschadhwaja) Hearing the words of Vischwaamithra (that were spoken) with approval of Vasishta, (King) Janaka, cupping his hands in Anjali, then said the following words to the two 'tigers' of Muni-s= I consider this, (my) family, most blessed (& fortunate) in as much as (Vischwaamithra & Vasishta) who are 'Tigers' amongst Muni-s, are themselves *commending this alliance of my family as worthy enough (Poet uses the word=*Aagnyaapayatha - Commands. ofcourse Vasishta-Vishwaamithra's request is a Command.)

❍ ❍ ❍

११. एवं भवतु भद्रं वः कुशध्वजसुते इमे ।
पत्न्यौ भजेतां सहितौ शत्रुघ्नभरतावुभौ ॥

11. So Be It: Welfare to you May these two daughters (of my brother) Kuschadhwaja, be wives of these two, Bharatha & Schathrugna who are (ever) together.

❍ ❍ ❍

१२. एकाह्ना राजपुत्रीणां चतसृणां महामुने ।
पाणीन् गृह्णन्तु चत्वारो राजपुत्रा महाबला: ।।

12. Oh great Muni (Vischwaamithra)! The four mightily strong royal princes (Raama, Lakshmana, Bharatha, Schathrugna), May they hold the hands of the Princesses (in marriage) on the same day.

(Here is a case of Bridegroom's party asking for the hand of Bride; normally the custom in India is that bride seeks the groom! But then this alliance is unique Two very great men, Vashishta & Vischwaamithra - The Bramma Rishis- have the authority to speak on behalf of the bridegroom's father Dhascharatha. Further, it is an alliance between two great kings, Ayodhya & Mithila.)

❍ ❍ ❍

१३. उत्तरे दिवसे ब्रह्मन् फल्गुनीभ्यां मनीषिण: ।
वैवाहिकं प्रशंसन्ति भगो यत्र प्रजापति: ।।

13. Oh Braamin (Vischwaamithra)! Wise and devoted men value highly the marriages performed on the day of Uthra star Phalguni when Baga as Prajapathi as the Lord Patron presides.

❍ ❍ ❍

१४. एवमक्त्वा वच: सौम्यं प्रत्युत्थाय कृताञ्जलि: ।
उभौ मुनिवरौ राजा जनको वाक्यमब्रवीत् ।।

14. Having said thus pleasantly, he got up again, (this) king Janaka, and cupping his hands in reverence of Anjali, addressed the two foremost Muni-s (Vishwaamithra & Vasishta) the following words:

❍ ❍ ❍

१५. परो धर्मः कृतो मह्यं शिष्योऽस्मि भवतोः सदा ॥

15. Great Dharma was bestowed upon me I am ever your disciple.

❍ ❍ ❍

१६. इमान्यासनमुख्यानि आसातां मुनिपुङ्गवौ ।
यथा दशरथस्येयं तथाऽयोध्यापुरी मम ॥
प्रभुत्वे नास्ति संदेहो यथार्हं कर्तुमर्हथ ॥

16. This (My) Mithila is Dhascharatha's; And Ayodhya city is mine: Likewise may you two 'Tigers' of Muni-s occupy the foremost Thrones There is no uncertainty about your power & status You are (at perfect liberty) to do as you please (here).

❍ ❍ ❍

१७. तथा ब्रुवति वैदेहे जनके रघुनन्दनः ।
राजा दशरथो हृष्टः प्रत्युवाच महीपतिम् ॥

17. When the Vidheha king Janaka was speaking thus, the delighter of Raghu-s, King Dhascharatha, with great joy, replied to (Janaka) the lord of earth.

❍ ❍ ❍

१८. यथवामसफ्येयगुणौ भ्रातरौ मिथिलेश्वरौ ।
ऋषयो राजसङ्घाश्च भवद्भ्यामभिपूजिताः ॥

18. You two brothers, the lords of Mithila, possess innumerable virtues; The Rishi-s, and the congregation of kings have all been duly honoured.

❍ ❍ ❍

१९. स्वस्ति प्राप्नुहि भद्रं ते गमिष्यामि स्वमालयम् ।
श्राद्धकर्माणि सर्वाणि विधास्यामीति चाब्रवीत् ॥

19. May you obtain Swasthi (Peace & welfare); Welfare to you; I am going (now) to my cottage, I will do all the Shraadha ceremonies; Thus he said, (this Dhascharatha to Janaka).

(The Shraadha ceremony is an elaborate set of Rituals done to please forefathers & celestials it is done on occasions of rejoicing as well on solemn occasions).

❍ ❍ ❍

२०. तमापृष्ट्वा नरपतिं राजा दशरथस्तदा ।
मुनीन्द्रौ तौ पुरस्कृत्य जगामाशु महायशाः ।।

20. Then the most famous Dhascharatha took leave of this king (Janaka) and left along with the great Muni-s.

❍ ❍ ❍

२१. स गत्वा निलयं राजा श्राद्धं कृत्वा विधानतः ।
प्रभाते काल्यमुत्थाय चक्रे गोदानमुत्तमम् ।।

21. Reaching his abode, king (Dhascharatha) did Shraadhdha ceremony as per norms; and getting up before sunrise, did the foremost (propitious) Godhaana (Haircuts, baths etc.).

❍ ❍ ❍

२२. गवां शतसहस्त्राणि ब्राह्मणेभ्यो नराधिपः ।
एकैकशो ददौ राजा पुत्रानुद्दिश्य धर्मतः ।।

22. And the lord of men king (Dhascharatha), for the sake of (welfare of) his sons, gave to Braamins, to every one, hundred thousand cows (as gifts), as per Dharma.

❍ ❍ ❍

२३. सुवर्णश‍ृङ्गाः संपन्नाः सवत्साः कांस्यदोहनाः ।
गवां शतसहस्त्राणि चत्वारि पुरुषर्षभः ।।

२४. वित्तमन्यच्च सुबहु द्विजेभ्यो रघुनन्दनः ।
ददौ गोदानमुद्दिश्य पुत्राणां पुत्रवत्सलः ।।

23 & 24.

(And he gifted): Cows with golden horns, well endowed (with form), along with calves, yielding milk as much as one desired, cows in four hundred thousand (he gave); This (Dhascharatha) the 'Bull' amongst men the delighter of Raghu-s who was deeply attached to his (four) sons, gave to Braamins many other items in lieu of Godhaana ceremony of his sons

❍ ❍ ❍

२५. स सुतैः कृतगोदानैर्वृतस्तु नृपतिस्तदा ।
लोकपालैरिवाभाति वृतः सोम्यः प्रजापतिः ॥

25. Surrounded by his sons who had finished The Godhaana ceremony, he appeared at that time, like the pleasant Prajaapathi (God Bramma) when surrounded by Lokpaals.

❍ ❍ ❍

Chapter 73

The Marriage of Seetha & others

१. यस्मिंस्तु दिवसे राजा चक्रे गोदानमुत्तमम् ।
तस्मिंस्तु दिवसे शूरो युधाजित्समुपेयिवान् ॥

1. On the day king (Dhascharatha) performed the foremost Godhaana ceremony (for his sons), on that day the brave Yudhaajith came there (to Mithila).

(Yudhaajith was the brother of Kaikeyi, the third wife of Dhascharatha & so he was uncle to Bharatha, the third son of Dhascharatha through his wife Kaikeyi.)

❍ ❍ ❍

२. पुत्रः केकयराजस्य साक्षाद्भरतमातुलः ।
दृष्ट्वा पृष्ट्वा च कुशलं राजानमिदमब्रवीत् ॥

2. He was the son of Kekeya king & (thus) was Bharatha's own uncle: Seeing the king and after enquiring about his welfare, he said:

❍ ❍ ❍

३. केकयाधिपती राजा स्नेहात्कुशलमब्रवीत् ।
येषां कुशलकामोऽसि तेषां संप्रत्यनामयम् ।।

3. Whose welfare you are desirous to know about, they are all well now; The chief of Kekeya, my (father &) king, with great affection, wishes your welfare.

❍ ❍ ❍

४. स्वस्त्रीयं मम राजेन्द्र द्रष्टुकामो महीपतिः ।
तदर्थमुपयातोऽहमयोध्यां रघुनन्दन ।।

4. Oh emperor! Oh delighter of Raghu-s (Oh Dhascharatha!): (My father), the king wishes to see the son of my sister (Kaikeyi) For this purpose, I had gone to Ayodhya.

❍ ❍ ❍

५. श्रुत्वा त्वहमयोध्यायां विवाहार्थं तवात्मजान् ।
मिथिलामुपयातांस्तु त्वया सह महीपते ।।

६. त्वरयाऽभ्युपयातोऽहं द्रष्टुकामः स्वसुः सुतम् ।
तस्य त्वं राजशार्दूल प्रीतिं कर्तुमिहार्हसि ।।

5 & 6.

Oh king (Dhascharatha)! (But) Hearing at Ayodhya that you had left for Mithila at once along with your sons for marriage, desirous of seeing my sister's son (Bharatha), I came (here to Mithila from Ayodhya) Oh Lion of kings! In this matter, may you please him (by sending Bharatha with me to see his grandfather).

❍ ❍ ❍

७. तस्य तद्वचनं श्रुत्वा मधुरं मधुराक्षरम् ।
अथ राजा दशरथः प्रियातिथिमुपस्थितम् ।।
दृष्ट्वा परमसत्कारैः पूजनार्हमपूजयत् ।।

7. Hearing his sweet speech with sweet words, King Dhascharatha, seeing his beloved guest who had come there & who deserved hospitality, honoured him with great hospitality.

❍ ❍ ❍

८. ततस्तामुषितो रात्रिं सह पुत्रैर्महात्मभिः ।
प्रभाते पुनरुत्थाय कृत्वा कर्माणि तत्त्ववित् ॥
ऋषींस्तदा पुरस्कृत्य यज्ञवाटमुपागमत् ॥

8. After spending the night with his most eminent sons, (King Dhascharatha) got up early morning; performed morning Rituals And he, who had knowledge of the Thathva (essence of) Shaasthra-s, accompanied by Rishi-s, entered The Yaaga Hall (Marriage hall).

❍ ❍ ❍

९. युक्ते मुहूर्ते विजये सर्वाभरणभूषितः ।
भ्रातृभिः सहितो रामः कृतकौतुकमङ्गलः ॥

9. Bedecked with all ornaments, Raama, accompanied by his brothers, tied (on his wrist) the auspicious 'Thread' at the auspicious time which (ever & surely) brings victory (& glory) (The Kowthgamangala ceremony is a very important ritual).

❍ ❍ ❍

१०. वसिष्ठं पुरतः कृत्वा महर्षीनपरानपि ।
पितुः समीपमाश्रित्य तस्थौ भ्रातृभिरावृतः ॥

10. Surrounded by brothers, and making (way for) Vasishta and other great Rishi-s to go in front, he approached his father & stood.

❍ ❍ ❍

११. वसिष्ठो भगवानेत्य वैदेहमिदमब्रवीत् ॥

11. And the Lord (Sage) Vasishta approached the Vidheha king (Janaka) and addressed him thus:

❍ ❍ ❍

१२. राजा दशरथो राजन् कृतकौतुकमङ्गलैः ।
पुत्रैर्नरवरश्रेष्ठ दातारमभिकाङ्क्षते ॥

12. Oh King! Oh foremost of men! (Oh Janaka)! King Dhascharatha, along with his sons (who are all ready)

having done the Kowthumangala (& other premarriage rituals), is eagerly awaiting the donor (The bride's father is the donor & the bridegroom's father is the recipient as per Indian tradition).

❍ ❍ ❍

१३. दातृप्रतिग्रहीतृभ्यां सर्वार्थाः प्रभवन्ति हि ।
स्वधर्मं प्रतिपद्यस्व कृत्वा वैवाह्यमुत्तमम् ।।

13. As all wealth & substance will spring forth for (you both), for The Donor & The Recipient, may you perform the (noble) foremost marriage (ceremony) and (thus) obtain your Dharma.

❍ ❍ ❍

१४. इत्युक्तः परमोदारो वसिष्ठेन महात्मना ।
प्रत्युवाच महातेजा वाक्यं परमधर्मवित् ।।

14. When told thus by the great soul Vasishta, the most brilliant, the most exalted (Janaka) who was foremost man of Dharma, replied with these words.

❍ ❍ ❍

१५. कः स्थितः प्रतिहारो मे कस्याज्ञा संप्रतीक्ष्यते ।
स्वगृहे को विचारोऽस्ति यथा राज्यमिदं तव ।।

15. (King Janaka is so happy with this alliance that he expresses his feelings thus) Who is the gate keeper who stands (between me & you)! As this is your kingdom, where (is the need) for consideration and hesitation (to enter) in your own house! Whose orders are you awaiting (when you can order about).

❍ ❍ ❍

१६. कृतकौतुकसर्वस्वा वेदिमूलमुपागताः ।
मम कन्या मुनिश्रेष्ठ दीप्ता वह्निरिव ।।

16. Oh foremost Muni (Vasishta)! My daughters (including the daughters of my brother), wearing ceremonial

threads & necklaces have come to The Marriage Mound, shining like rays of fire

❍ ❍ ❍

१७. सज्जोऽहं त्वत्प्रतीक्षोऽस्मि वेद्यामस्यां प्रतिष्ठित: ।
अविघ्नं क्रियतां राजन् किमर्थमवलम्बसे ।।

17. Oh king (Dhascharatha)! I am awaiting you at this ceremonial mound ready (for marriage ceremony): Why are you waiting May the ceremony proceed without hindrance.

❍ ❍ ❍

१८. तद्वाक्यं जनकेनोक्तं श्रुत्वा दशरथस्तदा ।
प्रवेशयामास सुतान् सर्वानृषिगणानपि ।।

18. Hearing the words spoken by Janaka, Dhascharatha then made his sons, the congregation of Rishi-s and all others enter (the hall).

❍ ❍ ❍

१९. ततो राजा विदेहानां वसिष्ठमिदमब्रवीत् ।
कारयस्व ऋषे सम्यगृषिभि: सह धार्मिकै: ।।
रामस्य लोकरामस्य क्रियां वैवाहिकीं प्रभो ।।

19. Then (Janaka) the king of Vidheha, addressed Vasishta thus: Oh Rishi! Oh Lord! You must perform the marriage ceremony of Raama the delighter of the world perfectly, (as per norms), along with these Rishi-s who are men of Dharma.

❍ ❍ ❍

२०. त्वया न विदितं किञ्चिन्नास्ति ब्रह्मविदां वर ।
तस्मात्त्वमेव ब्रह्मर्षे अशेषं कर्तुमर्हसि ।।

20. Oh foremost amongst men knowing Brammam! Oh Bramma Rishi! (Oh Vasishta)! There is nothing that is not known to you Therefore you alone should perform without leaving out anything.

❍ ❍ ❍

२१. तथेत्युक्त्वा तु जनकं वसिष्ठो भगवानृषिः ।
विश्वामित्रं पुरस्कृत्य शतानन्दं च धार्मिकम् ।।
२२. प्रपामध्ये तु विधिवद्वेदिं कृत्वा महातपाः ।
अलञ्चकार तां वेदिं गन्धपुष्पैः समन्ततः ।।
२३. सुवर्णपालिकाभिश्च छिद्रकुम्भैश्च सामुरैः ।
अमुराढ्यैः शरावैश्च धूपपात्रैः सधूपकैः ।।
२४. शफ्पात्रैः स्रुवैः स्रुग्भिः पात्रैरर्घ्याभिपूरितैः ।
लाजपूर्णैश्च पात्रीभिरक्षतैरभिसंस्कृतैः ।।

21 to 24.

(Vasishta performs The rituals of marriage- stanzas) Rishi Vasishta, saying "So Be It" to the lord (king) Janaka before (& in presence of) Schathanandh the man of Dharma, & before Vischwaamithra, this (Vasishta) the man of great penance, prepared Fire over the Mound in the middle of the hall as per norms, He decorated the Mound with sweet smelling flowers all around With many gold pots (kept there) (There were) Water vessels with side holes: Vessels with flanges & with supports: Vessels full with incenses & scents: Pots full with seedlings & sprouts Vessels made of conch shells; Ladles called Sruva-s, wooden spoons; pots full with water for Arghya rituals: Pots filed up with puffed grains (& the like): Pots filled with various seeds.

❍ ❍ ❍

२५. दर्भैः समैः समास्तीर्य विधिवन्मन्त्रपूर्वकम् ।
अग्निमाधाय वेद्यां तु विधिमन्त्रपुरस्कृतम् ।।
जुहावाग्नौ महातेजा वसिष्ठो भगवानृषिः ।।

25. The most brilliant Lord sage Vasishta spread with equivalent numbers of Dharbha grass as per norms, reciting chants and he then lit the Fire on the Mound with prayers and chants and then performed Fire Oblations on the (holy) Fire.

❍ ❍ ❍

२६. ततः सीतां समानीय सर्वाभरणभूषिताम् ।
श्रियं पद्मवियुक्तां वै केशवाफ्च्युतामिव ॥
२७. विद्युत्प्रभां विशालाक्षीं नीलकुञ्चितमूर्धजाम् ॥
२८. हंसामितेन क्षौमेण किञ्चित्पीतेन संवृताम् ।
वासितेनोत्तरीयेण सुरक्तेन सुसंवृताम् ॥
२९. समक्षमग्ने: संस्थाप्य राघवाभिमुखे तदा ।
अब्रवीज्जनको राजा कौसल्यानन्दवर्धनम् ॥

26 to 29.

(Seetha's presence described by poet Vaalmeeki) Then (Janaka) brought Seetha who was decorated with all ornaments, who was resplendent as though she was (like) Goddess Lakshmi 'slipping out' from the body of (God Vishnu the) Keschava she was wide eyed: Bright like lightning: her hair was dark blue she was dressed in silken robe, somewhat yellow in color, with figure of swan painted on it; her upper garment which covered her, was red and well scented (Such a Seetha) was brought up before The Fire Mound and she was stationed in front of (Raama) the Raaghava: Then king Janaka addressed (Raama) who (ever) increased the joy of (his mother) Kowsalya.

❍ ❍ ❍

३०. इयं सीता मम सुता सहधर्मचरी तव ।
प्रतीच्छ चैनां भद्रं ते पाणिं गृह्णीष्व पाणिना ॥
३१. पतिव्रता महाभागा छायेवानुगता तव ।
इत्युक्त्वा प्राक्षिपद्राजा मन्त्रपूतं जलं तदा ॥

30 & 31.

=This Is Seetha, My Daughter: She Will Always Be With You In (your) Duties Of Dharma: Accept Her: Welfare To You Clasp Her Hand With Your Hand She Is Most Virtuous: Most Illustrious: She Will Follow You Like A Shadow= Saying thus, the king (Janaka) sprinkled water with recitation of chants.

(These two stanzas are considered very propitious: Describes the qualities of a good wife)

❍ ❍ ❍

३२. प्रक्षिप्ते सलिले भूमौ गगने चोत्थिताः स्वनाः ।
साधु साध्विति देवानामृषीणां वदतां तदा ।।
३३. देवदुन्दुभिनिर्घोषाः पुष्पवृष्टिर्महत्यभूत् ।।
32 & 33.

When water was sprinkled on earth, there arose a roar in the entire sky! At that time, the Dheva-s & Rishi-s said: (acclaimed): = Excellent, Excellent:= A shower of flowers (fell) with sounds from celestial Dhundhubi drums (reverberating all around).

❍ ❍ ❍

३४. एवं दत्त्वा तदा सीतां मन्त्रोदकपुरस्कृताम् ।
अब्रवीज्जनको राजा हर्षेणाभिपरिप्लुतः ।।

34. And king Janaka, overwhelmed with joy, gave Seetha (in marriage to Raama) thus, with water offerings & with (recitations) of chants Then he said:

❍ ❍ ❍

३५. लक्ष्मणागच्छ भद्रं ते ऊर्मिलामुद्यतां मया ।
प्रतीच्छ पाणिं गृह्णीष्व मा भूत्कालस्य पर्ययः ।।

35. Oh Lakshmana! Come! Welfare to you: Accept Oormila, (my daughter) brought up by me Hold her hand (by your hand) There should be no delay.

❍ ❍ ❍

३६. तमेवमुक्त्वा जनको भरतं चाभ्यभाषत ।
गृहाण पाणिं माण्डव्याः पाणिना रघुनन्दन ।।

36. After saying thus to him, Janaka said to Bharatha: = Oh darling of Raghu-s; Clasp the hand of Maandvi with your hand=

❍ ❍ ❍

३७. शत्रुघ्नं चापि धर्मात्मा अब्रवीज्जनकेश्वरः ।
श्रुतकीर्त्या महाबाहो पाणिं गृह्णीष्व पाणिना ॥

37. And further, the noble soul man of Dharma, king Janaka, then said to Schathrugna: Oh mighty limbed (Schathrugna)! You clasp the hand of Schruthakeerthi with your hand.

❍ ❍ ❍

३८. सर्वे भवन्तः सौम्याश्च सर्वे सुचरितव्रताः ।
पत्नीभिः सन्तु काकुत्स्था मा भूत्कालस्य पर्ययः ॥

38. Let there be no waste of time: All you Kaakuthsa-s are very pleasant (men): May you all be steadfast in your vows along with your wives, and practise good conduct.

❍ ❍ ❍

३९. जनकस्य वचः श्रुत्वा पाणीन्पाणिभिरस्पृशन् ।
चत्वारस्ते चतसृणां वसिष्ठस्य मते स्थिताः ॥

39. Hearing Janaka's words, all these four (sons of Dhascharatha) clasped the hands of the four girls with their hands (respectively), (ever) abiding by Vasishta's (desire and) intentions.

❍ ❍ ❍

४०. अग्निं प्रदक्षिणीकृत्य वेदिं राजानमेव च ।
ऋषींश्चैव महात्मानः सभार्या रघुसत्तमाः ॥
यथोक्तेन तदा चक्रुर्विवाहं विधिपूर्वकम् ॥

40. These most eminent & foremost Raghu-s, along with their wives, went round The Fire, The Mound, the King, The Rishi-s, in cirumbambulation Then as per custom and as per Shaasthra-s, they married.

❍ ❍ ❍

४१. काकुत्स्थैश्च गृहीतेषु ललितेषु च पाणिषु ।
पुष्पवृष्टिर्महत्यासीदन्तरिक्षात्सुभास्वरा ॥
दिव्यदुन्दुभिनिर्घोषैर्गीतवादित्रनिःस्वनैः ॥

41. When the hands of these (lovely)girls were clasped by the (four) Kaakuthsa-s, there was a great shower of flowers from the Sky, to the accompaniment of music, Instrumental strains and beatings of the celestial Dhundhubi drums

❍ ❍ ❍

४२. ननृतुश्चाप्सरःसङ्घा गन्धर्वाश्च जगुः कलम् ।
विवाहे रघुमुख्यानां तदद्भुतमिवाभवत् ।।

42. The (celestial) Apsara maidens danced: Ghandhrva-s sang softly; such wonderful things happened during the wedding of these foremost Raaghava-s.

❍ ❍ ❍

४३. ईदृशे वर्तमाने तु तूर्योद्धुष्टनिनादिते ।
त्रिरग्निं ते परिक्रम्य ऊहुर्भार्या महौजसः ।।

43. With musical strains & dance rhythms reverberating thus, these most radiant (sons of Dhascharatha) went round the Fire thrice, and clasped their wives.

❍ ❍ ❍

४४. अथोपकार्यां जग्मुस्ते सदारा रघुनन्दनाः ।
स्वानि यानानि चारोप्य तां पुरीं प्रययुस्तदा ।।

44. Then they (all) left to their (respective) camps; (But) these darlings of Raghu-s, accompanied by their wives, got on to their respective chariots and roamed about the city (of Mithila - for sight seeing & to be seen by the multitude of citizens of Mithila).

❍ ❍ ❍

४५. प्रीयमाणो दशरथः पुत्रान् पुत्रवतां वरः ।
राजाऽप्यनुययौ पश्यन् सर्षिसङ्घः सबान्धवः ।।

45. King Dhascharatha who was most (fortunate) amongst those who had sons, went along happily with the Rishi-s and his relatives, all (the time) looking at his sons.

(Note: Poet Vaalmeeki does not elaborate the Rituals performed during the marriage nor has he indicated the 'source' & 'authority' for the elaborate ceremonies during marriage In post Vedhic period, we have some sources & authority from Gobhila & Paaraskara & others And there seems to be some doubt whether Dhascharatha's wives attended their sons' wedding at all.)

Chapter 74

The Encounter with ParaschuRaama

१. अथ रात्र्यां व्यतीतायां विश्वामित्रो महामुनि: ।
आपृष्ट्वा तौ च राजानौ जगामोत्तरपर्वतम् ।।
आशीर्भि: पूरयित्वा च कुमारांश्च स राघवान् ।।

1. The great Muni (Vischwaamithra), when night had ended, (after marriage of Raama & others) and after 'filling' the young Raaghava-s (Raama and his brothers) with his blessings, took leave of the (two) kings (Janaka & Dhascharatha) and went to northern mountain (of Himaalya-s to do more penance).

(Readers may be somewhat surprised that Poet Vaalmeeki devotes just this stanza for Vischwaamithra who had done so much for Raama & for Dhascharatha;'s family. There is not even a word of thanks from Dhascharatha!)

❍ ❍ ❍

२. विश्वामित्रे गते तस्मिन् राजा च जगतीपति: ।
अयोध्याधिपति: श्रीमान् वैदेहं मिथिलाधिपम् ।।
आपृष्ट्वाऽथ जगामाशु राजा दशरथ: पुरीम् ।।

2. Soon after the departure of this Vischwaamithra, the lord of earth, the ruler of Ayodhya, this king, this resplendent Dhascharatha, taking leave of the Vidheha

king (Janaka) the lord of Mithila, left for (his) city (of Ayodhya with his sons, daughters in law and his entourage.)).

❍ ❍ ❍

३. गच्छन्तं तं तु राजानमन्वगच्छन्नराधिपः ।।

४. अथ राजा विदेहानां ददौ कन्याधनं बहु ।।

५. गवां शतसहस्राणि बहूनि मिथिलाधिपः ।
कम्बलानां च मुख्यानां क्षौमकोट्यम्बराणि च ।।

3 to 5.

King (Janaka) followed this king (Dhascharatha) for some distance.Then this king of Vidheha, gave as dowry, plenty of cows, foremost blankets, many thousands of silken robes and millions of dresses.

❍ ❍ ❍

६. हस्त्यश्वरथपादातं दिव्यरूपं स्वलंकृतम् ।
ददौ कन्यापिता तासां दासीदासमनुत्तमम् ।।

6. (Janaka), the father of the brides, gave celestial looking wonderfully decorated horses, elephants, chariots and Infantry men and also foremost servants & maids.

❍ ❍ ❍

७. हिरण्यस्य सुवर्णस्य मुक्तानां विद्रुमस्य च ।
ददौ परमसंहृष्टः कन्याधनमनुत्तमम् ।।

7. And he gave as dowry foremost gifts of gold, silver, pearls, gems etc. with great joy.

❍ ❍ ❍

८. दत्त्वा बहुधनं राजा समनुज्ञाप्य पार्थिवम् ।
संपूज्य मङ्गलाशीर्भिः कुमारान् रघुनन्दनान् ।।
प्रविवेश स्वनिलयं मिथिलां मिथिलेश्वरः ।।

8. After giving many things and taking leave of king (Dhascharatha) and honouring these young sons of Raghu clan with auspicious blessings, the ruler of

Mithila, this king (Janaka), went back to his abode in Mithila.

❍ ❍ ❍

९. तस्मिन् प्रविष्टे नगरं जनके जगतीपतिः ।
राजाऽप्ययोध्याधिपतिः सह पुत्रैर्महात्मभिः ॥
ऋषीन्सर्वान्पुरस्कृत्य जगाम सबलानुगः ॥

9. After this Janaka had gone back, the lord of Earth, the ruler of Ayodhya, king (Dhascharatha), accompanied by his armed forces and his followers, started, along with his most eminent sons and accompanied by all the Rishi-s (to get back to Ayodhya).

❍ ❍ ❍

१०. वाहिनीं महतीं कर्षन् कीर्तिमांश्च ययौ तदा ॥

10. The renowned king went along, leading his mighty army.

❍ ❍ ❍

११. गच्छन्तं तं नरव्याघ्रं सर्षिसङ्घं सराघवम् ।
घोराः स्म पक्षिणो वाचो व्याहरन्ति ततस्ततः ॥

11. When this 'tiger' of men' (Dhascharatha) was going along with the multitude of Rishi-s and with (his sons, the) the Raaghavas, the birds were screaming gruesomely, hither & thither.

❍ ❍ ❍

१२. भौमाश्चैव मृगाः सर्वे गच्छन्ति स्म प्रदक्षिणम् ॥

12. All the animals on earth were going round & round (in circle).

❍ ❍ ❍

१३. तान्दृष्ट्वा राजशार्दूलो वसिष्ठं पर्यपृच्छत ॥

13. (Dhascharatha) the 'Lion' amongst men observing all this, asked Vasishta.

❍ ❍ ❍

१४. असौम्याः पक्षिणो घोरा मृगाश्चापि प्रदक्षिणाः ।
किमिदं हृदयोत्कम्पि मनो मम च सीदति ।।

14. The Birds are cheerless: The animals are going round in circles, gruesomely: My mind is also dejected What is this that makes my heart tremble?

❍ ❍ ❍

१५. राज्ञो दशरथस्यैतत्गछुत्वा वाक्यं महानृषिः ।
उवाच मधुरां वाणीं श्रूयतामस्य यत्फलम् ।।

15. Hearing the words of King Dhascharatha, the great Rishi spoke words sweetly: May you listen to what the 'Fruit', (the cause) of all is.

(Vasishta tells the frightened Dhascharatha when he saw bad omens on the way to Ayodhya: Dont worry, everything will be all right, says Vasishta.)

❍ ❍ ❍

१६. उपस्थितं भयं घोरं दिव्यं पक्षिमुखाच्च्युतम् ।
मृगाः प्रशमयन्त्येते सन्तापस्त्यज्यतामयम् ।।

16. These animals are allaying to the gruesome impending dangers that are indicated through these birds: (Surely) there is Divine (Sanction to all this): (Therefore) May this torment (of yours) be abandoned.

❍ ❍ ❍

१७. तेषां संवदतां तत्र वायुः प्रादुर्बभूव ह ।
कम्पयन्मेदिनीं सर्वां सपर्वतवनां महान् ।।

17. While they were conversing, there arose a mighty Gale (Vaayu) which shook the entire earth along with mountains & forests.

❍ ❍ ❍

१८. तमसा संवृतः सूर्यः सर्वा न प्रबभुर्दिशः ।
भस्मना चावृतं सर्वं संमूढमिव तद्बलम् ।।

18. Sun was covered by darkness: All the directions were

not visible: His entire Army was perplexed and covered by dust.

❍ ❍ ❍

१९. वसिष्ठश्चर्षयश्चान्ये राजा च ससुतस्तदा ।
सरसंज्ञा इव तत्रासन्सर्वमन्यद्विचेतनम् ॥

19. Vasishta, other Rishi-s, his sons & the king were not bewildered (But) there, at that time, all others were bewildered.

❍ ❍ ❍

२०. तस्मिंस्तमसि घोरे तु भस्मच्छन्नेव सा चमूः ।
ददर्श भीमसमाशं जटामण्डलधारिणम् ॥
२१. भार्गवं जामदग्न्यं राजवंशविमर्दनम् ।
कैलासमिव दुर्धर्ष कालाग्निमिव दुःसहम् ॥
२२. ज्वलन्तमिव तेजोभिर्दुर्निरीक्षं पृथग्जनैः ।
स्कन्धे चासज्य परशुं धनुर्विद्युद्गणोपमम् ॥
प्रगृह्य शरमुख्यं च त्रिपुरघ्नं यथा शिवम् ॥

20 to 22.

(ParaschuRaama appears & confronts Raama) At that terrible 'Darkness', the Army that was covered by dust saw a terrible looking (person) with matted hair. He was from Bhrighu family; was Jamadhagni's son: A destroyer of the Kshathriya caste; Unapproachable like mount Kailaash (in Himaalayas); He was unbearable like Fire at Pralaya (appeared like) As though burning by his own brilliance: Could not be looked at by ordinary men; On his shoulders (he had) an axe: Was wielding a bow that was like 'Streak of Lightning'; Was carrying in his hand foremost weapons (arrows etc.): He was like God Schiva who burnt up Thripura.

❍ ❍ ❍

२३. तं दृष्ट्वा भीमसमाशं ज्वलन्तमिव पावकम् ।
वसिष्ठप्रमुखाः सर्वेजपहोमपरायणाः ॥

२४. सङ्गता मुनयः सर्वे संजजल्पुरथो मिथः ।
कच्चित्पितृवधामर्षी क्षत्रं नोत्सादयिष्यति ॥

23 & 24.

Vasishta & other Rishi-s for whom prayers & Fire Rituals had taken refuge, saw this terrible looking (man) who was burning like fire; (and seeing him) all the sages who were together, conversed (& discussed) amongst themselves saying: = Out Of Revenge over His Father's Killing, Is He Going To Destroy The (Entire) Kshathriya Race, or What?

❍ ❍ ❍

२५. पूर्वं क्षत्रवधं कृत्वा गतमन्युर्गतज्वरः ।
क्षत्रस्योत्सादनं भूयो न खल्वस्य चिकीर्षितम् ॥

25. Having done destruction upon the Kshathriya-s before, he had given up his wrath and was also cured of 'The Fever' (of revenge): The destruction of the Kshathriya-s should not be desired by him (now) again, surely =

❍ ❍ ❍

२६. एवमुक्त्वाऽर्घ्यमादाय भार्गवं भीमदर्शनम् ।
ऋषयो राम रामेति मधुरं वाक्यमब्रुवन् ॥

26. Having said thus, the Muni-s, taking Arghya (waters) addressed this terrible looking person of Bhrighu family: With sweet words Oh Raama! Oh Raama! (they said & welcomed this ParaschuRaama - not to be confused with Raama, son of Dhascharatha).

❍ ❍ ❍

२७. प्रतिगृह्य तु तां पूजामृषिदत्तां प्रतापवान् ।
रामं दाशरथिं रामो जामदग्न्योऽभ्यभाषत ॥

27. Accepting the honour from these Rishi-s, the glorious son of Jamadhagni, this Raama (the Paraschu-Raama), then spoke (& he spoke only) to Raama, the son of Dhascharatha, there.

(Note: Paraschu-Raama, usually called Raama (not to be confused with Raama the son of Dhascharatha) is a Braamin by birth. As his name suggests, he is a mighty wielder of axe His father sage Jamadhagni was killed by a Kshathriya king. From that time he developed an intense hatred for the (Warrior caste) the Kshathriya. He was a terror to many kings who were mostly Kshathriya-s. Now he waylays Dhascharatha on his way back to Ayodhya. But his purpose is different. He wants to confront not Dhascharatha but his son Raama and only Raama. Read next chapter.)

❍ ❍ ❍

Chapter 75

The Stringing up of The Vishnu Bow

(ParaschuRaama the great Braamin sage versus the Kshathriya Raama; The Confrontation: ParaschuRaama addresses Raama.)

❍ ❍ ❍

१. राम दाशरथे वीर वीर्यं ते श्रूयतेऽद्भुतम् ।
धनुषो भेदनं चैव निखिलेन मया श्रुतम् ॥

1. Oh son of Dhascharatha! Oh Raama, the brave! It is heard that your valour is a marvel: The breaking of the Bow (at Mithila by you) was heard by me also in detail.

❍ ❍ ❍

२. तदद्भुतचिन्त्यं च भेदनं धनुषस्त्वया ।
तच्छ्रुत्वाऽहमनुप्राप्तो धनुर्गृह्यापरं शुभम् ॥

2. Hearing about the breaking of the Bow (at Mithila) by you & that it was a marvel and unimaginable, I took with me another foremost (auspicious) Bow and

came here (to meet you on your way to Ayodhya from Mithila).

❍ ❍ ❍

३. तदिदं घोरसमाशं जामदग्न्यं महद्धनु: ।
पूरयस्व शरेणैव स्वबलं दर्शयस्व च ॥

3. (ParaschuRaama throws a challenge to Raama): You now string up this mighty Bow, which is gruesome and which was obtained from (my father) Jamadhagni: Exhibit your own strength.

❍ ❍ ❍

४. तदहं ते बलं दृष्ट्वा धनुषोऽस्य प्रपूरणे ।
द्वन्द्वयुद्धं प्रदास्यामि वीर श्लाघ्यमिदं तव ॥

4. After seeing your strength in your stringing up this Bow, I will then offer you a combat, a twosome combat (between us) This will be commendable to you, oh brave (Raama).

❍ ❍ ❍

५. भीतो यदि धनुस्त्यक्त्वा निर्जितोऽस्मीति वा वद ।
अथवा द्वन्द्वयुद्धं मे दाता त्वं वै न संशय: ॥

5. Otherwise, throwing away the Bow, say: "I Am Scared; I Am Defeated" (or say=I accept defeat & surrender=) Or else, (string up the Bow) and then you become the one who bestows a Twosome Combat with me: No doubt: (only then you will be worthy of a fight with me).

❍ ❍ ❍

६. तस्य तद्वचनं श्रुत्वा राजा दशरथस्तदा ।
विषण्णवदनो दीन: प्राञ्जलिर्वाक्यमब्रवीत् ॥

6. Then hearing his words, king Dhascharatha whose face was downcast and who became 'feeble', addressed the following words with his (hands in) Anjali.

❍ ❍ ❍

७. क्षत्ररोषात्प्रशान्तस्त्वं ब्राह्मणानां च सन्निधौ ।
बालानां मम पुत्राणामभयं दातुमर्हसि ॥

7. (It is Dhascharatha who speaks, although it is Raama he addressed) You have become tranquil, having given up wrath against the Kshathriya-s You should bestow peace & security to these sons (of mine who are but) boys, before these Braamins (here).

❍ ❍ ❍

८. भार्गवाणां कुले जातः स्वाध्यायव्रतशालिनाम् ।
सहस्राक्षे प्रतिज्ञाय शस्त्रं निक्षिप्तवानसि ॥

8. Born in the family of Bhrighu-s, treating the study of Vedha-s as a vow for you, you had cast aside weapons (& wrath) as per the promise given to the thousand eyed Indhra (long ago).

❍ ❍ ❍

९. स त्वं धर्मपरो भूत्वा कश्यपाय वसुन्धराम् ।
दत्त्वा वनमुपागम्य महेन्द्रकृतकेतनः ॥

9. Such as you are, ever intent on Dharma (& Dharma alone) you gave the entire earth, (the entire conquest by you), to Kaaschyapa and went away to forest and made Mahendhra mountain your abode (When that is the case, why are you here, now, trying to 'kill' Kshathriya-s like us, asks Dhascharatha).

❍ ❍ ❍

१०. मम सर्वविनाशाय संप्राप्तस्त्वं महामुने ।
न चैकस्मिन्हते रामे सर्वे जीवामहे वयम् ॥

10. If this one, this (my son) Raama dies (at your hands), all of us will not live: Oh great Muni (ParaschuRaama)! You have come here to destroy me totally, (I fear greatly).

❍ ❍ ❍

११. ब्रुवत्येवं दशरथे जामदग्न्यः प्रतापवान् ।
अनादृत्यैव तद्वाक्यं राममेवाभ्यभाषत ।।

11. While Dhascharatha was saying thus, the glorious (ParaschuRaama) the son of Jamadhagni, showing scant regard (for Dhascharatha) spoke to Raama (and Raama) only.

❍ ❍ ❍

१२. इमे द्वे धनुषी श्रेष्ठे दिव्ये लोकाभिविश्रुते ।
दृढे बलवती मुख्ये सुकृते विश्वकर्मणा ।।

12. (ParaschuRaama ignores Dhascharatha but speaks to Raama) These two Bows were created by (the divine architect) Vischwakarma: They are foremost, divine, renowned in all the worlds Tough, strong, meritorious & well made.

❍ ❍ ❍

१३. अतिसृष्टं सुरैरेकं त्र्यम्बकाय युयुत्सवे ।।

13. One was passed on to Thryambak (Schiva, The Rudhra) who desired to do war, (was passed on) by the Dheva-s.

❍ ❍ ❍

१४. त्रिपुरघ्नं धनुःश्रेष्ठं भग्नं काकुत्स्थ यत्त्वया ।
इदं द्वितीयं दुर्धर्षं विष्णोर्दत्तं सुरोत्तमैः ।।

14. Oh (Raama)The Kaakuthsa! That foremost Bow which could destroy Thripura, was broken by you (at Mithila); This (Bow with me) the second one, which is uncrushable, was given by Dheva-s to God Vishnu.

❍ ❍ ❍

१५. तदिदं वैष्णवं राम धनुः परपुरञ्जयम् ।
समानसारं काकुत्स्थ रौद्रेण धनुषा त्विदम् ।।

15. Oh Kaakuthsa, Oh Raama! Such a one, this Vishnu Bow, will conquer enemy's fortress (cities etc) This (Bow) is also equally matched with Rudhra's (Schiva's) Bow.

❍ ❍ ❍

१६. तदा तु देवता: सर्वा: पृच्छन्ति स्म पितामहम् ।
शितिकण्ठस्य विष्णोश्च बलाबलनिरीक्षया ॥

16. With a view to behold and assess the relative strength of Schithi kanta, (the dark necked Rudhra,God Schiva) and God Vishnu, all the Dheva-s asked God Bramma.

❍ ❍ ❍

१७. अभिप्रायं तु विज्ञाय देवतानां पितामह: ।
विरोधं जनयामास तयो: सत्यवतां वर: ॥

17. The foremost amongst those who are men of truth, God Bramma, the Pithaamaha, realising the intentions of the Dheva-s, created an Enmity between them: (between the Gods Schiva-Vishnu).

(Even celestials are not free from pettiness; God Bramma was a silent spectator to the great havoc caused by all this.)

❍ ❍ ❍

१८. विरोधे च महद्युद्धमभवद्रोमहर्षणम् ।
शितिकण्ठस्य विष्णोश्च परस्परजिगीषिणो: ॥

18. Owing to enmity, desirous of killing the other, a mighty war ensued, causing hair raising (fear) between (Gods) Schithikanta (Schiva) & Vishnu.

❍ ❍ ❍

१९. तदा तु जृम्भितं शैवं धनुर्भीमपराक्रमम् ।
हुंकारेण महादेव: स्तम्भितोऽथ त्रिलोचन: ॥

19. Then, the terribly powerful Schiva's Bow was broken by a mere 'Hum' sound (emanating from Vishnu's breath); And the Three eyed (Schiva) the Mahaadheva became stunned.

❍ ❍ ❍

२०. देवैस्तदा समागम्य सर्षिसङ्घै: सचारणै: ।
याचितौ प्रशमं तत्र जग्मतुस्तौ सुरोत्तमौ ॥

20. At that time, these two foremost Dheva-s (Schiva & Vishnu) were begged by Dheva-s who had come together with a congregation of Muni-s and with Chaarana-s: And they (Schiva and Vishnu), obtained peace & tranquillity (ending their conflict).

❍ ❍ ❍

२१. जृम्भितं तद्धनुर्दृष्ट्वा शैवं विष्णुपराक्रमैः ।
अधिकं मेनिरे विष्णुं देवाः सर्षिगणास्तदा ॥

21. Then, the Dheva-s who were with multitude of Rishi-s, seeing Schiva's Bow broken by the power of Vishnu, considered Vishnu as more (powerful).

❍ ❍ ❍

२२. पूजयित्वा ततो विष्णुनामन्त्र्य च पिनाकिनम् ।
ब्रह्मेन्द्रादीन् पुरस्कृत्य नाकपृष्ठं ययुस्तदा ॥

22. Saluting Vishnu and honouring him, they all went away to heaven, accompanied by Bramma, Schiva & Indhra.

❍ ❍ ❍

२३. धु रुद्रस्तु संक्रुद्धो विदेहेषु महायशाः ।
देवरातस्य राजर्षेर्ददौ हस्ते ससायकम् ॥

23. The most famous & wrathful Rudhra (Schiva) then gave and entrusted (his) Bow at the hands of the royal sage Dhevaraatha at Vidheha, along with the weapons.

❍ ❍ ❍

२४. इदं च वैष्णवं राम धनुः परपुरञ्जयम् ।
ऋचीके भार्गवे प्रादाद्विष्णुः संन्यासमुत्तमम् ॥

24. Oh Raama! And God Vishnu also gave the Vishnu Bow which can destroy enemy's fortress, as a foremost trust to Richika of Bhrigu clan.

❍ ❍ ❍

२५. ऋचीकस्तु महातेजाः पुत्रस्याप्रतिकर्मणः ।
पितुर्मम ददौ दिव्यं जमदग्नेर्महात्मनः ।।

25. And the most brilliant Richika gave this divine Bow to his son, the great soul Jamadhagni who is my father, a man of incomparable deeds.

❍ ❍ ❍

२६. न्यस्तशस्त्रे पितरि मे तपोबलसमन्विते ।
अर्जुनो विदधे मृत्युं प्राकृतां बुद्धिमास्थितः ।।

26. When my father having given up all weapons was in a state of penance (absorbed in penance), one Arjuna of vulgar mind killed him.

(Thus ParaschuRaama took revenge on all kshathriya-s because this Arjuna, a Ksharhriya king, killed his Braamin father.)

❍ ❍ ❍

२७. वधमप्रतिरूपं तु पितुः श्रुत्वा सुदारुणम् ।
अमर्षोमे महानासीत्सर्वलोकभयप्रदः ।।
२८. क्षत्रमुत्सादयन्रोषाज्जातं जातमनेकशः ।।

27 & 28.

When I heard of the cruel & odious killing of my father, great indignation seized (me) which caused great fear amongst all the worlds: In wrath, I destroyed Kshathriya-s as they were being born & born, many many times: (I went around the world and killed the kshathriya-s).

❍ ❍ ❍

२९. पृथिवीं चाखिलां प्राप्य कश्यपाय महात्मने ।
यज्ञस्यान्ते तदा राम दक्षिणां पुण्यकर्मणे ।।
३०. दत्त्वा महेन्द्रनिलयस्तपोबलसमन्वितः ।
स्थितोऽस्मि तस्मिंस्तप्यन्वै सुसुखं सुरसेविते ।।

29 & 30.

Oh Raama: At the end of my Yaaga, having obtained all the Earth (by conquering Kshathriya kings & others), I gave as 'Dakshina' (Fee) for service (all this), to the great soul Kaaschyapa, the doer of Holy Deeds Having given (all of mine), I reached Mahendhra mountain, engulfed by the power of penance, firm, (resolute in doing penance) (living) happily there which is inhabited by Dheva-s, (ever) doing penance there.

❍ ❍ ❍

३१. श्रुत्वा तु धनुषो भेदं विस्मितानां नभस्तले ।
भाषतां देवसङ्घानां ततोऽहं द्रुतमागतः ॥

31. (I overheard) Recently the conversation in the sky amongst the Dheva-s who were wonder struck; Hearing about the breaking of the Bow (by you at Mithila) I came here quickly.

❍ ❍ ❍

३२. तदिदं वैष्णवं राम पितृपैतामहं महत् ।
क्षत्रधर्मं पुरस्कृत्य गृह्णीष्व धनुरुत्तमम् ॥

32. (Let me test your bravery, ParaschuRaama tells Raama): Oh Raama! Take this great & foremost Vishnu Bow which had been used by forefathers, thus honouring the (so called) Kshathriya Dharma (of yours)!

❍ ❍ ❍

३३. योजयस्व धनुःश्रेष्ठे शरं परपुरञ्जयम् ।
यदि शक्नोषि काकुत्स्थ द्वन्द्वं दास्यामि ते ततः ॥

33. Oh (Raama) the Kaakuthsa! String up the Bow, this Foremost Bow with one weapon that can destroy enemy's fortress; If you are capable (of doing this) then I will offer myself for a twosome combat with you.

(Note: Here is a case of a caste war! The Kshathriya is the warrior caste & the Braamin is considered 'weak' & good enough only for study of Vedha-s and the like! The

Braamin Raama (The Paraschu-Raama) confronts the Kshathriya Raama, the prince of Ayodhya: Secondly, it is interesting that even the Gods sometimes lose their composure & bearing: they behave like mortals! Ah!)

Chapter 76

ParaschuRaama's Defeat

१. तच्छ्रुत्वा जामदग्न्यस्य वाक्यं दाशरथिस्तदा ।
गौरवाद्यन्त्रितकथः पितू राममथाब्रवीत् ॥

1. Hearing these words from (ParaschuRaama) the son of Jamadhagni, (Raama), the son of Dhascharatha, curbing himself in speech out of respect to his father, addressed Raama, the Paraschu-Raama.

❍ ❍ ❍

२. श्रुतवानस्मि यत्कर्म कृतवानसि भार्गव ।
अनुरुध्यामहे ब्रह्मन् पितुरानृण्यमास्थितः ॥

2. Oh Braamin (ParaschuRaama) of Bhrighu family! I have heard about the deeds (done by you) out of your steadfastness in discharging the debt to your (dead) father. I will act accordingly.

❍ ❍ ❍

३. वीर्यहीनमिवाशक्तं क्षत्रधर्मेण भार्गव ।
अवजानासि मां राम पश्य मेऽद्य पराक्रमम् ॥

3. Oh Raama (the ParaschuRaama) of the Bhrighu family! You are treating me with contempt as though I lack bravery and am incompetent Now You will See My Prowess As Per (my) Kshathriya Dharma!

❍ ❍ ❍

४. इत्युक्त्वा राघवः क्रुद्धो भार्गवस्य वरायुधम् ।
शरं च प्रतिजग्राह हस्ताल्लघुपराक्रमः ॥

4. Saying thus, (Raama) the Raaghava who was in anger, reaching out (moving in) quickly and took this foremost Bow along with the weapon from the hands of this Bhaargava (ParaschuRaama with ease & minimum effort).

❍ ❍ ❍

५. आरोप्य तद्धनू रामः शरं सज्यं चकार ह ।
जामदग्न्यं ततो रामं रामः क्रुद्धोऽब्रवीद्वचः ॥

5. Bending the Bow, he fixed this weapon (after stringing it up); Then the angry Raama addressed Raama, (The Paraschu Raama) the son of Jamadhagni, these words.

❍ ❍ ❍

६. ब्राह्मणोऽसीति पूज्यो मे विश्वामित्रकृतेन च ।
विश्वामित्रः पूजनीयस्तदीयस्त्वं द्विजोत्तम ॥
तस्माच्छक्तो न ते राम मोक्तुं प्राणहरं शरम् ॥

6. Oh foremost Braamin! Oh Raama (the ParaschuRaama)! Vischwaamithra is (ever) to be honoured (by me) And you are Vischwaamithra's "clan" and further a Braamin: Therefore you are to be honoured by me So I am not able to discharge the weapon that can take away your life (Raama the kshathriya tells this Raama the Braamin that he wont kill him because he has such a regard for his teacher & mentor Vischwaamithra, the Bramma Rishi).

❍ ❍ ❍

७. इमां वा त्वद्गतिं राम तपोबलसमार्जिताम् ।
लोकानप्रतिमान्वा ते हनिष्यामि यदिच्छसि ॥

7. Oh Raama (the ParaschuRaama)! (Tell me) What you desire & I will crush it This, your mobility obtained by the power of your penance or your incomparable worlds (obtained by you) (What will it be, asks Raama I can make you lame, says Raama).

❍ ❍ ❍

८. न ह्ययं वैष्णवो दिव्यः शरः परपुरञ्जयः ।
मोघः पतति वीर्येण बलदर्पविनाशनः ॥

8. This weapon is God Vishnu's: It is divine; It will destroy power & arrogance It will destroy enemy's fortress Therefore this will not fall down (now) wasting away its power

(Readers to note: This being a divine weapon, must be discharged once fixed on to divine Bow that is strung up So Raama the Kshathriya asks Raama the Braamin, what will it be?)

❍ ❍ ❍

९. इति ब्रुवति काकुत्स्थे भार्गवं प्रति रोषिते ।
वरायुधधरं रामं द्रष्टुं सर्षिगणाः सुराः ॥
पितामहं पुरस्कृत्य समेतास्तत्र सङ्घशः ॥
१०. गन्धर्वाप्सरसश्चैव सिद्धचारणकिन्नराः ।
यक्षराक्षसनागाश्च तद्द्रष्टुं महदद्भुतम् ॥

9 & 10.

While Raama the Kaakuthsa was talking like this in wrath to Bhaargava (ParaschuRaama), the Dheva-s along with Rishi-s, accompanied by God Bramma, came there to see Raama who was wielding this foremost weapon, Together with Apsara-s, Ghandharva-s, Sidha-s, Chaarana-s, kinnara-s, Yaksha-s, Demons-, Naaga-s, all came to see this marvel (The marvel of confrontation between the two 'Raama-s').

❍ ❍ ❍

११. जडीकृते तदा लोके रामे वरधनुर्धरे ।
निर्वीर्योजामदग्न्योऽसौ रामो राममुदैक्षत ॥

11. At that time when Raama wielded this foremost Bow (with divine weapon), the world was stunned; And this Raama (ParaschuRaama) the son of Jamadhagni, stared at Raama, having lost all his power.

❍ ❍ ❍

१२. तेजोऽभिहतवीर्यत्वाज्जामदग्न्यो जडीकृतः ।
रामं कमलपत्राक्षं मन्दं मन्दमुवाच ह ॥

12. His power snatched away by the brilliance (of Raama), this ParschuRaama the son of Jamadhagni, became stunned and he addressed Raama whose eyes were like lotus petals, slowly & slowly (with a faltering, feeble voice).

❍ ❍ ❍

१३. त्राहि त्राहि महाबाहो श्रृणु राम वचो मम ।
राजसूये कृते पूर्वं यज्ञे दशरथात्मज ॥

१४. कश्यपाय मया दत्त्वा यदा पूर्वं वसुन्धरा ।
विषये मे न वस्तव्यमिति मां कश्यपोऽब्रवीत् ॥

13 & 14.

Oh Raama, the mighty limbed son of Dhascharatha! Save Me, Save Me! (Please) Listen to my words; Long ago when Raajasooya Yaaga was going on, the world was gifted away to Kaaschyapa by me And Kaaschyapa told me; "You should not live in my dominion (any more)."

❍ ❍ ❍

१५. सोऽहं गुरुवचः कुर्वन् पृथिव्यां न वसे निशाम् ।
कृता प्रतिज्ञा काकुत्स्थ कृता भूः कश्यपस्य ह ॥

15. Oh (Raama) the Kaakuthsa! And (such) commitment was made (by me); The 'world' (that was mine) was given to Kaaschyapa: Such as I am, I do not live at night on earth, honouring my Guru (Kaaschyapa's) words.

❍ ❍ ❍

१६. तदिमां मद्गतिं वीर हन्तुं नार्हसि राघव ।
मनोजवं गमिष्यामि महेन्द्रं पर्वतोत्तमम् ॥

16. Oh brave (Raama) the Raaghava! Therefore this, my mobility, you should not destroy: I will go with

the speed of mind, to the foremost of mountains, Mahendhra.

(Poor ParaschuRaama! He was not allowed to stay even a night on flat earth by Kaaschyapa He had thus become a wanderer & ultimately took refuge in the high peaks of Himaalya-s-Mahendhra mountain He begs Raama not to take away his mobility.)

❍ ❍ ❍

१७. लोकास्त्वप्रतिमा राम निर्जितास्तपसा मया ।

जहि ताञ्छरमुख्येन मा भूत्कालविपर्ययः ।।

17. Oh Raama! By (power of my) penance, incomparable worlds were 'conquered' by me Now, at the point of weapons (Gun!) you (enjoy &) conquer all this Dont waste time.

❍ ❍ ❍

१८. अक्षयं मधुहन्तारं जानामि त्वां सुरोत्तमम् ।।

१९. धनुषोऽस्य परामर्शात्स्वस्ति तेऽस्तु परन्तप ।।

18 & 19.

(And this Braamin Paraschuraama realises who this Kshathriya Raama really is. He knows this Raama as Incarnation of God Vishnu on earth; very few knew this at that time): Oh Tormentor of Enemies (Raama)! I Know You As Destroyer of Madhu You Are The Foremost of Dheva-s And The Imperishable By The Stringing Up Of The (Vishnu) Bow, (I Know You As God Vishnu on Earth, As Raama) Welfare to You.

❍ ❍ ❍

२०. एते सुरगणाः सर्वे निरीक्षन्ते समागताः ।

त्वामप्रतिमकर्माणमप्रतिद्वन्द्वमाहवे ।।

20. All the multitude of Dheva-s have come here together and are watching you who are without any one equal to you in war and you are one who has no one comparable to you in deeds.

❍ ❍ ❍

२१. न चेयं मम काकुत्स्थ व्रीडा भवितुमर्हति ।
त्वया त्रैलोक्यनाथेन यदहं विमुखीकृतः ॥

21. Oh (Raama) the Kaakuthsa! I lost 'Face' before you who are (verily) the lord of all the Three Worlds Therefore I am not to be ashamed of myself by this (defeat at your hands).

❍ ❍ ❍

२२. शरमप्रतिमं राम मोक्तुमर्हसि सुव्रत ।
शरमोक्षे गमिष्यामि महेन्द्रं पर्वतोत्तमम् ॥

22. Oh Raama) of good vows! Release (now) the incomparable weapon (from the divine stringed up Bow) When weapon is discharged, I will go away (for good) to the foremost mountain of Mahendhra.

❍ ❍ ❍

२३. तथा ब्रुवति रामे तु जामदग्न्ये प्रतापवान् ।
रामो दाशरथिः श्रीमांश्चिक्षेप शरमुत्तमम् ॥

23. As soon as he heard this from (ParaschuRaama) the son of Jamadhagni, the glorious & resplendent Raama the son of Dhascharatha, discharged the foremost weapon.

❍ ❍ ❍

२४. स हतान्दृश्य रामेण स्वांल्लोकांस्तपसाऽऽर्जितान् ।
जामदग्न्यो जगामाशु महेन्द्रं पर्वतोत्तमम् ॥

24. Seeing all the worlds that he conquered, (Earned), through penances snatched away by Raama (the son of Dhascharatha), (ParaschuRaama), the son of Jamadhagni, at once left for the foremost mountain of Mahendra.

❍ ❍ ❍

२५. ततो वितिमिराः सर्वा दिशश्चोपदिशस्तथा ।
सुराः सर्षिगणा रामं प्रशशंसुरुदायुधम् ॥

25. At that time, all the regions and likewise all the sub-

regions (shone bright), with darkness gone The congregation of Rishi-s & Dheva-s extolled Raama who had raised the Bow high up.

❍ ❍ ❍

२६. रामं दाशरथिं रामो जामदग्न्यः प्रशस्य च ।
तत: प्रदक्षिणं कृत्वा जगामात्मगतिं प्रभुः ॥

26. And Lord Raama, (this ParaschuRaama) son of Jamadhagni (also), then extolled Raama the son of Dhascharatha, after doing circumbambulation And he went away to his own place. (His crusade against the Kshathriya was over And Raama the Kshathriya had once and for all destroyed the wrath & arrogance of this great Braamin ParaschuRaama.)

❍ ❍ ❍

Chapter 77

The Return to Ayodhya

(King Dhascharatha accompanied by his sons, daughters in law, ministers, army, Rishi-s and others return to Ayodhya from Mithila. This is the last chapter of The First Book, The Baala Kaanda.)

❍ ❍ ❍

१. गते रामे प्रशान्तात्मा रामो दाशरथिर्धनुः ।
वरुणायाप्रमेयाय ददौ हस्ते महायशाः ॥

1. After Raama (ParaschuRaama) had gone away, this most famous Raama the son of Dhascharatha, whose mind was tranquil, handed over this incomparable Bow into the hands of Lord Varuna.

❍ ❍ ❍

२. अभिवाद्य ततो रामो वसिष्ठप्रमुखानृषीन् ।
पितरं विह्वलं प्रोवाच रघुनन्दनः ॥
३. प्रणयन् मनसो वृत्तिं पितुः स परमात्मवान् ॥

2 & 3.

Bowing before Vasishta & others and also before the Rishi-s, the darling of Raghu-s, seeing his father agitated and noticing also the state of the mind of his father (Dhascharatha), (this Raama) who was totally composed, spoke to him.

❍ ❍ ❍

४. जामदग्न्यो गतो रामः प्रयातु चतुरङ्गिणी ।
अयोध्याभिमुखी सेना त्वया नाथेन पालिता ॥

4. (Dhascharatha was so scared of the terrible ParaschuRaama that during their 'encounter' and subsequent 'defeat' of ParaschuRaama at the hands of his son, he rarely opened his eyes!)

(Oh Father)! Raama, (the ParaschuRaama), the son of Jamadhagni is gone (for good)! Let the Foursome Army (of ours) move on to Ayodhya (now), this Army that is protected by you, the protector.

❍ ❍ ❍

५. संदिशस्व महाराज सेनां त्वच्छासने स्थिताम् ।
शासनं काङ्क्षते सेना चातकालिर्जलं यथा ॥

5. Oh great king (Dhascharatha)! Like Water birds (awaiting rain) waters, your army is awaiting your command, Command your Army that is under your command.

❍ ❍ ❍

६. रामस्य वचनं श्रुत्वा राजा दशरथः सुतम् ।
बाहुभ्यां संपरिष्वज्य मूर्ध्न्युपाघ्राय राघवम् ॥
७. गतो राम इति श्रुत्वा हृष्टः प्रमुदितो नृपः ।
पुनर्जातं तदा मेने पुत्रमात्मनमेव च ॥

6 & 7.

Hearing Raama's words, king Dhascharatha hugged his son (Raama the) Raaghava, with his hands & kissed him on his (forehead) And hearing Raama (the ParaschuRaama) had gone away, king (Dhascharatha) was very happy, greatly exhilarated with joy and considered that he and his son were reborn!

❍ ❍ ❍

८. चोदयामास तां सेनां जगामाशु ततः पुरीम् ॥

९. पताकाध्वजिनीं रम्यां तूर्योद्घुष्ठनिनादिताम् ।
सिक्तराजपथां रम्यां प्रकीर्णकुसुमोत्कराम् ॥

१०. राजप्रवेशसुमुखैः पौरैर्मङ्गलवादिभिः ।
संपूर्णां प्राविशद्राजा जनौघैः समलंकृताम् ॥

8 to 10.

(The Return to Ayodhya: How the city looked to receive king Dhascharatha and his sons with their brides.)

The king then commanded his Army and at once they left The city was beautiful; was full of banners & flags: Reverberating with sounds of Thoorya drums etc. the beautiful roads cleansed with (river) water: with flowers strewn: The king entered such a city (of his) which was well decorated by the multitude of citizens, which was full of men rendering blessings (to the princes & brides), which was crowded with citizens whose faces were cheerful because of their king's return.

❍ ❍ ❍

११. पौरैः प्रत्युद्गतो दूरं द्विजैश्च पुरवासिभिः ।
पुत्रैरनुगतः श्रीमान् श्रीमद्भिश्च महायशाः ॥

१२. प्रविवेश गृहं राजा हिमवत्सदृशं प्रियम् ।
ननन्द सजनो राजा गृहे कामैः सुपूजितः ॥

11 & 12.

Received by citizens & Braamin residents of the city

who went far out (of the city) to receive him who was most famous, who was resplendent, and who was accompanied by his pleasant sons, king Dhascharatha entered his beautiful palace that was like Himaalya-s; 'Honoured' with all the 'Desirables' in the palace, king rejoiced with his folks.

❍ ❍ ❍

१३. कौसल्या च सुमित्रा च कैकेयी च सुमध्यमा ।
वधूप्रतिग्रहे युक्ता याश्चान्या राजयोषितः ॥
१४. रामं च लक्ष्मणं चैव शत्रुघ्नं भरतं तथा ।
आर्चयन् मङ्गलाशीर्भिर्मङ्गलैरभ्यपूजयन् ॥
उपाहारैश्च संहृष्टाः कुमारानभिपूज्य च ॥

13 & 14.

(The mothers of these princes & other ladies bless their wives: There is a feeling that the mothers did not visit Mithila for wedding of their sons):

(Dhascharatha's) Wives Kowsalya, Sumithra & the slender waisted Kaikeyi and other ladies were all engaged in receiving, (welcoming), the young brides with great joy They honoured the sons, Raama, Lakshmana, Bharatha, & Schathrugna and they extolled them with benediction They honoured with flowers in abundance.

❍ ❍ ❍

१५. ततः सीतां महाभागामूर्मिलां च यशस्विनीम् ।
कुशध्वजसुते चोभे जगृहुर्नृपपत्नयः ॥

15. Then the king's wives led the most illustrious Seetha, the most famous Oormila and also the two daughters of Kuschadhwaja.

❍ ❍ ❍

१६. मङ्गलालम्भनैश्चैव शोभिताः क्षौमवाससः ।
देवतायतनान्याशु यथार्हं प्रत्यपूजयन् ॥

16. Wearing silken dress, putting on auspicious marks (& ornaments) shining (bright), they all at once worshipped the Deities as per norms.

❍ ❍ ❍

१७. अभिवाद्याभिवाद्यांश्च सर्वा राजसुतास्तदा ।
स्वं स्वं गृहं समासद्य कुबेरभवनोपमम् ।।
१८. गोभिर्धनैश्च धान्यैश्च तर्पयित्वा द्विजोत्तमान् ।
रेमिरे मुदिताः सर्वा भर्तृभिः सहिता रहः ।।

17 & 18.

Then after bowing (& paying respects) to those who were to be bowed to, they, these Royal princesses went to their respective palaces that were like Kubhaera's abode And they pleased the foremost Braamins with (gifts of) Cows, gold coins, grains etc. Then, along with their husbands, they all enjoyed (life) in privacy.

❍ ❍ ❍

१९. कुमाराश्च महात्मानो वीर्येणाप्रतिमा भुवि ।
कृतदाराः कृतास्त्राश्च सधनाः ससुहृज्जनाः ।।
२०. शुश्रूषमाणाः पितरं वर्तयन्ति नरर्षभाः ।
काले काले तु नीतिज्ञास्तोषयन्तो गुरुं गुणैः ।।

19 & 20.

The 'Bulls' amongst men', these most eminent youths were incomparable in valour; they had obtained (knowledge of) weapons; possessed all wealth; were amongst good friends they did reverential service to their father; they had knowledge of Law; they pleased their Guru (teachers) from time to time by their noble qualities (& deeds); They lived (happily).

❍ ❍ ❍

२१. कस्यचित्त्वथ कालस्य राजा दशरथः सुतम् ।
अभिवादयितुं प्राप्तं श्यामं कमललोचनम् ।।
अक्लिष्टकारिणं शूरं परसैन्यविमर्दनम् ।।

२२. विनयं देहयोगेन संप्राप्तमिव संस्थितम् ।
भरतं कैकयीपुत्रमब्रवीद्रघुसत्तमः ॥

21 & 22.

After some days, king Dhascharatha (saw) his son who had come to pay his respects to him, who was of darkish hue, whose eyes were like lotus, who was brave and who could destroy enemy's army and who could do deeds without any weariness who was endowed with modesty as though it was 'born' along with his body; Such a son (Bharatha), the son of (his third wife) Kaikeyi, this (Dhascharatha), the foremost of Raghu-s, addressed.

❍ ❍ ❍

२३. अयं केकयराजस्य पुत्रो वसति पुत्रक ।
त्वां नेतुमागतो वीर युधाजिन्मातुलस्तव ॥
२४. प्रार्थितस्तेन धर्मज्ञ मिथिलायामहं तदा ।
ऋषिमध्ये तु तस्य त्वं प्रीतिं कर्तुमिहार्हसि ॥

23 & 24.

(Dhascharatha addresses his son Bharatha) Oh my son the brave (Bharatha)! Your uncle, the son of Kekeya king who has come here to take you with him (to your maternal grandfather's place), this Yudhajith is (still) staying (here) (When we were) At Mithila, I was requested by him in presence of Rishi-s at that time: Oh knower of Dharma (my son Bharatha)! In this matter, you should satisfy his wish (to go along with him to Kekeya).

❍ ❍ ❍

२५. श्रुत्वा दशरथस्यैतद्भरतः कैकयीसुतः ।
अभिवाद्य गुरुं रामं परिष्वज्य च लक्ष्मणम् ॥
गमनायाभिचक्राम शत्रुघ्नसहितस्तदा ॥

25. Hearing thus from (his father) Dhascharatha, Bharatha the son of Kaikeyi, then bowed to his Guru (his teacher-

father) and to (his brother) Raama and after hugging Lakshmana, prepared to leave, accompanied by (his other brother) Schathrugna

❍ ❍ ❍

२६. आपृच्छ्य पितरं शूरो रामं चाक्लिष्टकारिणम् ।
मातृश्चापि नरश्रेष्ठः शत्रुघ्नसहितो ययौ ॥

26. After taking leave of his father and Raama who ever did tasks without any weariness at all, and (after taking leave of) his mothers (mother Kaikeyi & step mothers Kowsalya, Sumithra & others) this brave foremost man (Bharatha) left with (his brother) Schathrugna.

❍ ❍ ❍

२७. युधाजित्प्राप्य भरतं सशत्रुघ्नं प्रहर्षितः ।
स्वपुरं प्राविशद्वीरः पिता तस्य तुतोष ह ॥

27. And taking Bharatha & Schathrugna with him, Yudhaajith, with great joy, went to his city And there, his great father became mightily pleased (to see his grandson Bharatha & Schathrugna).

❍ ❍ ❍

२८. गते च भरते रामो लक्ष्मणश्च महारथः ।
पितरं देवसमाशं पूजयामासतुस्तदा ॥

28. After Bharatha had left, Raama and the great warrior (& charioteer) Lakshmana (served &) honoured their father who was like a Dheva.

❍ ❍ ❍

२९. पितुराज्ञां पुरस्कृत्य पौरकार्याणि सर्वशः ।
चकार रामो धर्मात्मा प्रियाणि च हितानि च ॥

29. The noble soul man of Dharma Raama, ever followed his father's orders and performed the duties of his kingdom pleasantly and beneficially in every way.

❍ ❍ ❍

३०. मातृभ्यो मातृकार्याणि कृत्वा परमयन्त्रितः ।
गुरूणां गुरुकार्याणि काले कालेऽन्ववैक्षत ।।

30. Raama who was greatly duty bound, did service time & again, for the mothers, (mother Kowsalya & step mothers Sumithra & Kaikeyi) that are to be done for a mother (by a devoted son): Did service for teachers that are to be done for a teacher (by a devoted student) He showed great consideration.

❍ ❍ ❍

३१. एवं दशरथः प्रीतो ब्राह्मणा नैगमास्तथा ।
रामस्य शीलवृत्तेन सर्वे विषयवासिनः ।।

31. By such good conduct of Raama, king Dhascharatha was very pleased; Likewise the Braamins, citizens, and subjects living in villages, all of them (in the kingdom).

❍ ❍ ❍

३२. तेषामतियशा लोके रामः सत्यपराक्रमः ।
स्वयंभूरिव भूतानां बभूव गुणवत्तरः ।।

32. Like God Bramma to His Creations, this Raama who was very famous and who was truly valiant, appeared in the world, endowed with foremost qualities.

❍ ❍ ❍

३३. रामस्तु सीतया सार्धं विजहार बहूनृतून् ।
मनस्वी तद्गतस्तस्या नित्यं हृदि समर्पितः ।।

33. The good hearted Raama who was always in her heart, whose attentions were towards her, enjoyed many *moments with Seetha. (*Poet uses word Rithu-Seasons. We have 'used' moments.)

❍ ❍ ❍

३४. प्रिया तु सीता रामस्य दाराः पितृकृता इति ।
गुणाद्रूपगुणाच्चापि प्रीतिर्भूयोऽभ्यवर्धत ।।
३५. हृदयं चैव जानाति प्रीतियोगि परस्परम् ।।

34 & 35.

Entwined in Love, their feelings were mutual. (their hearts were one) As Seetha was offered to Raama by her father and as she was his beloved and as she was endowed with beauty and also with (good) qualities, great affection grew between them.

❍ ❍ ❍

३६. तस्याश्च भर्ता द्विगुणं हृदये परिवर्तते ।
अन्तर्जातमपि व्यक्तमाख्याति हृदयं हृदा ॥

36. In her heart her husband (Raama) lived 'Doubly'; (Raama's heart was in hers; and her heart was with Raama) Mind (and feelings, going) along with mind (and feelings of the other). The inborn feelings of one's heart was clearly perceived by the other.

❍ ❍ ❍

३७. तस्य भूयो विशेषेण मैथिली जनकात्मजा ।
देवताभिः समा रूपे सीता श्रीरिव रूपिणी ॥

37. Beautiful like Goddess (Lakshmi) in form, she was (comparable to and) equal to Deities: This Seetha the daughter of Janaka, shone even more by him (by Raama's side).

❍ ❍ ❍

३८. तया स राजर्षिसुतोऽभिरामया समेयिवानुत्तमराजकन्यया ।
अतीव रामः शुशुभेऽतिकामया विभुः श्रिया विष्णुरिवामरेश्वरः ॥

38. Like The Eternal Lord, the All Pervading God Vishnu along with (His consort) Goddess Lakshmi, this Raama the son of Royal Sage (Dhascharatha) shone most brilliantly along with the most beautiful and most endearing (Seetha), the daughter of the foremost king (Janaka)

(Note: We come to The End of The First Book of Vaalmeeki: The Baala Kaanda: This Book ends with a happy note. How none was happier than the old King

Dhascharatha who was enjoying life with his four noble sons. But The 'Drama' is reserved for The Second Book, The Ayodhya Kaanda).

❍ ❍ ❍